Harbottle's Dictionary of Battles

Harbottle's Dictionary of Battles

Second Revised Edition
by
George Bruce

GRANADA
London Toronto Sydney New York

Granada Publishing Limited
Frogmore, St Albans, Herts AL2 2NF
and
3 Upper James Street, London W1R 4BP
866 United Nations Plaza, New York, NY 10017, USA
117 York Street, Sydney, NSW 2000, Australia
100 Skyway Avenue, Rexdale, Ontario M9W 3A6, Canada
PO Box 84165, Greenside, 2034 Johannesburg, South Africa
CML Centre, Queen & Wyndham Streets, Auckland 1, New Zealand

Copyright © George Bruce 1971, 1979

ISBN 0 246 11103 8

First published in Great Britain 1904
Revised edition published by Hart-Davis, MacGibbon Ltd 1971 (ISBN 0 246 64031 6)
Second edition published by Granada Publishing 1979

Printed and bound in Great Britain by
William Clowes (Beccles) Limited
Beccles and London

Granada ®
Granada Publishing ®

Foreword

Brigadier Peter Young, DSO, MC, MA, FSA, FRHistS, FRGS

T. B. Harbottle's *Dictionary of Battles* has long been a standard reference work. Since its first publication in 1904, the dictionary has provided student and scholar alike with concise and accurate information on literally thousands of engagements. This new edition has been revised and brought up to date by George Bruce, whose efforts have expanded the dictionary without detracting from Harbottle's original far-ranging scholarship. Each individual entry supplies the reader with substantial information. It gives the name of the battle and the campaign of which it was part, together with a brief résumé of the course of the action. In most instances casualty figures too are included. Many battles bedevil the historian by being known by a variety of names. The dictionary diminishes this problem by giving the alternative titles of an action. Thus, the great Prussian victory in the Austro-Prussian War of 1866 is to be found under Koeniggrätz, with an alternative listing under Sadowa.

It must be remembered that any reference work which covers the history of warfare from the earliest times to the present day can only do so in limited depth. Space alone makes detailed treatment impossible. The political background to the war in question, the strategy of the campaign and a spirited account of the course of the action must all be left to specialist works with a much narrower field. So too must the more delicate tasks of interpretation and comment.

The *Dictionary of Battles* moves deftly from Negapatam to Naxos, from Forum Terebronii to Fredericksburg. It deals with contests on both land and sea. Engagements as epochal as Waterloo and Gettysburg, Sedan and Trafalgar are not allowed to obscure such lesser fights as the Battle of Gislikon, an almost bloodless encounter in the Swiss civil war of 1847. The time-scale ranges from classical antiquity to the recent past. The geographical breadth is as wide; engagements in all continents receive attention.

The dictionary provides readers of widely-differing backgrounds with an accessible and comprehensive source of information on the conflicts which have for so long been a feature of history. There is, indeed, every sign that they will remain so.

PETER YOUNG

Preface

Thomas Benfield Harbottle compiled this *Dictionary of Battles* about seventy-five years ago. Mr Harbottle was also the author of a *Dictionary of Historical Allusions*, a *Dictionary of Classical Quotations*, and, with Colonel Philip Hugh Dalbiac, co-author of a *Dictionary of French and Italian Quotations*. Just as his *Dictionary of Battles* was going to press, in 1904, Mr Harbottle died and upon Colonel Dalbiac fell the task of correcting proofs and preparing the index. In his foreword Colonel Dalbiac remarked that he had been unable in the time available to check all the references in the dictionary with the original sources; and should any printer's errors or varieties of spelling remain he should be blamed, since he could never hope to equal his departed friend's patience in research, depth of knowledge and accuracy in compilation. After the considerable amount of editing, revision and up-dating of this dictionary that I have undertaken, I echo the last clauses of Colonel Dalbiac's remark. Mr Harbottle would have put into it several years' work and a huge amount of knowledge, but a small edition only was published, by Swann Sonnenschein & Company, a little-known firm who not long afterwards went into voluntary liquidation. I found a copy, saw its usefulness, arranged for its publication and began the necessary work of revising and bringing up-to-date. Alterations and changes in the text I confined to matters of fact. I standardized the sequence of fact in each battle reference, but I did not change either Mr Harbottle's spelling of place names, or his style. Thus, in battles before the twentieth century, occasionally the enemy are 'slain', 'utterly routed', 'signally defeated', or 'driven from the field in confusion'.

Battle is usually defined today as combat between large or relatively large armed forces on land or sea or in the air, and it is in this sense that this work is a dictionary of battles, not of political events associated with them, though reference is necessarily made to these. Battle has been defined fairly broadly to include—where they are significant—sieges, like Multan; raids, like Dieppe; and relatively minor actions of, for example, the Napoleonic Wars, the American Civil War, the American Revolutionary War, mainly because these minor actions represent the tactical moves which so often led up to the main battles. Throughout, battles are listed in alphabetical order by place names—with a few well-known exceptions—the entry for each battle stating the war or campaign of which it was part; the date it began; who commanded how many men on each side; the tactics and sometimes the weapons employed; to whom went victory; the casualties, and, where it can be said, what was the ultimate outcome. After each entry, cross-references name associated battles, where this is possible. The index lists both personal names and wars, with the page numbers of component battles. Battles of the twentieth century I have described rather more fully than those up to 1900 compiled by Mr Harbottle, but I have omitted the so-called emergency of the post-war years in Malaya (now Malaysia), the uprising in Algeria and the civil wars in The Congo and Biafra, mainly because these were characterized by guerrilla warfare without notable battles.

GEORGE BRUCE

Acknowledgements

For his valuable advice I wish to thank my
friend Brigadier Peter Young, DSO, MC,
MA, FSA, FRHistS, FRGS, late of the
Department of Military History, Royal
Military Academy, who has written the
foreword to the dictionary; also Mr King,
Librarian, and the staff of the War Office
Library; and the staff of the London Library.

A

Aachen *World War II*

The first German city captured by the Allies, after an eight-day house-to-house battle during October 13 to 20, 1944, between XIX and VII Corps of General Courtney Hodges US First Army and German Nazi forces under General Hermann Balck. *See* The Rhineland.

Abensberg *Napoleonic Wars*

April 20, 1809, between the French and Bavarians under Napoleon, about 90,000 strong, and 80,000 Austrians under the Archduke Charles. On the French left, Marshal Lannes' corps drove back the Austrians after a feeble resistance. In the centre the Bavarians were hard pressed, but eventually Napoleon succeeded in turning the Austrian flank, exposed by the defeat of their right, and Charles was forced to retreat. The Austrians lost 7,000, the French and Bavarians about 3,000 killed and wounded. *See* Oporto, Sacile, Eckmühl.

Aberdeen *English Civil War*

September 13, 1644, between the Covenanters, 3,000 strong under Lord Burleigh, and the Royalists, about 1,500 strong under the Marquis of Montrose. The Covenanters were put to flight, and no quarter being given, they lost heavily before reaching Aberdeen. The Royalist losses were insignificant. *See* Tippermuir.

Abraham, Plains of,

see Plains of Abraham

Abu Hamed *British Sudan Campaigns*

August 7, 1897, when the Dervish entrenchments outside Abu Hamed were stormed by a Sudanese Brigade, with two guns Royal Artillery, under Major-General Hunter. The Mahdist garrison was driven through the town, losing heavily, and their commander, Mohammed Zain, captured. The Egyptian loss was 80 killed and wounded, including four British officers. *See* Atbara, Khartoum, Abu Klea.

Abukir I *French Revolutionary Wars*

July 25, 1799, Napoleon attacking the position held by Mustapha Pasha IV, who had recently landed in Egypt at the head of 18,000 Turks. The French, 7,700 strong, were completely successful, two-thirds of the Turkish troops being killed or driven into the sea, while 6,000, with the Pasha, surrendered. *See* Nile.

Abukir II *British Invasion of Egypt*

March 8, 1801, when 5,000 British under General Sir Ralph Abercromby disembarked on the beach at Abukir, in the face of a force of 2,000 French under General Friant. The landing was effected under a heavy musketry and artillery fire, which cost the assailants 1,100 killed and wounded. The French were driven from their positions with a loss of 500 men. *See* Alexandria, Acre III.

Abu Klea *British Sudan Campaigns*

January 17, 1885, between a British force, 1,500 strong, under General Sir Herbert Stewart, and 12,000 Mahdists, of whom about 5,000 actually attacked. The British square was broken at one corner, owing to the jamming of a Gardner gun, and the Mahdists forcing their way inside, a desperate hand-to-hand conflict followed. Eventually the assailants were driven off, and the square reformed. The British loss was 18 officers, among them Colonel Frederick Burnaby, and 150 men. In the immediate vicinity of the square, 1,100 Arab dead were counted. *See* Khartoum, Atbara, Abu Kru, Omdurman.

Abu Kru *British Sudan Campaigns*

January 19, 1885, between 1,200 British troops under General Sir Herbert Stewart, and a large force of Mahdists. The Mahdists attacked a short distance from the Nile, and the British square moved towards the river, repelling all assaults successfully till they reached the Nile. The British losses were 121, including Stewart, mortally wounded. This action is also known as the battle of Gubat. *See* Khartoum, Atbara, Omdurman.

Acapulco *Mexican Liberal Rising*

August 9, 1855, between the Mexican Government troops under General Santa

Anna, and the Liberals under Juárez. Santa Anna was totally routed and fled from the country. *See* La Puebla, Calpulalpam.

Accra I *First British-Ashanti War*

1824, between 10,000 Ashantis and a force of 1,000 British under General Sir Charles McCarthy, in what was formerly the Gold Coast, and is now Ghana. The British were surrounded and routed by the Ashantis, McCarthy being killed. *See* Accra II.

Accra II *First British-Ashanti War*

In 1825, between 15,000 Ashantis and 400 British troops, with 4,600 native auxiliaries. The Ashantis were defeated, and the king compelled to abandon his move on Cape Coast Castle. Kumasi was captured in 1874 and the country annexed in 1901. *See* Amoaful.

Acragas *Second Carthaginian Invasion of Sicily*

This fortress (now Agrigentum) was besieged 406 BC, by the Carthaginians under Hannibal, the garrison being commanded by Dexippus the Spartan. Early in the siege an epidemic in the Carthaginian camp killed Hannibal, who was succeeded by his cousin, Himilco. A relieving army of 35,000 Syracusans under Daphnaeus fought a pitched battle with the Carthaginians beneath the walls of the city, and succeeded in seizing and holding one of their camps, but shortly afterwards dissension broke out in the garrison, and many of the foreign mercenaries deserting, the citizens, after a siege of eight months, left the place. The Carthaginians at once occupied the fortress. *See* Syracuse, Selinus.

Acre I *Third Crusade*

Siege was laid to this city by the Christians in August, 1189, and it was obstinately defended by the Saracens for two years, during which the Crusaders were said to have lost 120,000 men. In June, 1191, the besiegers were reinforced by an English army under King Richard I (Coeur de Lion), and in the following month the garrison surrendered. *See* Arsouf, Jerusalem III.

Acre II *Crusader-Turkish Wars*

The city remained in the hands of the Christians till May 19, 1291, when it was captured by the Muslims under Malek al Aschraf, Sultan of Egypt. The last stronghold in the Holy Land thus passed out of the keeping of the Christians. *See* Tunis II.

Acre III *French Revolutionary Wars*

The city was besieged March 17, 1799, by the French under Napoleon, and defended by the Turks under Djezzar (the Butcher) and a small force of British seamen under Captain Sir Sidney Smith RN. An assault on the 28th was repulsed with loss, and then a threatened attack by a Syrian army forced Napoleon to withdraw a large portion of his troops. On the resumption of the siege, no less than seven more assaults were delivered, while the French had to meet eleven sallies of the besieged, but they were unable to effect a lodgment, and on May 21 Napoleon reluctantly raised the siege. The fall of Acre would have placed the whole of Syria, and possibly of the Turkish empire, in the hands of the French. *See* Abukir, Pyramids.

Acre IV *Egyptian Revolt*

Mehemet Ali of Egypt having refused to accept the conditions imposed upon him by the Quadrilateral Alliance, Acre (now in Israel) was shelled, November 3, 1840, by a combined British and Turkish fleet under Admiral Sir R. Stopford, and the town laid in ruins. The Egyptians withdrew, and came to terms. *See* Nizib, Koniah.

Acs *Hungarian Rising*

July 2, 1849, between 25,000 Hungarians, under General von Görgey, and the Russo-Austrian army, greatly superior in numbers, under Prince zu Windischgrätz. The allies attacked the entrenched camp of the Hungarians, outside Komorn, while the Hungarians made an attempt to turn the allied left. Both attacks were repulsed, and the battle was undecided. *See* Kapolna, Schwechat, Sárkány.

Actium *Wars of the Second Triumvirate*

September 2, 31 BC, between the fleet of Antony, 480 galleys, and that of Octavius, about 400, but much lighter and less well

10

manned than those of Antony. The battle was fiercely contested, with varying fortune; but at a critical moment Cleopatra ordered the Egyptian admiral to make sail, and with 60 galleys withdrew from the fight. She was followed by Antony, and his fleet, discouraged by his flight, surrendered after ten hours' fighting. The Octavians captured 300 galleys, and 5,000 Antonians fell in the action. A few days later Antony's land army of 120,000 men laid down their arms. Octavius became the first ruler of the Roman Empire. *See* Naulochus.

Acultzingo *Franco-Mexican War*

April 28, 1862, between the French, 7,500 strong, under General Lorençez, and the main Mexican army, about 10,000, under General Zaragoza. The Mexicans held a strong position in the Cumbres Pass, from which they were driven by the French, and forced to retire upon La Puebla. *See* La Puebla I and II, Calpulalpam.

Admagetobriga *Gallic Tribal Wars*

61 BC, between the Sequani under Ariovistus, and the Haedui under Eporedorix. The Haedui were defeated, with the loss of the flower of their chivalry, and were compelled to give hostages and pay tribute to Ariovistus. *See* Bibracte.

Adrianople I *Fourth Crusade*

April 15, 1205, between the crusaders under the Latin Emperor, Baldwin I, and the revolted Bulgarians under their chief, Kaloyan, at Adrianople (Edirne). The Bulgarian cavalry fled, and lured the Latin horse in pursuit. Then turning upon them, they routed them with the loss of their leader, the Comte de Blois, and in the end the crusaders were completely defeated and the Emperor captured. *See* Constantinople II.

Adrianople II *First Balkan War*

February 3, 1913, between Bulgaria (King Ferdinand) and Turkish nationalists led by Enver Pasha, for the possession of Adrianople (Edirne), ceded to Bulgaria in the armistice of December 1912. The Bulgarians captured the city on March 26 and a treaty was signed in London on May 30. The city was reoccupied and kept by Turkey in the Second Balkan War. *See* Kumanovo.

Aduatuca *Gallic Wars*

52 BC, when a Roman force of 9,000 men under Titurius Sabinus was attacked in its camps by the Eburones under Ambiorix. The assault failed, but an offer by Ambiorix of a safe passage to the nearest Roman station was accepted. On the march the Romans were treacherously attacked by the Eburones and cut to pieces, Sabinus being among the slain. *See* Avaricum.

Aduwa *Italian Invasion of Ethiopia*

March 1, 1896, when the Italian force under General Baratieri attacked the Shoan army, strongly posted in difficult country, and was routed with enormous loss. Italy recognized Ethiopian independence in the Treaty of Addis Ababa in October. *See* Agordat.

Adwalton Moor *English Civil War*

June 30, 1643, when the Parliamentarians, numbering 4,000, with a levy of armed peasants, were defeated by 10,000 Royalists under the Earl of Newcastle. Lord Fairfax, who commanded the Parliament force, succeeded in reaching Hull. The battle is also known as that of Atherton Moor. *See* Chalgrove Field.

Ægina *Third Messenian War*

458 BC, between the Athenian fleet, and that of Ægina, aided by the Peloponnesian States. The Athenians were victorious, capturing 70 ships, and landing they invested Ægina, which fell into their hands after a siege of a little less than two years. *See* Tanagra.

Ægospotami *Peloponnesian War*

405 BC, between 180 Athenian triremes, under Conon, and 170 Peloponnesian ships under Lysander. The Athenian fleet was lying at Ægospotami, opposite Lampsacus, where Lysander was stationed. For four days in succession the Athenian admiral crossed the straits, and endeavoured, but in vain, to bring on a general action. On the fifth day Lysander waited till the Athenians had returned to their anchorage, and then, making a sudden dash across the straits, caught them unprepared, and seized all but 20 ships, putting to death all the Athenians who were captured. This disaster destroyed the naval power of Athens, and was soon followed by the end of

the Peloponnesian War. *See* Cunaxa, Haliartus.

Ægusa *First Punic War*

March 10, 241 BC, between the Roman fleet of 200 quinqueremes under C. Lutatius Catulus, and a Carthaginian fleet under Hanno despatched to relieve the town. The action was fought in heavy weather, and the Roman sailors being far better trained than their opponents, Catulus gained a signal victory, capturing 70 and sinking 50 of the enemy's ships. The victory ended the First Punic War. *See* Drepanum.

Agendicum *Gallic War*

52 BC, between the Romans under Labienus, and the Celts under Camulogenus. Labienus was endeavouring to effect a junction with Caesar, which the Celts were opposing, and Labienus, crossing the Marne in face of their army, inflicted upon them a severe defeat, in which Camulogenus fell. *See* Alesia.

Agincourt *Hundred Years' War*

October 25, 1415, between 25,000 French, under the Constable d'Albret, and about 5,700 English, mostly archers, under King Henry V. The archers protected their front with a palisade of stakes, which broke the charge of the French men-at-arms, and the French army was routed with a loss of 8,000 slain, including the Constable and the Dukes of Alençon, Brabant and Bar, and 2,000 prisoners, including the Duke of Orleans and Marshal Boucicuaut. The English lost only 400, among whom were the Duke of York and the Earl of Oxford, but instead of marching on Paris, Henry withdrew to Calais. *See* Rouen.

Agnadello *War of the League of Cambrai*

May 14, 1509, between 30,000 French under Louis XII and Marshal Trivulzio, and 35,000 Venetians under General Alviani. The Venetians were defeated with a loss of 6,000 men and 20 guns, Alviani being taken, and in consequence of his victory, Louis XII occupied all the territory assigned to him by the League, up to the Mincio. *See* Garigliano.

Agordat *Italian Sudan Campaigns*

December 21, 1893, between 2,200 Italians, and local troops, under General Arimondi, and

11,500 Mahdists under Ahmed Ali, who had invaded Italian territory. The Mahdists were routed with a loss of about 3,000 men. The Italians lost 13, and 225 tribesmen killed and wounded. *See* Aduwa.

Agra I *Farrukhsiyar's Rebellion*

1713, between Jahandar Shah, with 70,000 troops, under Zulfikar Khan, and the rebels under Jahandar's nephew, Farrukhsiyar. After a stubborn fight, the rebels overpowered the Imperial troops, and Jahandar Shah was captured and put to death by Farrukhsiyar, who ascended the throne, to be executed by his brothers in 1719.

Agra II *Second British-Maratha War*

The fortress was besieged October 4, 1803, by the British under General Lake, and was defended by a garrison of Sindhia's troops, 6,000 strong, who held the citadel, while seven additional battalions were encamped in the town. The latter force was attacked on the 10th and routed, losing 26 guns, while the survivors, 2,600 in number, surrendered on the following day. On the 17th the batteries opened fire on the citadel, and on the 18th the garrison surrendered. *See* Aligarh, Delhi III.

Agra III *Indian Mutiny*

On August 2, 1857, the British garrison holding Agra sallied out to attack a body of 10,000 rebels encamped within four miles of the city. The Kotah contingent, which formed a portion of the British force, deserted to the rebels, and the British troops, hard pressed and short of ammunition, were driven back into Agra, and forced to take refuge in the fort. In October of the same year Colonel Greathed's column of four battalions and two cavalry regiments encountered close to Agra a force of 7,000 rebels. The rebels at first held their own, but were eventually put to flight. *See* Delhi V, Cawnpore I.

Ahmadabad *First British-Maratha War*

This strong fortress, garrisoned by 8,000 Arabs and Sind Infantry, and 2,000 Marathas, was taken by assault by a British force under General Goddard, February 15, 1780. The British lost 106 killed and wounded. *See* Agra II, Aras, Bassein, Gwalior.

12

Ahmadnagar *Mughal Invasion of the Deccan*

Besieged in 1593 by the Mughals under Mirza Khan, one of Akbar's generals, and defended by a garrison of Deccanis under Chand Bibi, ex-Queen of Bijapur. A practicable breach having been effected, the garrison was disposed to surrender, but Chand Bibi, heading the defenders, superintended the repair of the breach, and succeeded in holding out until a peace was signed in 1596 by which Akbar Khan agreed to leave Ahmadnagar unmolested. In 1600, on the death of Chand Bibi, Akbar took Ahmadnagar.

Ahmed Khel *Second British-Afghan War*

1880, when a British force under General Stewart on the march to Ghazni was attacked by about 15,000 Ghilzis. A rush of 3,000 Ghazis (religious fanatics) was successfully repulsed, and the enemy defeated and driven off, leaving 1,000 dead on the field. The British lost 17. *See* Maiwand.

Aiguillon *Hundred Years' War*

This fortress was besieged by the French under John, Duke of Normandy, in May, 1347, and was defended by a small English garrison under Sir Walter Manny, who held out till the end of August, repelling numerous assaults. The defeat of Crécy then forced the Duke of Normandy to lead his army northward, and he was compelled to raise the siege. *See* Crécy.

Aisne I *World War I*

September 13, 1914. Having in September 1914 lost the first battle of the Marne, the German armies retreated to a strong position on the crest of the high plateau north of the Aisne. Under the supreme command of General von Falkenhayn, General von Kluck led the 1st, General von Heeringen the 7th and General von Bülow the 2nd Armies, from west to east. General Joffre, commanding the Allied armies, unaware of the German change from a war of movement to trench warfare, decided on a frontal assault and attacked with the allied left-wing armies made up of the 6th, General Maunoury; the British Expeditionary Force, General Sir John French; and the 5th, General Franchet d'Esperey.

Under heavy fire they mostly crossed the Aisne over pontoon bridges on September 13, and next day assaulted the strong German positions on the plateau above them, making considerable gains. Violent German counter-attacks next day, helped by an artillery barrage from prepared positions, forced Maunoury's 6th Army back to within a few hundred yards of its starting place on the Aisne. Allied counter-attacks again took them forward, but soon the battle resolved itself into an artillery duel. August 18, when the Allies were hard pressed at Reims and beating in vain against the whole German line, marked the end of the battle, for Joffre and his generals had learned the uselessness of a frontal assault by infantry without strong artillery bombardment. The Aisne battle marked the transition from a war of movement in World War I to stabilized trench warfare. *See* Marne I, Ypres I.

Aisne II *World War I*

April 16, 1917, when General Nivelle, C-in-C the Western Front, attacked on a 50-mile front along the River Aisne between Soissons and the River Suippe, in Champagne, with the French 5th and 6th armies, hoping to break through to Laon. Entrenched in fortified positions on the northern slopes of the Aisne, gunners of the German 1st and 7th armies knocked out about 150 French tanks, stopped the offensive after small gains, and counter-attacked next day. Reinforced by the 10th army, the French could still make no progress against the unyielding German defence, a month's fighting failed to give them their first day's objectives, and the battle petered out. Pétain had succeeded Nivelle as C-in-C on April 28. Casualties of 100,000 upwards caused defeatism and mutiny, 23,385 men being found guilty, 55 shot. Marshal Joffre was sent to the US to enlighten the President and had it not been for American intervention France might well have negotiated a compromise peace with Germany. *See* Arras II, Messines.

Aisne III *World War I*

May 27, 1918, when General von Ludendorff, after one of the war's heaviest bombardments, attacked with 41 divisions of the 1st and 7th armies along the Soissons to Reims front, thinly held by four British and four French divisions. The British held their sector, but the French, driven back behind the Aisne, obliged them to withdraw behind it. By May 29, the Germans had taken Soissons, soon reaching the Marne between Château-Thierry and Dormans. During three days they had advanced 10 miles a day, taking 40,000 prisoners. American troops, rushed in as reserves, captured the critical point of Cantigny, the British recaptured Bligny, south-west of Rheims, and also drove the Germans back south-west of Château-Thierry. The American 2nd Division then recaptured Belleau Wood. The German 35-mile advance ended on June 6. They took 55,000 prisoners and 450 guns. Casualties on both sides were heavy. *See* Lys River.

Aix, Île d' *Seven Years' War*

March 4, 1758, when a British squadron of seven sail, under Sir Edward Hawke, attacked a French squadron of five ships of the line and six frigates, convoying forty transports, and drove them ashore on the Île d'Aix. This delayed the French expedition to North America, and facilitated the capture of Cape Breton. *See* Quiberon Bay.

Aix-la-Chapelle *French Revolutionary Wars*

March 3, 1795, between the French under General Miranda and the Austrians under the Prince of Saxe-Coburg. The French were totally defeated, and fled in disorder, with a loss of 3,500 killed and wounded and 1,500 prisoners. *See* Fleurus III, Montenotte.

Aiznadin *Muslim Invasion of Syria*

July 30, 634, between 45,000 Muslims under Khaled and 70,000 Imperial troops under Werdan. The Imperialists were routed with great slaughter, leaving Khaled to prosecute the siege of Damascus. The Muslims admitted a loss of only 470. *See* Damascus I.

Aladja Dagh *Russo-Turkish War*

1877, between the Russians under General Loris-Melikov, and the Turks under Mukhtar Pasha. The Russians were victorious, and

Mukhtar was compelled to take refuge under the walls of Erzeroum. *See* Plevna, Kars.

Alam el Halfa *World War II*

August 30, 1942, when General Rommel's *Afrika Korps*, after its advance across Cyrenaica, made a desperate attempt, 17 days after General Montgomery's taking over command of the British 8th Army, to break through the so-called Alamein Line to Cairo. Forewarned by RAF reconnaissance, the British laid deep and intricate mine fields, set up strong artillery positions and, aided by aerial bombing, stopped the attack by Rommel's three armoured divisions in a four-day battle. Rommel then acknowledged defeat and withdrew to a defensive position. The British lost 1,750 men in this important battle and the Germans considerably more. *See* El Alamein I, II.

Alamo, Storming of the *Texan Rising*

On February 22, 1836, General Santa Anna, with the advance guard of the Mexican army, appeared before the walls of the Alamo, a fortified mission station held by 145 Texans under Colonel Travis, who replied to a summons to surrender by a cannon shot. On March 1 the garrison was reinforced by 30 men, Santa Anna's force at this date being 3,000. On the 6th, 2,500 Mexicans assaulted the fort, and at the third attempt effected an entrance. The building was defended room by room, the church within the enclosure being the last building captured, when all the survivors were put to the sword. The victory cost the Mexicans 400 killed and many wounded. 'Remember the Alamo' became the watchword of the Texans. Texas proclaimed its independence on March 2 at Washington.

Aland *Great Northern War*

July, 1714, between the Russian fleet of 30 ships of the line and 180 galleys under Admiral Apraxin, and the Swedish, about one-third of that strength, under Admiral Erinschild. The Swedes sought to prevent the landing of a Russian force on the island of Aland, and fought an unequal combat for three hours, when they were overpowered and forced to retire. The Czar, Peter the Great, who was serving under Apraxin as Rear-Admiral, captured Erinschild's flagship. *See* Stralsund II.

Alarcos *Spanish-Muslim Wars*

July 19, 1195, between the Moors under Yakub el Mansur, and the Spaniards under Alfonso VIII of Castile. The Spaniards were utterly routed, and very few escaped to Calatrava. The Moors claimed to have taken 30,000 prisoners. *See* Ucles.

Albania *Italian Fascist Invasion*

April 7, 1939, Mussolini's navy shelled coastal towns, landed troops and quickly occupied the entire country, whose armed forces were ill-equipped to resist. This seizure of a small primitive state was one of the events which, indirectly, led to Britain's re-arming and eventual declaration of war against Germany. *See* The Balkans.

Albuera *Peninsular War*

May 16, 1811, between the allied British, Portuguese and Spanish forces, plus a small number of German infantry, 35,000 men altogether, under the command of General (later Lord) Sir William Carr Beresford, and 25,000 French under Marshal Soult. Wellington was absent, having fought the battle of Fuentes de Onoro 11 days before. Beresford, a brave but not very skilful commander, was moving cautiously towards Badajoz, when 15 miles south-east of it Marshal Soult's forces attacked his position on the ridge of Albuera. The Spanish and Portuguese forces fled and defeat was only averted by the steadiness of the British, especially of the Fusiliers, who came into action when the day seemed lost, and drove the French from the field, at great cost to themselves. Of the 7,640 British, 3,930 were killed or wounded. The French lost over 8,000, including five generals. Wellington first re-organized his army, then until the end of the year established a distant blockade of Marshal Marmont's base at Ciudad Rodrigo before laying siege to it.

Alcántara I *Spanish Conquest of Portugal*

In 1580 Philip II of Spain sent the Duke of Alva with an army into Portugal to support his claim to the throne after the death without an heir of Portugal's King Henry. At Alcántara on the Tagus, on August 25, the Spanish routed a disorganized force of citizens and peasants led by a rival claimant, Dom Antonio, and seized Lisbon. Portugal was from then on, until 1640, ruled from Madrid.

Alcántara II *War of the Spanish Succession*

1706, when a force of British and Portuguese under Lord Galway attacked and drove out of Alcántara the garrison, consisting of a portion of Marshal Berwick's army. Ten French battalions laid down their arms, and 60 guns were captured. *See* Ramillies.

Alcolea *Isabel II of Spain Deposed*

September 28, 1868, when Francisco Serrano's revolutionary forces rising against Queen Isabel's oppressive rule, defeated the royal army at Alcolea, on the Guadalquivir. Isabel fled to France and a provisional government ruled until Amadeo I came to the throne in 1871.

Aleppo I *Muslim Invasion of Syria*

This city was besieged by the Muslims under Abu Obeidah and Khaled-ibn-al-Walid in 638, and it almost immediately surrendered, but the garrison retired to the citadel, where under Youkinna it maintained a stubborn defence for five months, and caused heavy loss to the besiegers. At last the citadel was taken by surprise and Youkinna became a convert to Mohammedanism. This was the last serious resistance offered in Syria to the invading Muslims. *See* Aiznadin, Muta, Damascus I.

Aleppo II *Tatar Invasion of Syria*

November 11, 1400, between the Tatars under Tamerlane, and the Turks under the Syrian Emirs. Instead of standing a siege, the Emirs sallied out to meet Tamerlane in the open field, and suffered a disastrous defeat. They were driven back to Aleppo with the loss of many thousands, and a few days later the Tatars sacked the city and captured the citadel. *See* Damascus II.

Aleppo III *Ottoman Wars*

1516, between the Turks under Selim I, and the Egyptians under the Mameluke Sultan,

Tooman Bey. After a bloody battle, the Egyptians were utterly routed, Selim added the whole of Syria to the Ottoman dominions and advanced on Egypt. *See* Cairo.

Alesia *Gallic War*

Siege was laid to the town by the Romans under Caesar, 52 BC, and it was defended by the Gauls, numbering 80,000 infantry and 15,000 cavalry under Vercingetorix, the Romans being about 50,000 strong. An attempt was made by the Belgi, with an even bigger army, to relieve the town, but they were met and routed by Labienus with terrific slaughter. This disaster so discouraged the garrison that the town immediately surrendered, Vercingetorix being sent a prisoner to Rome, where five years later he was beheaded as a rebellious subject. The Roman conquest of Gaul was now complete. *See* Agendicum.

Alessandria *French Revolutionary Wars*

June 18, 1799, between the French, 14,000 strong under General Moreau, and the Imperialists under General Bellegarde. The French gained a signal victory, the loss of the Imperialists being 1,500 men and five guns. *See* Acre III.

Aleutian Islands *World War II*

June 3, 1943, Japanese carrier-borne bombers made a diversionary attack on Dutch Harbour, the US air and naval base in the Aleutian island of Unalaska, and three days later Japanese troops seized the islands of Kiska and Attu. On May 11, 1943, the US 7th Infantry Division under General Brown landed in three places and after fighting in bitter cold finally defeated the enemy on May 30, losing 552 killed and 1,140 wounded. Only 28 Japanese were captured, 2,350 being killed or taking their own lives. When on August 15, a force of 29,000 US troops and 5,300 Canadians landed on Kiska, they found the Japanese had secretly abandoned it, three days earlier. *See* Midway, Solomon Islands, Tarawa-Makin.

Alexandria I *Muslim Invasion of Egypt*

This city, the capital of Egypt, was besieged by the Muslims, under Amrou, in 642, and after a defence of fourteen months, in the course of which the besiegers lost 23,000 men, surrendered, leaving the victors undisputed master of Egypt. *See* Tripoli.

Alexandria II *British Invasion of Egypt*

March 21, 1801, between the French under General Menou, and the British expeditionary force of 14,000 under General Sir Ralph Abercromby. The French cavalry charged the British right, but were repulsed, and after hard fighting the French were defeated and driven under the walls of Alexandria. Among those who fell was Abercromby, mortally wounded. Egypt was given back to the rule of Selim III, the Turkish sultan. *See* Abukir, Hohenlinden.

Alexandria III *Egyptian Revolt*

In 1881 Colonel Arabi Pasha organized a revolt against England and France, who controlled the Suez Canal and administered Egypt's finances. Arabi Pasha having refused to cease work upon the forts of Alexandria, Admiral Sir Beauchamp Seymour, who had under his command a fleet of eight battleships and five gunboats, decided to shell them. France refused to co-operate. The British opened fire on the morning of July 11, 1882, and the bombardment continued till the evening of the 12th, when the forts were totally destroyed and the garrison abandoned the city. *See* Tel-el-Kebir, Kassassin.

Alford *English Civil War*

July 2, 1645, between the Royalists under the Marquis of Montrose, and the Covenanters under General Baillie. Baillie crossed the Don to attack Montrose, whom he imagined to be in retreat, but who was really waiting for him in a well-chosen position. The attack was repulsed, the Covenanters being routed with heavy loss. *See* Naseby.

Algeçiras Bay *French Revolutionary Wars*

July 8, 1801, between a British squadron of seven ships of the line, one frigate and one brig, under Admiral Sir James Saumarez, and a French squadron of three line-of-battle ships and one frigate, under Admiral Linois. The French were aided by the Spanish gunboats and the shore batteries, and Saumarez lost the *Hannibal*, which ran ashore, and was captured by the French. The British lost 121 killed and 240 wounded, the French 306 killed. On July 12, the French squadron, which had been reinforced meanwhile by five Spanish ships of the line, was again attacked by Saumarez, who succeeded in capturing the *St Antoine* and blowing up the *Hermenegilda*. The British lost 17 killed and 100 wounded; the allies, 2,000, chiefly in the *Hermenegilda*. *See* Alexandria II

Alghero *Aragonese Conquest of Sardinia*

1353, between the Aragonese under Pedro IV (the Great) and the Genoese. Pedro won a complete victory, driving the Genoese out of the island of Sardinia, the whole of which island became an appanage of the Crown of Aragon for nearly 400 years.

Algiers I *Spanish-Algerine War*

This city was attacked July 8, 1775, by a Spanish force of 51 ships of war and 26,000 men under Don Pedro de Castijon and Count O'Reilly. After a severe conflict, the Spaniards failed to dislodge their opponents, and retired, with a loss of over 3,000 killed and wounded. The Algerines lost about 5,000.

Algiers II, Bombardment of

In 1816 Lord Exmouth, in command of 19 British warships, and accompanied by six Dutch ships under Admiral Van Capellan, bombarded the forts of Algiers, mounting 500 guns. The bombardment lasted for about eight hours, and resulted in the destruction of the forts and a large part of the city. The Bey then gave way, and agreed to the total abolition of Christian slavery in his dominions. The losses of the allies amounted to 885 killed and wounded; that of the Algerines to over 6,000.

Alhama *Spanish-Muslim Wars*

This fortress, one of the ring of strong places protecting the Moorish capital, Granada, was surprised by a small party of Spaniards, under Juan de Ortiga, in the early morning of February 28, 1482. They scaled the ramparts unperceived, and opened the gates to the Spanish army. The garrison continued to defend the streets obstinately, and it was only after hard fighting that the Spaniards mastered the town. An attempt was made to recapture the place by Abul Hasan, King of Granada, who set down before it with 50,000 Moors on March 5, 1482. The garrison, under the Marquis of Cadiz, made a gallant defence, and on the 29th, Abul Hasan, alarmed by the approach of a strong relieving army under Ferdinand, raised the siege. *See* Loja.

Alhandega *Spanish-Muslim Wars*

In 939, between the Moors under Abd al Rahman, and the Christians under Ramiro II of León. The Moors, 100,000 strong, were besieging Zamora, when they were attacked by Ramiro, who, aided by a sortie of the garrison, utterly routed them. In the battle 20,000 Moors fell, and 40,000 are said to have drowned in the moat surrounding the city. *See* Zamora.

Alicante *War of the Spanish Succession*

On June 29, 1706, Alicante was taken by a British squadron of five ships under Admiral Sir George Byng. The fleet attacked the city walls, while the suburbs were occupied by a landing party of marines under Sir John Jennings. The place was captured with a loss to the British of 30 killed and 80 wounded. *See* Barcelona.

Aligarh *First British-Maratha War*

This fortress, the arsenal of Sindhia of Gwalior, near Agra, was captured August 29, 1803, by the 76th Highlanders under Colonel Monson, forming part of General Lake's army. The place was strongly fortified and surrounded by a ditch 100 feet wide, containing 10 feet of water. The Highlanders carried the fortress by storm, blowing in the main gate, and fighting their way from room to room till it was captured. Two hundred and eighty-one guns were taken. The British loss amounted to 223 killed and wounded. *See* Agra, Delhi, Bassein, Gwalior.

Aliwal *First British-Sikh War*

January 28, 1846, between General Sir Harry Smith's 12,000-strong British-Indian force, and 20,000 Sikh troops under Runjur Singh, entrenched between the Punjab villages of Aliwal and Bhundri, with the river Sutlej a mile behind. Smith's infantry drove the Sikhs out of Aliwal, then despite counter-attacks, rolled up their line, with strong cavalry and artillery support, and drove the enemy pell-mell into the river. The British took 67 guns, lost 564 killed and wounded. 3,000 Sikhs were killed, or missing. *See* Sobraon, Ferozeshah, Chilianwala, Multan, Gujerat.

Aljubarotta *Spanish-Portuguese Wars*

August 14, 1385, between the 30,000 Castilians, under King John I, in support of the claim of Beatrix of Castile to the throne of Portugal, and the 6,880 Portuguese under the Regent John. The Portuguese inflicted a crushing defeat upon the Spaniards, and John I was compelled to withdraw his troops, and renounce his sister's claim.

Alkmaar I *Netherlands War of Independence*

Siege was laid to this town August 21, 1573, by 16,000 Spaniards under Don Federico de Toledo. It was defended by a garrison of 800 soldiers and 1,300 armed burghers. On September 18, an assault was delivered, which was repulsed, with a loss to the besiegers of 1,000 men, while only 37 of the garrison fell. The opening of the dykes at last rendered the position of the Spaniards most precarious, and on October 8 the siege was raised. *See* Haarlem, Leyden.

Alkmaar II *French Revolutionary Wars*

October 2, 1799, between 30,000 British and Russians under the Duke of York and the French, in about equal strength, under General Brune. The action began by the Russians driving in the French advanced posts. Meanwhile, the Duke of York had outflanked them, and as soon as he was in position a simultaneous attack on the French left and centre forced Brune to abandon the key of his position, Alkmaar, which was at once occupied by the allies. *See* Zürich, Stockach.

Allia, The *First Invasion of the Gauls*

July 18, 390 BC, between the Romans, 40,000 strong, under Quintus Sulpicius, and the Gauls, about equal in numbers, under Brennus. The Romans took post on the Allia to check the advance of the Gauls on Rome. Here they were attacked by Brennus, who routed the right wing, where the younger soldiers were posted, then broke the Roman centre and left, putting them to flight with enormous loss and going on to sack Rome. *See* Veii.

Alma *Crimean War*

September 20, 1854, between the Russians, 40,000-strong, under General Prince Aleksandr Mentschikov, and the allied British and French armies, commanded by General Lord Raglan and Marshal Jacques St Arnaud, supported by the Turks, altogether 63,000-strong. Following the declaration of war by Great Britain on March 28 and France on March 27, in their new-found *entente*, the allies had landed at Yevpatoria, in Kalamita Bay, intending to attack the Russian naval base at Sevastopol, 60 miles south. General Mentschikov deployed his troops near the Alma river to block the allies, who immediately attacked. The bulk of the hard fighting fell upon the British 2nd and Light Divisions and the Guards, who carried the heights held by the Russians at the point of the bayonet and routed them.
The Russians lost 1,800 killed and 4,700 prisoners, many of them wounded. The British lost 365 killed, 1,650 wounded, the French 63 killed, 560 wounded. Marshal St Arnaud died of cholera after the battle and was succeeded by General Canrobert. The road to Sevastopol was now open and an attack could not have been resisted, but instead the allies made a leisurely advance round to the south of the city where they established camp. Meanwhile, General Count Totleben fortified the city strongly. *See* Sevastopol, Balaclava.

Almansa *War of the Spanish Succession*

April 25, 1707, between the French under Marshal Berwick (the natural son of James II of England and the Duke of Marlborough's sister Arabella), and the British and Portuguese under Lord Galway and the Marqués das Minas. Galway, though inferior in cavalry, attacked at first with success, but the Portuguese on the right broke and fled, and the British centre, attacked in front and flank simultaneously, was routed by Berwick and forced to surrender. As a consequence of this defeat, the whole of Spain was lost to Archduke Charles of Austria with the exception of Catalonia. *See* Barcelona, Stollhoffen, Almenara.

Almenara *War of the Spanish Succession*

July 10, 1710, when the British contingent of the Archduke Charles' army, under General Stanhope, attacked and defeated the Spaniards under Philip V, after severe fighting. So complete was the rout that Philip's army was only saved by the fall of night from complete destruction. *See* Brihuega, Denain.

Almorah *British-Gurkha War*

April 25, 1815, when 2,000 British regulars under Colonel Nicolls and a force of irregular troops under Colonel Gardiner assaulted and captured the heights of the town of Almorah. The result of this victory was the surrender of the province of Humaon and all its fortresses. *See* Jitgurh, Mukwanpur, Kalunga.

Alnwick *Anglo-Scottish Wars*

November 13, 1093, between the Scots under Malcolm Canmore and the English. The Scots were totally defeated, and Malcolm and his eldest son Edward slain in the battle.

Alresford *English Civil War*

March 29, 1644, between the Royalists under the Earl of Brentford and General Sir Ralph Hopton, and the Parliamentarians under General Sir William Waller. The Parliament forces were victorious, but their losses were so severe that Waller was unable to follow up his advantage, and the Royalists made an orderly retreat.

Alsen *Schleswig-Holstein War*

This island, in which the Danish garrison of Düppel had taken refuge, was captured by the Prussians, who crossed from the mainland in boats on the night of June 29, 1864, and under a heavy fire carried the Danish entrenchments, and compelled them to surrender. This was the last engagement of the war. *See* Düppel.

Altendorf *Thirty Years' War*

August 24, 1632, between King Gustavus II of Sweden, with 40,000 Swedes and Germans, and the Imperialists, of about equal numbers, under General von Wallenstein. Wallenstein was very strongly posted on the hill and in the ruined castle of the Altenwald, and after a day spent in fruitless assaults, the King was forced to retire, having lost about 2,300 in killed and wounded. The defenders admitted a loss of 70 officers and 2,000 men killed, besides wounded and prisoners. *See* Lützen.

Alto Pascio *Guelfs and Ghibellines*

1325, between the Ghibellines under Castruccio Castracane of Lucca, and the Florentine Guelfs. The Florentines were defeated with heavy loss, among the trophies taken by Castracane being the *carroccio* of Florence. *See* Corte Nuova, Monte Aperto, Campaldino.

Amakusa *Revolt of the Christians in Japan*

February 28, 1638, the castle of Hara, on the island of Amakusa, held by 30,000 Christian rebels under Masada Shiro, was captured after very hard fighting by 125,000 troops of the Shogun, Yoshimune, under Matsudaira Idzu-no-Kami. The defenders set fire to the castle, and perished to the last man, either in the flames or by the sword. Until 1873 Japan forbad Christianity under pain of death.

Amalinde *Kaffir Wars*

1818, between the Gaikas and the forces of Ndlambi, in which the former were utterly routed. *See* Amatola Mountain.

Amatola Mountain *Kaffir Wars*

1846, between the Kaffirs under Sandilli, and

the British and Cape troops under Colonels Campbell and Somerset. Sandilli was totally defeated, but, rallying his forces, he made a successful attack on the British baggage train, the loss of which forced them to retire. *See* Amalinde.

Ambate *Conquest of Peru*

1532, between the two Peruvian chiefs, Atahualpa and Huascar, in which the latter suffered a complete defeat. *See* Cuzco, Anaquito.

Ambracian Gulf *Corcyrean-Corinthian War*

435 BC, when a Corinthian fleet of 75 ships attempted the relief of Epidamnus, which was besieged by the Corcyreans, and was defeated with heavy loss by 80 Corcyrean triremes.

Ambur I *Carnatic War*

1749, between the army of Anwar-ud-din, Nawab of Arcot, 20,000 strong, and the combined forces of Muzuffer Jung and Chunda Sahib, aided by a French contingent under M. d'Auteil. Anwar-ud-din was defeated and slain, and Muzuffer Jung assumed the title of Subahdar of the Deccan, Chunda Sahib that of Nawab of Arcot. *See* Arcot, Pondicherry.

Ambur II *First British-Mysore War*

This strong fortress was held by a garrison of 500 Sepoys, under Captain Calvert, and a detachment of Mysore troops under Mukhlis Khan, who had assumed the status of an independent chief, but being suspected of intriguing with Hyder Ali, was arrested by Calvert. Hyder laid siege to the place November 10, 1767; but Calvert, now secure from treachery within, held out with his small garrison till December 6, when the approach of a relieving force obliged Hyder to raise the siege. *See* Trincomalee II.

Amida *Roman-Persian Wars*

This fortress, defended by a Roman garrison, was besieged and after a vigorous defence taken by storm by the Persians under Sapor II in 359. The garrison and inhabitants were put to the sword. The siege, which lasted 73 days, cost the Persians 30,000 men, and so

weakened Sapor that he was compelled to relinquish his designs upon the Eastern Empire. *See* Singara.

The fortress was again besieged by the Persians under Kobad in 503, being defended as before by a Roman garrison. After a defence of three months, which cost the besiegers 50,000 men, a weakly defended tower was surprised at night, and on the following day the Persians, headed by their king, scaled the walls, and massacred a reported 80,000 of the garrison and inhabitants. *See* Maogamalcha.

Amiens I *Franco-Prussian War*

November 27, 1870, between the French under General Faure, and the Germans under General von Manteuffel. The French were compelled to abandon the city, having already capitulated at Metz. The French lost 1,383 killed and wounded, and 1,000 missing; the Germans, 76 officers and 1,216 men. *See* Sedan, Metz.

Amiens II *World War I*

August 8, 1918, when Marshal Foch, Allied C-in-C, launched his second offensive of the year against General von Ludendorff's armies, already weakened by the Second Battle of the Marne. Under Britain's Field Marshal Sir Douglas Haig, this attack was intended to force back the German bulge towards Amiens and free the Paris–Amiens railway and the northern coal mines. General Sir John Rawlinson's 4th Army of three Canadian, two Australian, one American and two British divisions with four altogether in support, 400 tanks and three British cavalry divisions, as well as General Daubeny's left wing of the French 1st Army, attacked first on a 14-mile front. Facing them initially were seven German divisions composed of the left of General von der Marwitz's 2nd Army and the right of General von Hutier's 15th Army, with about nine divisions of Prince Rupprecht in reserve. Led by an intense but short artillery barrage, the 4th Army achieved brilliant tactical surprise, penetrated 10 miles into enemy-held country and by 3 pm had taken 6,000 German prisoners and 100 guns, a performance surpassed the next day, when another 24,000 prisoners and 200 guns were taken. On the 10th General Georges Humbert's

French 3rd Army drove the Germans from Montdidier in the south, thus freeing the Paris–Amiens railway for traffic. By August 15, the entire Lassigny *massif* was in Rawlinson's hands; he had direct observation over the enemy's communications throughout the southern front in the region and over the northern plain. The first phase of the Allied offensive, the Battle of Amiens, had ended. The Germans lost some 33,000 prisoners, and more than 40,000 killed and wounded. British and Commonwealth losses were 22,000 and French 24,000. *See* Marne II.

Amoaful *Second British-Ashanti War*

January 31, 1874, when the British expeditionary force under General Sir Garnet Wolseley defeated the Ashantis after a desperate resistance, which cost the British 16 officers and 174 men killed and wounded. The 42nd Regiment, which led the attack, lost nine officers and 105 men. *See* Accra I & II.

Amorium *Muslim Invasion of Asia Minor*

Fought 838, between the Muslims under the Caliph Motassem, and the Greeks under Theophilus. Thirty thousand Persian horsemen, serving under the Emperor, succeeded in breaking the line, but the Greeks themselves were overthrown by the Muslims, and the day ended in a complete rout of the Imperial Army. Motassem then laid siege to Amorium, and after a defence of 55 days, which cost the besiegers 70,000 men, the gates were opened by treachery, and 30,000 Christians were massacred. *See* Mount Taurus.

Amphipolis *Great Peloponnesian War*

March 422 BC, between 1,500 Athenians, with a contingent of allies under Cleon, and the Spartans, 2,000 hoplites, besides light armed troops, under Brasidas. Cleon advanced to attack Amphipolis, but finding the garrison preparing for a sortie, wheeled about and commenced to retreat. He was at once assailed by Brasidas, and his left fled without striking a blow. The Athenian right and centre offered some resistance, but in the end were routed with heavy loss. Both Brasidas and Cleon fell, the latter while fleeing from the field. *See* Cynossema, Syracuse, Delium.

Amstetten *Napoleonic Wars*

November 5, 1805, when the Austrians retiring on Vienna fought a rear-guard action against Marshal Murat's cavalry and a portion of Marshal Lannes' corps, in which they were defeated with a loss of 1,000 killed, wounded, and prisoners. *See* Austerlitz.

An Lao Valley,

see Vietnam War

Anaquito *Conquest of Peru*

January 8, 1546, between the troops of the Viceroy, Blasco Nuñez, and those of Gonzalo Pizarro. Pizarro gained a signal victory, the Viceroy being among the slain, and in consequence the Government of Peru fell into Pizarro's hands. *See* Cuzco, Ambate.

Ancona *Italian Wars of Independence*

This town was attacked, September, 1860, by the Piedmontese fleet of 13 warships under Admiral Persano, and the army of General Cialdini. It was defended by a small Papal garrison under La Moricière, and after a resistance of over a week, at the end of which time Persano forced the boom guarding the harbour, capitulated. *See* Calatafimi.

Ancrum Moor *Anglo-Scottish Wars*

February 17, 1545, between the English under Sir Ralph Evers, and the Scots under the Earl of Angus. The Borderers who had joined the English deserted, with the result that the Scots were victorious.

Ancyrae

Fought 242 BC, between the Syrians under Seleucus Callinicus, and the rebels under his brother Hierax, aided by a large contingent of Gauls. After a desperate struggle, in which Hierax nearly lost his life at the hands of his barbarian auxiliaries, Seleucus was utterly routed.

Angora *Tatar Invasion of Asia Minor*

June 20, 1402, between the Tatars under

Tamerlane, and the Turks under Bajazet I. The numbers engaged were variously estimated at from one to two millions, Tamerlane, it is said, having at least 800,000 men in the field. The Turks were totally defeated, Bajazet and one of his sons being captured, while another son was killed. *See* Baghdad, Nicopolis.

Angostura I *American-Mexican War*

February 21, 1847, between the Mexicans under General Santa Anna and the Americans under General Scott, when the Mexicans were totally defeated. *See* Buena Vista.

Angostura II *Paraguayan War*

December 22 to 27, 1868, between the Paraguayans under Lopez, and the allied armies of the Argentine Republic, Brazil, and Uruguay. Lopez held his position for six days against the greatly superior forces of the allies, but was then compelled to retire, leaving in the hands of the enemy 1,000 prisoners and six guns. *See* Humaita, Curupayti.

Antietam *American Civil War*

September 17, 1862, between the main Confederate army under General Lee, and the Federals under General McClellan. On the morning of the 17th Lee had only 35,000 men on the ground against McClellan's 84,000. The Federals strongly attacked Lee's left, and after a stubborn fight drove it back, but reinforcements arriving, Lee resumed the offensive, and recovered his lost positions. On the following day neither side was disposed to resume the struggle, and the battle was therefore indecisive. The Federals lost 12,460 men; the Confederates 13,700. *See* Bull Run, Fredericksburg, Harper's Ferry.

Antioch I *Syrian Wars*

244 BC, between the Syrians under Seleucus Callinicus and the Egyptians under Ptolemy Energetes. Seleucus was routed and compelled to take refuge within the walls of Antioch. *See* Raphia.

Antioch II *First Crusade*

The city was besieged, October 21, 1097, by the Crusaders under Godefroi de Bouillon, and defended by a Saracen garrison under Baghasian. The siege was unskilfully conducted, and provisions and munitions ran short in the Christian camp, with the result that the place held out till June 3, 1098, when it was taken by stratagem. An indiscriminate massacre followed, in which 10,000 of the defenders perished. On the 28th of the same month the Crusading army was attacked outside Antioch by a force of Saracens under Kirboga. Kirboga concentrated his attack against one wing of the Christians, and outflanked it, but was then assailed by the main body, and driven off with heavy loss. *See* Jerusalem, Ascalon.

Antium *War of Chioggia*

May 30, 1378, when Vittorio Pisano, with 14 Venetian galleys, defeated the Genoese fleet under Fieschi. The Genoese lost six ships, and Fieschi was taken prisoner. *See* Chioggia.

Antwerp I *Netherlands War of Independence*

This city was sacked by the Spaniards, November 4, 1576. It was defended by 6,000 troops, mostly Walloons, who offered little resistance to the 5,600 Spaniards under Sancho d'Avila, who formed the attacking force. Having effected an entrance, the Spaniards proceeded to massacre the inhabitants, of whom 8,000 are said to have died, an event they called the Spanish Fury. *See* Maastricht, Zutphon.

Antwerp II *Liberation of Belgium*

When Holland refused to recognize the London Protocol creating Belgium an independent State, the French laid siege to Antwerp, which was still occupied by the Dutch, in November, 1832. The city, which was defended by General Chassé, held out till December 23, when, the citadel being demolished by French fire, it was forced to capitulate.

Antwerp III *World War I*

In August 1914, the battle of the River Aisne had tended to stabilize the western front. Germany and the Allies both sought to ban each other access to the North Sea by seizing the Belgian coast, especially Antwerp. Germany had occupied Brussels on August 20, and the small 150,000-strong Belgian army fell back north-west to Antwerp, then, in three successive sorties drove the Germans from Malines, re-captured Alost, north-west of Brussels, and struck at Cortenberg, between Brussels and Louvain. The German command answered with atrocities against Belgian civilians, women and children, and with a siege of Antwerp on September 28. Their howitzers knocked out the old forts around Antwerp, and by October 6 the Germans advanced, the civilian population was evacuated, the Belgian army escaped south-west along the coast and the Germans entered Antwerp on October 10, 1914. *See* Ypres I, Aisne I, Namur.

Anzio *World War II*

January 22, 1944, when 50,000 British and American troops (1st British Division, 3rd US Division as spearhead; 5th and 56th British, US 1st Armoured and 45th Infantry, in support) under Major-Gen. Lucas landed at Anzio, 30 miles south of Rome, and 70 miles behind the German lines in Italy, to cut their lines of communication with Rome. Instead of pushing inland with this object, Gen. Lucas dug-in to consolidate his beach-head, 7 miles deep and about 15 long. The German 14th Army under General von Mackensen raced up, attacked the beach head with four divisions and some 450 guns, and successfully contained it. Not until May 23, after Cassino had fallen, did the reinforced VI Corps break out from Anzio. American and British losses were some 7,000 killed, wounded and missing. *See* Gustav-Cassino Line, Gothic Line.

Aong *Indian Mutiny*

July 15, 1857, between the British relieving force under General Sir Henry Havelock and the mutineers who were opposing their advance on Cawnpore. The rebels were defeated and driven from their entrenchments. *See* Delhi, Cawnpore I.

Appomattox River *American Civil War*

April 9, 1865, when General John Gordon's 1,600 infantry of General Robert E. Lee's

exhausted Confederate Army of Northern Virginia, about 30,000 strong, attacked the combined Federal forces of General Charles Griffin's V Corps, General Philip Sheridan's cavalry corps and General Edward Ord's Army of the James, which at Appomattox Station blocked his desperate attempt to retreat to Lynchburg. Lee's last attack was defeated by the far stronger Federal forces and at 4 pm on this historic day he surrendered at Appomattox Court House to General Ulysses S. Grant, the Federal commander. When on April 18, in North Carolina, General Joseph Johnston's Confederate army surrendered and on May 26 General Edmund Kirby Smith's forces laid down their arms at Shreveport, the American Civil War, which had raged since 1861, was at an end. *See* Five Forks.

Aquae Sextiae *Cimbric War*

102 BC, when the Teutones under the king, Teutobod, were totally routed by the Romans under Marius. *See* Arausio.

Aquidaban *Paraguayan War*

The last stand of the Paraguayans against the allied armies of the Argentine Republic, Brazil, and Uruguay, May 1, 1870. Lopez, with a small force of Paraguayans and 5,000 Indians, met the attack of the allies under General Camera on the banks of the Aquidaban, and after a bloody engagement, in which he and the Vice President Sanchez fell, his army was cut to pieces, and the war ended. During the war the population of Paraguay was reduced from 1,500,000 to 221,000, of whom only 29,000 were males over fifteen years of age. *See* Parana.

Aquileia *Roman Civil Wars*

September 5 and 6, 394, between Theodosius, Emperor of the East, and Eugenius, the usurping Emperor of the West, whose army was commanded by Arbogastes. The first day's fighting went against Theodosius, who was saved only by darkness from a severe reverse, but during the night a force sent by Arbogastes to secure the passes in Theodosius' rear, deserted to his standard, and thus reinforced and aided by a dust storm which blew in the faces of his antagonists and disordered their ranks, he on the following day gained a signal victory. *See* Pollentia.

Aras *First British-Maratha War*

May 18, 1775, between Raghunath Rao, the claimant to the Peshwaship, with 20,000 Marathas, and 2,500 British troops under Colonel Keating; and the army of the Maratha chieftains, 25,000 strong under Hari Pant Phunhay. Raghunath's undisciplined levies fled, and threw the British line into confusion; but the troops rallied, and after hard fighting repulsed the Marathas with heavy loss. The British lost 222, including 11 officers. *See* Bassein, Gwalior.

Arausio *Fourth Gallic Invasion*

105 BC, when the Gauls under Boiorix totally routed two consular armies under Caepio and Cn. Mallius Maximus. It was said that 80,000 Romans fell. *See* Aquae Sextiae.

Arbela *Alexander's Asiatic Campaigns*

October 1, 331 BC, between 47,000 Macedonians under Alexander the Great, and the Persian army, three or four times as numerous, under Darius Codomannus. Alexander, who led the Macedonian right wing, forced a passage between the Persian left and centre, and attacked the centre on the flank. After a stubborn resistance, and though meanwhile the Macedonian left had been hard pressed, the Persians gave way, and Darius taking to flight, the whole army fled in confusion, and was routed with enormous loss, especially at the passage of the Lycas, which barred their retreat. This victory made Alexander master of Asia. *See* Gaza, Hydaspes.

Arcis-sur-Aube *Napoleonic Wars*

March 20, 1814, between 23,000 French under Napoleon, and 60,000 allies under Prince Schwartzenberg. The French made a gallant stand against superior numbers, and in the end effected an orderly retreat, with a loss of about 2,000. The allies, whose losses were considerably heavier, now marched on Paris. *See* Paris, Laon, Reims.

Arcola *French Revolutionary Wars*

November 15, 16 and 17, 1796, between the main Austrian army under General Alvinzi, 20,000 strong, and 18,000 French under

Napoleon. Napoleon's object was to drive back Alvinzi before he could effect a junction with General Baron Davidovich, who was descending from the Tirol. The village of Arcola was occupied on the 15th, after severe fighting, in which Napoleon was in great personal danger on the bridge, but it was evacuated during the night. On the 16th Napoleon again attacked the village, but the Austrians held their ground. On the 17th he turned the position, and Davidovich still remaining inactive, Alvinzi was driven back, with losses variously estimated at from 6,000 to 18,000. The French also lost heavily. *See* Caldiero, Mantua.

Arcot *Carnatic War*

This fortress was captured by Ensign Robert Clive (Lord Clive), with a force of 200 Europeans and 300 Sepoys, in August, 1751. The garrison, 1,100 strong, offered no resistance, but marched out on Clive's approach. In the course of the autumn Arcot was beleaguered by an army of 10,000 Indians and 150 French under Chunda Sahib, the French nominee for the Nawabship of Arcot. Against this overwhelming force, Clive, whose garrison had been reduced by sickness to 120 Europeans, and less than 200 Sepoys, held out for seven weeks, till the approach of a Maratha army forced Chunda Sahib to raise the siege. The garrison had 45 Europeans and 30 Sepoys killed. French advance in India was checked. *See* Madras, Calcutta, Ambur.

Ardennes I *World War I*

One of four great interlocking battles between France and Germany during the first month of the war, the other three being Lorraine, Charleroi and Mons. As part of Plan 17, France's General Joffre launched General Ruffey's 3rd Army and General de Langle de Cary's 4th Army into the wooded Ardennes centre of the battle front. On August 21, 1914, in a dense early morning mist, the French first clashed with Crown Prince Friedrich Wilhelm's 5th and Duke Albrecht of Württemberg's 4th German Armies. After two days of bitter fighting Ruffey withdrew his force back across the Meuse and thence to the fortified region around Verdun, for which he was swiftly demoted. De Langle de Cary's 4th Army, having first punched back the Germans between Stenay and Sedan

24

withdrew to the Upper Marne. *See* Battle of the Frontiers.

Ardennes II *World War II*

On December 16, 1944, when, on Hitler's personal orders, the newly created German reserve armies of 250,000 men and 1,100 tanks of Field Marshal Model's Army Group B were flung into a desperate winter offensive with the aim of retaking the Allied supply bases of Liège and Antwerp, and splitting their armies in the north from those in central France. General Sepp Dietrich's 6th Panzer Army, with von Manteuffel's 5th Panzer on the left and General Brandenberger's 7th on the right, a total of 20 divisions, in a surprise attack of great violence on a 50-mile front from Monschau to Echternach, forced General Courtney Hodges' US 1st Army back in disarray and advanced west towards the Ardennes.

But farther north, near Malmedy, General Leonard Gerow's US 5th Corps after falling back, stopped the enemy advance towards Liège after three days' hard fighting. Von Manteuffel's 5th Panzer had meantime shattered US General Troy Middleton's 8th Corps, which was stretched over a long front, two panzer corps breaking through the US 28th Division and advancing west to reach Houffalize and Bastogne on December 20. The US 101st Airborne Division was brought forward to help General McAuliffe hold this vital road junction, which German infantry surrounded, while the panzer units drove on to the west and north-west towards the river Meuse. On the south of the front, near Echternach, General Brandenberger's 7th Army was stopped, after some progress, by the US 4th Infantry and 9th Armoured Division.

The German advance towards the west had by now split the US 1st and 9th Armies north of the salient from their 12th US Army Group Headquarters, and to overcome communication problems, Field Marshal Montgomery, in command of British 21st Army Group, was now also given command of these two US armies. At the same time General Patton's 3rd Army advanced north to attack the southern flank of the German salient with the special purpose of relieving the hard-pressed road junction of Bastogne. Meantime, General von Manteuffel's spearhead had advanced far west and on December 24

clashed with the British 29 Armoured Brigade and the US 2nd Armoured Division in the region of Dinant and Celles, only four miles from the Meuse. Here their advance was stopped. By December 25 Allied units had blocked all routes to the River Meuse. The next day Bastogne was relieved. Better weather near the end of December enabled some 5,000 Allied aircraft to smash the German road convoys stretched bumper to bumper to their frontier and thus isolate the enemy battlefront units.

The Allied counter-attack began on January 3, when Montgomery attacked with the US 7th Corps (General Collins) and the next day with the British 30th Corps (General Brian Horrocks) in the north. The enemy now tried a new offensive in the south-west, but dogged American defence of Bastogne and its road network became the stumbling block and faced with failure Model began a stubborn retreat. British 6th Airborne Division patrols linked up with those of the 3rd US Army at St Hubert on January 11 and by January 16 the 1st and 3rd US Armies made contact and at Houffalize, thus reducing the salient to a mere bulge.

The battle finally ended on January 28, at a cost to the Allies of 76,900 killed and wounded and to the Germans of 70,000 killed and wounded, 50,000 prisoners and about 600 tanks and 1,600 aircraft. It had delayed the Allied Rhineland offensive six weeks, but at very great cost to the reserves Field Marshal Model had built up to try to meet the Russian spring offensive. *See* Rhineland, Ukraine.

Argaon *Second British-Maratha War*

November 28, 1803, between the British under General Lord Wellesley (later the Duke of Wellington) and the forces of the Rajah of Berar, under Sindhia of Gwalior. Three of Wellesley's battalions, which had previously fought well, on this occasion broke and fled, and the situation was at one time very serious. Wellesley, however, succeeded in rallying them, and in the end defeated the Marathas, with the loss of all their guns and baggage. The British lost 346 killed and wounded. This victory ended the Second Maratha War and increased the territory of British India. *See* Assaye, Laswari.

Argentaria *Invasion of the Alemanni*

May 378, between the Romans under Gratianus and the Alemanni under Priarius. The Alemanni were overwhelmed by the Roman legionaries, though they stood their ground bravely, and only 5,000 escaped from the field. Priarius was slain. *See* Argentoratum.

Argentoratum *Invasion of the Alemanni*

August, 357, between 13,000 Romans under Julian, and a vastly superior army of Alemanni under Chnodomar. The Romans attacked the German lines shortly before nightfall, after a long march, and though the right wing, under Julian, was at first driven in, they were rallied by their general, and the left and centre pressing on, the Alemanni were totally routed, with a loss of 6,000, in addition to those who fell in the fight. The Romans lost four tribunes and 243 soldiers only. Chnodomar was taken prisoner. *See* Amida, Châlons.

Arginusae *Great Peloponnesian War*

406 BC, between 150 Athenian triremes under Thrasyllus and other generals, and 120 Peloponnesian ships under Callicratidas. The Peloponnesians were routed, with a loss of 70 vessels, sunk or taken, and Callicratidas slain. The Athenians lost 25 ships with their crews, and the generals were brought to trial for not having taken proper steps to rescue the men of the disabled ships. They were convicted, and six of them, including Thrasyllus, executed. This victory temporarily restored to Athens the command of the sea. *See* Cyzicus, Ægospotami.

Argos *Roman Invasion of Greece*

195 BC, between Nabis of Sparta, with 15,000 men, and 50,000 Romans and Macedonians under Flaminius. Nabis was totally defeated, and though allowed to retain Sparta, was compelled to restore to the Archaean League all his foreign possessions. *See* Cynoscephalae II.

Arikera *Second British-Mysore War*

May 13, 1791, between the British under General Lord Cornwallis, and the forces of Tippu Sahib. The latter was encamped between Arikera and Seringapatam, and was attacked by Cornwallis, who attempted to surprise him by a night march, but was foiled by heavy rain. A frontal attack on Tippu's position was, however, successful, and, aided by a flank movement, resulted in the total defeat of the Mysore troops, with a loss of over 2,000. The British loss amounted to 500. This is also known as the battle of Carigat. *See* Laswari.

Arius, The *Wars of the Hellenistic Monarchies*

214 BC, between the Syrians under Antiochus the Great, and the Parthians and Bactrians under Arsaces II, and Euthydemus. Antiochus was severely wounded, but remained at the head of his troops, and completely routed the enemy with enormous loss. *See* Raphia.

Arkenholm *Douglas Rebellion*

May 12, 1455, between the troops of James II of Scotland and the rebels under the Douglas brothers. The rebels were completely defeated. Archibald Douglas was killed, Hugh captured, and James, Earl of Douglas, forced to take refuge in England. *See* Harlaw.

Arklow *Irish Rebellion*

June 9th, 1798, when General Needham, with about 1,400 Militia and Volunteers, defended the town from the attack of 27,000 insurgents led by Billy Byrne and Edward Fitzgerald. The ill-armed insurgents were defeated, and their intended advance on Dublin prevented. *See* New Ross.

Armada, The *Anglo-Spanish War*

The fight with the Spanish Armada in the Channel began on Sunday, July 21, 1588, and lasted with intervals until the 30th. The Armada consisted of 125 ships (68 fighting ships, 32 light craft, 25 store ships), carrying 20,000 soldiers, under the command of the Duke of Medina Sidonia. The English fleet numbered 197 in all, but only 34 were Queen's ships, and of these only eight were over 600 tons burden. Lord Howard of Effingham commanded, with Admirals Drake and Hawkins as his lieutenants. The English vessels hung on to the flanks of the Spanish ships as they sailed up channel, harassing them in every way, and doing considerable damage, until the Armada anchored in Calais roads. Here many of their finest vessels were captured or destroyed by English fire-ships. On the 30th Medina Sidonia decided to sail northwards and escape around Scotland and Ireland into the Atlantic. Storms wrecked three ships off western Scotland and 25 off western Ireland. About one half of the Armada reached Spain. *See* Cadiz.

Arnee I *Carnatic War*

1751, shortly after the relief of Arcot, between 900 British troops under Clive, with 600 Maratha horse under Basin Rao, and a French force of 4,800, including 300 Europeans, who were in charge of a convoy of treasure. Clive took up a position in swampy ground, crossed by a causeway along which the convoy must pass, The French were thrown into disorder, and forced to retreat, but night saved them from complete destruction. The treasure was captured. *See* Arcot, Ambur.

Arnee II *First British-Mysore War*

An indecisive action fought June 7, 1782, between the British under Sir Eyre Coote, and the Mysore troops under Hyder Ali. *See* Aras.

Arnhem *World War II*

September 17, 1944, in a bid to outflank the northern wing of the Siegfried Line and end the war more speedily, three airborne divisions, the 101st US, the 82nd US and the 1st British were dropped from Nijmegen to Arnhem. The US landings at Eindhoven and Nijmegen successfully secured bridges over the rivers Maas and Waal, but the 1st Airborne were dropped too far from the Arnhem bridge to be able to seize it at once, and the German 9th SS Panzer Division counter-attacked violently. Bad weather stopped airdrops of ammunition, supplies and reinforcements, while the Guards Armoured Division made only slow progress in their drive north to relieve them by land. Only by September 21 did weather permit about two-thirds of the Polish Parachute Brigade to be dropped near Elst, south of Arnhem, but they failed to make contact with the 1st Airborne, on the other side of the Lower Rhine. By September 25 the hard-pressed 1st Airborne could fight no longer and during the night of September 25 to 26 some 2,400 survivors were withdrawn across the river in assault boats.

Of the 10,000 who went in 1,130 were killed and 6,450 made prisoner. German losses were 3,300 killed and wounded. Though Arnhem failed in its major objective, the bridges over the Waal and Maas were held, so the operation succeeded in part. *See* Rhineland.

Arques *French Religious Wars*

September 21, 1589, between 5,000 Huguenots under Henri IV of Navarre (later King), and 30,000 Leaguers under the Duc de Mayenne. The King had taken up a strong position, defended by marshy ground, and of such a nature that Mayenne could only bring against him 5,000 troops at a time, thus neutralizing the disparity of numbers. Mayenne repulsed attack after attack, with heavy loss to the Leaguers, and eventually was forced to withdraw, with the loss of about half his army. *See* Coutras.

Arrah *Indian Mutiny*

A house in Arrah was, in 1857, defended by a Mr Boyle, with 16 Englishmen and 60 Sikh police, against the attacks of three revolted Indian regiments, led by a Zemindar named Kur Singh. This small garrison held out from July 25 till August 3, when they were relieved by a small field force under Major Vincent Eyre. *See* Lucknow, Cawnpore I, Delhi.

Arras I *Wars of Louis XIV*

This town, held by a French garrison, was besieged August, 1654, by the Spaniards under the Great Condé. On the 24th a relieving army under the Vicomte de Turenne attacked the Spanish lines, and totally routed them with a loss of 30,000 men. Condé succeeded in rallying the remainder of his army, and made a masterly retreat to Cambrai. *See* Lens.

Arras II *World War I*

In April 1917, the British, under Field Marshal Haig, attacked Arras seven days before the new French C-in-C General Nivelle's big offensive on the River Aisne front, southern pivot of the Siegfried Line. The main object of the British attack as conceived at Allied HQ was simply to draw German reserves away from the Aisne and make Nivelle's grand offensive easier. For four days from April 4, 2,800 British guns bombarded all the enemy positions, especially their artillery batteries, while aircraft of both sides engaged in dog-fights for air mastery. On Easter Monday, April 9, General Byng's Canadian Corps on the left seized part of Vimy Ridge after three hours' hard fighting. Next to them, General Ferguson's 17th Corps advanced on Thelus. In front of Arras, General Haldane's 6th Corps over-ran Blangy and farther south the 7th Corps took the fortress called the Harp. By the evening of April 11, the British had taken 12,000 prisoners and 150 guns and had broken through the German defences on all their front. Counter-attacks were mostly thrown back and on April 16 General Nivelle launched his big offensive, which, however, failed to reach expectations.

Haig, therefore, pressed his own offensive towards Douai and Cambrai. By the end of May, towards the end of the battle, the British had taken 20,000 prisoners, 257 guns, 227 mortars, 470 machine guns and seized as well the northern six miles of the Siegfried Line. German casualties were 75,000, British 84,000. It was one more stage in the war of attrition. *See* Aisne II, Ypres III.

Arretium *Etruscan War*

283 BC, when the consular army of L. Caecilius Metellus, marching to the relief of Arretium, which the Etruscans were besieging, met with a disastrous defeat. Thirteen thousand, including Metellus, were slain, and the rest made prisoners.

Arroyo Grande *Uruguayan Civil War*

1842, between Argentine troops under Oribe, and the Uruguayans under Ribera, leader of the Colorado party. Ribera was totally defeated, and Oribe proceeded to lay siege to Montevideo. *See* Montevideo.

Arsouf *Third Crusade*

September 7, 1191, between the English Crusaders under King Richard I (Cœur de Lion), and the Saracens, 300,000 strong under Saladin. The Saracens made a desperate onslaught on the English, and both their wings gave way, but the centre under the king stood firm and finally drove back the Saracens in great disorder, with a loss of 40,000 men. But Richard sailed for England in October and the Holy City stayed in possession of the Saracens. *See* Acre.

Artois *World War I*

On May 9, 1915, after an intense artillery bombardment, General Joffre let loose a powerful offensive on a six-mile front north of Arras, forcing the German front back some three miles and seizing part of Vimy Ridge. Enemy counter-attacks expelled the French and thereafter until the battle ended on June 18, both sides engaged in a war of attrition. The French lost nearly 100,000 killed and wounded, the Germans 77,000. *See* Ypres II, Champagne.

Artois-Loos *World War I*

General Joffre planned an offensive in Champagne to break German communications from east to west along the Aisne and thus force them to retreat from their front on the Oise and Somme. The British, with their smaller forces, were to mount a smaller attack. On September 25, 1915, after a heavy artillery bombardment, General de Langle de Cary's 4th Army spearheaded an attack which carried much of the German first and part of their second lines of defence. German counter-attacks under von Falkenhayn checked further advances. Farther north from La Bassée Canal to Lens and in front of Loos, the British 1st Army advanced and even penetrated the rearward German lines, but Headquarters failed to have reserves at hand and here too German counter-attacks succeeded. French casualties were 120,000, British 50,000 and German 165,000. The front relapsed into the position of the year before. *See* Champagne, Verdun.

Ascalon *First Crusade*

Fought August 19, 1099, between the Crusaders under Godefroi de Bouillon, and the Saracens under Kilidj Arslan. The Crusaders gained a signal victory, and for a time the Muslim resistance to the Christian occupation of the Holy Land came to an end. *See* Antioch, Jerusalem.

Asculum I *Pyrrhus' Invasion of Italy*

279 BC, between 45,000 Romans under Sulpicius Saverrio and P. Decius Mus, and the Epirots, with their Italian allies, in about equal force. The Romans fought to raise the siege of Asculum, but were finally routed by the Epirot cavalry and elephants, and driven

back to their camp with a loss of 6,000. The Epirots lost 3,500. Here is the origin of 'Pyrrhic victory'. *See* Beneventum.

Asculum II *Social War*

89 BC, between 75,000 Romans under Strabo, who was besieging the town, and 60,000 Italians under Judacilius, who had marched to its relief. The Romans were victorious, but Judacilius succeeded in throwing a considerable portion of his army into the beleaguered city. An offer of Roman citizenship to all Italians ended the war. *See* Tolenus.

A Shau,

see Vietnam War

Ashdown *Danish Invasion of Britain*

871, between the West Saxons under Æthelred and the Danes under Bag Secg and Halfdene. Largely owing to the brilliant leading of Alfred (the Great), who commanded one of the wings, the Danes, after a desperate conflict, which lasted throughout the day, were finally put to flight, having lost one of their kings and five jarls. *See* Reading.

Ashtee *Third British-Maratha War*

February 18, 1818, between the army of the Peshwa, Baji Rao, and the British under General Smith. The Peshwa fled before the action began, whereupon the Marathas broke and fled in confusion. *See* Asirghar, Kirkee, Sholapur.

Asiago *World War I*

Italy had made little impression on Austria's defences along the River Isonzo during the first year of the Austro-Italian conflict, and on May 15, 1916, Austria's C-in-C, Marshal Conrad von Hötzendorf, went over to the offensive on a line from Trento to Venice, with 15 divisions, aiming at Padua, about 20 miles west. General Brusati's 1st Italian Army fell back, Asiago and Arsiero both falling to the Austrians on May 31. General Cadorna, the Italian C-in-C, rushed up reinforcements, and by June 3 had checked the Austrian offensive, but 10 days later the Austrians advanced to within four miles of the rail link to Padua. At this critical moment they were forced to switch troops to the Russian front. The Italians counter-attacked and advanced again almost to the battle's starting line. Each side lost about 100,000 men killed and wounded. *See* Isonzo, Caporetto.

Asirghar *Third British-Maratha War*

This fortress, held by Jeswunt Rao, with a strong Maratha garrison, was besieged by a British force under Sir John Malcolm and General Doveton, March 18, 1819. On the 21st the garrison was driven into the upper fort, and after a continuous bombardment, Jeswunt Rao surrendered April 7. The British loss during the siege was 313 killed and wounded; that of the garrison somewhat less. *See* Ashtee, Kirkee, Sholapur.

Askultsik *Ottoman Wars*

August 1828, between 30,000 Turks and the Russians, 17,000 strong, under General Paskevich. The Turks were routed, and their camp, with all artillery and baggage, captured. Paskevich then laid siege to the town, which was defended by a garrison of 50,000 men, and after a siege of three weeks, carried it by storm August 28. *See* Varna.

Aspendus *Wars of the Hellenistic Monarchies*

191 BC, between the Syrian fleet of Antiochus the Great, under Hannibal, and a Rhodian squadron under Eudamus. Though Hannibal was in superior force, he suffered a severe defeat. *See* Thermopylae II.

Aspern *Napoleonic Wars*

May 21 and 22, 1809, between 48,000 French with 144 guns, under Napoleon, and 95,000 Austrians under the Archduke Charles with 264 guns. The battle commenced about four pm on the 21st by an attack on the French position at Aspern, and at nightfall the Austrians had established a lodgement in the village. On the 22nd, both armies having been reinforced during the night, the combat was renewed round Aspern, which was taken and retaken ten times, while Essling was the scene of an equally desperate conflict. Towards evening the bridge by which Napoleon had crossed the Danube was swept away, and Napoleon was compelled to retire. Each side lost about 20,000 men, and both claimed the victory. Among the French who fell was Marshal Lannes. *See* Wagram, Raab.

Aspromonte *Italian Wars of Independence*

August 29, 1862, between a small force of 'Red Shirts' under Garibaldi, and the royal troops under General Pallavicini. After a short engagement, in which Garibaldi was wounded, the 'Red Shirts' laid down their arms. *See* Custoza.

Assaye *Second British-Maratha War*

September 23, 1803, when General Wellesley (later the Duke of Wellington) with 4,500 British and Indian troops routed the army of Sindhia of Gwalior, over 30,000 strong. All the camp equipment and 100 guns were taken. Wellington always considered this the bloodiest action, for the numbers engaged, that he ever fought. The British loss amounted to 1,566, or more than one-third of Wellesley's entire force. *See* Aligarh.

Assundun *Danish Invasions of Britain*

The last of the five battles fought in 1016 between the English under Edmund Ironside and the Danish invaders under Knut. Owing to the treachery of Ædric, who crossed over with the Hereford men in the course of the battle, the English were defeated, and Knut was proclaimed King. *See* Fulford.

Astrakhan *Turkish Invasion of Russia*

Siege was laid to this town, 1569, by the Turks under Selim II, who required it as a base for his projected invasion of Persia. It was held by a small Russian garrison, which made an obstinate defence, and was finally relieved by an army despatched to its assistance by Ivan the Terrible, which attacked the Turkish lines, and routed them. *See* Szigeth.

Atahualpa *Conquest of Peru*

1531, between 160 Spaniards under Pizarro, and 30,0000 Peruvians, forming the escort of the Inca, Manco-Capac. The battle was nothing but a butchery, Pizarro, who had invited the Inca to visit him, falling upon the unsuspecting Peruvians, seizing Manco-Capac, and slaughtering 4,000 men, without the loss of a single Spaniard. *See* Cuzco, Las Salinas.

Atbara *British Sudan Campaigns*

April 8, 1898, between the British and Egyptian army, 14,000 strong, under General Sir Herbert Kitchener, and 18,000 Mahdists. The Mahdists occupied an entrenched zareba on the Atbara, where they were attacked and utterly routed, with a loss in the zareba of 5,000 killed and 1,000 prisoners, while many more fell in the pursuit. The Anglo-Egyptian losses were 570 killed and wounded, including 29 British officers. *See* Khartoum, Omdurman.

Athenry *Conquest of Ireland*

1316, between the English under William de Burgh and Richard de Bermingham, and the O'Connors under their chieftain, Felim. The O'Connors were defeated, 11,000 of them falling in the battle. This is the last appearance of the O'Connors as a clan in Irish history.

Atherton Moor,

see Adwalton Moor

Atlantic I *World War I*

The German campaign to starve Britain out of the war by sinking merchant vessels carrying food across the Atlantic Ocean reached its climax in 1917, with the destruction, at a rate faster than the Allies could build, of 875,000 tons of shipping, over a half of it British. The belated use in May 1917 of naval convoys combined with submarine chasers attacking with depth charges began to save the day. Shipping losses were cut substantially, and German submarines knocked out. By the end of 1917 more merchant ships were launched in Allied yards than the Germans sank. The Battle of the Atlantic was won. *See* Coronel, Jutland.

Atlantic II *World War II*

In this four-year battle, 1940–1944, the Royal Navy and the RAF fought enemy U-boats, surface warships, aircraft, acoustic, magnetic and contact mines to defeat the attempt to starve Britain into surrender. Hitler declared a total blockade on August 17, 1940, with the announcement that neutral vessels sailing to Britain would also be sunk on sight. June 1, 1940 to July 1, 1941, Britain lost 899 ships; Allies and neutrals 471, a loss that exceeded by three times the joint production of British and US yards. From a weekly average of 1·2 million tons (not oil) in June 1940, imports fell to just over ·8 million by December. U-boats accounted for about half the total merchant vessels sunk, though by the end of 1940 the RN and the RAF had together destroyed 31 U-boats, leaving Hitler with only 22. In 1941 the German yards were turning out up to 18 a month and by August a fleet of over 100 was constantly in operation. Moreover, the battleships *Scharnhorst* and *Gneisenau* sank or took 22 merchant ships (115,600 tons) during February and March 1941, but in May 1941 the Navy sank the battleship *Bismarck* in the North Atlantic. In the first six months of 1942, Allied losses from U-boats alone rose to a crisis point of 900 ships (4 million tons), and reached a total of 1,664 ships (7,790,697 tons) for the year, 1,160 ships being U-boat victims. But the British introduction of Asdic underwater detection, radar, convoy escort by Navy 'support groups', long-range aircraft for Coastal Command, all helped to cut these losses in the future. Then, under Admiral Docnitz in 1943, the Nazis put forth their greatest effort with a fleet of 250 U-boats, and sank 500,000 tons of Allied Atlantic shipping. But a record number of U-boats were sunk— 67 from March to the end of May. It was more than Germany could take, for Doenitz then called in his fleet to rest and refit. This was a turning point, for June's total losses fell dramatically to 28,000 tons. Owing both to the defeat of the German blockade and to series production of Liberty ships in the US, new launchings by the end of 1943 were substantially exceeding losses. The RN sank the enemy battle cruiser *Scharnhorst* on December 26, 1943. The battle of the Atlantic was finally won by the end of 1944, but the U-boats fought on to the bitter end, during the last five weeks of the war sinking 10 ships (52,000 tons), for the loss of 23, with valuable crews. When Germany surrendered, 156 U-boats obeyed the orders of Doenitz and surrendered, 221 scuttled. Statistics tell little of the grim struggle for survival or of the awful deaths of merchant seamen, of whom 30,248 were lost. The RN lost 51,578 killed or missing. U-boats sank in all 2,828 Allied or neutral ships (14,687,231 tons) of which 11,500,000 tons were British. *See* Bismarck, Graf Spee.

Auerstadt,

see Jena

Aughrim *War of the English Succession*

July 12, 1691, between William III's troops, under General de Ginkel, and the French and Irish under St Ruth. The English struggled in vain to carry St Ruth's entrenchments, which were protected by a bog, but his flank was at last turned by the cavalry, which found a passage through the morass, and St Ruth was killed. The Irish then broke and fled, losing between 6,000 and 7,000. *See* The Boyne, Londonderry, Lagos.

Augsburg *Holy Roman Empire Wars*

900, between the Christian Germans and the invading Hungarians. The Christians fought gallantly, but were overwhelmed by the numbers of the barbarian cavalry.

Auldearn *English Civil War*

May 9, 1645, when Montrose and his Highlanders defeated a largely superior force of Covenanters under Sir John Hurry, who was marching northward to raid the lands of the Gordons. *See* Inverlochy.

Auray *Hundred Years' War*

September 27, 1364, between the partisans of John de Montfort, and those of Charles of Blois, the rival claimants to the Dukedom of Brittany. The English party, under Sir John Chandos, were besieging Auray, when they were attacked by the French, who were led by Bertrand du Guesclin. Chandos' position, however, was very strong, and the French were unable to make any impression upon it. Meanwhile they were thrown into utter confusion by an attack on their flank, and were ultimately routed, with heavy loss, Charles of Blois being among the slain. Bertrand du Guesclin was captured. De Montfort was shortly afterwards acknowledged by Charles V of France as Duke of Brittany. *See* Navarrete, Poitiers.

Aussig *Hussite War*

1426, between the Germans under the Emperor Sigismund, and the Taborites, the extreme section of the Hussites, under John Zisca. The Germans were signally defeated. *See* Deutschbrod.

Austerlitz *Napoleonic Wars*

December 2, 1805, between 60,000 Russians and 25,000 Austrians with 278 guns, under the Emperors of Russia and Austria with General Kutuzov, and 73,000 French with 139 guns under Napoleon. An attempt to turn the French flank failed, and led to the allies' left being cut off from their centre. Their left and centre were thus beaten in detail, and the right, which had at first held its own, was surrounded, and driven in disorder across a partially frozen lake, where many perished. The allies lost 27,000 killed, wounded, and prisoners, and a large number of guns. The French lost about 8,000. The battle is called The Battle of the Three Emperors, those of Russia, Austria and France being all present with their respective armies. Under the Treaty of Pressburgh, December 26, Francis II, Emperor of the Holy Roman Empire, lost much territory and became Francis I of Austria. In 1806, the Empire was abolished. *See* Jena, Saalfeld.

Avaricum *Gallic War*

This place (Bourges) was made the headquarters of the revolted Gauls under Vercingetorix, 53 BC, and was besieged by Caesar, with 50,000 Romans. It was strongly defended, but supplies ran short, and Vercingetorix attempted to withdraw his troops. In this he was unsuccessful, and the Romans, delivering a vigorous assault, took possession of the town, and massacred the garrison and inhabitants. *See* Agendicum.

Avus *Second Macedonian War*

198 BC, between 20,000 Macedonians under Philip, and two Roman legions under T. Quintius Flaminius. A force of 4,000

legionaries penetrated to the rear of Philip's camp, and when Flamininus attacked in front, they fell upon the Macedonian rear, and completely routed them, with a loss of 2,000. *See* Cynoscephalae.

Axarquia *Spanish-Muslim Wars*

March 20, 1483, between a Spanish force of 3,000 knights with about 2,000 infantry, under the Marquis of Cadiz, and a strong Moorish force under Abul Hasan. The Spaniards were marching through the defile of Axarquia, on their way to attack Malaga, when they were assailed in front and flank, and totally routed, losing 800 killed and 1,600 prisoners. *See* Granada, Malaga.

Ayacucho *Peruvian War of Independence*

December 9, 1824, between the patriots, 5,780 strong, under Sucre, and the Spaniards, 9,310 in number, under La José de Serna, the Spanish Viceroy. The latter were routed with a loss of 2,100 killed and wounded, and over 3,500 prisoners, including La Serna, in addition to 15 guns. The patriots lost 979. This engagement, which is also known as the Battle of Candorcanqui, practically decided the question of Peruvian independence. *See* Junin.

Aylesford *Jutish Invasion of Britain*

456, between the Jutes under Hengist and Horsa, and the Britons under Vortigern. Horsa was slain in the battle, but the Jutes were victorious.

Azimghur *Indian Mutiny*

April 15, 1858, between a British column, composed of three regiments of infantry and three of Sikh cavalry, under Sir Edward Layard, and the Dinapur mutineers, about 5,000 strong, under Kur Singh. The rebels were routed and dispersed, Kur Singh falling mortally wounded. *See* Gwalior.

Azores *Anglo-Spanish War*

August, 1591, a fleet of seven ships under Lord

Thomas Howard was driven from Flores by the Spanish fleet of 15 warships under Don Alfonso Bassano. The action was chiefly remarkable for the gallant fight made by Sir Richard Grenville in the *Revenge*, which, crippled and surrounded by the Spanish warships, maintained an unequal struggle for 15 hours, when her commander was mortally wounded, and she surrendered at daybreak. Two Spanish warships were sunk. *See* Armada, Cadiz.

B

Badajoz *Peninsular War*

On March 17, 1812, this fortress, believed impregnable, and held by a garrison of 4,900 French, Germans and Spaniards under General Phillipon, a fortifications expert, was besieged by four divisions of Wellington's army, the 3rd, 4th, 5th and Light, about 15,500 men with 5,000 Portuguese troops as well. Five hundred volunteers of the Light and 3rd Divisions having stormed Fort Picurina, an outer bastion, on March 25, Wellington's gunners were enabled to batter the main walls from it and by April 6 had made three breaches.

An assault was ordered that night. The first storming parties were blown to pieces by mines in the ditch and a bloody battle then followed, but the British failed to penetrate the breaches. At midnight, when a third of the Light Division had fallen, Wellington temporarily called off the attack and sent word to General Picton, whose 3rd Division was trying the seemingly impossible task of storming the castle on the other side, up walls 100 feet high in places, that he must succeed. At that moment a British bugle sounded from the castle, signalling that Picton's men were in. General Walker's 5th Division had also scaled ramparts nearby, found to be weakly held. Soon all were fighting their way through the town to take, in the rear, the French opposing Wellington's main assault. Surprised, the French surrendered and the entire town and fortress were in British hands, at a loss to them of nearly 5,000 killed or wounded. For 3 days the troops revenged themselves for their losses with an orgy of plunder, drunkenness, rape and murder, before order and discipline were restored. Wellington then advanced into Spain.

Baduli-ki-Serai *Indian Mutiny*

June 8, 1857, when a British force, under Sir Henry Barnard, defeated a large body of mutineers, who were opposing their march to Delhi. All the rebels' guns were captured. *See* Cawnpore I, Delhi.

Baghdad *Mongul Invasion of Mesopotamia*

This city was captured by the Monguls under Tamerlane, July 23, 1401. It was razed and the citizens were massacred. *See* Delhi, Meerut.

Bagradas *Wars of the First Triumvirate*

49 BC, between the Caesareans under Curio and the Numidians under Juba and Saburra, who adhered to the fortunes of Pompey. The Roman cavalry was cut to pieces, before the legionaries could come to its assistance, and eventually the Romans were surrounded, and cut down to a man, Curio being amongst the slain. This victory left the Pompeians masters of Africa. *See* Utica, Pharsalus.

Bahur *Seven Years' War*

August, 1752, between the French, numbering 2,500, including Indians, under M. Kirkjean, and 2,000 British troops, with 4,000 of Mohammed Ali's levies, under Major Stringer Lawrence. The French were totally defeated, losing heavily in men, guns and stores. This victory determined the Marathas, who were wavering, to throw in their lot temporarily with the British. *See* Calcutta.

Balaclava *Crimean War*

October 25, 1854, between 30,000 Russians under Prince Mentschikov, and the British under Lord Raglan. The Russians, having driven the Turks from their redoubts at Kadikoi, entered the valley of Balaclava, where they were encountered and driven back by the Heavy Cavalry Brigade under General Scarlett. Later in the day, acting under a mistaken order, Lord Cardigan leading the Light Brigade, charged the Russian guns at the head of the valley, and attacked their batteries. Having been shelled from all sides, however, he was compelled to retire with heavy loss. Of this mistaken feat of arms, General Bosquet is reported to have said, 'C'est magnifique, mais ce n'est pas la guerre.' Another feature of this singular battle was the repulse by the Highland Brigade, in line, of a charge of the Russian cavalry. The British losses were small, except in the Light Brigade, whose casualties amounted to 272 out of 673 who took part in the charge. *See* Sevastopol, Alma.

Balkans I *World War II*

Between October 28, 1940 and June 1, 1941, Germany occupied Rumania and Bulgaria without resistance. On October 28, 1940, Mussolini's Italy invaded Greece, which counter-attacked successfully, seizing Koritza (Albania). In February 1941, Greece accepted the aid of a small British and Commonwealth force of about five divisions from North Africa. Germany intervened on April 6, 1941, and attacked Yugoslavia and Greece with 33 divisions and the *Luftwaffe*. Belgrade fell on April 13, and four days later King Peter's Government surrendered. The Greek Government surrendered on April 24, some 43,000 British and Commonwealth troops being evacuated, mostly to Crete, and about 11,000 with much equipment being left behind. Germany's invasion of Greece delayed by some five weeks its attack on Soviet Russia. Germany attacked Crete on May 20. *See* Crete.

Balkans II *World War II*

Rumania fell to the Russians under General Tolbukin in August 1944; Bulgaria in September, and, with the considerable help of Tito's partisans, Yugoslavia in October. *See* Ukraine.

Ball's Bluff *American Civil War*

October 21, 1861, between the Federals under General Stone, and the Confederates under General Evans. The Federals crossed the Potomac to attack the Southern position, but were repulsed, and driven back over the river in confusion losing 1,100 killed and wounded, 700 prisoners and the only three guns which they had succeeded in taking across. The Confederates lost 155 only. *See* Bull Run.

Ballymore *Irish Rebellion*

June 3, 1798, when Colonel Walpole, with 500 Royal troops, on the march to Enniscorthy, was surprised and overpowered by a body of rebels under Father Murphy. Walpole was killed and the majority of his force were cut to pieces. *See* Gibbel Rutts, Dunganhill.

Baltimore *Anglo-American War of 1812*

This city was attacked September 11, 1814, by a British fleet of ten sail, under Admiral Sir Alexander Cochrane, and a land force of 3,270 under General Ross, who fell during the action. The Americans, 17,000 strong, under General Winder, were defeated, but the British retired on the evening of the 13th. The British lost 46 killed and 300 wounded, the Americans, 20 killed, 90 wounded, and 200 prisoners. *See* Bladensburg.

Bamian *Tatar Invasion of Kharismia*

This city was invested by the Monguls under Genghis Khan in 1221, and after an obstinate defence, lasting several months, was taken by storm. Genghis, who had seen a favourite grandson killed during the progress of the siege, gave orders that neither woman nor child was to be spared, and the whole city with its inhabitants was wiped out.
Once a kingdom with great possessions, Kharismia, now Khorezm, is a province of Uzbek SSR. *See* Otrar.

Banda *Indian Mutiny*

April 19, 1858, between a force of rather over 1,000 British troops under General Whitlock, and 7,000 mutineers under the Nawab of Banda. The rebels were routed. *See* Gwalior, Jhansi.

Banda Islands *French Revolutionary Wars*

These islands, forming part of the Dutch East Indian possessions, were captured March 8, 1796, by a British squadron under Admiral Peter Rainier. *See* St Lucia.

Bands, The *Danish Invasion of Scotland*

Fought 961, between the Scots under their king, Indulph, and the Danish pirates who were defeated. Indulph fell in the battle. *See* Kinloss.

Bangalore *Second British-Mysore War*

This place was besieged by the British under Lord Cornwallis, March 5, 1791, and notwithstanding numerous efforts to relieve it on the part of Tippu Sahib, it was taken by storm on the night of the 21st, Tippu's final attempt being beaten off by the reserve with heavy loss. *See* Seringapatam.

Bannockburn *Wars of Scottish Independence*

June 24, 1314, between the Scots under Robert Bruce, and the English invaders under King Edward II. Bruce's position was partly covered by a marsh, and further strengthened by pitfalls, in which the English cavalry were entrapped, and defeated with great loss. The English king escaped with difficulty, the invasion was abandoned and Scottish independence assured. *See* Loudon Hill.

Bapaume *Franco-Prussian War*

January 3, 1871, between the French under General Faidherbe, and the Germans under von Goeben. The result was indecisive, and though the French gained some tactical successes, strategically it was an advantage to the Germans, as General Faidherbe was compelled to desist from his attempt to raise the siege of Péronne. The Germans lost 52 officers and 698 men; the French 53 officers and 1,516 men killed and wounded, and 550 prisoners. *See* Coulmiers, Le Mans.

Barbosthenian Mountains *Wars of the Achaean League*

192 BC, between the Spartans under Nabis, and the Achaean League under Philopoemen. Nabis was totally routed, with the loss of three-fourths of his troops. *See* Larissus, Leucopetra.

Barcelona I *War of the Spanish Succession*

This city, which was held for Philip V of Spain by a Spanish garrison, was besieged September 14, 1705, by the British under the Earl of Peterborough. After a short bombardment, it surrendered, October 9. *See* Almansa, Blenheim.

Barcelona II *Spanish Civil War*

December 23, 1938, General Franco launched six armies, including four Italian divisions, in a broad offensive against the Republicans under General Sarabia on a front stretching from the northern Pyrenees to the River Ebro. The Republicans were driven back in an easterly direction towards Barcelona, itself under severe attack from the air. Tarragona was taken by General de Yagüe's Moroccan forces on January 14, 1939. Ten days later, on January 24, an almost deserted Barcelona fell to the Nationalists. More than 200,000 Republican troops and some 225,000 civilians fled across the frontier into France. *See* Ebro River, Madrid.

Bardia *World War II*

January 3, 1941, when General O'Connor's British XIII Corps, having crossed into Libya after its victory at Sidi Barrâni, surrounded some 45,000 of Marshal Graziani's Italian 10th Army. The 7th Armoured Division penetrated the defences of the Italians, who resisted for two days, suffering heavy casualties. The British, whose casualties were light, took nearly 40,000 prisoners. O'Connor's force then moved west for its attack on Tobruk. *See* Sidi Barrâni, Tobruk I.

Barnet *Wars of the Roses*

April 14, 1471, between the Yorkists under King Edward IV, and the Lancastrians under the Earl of Warwick. Warwick prepared to attack the king as he issued from Barnet, but Edward came out during the night and took up a position opposite Warwick unseen. The left of the Yorkists was outflanked and beaten, but their right outflanked and defeated the Lancastrian left, and then fell upon and routed the centre. Warwick was slain. The losses on the two sides are said to have amounted in all to 1,000 killed. *See* Tewkesbury.

Barossa *Peninsular War*

In the course of the operations for the relief of Cadiz, General Graham, with 4,000 British troops, defeated Marshal Victor with 9,000 French, March 5, 1811. The French lost 2,000 killed and wounded, as well as two generals, 400 prisoners and six guns. The British losses amounted to 50 officers and 1,160 men. A large Spanish force under General La Peña stood idly by, and took no part in the action. *See* Albuera, Badajoz.

36

Barquisimeto *Colombian War of Independence*

Fought 1813, between the Colombian patriots under Simon Bolívar, and the Spanish Royalists, Bolívar gaining a complete victory. *See* Boyacá, Carabobo.

Basing *Danish Invasion of Britain*

A victory of the Danish invaders in 871 over the West Saxons. *See* Ashdown, Reading.

Bassano *French Revolutionary Wars*

September 8, 1796, when Napoleon, who had on the previous day destroyed the Austrian vanguard at Primolano, fell upon the main body of Field Marshal von Wurmser's army. The assault on the town of Bassano was delivered by General Augereau's division on the right, and General Masséna's on the left, and the French utterly routed the Austrians, von Wurmser narrowly escaping capture. Six thousand men laid down their arms, and when von Wurmser collected his scattered forces, he had but 16,000 left out of the 60,000 with which he had started the campaign. *See* Caldiero.

Bassein *First British-Maratha War*

This place, held by a Maratha garrison, was besieged by a British force under General Goddard, November 13, 1780. A serious attempt was made to relieve the garrison, but the defeat of the relieving force by Colonel Hartley at Dugaar, on December 10, completely discouraged the defenders, and they surrendered on the following day. *See* Gwalior.

Basra *Islamic Wars*

Fought in 665 between the Caliph Ali, at the head of 29,000 Muslims, and the rebel Arabs in superior force, under Telha and Zobin. The rebels were defeated with heavy loss, Telha and Zobin being slain, and Ayesha, the widow of the Prophet, who had espoused their cause, captured. This victory is known to Muslims as the Day of the Camel, 70 men, who in succession held the bridle of the camel on which Ayesha was mounted, being killed in the fight which raged round her. *See* Siffin, Medina, Bosra.

Bastogne *World War II*

December 15, 1944, the German 5th and 6th Panzer armies, about 250,000 men, and nearly 1,000 tanks, launched a major offensive in the Ardennes sector, held by only four tired American divisions over an 80-mile stretch, with the object of trying to pierce the American centre, cross the Meuse and drive north to Brussels and Antwerp, cutting British lines of communication and forcing them to withdraw from the continent, as at Dunkirk. General Hasso von Manteuffel's 5th Army shattered General Middleton's US VIII Corps, broke through the 28th division sector and reached the outskirts of Bastogne, a vital road junction, on December 18. Under General McAuliffe, Bastogne held out, reinforced by the US 101st Airborne Division, until the arrival of General Patton's US 3rd Army, which on December 30 met von Manteuffel's forces in a head-on battle in bitter snowstorms. When it died down, with Bastogne still secure, the Germans were spent. On December 8 they began to withdraw. *See* Ardennes II.

Bataan-Corregidor *World War II*

Three days after Pearl Harbor on December 7, 1941, Japan invaded the Philippines with a preliminary bombardment of airfields that knocked out many US aircraft, then landed in Luzon. General MacArthur withdrew his 19,000 American troops and 21,000 Philippinos into the Bataan peninsula, with half-rations and a shortage of ammunition and medical supplies.
On January 10, General Masaharu Homma's 14th Army attacked and drove back the US forces, MacArthur, next day, being taken off by torpedo boat on President Roosevelt's orders to Mindanao, and thence to Australia, as commander of the South-West Pacific area. On March 31 the Japanese broke through the US lines and on April 9 General King ordered his 12,000 American troops and 55,000 Philippinos to surrender. The prisoners were sent on the notorious death march to the north of Luzon. General Wainwright held out in the old fortress on Corregidor until May 6, 1941. *See* Coral Sea, Leyte.

Batavia *Napoleonic Wars*

This town (Djakarta) was captured by the British under Sir Samuel Auchmuty, with

10,000 troops, August 26, 1811. The French
and Dutch garrison had abandoned the town,
and occupied a strong position at Fort
Cornelius, in the immediate neighbourhood.
The British stormed the entrenchments, with
a loss of 872 killed and wounded, whereupon
the survivors of the garrison laid down their
arms.

Batoche *Riel's Second Rebellion*

May 9 to 12, 1885, when 750 Canadians under
General Middleton gradually drove back and
finally defeated Riel's force of half-breeds
and Indians, with a loss of 224. The Canadians
lost only 54 killed and wounded. Riel
surrendered on the 15th, was tried and
executed.

Battle of Britain,

see Britain, Battle of

Bautzen *Napoleonic Wars*

May 20 and 21, 1813, between 115,000
French under Napoleon, and the Prussians
and Russians, 100,000 strong, under General
Blücher and Count Wittgenstein. The allies
were strongly posted in and around Bautzen,
while their front was protected by the River
Spree. On the 20th Napoleon forced the
passage of the Spree, and seized Bautzen after
severe fighting, driving the allies from their
first line of defence. On the 22nd he attacked
the second line, while a flank march of
Marshal Ney's corps drove in their right flank,
and captured all their positions. The allies
retired in good order, lack of cavalry
preventing Napoleon from pushing his
advantage. The allies lost 15,000 killed and
wounded in the two days; the French 13,000.
See Lützen II, Vitoria, Gross-Beeren.

Bavay *Gallic Wars*

57 BC, between the Romans, 50,000 strong,
under Caesar, and a large force of Gauls,
drawn from the Nervii, Viromandui, Atrebates
and other tribes. The Gauls attacked as the
Romans were pitching their camp on the
banks of the Sambre, but, although surprised,
the legionaries stood their ground, and utterly
routed their assailants. The Nervii, in
particular, were practically annihilated. *See*
Aduatuca, Agendicum.

Baylen *Peninsular War*

July 19, 1808, between 15,000 Spaniards
under General Castaños, and 20,000 French
under General Dupont. The French were
totally defeated with a loss of over 2,000 men,
and Dupont surrendered with his whole army.
See Vimeiro.

Baza *Spanish-Muslim Wars*

This fortress, one of the outposts of Granada,
was besieged by King Ferdinand, with 95,000
Spaniards, in June 1489, and was held by a
strong Moorish garrison under Sidi Yahye.
The town was gallantly defended until
December 4, when it surrendered. *See*
Granada II.

Beachy Head *War of the English Succession*

A naval action fought between June 30 and
July 10, 1690, between a combined English
and Dutch fleet of 73 sail under Lord
Torrington, and a French fleet of 78 ships
under Admiral Comte de Tourville, which
had been despatched to create a diversion in
favour of James II in Ireland. The allies
were defeated, the Dutch losing six and the
British one ship. *See* Fleurus II, La Hogue.

Beaugé *Hundred Years' War*

March 22, 1421, between the English under
the Duke of Clarence, and the Armagnacs,
aided by the Scottish mercenaries, resulting
in one of the few defeats sustained by the
English during the French wars. The Duke
and his immediate following, charging ahead
of his troops, vigorously attacked the Scottish
outposts, and, becoming separated from the
main body, was surrounded and slain, all his
nobles being either killed or captured. The
bodies were afterwards recovered by the
English archers, but the defeat was complete.
See Cravant, Rouen.

Beaumont *Franco-Prussian War*

August 30, 1870, between the Fifth French
Corps d'Armée under General de Failly, and
the Fourth and Twelfth German Army Corps
under the Crown Prince of Saxony. The
French were surprised in their cantonments,

and were driven back upon Monzon, with a loss of 4,800 men and 42 guns. The Germans lost about 3,500. *See* Sedan.

Beaune-la-Rolande *Franco-Prussian War*

November 28, 1870, between 9,000 Germans under the Grand Duke of Mecklenburg, and 60,000 French under General Crouzat. The French assailed the German position, but, notwithstanding the disparity of numbers, the Germans succeeded in maintaining their ground, after a desperate encounter, driving off their assailants with a loss of 8,000 men. The Germans lost 37 officers and 817 men only. *See* Metz.

Beauséjour *Seven Years' War*

This fort in Nova Scotia, held by a garrison of 460 men under Duchambon de Vergor, was invested June 4, 1755, by 2,000 Massachusetts volunteers and a small force of regulars under Colonel Monckton. On the 14th the besiegers opened fire, and on the 16th the garrison surrendered. *See* Lake George.

Beaver's Dam Creek,

see Seven Days' Battle

Beda Fomm *World War II*

February 5-7, 1941, when General O'Connor, in the first British offensive against Italy in Libya, after taking Tobruk pursued the retreating Italian 10th Army, advancing the 6th Australian Infantry along the coast road, while the 7th Armoured Division raced across the desert, re-entering the coast road at Beda Fomm on February 5, thus cutting off the Italian retreat. After two days' fighting, the Italians, 20,000 strong, surrendered with the loss of 84 tanks. In the 62 days since the start of the offensive in Egypt, the small British force, about two divisions, had destroyed 10 Italian divisions, taken over 130,000 prisoners, 380 tanks and 850 guns, losing only 500 killed, 1,380 wounded, 55 missing. But the victory was short-lived. Rommel entered the North African theatre with the Afrika Korps while British forces were weakened to provide reinforcements for Greece. *See* Tobruk I, Tobruk II.

Bedr *Islamic Wars*

Fought in 623, and notable as the first military exploit of Mohammed, who, with only 313 followers, routed a force of 950 Koreish, who had been sent out to meet and protect a caravan of 1,000 camels, with which was their chief, Abu Sophian. After his victory, Mohammed pursued and captured the caravan. *See* Basra, Siffin, Bosra.

Bedriacum *Civil Wars of the Roman Empire*

April 19, 69, between the legions of the Emperor Otho and the Vitellians under Fabius Valens. The Imperial troops were utterly routed, and driven back to their camp, which they surrendered to the Vitellians on the following day. *See* Cremona II.

Bega *Ottoman Wars*

1696, between the Turks, under Mustapha II, and the Imperialists, when the Turks gained a complete victory. *See* Peterwardein, Belgrade I.

Belgrade I *Ottoman Wars*

Siege was laid to this city by a large Turkish army under Mohammed II, the defence being in the hands of the Hungarians under John Hunyadi. After a gallant resistance of 40 days, the Turks were compelled to raise the siege, September 4, 1456. This was Hunyadi's last exploit, and he died a month later. Mohammed was wounded in the course of the siege. *See* Constantinople V.

Belgrade II *Ottoman Wars*

August 16, 1717, between 40,000 Austrians under Prince Eugène, and 180,000 Turks under the Grand Vizier, Ibrahim Pasha. The Turks were entrenched in and around Belgrade, and were attacked by Eugène at night. His right wing lost touch and were in danger of being overwhelmed, but were rescued by the Prince. The main attack was completely successful, and the Turks were driven out of their positions with a loss of 15,000 killed and wounded, and 166 guns. The Austrians lost about 5,500, among those who fell being Marshal Hauben. *See* Peterwardein.

Belgrade III *Ottoman Wars*

On October 8, 1789, the city was surrendered by the Turks, after a brief siege, to an

39

Austrian army under General Laudon. *See* Focsani.

Belle-Île-en-Mer I *Seven Years' War*

November 20, 1759, between a British fleet of 27 ships of the line and six frigates under Admiral Sir Edward Hawke, and a French fleet of 20 ships of the line and six frigates under Marshal de Conflans. The French were completely defeated, losing six ships and a large number of men. The British lost two ships ashore, and 58 killed and 251 wounded. *See* Quiberon Bay, Madras.

Belle-Île-en-Mer II *Seven Years' War*

On June 7, 1761, the island was captured by 8,000 British troops under General Hodgson, convoyed by the fleet under Admiral Keppel. After a first repulse, the troops made good their landing, and the garrison of Palais, the principal town, at once capitulated. The island was restored to France in 1763. *See* Martinique.

Belle-Île-en-Mer III *French Revolutionary Wars*

June 23, 1795, between a British fleet of 17 battleships under Lord Bridport, and a French squadron. The French endeavoured to escape, but the British gave chase, and captured three ships, with a loss of three killed and 113 wounded. The French lost about 700. *See* Martinique.

Belleau Wood *World War I*

June 6, 1918, when General Bundy's 2nd US Division attacked General Ludendorff's greatly superior German force in this mile-square wood and cleared it after more than three weeks' fighting in the first major German-American encounter of the war. American losses were 1,811 killed and about 7,000 wounded. *See* Aisne III.

Bellevue *Franco-Prussian War*

October 18, 1870, when Marshal Bazaine attempted to break through the lines of the Germans investing Metz. He was unsuccessful, and was driven back into the city with a loss

of 64 officers and 1,193 men. The Germans lost 75 officers and 1,703 men. *See* Metz, Sedan.

Belmont *Second Boer War*

November 23, 1899, between a Boer commando, about 3,000 strong, occupying a strong position on the hills near Belmont, and Lord Methuen's division of 71 battalions of infantry and a regiment of cavalry. The Boer position was carried by a frontal attack, which cost the assailants 28 officers and 270 men. The Boers lost about 300 killed and wounded, and 50 prisoners. *See* Kimberley.

Benburb *Great Irish Rebellion*

June 5, 1646, when 5,500 Irish rebels under Owen Roe O'Neill, totally routed the Scottish army under General Monro. The Scots left 3,000 dead upon the field, and the fugitives were ruthlessly butchered by the Irish in their flight, but the battle decided nothing. *See* Dunganhill.

Bender *Ottoman Wars*

This place, held by a Turkish garrison, was besieged by the Russians under Count Panin, August, 1768. After a defence of two months, the place was taken by storm, and the garrison put to the sword. *See* Belgrade III.

Benevento *Franco-Italian Wars*

February 26, 1266, between the Neapolitans, under Manfred, the usurper of the crown of the Two Sicilies, and the French under Charles I of Anjou. After a bloody engagement, in which Manfred was slain, the Neapolitans were utterly routed, and Charles of Anjou was proclaimed King of Naples and Sicily. *See* Tagliacozzo.

Beneventum I *Pyrrhus' Invasion of Italy*

275 BC, when Pyrrhus with a strong force of Epirots and Italians made a night attack upon the consular army of M. Curius Dentatus, encamped in a strong position near Beneventum. Pyrrhus was repulsed with considerable loss, including eight elephants. Encouraged by this success, the Romans shortly afterwards advanced to meet Pyrrhus

in the open plain, and were at first driven back by the elephants, but rallying, they drove these back through Pyrrhus' lines, and disordered the Epirot phalanx, then a charge of the legionaries completed the rout. This was Pyrrhus' last serious attack against the Roman power, and he soon afterwards left Italy. *See* Asculum.

Beneventum II *Second Punic War*

214 BC, between 18,000 Carthaginians under Hanno, and 20,000 Romans under Tiberius Gracchus. Hanno's troops were routed, his infantry being cut to pieces, and he himself escaping with difficulty, with a portion of his cavalry. *See* Syracuse III, Capua.

Beneventum III *Second Punic War*

212 BC, when a Roman consular army under Cn. Fulvius, stormed Hanno's camp, three miles from Beneventum, at daybreak, and surprising the Carthaginians, routed them with heavy loss and captured all the corn and supplies intended for the revictualling of Capua. *See* Syracuse III, Capua.

Bennington *American Revolutionary War*

August 16, 1777, between a British and German force under Colonel Baum, and the New Hampshire troops under General Stark. Baum had been ordered to seize the American magazines at Bennington, but found the place too strong, and asked for reinforcements. Meanwhile, they were surrounded and attacked by Stark. The British and Germans fought till their ammunition was exhausted and many were killed, then surrendered, while Baum was killed trying to cut his way through the American lines. *See* Stillwater, Ticonderoga.

Berea *Kaffir Wars*

December 20, 1852, between the British under General Cathcart, about 2,500 strong, and the Basutos, many thousands in number, under Moshesh. The British, after hard fighting, at first succeeded in holding their ground, but on the following day retreated to the entrenched camp on the Caledon, having lost 37 killed and 15 wounded.

Berestecko *Polish-Cossack War*

June 28–30, 1651, between the Poles, 100,000 strong under John II, and a large army of Cossacks, Lithuanians, and Ukraine Tartars, 300,000 in all, under Bogdan Chmielnicki. The Poles were completely victorious, defeating Bogdan with enormous loss.

Berezina *Napoleonic Wars*

On November 28, 1812, the French Grande Armée in retreat from Moscow, was attacked by the Russians under Admiral Chitchagov and General Wittgenstein. The former, on the right bank, assailed Napoleon, who had already crossed the river, while Wittgenstein attacked Marshal Victor's troops, which formed the French rearguard. The attack on Napoleon was repulsed, but on the other side of the river the Russian onslaught caused a panic among those who were waiting to cross, and though the rearguard made a brave resistance, the losses among the stragglers and others were enormous. The official Russian report said that 36,000 bodies were recovered from the Berezina after the thaw. *See* Maloyaroslavets, Lützen.

Bergen *Seven Years' War*

April 13, 1759, between the French under the Duc de Broglie, and the Hanoverians, about 40,000 strong, under Ferdinand of Brunswick. The French gained a signal victory, and retained possession of Bergen, the recapture of which was the object of Ferdinand's advance. *See* Crefeld, Minden.

Bergen-op-Zoom I *War of the Austrian Succession*

This fortress, held by a garrison of Dutch and English under Cronstrun, was besieged July 15, 1747, by 25,000 French under Count Löwendahl. The besieged made numerous vigorous sorties, inflicting heavy losses upon the French, but on September 17 the besiegers by an unexpected assault, effected a lodgement, and after severe fighting captured the place. The French lost 22,000 men during the siege; the garrison 4,000. A Scottish brigade in the Dutch service specially distinguished itself, losing 1,120 out of a strength of 1,450. *See* Lauffeld.

41

Bergen-op-Zoom II *French Revolutionary Wars*

In the outskirts of the town, September 19, 1799, between 35,000 British and Russians under the Duke of York, and the French under Vandamme. The Russians on the right met with disaster, their commander, General Hermann, with nearly all his division, being taken prisoner, but the British repulsed the French attack with heavy loss. The victory, however, was not of much advantage to the allies, who were forced to continue their retreat to Zijp. The French lost about 3,000 killed and wounded, and the British 500 only, but the Russian casualties amounted to 3,500, while they also lost 26 guns. *See* Alkmaar II, Zürich, Stockach.

Bergfried *Napoleonic Wars*

February 3, 1807, when General Leval's division of Marshal Soult's corps forced the bridge of Bergfried, and carried the village, driving out the Russians after a short and sharp encounter, with a loss of about 1,200 men. The French lost 700. *See* Eylau.

Berlin *World War II*

In April 1945, three Russian Army Groups and two tank armies totalling 1,593,000 men, commanded by Marshal Zhukov in the centre, with Marshal Koniev in the south and Marshal Rokossovski in the north, had deployed for their great offensive on Berlin. Already, in March, troops of Zhukov's 1st Army Group had forced a bridgehead 30 miles long by 10 wide across the Oder at Kostrzyn, about 45 miles east of the city. They were faced in the east by General Busse's depleted 9th Army, with a mere 744 guns, 600 AA guns used as field artillery and 700 tanks, for Hitler had ordered five panzer divisions to the south to check what he believed would be the main Russian attack against Prague.
After an intense artillery barrage from 20,000 guns at 4.30 am on April 16, the Russian 8th Guards Army led the assault, supported by 6,500 fighters and bombers, but Col-General Heinrici, commanding this front, saved his forces by secretly withdrawing them to the second line of defence, the Seelow Heights, where the 56th Panzer Corps (Lt. General Weidling) fought a desperate battle to stem Zhukov's advance.

Meantime, in the south, Marshal Koniev's 1st Ukrainian Army Group, after a more effective artillery attack, crossed the river Neisse on an 18-mile front, penetrated 10 miles through the German defences and fought their way north towards Zossen, German High Command HQ, and Berlin. On April 20, Rokossovski's 3rd Army Group attacked General von Manteuffel's 3rd Panzer Army from the north. Russian shells crashed into Berlin at 11.30 am on April 21, General Busse's troops to the east were encircled, and on April 22, Zossen fell to Gen. Rybalko's 3rd Guards Tank Army.
Zhukov's and Koniev's armies, hammering the city with artillery shells from the east and the south, drove the desperate German forces before them through a trail of street battles and ruins. On May 1 Zhukov's forces won the honour of planting the Red Flag on the ruined Reichstag building, and the next day Lt. Gen. Weidling, to whom Hitler had given charge of the city's defences before committing suicide, formally surrendered Berlin and its remaining 140,000 defenders. (It is fair to say that decisions taken first by President Roosevelt, and later by General Eisenhower, long before the battle, led to the change in Allied policy that enabled the Russians to enter Berlin first.) *See* Ukraine, The Rhine.

Berwick-on-Tweed *Wars of Scottish Independence*

March 28, 1296, after King John de Baliol of Scotland refused to supply men and arms for King Edward I's war against Gascony, instead forming a defensive alliance with France. Edward marched an army north and attacked the Scottish border town of Berwick, a centre then of international trade. Overwhelming the citizens' clumsy defences, his trained soldiers brutally slaughtered thousands and changed the prosperous city overnight into a smoking charnel house, which he later fortified and used as a military base. *See* Dunbar.

Béthune *War of the Spanish Succession*

This small fortress, held by a French garrison of 3,500 under M. du Puy Vauban, was invested July 14, 1707, by the Imperialists, with 30 battalions under Count Schulemburg. Vauban made a most skilful and gallant defence, lasting 35 days, when, the garrison being reduced to 1,500 men, he was compelled to surrender. This little place cost the allies 3,500 in killed and wounded. *See* Stolhoffen, Almansa.

Betioca *Colombian War of Independence*

1813, between the Colombian patriots under Simon Bolívar, and the Spanish royalists, Bolívar gaining a complete victory. *See* Boyacá, Caracha.

Betwa, The *Indian Mutiny*

April 1, 1858, between 1,200 British under Sir Hugh Rose, forming part of the force besieging Jhansi, and 20,000 rebels, chiefly belonging to the Gwalior contingent, under Tantia Topi. The enemy was thrown into confusion by a charge of cavalry on the flank, and, being then attacked with the bayonet, broke and fled, leaving 1,000 dead on the field and all their guns. *See* Cawnpore.

Beylan *Egyptian Revolt*

1831, between the Syrians and Egyptians under Ibrahim Pasha, and the Turks, the latter being completely defeated. *See* Acre IV.

Beymaroo *First British-Afghan War*

November 23, 1841, when a detachment of General Elphinstone's Kabul force, under Brigadier Shelton, attempted to dislodge a large body of Afghans, posted near Beymaroo village. Elphinstone allowed the detachment one gun only, which, being well served, kept the Afghans at bay, but soon overheating stopped its use, whereupon the Afghans attacked, caused a panic and a disorderly flight to the British camp, with many casualties. *See* Jellalabad.

Bezetha *Jewish Wars of Roman Empire*

October, 66, when the Romans under Cestius Gallus were attacked by the populace of Jerusalem, and driven out of their camp, with a loss of 6,000 men and all their baggage and siege train. *See* Jotapata.

Bhurtpore I *Second British-Maratha War*

This city, garrisoned by about 8,000 of the Rajah's troops, was besieged by General Lake, January 4, 1805. Finding that his siege train was inadequate to reduce the town by the ordinary methods, Lake determined to carry it by storm. Four successive assaults were made, but without success, and on April 21 Lake was obliged to withdraw, having lost 3,200 men. *See* Farrukhabad.

Bhurtpore II *Second Siege of*

The city was again besieged by the British under Lord Combermere in 1827, a dispute having taken place as to the succession, and the Rajah who was under British protection having been expelled. After a bombardment of two months, which had little effect on the fortress, it was taken by assault.

Biberac *French Revolutionary Wars*

October, 1796, between the French under General Moreau, and the Austrians under the Archduke Charles, who had previously defeated General Jourdan at Würtzburg, and now turned upon Moreau, who was retreating through the Black Forest, Moreau severely defeated the Austrians, and continued his retreat unmolested. *See* Würtzburg.

Bibracte *Gallic Wars*

58 BC, between the Romans under Caesar and a largely superior force of Helvetii. The battle was a momentous one, for a defeat to Caesar meant destruction. He therefore sent away all his officers' horses, giving them to understand that they must stand their ground to the last. In the event, the Helvetii were totally routed, and compelled to submit to the domination of Rome. *See* Mühlhausen.

Bilbao I *First Carlist War*

This fortress was besieged by the Carlists, November 9, 1836, and was defended by a small Cristino garrison. The besiegers took possession of some of the suburbs, which were recaptured by a sortie. Finally, after several unsuccessful attempts, Espartero, at the head of about 18,000 Cristinos, drove off the besiegers, December 25, and relieved the city, capturing the Carlist artillery of 25 pieces. In the action the Cristinos lost 714 killed and wounded, while the losses of the garrison during the siege amounted to about 1,300. *See* Huesca.

Bilbao II *Spanish Civil War*

March 31 to June 19, 1937, when Franco's General Mola launched an offensive against this industrial city and Basque stronghold with 50,000 troops, forcing back General de la Encomienda's 39,000 under-armed men beyond the so-called Ring of Iron defences. By June 12 the Nationalists penetrated these defences, civilians were evacuated and during the night of June 17 the Basque troops abandoned it. The Nationalists entered on June 19. *See* Santander.

Bingen *Gallic Revolt*

In the year 70, Petilius Cerialis, who, with four Roman legions, had crossed the Alps from Switzerland, surprised the revolted Gauls under Tutor, in their camp at Bingen. The Gallic legionaries in Tutor's army deserted to the Romans, and Tutor was totally defeated.

Biruan *Tatar Invasion of Kharismia*

Fought 1221, between 80,000 Tatars under Katuku, and the troops of Jellalladin, Sultan of Kharismia (now Khorezm), 60,000 strong. The Tatars were routed and driven from the field in confusion. *See* Bokhara, The Indus.

Bismarck *World War II*

May 27, 1941, when Germany's battleship *Bismarck*, 45,000 tons, commanded by Admiral Lutjens and believed to be the most powerful battleship afloat, having three days earlier sunk the cruiser *Hood* and badly damaged the battleship *Prince of Wales*, off Greenland, was attacked 400 miles off Brest by the battleships *King George V* and *Rodney*, and the cruisers *Dorset* and *Norfolk*, plus the aircraft carrier *Ark Royal's* obsolete *Swordfish* torpedo-bombers. The *Bismarck* fought heroically, but blasted by both torpedoes and shells, she sank at 10.36 am with colours flying, 2,000 of her crew, including Lutjens, going down with her. *See* Atlantic.

Bismarck Sea *World War II*

March 2–5, 1943, when aircraft of the 5th US Air Force and the RAAF attacked a 16-ship Japanese convoy carrying troop reinforcements to New Guinea, sinking all eight of the troopships and four destroyers, so that only 1,000 out of 7,000 men reached their destination. *See* New Guinea, Rabaul.

Bitonto *War of the Polish Succession*

May 25, 1734, between the Imperialists, 10,000 strong, and the Spaniards under General Mortemar. The Imperialists were driven from a strong position, with heavy loss, and the victory resulted in the establishment of Spanish rule throughout the Neapolitan provinces. *See* Parma.

Blackheath *Flammock's Rebellion*

June 22, 1497, between the royal troops under King Henry VII and the rebels under Flammock and Lord Audley. The rebels were defeated with a loss of 2,000 killed, and all their leaders were captured and executed. *See* Bosworth Field.

Black Rock *War of 1812*

1814, between 1,400 British troops under General Riall, and a force of 2,000 American Indians, occupying a strong position at Black Rock. The British stormed the entrenchments and dispersed the enemy, following up their success by the seizure of Buffalo. *See* Bladensburg.

Blackwater *O'Neill's Rebellion*

August 14th, 1598, between 5,000 Irish rebels under Hugh O'Neill, and 5,000 English under Sir Henry Bagenal, the English Marshal. Bagenal was defeated with a loss of 1,500 and all his ammunition and baggage, while he himself was killed. Also known as the Battle of the Yellow Ford. *See* Dunganhill.

Bladensburg *War of 1812*

August 24, 1814, between the British under General Ross, and the Americans under General Winder, who was opposing the British advance upon Washington, and had taken up a position which commanded the only bridge over the Potomac. Ross attacked with a portion of his force, under Thornton, and having carried the bridge, a combined assault upon the main position resulted in a signal defeat of the American army, which broke and fled. Ross entered Washington the same evening. *See* New Orleans.

Blanquefort *Hundred Years' War*

November 1, 1450, when the English made a sally from Bordeaux to repel a marauding band under Amanien. The English cavalry, advancing too rapidly, became separated from the main body, and were cut off. Amanien then fell upon the infantry, who, being unsupported, were overwhelmed and almost annihilated. So great was the slaughter that the day was long known in Bordeaux as the 'Mal Journée'. *See* Castillon.

Blenheim *War of the Spanish Succession*

August 13, 1704, between the 52,000 English and Imperialists, under the Duke of Marlborough and Prince Eugène of Savoy, and the 56,000 French and Bavarians under Marshals Tallard and Marsin, and the Elector of Bavaria. With the Danube on its right, the Franco-Bavarian army was deployed for three miles along the top of a rise, from the strongly fortified villages of Blenheim, to Oberglau to Lutzingen, behind marshy land crossed by a stream, the Nebel. It was a strong position, and Marshal Tallard expected the allies to retreat, rather than attack, in face of it.

But after an overnight surprise march Marlborough and Eugène arrived early before the enemy lines. Eugène then attacked the enemy's far right near Lutzingen, while Marlborough made diversionary attacks on Blenheim and Oberglau to pin down the defenders with smaller numbers. This achieved, he launched the main body of his troops, 90 cavalry squadrons and 23 battalions of infantry, with numerous guns, against Tallard's 55 cavalry squadrons and nine infantry battalions. After an initial setback, Marlborough's guns destroyed the French infantry with grapeshot. His cavalry then shattered the French cavalry, breaking their lines and driving 30 squadrons of them into the Danube.

Prince Eugène had meanwhile held the attacks of Marsin and the Elector and, after

Marlborough's charge, he assumed the offensive, routing the French right and centre. The Franco-Bavarian army lost about 40,000, including 16,000 prisoners, among whom was Marshal Tallard. The allies lost about 12,000. It was the decisive battle of the war. *See* Ramillies, Turin, Stolhoffen.

Bloemfontein *Second Boer War*

March 31, 1900, when, after his victory at Paardeberg, General Lord Roberts, with a reinforced army, defeated the Boers and drove them out of this city, capital of the Orange Free State. Advancing north, the British sieged Kroonstad on May 12 and on May 24 annexed the entire State. *See* Paardeberg.

Blore Heath *Wars of the Roses*

September 23, 1459, between the Yorkists under the Earl of Salisbury, and the Lancastrians under King Henry VI. The former, who were inferior in numbers, were attacked by Henry, who crossed a brook before the assault. As the Lancastrians were reforming after the crossing, the Yorkists charged down upon them and dispersed them with heavy loss. *See* Mortimer's Cross, Bosworth Field.

Blueberg *Napoleonic Wars*

On January 8, 1806, a British force 6,600 strong, under General Baird, which had just landed at Saldanha Bay, was attacked by the Dutch and French under General Janssens, issuing from Cape Town. The British gained a signal victory, in which they lost 212 killed, wounded and missing, while their opponents' losses amounted to about 300. Baird at once occupied Cape Town.

Boadicea, defeat of,

see Boudicca, defeat of

Bois-le-Duc *French Revolutionary Wars*

November 12, 1794, between the French and Austrians under the Duke of York, and the French under General Moreau. Moreau's object was to enter Holland at a period when the dykes would be no obstacle to his advance, and for the purpose he endeavoured to cross the Meuse at Fort Crèvecœur, near Bois-le-Duc. The allies, however, disputed his passage so vigorously that Moreau was forced to retire, and give up his project. *See* Fleurus III.

Bokhara *Tatar Invasion of Kharismia*

This city was besieged by the Tatar army under Genghis Khan in March, 1220, and was held by a Kharismian garrison. On the approach of the Tatars, however, the Kharismian general, with the whole garrison, 20,000 strong, fled from the place, and the Bokhariots, having no means of defending themselves, opened the gates to Genghis. The Governor held out for a short time in the citadel, which was finally fired and destroyed. *See* Biruan.

Borghetto *French Revolutionary Wars*

May 30, 1796, in the course of Napoleon's pursuit of General Baron de Beaulieu. The French crossed the Mincio at Borghetto, having previously repaired the bridge under a heavy fire, and forced the Austrians to evacuate Peschiera, with a loss of 500 prisoners, besides killed and wounded. *See* Lodi, Brig of, Mantua.

Bornholm *Northern War*

Fought 1676, between the fleet of Charles XI of Sweden, and a combined Dutch and Danish squadron. The Swedes were utterly routed, a disaster which was followed by the loss of Helsingborg, Landscroon, and other fortresses. *See* Kiöge.

Bornhöved *Wars of Scandinavia*

1227, between the Danes under Valdemar II, and the insurgents of the province of Dithmarsh, who had risen against the Danish dominion. The royal troops were totally routed, and, as a consequence, the province was lost to the Danish crown.

Borodino *Napoleonic Wars*

September 7, 1812, between Marshal Prince Kutuzov's 120,800 Russians with 640 guns and Napoleon's 130,000 men with 587 guns. The Russians were entrenched in a very strong position on high ground east to west astride the Moscow road and along the river Kolotza as far as a redoubt on still higher ground a mile south of the village of Borodino, and thence south to the village of Utitsa, their left flank. The French, two miles to the west, began with an artillery bombardment at 6 am then advanced on their right and took some of the Russian fieldworks, which were retaken, and for three hours the battle moved back and forth. The French 5th Corps took the village of Utitsa but made no progress up the heights beyond.

Napoleon sent in reinforcements and drove the Russians back in the Semanovski sector in the centre and later at 3 pm carried the fieldwork called the Great Redoubt, but the Russian guards retook it. The French attacked with 200 guns, assaulted again with cavalry support and took it again. The Russians again counter-attacked repeatedly, then late in the afternoon retired exhausted to a ridge to the rear of their first position and the French to the position they held before the battle.

Napoleon, who had won a technical victory, entered Moscow unopposed a week later, but Kutuzov was able to withdraw 90,000 men from the battlefield, having lost 15,000 killed and about 25,000 wounded. Prince Bagration was among the killed. French losses were 30,000, including 12 generals killed. *See* Maloyaroslavets, Smolensk.

Boroughbridge *Rebellion of the Marches*

March 16, 1322, between the Royalists under King Edward II, and the rebels under Earls Hereford and Lancaster. The rebels, falling back before the king, were surprised by another force while crossing the bridge at Boroughbridge, and were utterly routed. Hereford was killed, and Lancaster, with several hundred barons and knights, surrendered. *See* Mytton.

Borysthenes The *Russo-Polish Wars*

Fought 1512, when the Poles under Sigismund I defeated an army of Muscovites, 80,000 strong, with enormous slaughter.

Bosra *Muslim Invasion of Syria*

This strong fortress in Syria was besieged,

632, by 4,000 Muslims under Serjabil. A sortie of the garrison nearly caused their destruction, but they were rescued by the arrival of 1,500 horse under Khaled. After a brief interval, the whole of the garrison marched out of the city to give battle, but were defeated by Khaled with a loss to his troops of 250 men only, and the city was shortly afterwards betrayed by Romanus, the Governor. *See* Siffin, Basra.

Bosworth Field *Wars of the Roses*

August 21, 1485, between Richard III and Henry Duke of Richmond (Henry VII). Richmond had received a promise from Lord Stanley and his uncle that they would desert during the battle, and, after holding aloof for some time, they came over, with their followers, at a critical moment of the engagement, and Richard was routed and killed. He fought to the end, and among others who fell with him were the Duke of Norfolk and Lord Ferrers. The Wars thus ended and Henry VII was crowned. *See* Tewkesbury, Stoke.

Bothwell Bridge *Covenanters' Rising*

June 22, 1679, when the Royal troops, under the Duke of Monmouth, defeated the Covenanters with much bloodshed. *See* Rullion Green.

Boudicca, defeat of *Roman Occupation of Britain*

In the year AD 61, Suetonius, with 10,000 legionaries, totally routed an enormous host of Britons under Boudicca, Queen of the Iceni, who had sacked Camelodunum, and taken Londinium and Verulamium. The Britons lost 80,000 killed, and Boudicca took poison on the battlefield. *See* Camelodunum.

Boulogne *Anglo-French Wars*

Siege was laid to the town by the English under Henry VIII, September 14, 1544. It was defended with much courage, and, in the face of enormous difficulties, for two months, when it was forced to surrender, the inhabitants being allowed to march out with their arms and property. *See* Guinegate.

Bourbon *Napoleonic Wars*

On July 8, 1810, this island was captured by a British squadron of five ships under Commodore Rowley, with a detachment of troops under Colonel Keatinge. The British lost 22 killed and 79 wounded.

Bouvines *Anglo-French Wars*

July 27, 1214 between the French under Philip Augustus, and the Germans, Flemish and English under Otho IV, the numbers engaged on both sides being considerable. The French gained a signal victory, which broke up the coalition and rendered the position of Philip Augustus secure. *See* Damme.

Bovianum *Second Samnite War*

305 BC, between the Romans under Titus Minucius, and the Samnites under Statius Gellius. Gellius attempted to relieve Bovianum, which the Romans were besieging, and was totally defeated, though Minucius fell in the battle. This defeat broke the Samnite power, and they sued for peace in the following year, leaving Rome without dispute the first power in Italy. *See* Caudine Forks.

Boyacá *Colombian War of Independence*

August 7, 1819, between the Colombian patriots under Bolívar, and the Spanish Royalists, 2,500 strong, under Colonel Barreiro. Bolívar crossed the Cordilleras, under incredible difficulties, and, eluding Barreiro, took up a position at Boyacá, cutting him off from his base at Bogotá. The Spaniards attacked him, and were routed, Barreiro and 1,600 men being captured. Colombia was free. *See* Carabobo, Caracha.

Boyne, The *War of the English Succession*

July 1, 1690, between the 36,000-strong forces of William III, and the 25,000 Irish under James II. William and the elder Schomberg, Duke Frederick, attacked the front of James's position, while the younger Schomberg, Count Treinhard, crossed the Boyne a few miles higher up, and attacked him in the flank. William forced the passage of the river, and drove the Irish from their entrenchments at a cost of 500 killed and wounded, including the elder Schomberg. The Irish lost 1,500. It was the decisive battle of the war. *See* Londonderry.

Braddock Down *English Civil War*

January 19, 1643, between the Royalists under Sir Ralph Hopton, and the Parliamentary forces under General Ruthven. The latter had crossed the Tamar and occupied Liskeard, without adequate support, and was defeated by the Royalists with heavy loss. *See* Stratton.

Bramham Moor *Northumberland's Rebellion*

February 20, 1408, when Sir Thomas Rokeby, High Sheriff of Yorkshire, defeated the Earl of Northumberland, who had again raised the standard of rebellion in the North. The Earl was killed, and the rebellion subsided. *See* Shrewsbury, Homildon Hill.

Brandywine *American Revolutionary War*

September 11, 1777, between 18,000 British under General Howe, and 8,000 Americans under Washington. The British general made a flank movement with a large portion of his force, whereupon Washington attacked the British in the front, but, being ill supported by General John Sullivan, he was driven back, and forced to retreat, with a loss of 900 killed and wounded and 300 prisoners. The British lost 590 killed and wounded. They seized Wilmington. *See* Princeton.

Breitenfeld I,

see Leipzig

Breitenfeld II *Thirty Years' War*

November 2, 1642, between the Imperialists under the Archduke Leopold and General Piccolomini, and the Swedes under Field-marshal Torstenson. The latter, who were in retreat, were caught by the pursuing Austrians at Breitenfeld, but turning upon them, they offered a desperate resistance, and finally drove them from the field, totally routed, with a loss of 10,000 men. *See* Rocroi.

Brenneville *Anglo-French Wars*

August 20, 1119, between a small body of English cavalry under King Henry I, and a similar French force under Louis VI. Though only about 900 men were engaged, and very few killed, the fight was considered a decisive victory for the English, and Louis shortly afterwards made peace, conceding Henry's terms.

Brentford *English Civil War*

November 12, 1642, between the Royalists under Lord Forth and Prince Rupert, and a Parliamentary force under Colonel Denzil Holles. Three regiments stationed at Brentford were driven out of their entrenchments by the Royalists, losing 1,500 prisoners and 11 guns. *See* Edgehill.

Brescia *Italian Rising*

This city, where the populace had risen and shut up the small Austrian garrison in the citadel, was carried by assault by General Haynau, with about 4,000 Austrians, March 31, 1849. Carrying the Porta Torrelunga, he fought his way from barricade to barricade, till, by the evening of April 1, the resistance of the citizens was overcome. The Austrians lost 480 killed, including General Nugent, and many wounded. The wholesale executions ordered by Haynau after the capture earned for him the soubriquet of the Hyaena. *See* Novara, Venice.

Breslau *Seven Years' War*

November 22, 1757, between 70,000 Austrians under Prince Charles of Lorraine, and 20,000 Prussians under the Prince of Bevern. The Prussians, who were encamped under the walls of Breslau, were driven into the city with a loss of 5,000 killed and wounded, 3,600 prisoners, including the Prince of Bevern, and 80 guns. They evacuated the city at once, leaving a garrison of 6,000, which surrendered two days later. The Austrians lost 8,000 killed and wounded. *See* Rossbach, Leuthen.

Brest *War of the Holy League*

August 10, 1512, between the English fleet of 45 sail under Lord Edward Howard, and the French fleet of 39 sail under Jean de

Thenouënel. The French ships were driven into Brest, or along the coast, with heavy loss. The English lost two ships and 1,600 men. *See* Ravenna.

Brienne *Napoleonic Wars*

January 29, 1814, between 18,000 French under Napoleon, and about 30,000 Russians and Prussians under Marshal Blücher. The allies were driven from their positions, and the Château de Brienne taken. After nightfall a determined attempt to retake the château was made by the Russians under General Sachen, but they failed to dislodge the French. The allies lost about 4,000; the French 3,000 killed and wounded. *See* Hanau.

Brig of Dee *Bishops' Wars*

June 18, 1639, between the Scottish Covenanters, 2,300 strong, and the Royal troops under Lord Aboyne. The bridge itself was barricaded and held by 100 sharpshooters, under Colonel Johnstone, and Montrose, who led the Covenanters, finding the defences too strong, succeeded by a stratagem in drawing off the main body of the defenders, whereupon he forced a passage. The losses on both sides were very small.

Brihuega *War of the Spanish Succession*

December 9, 1710, between the British under James, Earl of Stanhope, and the French under the Duc de Vendôme. Stanhope, who was retreating from Madrid to Catalonia, was surprised and surrounded, and, though he made a gallant stand, fighting till all his powder was spent, and then leading a bayonet charge, his force was at last reduced to 500 men, when he surrendered. *See* Turin, Toulon, Malplaquet.

Brill *Netherlands War of Independence*

This fortress was captured from the Spaniards by the Beggars of the Sea, about 400 strong, under De la Marck and Treslong, April 1, 1572. It was the first success of the Netherlands patriots in their struggle against Spanish rule, and may be said to have laid the foundation of the Dutch republic. *See* Haarlem.

Bristoe Station *American Civil War*

October 14, 1863, when General Ambrose Hill's Confederate troops marched to attack General William French's Federals, but instead met a hail of fire from General Warren's troops concealed behind a railway embankment, and lost some 1,900 killed and wounded. *See* Gettysburg.

Britain, Battle of *World War II*

From July 10, 1940, when bomber squadrons of Germany's 2,830-strong *Luftwaffe* began attacking Channel shipping in readiness for Operation *Sealion*, the projected invasion of Britain by some 20 divisions. Earlier in July, Hitler had issued orders for the 'interdiction of the Channel to merchant shipping' and 'the destruction of the RAF'. The RAF, commanded by Air Chief Marshal Sir Hugh Dowding, had then about 600 fighters, Hurricanes except for 120 Spitfires plus a few Defiants and Blenheim night fighters. Goering's air force totalled 1,300 Messerschmitt-109 fighters, 180 Messerschmitt-110 fighter-bombers and 1,350 Heinkel bombers. From August 8, 1940, the *Luftwaffe* switched its attack to Channel and south-east coast ports and airfields, reaching a peak with an attack there and in the north with about 940 aircraft on August 15. Nazi losses were invariably heavy, on this day 76 being shot down at a cost to the RAF of 34 fighters and 21 bombers destroyed in the air and on the tarmac.

The brilliant, tough fighting of 'the few', as pilots of Fighter Command were called, caused a switch in German tactics to attacks on RAF airfields, aircraft factories, radar stations and gun sites, which destroyed in the air or on the ground 466 fighters plus 103 pilots killed and 128 wounded, a critical 25 per cent of pilot strength. But during these two weeks (August 24 to September 6) German losses were twice as high. Defeated in their attempt to break Britain's air arm, the Nazis turned to 'terror' daylight air raids on London, some 320 Heinkel bombers escorted by 600 fighters launching the first attack between 5 and 6 pm on September 7 and another 250 from 8.10 pm until 4.30 am, followed next day by another 200 fighter-escorted bombers. These massive daylight attacks reached a peak on September 15, when Goering sent over 400 bombers, but heavy losses—60 on this

occasion—forced him to change to night attacks.
With an average strength of 200 bombers, these raids went on for 57 nights non-stop. On October 15 an estimated 400 bombers showered London with 380 tons of HE bombs and 70,000 incendiaries. Fighter Command fought them off with a few squadrons of radar-guided night fighters and some 2,000 mobile AA guns. Legions of auxiliary firemen and civil defence workers quelled the flames and dug out victims from bombed buildings. The Battle of Britain may be said to have ended on October 12, when Hitler cancelled Operation *Sealion*. The RAF had given Nazi Germany its first defeat, at a cost of 915 aircraft and 481 men killed, wounded or missing. The Germans admitted 1,733 of their aircraft lost, the RAF claimed 2,698. Over 43,000 people were killed in the Battle. *Luftwaffe* bombing attacks went on in diminished scale into 1941, the last big raid occurring on May 10, five weeks before Hitler's attack on the USSR. *See* Atlantic II.

Brittany, Action off *Gallic War*

This, the first sea fight in the Atlantic, was fought 56 BC, between the Roman fleet under Brutus, and the fleet of the Veneti, consisting of 220 galleys. The Romans were victorious, and the surrender of the Veneti and the whole of Brittany quickly followed.

Bronkhorst Spruit *First Boer War*

The opening engagement of the war, when, on December 20, 1880, a British column, 259 strong, under Colonel Anstruther, was ambushed by 150 mounted Boers under Joubert, and defeated with a loss of 155 killed and wounded. The Boers stated their losses at two killed and five wounded only. *See* Majuba.

Brooklyn *American Revolutionary War*

August 27, 1776, between 30,000 British under Sir William Howe, and the Americans, about 11,000 strong, under General Putnam. The Americans were completely defeated, with a loss of about 2,000 killed and wounded. The British lost 65 killed and 255 wounded. *See* Cape Henry.

Brunanburh *Danish Invasion*

In 937, when Æthelstan defeated with great slaughter the combined armies of Anlaf the Dane, Owen of Cumberland, and Constantine III of Scotland. *See* Kinloss.

Bucharest *Ottoman Wars*

In 1771, between the Turks under Mousson Oglou, and the Russians under General Romanzov. The Turks were totally defeated. *See* Ceşme, Focsani.

Buena Vista *American-Mexican War*

February 22, 1846, between 18,000 Mexicans under General Santa Anna, and 4,500 Americans under General Zachary Taylor. The Americans occupied a series of heights commanding the Angostura pass, and were there attacked by Santa Anna, who failed to dislodge them, the day ending with the combatants occupying the same ground as in the morning. On the 23rd, however, Santa Anna retired. The Americans lost 746 killed and wounded; the Mexicans admitted a loss of 1,500 killed, but it was probably heavier. *See* Monterrey.

Buenos Aires I *Napoleonic Wars*

This city was captured June 27, 1806, by a *coup de main*, by a British force, 1,700 strong, under General Beresford, aided by a small squadron under Sir Home Popham. Beresford, however, was not strong enough to hold the place, and before reinforcements could arrive he was defeated by the South Americans under General Liniers, with a loss of 250 killed and wounded, and compelled to surrender with his whole force. *See* Cape Finisterre III.

Buenos Aires II *Napoleonic Wars*

July 5, 1807, when 9,000 British troops under General Whitelocke assaulted the city. They penetrated into the streets, but suffered terrible losses from the defenders' fire from windows and roofs, and, Whitelocke proving a most incapable leader, were forced to surrender and evacuate the whole of the River Plate region. *See* Buenos Aires I, Cape Finisterre III.

Buenos Aires III *Mitre's Rebellion*

November 6, 1874, between the Argentine

Government troops under Sarmiento, and the rebels under Mitre and Aredondo. The rebels were defeated, and Mitre forced to surrender.

Bull Run I *American Civil War*

July 21, 1861, between 35,000 Federals under General McDowell, and 20,000 Confederates under General Beauregard. The Confederates occupied a position extending for about nine miles along the southern bank of the Bull Run, and an attempt to turn and drive in their left was at first successful, but, being rallied by General Beauregard, they assumed the offensive and totally routed the Northerners, with a loss of 1,492 killed and wounded, 1,600 prisoners, and 28 guns. The Confederates lost 1,752. The Confederate Colonel Thomas Jackson earned the name 'Stonewall Jackson' for his brigade's firm stand. *See* Rich Mountain.

Bull Run II *American Civil War*

August 30, 1862, between the Confederates under Stonewall Jackson, and the Federals under General Pope. The Federals attacked Jackson's position, which he maintained till evening, when, the Federal left giving way, he ordered a general advance, and drove the enemy from the field with heavy loss. Over 7,000 prisoners were taken. *See* Harper's Ferry.

Bunker's Hill *American Revolutionary War*

June 17, 1775, when 2,000 British troops, forming a portion of General Gage's army, dislodged the Americans holding Breed's Hill and Bunker's Hill, on the outskirts of Boston. The position was stubbornly contested, the assailants losing 800 men. American losses were some 410 killed and wounded. *See* Lexington.

Burlington Heights *War of 1812*

May 5, 1813, when the British under Colonel Procter were attacked by 1,300 Americans under General Clay, while engaged with another American force holding Burlington Heights. The Americans broke the British line and seized their guns, but Procter, who had only 1,000 men, with some Indian auxiliaries, rallied his troops and routed Clay, with a loss of nearly 1,000 killed, wounded and captured. *See* Lake Erie.

Burma I *World War II*

January 16, 1942, when Japan's 15th Army invaded Burma, then part of the British Commonwealth, overwhelming the British-Indian 17th Division, the 1st Burma Division and the two Chinese Divisions commanded by the American General Joseph Stilwell. Rangoon fell on March 9, Toungoo on March 31 and Mandalay on May 1. By May 20 all Burma was effectively occupied. Aircraft from India flew out over 8,000 wounded and sick, while the remnants of the British forces retreated through mountainous tropical jungle to Assam, India. British-Indian losses were 13,000 killed, wounded and missing. The Japanese lost 4,500 killed and wounded. *See* Malaya, Singapore.

Burma II *World War II*

In 1943 the Allies began a counter-offensive in Burma with the additional objective of opening an overland supply route to China. The British 15th Corps attacked down the Arakan coast to try to recapture Akyab, on the Bay of Bengal, but was held by the Japanese 28th Army. Farther north Brigadier Orde Wingate's guerrilla force cut the Mandalay–Myitkyina railway in more than 70 places. In August 1943, South-East Asia Command, set up under Lord Louis Mountbatten, launched three offensives. General Stilwell's two Chinese divisions (about 12,000 combatants) advanced from the north, the Chindit guerrillas operated behind the Japanese lines in central Burma, and, most important, General Slim's 14th British Army launched an offensive with the aim of retaking Akyab. General Mutaguchi counter-attacked the British in March 1944 at Imphal, but Allied ground and air superiority won the day and the Japanese were defeated with a loss of 12,500 killed and wounded by June 22. Myitkyina airfield was recaptured on May 17, the town on August 3. After the monsoon, the 14th Army took Akyab on January 3, 1945, Mandalay on March 20, then, after Prome and Pegu, Rangoon on May 3, 1945, thus freeing Burma from Japanese domination. *See* Malaya.

Burns Hill *Kaffir Wars*

In 1847, between the Kaffirs under Sandilli, and a small British force sent to arrest that chief. The British were greatly outnumbered, and were defeated and forced to retreat.

Busaco *Peninsular War*

Fought by General Lord Wellington (formerly Sir Arthur Wellesley) on September 27, 1810, to secure his retreat to Torres Vedras. Having occupied the far side of a ridge on the heights of Busaco with 25,000 British and the same number of Portuguese, he was attacked five times successively by 65,000 French under Marshal André Masséna. The actual assaults were delivered by the corps of Marshal Ney and General Reynier, but after much fierce fighting they failed to dislodge the British and were driven off with a loss to them of 4,500 killed or wounded. Wellington lost 1,300 killed and wounded. He then withdrew his army into previously fortified lines at Torres Vedras by October 10. Masséna, finding them too strong to attack, withdrew into winter quarters. Deprived of food for his men and harried by British hit-and-run tactics, he lost a further 20,000 men captured or dead from starvation or sickness before he retreated into Spain early in 1811. Wellington had now freed Portugal from French occupation except for Almeida, near the frontier. *See* Fuentes de Oñoro, Talavera.

Buxar *British Conquest of Bengal*

October 23, 1764, in India, between 7,000 British troops and sepoys under Major Monro and the army of Oude, 40,000 strong, under Siraj-ud-Daula, who was accompanied by the Great Mogul, Shah Akkam. The British gained a signal victory, Daula abandoning his camp with a loss of 4,000 men and 130 guns. The British lost 847 killed and wounded. The battle opened the way to the East India Company's domination of India. *See* Plassey, Calcutta.

Buzenval *Franco-Prussian War*

A sortie from Paris under General Trochu on January 19, 1871. The French, advancing under cover of a fog, established themselves in the Park of Buzenval, and occupied St Cloud, where they maintained their position throughout the day. At other points, however, they were less successful, and, on the morning of the 20th, the force at St Cloud, finding itself unsupported, was obliged to retire, and all the captured positions were abandoned. The Germans lost 40 officers and 570 men; the French 189 officers and 3,881 men. This sortie is also known as the Battle of Mont Valérien. *See* Sedan, Metz.

Byzantium I *Civil Wars of the Roman Empire*

In 318 BC, between the Macedonian fleet under Antigonus, and that of the Asiatic rebels under Clytus. The Asiatics were surprised at anchor, most of the crews being ashore, and, after a feeble defence, the whole of their fleet was destroyed or captured, with the exception of the admiral's galley, in which Clytus succeeded in escaping.

Byzantium II *Civil Wars of the Roman Empire*

In 323 the city was besieged by Constantine the Great after his victory over Licinius at Hadrianopolis. Licinius, finding the place difficult of defence, crossed into Asia and collected an army to raise the siege. He was, however, defeated at Chrysopolis, and Byzantium surrendered in 324. Constantine was proclaimed Emperor of the united Empire, and Byzantium, under its modern name of Constantinople, was made the capital. *See* Adrianople.

C

Cabala *Second Carthaginian Invasion of Sicily*

379 BC, between the Syracusans under Dionysius, and the Carthaginians under Mago. The latter were totally defeated and Mago killed. *See* Syracuse.

Cabria *Third Mithridatic War*

72 BC, between three Roman legions under Lucullus, and the Pontic army under Diophantus and Taxiles. The Pontic cavalry, on which Mithridates chiefly relied, was overwhelmed by Fabius Hadrianus, and the king was driven out of Pontus, which was erected into a Roman province. *See* Cyzicus, Tigranocerta.

Cadesia *Muslim Invasion of Persia*

In 636, between 30,000 Muslims under Said, the lieutenant of the Caliph Omar, and 120,000 Persians under Rustam. Throughout the first day the Persians, superior in numbers, but far inferior in warlike qualities, sustained the attacks of the Muslims without losing ground, but on the following day Rustam was slain, and his followers, losing heart, were driven headlong from the field, with fearful slaughter. The Muslims lost 7,500 in the battle. *See* Yarmuk, Jerusalem, Aleppo.

Cadiz *Anglo-Spanish War*

On April 29, 1587, Sir Francis Drake, with between 30 and 40 English ships, entered Cadiz Bay, and destroyed over 100 Spanish vessels. This exploit Drake described as 'Singeing the King of Spain's beard'. *See* Armada.

Cadsand *Hundred Years' War*

November 10, 1357, between 2,500 English under the Earl of Derby, and 5,000 Flemings in the French service. The Flemings were defeated with a loss of 1,000 men. *See* Auray, Poitiers.

Caen Area *World War II*

After D-Day Field-Marshal Montgomery planned to tie down as many Panzer divisions as possible in this area so as to make it easier for the Americans to break out at St Lô. The Germans concentrated six infantry divisions, seven Panzer divisions and three Nebelwerfer brigades (670 tanks) to oppose the British 2nd Army's 10 infantry, three armoured and one airborne division plus six armoured brigades (1,350 tanks). Three battles followed: first, June 10–15, when the British tried to encircle the city: second, June 25–29, when 8th Corps successfully drove back German armour and cut the Caen–Falaise road: third, July 7 after a heavy bombardment, which caused many civilian casualties. The British then fought their way into the city on July 8 and continued their attacks east and west of the Orne to keep the Panzers in this sector, so that the Americans at St Lô finally faced only 100 enemy tanks and nine divisions, and were able to break out. British casualties up to July 19: 6,010 killed, 28,690 wounded. German to July 23, 116,863 killed and wounded (Normandy Front). *See* St Lô.

Cairo *Ottoman Wars*

January 22, 1517, between the Turks under Selim I, and the Egyptians under the Mameluke Sultan, Tooman Bey. The Egyptians were utterly routed and Cairo taken, 50,000 of the inhabitants being massacred. Tooman Bey, the last of the Mamelukes, was hanged before the city gates, and Egypt annexed to the Ottoman Empire. *See* Rhodes, Aleppo III.

Calafat *Crimean War*

This position, strongly entrenched and held by 30,000 Turks under Ahmed Pasha, was invested by the Russians, 40,000 strong, under General Anrep, about the middle of February, 1854. The Russians delivered assault after assault upon the place, without effect, and finally withdrew their forces in May; having suffered a loss from disease, privation, and battle of 20,000 men. The Turks lost 12,000. *See* Inkerman, Kars.

Calais I *Hundred Years' War*

Siege was laid to this fortress in August 1346 by the English under King Edward III. The citizens made a brave defence, holding out for nearly a year, but at last were forced to surrender August 4, 1347. In the course of the siege, six burgesses offered themselves to the king as ransom for their fellow citizens; but their lives were spared on the intercession of Queen Philippa. *See* Crécy.

Calais II *Anglo-French Wars*

The last English stronghold in France was captured by the French under the Duc de Guise, January 6, 1558, after a siege of seven days only. Queen Mary is said to have exclaimed, on hearing the news, that at her death the word 'Calais' would be found engraven on her heart, but Calais fell because Mary, dominated by her husband Philip II of Spain, sent no money or men for its defence. *See* Boulogne, Gravelines.

Calatafimi *Italian Wars of Independence*

May 15, 1860, between Garibaldi's 'Thousand Volunteers', with a few thousand Sicilian 'Picciotti' and 4,000 Neapolitans under General Landi. The Neapolitans were driven back with heavy loss, and retreated in disorder to Palermo. Garibaldi lost, of his thousand, 18 killed and 128 wounded. *See* Solferino, Milazzo.

Calcutta *Seven Years' War*

Siege was laid to the city June 16, 1756, by Siraj-ud-Daula, Nawab of Bengal, with a large force. The garrison, consisting of 514 regulars and militia, and 1,000 matchlock men, under Captain Minchin, was quite inadequate to man the defences, and it was decided to abandon the city, remove all non-combatants to the ships, and only defend the fort. The Governor, Mr Drake, was among those who left the place, accompanied by Captain Minchin, who deserted his post, as did many of the militiamen. Only 190 remained for the defence of the fort. An assault was repulsed, with a loss to the defenders of 95 killed and wounded, but on

the 20th the little garrison surrendered. The survivors were thrust into a small room, known as the Black Hole, and out of 146 only 23 survived. *See* Arcot, Plassey.

Caldiero I *French Revolutionary Wars*

November 12, 1796, between the French under Napoleon and the Austrians under General Alvinzi. Napoleon attacked the Austrian position, and, for the first time in the campaign, suffered a reverse, eventually, after severe fighting, retiring with a loss of 3,000. Within the week, however, this defeat was avenged by the victory of Arcola. *See* Arcola, Bassano.

Caldiero II *Napoleon's Italian Campaigns*

On October 30, 1805, Marshal Masséna, with 37,000 French, encountered the Austrians, 50,000 strong, under the Archduke Charles, strongly posted in the village and on the heights of Caldiero. Masséna attacked and carried the heights, but the village held out until nightfall. During the night the Archduke removed his baggage and artillery, leaving a corps of 5,000 men, under General Hillinger, to protect his retreat, which force was captured on the following day. The Austrians lost 3,000 killed and wounded, and, including Hillinger's corps, 8,000 prisoners; the French about 4,000 killed and wounded. *See* Ulm.

Calicut *Second British-Mysore War*

December 10, 1790, between 9,000 Mysore troops under Hussein Ali, and a British force of one European and two native regiments under Colonel Hartley. Hussein Ali occupied a strong position in front of Calicut, which was attacked and carried by Hartley with a loss of 52 only. The enemy lost 1,000 killed and wounded, and 2,400 prisoners, including their commander. *See* Porto Novo, Seringapatam.

Callao I *Peruvian War of Independence*

On the night of November 5, 1820, Lord

Cochrane, who with three Chilean frigates was blockading the Spaniards in Callao, rowed into the harbour with 240 seamen and marines, and cut out the Spanish frigate *Esmeralda* from under the 300 guns of the shore batteries. He lost in the enterprise 41 killed and wounded, while the whole of the crew of the *Esmeralda*, including the Spanish Admiral, was captured or killed. *See* Callao II, Ayacucho, Junín.

Callao II *Peruvian War of Independence*

The town was bombarded by the Spanish fleet of 11 warships, May 2, 1866. The Peruvian batteries replied vigorously, and, after severe fighting, drove off the Spanish ships with a loss of 300. The Peruvians lost 1,000 killed and wounded. *See* Callao I, Ayacucho, Junín.

Calpulalpam *Mexican Liberal Rising*

December 20, 1860, between the Mexican Government troops under Miramón, and the Liberals under Juárez. The Liberals won a signal victory which opened the way to Mexico City, and brought about the downfall of Miramón's administration. *See* La Puebla, Acapulco.

Calven, The *Swiss-Swabian War*

May 22, 1499, between 6,300 men of the Grisons under Benedict Fontana, and 15,000 Imperialists under Maximilian I. The Swiss carried the Austrian entrenchments, and drove them out with heavy loss. *See* Frastenz.

Cambrai *World War I*

November 20 to December 7, 1917, when Brigadier-General Elles's Tank Corps spearheaded the world's first massed tank attack — on the two-miles-deep Hindenburg Line west of Cambrai. The 434 tanks, of which 378 were fighting ones, the others for specialized support, were inadequately backed by six infantry divisions and 40,000 cavalry of General Byng's Third Army. Field Marshal Haig's object was to penetrate the enemy line, then take it in reverse westwards and northwards so as to end the stalemate of trench warfare.

By 11 am November 20, the tanks, followed by infantry, had broken through General von der Marwitz's Second Army in the entire Hindenburg main, reserve and final systems on a six-mile front, being held up only at Flesquières village. The road to Cambrai, a key point, was now open but the cavalry, unable to cross the Scheldt canal at Masnières, where the bridge was down, made no attempt to cross at Marcoing, a mile east, and the chance to exploit the tanks' historic breakthrough was totally lost. With Bourlon Wood and the Bapaume–Cambrai road not yet taken, the attack slowed from the next day onwards, the infantry playing the main role.

On November 30, when many tanks were out of action, General Ludendorff ordered a counter-attack with 16 fresh divisions. A storm of gas shells hit the British lines. Soon much of their gains were lost and Haig ordered a withdrawal from December 4 to 7 to shorten the salient. What could have been a decisive battle ended with little gain, owing to poor generalship and the use of cavalry to exploit, rather than light tanks. British losses were 40,000 killed and wounded, 6,000 taken prisoner. German losses 50,000 killed and wounded, 11,000 taken prisoner. *See* Ypres III, Somme II.

Cambrai-St Quentin *World War I*

The first phase of the final Allied offensive was fought from September 27 to 30, 1918, when the British 1st, 2nd, 3rd, and 4th Armies took 26,500 prisoners and 340 guns in their attacks on the German Cambrai-St Quentin positions, and the French 1st Army gained an equivalent triumph. Several US Army divisions supported the British 4th Army's successful attack on September 29 on the canal to the north of St Quentin. The 3rd Army drove into the western suburbs of Cambrai, while the Canadians threatened to outflank it from the north. On October 1 the Germans gave up St Quentin to the French. Other gains by the New Zealanders and Canadians led to the fall of the Hindenburg line. On October 8 began the final phase of the battle. The Selle line was taken between October 18 and 20. On the 16th Ludendorff resigned and was replaced by General Groener, while the German armies in the north were driven back beyond the Scheldt

55

on a front of 20 miles. The success of the
Cambrai-St Quentin battle paved the way for
the startling Allied advances along the entire
front later in November which led to the
German surrender. *See* Amiens II, Meuse.

Cambuskenneth,

see Stirling Bridge

Camden *American Revolutionary War*

August 16, 1780, between 2,240 British under
General Cornwallis, and the Americans under
Generals Gates and de Kalb. Cornwallis had
concentrated about 2,000 men at Camden,
and though the Americans numbered 5,000
they were of very inferior quality. After a
small affair of outposts, the British attacked
the American levies, who were unable to face
the steady attack of the regulars, and fled
with heavy loss. Among the killed was de Kalb.
The British lost 312 killed and wounded.
See Guilford Courthouse.

Camelodunum *Second Invasion of Britain*

Fought 43, between the Romans under the
Emperor Claudius, and the Britons under
Caractacus. The Britons were routed, and
Camelodunum, Caractacus' capital, taken.
See Boudicca.

Camerinum *Third Samnite War*

298 BC, between two Roman legions under
Lucius Scipio, and the Samnites under Gellius
Equatius, aided by a force of Gauls. Scipio,
who had been stationed near Camerinum to
watch the pass through which the Gauls
were expected to cross the Apennines, was
unable to prevent the junction of the two
armies, and was totally defeated, one of his
legions being cut to pieces. *See* Bovianum.

Campaldino *Guelfs and Ghibellines*

June 11, 1289, between the Guelfs of Florence
and the Ghibellines who had been expelled
from the city. The latter were utterly routed,
and this defeat put an end to their power in
Florence. The battle is notable for the
presence of Dante in the ranks of the victors.
See Alto Pascio, Corte Nuova, Monte Aperto.

Campen *Seven Years' War*

October 18, 1759, between the Prussians
under the Prince of Brunswick, and the
French under General de Castries, when the
Prussians were defeated with a loss of 1,600
men. *See* Bergen, Crefeld.

Camperdown *French Revolutionary Wars*

Fought between the British fleet, 16 line of
battle ships, under Admiral Duncan, and the
Dutch, in equal force, under Admiral de
Winter, October 11, 1797. The Dutch fleet
was on its way to cooperate with the French
in a landing in Ireland, and was intercepted
by Duncan, who at once gave battle. The
British fleet, in two lines, broke through the
Dutch line, and, in the general action which
followed, captured eight ships, including the
flagship, the *Vrijheid*. The British lost 1,040
killed and wounded, the Dutch 1,160 and
6,000 prisoners. *See* Cape St Vincent,
Vinegar Hill.

Campo Santo *War of the Austrian Succession*

February 8, 1743, between the Spaniards
under Mortemar, and the Imperialists under
Count Traum. Mortemar was endeavouring
to effect a junction with the army of the
Prince de Conti, and though the action was
undecided, its results were in favour of the
Imperialists, who prevented the two armies
from joining hands. *See* Dettingen, Mollwitz.

Campus Castorum *Revolt of Vitellius*

In 69, between the revolted legionaries,
70,000 strong, under Fabius Valens and
Alienus Caecina, and the army of the Emperor
Otho under Suetonius Paulinus. The Imperial
troops gained some advantages, but Suetonius
did not consider himself strong enough to
follow it up, and was relieved of his command
by Otho. *See* Bedriacum.

Candia *Candian War*

Siege was laid to this town (Heraklion) by the Turks under Jussuf, the Capitan Pasha, in 1648, and was defended by a small garrison of Venetians, under Luigi Moncenigo. So vigorous was the defence that the Turks lost 20,000 men in the first six months of the siege. The siege lasted over twenty years, the place being from time to time revictualled and reinforced by the Venetians and the French, but it was finally surrendered by Morosini, September 27, 1669.

Canea *Candian War*

This town, in northern Crete, also known as Khania, was besieged June 24, 1644, by 50,000 Turks under Jussuf, the Capitan Pasha, and defended by a small force of Venetians and Candians, who held out until August 22, repulsing numerous assaults, which cost the Turks 20,000 men. *See* Candia.

Cannae *Second Punic War*

August 3, 216 BC, between 85,000 Romans under Varro, and about 50,000 Carthaginians under Hannibal. Hannibal, though outnumbered in infantry, was much superior in cavalry. The Romans were drawn up with the sea in their rear, and were attacked and broken by the Carthaginian horse. The infantry followed up the attack, and, flight being impossible, the Romans were slaughtered where they stood, 50,000 falling, including the Consul Æmilius, 25 superior officers, and 80 senators. The Carthaginians lost 5,700. *See* Capua.

Cape Bona *Wars of the Western Roman Empire*

In 468, between the Roman fleet of 1,100 galleys and transports under Basiliscus, and the fleet of the Vandals under Genseric. The Romans were lying at anchor, having landed their troops, and Genseric, taking advantage of a favourable wind, sent in a fleet of fireships following them up by a determined attack. More than half the Roman ships were destroyed, Basiliscus escaping with difficulty. *See* Hippo.

Cape Finisterre I *War of the Austrian Succession*

May 3, 1747, between a British fleet of 16 sail under Admiral Anson, and a French fleet of 38 sail under Admiral de la Jonquière. The French were completely defeated, losing 10 ships and nearly 3,000 prisoners. *See* Toulon.

Cape Finisterre II *War of the Austrian Succession*

October 2, 1747, when a British fleet of 14 ships under Admiral Hawke attacked a French fleet of nine battleships under Admiral de l'Etenduère. The French were signally defeated, losing four ships. The British lost 598 killed and wounded. *See* Roucoux.

Cape Finisterre III *Napoleonic Wars*

July 22, 1805, between a British fleet of 15 sail of the line under Rear Admiral Sir Robert Calder, and the combined French and Spanish fleets returning from the West Indies, under Admiral de Villeneuve. The French fleet, consisting of 20 battleships, was attacked by Calder, who captured two ships. Fogs and light airs prevented him from following up his advantage next day, for which he was tried by court-martial, censured, but later made Admiral. The British loss was 183 killed and wounded, the French losing 149 killed and 327 wounded. *See* Copenhagen, Ulm, Trafalgar.

Cape Henry *American Revolutionary War*

March 16, 1781, between a British fleet of eight ships of the line and three frigates under Vice-Admiral Arbuthnot, and a French squadron stronger by one frigate. The French were forced to retire, the British losing 30 killed and 64 wounded. *See* Brooklyn.

Cape Passero *War of the Quadruple Alliance*

July 31, 1718, between a British fleet of 21 ships under Admiral Sir George Byng, and a Spanish fleet of 29 ships under Don Antonio Castañeta. Byng attacked the Spaniards in the Straits of Messina, and, after a very severe action, in which both sides lost heavily, captured or destroyed no less than 15 of the Spanish ships. Castañeta died of wounds received in the action. This battle is also known as the Battle of Messina.

Cape St Vincent *French Revolutionary Wars*

February 14, 1797, between a British fleet of 15 ships of the line and five frigates under Sir John Jervis, and a Spanish fleet of 26 sail of the line and 12 frigates under Admiral Don Juan de Langara. In spite of their superior numbers, the Spaniards were totally defeated, losing four ships and over 3,000 prisoners, in addition to heavy losses in killed and wounded. The British lost 74 killed and 227 wounded. For this signal victory, Jervis was created Lord St Vincent. Nelson, then commodore, by independently attacking 18 Spanish warships who tried to escape northward, was largely responsible for the victory. He was made a Knight of the Bath. *See* Camperdown, Nile.

Caporetto *World War I*

October 24 to November 7, 1917, when seven German and eight Austrian divisions under General von Bülow attacked General Capello's mutinous 2nd Italian Army in snow after a heavy five-hour artillery preparation. Between Zaga and Auzza the 2nd Army broke at once, forcing the retreat as well of the Italian 3rd and 4th Armies. By dawn von Bülow's forces had crossed the Isonzo and the Italian frontier, taking 100,000 prisoners, many with white flags, and 700 guns. The Italians fell back to the Piave river line. The Austrians seized dominating heights between the Piave and the Brenta rivers and a bridgehead across the Piave at Zenson. They were finally held with the aid of five British and six French reinforcement divisions after a four-day battle, December 11–15, in the Brenta valley. At Caporetto and later, the Italians lost more than 300,000 men taken prisoner, some 40,000 killed and wounded, besides 3,000 guns of all types. *See* Isonzo, Asiago, Piave River.

Caprysema *First Messenian War*

743 BC, between the Spartans and Corinthians, and the Messenians with their allies from other Peloponnesian states under Cristomenes.

The Spartans were routed, and, but for the eloquence of Tyrtacus, would have abandoned the struggle. *See* Cecryphalea.

Capua *Second Punic War*

Besieged in the autumn of 212 BC, by 60,000 Romans under Q. Fulvius and Appius Claudius. The Romans formed a double wall of circumvallation round the city, and, early in the winter, their defences were attacked by the garrison from within and Hannibal from without, but with no success. Hannibal then attempted to draw the besiegers from their position by marching upon Rome, but only a small portion of the besieging force followed him. It being thus found impossible to relieve the city, it shortly afterwards surrendered. *See* Metaurus.

Carabobo *Venezuelan War of Independence*

June 24, 1821, between the Colombian patriots, 8,000 strong, under Bolívar, and the Spanish Royalists, about 4,000 under General La Torre. The Royalists were utterly routed, barely 400 reaching Porto Cabello. This battle determined the independence of Venezuela. *See* Boyacá.

Caracha *Colombian War of Independence*

In 1813, between the Colombian Patriots under Bolívar and the Spanish Royalists, Bolívar gaining a complete victory. *See* Boyacá.

Caraguatay *Paraguayan War*

August, 1869, between the Paraguayans under López, and the Brazilians under the Comte d'Eu. After a stubborn engagement the Brazilians were victorious. *See* Aquidaban.

Carbiesdale *English Civil War*

April 27, 1650, between the Royalists of Orkney, 1,000 strong, with 500 Swedish mercenaries, and a small Parliamentary force under Colonel Strachan. General the Marquis of Montrose, who commanded the Royalists, saw his troops broken by the Parliamentary horse, only the Swedes offering any serious resistance. The Royalists lost 396 killed and wounded and over 400 prisoners, while

Strachan had lost only two wounded. This was Montrose's last fight, and he was soon afterwards captured and hanged at Edinburgh on May 21. *See* Dunbar.

Carenage Bay *American Revolutionary War*

In 1778, between the French under the Comte d'Estaing, and the English under Admiral Barrington and General Meadows. The French were defeated, and the British seized the island of St Lucia. *See* Minorca.

Carigat,

see Arikera

Carlisle *Jacobite Rebellion of the Forty-five*

This city was besieged by the Jacobites under the Young Pretender, November 9, 1745, and was defended by the Duke of Cumberland and the Westmorland Militia, with a small force of regulars, under Colonel Durand. The besiegers opened fire on the 13th, and on the evening of the 14th Durand surrendered. *See* Culloden, Prestonpans.

Carnoul *Persian Invasion of India*

In 1739, between the Persians under Nadir Shah, and the Mughals under the Emperor Mohammed Shah and his Grand Vizier, Nizam-ul-Mulk. The Persian veterans completely defeated the raw Mughal levies, and Nadir Shah shortly afterwards occupied and sacked Delhi, carrying off, it was said, jewels and coin to the value of thirty millions sterling. *See* Panipat III.

Carpi *War of the Spanish Succession*

July 1701, between the Imperialists under Prince Eugène, and the French army in Lombardy, under Marshal Catinat. The French were badly defeated, and, in consequence, Catinat was recalled from the command. *See* Cremona III.

Carrhae *Parthian War*

53 BC, between the Romans, 6,000 strong, under Publius Crassus, and the Parthians under Sillaces. The Parthians, entirely cavalry, adopted their usual tactics of retiring and drawing their foes in pursuit. As the heavily armed legionaries became strung out across the plain, they turned upon them and cut them down in detail. Of the division, 6,000 strong, which actually came into action, 500 were made prisoners, and the rest, including Crassus, killed. *See* Alesia.

Carrical *Seven Years' War*

An action was fought off this town in India, on August 2, 1758, between a British squadron under Admiral Pococke, and the French under Comte d'Aché. After a severe engagement, the French fleet drew off, but the English pursuit, owing to damaged rigging, was ineffectual, and d'Aché reached Pondicherry without the loss of a ship. *See* Fort St David.

Carthage I *Third Punic War*

In 152 BC siege was laid to this city by a Roman consular army under Manius Manilius, aided by a fleet under L. Censorinus. The Carthaginian army under Hasdrubal was encamped outside the walls, and greatly hindered the operations of the Romans, who would have made little progress but for the efforts of Scipio Æmilianus, then a military tribune. In 148 BC, Scipio was made consul, and appointed to the command, and he succeeded in completely blockading the city, which, after an obstinate resistance lasting six years, was captured 146 BC and razed to the ground. *See* Numantia.

Carthage II *Byzantine Empire Wars*

September 14, 533, between the Vandals under Gelimer, about 160,000 strong, and the Romans under Belisarius, far inferior in numbers. Gelimer divided his army into three, of which he led one portion to attack the main body of the Romans. The action was precipitated, however, by the hasty attack by Ammatas of the vanguard, wherein he was routed with heavy loss. Gelimer then fell upon the pursuing Romans, but Belisarius coming up, the Vandals were put to flight, and the Romans gained a complete victory. On the following day Carthage opened her gates to the victors. *See* Rome IV.

59

Carthagena *War of the Austrian Succession*

This port was blockaded March 9, 1741, by a British fleet under Admiral Vernon. An unsuccessful attack was made upon the forts, and eventually Vernon, having lost 3,000 men during the operations, withdrew April 9. *See* Mollwitz.

Casal *Wars of Louis XIV*

April 1640, between the French, 10,000 strong, under Harcourt, and the Spaniards, numbering 20,000, who were besieging Casal. Harcourt pierced the Spanish lines and totally defeated them, with a loss of 3,000 killed and wounded, 800 prisoners, and 18 guns. *See* Dunes, Marsaglia.

Casilinum *Byzantine Empire Wars*

In 554, between 18,000 Imperial troops under Narses, and the Franks and Alemanni, 30,000 strong, under Buccelin. The Romans won a signal victory, and are said by the chroniclers to have exterminated the invading army with a loss to themselves of 80 only. Buccelin fell in the battle. *See* Taginae, Rome IV.

Cassano *War of the Spanish Succession*

August 16, 1705, between the French under the Duc de Vendôme, with 35 battalions and 45 squadrons, and the Imperialists under Prince Eugène. The Prince, with greatly inferior numbers, attacked the French in a strong position, which he succeeded in carrying as the night fell. The Imperialists lost about 4,000; the French about 5,000. *See* Luzzara, Blenheim.

Cassino *World War II*

The German Gustav Line, which ran from the Garigliano river estuary on the west coast to just south of Pescara on the Adriatic, was held by Field Marshal Kesselring with nine divisions out of his total of 18 in Italy. General Alexander had the seven Commonwealth divisions of the 8th Army, and the US 5th Army of five American, five British, two French and one Polish divisions. From January 29 to February 4, 1944, the US 3rd division failed after a desperate attack to take the key point of

Cassino, dominated by the ancient mountaintop monastery of St Benedict. It was decided to obliterate the monastery by bombing, carried out after a warning, on February 15, when 546 tons of bombs turned it into rubble. An attack carried out as the bombing ended failed as well, the Germans being dug-in in deep bunkers. On March 15 British-Indian and New Zealand troops seized a foothold in the ruins, but this attack too was halted. Finally, on May 11, Cassino was outflanked by the Polish Corps and taken from the rear six days later. The Allies lost more than 2,500 killed and wounded. *See* Anzio, Salerno.

Castelfidardo *Italian Wars of Independence*

September 18, 1860, between the Papal troops under General La Moricière, about 8,000 strong, and the Sardinians, 40,000 strong, under General Cialdini. The Papal army was totally routed, and La Moricière assembled 300 infantry, with which he retreated to Ancona. *See* Milazzo.

Castella *Peninsular War*

April 13, 1813, between 17,000 allied troops under General Sir John Murray, and 15,000 French under Marshal Suchet. The French were defeated. The allies lost 600 killed and wounded; the French, according to Suchet, 800, according to Murray, 3,000, but the former figure is probably nearer to the truth. *See* Vitoria.

Castelnaudary *French Civil Wars*

September 1, 1632, between the troops of Louis XIII and the rebel nobles under the Duc de Montmorenci. The rebels were routed, and Montmorenci taken prisoner.

Castiglione I *War of the Spanish Succession*

September 8, 1706, between the Imperialists under the Prince of Hesse, and the French under General de Medavi. The Prince was besieging Castiglione, when he was attacked by the French, and totally defeated, with a loss of 8,000 killed, wounded, and missing. *See* Turin, Denain.

Castiglione II *French Revolutionary Wars*

August 3, 1796, between the French under Napoleon and the Imperialists under Field Marshal Count von Wurmser. Napoleon with 25,000 men advanced upon Lonato, while General Augereau with the 3rd Division moved upon Castiglione. Lonato was carried by assault and the Austrian army cut in two. One part, under General Bazalitch, effected a retreat to the Mincio, but the other part was cut up by a French division under General Guyeaux, and Marshal Junot's dragoons, near Salo, losing 3,000 prisoners and 20 guns. In the action fought near Castiglione on August 5 the Austrians were defeated with a loss of 2,000 men and driven back upon Mantua. *See* Mantua.

Castillejos *Spanish-Moroccan War*

January 1, 1860, when the advance guard of the Spanish army under General Prim defeated a strong force of Moors after severe fighting. The victory opened the road to Tetuán. *See* Guad-el-Ras.

Castillon *Hundred Years' War*

July 17, 1453, the last battle of the Hundred Years' War. The English, under John Talbot, Earl of Shrewsbury, marched to the relief of Castillon and attacked the lines of the besiegers, but were taken in flank by a sortie from the French entrenchments and totally defeated, Talbot being killed. On October 19 following, Bordeaux opened her gates to the French. Calais was now the sole English possession in France. *See* Formigny.

Caudine Forks *Second Samnite War*

321 BC, when a Roman force under T. Venturius Calvinus was trapped by the Sabines under Pontius, in the narrow pass of Caudium. The Romans fought till nightfall, suffering heavy loss, and next day, finding every exit from the pass barred, the survivors surrendered. This defeat stimulated the evolution of the Roman legion as a military unit. *See* Bovianum.

Cawnpore I *Indian Mutiny*

The residency of Cawnpore was invested by the mutineers June 6, 1857, and defended by a small garrison until June 24, when the survivors, about 450 in number, surrendered under promise from the Nana Sahib of a safe conduct to Allahabad. They were, however, fired upon as they took to the boats, and only a few escaped. The survivors of this massacre were afterwards murdered in cold blood by order of the Nana Sahib. *See* Lucknow, Gwalior, Delhi V.

Cawnpore II *Indian Mutiny*

December 6, 1857, between the British under General Sir Colin Campbell, and 25,000 rebels, including the Gwalior contingent. The mutineers were routed at all points, and fled, pursued by the cavalry for 14 miles, suffering heavy loss. Out of 36 guns, 32 were captured. The British lost 99. *See* Lucknow, Delhi.

Cecryphalea *Third Messenian War*

A naval action, fought 458 BC between the Peloponnesians and the Athenians, in which the latter were victorious.

Cedar Creek *American Civil War*

October 19, 1864, between 17,000 Confederates under General Early, and about 31,000 Federals under General Sheridan. Under cover of a fog, Early turned Sheridan's right, capturing 18 guns, but Sheridan, rallying his broken right wing, totally routed the Confederates, who had been engaged in plundering the captured camp. The Federal losses were the heavier, but Sheridan captured 22 guns, besides retaking the 18 he had lost at the beginning of the action. *See* Fisher's Hill.

Cedar Mountain *American Civil War*

August 9, 1862, between 20,000 Confederates under Jackson, and about 9,000 Federals under General Pope. The strong Confederate position was assailed at 5 pm, and successive attacks were repulsed until late in the evening, when the fighting ceased. The Federals lost about 2,800 killed, wounded, and missing; the Confederates, 800 or 900. *See* Seven Days' Battle, Fair Oaks.

Cepeda *Argentine Civil War*

October 23, 1859, between the troops of the Argentine Confederation under Justo de Urquiza, and those of the State of Buenos Aires, under Mitre. Urquiza was victorious, and in the following month Buenos Aires entered the Confederation. *See* Monte Caseros.

Cephisus

Fought 1307, between the Catalan 'Great Band' 9,500 strong, and the troops of Walter de Brienne, Duke of Athens, 15,000 in number. The Catalans surrounded their camp with an artificial inundation into which the Duke's cavalry rode unsuspectingly and were cut to pieces, de Brienne being among those killed.

Cerignola *Franco-Spanish Wars in Italy*

In 1503, between the Spaniards under Gonsalvo de Cordova and the French under the Duc de Nemours. The French were totally defeated and Nemours killed. Naples was occupied by the Spanish. *See* Garigliano.

Cerisolles *Wars of Charles V*

April 28, 1544, between the French under François de Bourbon and the Imperialists under du Gast, the French gaining a complete victory. *See* Pavia IV, Rebec.

Ceşme *Ottoman Wars*

July 7, 1770, between the Russian fleet of 50 sail under Count Alexis Orloff and the Turkish fleet of nearly 100 ships of the line under Hassan Bey. With the exception of one ship, which was captured, the whole of the Turkish fleet was destroyed. *See* Focsani.

Chacabuco *Chilean War of Independence*

February 12, 1817, between the Chilean patriots under San Martin and the Spanish royalists. The Chileans won a complete victory. *See* Maypo.

Chaeronea I *Amphictyonic War*

August 338 BC, between the Macedonians under Philip, and the Athenians and Thebans under Charles and Theagenes respectively. Philip had 30,000 foot and 2,000 horse, the latter led by Alexander, then a lad of eighteen; the allies were slightly fewer in number. Philip reinforced his right wing, which was opposed by the Athenians, and sent his heavy cavalry against the Thebans, on the allied right. Their charge broke the Theban ranks, and they then attacked the Athenians in flank and rear. A hopeless rout ensued, the Theban 'Sacred Band' dying where they stood. The Athenians lost 6,000 killed and 2,000 prisoners. The Thebans were almost annihilated. *See* Thebes.

Chaeronea II *First Mithridatic War*

86 BC, between the Romans under Sulla, 30,000 strong, and the troops of Pontus, 90,000 in number, under Archelaus. The Romans were completely victorious. *See* Orchomenus.

Chalcedon *Third Mithridatic War*

74 BC, between the Roman fleet, under Rutilius Nudo, and that of Pontus. The Romans sallied out of the harbour, but were driven back, and the Pontic fleet then broke the chain protecting the entrance and destroyed the whole of the Roman ships, 70 in number. *See* Cabria.

Chalgrove Field *English Civil War*

A cavalry skirmish fought June 18, 1643, between 1,850 Royalists under Prince Rupert, and about 1,000 Parliamentarians under Sir Philip Stapleton and notable only for the fact that John Hampden was killed in the affair.

Châlons I *Revolt of the Legions of Aquitaine*

Fought 271, between the troops of the Emperor Aurelian, and the revolted legions under Tetricus. Tetricus, who was only a puppet in the hands of his soldiers, concerted measures with Aurelian for their destruction, and so posted his forces as to give the

Emperor the advantage, after which he deserted, with a few followers. The revolted legionaries fought desperately, but were cut to pieces.

Châlons II *Invasion of the Alemanni*

July 366, between the Romans under Jovinus, and the Alemanni under Vadomair. After an obstinate engagement, lasting throughout the day, the Alemanni were routed with a loss of 6,000 killed and 4,000 prisoners. The Romans lost 1,200. *See* Argentoratum, Tigris.

Châlons III *Wars of the Western Roman Empire*

In 451, between the Romans and the Visigoths under Actius and Theodoric respectively, and the Huns under Attila. The battle was fought on an open plain, and while the right and centre of the allies withstood Attila's onslaught, the Visigoths on the left made a furious charge, in which Theodoric fell, and totally routed the right of the Huns. Attila then withdrew to his camp, having suffered heavy loss, and prepared to resist the attack of the allies on the following day. Actius, however, did not renew the conflict, and allowed Attila to retreat unmolested. *See* Hippo, Rome II.

Châlons IV *'Little' Battle of*

Arising out of a tournament in 1274, in which the life of Edward I was endangered by foul play, a fight in earnest took place between the English and French knights present. The French were worsted, and a considerable number slain. This fight is called the 'Little' Battle of Châlons.

Champagne *World War I*

On September 25, 1915, after an intense artillery bombardment, General de Langle de Cary's 4th and General Pétain's 2nd French Armies attacked the German lines in Champagne to try to break their communications from east to west along the Aisne. Some success followed this first attack, the French taking thousands of prisoners and scores of guns. Two successive French attacks were less successful and on October 30 German counter-attacks recovered much ground and their lost rail

communications in the region. The battle ended on November 6, with the French holding advances of up to 2½ miles in some places on a 15-mile front, which gave them no worthwhile advantage. French casualties amounted to 145,000 killed or wounded. They also took 25,000 German prisoners and about 160 guns. *See* Artois and Artois-Loos.

Champaubert *Napoleonic Wars*

February 10, 1814, when Napoleon with his main army, by an extraordinary forced march through a difficult country, fell upon Blücher's army marching upon Paris, via Châlons. Blücher was advancing in three divisions, and Napoleon attacked the second of these, under General Alsusieff, and completely dispersed it, taking 2,000 prisoners and all the guns. On the following day he encountered General Sachen, who with 20,000 men formed the advance guard, and defeated him at Montmirail, with a loss of 6,000, forcing him to abandon the main road and retire on Château-Thierry. On the 13th he encountered General Count Yorck, with 30,000 Russians and Prussians at Château-Thierry, driving him out with heavy loss, including 3,000 prisoners, while finally on the 14th he turned on the main body under Blücher himself, who, not being sufficiently strong to face the main French army, was compelled to retire, which he did in good order, after losing 3,000 in killed, wounded, and prisoners. This flank march is considered one of Napoleon's most brilliant achievements. *See* La Rothière.

Chancellorsville *American Civil War*

May 2, 3 and 4, 1863, between 53,000 Confederates under General Lee and 75,000 Federals under General Hooker. Lee, though largely outnumbered, detached half his force under Jackson to turn Hooker's right, while he contained the Federals with the rest of his army. Jackson's march was successfully carried out, and on the afternoon of the 2nd he commenced his attack, routing the Federal 11th Corps. This success, however, cost the Confederates dear, for Jackson's staff was mistaken in the dusk for that of a Federal general, and was fired into by a South Carolina regiment, and Jackson mortally wounded. On the 3rd the attack was renewed in front and flank, with further success for the Confederates, while on the 4th the Federals were driven off, and Hooker forced to recross the Rappahannock on the 5th. The Confederates lost about 10,000 men; the Federals about 18,000 including 7,650 prisoners. *See* Fredericksburg.

Chanda *Third British-Maratha War*

This fortress, the chief stronghold of the Rajah of Nagpur, was besieged by a British force under Colonel Adams, May 9, 1818. It was defended by over 3,000 of the Rajah's troops, but after two days' bombardment the place was taken by storm, with small loss to the assailants, while the garrison had 500 killed, including the commandant. *See* Kirkee.

Chandernagore *Seven Years' War*

Besieged March 14, 1757, by Clive, with 2,000 East Indian Company's troops, and defended by 600 Frenchmen and 300 Sepoys. On the 19th three British ships under Admiral Watson arrived, and on the 24th a joint attack by sea and land resulted in the capture of the place. *See* Madras.

Chapultepec *American-Mexican War*

September 13, 1847, when three American divisions attacked the hill of this name, held by some 4,000 Mexicans, cleared it and that night went on to storm and take Mexico City itself, to which Chapultepec commanded the approaches. *See* Buena Vista.

Charasiab *Second British-Afghan War*

October 6, 1879, when Sir Frederick Roberts attacked a force of Afghans and Ghilzais, who were massed on the road by which a convoy was approaching from Zahidabad, under General Macpherson. The enemy was routed and dispersed, and the convoy reached camp safely. *See* Maiwand, Kandahar.

Charenton *War of the Fronde*

February 8, 1649, between the Royal troops, 8,000 strong, under the Great Condé, and the forces of the Paris Parliament under Clauleu. Condé gained a complete victory, driving the Frondeurs from all their entrenchments, and forcing them back upon Paris with heavy loss, including 100 officers. Among the slain was Clauleu. *See* Palais Gallien, Porte St Antoine.

Charleston *American Civil War*

The siege of this town began on April 6, 1863, on which day the Federal fleet crossed the bar. On the 7th an attack was made upon Fort Sumter by nine ironclads under Admiral Dupont, which was repulsed with a loss of one ship and the disabling of several others. The defenders lost two men only. On July 10th and 11th a land force attacked Fort Wagner, but was repulsed with loss. On the 18th an assault by three brigades under General Seymour was also repulsed with enormous loss; and preparations were then made for a sap. On September 5, after a very heavy bombardment, Fort Wagner proved to be untenable, and, with the works on Morris Island, was abandoned, but the besiegers failed in all their attempts on Fort Sumter, and the inner defences. From this time the siege became a mere blockade of the port, until, on the approach of Sherman's army, the garrison, then 9,000 strong, evacuated the city, February 18, 1865. *See* Chancellorsville, Gettysburg.

Chateauguay *War of 1812*

October 26, 1813, between the Americans, 7,000 strong, under General Hampton, and a force of Canadian Militia, far inferior in numbers, who were strongly posted near Chateauguay. The Americans attempted to storm the Canadian lines, but the Canadians made a most gallant defence, and repulsed them with heavy loss. *See* Chrysler's Farm.

Château-Thierry,
see Champaubert

Chattanooga *American Civil War*

November 24 to 27, 1863, between 56,000 Federals under General U. S. Grant, and the Confederate Army of the West, 64,000 strong, under General Bragg. The attack on the Confederate lines began on the 27th, the Federals capturing Look Out Mountain, on their extreme left. They advanced unseen through a thick fog, to the upper slopes, and drove out the defenders, whence this action is known as the 'Battle Above the Clouds'. On the following day Braxton Bragg's centre was pierced, while fighting of the 26th and 27th was in the nature of severe rearguard actions. The Federals lost 5,286 killed and wounded, and 330 missing. The Confederates lost fewer in killed and wounded, but they left in the hands of the Federals 6,142 prisoners, 40 guns and 7,000 rifles. Also called the 'Battle of Missionary Ridge'. *See* Chickamauga.

Che-mul-pho *Russo-Japanese War*

February 8, 1904, between a Japanese squadron of four protected cruisers, convoying transports, under Admiral Uriu, and a Russian cruiser and gunboat which sought to oppose the landing. After a smart action the cruiser was blown up to avoid capture, and the gunboat destroyed, the Russians losing 504 killed and wounded. The Japanese suffered no material damage. *See* Port Arthur.

Cheriton *English Civil War,*

see Alresford

Chetaté *Crimean War*

January 6 to 9, 1854. On the 6th the advanced Russian post of 6,000 men at Chetaté, under General Fischbuch, was attacked by 6,000 Turks under Ahmed Pasha. After heavy fighting, in which the Russians lost 3,000 killed or wounded, and many prisoners, and the Turks 1,000, the Russians were driven out of the village. On the following days the Russians made desperate attempts to recover the position, General Anrep, on the 9th, bringing up some 20,000 men from Cragova. All their efforts, however, failed, and the three days' fighting cost them a further 2,000 men, the Turks losing about 1,000. *See* Alma, Sevastopol.

Chevilly *Franco-Prussian War*

September 30, 1870, when a sortie from Paris under General Vinoy was repulsed by the Sixth German Corps under von Tümpling, with a loss of 74 officers and 2,046 men. The Germans lost 28 officers and 413 men killed and wounded. *See* Sedan.

Chevy Chase,

see Otterburn

Chiari *War of the Spanish Succession*

September 1, 1701, between the Imperialists, about 28,000 strong, under Prince Eugène, and the French and Spaniards under the Duke of Savoy. The Prince occupied the small town of Chiari, where he was attacked by the allies, who, after two hours' hard fighting, were repulsed with a loss of nearly 3,000. Owing to the strength of their position, the Imperialists lost 117 only. *See* Cremona.

Chickahominy *American Civil War*

June 3, 1864, between the Federal Army of the Potomac under General Grant, and the Confederate army of Virginia under General Lee. Grant attacked the Southerners' entrenchments, with the object of forcing the passage of the Chickahominy, and his first onslaught met with some success, but the Confederates, rallying, drove back their assailants to their original position with heavy loss. All further attempts on Lee's lines failed, and the Federals were finally repulsed with a loss of over 13,000 killed, wounded and missing. The Confederates lost about 6,000. *See* Spotsylvania.

Chickamauga *American Civil War*

September 19 and 20, 1863, between the 66,000-strong Confederate Army of the West under General Braxton Bragg, and the 58,000 Federals under General Rosecrans. On the 19th the Confederates attacked along the whole line and drove back their opponents, cutting them off from the river, and forcing them to bivouac for the night in a waterless country. On the 20th the attack was renewed, and though Bragg's right was repulsed, he was elsewhere successful, and by nightfall Rosecrans was in full retreat. Bragg however, failed to follow up his victory, and allowed Rosecrans to retire on Chattanooga unmolested. The Federals lost 16,351 men killed, wounded or missing, and 36 guns; the Confederates about 12,000. *See* Chattanooga.

Chilianwala *Second British-Sikh War*

January 14, 1849, between the 12,000 strong British-Indian force, with 60 guns, under Lord Gough, and the Sikhs, 40,000 strong, with 62 guns, under Shir Singh. The battle was evenly contested, and though in the end Lord Gough drove the Sikhs from the field, he lost 2,300 men killed or wounded in three hours and was compelled to retire after the action owing to lack of water. *See* Gujerat.

Chiloe *Chilean War of Independence*

On January 19, 1826, the small group of islands, held for the Spanish crown by a garrison under Quintanella, was surrendered to a force of Chileans, 4,000 strong, with a small squadron of warships under Freyre. *See* Chacabuco.

Chingleput *Carnatic War*

This fortress, near Madras, defended by a French garrison of 40 Europeans and 500 troops, was captured, 1752, by Ensign Robert Clive, with a force of about 700 recruits and Sepoys. *See* Arcot.

Chioggia *War of Chioggia*

This city, which had been captured by the Genoese from Venice, was besieged by the Venetians under Admiral Pisano and defended by Luciano Doria, who was killed during the siege. It made an obstinate resistance, but was forced to surrender June 24, 1380, the Venetians capturing 19 Genoese galleys and 4,000 prisoners. This disaster broke the power of the Genoese Republic for many years. *See* Pola.

Chios I *Social War*

Chios having risen against Athenian rule in 357 BC, a fleet of 60 ships under Chabrias and Chares was sent to reduce it. A force having been landed, a joint attack was made by the fleet and the army, but in attempting to enter the harbour, the galley of Chabrias, which led the way, was surrounded and overpowered, Chabrias falling. The troops were then withdrawn, and the attack abandoned. *See* Embata, Tolenus.

Chios II *Wars of the Hellenistic Monarchies*

201 BC, between the Macedonian fleet, 48 triremes and some smaller vessels under Philip, and the combined fleets of Rhodes and Pergamus under Theophiliscus and Attalus. Philip was defeated with the loss of half his ships, 3,000 killed and 5,000 prisoners.

The allies lost six ships and 800 men. *See* Thermopylae.

Chippenham *Danish Invasions of Britain*

January, 878, when a strong force of Danes under Guthrum attacked with great slaughter King Alfred's army of Wessex during a Twelfth Night festival. Alfred became a fugitive at Athelny, in Somerset, and the Danes were supreme in southern England. Later, from his hiding place King Alfred ordered a mobilization to take place in May for an attack on the Danes. *See* Ethandun.

Chippewa *War of 1812*

July 5, 1814, between 4,000 Americans under General Jacob Brown, and 2,400 British, 1,500 being regulars, under General Riall. Riall attacked Brown in a strong position at Chippewa, and was repulsed with considerable loss. *See* Chrysler's Farm.

Chizai *Hundred Years' War*

July, 1372, between the French under Bertrand du Guesclin, and the English under Thomas Hampton. Du Guesclin, who was engaged in the siege of Chizai, was attacked by the English, in about equal force to his own, and, after a long and bloody engagement, totally defeated them, and captured the town. The reverse cost Edward III Saintonge and Poitou. *See* La Rochelle, Margate.

Choczim *Ottoman Wars*

Fought 1769, between the Russians under Prince Galitzin, and the Turks under Mohammed Emin Pasha. The Russians, who were endeavouring to capture Choczim by a *coup de main*, were met and defeated by the Turks with considerable loss. *See* Stavrichani.

Chong-ju *Russo-Japanese War*

The first encounter between the land forces of Russia and Japan, April, 1904, when the advanced guard of the First Japanese Army came in contact with a force of Cossacks under General Mischtchenko, and after a brisk engagement drove them back and occupied Chong-ju. The losses on both sides were small. *See* Port Arthur.

66

Chorillos *Peruvian-Chilean War*

January 13, 1861, between the Chileans under General Baquedano and the Peruvians under General Caçeres. The Peruvians were totally defeated with a loss of 9,000 killed and wounded, and 2,000 prisoners. The Chileans lost 800 killed and 2,500 wounded.

Chotusitz *War of the Austrian Succession*

May 17, 1742, between the Austrians under Prince Charles of Lorraine, and the Prussians under Frederick the Great. The numbers were about equal, but the steadiness of the Prussian infantry eventually wore down the Austrians, and they were forced to retreat, though in good order, leaving behind them 18 guns and 12,000 prisoners. The killed and wounded numbered about 7,000 on each side and the Austrians made 1,000 prisoners. *See* Dettingen, Toulon.

Christianople *Danish-Swedish Wars*

The first military exploit of Gustavus Adolphus of Sweden, who, during the war of 1611, made a night assault on this fortress with 1,500 men, and blowing in the gate, captured the place without losing a man. *See* Wimpfen, Wiesloch.

Chrysler's Farm *War of 1812*

November 11, 1813, between 800 British under Colonel Morrison, and about 3,000 Americans under General Boyd. The Americans were defeated with a loss of 249 killed and wounded and 100 prisoners. The British lost 203. *See* Chippewa.

Chrysopolis *War of the Two Empires*

Fought in 324 between 60,000 troops under Licinius, Emperor of the East, and a force detached by Constantine from the siege of Byzantium. Licinius was totally defeated, with a loss of 25,000, and surrendered. The result of this victory was the reunion of the whole of the Roman Empire under one head. *See* Hadrianople, Hellespont.

Chunar *Hindu-Mughal Wars*

This fortress, which was held for Sher Khan Sur, Nawab of Bengal, was besieged by the Mughals under Humayun in 1538. This is the first siege in Indian history which was conducted according to the rules of war, and was notable for the use of artillery by both sides. After a siege lasting several months, the garrison was forced by famine to surrender.

Chu Pong-Ia Drang River,

see Vietnam War

Cibalis *War of the Two Empires*

October 8, 315, between Constantine the Great, with 20,000 men, and Licinius, Emperor of the East, with 35,000. Constantine was posted in a defile, where he was attacked by Licinius. The attack was repulsed, and Constantine followed the enemy into the open plain, where Licinius rallied his troops, and resumed the offensive. The day seemed lost, when a charge of the right wing, under Constantine in person, once more broke the Illyrians, and Licinius having lost 20,000 of his best troops, abandoned his camp during the night and retreated to Sirmium. *See* Heraclea.

Ciudad Rodrigo *Peninsular War*

This fortress, held by a French garrison of 2,000 men with 153 guns, was invested by General Lord Wellington on March 8, 1812, after a march through freezing snow with 35,000 men and a siege-train recently arrived from England. The artillery having made two breaches in the walls by January 14, Wellington ordered the 3rd and the Light Divisions to assault next evening in the dark at 7 pm, when the fortress was taken by storm.
Wellington lost 900 men wounded and 200 killed, including Generals Crauford and Mackinnon, in the hard fighting that took place. The French lost 300 killed or wounded, 1,500 prisoners and all their guns. Having taken this vital gateway into Spain from Portugal, Wellington wheeled his army south to march on the more formidable fortress of Badajoz. *See* Albuera, Badajoz.

67

Civitella *Norman Invasion of Italy*

Fought 1033, when 3,000 Normans under Robert Guiscard assailed and totally routed a miscellaneous force of Germans and Italians under Pope Leo IX. Only the Germans offered any serious resistance, but they were cut down to a man, and the Pope was overtaken in his flight and captured. *See* Rome VI.

Clissau *Swedish-Polish Wars*

July 13, 1702, between the Swedes, 12,000 strong, under Charles XII, and 24,000 Poles and Saxons under Frederick Augustus. The Saxons fought gallantly, but the demoralized Poles fled at the first onslaught, and in the end the Swedes gained a complete victory. Among those who fell was the Duke of Holstein, commanding the Swedish cavalry. *See* Dwina, The.

Clontarf *Norse Invasion of Ireland*

April 23, 1014, when the Scandinavian invaders were totally routed by the Irish of Munster, Connaught, Ulster and Meath, under Brian Boru in a battle just outside Dublin. The Norsemen are said to have lost 6,000 men. Brian Boru and his son fell in the battle. *See* Mortlack.

Clusium *Conquest of Cisalpine Gaul*

Fought 225 BC, when the Gauls utterly routed a Roman Army with a loss said to have amounted to 50,000 men.

Cnidus *Wars of Greek City States*

394 BC, between 120 Spartan triremes under Pisander and a largely superior Persian fleet under Pharnabazus, and Conon the Athenian. Pisander was defeated and slain, and his fleet destroyed. Persia thus re-established her power in the Greek cities of Asia, and the maritime power of Sparta was destroyed. *See* Coronea.

Cocherel *Hundred Years' War*

May, 1364, between the Navarrese under Jean de Grailli, known as Captal de Buch, aided by a force of English mercenaries under John Joel, and the French, 10,000 strong, under Bertrand du Guesclin. Du Guesclin, who was executing a strategic retreat, was attacked by the English, who were surrounded

and overpowered, Joel falling. De Grailli came to their aid, but was also overwhelmed and made prisoner, and the Navarrese, deprived of their leaders, laid down their arms. *See* Auray, Poitiers.

Coldharbour *American Civil War*

June 1, 1864, when General Lee's 59,000-strong Confederate army attacked this road junction 10 miles north east of Richmond, but were driven off after the arrival of Federal reinforcements. On June 3, General U. S. Grant, with his army reinforced to 108,000 men, ordered an assault against the Confederate right and centre, but it was repulsed with 7,000 Federal casualties. Confederate casualties were less than 1,200. *See* Petersburg.

Colenso *Second Boer War*

December 15, 1899, being the first action in Sir Redvers Buller's campaign for the relief of Ladysmith. Buller attempted to carry by a frontal attack the Boer position on the opposite side of the Tugela, and notwithstanding the gallantry of the troops, was compelled to retire, with a loss of 71 officers and 1,055 rank and file. Of this total the Irish Brigade lost about half. The Boers captured 10 guns. *See* Ladysmith.

Colline Gate *Civil War of Marius and Sulla*

82 BC, between the adherents of Sulla, and the Roman democrats and Samnites under Pontius, outside the walls of Rome. The battle was obstinately contested, but, after a fight lasting throughout the night, the insurgents were routed, and 4,000 prisoners taken. This victory of the aristocratic party ended the civil war. *See* Mount Tifata.

Colombey *Franco-Prussian War*

August 14, 1870, between Marshal Bazaine's retiring French army, and the advance guard of the First German Army Corps under General von Steinmetz. The French maintained most of their positions, but two of their divisions were overthrown, and Bazaine's retreat on Verdun was seriously delayed. The French lost about 7,000; the Germans 222 officers and 5,000 men. *See* Wörth, Mars-la-Tour.

Colombo *French Revolutionary Wars*

This town, in Ceylon, was captured from the Dutch in 1796, by a squadron of four British warships, and a small force of troops under Admiral Peter Rainier and Colonel Stuart.

Concha Rayada *Chilean War of Independence*

February, 1818, between the Spanish Royalists, 5,000 strong, under General Osorio, and the Chileans and Colombians under San Martin. The Spaniards gained a complete victory. *See* Chacabuco.

Concon *Chilean Civil War*

August 21, 1891, between 10,000 Congressists under General del Canto, and 11,000 Balmacedists under General Barbosa. Aided by the fire of three warships, the Congressists, who had landed unopposed on the 20th, stormed the entrenchments of the Balmacedists, and drove them out with a loss of 1,648 killed and wounded, and 1,500 prisoners. The victors lost 869. *See* Tacna.

Constantine *Conquest of Algeria*

This fortified city in Eastern Algeria, which, under Hadji Ahmad, had held out for six years against French rule, was invested by the French, 7,000 strong, under Marshal Clausel, in the autumn of 1836. Having no breaching pieces, Clausel essayed an assault, but was repulsed with a loss of 2,000 men, and abandoned the siege. In the following year General Damremont besieged Constantine October 6, with 10,000 men, and on the 12th, a breach having been effected, an assault was on the point of taking place, when Damremont was killed. His successor, General Valée, however, took the place by storm on the following day. *See* Isly.

Constantinople I *Muslim Invasion of Europe*

This city was besieged in 668, by the Saracens under Sophian, the lieutenant of the Caliph Moawiyeh. The Muslim fleet passed the Hellespont unopposed, but their attack upon the city was met with a most determined resistance. After keeping the field from April to September, Sophian retired into winter quarters, but renewed active operations during the following and five succeeding summers, without success, until, in 675, he finally abandoned the siege, having lost in its progress over 30,000 men.

In 716, the Saracens again laid siege to the city, with 120,000 men under Moslemeh, brother of the Caliph Suleiman. A fleet of 1,800 sail co-operated with the land forces, but was destroyed by the Greek fire ships, and thus obtaining the command of the sea, the citizens were relieved from all fear of famine, and repulsed all Moslemeh's assaults. After a siege of 13 months, the Saracens withdrew, following a defeat at the hands of a Bulgarian relieving army, in which they lost 22,000 men.

Constantinople II *Fourth Crusade*

The city was besieged July 7, 1203, by the French and Venetian Crusaders under Count Thibaut de Champagne. After a feeble defence, it was surrendered July 18, by the Usurper, Alexius, and occupied by the Crusaders, who restored Isaac Angelus to the throne, and withdrew.

In January 1204, the Crusaders again laid siege to Constantinople, and at the end of three months, in the course of which Isaac Angelus died, and Mourzoufle assumed the purple, they stormed and pillaged the city. Baldwin was then proclaimed first Latin Emperor of the East.

Constantinople III *Reconquest by Byzantines*

On July 25, 1261, Constantinople was taken by surprise by the troops of the Greek Emperor, Michael Palaeologus, under his lieutenant, Alexius Stragopulos. The Latin Emperor, Baldwin II, made no attempt at resistance, but escaped to the Venetian galleys, and the restoration of the Greek Empire was accomplished without opposition. *See* Arsouf, Adrianople.

Constantinople IV *Ottoman Invasion of Europe*

On June 10, 1422, Amurath II, with 50,000 Turks, laid siege to the city, which was defended by the Greek garrison under the Emperor Manuel. After a siege of two months, in which the Turks lost heavily in their numerous assaults, and in the defenders' sallies, Amurath was called away to Boursa by a domestic revolt, and raised the siege.

Constantinople V *Turkish Conquest*

On April 6, 1453, the Turks again laid siege to Constantinople with 60,000 men under Mohammed II. The garrison, consisting of 5,000 Greeks and 2,000 foreigners, though short of ammunition, made a gallant defence, but were overpowered by numbers in a general assault on May 29, and the city was captured. Constantine Palaeologus, the last Emperor of the East, was killed by an unknown hand, in the tumult which followed the storming of the ramparts. *See* Belgrade.

Copenhagen I *French Revolutionary Wars*

April 2, 1801, between the British fleet of 20 sail of the line, besides frigates, under Admirals Hyde Parker and Nelson, and the Danish fleet of 10 line of battleships, aided by the shore batteries. Nelson attacked with 12 ships, Parker remaining in reserve, but three of Nelson's vessels running aground, he met the Danish line with 9 only. The Danes offered a strenuous resistance, and Parker hoisted the signal to retire, but Nelson put the telescope to his blind eye, and refused to see the signal. The action continued until the Danish fire was silenced. The British lost 1,200 men, and had six vessels seriously damaged. The Danes had one ship destroyed, and the rest of their fleet completely disabled. This victory caused the dissolution of the league of the Northern Powers. *See* Cape Finisterre.

Copenhagen II *Napoleonic Wars*

The city was captured September 5, 1807, by 20,000 British troops under Lord Cathcart, after four days' bombardment of the forts and citadel by 27 ships of the line. The Danish fleet of 18 sail of the line, which was surrendered, would otherwise, under a secret clause of the Treaty of Tilsit, have been placed at the disposal of Napoleon. *See* Friedland.

Copratus, The *Wars of Alexander's Successors*

316 BC, between the Macedonians under Antigonus, and the Asiatics under Eumenes.

Each army was about 30,000 strong, and Eumenes fell upon the Macedonians as they were crossing the Copratus, and signally defeated them, though Antigonus was able to retreat in good order. *See* Gaza, Paraetakene Mountains.

Coral Sea *World War II*

May 8, 1942, when US Admiral Fletcher's naval task force, which included the carriers *Yorktown* and *Lexington*, challenged a Japanese flotilla in the Coral Sea escorting an invasion force headed for Port Moresby, New Guinea. For the first time in naval history, the battle was fought at long range by aircraft from the carriers. No warship sighted an enemy vessel. US aircraft sank the *Shoko* and the *Shokaku* with the loss of 33 out of 82 aircraft, while the Japanese sank the *Lexington*, a destroyer and a tanker at a cost of 43 out of 69 aircraft. But the Japanese fleet withdrew from the Coral Sea and Port Moresby was held. *See* New Guinea, Java Sea, Midway.

Cordova *Spanish-Muslim Wars*

August, 1010, between the Berbers under Suleiman, aided by the Spaniards under Sancho, Count of Castile, and the Moors of Cordova under Almudy. Almudy marched out of Cordova to meet the Berbers, but was utterly routed, with a loss of 20,000, including most of his principal Emirs. *See* Zamora.

Corinth I *Peloponnesian War*

429 BC, between 47 Peloponnesian ships under Cnemus, and 20 Athenian triremes under Phormio. Phormio, who was blockading the Gulf of Corinth, allowed Cnemus to pass into the open sea, and when disordered by the heavy weather prevailing, he attacked and completely defeated the Peloponnesians, capturing 12 ships. *See* Delium.

Corinth II *Corinthian War*

394 BC, between 14,000 Spartans, and 26,000 Athenians, Corinthians, Thebans and Argives. The allies were defeated, losing twice as many men as their opponents, but the Spartans, in spite of their victory, were obliged to retire, leaving the Isthmus in their possession. *See* Cnidus.

Corinth III *American Civil War*

October 3 and 4, 1862, between 22,000 Confederates under General Van Dorn, and the 23,000 Federals under General Rosecrans. Rosecrans was strongly entrenched at Corinth, where he was attacked on the 3rd and driven into his inner lines. The attack was renewed on the 4th, but an attempt to storm the entrenchments was repulsed, and the Federals, taking the offensive against the disordered Southerners, drove them from the field with a loss of 6,423 killed or wounded, and 2,248 prisoners. The Federals lost 2,359 killed, wounded, and missing. *See* Fredericksburg.

Coronea I *First Peloponnesian War*

447 BC, when an Athenian army under Tolmides, which had entered Boeotia to reduce certain of the Boeotian towns which had thrown off their allegiance to Athens, was encountered and totally defeated by a largely superior force of Boeotians. Almost all the surviving Athenians were captured, and, to secure their release, Athens resigned her claims over Boeotia. *See* Plataea.

Coronea II *Corinthian War*

394 BC, August, between the Athenians, Argives, Thebans and Corinthians, and the Spartans under Agesilaus. The Spartan right defeated the Argives, but their left fled before the Thebans, who then attacked the Spartan right, but, after a desperate struggle, were defeated. The Spartans, however, had suffered so severely that Agesilaus was compelled to evacuate Boeotia. *See* Cnidus.

Coronel *World War I*

November 1, 1914, when Rear-Admiral Cradock's squadron of three cruisers, the *Monmouth*, the *Good Hope* and the *Glasgow*, with the armed merchantman *Otranto*, met with Admiral von Spee's powerful squadron of two heavy cruisers, the *Scharnhorst* and the *Gneisenau* and three smaller cruisers off Coronel, Chile. The Germans got the range first, the *Good Hope* blew up and the *Monmouth* was sunk. The *Glasgow* and the *Otranto* escaped. *See* Falkland Isles.

Corrichie *Huntly's Rebellion*

In 1562, between the troops of Mary, Queen of Scots, and the Scottish rebels under the Earl of Huntly. The rebels, whose forces had been greatly reduced by desertions, were totally defeated, and Huntly slain.

Corte Nuova *Guelfs and Ghibellines*

In 1237, between the Imperialists under Frederick II, and the Lombard Guelfs under the leadership of the Milanese. Frederick won a signal victory, capturing the *carroccio* of Milan. *See* Monte Aperto, Tagliacozzo.

Corumba *Paraguayan War*

In 1877, between the Paraguayans and a Brazilian army corps which was endeavouring to enter Paraguay from the north-east. The Brazilians retired in disorder, being pursued for many miles, and suffering heavy loss. The battle is remarkable for the presence in the Paraguayan army of a corps of Amazons led by Eliza Lynch. *See* Aquidaban.

Corunna *Peninsular War*

January 16, 1809, between 14,000 British under Sir John Moore, and 16,000 French under Marshal Soult, who was endeavouring to prevent the British from embarking. The French attacks were uniformly repulsed, and the troops safely embarked, with a loss of about 800, including Sir John Moore. The French lost about 2,000. *See* Talavera.

Corupedion *Wars of the Hellenistic Monarchies*

281 BC, between the Macedonians under Lysimachus, and the Syrians under Seleucus. The two generals met in single combat, in front of their armies, and Seleucus, though 81 years of age, defeated and slew his ancient comrade in arms. The two armies then engaged, and the Syrians gained a complete victory. *See* Ipsus.

Coulmiers *Franco-Prussian War*

November 9, 1870, between 20,000 Germans under General von der Tann, and a largely superior French force under General d'Aurelle de Paladines. After maintaining their position for the greater part of the day, the Germans

71

were driven back, having lost 576 killed and wounded, 800 prisoners, an ammunition column and two guns. The French losses were about 1,500. *See* Paris, Sedan.

Courtrai *Flemish War*

July 11, 1302, between the French, mainly crossbowmen and cavalry, under Robert d'Artois, and the Flemings, mainly billmen under Guy de Namur. The French were utterly routed, and so great was the carnage among the French nobility and knighthood, that after the battle 800 gilt spurs from the dead were hung up as trophies in Courtrai cathedral. From this circumstance this battle is commonly known as the Battle of the Spurs. It demonstrated for the first time, that well-led billmen were a match for unsupported cavalry. *See* Mons-en-Pévèle.

Coutras *French Religious Wars*

In 1587, between the Huguenots under Henry of Navarre (later Henri IV) and the Catholics under the Duc de Joyeuse. The Catholic army was annihilated, Joyeuse being among the slain. *See* Montcontour.

Craonne *Napoleonic Wars*

March 7, 1814, between 40,000 French under Napoleon, and about 90,000 of the allies under Marshal Blücher. Blücher occupied a very strong position on the heights about Craonne, which was attacked and carried by Marshal Victor's and Marshal Ney's corps at the point of the bayonet. The French lost 5,500, the allies 5,000 killed and wounded. *See* Laon.

Cravant *Hundred Years' War*

July 31, 1423. A force of Armagnacs under the Earl of Buchan, Constable of France, with some Scottish mercenaries, was advancing upon Craonne, the capture of which town would secure Charles VII's communications with Champagne. They were attacked by the Burgundians and English under the Earl of Salisbury and defeated with heavy loss. Buchan was captured. *See* Beaugé.

Crayford *Jutish Invasion*

Fought 456 between the Jutes under Hengist, and the Britons under Vortigern. The Britons were defeated, and driven out of Kent.

Crécy *Hundred Years' War*

August 26, 1346, when a very inferior force of English under King Edward III defeated about 30,000 French under Philip VI. The battle is notable as being the first in which the 9,000 strong English army was mainly composed of infantry, and as proving the powerlessness of mounted men against the English archers. The French losses were 11 princes, 1,200 knights, and 10,000 of lesser ranks, a total exceeding the whole English force. *See* Calais.

Crefeld *Seven Years' War*

June 23, 1758, between 32,000 Hanoverians, Hessians and Brunswickers under Prince Ferdinand of Brunswick, and about 50,000 French under the Comte de Clermont. The French were totally defeated, with heavy loss. *See* Olmütz.

Cremona I *Second Gallic Invasion*

198 BC, when the Romans defeated with heavy slaughter an invading army of Gauls under Hamilcar, a Carthaginian. Hamilcar was slain.

Cremona II *Civil Wars of the Roman Empire*

December, 69, between the Vitellians, and the Flavians under Antonius Primus, 40,000 strong. The Vitellians, who were without a leader, having deposed their general, Caecina, were attacked in their camp, and after a hard fight, which lasted throughout the night, were totally routed. The victors sacked and burnt Cremona. *See* Bedriacum.

Cremona III *War of the Spanish Succession*

This city, held by a French garrison, was surprised by the Imperialists under Prince Eugène, February 1, 1702. The town was entered without the alarm being given, and many important officers, including Marshal Villeroy, were made prisoners. A portion of the garrison, however, still held out in the citadel, and made Eugène's tenure of the town precarious, and finally, on the approach of a relieving force under the Prince de Vaudemont, he was forced to withdraw his troops. The garrison lost 1,000 killed. *See* Landau, Vigo Bay, Luzzara.

Crete *World War II*

After the Nazi occupation of Greece in April 1941, some 27,000 British and Commonwealth troops supported by nine tanks, 35 aircraft and 45 field guns were evacuated to Crete to reinforce the garrison of three infantry battalions. Two ill-equipped Greek divisions were also brought in. After the Nazis blitzed the airfields May 19, the few remaining serviceable RAF aircraft were flown out, giving the Nazis almost total command of the air. May 20, German parachutists and glider-borne troops, commanded by Colonel-General Löhr, landed in large numbers, established a foothold against fierce resistance and captured Maleme airfield by May 21, the turning point of the battle. German aircraft streamed in with reinforcements, while fighters pounded the defenders from the air. By May 28 the battle was lost. The Royal Navy took off 14,900 men, leaving behind another 18,000. Some 11,000 Germans were killed in the bitter fighting or when their convoys were sunk by the Navy. Three Royal Navy cruisers, six destroyers and 29 other craft were lost, with 2,000 casualties. *See* Balkans I.

Crimisus *Third Carthaginian Invasion of Sicily*

June, 341 BC, between 10,000 Sicilians under Timoleon, and 70,000 Carthaginians, including the Sacred Band of 2,500 Carthaginian citizens of good birth, under Hamilcar and Hasdrubal. Timoleon attacked the Carthaginians while they were crossing the Crimisus, and routed and dispersed the Sacred Band before the main army had crossed. A heavy storm of rain in the faces of the Carthaginians came to the aid of the Sicilians, and after a severe struggle, they gained a signal victory, and the Carthaginians fled, leaving 10,000 dead in the field, and 15,000 prisoners. Many more were drowned trying to recross the river, but Carthage continued to hold Sicily. *See* Himera.

Cronion *Second Carthaginian Invasion of Sicily*

379 BC, between the Syracusans under

Dionysius, and the Carthaginians. The Syracusans were defeated, with enormous loss, and Dionysius forced to accept unfavourable terms of peace. *See* Syracuse.

Cropredy Bridge *English Civil War*

June 29, 1644, between the Royalists under Charles I, and a Parliamentary army under Sir William Waller. Waller crossed the Cherwell near Banbury with the object of cutting off the Royalists' rear, but was repulsed with considerable loss, including most of his guns. *See* Alresford.

Crosskeys *American Civil War*

A rearguard action, fought June 8, 1862, between 8,000 Confederates under General Ewell, and about 12,000 Federals under General John Frémont. Ewell was given the task of holding Frémont in check, while General Jackson marched to meet the Federals under Shields, who were endeavouring to effect a junction with Frémont. The Confederates held their ground, beating back their opponents with a loss of 664 killed and wounded. After the action, Ewell crossed the river, burning the bridge behind him, and Jackson was enabled to fall upon Shields with his whole force. *See* Fair Oaks.

Crotone *German Invasion of Italy*

Fought July 13, 982, between the Germans under Otho II, and the Greeks, aided by 40,000 Saracens under the Caliph of Egypt. After an obstinate engagement, Otho was totally defeated, losing many of his bravest knights. *See* Mühldorf.

Crotoye *Hundred Years' War*

In 1347, during the siege of Calais by King Edward III. The French fleet attempted to relieve the town, but was defeated and driven off with heavy loss by the English fleet. *See* Calais.

Cuaspad *Ecuador-Colombia War*

December 6, 1862, between the Ecuadorians under Flores, 6,000 strong, and 4,000 Colombians under Mosquera. The Ecuadorians were utterly routed, losing 1,500 killed and wounded, 2,000 prisoners, and all their guns.

Cuddalore I *American Revolutionary War*

June 13, 1783, when a portion of the British force under General Stewart attacked the French entrenchments in front of Cuddalore, India, and after hard fighting, drove the French into the town with a loss of 700 men and 13 guns. The British lost 1,013 killed and wounded. *See* Pondicherry V.

Cuddalore II *American Revolutionary War*

A naval action was fought off Cuddalore June 20, 1783, between a British squadron of 17 sail under Sir Edward Hughes, and 12 French ships under Admiral de Suffren. The French declined to come to close quarters, and after a long range action, in which Hughes lost 532 men, fighting was suspended at nightfall, leaving de Suffren in possession of the roads, and able to prevent the complete investment of Cuddalore. *See* Pondicherry V.

Culloden *Jacobite Rebellion of the Forty-five*

April 16, 1746, between the Royal troops under the Duke of Cumberland, and the Highlanders under the Young Pretender. The rebels were completely routed by the British regulars, and in addition to heavy loss in the field, suffered terribly in the pursuit, being ruthlessly cut down by the cavalry. Cumberland's cruelty on this occasion earned for him the title of 'Butcher'. The Royalists lost 309 killed and wounded. This battle is sometimes called the Battle of Drummossie Moor. It ended all chance of a Stuart restoration. *See* Prestonpans.

Cunaxa *Expedition of Cyrus the Younger*

401 BC, between the Persians, about 400,000 strong, under Artaxerxes, and the army of his brother Cyrus, consisting of 100,000 Orientals, with 14,000 Greek mercenaries, under Clearchus. The Greeks on the right wing drove back the Persian left, and Cyrus in the centre broke the king's bodyguard, which fled in disorder. While pursuing his brother, however, he was struck down, and his Orientals at once took to flight. The Greeks refused to surrender, and were allowed to retain their arms and march to the coast. This

expedition of Cyrus forms the subject of Xenophon's 'Anabasis'. *See* Ægospotami, Haliartus.

Curicta *Civil War of Caesar and Pompey*

49 BC, when the Caesarian fleet under Dolabella was totally destroyed by the Pompeian fleet under Marcus Octavius. This victory cut off the Caesarian army under Caius Antonius, which was quartered on the island of Curicta, and Antonius was forced to surrender. *See* Pharsalus.

Curupayti *Paraguayan War*

September 22, 1866, between the troops of Brazil, Argentine and Uruguay, under General Flores, and the Paraguayans under López. The allies were totally defeated, and Flores abandoned the army, returning to Montevideo. *See* Aquidaban.

Custoza *Italian Wars of Independence*

June 24, 1866, between 74,000 Austrians under the Archduke Albert, and 80,000 Italians under General La Marmora. La Marmora crossed the Mincio, and advanced against the Archduke, who was covering Verona. The Italians having to pass through a hilly country, the columns were much broken up, and as they debouched into the plain of Custoza, they were beaten in detail, and driven back by the Austrians, who gained a signal victory. The Austrians lost 4,650 killed and wounded; the Italians 720 killed, 3,112 wounded, and 4,315 prisoners. La Marmora was compelled to recross the Mincio. Franz Josef ceded Venice to Italy. *See* Novara.

Cuzco *Conquest of Peru*

This city was besieged 1536, by 100,000 Peruvians and was defended by 250 Spaniards under Juan and Gonzalo Pizarro. After a siege of five months, Almagro, to whom certain of the conquered territories had been assigned by the king of Spain, arrived with his troops, and attacked and totally routed the Peruvians. He then laid siege to the place on his own account, and shortly afterwards compelled Gonzalo Pizarro to capitulate. Juan died in the course of the siege.

Cyme *Etruscan-Greek Wars*

474 BC, between the fleet of Hiero, tyrant of Syracuse, and the Etruscan fleet, which was investing the Greek colony of Cyme. The Etruscans were routed, and from this defeat dates the rapid decline of the Etruscan power. *See* Himera I.

Cynoscephalae I *Wars of Greek City States*

July, 364 BC, between the Thebans and Thessalians under Pelopidas, and the forces of Alexander, Despot of Pherae. Both armies made a forced march to seize the heights of Cynoscephalae, and reached the spot almost simultaneously. The Theban cavalry drove back Alexander's horse, but lost time in the pursuit, and his infantry made good their position on the heights. However, after very hard fighting, they were dislodged, and Alexander completely routed, though Pelopidas fell in the battle. *See* Mantinea II.

Cynoscephalae II *Second Macedonian War*

197 BC, between the Romans, 20,000 strong, under Flaminius, and the Macedonians, in about equal force under Philip. The Roman vanguard, coming unexpectedly upon the enemy, was repulsed, but Flaminius bringing up the legionaries, the battle became more equal. On the right Philip, with half his phalanx, drove back the Romans, but his left wing was utterly routed, and the victorious Roman right then turned and attacked the Macedonian right in flank and rear, and won a complete victory. The Macedonians lost 13,000 killed and wounded. The Roman losses were small. *See* Thermopylae II.

Cynossema *Peloponnesian War*

411 BC, between 86 Peloponnesian ships under Mindarus, and 76 Athenian triremes under Thrasybulus and Theramenes. The Athenian centre was broken, but, in the moment of victory, Thrasybulus fell upon the Peloponnesians with the right wing, and totally routed them, while Thrasyllus on the left also drove off his adversaries, after hard fighting. *See* Amphipolis, Syracuse.

Cyssus *Wars of the Hellenistic Monarchies*

191 BC, between the Roman fleet of 105 triremes under Caius Livius, and the fleet of Antiochus, numbering 70 sail, under Polyxenides. Polyxenides sailed out of Cyssus to encounter the Romans, but was defeated with a loss of 23 ships, and forced to seek refuge at Ephesus. *See* Magnesia.

Cyzicus I *Peloponnesian War*

410 BC, when Alcibiades, with 86 Athenian ships, surprised the Peloponnesian Admiral Mindarus, who was besieging Cyzicus, in Asia Minor, and, after a hard fight, totally defeated him. Mindarus was slain, 60 triremes were taken or destroyed, and the Peloponnesian fleet was practically annihilated. *See* Cynossema.

Cyzicus II *First Mithridatic War*

88 BC, when the army of Mithridates, who was besieging Cyzicus, Asia Minor, was hemmed by the Romans under Lucullus, and though the latter, with inferior forces, did not venture on a pitched battle, he fought a series of minor engagements, in which he eventually destroyed the Pontic army, their losses amounting in the end to over 200,000 men. *See* Tigranocerta.

Czarnovo *Napoleonic Wars*

December 24, 1806, between the French under Napoleon, and the Russians, about 15,000 strong, under Count Tolstoy. Napoleon with Davout's corps, crossed the Ukra, and made a night attack upon the Russians, driving them out of Czarnovo with a loss of 1,600 and several guns. The French lost 700. *See* Jena.

Czaslau *War of the Austrian Succession*

In 1742, between the Prussians under Frederick the Great, and the Austrians under Prince Charles of Lorraine. The Prussians were driven from the field, but the Austrians abandoned the pursuit to plunder, and the king, rallying his troops, broke the Austrian main body, and defeated them with a loss of 4,000 men. *See* Chotusitz.

75

D

D-Day *Operation Overlord, World War II*

June 6, 1944, on a 30-mile length of the Normandy coast from the river Orne to the base of the Cotentin Peninsula, where the Allies established a bridgehead for the Second Front, General Montgomery commanding 21st Army Group (2nd British and 1st US Armies), General Hausser the German 7th Army of Rommel's Army Group B. The Allies' three airborne, seven infantry divisions, two commando and three armoured brigades were opposed by three German infantry and one Panzer divisions. Before D-Day, a month-long air bombardment of road and rail links and oil stores played havoc with enemy communications. Naval minesweepers then swept lanes through German minefields and shipped the two armies over in a fleet of 3,000 vessels of all kinds. Up to the last moment Calais was the pretended invasion place and much German armour was lured there. Allied airborne troops and parachutists landing in the June 6 early hours secured bridges and both flanks of the beaches—Omaha and Utah in the west for US forces; Sword, Juno and Gold for British and Canadians. The US 101st and 82nd Airborne Divisions landing at Utah, secured most of their objectives, after much confusion and hard fighting, as did the seaborne US 4th Division there, all of whom quickly linked up and by midnight secured an area 4 miles wide by 9 inland. At Omaha, the US 1st and 29th Divisions landed at the wrong places, suffered 3,000 casualties on the beach and by midnight had penetrated only a bit over a mile inland. To the east the British 50th Division landed at Gold, advanced and took Arromanches and Bayeux against strong German opposition; the 3rd Division landed on Sword, also advanced inland but failed to take its objective of Caen owing to strong 21st Panzer opposition, while the Canadians at Juno swept inland seven miles to within sight of the main Caen road. German reactions were slow, worsened by French sabotage of telephone links; and Hitler refused to launch the Panzers in reserve until it was too late. By the afternoon of June 7 victory in the D-Day battle had been won.

By June 12, the invaders had linked up to form a bridgehead 80 miles long by 10 deep. Allied casualties were 2,500 killed, mostly at Omaha; 8,500 wounded or missing. *See* Caen; St Lô.

Dak To,

see Vietnam War

Dalmanutha *Second Boer War*

August 21 to 28, 1900, when the position of the Boers from Belfast to Machadodorp covering the Delagoa Bay Railway, and extending over a line 30 miles long, was attacked on the west by Lord Roberts, and on the south by Sir Redvers Buller. On the 28th Buller entered Machadodorp, by which time the Boers, who were under General Botha, had been driven from all their positions. Kruger at once fled to Delagoa Bay. The British loss in the four days amounted to about 500. *See* Ladysmith.

Damascus I *Muslim Invasion of Syria*

This city was besieged by the Muslims under Khaled in 635, and was defended by a large garrison of Greeks and Romans. The city made an obstinate defence, and the defenders succeeded in sending a demand for help to Werdan, the general of Heraclius. Werdan's approach drew Khaled away from the place, and as he was retiring he was attacked by the garrison, whom he defeated with enormous loss. He then marched against Werdan, defeated him, and returned to prosecute the siege. After a gallant defence, the city, 70 days later, was taken by storm. *See* Yarmuk.

Damascus II *Tatar Invasion of Syria*

On January 25, 1401, Damascus was captured, through treachery, by the Tatars under Tamerlane. *See* Aleppo II.

Damascus III *World War I*

September 19, 1918, when General Allenby launched his mixed force of British, French, Indian and Arabs—12,000 cavalry, 57,000 infantry and 540 guns—against 11 Turkish divisions holding a front stretching from Jaffa east to the Jordan and down its eastern bank to the Dead Sea, in the line about 40,000 infantry, 4,000 cavalry and 430 guns. Only 12 days later, after the war's most outstanding campaign, advanced units of Allenby's force entered Damascus, having utterly routed the Turkish armies. Beirut fell on October 8, Baalbek on the 11th, Tripolis on the 18th and Aleppo on the 25th. Since September 19, Allenby's force had moved 300 miles northward, destroyed entirely the Turkish armies in Syria, taken 75,000 prisoners, 430 guns and huge quantities of stores. The Turkish Empire, which was to have been Germany's path to the Persian Gulf and Central Asia, was in ruins. Turkey surrendered to the Allies early in November. *See* Gaza III.

Damme *Wars of Philip Augustus*

April, 1213, when an English fleet of 500 vessels under the Earl of Salisbury attacked and dispersed a large fleet of French ships designed to support Philip Augustus' invasion of Flanders. The English captured 300 and burnt 100 vessels, and Philip Augustus was forced to abandon his design. *See* Bouvines.

Dan-no-ura *Taira War*

Fought 1185, between the forces of the Shogun, Yoritomo, under his brothers Noriyori and Yoshitsune, and the Taira Clan under Munemori, when the Taira were routed and dispersed. This defeat broke the power of the clan, and the Minamoto became the dominant clan in Japan.

Danzig I *Thirty Years' War*

This fortress was besieged by the Swedes under King Gustavus Adolphus in 1627, and was defended by a Polish garrison which successfully resisted all attempts to storm the place, until the truce of September 16, 1629. In a night attack on May 27, 1627, the King of Sweden was severely wounded, while in the autumn of the same year a sally was made from the port by the Danzig ships, which defeated the Swedish fleet under Admiral Stjernsköld, the Admiral being killed, one ship captured and one destroyed. *See* Dessau.

Danzig II *Napoleonic Wars*

On March 19, 1807, Marshal Lefebvre, with 18,000 French, laid siege to the city, which

was defended by a garrison of 14,000 Prussians, and 4,000 Russians under Marshal Kalkreuth. For complete investment it was necessary for Lefebvre to encompass a circuit of about 17 leagues, for which purpose his numbers were too few, and he made little progress. Receiving reinforcements, however, he opened his first parallel April 1, while on the 12th an important outwork was carried. On the 23rd the batteries opened fire, and on May 15 a determined effort to relieve the place was made by a force of 8,000 Russians, who were repulsed with a loss of 2,000, the French losing 400 only. From this point the city was left to its fate, and an assault was ordered for the 21st. Before this date, however, Marshal Kalkreuth signified his readiness to parley, and on May 26 the place was surrendered, the garrison being then reduced to 7,000 effectives. (Lefebvre was created Duc de Dantzig). *See* Eylau.

Danzig III *Napoleonic Wars*

After the Moscow retreat, General Rapp, with 30,000 French, mostly survivors of the Moscow campaign, was besieged in Danzig, January 1813, by the allies, 30,000 in number, under the Duke of Wurttemberg. Rapp made a strenuous defence, but his works were mastered one by one, and, finding his garrison dwindling rapidly from starvation and exposure, he surrendered November 29, 1813, by which date the defenders numbered only 18,000 men. *See* Lützen.

Dargai *British N.W. Frontier Campaign*

October 20, 1897, when a British brigade, under General Yeatman Biggs, stormed the heights, 50 miles from Peshawar, W. Pakistan, which were held by a large force of Afridis. The actual storming was accomplished by the Gordon Highlanders, and the British loss amounted to 37 killed and 175 wounded. Colonel Mathias' speech to the Gordons, before leading them to the charge was, 'Highlanders, the General says the position must be taken at all costs. The Gordons will take it.'

Dazaifu *Chinese Invasion of Japan*

In 1281, Hwan Buako, the General of Kublai Khan, at the head of 100,000 Chinese, and 10,000 Koreans, endeavoured to effect a landing at Dazaifu. The Japanese, however, kept them at bay for 60 days, at the end of which time the Chinese fleet was wrecked and dispersed by a typhoon. The survivors, under Chang Pak, took refuge in the island of Takashima, where they were attacked and cut to pieces by the troops of the Daimiyo of Choshiu, under Shoni Kagasuke, only 3,000 out of the vast host making their way back to China.

Dee, Brig of,

see Brig of Dee

Deeg I *First British-Maratha War*

Fought 1780, between the British, 6,000 strong under General Fraser, and the Marathas under Holkar of Indore, with 14 battalions of infantry, a numerous cavalry, and 160 guns. The Marathas were utterly routed, leaving 87 guns on the field. The British lost 643, including General Fraser, killed. *See* Ahmadabad.

Deeg II *Second British-Maratha War*

The fortress, which was held by a garrison of Holkar's troops, was besieged December 11, 1804, by the British under Lord Lake. After six days' bombardment, it was stormed on the 23rd, and the citadel captured on the following day. Over 100 guns were taken. *See* Farrukhabad.

Delhi I *First Tatar Invasion of India*

1297, between 200,000 Monguls under Kuttugh Khan, and 300,000 Delhi Muslims, with 2,700 elephants, under Ala-ud-Din. The Indian right wing, with a successful charge, broke the Monguls' left, but carried the pursuit too far. Meanwhile the right of the Mongul army assailed the Indian left and drove it from the field. Kuttugh Khan, however, had lost so heavily, that he was unable to follow up his advantage, and retreated with all speed from India. *See* Delhi II.

Delhi II *Second Tatar Invasion*

December 17, 1398, between the Monguls under Timur (Tamerlane) and the Delhi Muslims, under Mahmud Tughlak. Timur having crossed the Jumna to reconnoitre with an escort of 700 horsemen, was attacked by Mahmud with 5,000 cavalry. Timur repulsed the attack, and later, having brought his main body across the river, totally defeated Mahmud, and drove him into Delhi, which at once surrendered. The city was plundered, and Timur withdrew laden with spoil. *See* Meerut.

Delhi III *Second British-Maratha War*

September 11, 1803, between 4,500 British under General Lake, and 19,000 Marathas of Scindia's army under General Bourquin. The enemy occupied a strong position with the Jumna in their rear, and Lake, feigning a retreat, drew them from their lines, and then turning upon them drove them with the bayonet into the river, inflicting enormous loss upon them. The British lost 400. The battle increased British power and prestige in India. *See* Aligarh.

Delhi IV *Second British-Maratha War*

The city was invested October 7, 1804, by 20,000 Marathas, with 100 guns, under Jeswunt Rao Holkar, and was successfully defended for nine days by a small British garrison. At the end of this period, Holkar withdrew. So small was the garrison, that they were on constant duty on the ramparts, through the siege, without relief. *See* Agra.

Delhi V *Indian Mutiny*

After the outbreak at Meerut, Delhi became the rallying place of the mutineers, and on June 8, 1857, Sir Henry Barnard commenced the siege of the city. His force was too small for a complete investment, while the mutineers numbered 30,000, and could obtain continual reinforcements, and ample supplies. The garrison made constant sorties, and fighting was incessant at the outposts. On September 8 the breaching batteries opened fire, and on the 14th the final assault was made and the city entered. It was not, however, till the 20th that the Palace was taken, and all resistance was at an end. Among those who fell was General John Nicholson. *See* Cawnpore, Lucknow.

Delium *Peloponnesian War*

424 BC, between the Athenians under Hippocrates, 17,000 strong, and the Boeotians under Pagondas, 17,000 strong. The armies met on a plain before Delium, and after an obstinate encounter, in which the Thebans on the right overpowered the Athenians, while their left attack was repulsed, the appearance of a large body of cavalry on their flank alarmed the Athenians, who broke and fled. Hippocrates fell in the battle. *See* Amphipolis.

Delphi *Sacred War*

355 BC, between the Phocians, 5,000 strong, under Philomelus, and the Locrians. Philomelus, who had seized Delphi, attacked the Locrians on the heights above the sacred city, and routed them with heavy loss, many being driven over the precipice. *See* Neon.

Denain *War of the Spanish Succession*

July 24, 1712, when the camp of the allies, held by 10,500 men under the Earl of Albemarle, was attacked by 24,000 French under Marshal de Villars. Prince Eugène made an effort to relieve the Earl, but was unable to cross the Scheldt, and the allies were overwhelmed by superior numbers, only about 4,000 making good their retreat. Five generals were killed or captured. *See* Brihuega, Malplaquet.

Dennewitz *Napoleonic Wars*

September 6, 1813, between the French army of the north under Marshal Ney, and the allies under the Crown Prince of Sweden. Ney had detached General Bertrand's division to mask Dennewitz, while his main body marched past the position on the road to Berlin, but Bertrand delayed so long before Dennewitz, that what was intended for a demonstration became a serious action, in which the full force of both sides was engaged. The French were defeated with a loss of 10,000 men and 43 guns. *See* Gross-Beeren.

Deorham *Overlordship of Wessex*

In 577, when Ceawlin, King of Wessex, defeated the Welsh, and extended the borders of Wessex to the Bristol Channel, thus severing the Welsh nation into two parts.

See Fethanleag.

Dessau *Thirty Years' War*

April 25, 1626, between the German Protestants under Count von Mansfeldt, and the Imperialists, about 20,000 strong, under General von Wallenstein. Von Mansfeldt was attacking the fort of Dessau, on the Elbe, when von Wallenstein, approaching under cover of the woods, fell upon his flank, and totally routed him, killing or capturing nearly three-fourths of his army. *See* Stadtlohn.

Dettingen *War of the Austrian Succession*

June 27, 1743, between the British and Allies, 40,000 strong, under King George II, and 60,000 French under Marshal the Duc de Noailles. The Allies, who were retiring upon Hanau from Aschaffenburg, found their retreat cut off by the French, Dettingen being held by 23,000 men under General de Grammont, while the main body was on the opposite bank of the Maine. De Grammont left his lines to attack the Allies, whereupon George II put himself at the head of his troops, and led a charge which broke the French and drove them headlong into the river. Their losses in crossing were heavy, and they left 6,000 killed and wounded on the field. This was the last occasion on which the Sovereign led British troops in battle. *See* Mollwitz, Chotusitz.

Deutschbrod *Hussite War*

1422, between the Taborite section of the Hussites under John Zisca, and the Germans under the Emperor Sigismund. Zisca was completely victorious.

Devicotta *Carnatic War*

This fortress, held for Pertab Singh by a garrison of the Tanjore army, was captured in 1749, after three days' bombardment, by a British force of 2,300 men under Major Stringer Lawrence. An attack upon the breach, headed by Clive, was nearly disastrous, as the Sepoys hung back, and of the Europeans engaged, only Clive and three others escaped, but Lawrence arriving opportunely with the main column, the place was stormed. *See* Arcot.

Diamond Hill *Second Boer War*

June 11 and 12, 1900, when General Botha, with the main Boer army of 15,000 men, strongly entrenched about 15 miles from Pretoria, was attacked by Lord Roberts with 17,000 men and 70 guns, and driven from his position. The Boer lines were so extended that three distinct actions were in progress at the same time. The British lost 25 officers and 137 men killed and wounded. *See* Kimberley, Ladysmith.

Dien Bien Phu *French-Vietnamese War*

After seven years' fruitless fighting against the Communist Vietminh guerrillas, General Navarre, French C-in-C, sought a decisive pitched battle on what he thought was suitable ground, a valley three miles wide and nine long. Here in a series of strongpoints, he concentrated in November, 1953, 14,000 infantry and artillery, commanded by General de Castries. The Vietminh, led by General Giap, reacted swiftly, ringing the valley with 72,000 troops, with 200 guns and mortars, and in an offensive which began on March 13, 1954, poured in fire and quickly knocked out the only two airstrips, thereafter making the French dependent for ammunition and supplies on parachute drops. The Vietminh, tightening a circle of trenches round the defenders, attacked constantly with mortar and artillery fire, knocking out the strongpoints one by one. The French fought back as well as their acute shortage of ammunition would allow, but the last three strongpoints were over-run on May 7, when the defenders surrendered. The French lost 2,293 dead, 5,134 wounded, the rest, some 6,000, being prisoners. Vietnam was two months later split by international agreement into the Democratic Republic of North Vietnam, and the Republic of South Vietnam. *See* Vietnam War.

Dieppe *World War II*

August 19, 1942, between a 6,000-strong raiding force of the 2nd Canadian Division with three British Commando units and German defenders in strongpoints in cliffs and coastal buildings. The British tanks could not negotiate the sand and rubble of the beach and many of the assaulting troops were killed there. Lord Lovat's No. 4 Commando took its objective, a battery at Varengeville. The force withdrew after a nine-hour fight in which it lost 3,670 men killed, wounded and prisoner, as well as 27 tanks, many landing craft and 106 aircraft. The Germans lost 46 aircraft and about 500 men. Some lessons in invasion techniques were learned. *See* D-Day.

Dingaan's Day *Afrikaner-Zulu War*

December 16, 1838, between the Boers of the Transvaal, and the Zulus under Dingaan. The Zulus were totally routed, with heavy loss. The Boer losses were small.

Dipaea *Arcadian War*

471 BC, between the Spartans and the Arcadian League. The Arcadians were totally defeated, and Tegea, the head of the League, shortly afterwards submitted to Sparta.

Diu I *Portuguese in India*

This fortified Portuguese factory was besieged early in September, 1537, by a fleet of 76 Turkish galleys, and 7,000 soldiers under Suleiman, Pasha of Egypt, acting with whom was an army of 20,000 Gujeratis under Bahadur Shah, and Khojah Zofar, an Italian adventurer. The garrison of 600, under Antonio de Silveira, repulsed assault after assault, but were nearly at the end of their resources, when the false rumour of an approaching Portuguese fleet caused Suleiman to withdraw.

Diu II *Portuguese in India*

In 1545 Diu was again besieged by the Gujeratis, the garrison being commanded by Mascarenhas. Khojah Zofar, who led the besiegers, was killed in the course of the siege, and was succeeded by Rami Khan. The garrison, at the end of several months, was on the point of surrendering, owing to famine, when it was relieved by Juan de Castro, who signally defeated the Gujeratis, and raised the siege. *See* Goa.

Djerba *Ottoman Wars*

1560, between the fleet of Suleiman I, Sultan of Turkey, under Piycala Pasha, and the combined squadrons of Malta, Venice, Genoa and Florence. The Christian fleet was utterly routed, the Turks securing thereby the preponderance in the Mediterranean. *See* Malta.

80

Dniester *Ottoman Wars*

September 9, 1769, between the Russians under Prince Galitzin, and the Turks under Ali Moldovani Pasha. The Turks crossed the river in the face of the Russian army, and attacked their lines with great impetuosity. After severe fighting, however, they were beaten off, and forced to withdraw from Choczim. *See* Ceşme.

Dodecanese Islands *World War II*

After the surrender of Italy on September 9, 1943, General Maitland-Wilson, British commander in the Mediterranean, landed a battalion of British troops each on the islands of Cos, Leros and Samos. German parachutists recaptured Cos on October 3, and on November 12, attacked reinforced Leros in strength, taking it in four days' fighting, with 3,000 prisoners, some 1,200 Allied troops being taken off by sea. Six Allied destroyers were lost in this fruitless attempt to seize a base in the Aegean. *See* Balkans I, Crete.

Dodowah *First British-Ashanti War*

1826, between the Ashanti army, which had invaded the Gold Coast, and the British under Colonel Purdon. The Ashantis fought bravely, but were routed with heavy loss. *See* Accra, Amoaful.

Dogger Bank I *American Revolutionary War*

August 15, 1781, between a British fleet of seven battleships and six frigates, under Admiral Hyde Parker, and a Dutch fleet of equal strength under Admiral Zoutman. After a severe engagement, the Dutch bore away, and reached their port safely, the British fleet being too crippled to pursue. The British lost 109 killed and 362 wounded; the Dutch one ship, the *Hollandia*, 142 killed and 403 wounded. *See* Porto Praia Bay.

Dogger Bank II *World War I*

January 24, 1915, when Vice-Admiral Beatty with a British battle squadron of five battle cruisers clashed just after dawn with Rear-Admiral Hipper's squadron of four battle cruisers, both with attendant heavy cruisers and destroyers, in the North Sea, 60 miles east of England. Hipper, on sighting the

British, at once turned south-east towards Heligoland, hoping to lure them on to minefields and within reach of a waiting submarine flotilla. Beatty's fleet overhauled Hipper's, the *Lion*, Beatty's flagship, hit the *Blücher* at a range of 10 miles. The *Lion* attacked the *Seydlitz*, and the *Princess Royal* the *Derfflinger*. British gunnery was precise. By 11 am the *Blücher* was sinking, the *Seydlitz* and *Derfflinger* were both afire. Beatty's *Lion* was then hit by a shell which damaged her fuel system and compelled her to retire. Rear-Admiral Moore, in the *New Zealand* then took charge of the action, but soon broke it off while still winning for fear of the German minefields. In fact he was 40 miles, about $1\frac{1}{4}$ hours' sailing from them, during which time he could have sunk both the burning German battle cruisers, which consequently escaped. Only 14 British were killed and six wounded; no ships were lost. *See* Falkland Isles, Coronel.

Dollar *Danish Invasions of Scotland*

875, when the Danish invaders under Thorstem totally defeated the men of Alban under Constantine. The Danes subsequently occupied Caithness, Sutherlandshire, Ross and Moray. *See* Kinloss.

Dolni-Dubnik *Russo-Turkish War*

November 1, 1877, when General Gourko, with two divisions of the Russian guard, dislodged the Turks from the redoubt of Dolni-Dubnik, and forced them to retire upon Plevna. There was little actual fighting, the Turks retiring without much resistance, but the action is important, because the capture of the redoubt made the investment of Plevna complete. *See* Plevna.

Dominica *American Revolutionary War*

April 12, 1782, between the British fleet of 36 sail of the line, under Admiral Rodney, with Admiral Lord Hood second in command, and the French fleet of 33 sail under the Comte de Grasse. Rodney departed from the usual tactics of a ship-to-ship action, and broke the enemy's line, gaining a complete victory, and capturing or destroying five ships, while two more were captured within the next few days. The British lost 261 killed and 837 wounded. The French losses have been put as high as

15,000, but it is probable that they lost about 3,000 killed and wounded, while 7,980 were taken in the captured ships. This action is also known as the battle of the Saints. *See* Yorktown.

Domokos *Greek War of Independence*

May 17, 1879, between five Turkish divisions of the army under Edhem Pasha, and the Greeks under the Crown Prince of Greece, about 40,000 strong. The Greeks held their ground till late in the evening, when the right was outflanked, and forced to give ground, though, when the action ceased, the Turks had made no other advance. Edhem was prepared to renew the fight on the following day, but the Crown Prince found that the retirement of his right had rendered the position untenable, and retreated during the night. The Greeks lost 600 killed and wounded; the Turks about 1,800. *See* Missolonghi.

Donabew *First Burma War*

March 7, 1825, when General Cotton, with about 700 troops, attacked three strong stockades held by 12,000 Burmans under Maha Bandoola. The smallest of the three was carried, but Cotton's force was too small, and it was not till the 25th that Sir Archibald Campbell arrived, and, shelling the stockade, forced the Burmans to evacuate the position. Maha Bandoola was killed. *See* Kemendine.

Donauwörth *War of the Spanish Succession*

July 2, 1704, between the British and Imperialists under the Duke of Marlborough, and the French and Bavarians under Count Darco. Donauwörth, a fortress town, was dominated by a steep oval-shaped hill, the Schellenberg, held by 14,000 of Darco's troops. Marlborough, whose 65,000 forces heavily outnumbered the enemy's, made three strong diversionary attacks with small numbers of troops on the hill's western side, where the defences were strongest, knowing that an attack would be least expected there. Fearing a major attack, Darco was persuaded to reinforce that sector with his reserves. The Duke's right wing, under the Margrave of Baden, then attacked the weaker southern sector and drove back the defenders while Marlborough again stormed the western side,

this time in strength. During the battle that followed, the enemy were first driven from the hill and then the town, with 10,000 killed and wounded. The victors lost 1,400 killed and 3,800 wounded. With this town in his hands Marlborough was now much more strongly placed.

Dorylaeum *First Crusade*

June 31, 1097, between 70,000 Crusaders under Bohemond and Raymond of Toulouse, and 250,000 Saracens under the Sultan Soliman. The Saracens drove back Bohemond's division on their camp, which they proceeded to plunder, and, while so engaged, were attacked by Raymond and totally routed with a loss of 30,000. The Crusaders lost 4,000. *See* Antioch, Jerusalem.

Douai *War of the Spanish Succession*

This town was besieged by the allies under Prince Eugène, April 25, 1710, and was defended by a French garrison, 8,000 strong, under General d'Albergotti. It was obstinately defended, numerous sorties being made, but, the French army being unable to relieve it, d'Albergotti was forced to surrender June 26. The besiegers lost 8,000 killed and wounded. *See* Brihuega, Denain.

Douro *Peninsular War*

May 12, 1809, when 12,000 British under Wellesley (later the Duke of Wellington) crossed the Douro and drove the French under Marshal Soult out of Oporto. The French numbered about 24,000, of whom 5,000 were killed, wounded or captured, mainly during the pursuit. In the action itself, the French lost 500, the British, 116. *See* Oporto.

Dover *Anglo-Dutch Wars*

November 29, 1652, between a Dutch fleet of 95 sail, under Admiral Van Tromp, and an English fleet of 40 ships, under Admiral Blake. The Dutch were victorious, the English fleet being much cut up, two ships captured, six sunk. *See* Portland.

82

Downs, The *Anglo-Dutch Wars*

June 1, 2 and 3, 1666, between the English fleet under the Duke of Albemarle, and the Dutch under Admirals de Ruyter, Van Tromp and de Witt. After an obstinate fight, Albemarle, on the 3rd, retired, after setting fire to his disabled vessels, but the Dutch were too seriously crippled to pursue. *See* North Foreland, The Goodwins.

Drepanum *First Punic Wars*

249 BC, during the siege of Lilybaeum, between the Roman fleet of 123 galleys under Publius Claudius, and the Carthaginians under Adherbal. Claudius was defeated, losing 93 ships, 8,000 killed and 20,000 prisoners, while the victors did not lose a ship. *See* Lilybaeum.

Dresden *Napoleonic Wars*

August 26–27, 1813, between 70,000 French under Napoleon and 150,000 Russians, Prussians and Austrians, under Count Wittgenstein, General von Kleist, and Prince Schwartzenberg, respectively. The Emperors of Prussia and Austria, and the King of Prussia, were present on the field. Napoleon, who was in possession of Dresden, made his main attack upon the Austrian left, which was separated from the centre by the ravine of Planen. This attack, which was entrusted to Marshal Murat, was completely successful, and the Austrians were driven with heavy loss into the ravine. Meanwhile, the centre and right of the allies had been attacked with equal success, and finally they were driven from the field with a loss of 16,000 killed or wounded, 15,000 prisoners, and 40 guns. The French lost about 10,000. *See* Katzbach II.

Dreux *French Religious Wars*

1562, between the Huguenots under the Prince de Condé, and the Catholics under the Constable, Marshal Duc de Montmorency. The Constable, heading a charge of the Catholic cavalry, was overthrown and captured by Admiral de Coligny. The Catholics then fled, but the Huguenots, carrying the pursuit too far, were charged and routed by François de Guise, and Condé made prisoner. The victory thus rested with the Catholics. *See* Jarnac.

Driefontein *Second Boer War*

March 10, 1900, between the Boer Army covering Bloemfontein, under De Wet, and the British under Lord Roberts. The Boers occupied a position about seven miles in extent, which was attacked in front by Kelly-Kenny's division, and on the left flank by that of Tucker. The Boers were driven out and the road to Bloemfontein opened, at a cost to the British of 424 killed and wounded. The Boers left over 100 dead on the field. *See* Bloemfontein.

Dristen *Wars of the Byzantine Empire*

This strong post on the Danube was defended for fifty-five days in 973, by the Russians under Duke Swatoslaus, against the Greeks under the Emperor John Zimisces. At the end of that time the Russians were forced to surrender, thus ending their invasion of Byzantine territory.

Drogheda I *Great Irish Rebellion*

Siege was laid to this town, which was held by an English garrison under Sir Henry Tichborne, by the Irish rebels, under Owen Roe O'Neill, in December, 1641. The garrison held out successfully for three months, when O'Neill was compelled to raise the siege. *See* Benburb.

Drogheda II *Cromwell's Campaign in Ireland*

On September 3, 1649, siege was laid to the town by the 10,000-strong Parliamentary army under Oliver Cromwell, the garrison of 3,000 being led by James Butler, Marquis of Ormonde. An assault on the 10th was repulsed but on the 12th the town was stormed, and the garrison put to the sword. Four thousand soldiers and inhabitants were said to have perished. *See* Rathmines.

Drumclog *Covenanters' Rising*

June 11, 1679, when a party of Covenanters, under Balfour of Burleigh, defeated the royal troops under Claverhouse. *See* Bothwell Bridge.

Drummossie Moor,

see Culloden

Dubba *Sind Campaign*

March 24, 1843, between 5,000 British troops under Sir Charles Napier and 20,000 Beluchis under the Amir Shir Mohammed. The Beluchis were strongly posted behind a double nullah, which was carried by the British infantry, and the Beluchis were totally defeated. Sind (Pakistan) was annexed. *See* Meeanee, Hyderabad.

Duffindale *Kett's Rebellion*

The scene of the defeat of the rebels under Robert Kett, by the royal troops, under the Earl of Warwick, in 1549. *See* Farrington Bridge.

Dunbar I *Wars of Scottish Independence*

April 27, 1296, between the English, under King Edward I, and the Scots under the Earl of Athol. The Scots were defeated, with a loss of 10,000 men. This defeat led to the surrender of John de Baliol, to whom Edward had awarded the Crown of Scotland in 1292, and Edward was proclaimed King of Scotland. *See* Stirling Bridge, Falkirk, Berwick-on-Tweed, Dupplin.

Dunbar II *Wars of Scottish Independence*

This town was besieged, 1339, by the English, under the Earl of Salisbury, and was defended by Agnes, Countess of March, known as Black Agnes of Dunbar, whose husband, the Governor, was absent at the time. So vigorous was the defence, that Salisbury was compelled to withdraw from the siege.

Dunbar III *Cromwell's Scottish Campaign*

September 3, 1650, between 11,000 Parliamentarians under Cromwell, and the Scottish Royalists, 22,000 strong, under David Leslie. General Leslie left a strong position on the heights near Dunbar, to meet Cromwell, and was routed with a loss of 3,000 killed and wounded, and 10,000 prisoners. Cromwell's losses were small. *See* Carbiesdale.

Dundalk *Scottish Invasion of Ireland*

October 5, 1318, between the Scots under Edward Bruce, 3,000 in number, and the English and Irish under John de Bermingham. The Scots were totally defeated, Bruce, with about 30 of his knights, and over 80 men-at-arms, being killed, and the invasion came to an end. *See* Bannockburn.

Dundee,

see Talana Hill

Dunes *Wars of Louis XIV*

June 14, 1658, between the Spaniards, 14,000 strong, under Don John of Austria and the Great Condé, and the French in equal force under Marshal Vicomte de Turenne. A force landed from the English fleet launched the attack on the Spaniards, which was vigorously supported by de Turenne, and the Spaniards were totally defeated, with a loss of 4,000 killed, wounded and captured. Ten days later the town of Dunkirk capitulated. *See* Valenciennes.

Dunganhill *Great Irish Rebellion*

August 8, 1647, between the Irish rebels, and an English force under Colonel Michael Jones. The Irish were routed with a loss of 6,000. *See* Ballymore, Gibbel Rutts, Benburb.

Dunkeld *Jacobite Rising*

August 21, 1689, between the Highlanders under Colonel Cannon, and the Cameronian Regiment under Colonel Cleland. The fight took place in the town of Dunkeld, where the Cameronians held a house belonging to the Marquis of Athol. The Highlanders were unable to dislodge them, and eventually retired, Cannon being killed. *See* Killiecrankie.

Dunkirk *World War II*,

see Flanders

Dunsinane *Anglo-Scottish Wars*

1054, between the usurper, Macbeth, and the Anglo-Saxons under Siward, Earl of

Northumberland, who was supporting Malcolm Canmore, the son of the murdered Duncan. Macbeth was defeated, allegedly losing 10,000 men, and fled to the north. The Anglo-Saxons lost 1,500. *See* Alnwick.

Düppel *Schleswig-Holstein War*

This fortress, protected by an outer chain of ten redoubts, was invested by the Prussians, 16,000 strong, under Prince Frederick Charles, and the first parallel opened, March 30, 1864. The Danish garrison numbered 22,000. On April 17, after a heavy bombardment, the Prussians were launched at the first six of the chain of redoubts, and, after a brief resistance, captured them, the fortress being immediately afterwards surrendered. The Prussians lost 70 officers and 1,331 men, the Danes, including prisoners, 5,500. *See* Langensalza, Alsen.

Dupplin *Baliol's Rising*

August 12, 1332, between the Scottish barons, under Edward Baliol, son of the former king, and the forces of David, King of Scotland. Though largely outnumbered Baliol was victorious. With the support of Edward III of England, whose overlordship of Scotland he acknowledged, Baliol was crowned, thus causing a strong nationalist reaction. *See* Halidon Hill.

Durazzo *Norman Invasion of Italy*

This fortress, which was defended by a garrison of Greeks and Macedonians under George Palaeologus, was besieged by the Normans, under Robert Guiscard, July 17, 1081. On October 18, the besiegers, now reduced to 18,000, were attacked by a force of about 75,000 Greeks, under Alexius Comnenus, and after a terrible struggle, in which the Normans were almost overpowered, the victory rested with Guiscard. The Greeks lost about 6,000. On the Norman side, the Italian auxiliaries suffered heavily, but only

20 Norman knights were killed. Notwithstanding this disaster, the city still held out, and it was not till February 8, 1082, that a night surprise rendered the Normans masters of the place. *See* Rome VI.

Dürrenstein *Napoleonic Wars*

November 11, 1805, during Napoleon's advance on Vienna, when Marshal Mortier, with one French division, was attacked by 30,000 Russians, and would have been overwhelmed but for the timely arrival of another division. The French lost 3,000; the Russians about the same number. *See* Ulm, Austerlitz.

Dwina, The *Swedish-Polish War*

Fought 1701, between 15,000 Swedes under Charles XII, and 12,000 Saxons under Marshal von Stenau. Charles, who was marching upon Riga, found the passage of the Dwina barred by von Stenau. Having the wind at his back, he set fire to a large quantity of straw, crossed the river unperceived. He then attacked the Saxons, who, after an obstinate engagement, were defeated and driven from the field.

Dyle *German States' Wars*

Fought 896, between the Norman invaders, and the Germans under Arnulph, Emperor of Germany. The Normans were totally routed with enormous loss. *See* Montfaucon.

Dyrrachium *Civil War of Caesar and Pompey*

48 BC, between the Caesareans, under Julius Caesar, and the Pompeians, under Pompey. The latter having formed an entrenched camp some distance from Dyrrachium, Caesar interposed his army between the camp and the town. This interrupted Pompey's communications, and he, in consequence, attacked the Caesarean lines, which he forced at the cost of 1,000 men, and obliged Caesar to retire. *See* Pharsalus.

E

East Africa *World War II*

British Somaliland's 1,500-strong garrison having been forced to evacuate the territory in August 1941, General Wavell agreed with Generals Sir William Platt and Sir Alan Cunningham the campaign for defeating the Italians and reconquering East Africa. Platt crossed the Eritrean border from Kassala and defeated the Italians at the battle of Agordat on January 31, 1942. Some 30,000 crack Italian infantry took up a strong defensive position in the fortress of Keren. It fell to Platt's 4th and 5th British-Indian divisions on March 27, after a battle which cost the British 4,000 casualties and the Italians 3,000 killed. Asmara fell on April 1 and the Red Sea port of Massawa on April 4. Meanwhile, on February 10, Cunningham advanced with the 1st South African and the 11th and 12th African divisions, defeated a 30,000-strong Italian force near the coastal town of Gelib, Italian Somaliland, on February 22 and occupied the port of Mogadiscio three days later. After a remarkable advance 550 miles north along the Gerrer River valley, he occupied Jijiga in central Ethiopia, then turned west up the Madar pass and successively took Harrar and Diredawa, arriving in Addis Ababa on April 6, two days after the Italians had abandoned it. General Platt's force had meantime turned south to combine with Cunningham's against the remnants of the Duke of Aosta's 200,000-strong army. Seeing himself attacked from north and south, and being without water, Aosta surrendered at Amba Alagi on May 17. Ethiopia was thus restored to its rightful sovereign, Haile Selassie, whom the Italians had earlier driven out.

East Prussia *World War II*

During the Russian summer offensive of 1944, strong German forces under Marshal Busch resisted stubbornly the attacks of General Chernyakovski's 3rd and General Zakharov's 2nd White Russian Armies against this historic German province. The fighting shifted south to Warsaw and the Carpathians until Russia began her final offensive on January 12, 1945, along a 750-mile front. Rokossovski's 2nd White Russian Army Group drove north-west to the Baltic west of Danzig on January 26, thus isolating the Germans in East Prussia. It then turned east, took Danzig and attacked East Prussia from the south-west while the 3rd White Russian Army Group attacked from the east. Braunsberg fell on March 20 and after another 20 days' fierce fighting Königsberg (Kaliningrad) surrendered with 90,000 German defenders on April 9. *See* Poland-East Prussia.

Ebersberg *Napoleonic Wars*

May 3, 1809, when Marshal Masséna's corps stormed the bridge and castle of Ebersberg, which was held by about 30,000 Austrians under the Archduke Charles. After the bridge was captured, a terrible conflict followed in the streets of Ebersberg, and finally the Austrians were driven out, with a loss of about 3,000 killed and wounded, 4,000 prisoners and many guns. The French admitted a loss of 1,700 only. *See* Eckmühl.

Ebro River *Spanish Civil War*

From July 24–25 to November 18, 1938, General Modesto's 100,000 strong Republican army having crossed the Ebro river in an offensive against Nationalist General de Yagüe's Moroccan regular troops designed to link up Catalonia with the remainder of Republican Spain. The Republicans advanced nearly as far as Gandesa before troops under General Franco's own command stopped them on August 1. These, aided by German and Italian aircraft which then pounded the Republican lines, counter-attacked strongly and forced the enemy to surrender much of their gains. Franco's Nationalists then launched a powerful counter-offensive on October 30 and by November 18 had driven the last of the Republicans back to their start line across the Ebro. At the price of 33,000 killed or wounded, they had inflicted upon the Republicans 30,000 dead, 20,000 wounded and taken 20,000 prisoners. This defeat crippled Republican battle capability. *See* Madrid, Barcelona.

Eckmühl *Napoleonic Wars*

April 22, 1809, between 90,000 French, under Napoleon, and 76,000 Austrians, under the Archduke Charles. The Austrians occupied a position on the high ground above Eckmühl, from which they were dislodged after severe fighting, but the approach of night enabled the Archduke to draw off his troops in tolerable order towards Ratisbon, with a loss of about 5,000 killed and wounded, and 3,000 prisoners. The French loss was said to be 2,500. By this victory Napoleon cut the main Austrian army in two. *See* Aspern, Wagram.

Ecnomus *First Punic War*

256 BC, between 330 Roman galleys, with crews of 100,000 men, under L. Manlius Valso, and M. Attilius Regulus, and 350 Carthaginian ships under Hanno. After a hard-fought battle, in which the Romans lost 24 vessels, they defeated the Carthaginians, with a loss of 30 ships sunk and 64 captured, and drove the rest of the fleet to Carthage. *See* Mylae.

Edessa *Persian Wars*

Fought 259, between the Romans under Valerian, and the Persians under Sapor I. The Romans were totally defeated, and Valerian taken prisoner.

Edgehill *English Civil War*

The first battle of the Civil War, October 24, 1642, between the Royalists under King Charles I, and the Parliamentarians, under the Earl of Essex, each army being about 13,500 strong. The victory was claimed by both sides, but the advantage rested with the King, as the Parliamentarians failed to face Prince Rupert's cavalry, and the Royalists, who also took seven guns, were not prevented from continuing their march on London. *See* Brentford.

Edgeworth *Wars of the Roses*

July 26, 1469, between the Yorkists under the Earl of Pembroke, and the troops of the revolted Nevilles. The Lancastrians attacked Pembroke, whose troops were chiefly Welshmen, and, notwithstanding a stubborn resistance, defeated them with heavy loss, no less than 168 Welsh knights falling, besides rank and file. Edward IV, who was in the neighbourhood, though not present at the battle, was captured soon after. *See* Tewkesbury.

El Alamein I *World War II*

From July 1, 1942, when Field-Marshal Erwin Rommel's Afrika Korps, with 55 fit tanks and about 8,000 German and Italian infantry, tired after their victories at Gazala and Mersa Matrûh and their long advance east, attacked the centre of General Auchinleck's 8th Army position, running from the Egyptian coastal village of El Alamein about 40 miles south to the salt marches of the Qattara Depression. The German 90th Light Division was stopped by intense artillery fire, the weak 15th and 21st Panzers were driven back with the loss of 18 tanks, by the British 4th and 22nd Armoured Brigades. The Italians made no progress in the north. When Rommel attacked again in the centre next morning, Auchinleck counter-attacked to try to cut his line of retreat, fell short of this, but drove the enemy back and destroyed another 12 tanks, leaving them with only 26 against his own 119. But during the next two days, despite this inferiority Rommel managed to pull out his mobile formations and thereafter the battle petered out with both sides exhausted in the intense heat of the desert. Auchinleck had robbed Rommel of his last chance of taking Cairo and in this sense had won a decisive battle. He was however, replaced by General Montgomery. The British lost some 13,000 killed, wounded and prisoner, the Afrika Korps about the same. *See* Gazala, Mersa Matrûh, El Alamein II.

El Alamein II *World War II*

October 23–24, 1942, General Montgomery's 8th Army, reinforced to 200,000 men with 1,100 tanks and air superiority, fired an 800 gun barrage then attacked initially with XXX Corps Field Marshal Rommel's line, held by 96,000 Germans and Italians, with 500 tanks. XXX Corps infantry and following tanks were held up by extensive minefields and next day were hit hard by enemy artillery. X Corps, which then attacked, was similarly held up, but ordered nevertheless to fight its way out to the west, which proved impossible. After five days' hard fighting and slaughter the 8th

Army had lost 10,000 men without penetrating the enemy line. On October 30–31, Montgomery, authorized to carry on without counting the cost, launched another offensive and, backed strongly by the RAF succeeded in penetrating the enemy's defended zone, breaking through and attacking his flanks. On November 3 Rommel began to disengage, was held up for 36 hours by a Führer stand-fast order, then began to withdraw again and continued for 1,500 miles with the 8th Army in pursuit, a retreat which ended finally with total Axis defeat in Tunisia. El Alamein II was thus one of the World War II's decisive battles. Axis losses were said to be 2,300 killed, 5,500 wounded, 30,000 taken prisoner, but reliable British sources put their killed and wounded as high as 20,000. See Tunisia.

Elandslaagte *Second Boer War*

October 21, 1899, between a strong Boer force under General Koch, and three battalions and five squadrons of British troops, with 12 guns, under General French. The Boers occupied a strong position, on high ground near the Ladysmith-Dundee railway, from which they were driven by the infantry and Imperial Light Horse (dismounted) with a loss of 250 killed and wounded, and 200 prisoners, including Koch. The British lost 35 officers and 219 men. See Ladysmith.

Elands River *Second Boer War*

August 4, 1900, a force of 400 Australians, under Colonel Hore, were surrounded by 2,500 Boers, with six guns. The Australians occupied an exposed kopje, with no water nearer than the river half-a-mile away. Their Maxim gun became unserviceable, an attempt by General Carrington to relieve them failed, and so severe was the Boer fire that, in 11 days, 1,800 shells fell within their lines. They held out, however, till August 15, when they were relieved by Lord Kitchener, having lost 75 killed and wounded, and nearly all their horses. See Spion Kop.

El Caney *Spanish-American War*

July 1, 1898, when 12,000 Americans, under General Shafter, captured from the Spaniards,

after heavy fighting, the strong position of El Caney and San Juan Hill, commanding Santiago de Cuba. The Spaniards made various attempts on the 2nd and 3rd to dislodge them, but without success. The American losses during the three days amounted to 115 officers and 1,570 men killed and wounded. See Manila, Santiago de Cuba.

Elchingen *Napoleonic Wars*

October 14, 1805, when Marshal Ney's corps, after repairing the bridge of Elchingen under fire, stormed and captured the convent and village, driving out 20,000 Austrians, and taking 3,000 prisoners and a number of guns. See Ulm.

Elena *Russo-Turkish War*

1877, between the Russians under Loris-Melikov, and the Turks under Mukhtar Pasha, in which the former were victorious. See Plevna.

Elinga *Second Punic War*

206 BC, between 75,000 Carthaginians, under Hanno, and 48,000 Romans under Scipio Africanus. The battle was fought on the open plain in front of Hanno's camp, and resulted in a complete victory for the Romans. This battle, which is also known as the battle of Silpia, ended the Carthaginian domination in Spain. See Metaurus.

Elk Horn,

see Pea Ridge

Ellandune *Rise of Wessex*

In this battle, fought 825, the Mercians under Beowulf, were totally routed by the West Saxons under Egbert, who became the first King of England.

Elleporus *Italiot Invasion of Sicily*

389 BC, between the Sicilians, 23,000 strong,

under Dionysius of Syracuse, and the Italiots, 17,000 strong, under Heloris. Dionysius attacked the Italiot vanguard, under Heloris himself, on the march, and the Italiot army, coming into action in detachments, was beaten piecemeal, and finally routed with heavy loss. The survivors, 10,000 in number, surrendered, and were allowed to go free. Heloris was slain. *See* Cabala.

El Teb I *British-Sudan Campaigns*

February 4, 1884, when a column of 3,500 Egyptian troops under Baker Pasha, marching to relieve Sinkat, was overwhelmed, and practically annihilated by 12,000 Sudanese under Osman Digna. The Egyptians lost 2,360 killed and wounded. *See* Khartoum, Omdurman.

El Teb II,

see Trinkitat

Embata *Social War*

356 BC, when an Athenian fleet of 120 sail, under Chares, designed to attack the Chians, with 100 galleys, in the straits between Chios and the mainland. The day proving stormy, however, his colleagues Iphicrates and Timoleon declined the enterprise as too hazardous, and Chares attacking alone, with a third of the fleet, was defeated with heavy loss. *See* Chios.

Emesa *Wars of the Roman Empire*

Fought 272, between the Romans under Aurelian, and the Palmyrenians under Zenobia. Zenobia was completely defeated, and forced to retire within the walls of Palmyra, to which Aurelian at once laid siege. *See* Pavia, Palmyra.

Empingham *Wars of the Roses*

March 12, 1470, when King Edward IV totally routed the northern rebels, under Sir Robert Wells. The battle is called 'Loosecoat Field', from the precipitate flight of the rebels, who threw off their upper garments to flee the faster. *See* Bosworth Field.

Engen *French Revolutionary Wars*

May 3, 1800, between the 56,000 French under General Moreau, and 110,000 Austrians under General Baron Kray. Moreau had crossed the Rhine on the 1st, and was advancing through the Black Forest, and the battle was in reality two distinct actions. Moreau's right, 25,000 strong, under General Lecourbe, overtook the Austrian rearguard, and drove them into and through Stockach, capturing 4,000 prisoners, and a large depot of munitions and stores. Moreau in the centre was attacked at Engen by 40,000 Austrians, under Kray, whom he repulsed with a loss of 2,000 killed and wounded, and 5,000 prisoners. The French lost 2,000 killed and wounded. *See* Marengo.

Englefield *Danish Invasions of Britain*

In 871, the first of the series of battles between the West Saxons and the Danish invaders. The former, under their king, Æthelred, defeated the Danes. *See* Ashdown, Reading.

Entholm *Northern Wars*

June 11, 1676, between the Danish fleet, under Admiral van Tromp, and Swedes. The Swedes were defeated with very heavy loss in ships and men. *See* Kiöge.

Ephesus I *Ionian War*

499 BC, between the Athenians and Ionians, under Aristagoras, and the Persians, under Artaphernes. The Greeks, who were retreating to the coast after burning Sardis, were overtaken by the pursuing Persians, under the walls of Ephesus, and signally defeated. The Athenians thereupon withdrew their fleet, and took no further part in the war. *See* Lade.

Ephesus II *Gallic Invasion of Asia*

262 BC, between the Syrians, under Antigonus, and the Gallic invaders. Antigonus was disastrously defeated.

Erbach *French Revolutionary Wars*

May 15, 1800, between 15,000 French under General Sainte-Suzanne, and 36,000 Austrians under General Baron Kray. The Austrians, who had 12,000 cavalry, attacked vigorously, but the French, through driven back at certain points, were not routed, and held to their main positions for 12 hours, until the approach of St Cyr's corps forced the Austrians to retire. Both sides lost heavily in the action. *See* Marengo.

Espinosa *Peninsular War*

November 10, 1808, between 18,000 French under Marshal Victor, and 30,000 badly armed Spaniards under General Blake. The Spaniards were routed, and Blake's army scattered. The French lost about 1,100 men.

Essling,

see Aspern

Etampes *Rise of France*

In 604, between the Burgundians, under Queen Brunehilde, and the Neustrians under Clothaire II. The latter were totally defeated.

Ethandun *Danish Invasions of Britain*

In 878, between the West Saxons, under Alfred, and the Danes, under Guthrum, following the victory at Chippenham. The Danes were totally defeated, and Alfred's victory was followed by the Peace of Wedmore which lasted for fifteen years. *See* Tettenhall, Chippenham.

Eurymedon, The *Third Persian Invasion*

466 BC, between the Persian fleet and army, and the Athenians and Delians, under Cimon. The Greeks were victorious both by land and sea, defeating the Persian fleet with a loss of 200 ships, and routing the land army with great slaughter. This victory secured the adhesion of the south of Asia Minor to the Athenian Confederacy. *See* Cunaxa.

Eutaw Springs *American Revolutionary War*

September 8, 1781, between the British garrison of Charleston, under Colonel Stewart, and the Americans, under General Greene. The British were at first driven back, but rallying carried the American positions, but with a loss of 700, which so weakened them that they were unable to profit by the victory. *See* Yorktown.

Evesham *Barons' War*

August 4, 1265, between 8,000 royalists under Prince Edward, and the Barons with 5,350 men under Simon de Montfort. The Barons were taken by surprise, having at first mistaken Edward's army for reinforcements under young de Montfort, and were totally defeated, Simon de Montfort falling. This defeat ended the Barons' War and led to the restoration of King Henry III. *See* Lewes.

Eylau *Napoleonic Wars*

February 8, 1807, between 53,000 French with 200 guns under Napoleon, and 72,000 Prussians and Russians, with 400 guns under Marshal Bennigsen. Napoleon attacked at daybreak, all along the line, but could at first make no impression on the Russian infantry, Marshal Augereau's 7th Corps being slaughtered during a snowstorm. Later in the day Marshal Davout all but succeeded in turning the Russian left, but the opportune arrival of a Prussian corps under General von Lestocq enabled the Russians to repulse him, and after a bloody engagement, which lasted till ten pm, both armies retained their original positions. On the following day the Russians retired unmolested. The French lost about 10,000; the Russians and Prussians about 25,000 killed and wounded. *See* Pultusk, Danzig.

F

Faenza *Wars of the Byzantine Empire*

In 541, between 20,000 Roman legionaries, and the Goths under Totila, King of Italy. The Romans made no attempt to resist the onslaught of the Goths, but throwing down their arms fled ignominiously, giving the Goths an easy victory. *See* Rome IV.

Fair Oaks *American Civil War*

May 31, and June 1, 1862, between the 41,000 Federals under McClellan and the 35,000 Confederates under General Johnston. McClellan was advancing upon Richmond, and his left wing was attacked in the afternoon of the 31st, and notwithstanding the arrival of Sumner's corps in support, was driven back for two miles. On the 1st the Federals recovered the ground they had lost, but made no further progress, and at the end of the day the Confederates, who were largely outnumbered, were permitted to retire unmolested. The Federals lost over 5,000 killed and wounded, the Confederates about 6,000. This is also called the Battle of Seven Pines. *See* Cedar Mountain, Seven Days' Battle.

Falkirk I *Wars of Scottish Independence*

July 22, 1298, between 18,500 English under Edward I, and 10,200 Scots under Sir William Wallace. The Scots were strongly posted behind a bog, which at first greatly hampered the English attack. In the end, however, the English archers overcame the Scottish defence, and a final charge routed them. Wallace escaped but was a fugitive for the rest of his life. Casualties: about 5,000 Scottish infantry and 40 knights; 200 English cavalry. *See* Dunbar, Stirling Bridge.

Falkirk II *Jacobite Rebellion of the Forty-five*

January 17, 1746, between the rebel Highlanders, 8,000 strong, under the Young Pretender, Prince Charles, and a force of 8,000 British troops, with 1,000 Campbells under General Hawley. The charge of the Highlanders broke the British line, and they were driven headlong from the field, with a loss of 600 killed and wounded, 700 prisoners, seven guns, and all tents and baggage. The rebels lost 120 only. This was the last Jacobite victory. *See* Prestonpans, Culloden.

Falkland Isles *World War I*

After the British naval defeat at Coronel, Chile, Admiral Sturdee's squadron of two battle cruisers and five light cruisers steamed hastily to the South Atlantic, arriving at the Falkland Isles, off the coast of Patagonia, 24 hours before Admiral von Spee's five cruisers and three supply ships. While the British warships were coaling, Admiral von Spee's squadron sighted them and steamed off, but Sturdee's vessels gave chase and in the ensuing battle on December 8th, 1914, sank the *Scharnhorst*, *Nürnberg*, *Leipzig* and *Gneisenau*, von Spee, his two sons and some 2,000 sailors being killed or drowned. The cruiser *Dresden* and an auxiliary German vessel escaped. German commerce raiders being thus cleared from these outer seas, the British fleet was able to concentrate nearer home. *See* Coronel.

Famagusta *Cyprus War*

This town was besieged by the Turks under Mustapha Pasha, on September 18, 1570, and was defended by 7,000 men, half Venetians, half Cypriots, under Marcantonio Bragandino. The garrison held out until August 6, 1571, when it capitulated, marching out with the honours of war. After the surrender, however, Mustapha murdered in cold blood Bragandino and four of his lieutenants, then slaughtered the entire garrison. The Turks allegedly lost 40,000 men in the course of the siege. *See* Lepanto.

Farquhar's Farm *Second Boer War*

October 29, 1899, between the main Boer army, under Joubert, and the garrison of Ladysmith, under Sir George White. The Boer position covered about eight miles, and White attacked in three columns, one of which, detached to the left to hold a position at Nicholson's Nek, was overwhelmed and surrendered. The Boers meanwhile developed a strong attack against the British right, and

White, having no guns capable of coping with the heavy Boer ordnance, ordered a retreat. This was effected in good order, and was greatly aided by the opportune arrival of two heavy naval guns, under Captain Hedworth Lambton. The British lost 317 killed and wounded, and 1,068 missing. The Boer losses are unknown, but were certainly small. *See* Magersfontein.

Farrington Bridge *Arundel's Rebellion*

July 27, 1549, between a small force of Cornish rebels, and an equal number of Royal troops under Lord Russell. The rebels were defeated and driven from the field, but there was no pursuit. Each side lost about 300. *See* Duffindale.

Farrukhabad *Second British-Maratha War*

November 14, 1804, between a small British force under Lord Lake, and an army of 60,000 Marathas under Jeswunt Rao Holkar. Holkar was signally defeated with heavy loss. The British casualties were two killed and 20 wounded. *See* Bhurtpore.

Faventia *Civil War of Marius and Sulla*

82 BC, between the consular army of Norbanus, and the Sullans under Metellus. Norbanus attacked here (Faenza) with his army wearied by a long march, and his force was totally broken up, only 1,000 remaining with the eagles after the battle. Sulla became dictator of Rome. *See* Mount Tifata.

Fehrbellin *Swedish Invasion of Brandenburg*

June 28, 1675, between the Swedes, under Charles XI, and the Brandenburgers, 15,000 strong, under the Elector, Frederick William. The Swedes were totally defeated, and forced to evacuate Brandenburg. *See* Kiöge.

Ferkeh *British-Sudan Campaigns*

June 7, 1896, between 9,500 Egyptian troops, with a British horse battery, under Sir Herbert Kitchener, and 4,000 Mahdists under the Emir Hamada. Kitchener, by a night march, surprised the Mahdists in their camp, and after two hours' fighting, drove them out with a loss of 1,500 killed and 500 prisoners. Of 62 Emirs present in the camp, 44 fell and four were captured. The Egyptians lost 20 killed and 81 wounded. *See* Khartoum.

Ferozeshah *First British-Sikh War*

December 21, 1845, between 50,000 Sikhs with 108 guns, under Lal Singh and 18,000 British and Indian troops, with 65 guns, under Sir Hugh Gough. Disagreement between Gough and Lord Harding, the Governor-General, who was present, prevented Gough from attacking the fortified Sikh camp until dusk. In a bloody battle his troops drove the Sikhs back, but at nightfall he ordered a withdrawal, the Sikhs re-entered their camp and shelled the exposed British. But there was treason among the Sikh leaders and the British were spared certain defeat next day by the sudden retirement of a fresh Sikh army under Tej Singh. British losses: 694 killed; 1,721 wounded. *See* Aliwal, Sobraon, Chilianwala, Gujerat.

Ferrara *Napoleon's Hundred Days*

April 12, 1815, when Marshal Murat, with 50,000 Italians, endeavoured to force the passage of the River Po in the face of an Austrian army, under General Bianchi. He was repulsed with heavy loss, and forced to retreat southward. *See* Ligny.

Ferrybridge *Wars of the Roses*

March 28, 1461, shortly before the battle of Towton, when a force of Lancastrian cavalry, under Lord Clifford, defeated the Yorkists, under Lord Fitzwalter, who was endeavouring to secure the passage of the Aire at Ferrybridge. Lord Fitzwalter was killed. *See* Towton, Mortimer's Cross.

Fethanleag *Saxon Conquests*

In 584, between the West Saxons, under Ceawlin, and the Britons under Cutha. The Britons were defeated. *See* Deorham.

Finland,

see Mannerheim Line

Fish Creek *Riel's Second Rebellion*

April 24, 1885, when General Middleton,
with 400 Canadians, attempted to drive the
rebels, 280 strong, from a strong position
near Fish Creek. After losing 50 men,
Middleton withdrew. The rebels lost 29
killed and wounded. *See* Batoche.

Fisher's Hill *American Civil War*

September 22, 1864, between 30,000 Federals,
under General Sheridan, and 8,000
Confederates, under General Early. The
Confederates were defeated and driven from
their position with a heavy loss in prisoners
and 11 guns. *See* Cedar Creek, Gettysburg.

Five Forks *American Civil War*

April 1, 1865, when Federal General Sheridan's
12,000 cavalry, aided by General Warren's
V Corps (16,000 men), attacked Confederate
General Pickett's 19,000 infantry and cavalry
at this road junction, routing them and taking
about 5,000 prisoners. This defeat forced
Confederate General Robert E. Lee to
withdraw from Petersburg and Richmond
the next day. *See* Petersburg, Appomattox
River.

Flanders *World War II*

4 am April 10, 1940, the Nazi *blitzkrieg* began
with German parachutists seizing bridges and
airfields in Holland and Belgium, while two
German army groups and one Panzer army
over-ran Dutch and Belgian forces on the
right and crossed the Meuse at Maastricht.
Holland's 10 divisions fought back, lost
100,000 men, a quarter of their strength, and
surrendered on May 14, the day Rotterdam
was blitzed. The BEF (13 divisions) joined
Belgium's 17 divisions and the French 1st
Army on the Dyle River on May 13, but
were forced back behind the Scheldt by May
19.
General Guderian's tanks broke through on a
50-mile front between Namur and Sedan and
in seven days smashed over 200 miles west to
Abbeville. Boulogne fell May 25, Calais, May
26, thus cutting British communications.
Withdrawal was ordered and the Admiralty
began Operation Dynamo, evacuation via
Dunkirk, at 6.57 pm May 26. Here the
French 16th Corps held a 10-mile and the
BEF a 45-mile front surrounding the blazing
town.
The evacuation, carried out in an inferno of
bombardment, lasted nine days. Including
120,000 French, 338,226 men were brought
back to Britain in an armada of 860 small
vessels, some 240 of which were sunk.
Numerous warships played a big part, six
destroyers being sunk and 19 badly damaged.
More than one million Allied troops were
taken prisoner in the Flanders *blitzkrieg*, a
battle the Allies lost largely owing to their
belief in positional as against mobile warfare.
See France.

Fleurus I *Thirty Years' War*

August 29, 1622, between the Spaniards,
under General di Spinola, and the Palatinate
troops, under Count von Mansfeldt and
Christian of Brunswick. The Germans were
endeavouring to retreat into Holland after
their defeat at Hoechst and were intercepted
by the Spaniards, through whom they tried
to fight their way. In this effort the infantry
was almost entirely cut to pieces, but about
7,000 cavalry reached Breda with the two
generals. *See* Dessau, Stadtlohn.

Fleurus II *Wars of the Grand Alliance*

July 1, 1690, between the French, under
Marshal Luxembourg, and the Germans and
Dutch under the Prince of Waldeck. The
French gained a signal victory, the allies being
driven from the field in disorder with a loss
of 14,000 killed and wounded, and 49 guns.
See Staffarda, Beachy Head.

Fleurus III *French Revolutionary Wars*

June 25, 1794, between the Austrians, 50,000
strong, under the Duke of Coburg, and 70,000
French, under General Jourdan. The
Austrians attacked, and after a severe
engagement, were repulsed and compelled
to fall back in the direction of Brussels to
cover that city. *See* Montenotte, Tourcoing.

Flodden *Anglo-Scottish Wars*

September 9, 1513, when the English, under the Earl of Surrey, attacked the Scots, under James IV, in a strong position on the hill of Flodden. The position was turned by the English left wing, under Stanley, and the Scots totally defeated with heavy losses. James and all his principal nobles fell. *See* Guinegate.

Florence *Wars of the Western Roman Empire*

This city was besieged in 406, by the German invaders under Radagaisus, and was almost on the verge of starvation, when the approach of Stilicho at the head of a large Roman army, encouraged the defenders to further resistance. The besiegers, in fact, now became the besieged, for Stilicho surrounded their camp, and starved the Germans into surrender. *See* Rome II.

Flushing *Walcheren Expedition*

This town was besieged by the British under Lord Chatham and surrendered after a feeble defence, August 16, 1809.

Focsani *Ottoman Wars*

July 21, 1789, between the Turks, under Yusuf Pasha, and the Russians and Austrians under Field Marshal Count Suvorov and the Prince of Saxe-Coburg. The allies stormed the Turkish entrenched camp and drove out the Turks with a loss of 2,000 men. *See* Rimnitz.

Fontenoy *War of the Austrian Succession*

May 11, 1745, between 50,000 British, Dutch and Austrian troops, under the Duke of Cumberland, and 70,000 French under Marshal Saxe. The Duke endeavoured to relieve Tournai, which the French were besieging, and the British troops captured the heights on which the French were posted. The Prince of Waldeck, however, who commanded the Dutch, failed to support the Duke, and the French being reinforced, the trenches were retaken, and the Allies beaten back, losing 6,500 men. Tournai fell shortly afterwards. *See* Hohenfriedberg.

Formigny *Hundred Years' War*

April 25, 1450, when the newly landed English reinforcements under Kyrielle were totally defeated, and almost annihilated, by the French under the Comte de Clermont. This defeat practically put an end to the English domination in the north of France. *See* Rouen, Patay, Castillon.

Fornham St Geneviève *Rebellion of the Princes*

In 1173, between the supporters of the rebel princes under Robert de Beaumont, and the forces of Henry II under the Justiciary, Richard de Lucy. The rebels were defeated.

Fornovo *Franco-Italian Wars*

July 6, 1495, between 34,000 Venetians and Mantuans under Francisco de Gonzaga of Mantua, and 8,000 French and Swiss under Charles VIII. The French were attacked as they were retiring, but succeeded in repulsing the Italians at a cost of only 100 of all ranks, while the assailants lost 3,500 killed and wounded. *See* Cerignola.

Fort Donelson *American Civil War*

February 15, 1862, when Confederate General Pillow and General Floyd, holding Fort Donelson with 12,000 men against Federal General U.S. Grant's 25,000 men, successfully attacked Grant's right wing in an effort to create an escape route. General Floyd's courage then failed him, and he ordered the victorious force back to its first position. The Federals then advanced, Generals Floyd and Pillow fled and next day 11,000 Confederates surrendered unconditionally to General Grant. Confederate casualties were 500 killed and 2,100 wounded. *See* Pea Ridge.

Fort Frontenac *Seven Years' War*

This place, held by about 110 French troops, under Noyan, was captured by Colonel Bradstreet with 3,000 Colonials, August 27, 1758. The capture was of extreme importance, as it robbed the French of the control of Lake Ontario, and severed their communications with their posts on the Ohio. *See* Fort William Henry.

Fort St David I *Seven Years' War*

This fortress, in India, was besieged, May 14, 1758, by a French force under Lally-Tollendal, and defended by a garrison of 800 British and 1,600 Indian troops. The defence was not energetically conducted, and, on the arrival in the roads of a French fleet under Comte d'Aché, the garrison surrendered June 2. *See* Plassey, Madras.

Fort St David II *Seven Years' War*

A naval action was fought off this place, April 29, 1758, between seven British ships under Admiral Pococke, and a squadron of French vessels under Comte d'Aché. After a short and indecisive engagement, the French sheered off, but the British were too severely damaged in the rigging to give chase. The French lost one ship, driven ashore. *See* Plassey, Madras.

Fort William Henry *Seven Years' War*

This fort, held by 2,200 British and Colonial troops under Colonel Monro, was besieged, August 4, 1757, by General Marquis de Montcalm, with 6,000 French and Canadians and 1,600 Indians. Montcalm's batteries opened on the 6th, and on the 9th, having lost 300 killed and wounded, and nearly all his guns being disabled, Monro surrendered. He was to be permitted to retire unmolested to Fort Edward, but the French were unable to control their Indian allies, who attacked the unarmed column as it retired. Before order was restored, some 50 had been killed, and 400 carried off prisoners by the Indians. *See* Oswego.

Forum Terebronii *First Gothic Invasion of the Roman Empire*

In 251, between the Romans under Decius, and the Goths under Cuiva. The Gothic army was drawn up in three lines, and the legionaries overthrew the two first, but, in attacking the third, they became entangled in a morass, and were utterly routed. Decius and his son were slain. *See* Philippopolis.

France 1940 *World War II*

After the débâcle in Flanders and the evacuation of the BEF at Dunkirk, France had only 65 weak, demoralized divisions against 140 German. And on June 5, 1940, as Dunkirk ended, the German 4th Army attacked west, reaching Rouen June 9; the 6th Army tore down the Oise Valley north of Paris; General von Rundstedt's three armies attacked in the centre, while General von Kleist's and General Guderian's panzers crossed the Marne at Château-Thierry and Châlons respectively, splitting and overwhelming the French, who abandoned their Maginot Line fortifications, June 14–15, opening the way to north-east France to the German 1st and 7th armies. All the time, the *Luftwaffe* divebombed and machine-gunned the refugee-choked roads. The 4th Army swept west to Cherbourg by June 18, thence on into Brittany. Von Kleist's armour took Dijon on June 16, then turned south to Lyon, while Guderian's reached Nancy and the Swiss border. The French government declared Paris an open city on June 11 and fled to Bordeaux. The Nazis goose-stepped into the capital on June 14. Marshal Pétain surrendered on June 17 and this took place formally on June 22 at Compiègne. In their 9-week campaign in Flanders and France since April 10, the Nazis had lost 27,000 killed, 111,000 wounded and 18,500 missing. They claimed to have taken nearly two million French prisoners. At this time, of all the nations in the world, only Britain and the Commonwealth opposed the Nazis, who were already planning an invasion. *See* Flanders; Britain, Battle of.

Frankenhausen *Peasants' War*

May 15, 1525, between the troops of Saxony, Hesse and Brunswick, and the revolted peasants under Thomas Münzer. The peasants were utterly routed, and Münzer captured and hanged out of hand. This put an end to the rising. *See* Mühlberg.

Frankfort-on-Oder *Thirty Years' War*

This town held by Emperor Ferdinand II's Independency, was taken by storm by King Gustavus Adolphus II, at the head of 13,000

Swedes, April 13, 1631. General Count Montecucculi, who was in the town, escaped with a portion of the cavalry, but 1,800 of the Imperial garrison were killed, and 800 captured, with 30 standards and 18 heavy guns. *See* Magdeburg.

Franklin *American Civil War*

November 30, 1864, between 30,000 Federals under General Schofield, and 40,000 Confederates under General Hood. Schofield occupied a strong position covering Nashville, where he was attacked by Hood, who penetrated his lines. The Federals, however, rallied, and recaptured the lost positions and after nightfall, Schofield was enabled to cross the Harpeth in good order, and effect a junction with General Thomas. The Confederates lost about 4,500; the Federals, 1,500 killed and wounded and 1,000 prisoners. *See* Nashville.

Frastenz *Swiss-Swabian War*

April 20, 1499, when the Swiss, under Heinrich Wolleb, attacked the Austrians who occupied a strongly entrenched position, and drove them out with a loss of 3,000 killed. Wolleb, who led the charge, was the first to fall on the Swiss side. *See* Calven.

Fraubrunnen *Invasion of the 'Guglers'*

January, 1376, between the Bernese, and the 'Guglers', French and English mercenaries, under Baron Ingelram von Coucy, who claimed the Canton of Aargau in right of his mother. The 'Guglers' were totally routed, and compelled to retire from Switzerland. *See* Sempach.

Frauenstadt *Russo-Swedish Wars*

February 12, 1706, between 10,000 Swedes under Marshal Reinschild, and 20,000 Russians and Saxons under General Schulemburg. The battle did not last a quarter of an hour, for the allies fled without making any resistance. No less than 7,000 loaded muskets were picked up on the battlefield. *See* Pultusk.

Fredericksburg *American Civil War*

December 13, 1862, between 120,000 Federals under General Burnside, and 70,000 Confederates under General Lee. The Confederates, who occupied a range of heights fringing the Rappahannock River, were attacked by the Federals, whom they repulsed after hard fighting, with a loss of 13,771 killed and wounded. The Confederates lost 5,200, but Lee, owing to his inferior numbers, did not feel strong enough to push his victory home, and allowed Burnside to evacuate Fredericksburg unmolested. *See* Antietam.

Fredrikshald *Great Northern War*

This fortress, the strongest in Norway, was besieged by the Swedes, under Charles XII, early in December, 1718. On the 11th, as he was inspecting the advanced batteries, the king was struck by a round shot, and fell dead. The Swedes at once raised the siege and eventually concluded the war, ceding the eastern Baltic lands to Russia, ending their domination of the Baltic. *See* Stralsund.

Freiburg *Thirty Years' War*

August 3, 5 and 9, 1644, between 20,000 French under the Great Condé and the Vicomte de Turenne, and 15,000 Bavarians under Baron von Mercy. On the 3rd, Turenne, after a long flank march, attacked the Bavarians on the flank, while Condé assailed their front, at 5 pm. When night fell, the Bavarians were giving way, and during the night Mercy retired to a fresh position. Here he was attacked on the 5th, but held his ground throughout the day, the French losing twice as many men as their opponents. Three days later, Mercy found it necessary to retreat, and on the 9th he was attacked while retiring by a force of cavalry. This he repulsed but Condé, coming up, rescued his cavalry, and drove the Bavarians headlong before him, capturing all their artillery and baggage. *See* Lens.

Freteval *Anglo-French Wars*

Fought 1194, between the English under Richard Coeur de Lion, and the French under Philip Augustus. Richard gained a complete victory. *See* Gisors.

Friedland *Napoleonic Wars*

June 14, 1807, between 80,000 French under Napoleon, and 60,000 Russians under General Bennigsen. The battle began at 3 am, at which time only Marshal Lannes' corps was on the field. Bennigsen at first contented himself with an artillery duel, and did not attack in force till 7 am, when a mere 26,000 French were in position. These held their ground till the arrival of Napoleon, who with his fresh troops launched an attack against the Russian columns massed in a bend of the river Alle, drove large numbers of them into the river, and occupied Friedland after hard fighting. It was 10 pm before the Russians were finally driven from the field, having lost 18,000 killed or wounded and 10,000 prisoners. The French lost between 7,000 and 8,000 killed or wounded. This victory was followed by the signing of the Peace of Tilsit, signed on a raft on the river Niemen on June 25. *See* Copenhagen.

Frontiers, Battle of the *World War I*

Four Battles: Lorraine, which influenced Ardennes, which affected Charleroi, which in turn had an impact on Mons. On August 20, 1914, the German Schlieffen Plan offensive under von Moltke clashed with the French Plan 17, under General Joffre, and for five days two great army groups battled from Mons, in Belgium, to the Swiss frontier, along the German, Luxembourg and Belgian frontiers with France — Germany's seven armies against France's five and Britain's one. Lorraine: the French 1st and 2nd armies, began their offensive on August 14, crossed the frontier into Germany next day and advanced to Sarrebourg and Morhange, Field Marshal von Moltke forbidding his 6th and 7th armies to counter-attack because he wanted the French to commit themselves so deeply here that they would be unable to pull out to support French armies in the north, where the Schlieffen Plan was getting under way. Only when signs came of French disengagement did the Germans counter-attack, on August 20, and defeat the French in the battle of Sarrebourg. On August 23, Prince Rupprecht of Bavaria began a counter-offensive and routed the French XV and XVI corps, but were then held by XX corps, at the battle of Morhange. The French finally stabilized their front along the line Nancy, Charmes, Epinal. Here they held until the battle of the Marne on September 5. Ardennes: August 21, when the French 3rd and 4th armies launched Plan 17's offensive against the German centre, clashed with the German 4th and 5th armies and, after two days' heavy fighting, fell back and retreated to Verdun, Stenay and Sedan on August 23–4. Charleroi: August 21, General von Bülow's 2nd army crossed the Sambre between Namur and Charleroi, taking Charleroi next day despite the fierce resistance of units of General Lanrezac's 5th army, whom the Germans drove back in a south-westerly direction, opening a gap between them and the British, then deploying at Mons. August 22–23, General von Hausen's 3rd army crossed the Meuse and assaulted Lanrezac's right wing, unprotected owing to the retreat of the French 4th army in the Ardennes. Lanrezac retreated in time, at a cost of 5,000 casualties, then counter-attacked briefly on August 29 and checked the German advance, only to be forced to retreat again to protect his exposed left wing. Mons: August 23, General Sir John French's British Expeditionary Force, 70,000 men, 300 guns, deploying behind the Mons canal, was attacked by General von Kluck's 1st Army, 160,000 men, 600 guns, during its Schlieffen Plan manoeuvre south towards France. The heavily outnumbered British held the Germans for nearly 10 hours before retreating. A grave defeat for France and Britain, the battles ensured that the war would be fought on French territory. *See* Namur, Marne.

Fuentes de Oñoro *Peninsular War*

May 5, 1811, in the course of Marshal Masséna's attempt to relieve Almeida. General Lord Wellington had earlier launched two armies to attack the Napoleonic forces in Spain, one towards Badajoz, under General Sir William Carr Beresford, and the other under himself along the northerly route, via Salamanca, with 32,000 British and Portuguese forces plus about 2,000 German cavalry. Finding the Portuguese town of Almeida, near the frontier, held by the French, he laid siege to it. Masséna then left Ciudad Rodrigo to relieve it, but Wellington marched his forces to a strong position behind Fuentes de Oñoro, just inside Spain. After a first badly planned attack on May 3, which Wellington's men easily repulsed, Masséna assaulted again on May 5, with 30,000 troops and 36 guns. During a hard-fought day-long battle, in which the issue, when doubtful, was turned by the British horse-drawn artillery, Wellington's men finally drove the French from the field, with 2,250 killed and wounded at a cost to them of 1,400 men. 'If Boney had been there we would have been damnably licked,' Wellington reputedly said. *See* Busaco, Albuera.

Fulford *Norse Invasion of Britain*

September 20, 1066, between the Norsemen under Harold Hardrada, King of Norway, the English under Earls Edwin and Morcar. The English were defeated. *See* Assundun.

Fushimi *Japanese Revolution*

In 1868, between the troops of Aizu and Kuwana, under the Shogun, Yoshinobu, and the anti-foreign clans of Satsuma and Choshu, who gained a complete victory. In 1869 the new 'Imperial System' was established.

Futteypore *Indian Mutiny*

July 12, 1857, between a strong force of rebels, and the British troops under General Sir Henry Havelock, who was marching to the relief of Lucknow. The rebels were completely defeated, losing 11 guns. No British and only a few loyal Indian troops were killed. *See* Cawnpore, Lucknow.

G

Gadebesk *Danish-Swedish Wars*

December 20, 1712, between the Swedes, 12,000 strong, under General Steinbock, and 24,000 Danes and Saxons. The allies occupied a position protected by marshy ground, where they were attacked by the Swedes, and, after three hours' hard fighting, driven from their entrenchments with heavy loss. *See* Stralsund.

Gaines' Mill,

see Seven Days' Battle

Galicia *World War I*

From August 10, 1914, when General Dankl's Austrian 1st Army crossed the Polish frontier in a major offensive against the Russian province of Galicia, clashing with General Ivanov's Russian 4th Army, which made a strategic retirement, 25 miles south of Lublin. Mobilization having been completed, General Russki's Russian 3rd Army crossed the Galician border near Brody, threatening the Austrians from the east while General Brusilov's 8th Army from Odessa advanced on a convergent path to the south.

By August 27 they were linked, and advancing on a 200-mile front towards the road and rail junction of Lemberg (Lvov), driving before them the Austrian 3rd and part of the 2nd armies. Capturing Tarnopol August 27, Brusilov then occupied Halicz and wheeled north to Lemberg, which, after a fierce 3-day battle fell on September 3, the Russians taking 100,000 prisoners. On September 4 the Austrians counter-attacked against the Russian centre, but were repulsed with losses, the Russians then going over to the offensive from the Vistula to the upper Dniester, penetrating the Austrian right, General Auffenberg's 4th army, at Rava Russka, and routing it.

The entire Austrian force retreated south-west in disorder as far as Cracow. The Russians took over 120,000 Austrian prisoners and besieged another 100,000 men in Przemyśl. Austrian casualties were about 110,000 killed or wounded. This Russian victory opened the way for another offensive against Cracow. *See* Gumbinnen, Warsaw.

Gallipoli *World War I*

From April 25, 1915, to January 10, 1916, when, by landings along the western and southern sides of the Gallipoli Peninsula, the Allies hoped to capture Istanbul and join Russia in an offensive from the east. For by command of the Dardanelles waterway, linking the Black Sea with the Mediterranean, Turkey was able to stop the Allies joining forces in the war against Germany, Austria-Hungary and Turkey.

British and French naval bombardment of the Dardanelles forts was at first tried, but this failed owing to minefields, and there were no landings. General Hamilton was then given command of 13 British and Commonwealth divisions, with a French corps, totalling eventually 490,000 men, who would be opposed by General Liman von Sanders' 20 Turkish divisions. Bungling and inefficiency dogged the expedition and 40 days were needed to launch the attack, once the island of Mudros had been chosen as the base, thus enabling the enemy to prepare.

Eventually, on April 25, some 75,000 men were landed on the Peninsula's southern tip, another 35,000 at Cape Helles plus 35,000 Anzacs further up the west coast, but the Turks held their main positions and under Colonel Kemal (later Kemal Ataturk), counter-attacked. By May 8 Hamilton had lost about a third of his men in the fierce fighting and there were signs of a stalemate, but resisting calls for evacuation he ordered his army to dig in. Another landing of 25,000 men at Suvla Bay on August 6 failed largely owing to the apathy of General Stopford, who slept on a ship at the critical time. A stalemate like that of the western front developed. Hamilton was replaced on November 22 by General Munro, and finally the Cabinet in London agreed to withdrawal. Suvla Bay and Anzac Cove were evacuated by the Navy on December 20 and Cape Helles on January 9–10, after another general action, but no lives were lost in this skilful withdrawal, the only success in the entire campaign. British and French casualties were about 250,000 and those of Turkey probably about the same.

99

Garigliano I *Franco-Spanish Wars in Italy*

November 8, 1503, between the Spaniards, 12,000 strong, under Gonsalvo de Cordova, and the French, in greatly superior force, under Francisco de Gonzaga of Mantua. Gonzaga, wishing to pass the Garigliano, had thrown a bridge over it, and proceeded to cross in face of the Spanish army. After very severe fighting, the French drove back the Spaniards, and made good the passage of the river. *See* Garigliano II, Cerignola, Seminara.

Garigliano II *Franco-Spanish Wars in Italy*

December 28, 1503, between the Spaniards, about 15,000 strong, under Gonsalvo de Cordova, and the French, slightly superior in number, under the Marquis of Saluzzo. Gonsalvo crossed the Garigliano at two points, and fell upon the French, who were retiring on Gasta. After hard fighting the French were utterly routed, leaving 4,000 dead on the field. The Spanish loss is unknown. Louis XII of France sought peace terms as a result of this defeat. *See* Cerignola, Seminara.

Garigliano III *Italian Wars of Independence*

October, 1850, between the Italian patriots under Colonel Cialdini, and the Neapolitans under Francis II of Naples. The patriots were victorious. *See* Venice, Magenta.

Gate Pah *Maori British War*

April 27, 1864, when 1,700 British soldiers and blue-jackets, under General Cameron, attacked the Maori stockade known as the Gate Pah. After a short bombardment, 600 men forced their way into the stockade, but were repulsed. On the following day it was found that the stockade had been evacuated. The British lost 14 officers, and 98 men killed and wounded. Only 30 dead and wounded Maoris were found in and near the Pah.

Gaulauli *Indian Mutiny*

May 22, 1858, between a British column under Sir Hugh Rose, and 20,000 rebels under Tantia Topi, the Rani of Jhansi, and other rebel leaders. The overwhelming numbers of the rebels at first gave them the advantage, but a bayonet charge broke them, and they fled in disorder with heavy loss. This victory was followed by the recovery of Calpi. *See* Cawnpore.

Gaza I *Alexander's Asiatic Campaigns*

This city, defended by a Persian garrison, under Batis, was besieged by Alexander the Great, October 332 BC. Utilizing the engines he had employed against Tyre, he succeeded, after some weeks, in breaching the walls, and, after three unsuccessful assaults, carried the city by storm, the garrison being put to the sword. Alexander was now able to march on Egypt. *See* Arbela.

Gaza II *Wars of Alexander's Successors*

312 BC, between the Syrians and Egyptians, under Seleucus and Ptolemy Soter, 25,000 strong, and an equal force of Macedonians under Demetrius Poliorcetes. The Macedonians were routed, losing 5,000 killed, 8,000 wounded, and all their treasure and baggage.

Gaza III *World War I*

March 26, 1917, when General Murray's British Empire troops moved into Palestine (now Israel and Jordan) and attacked General Kress von Kressenstein's 17,000 Turks with three infantry and two cavalry divisions, under General Dobell. British supplies, including water, had to be transported from Suez. The Turks in Gaza fought back strongly and although the British reached its northern outskirts night fell with it still in enemy hands. The British cavalry mistakenly withdrew; General Dobell had to order a general retirement. Next day von Kressenstein's Turks, reinforced, drove back the British, killing or wounding about 3,800 for losses of 2,400. *See* Gaza IV.

Gaza IV *World War I*

In a second battle on April 17, 1917, a frontal attack against numerically superior forces, the British were stopped and withdrew two days later, having lost 6,400 killed or wounded. General Dobell then resigned owing to ill health, and on June 28 General Allenby took

100

over from General Murray. After the successes of the Sinai campaign, Gaza was a temporary setback to British arms in the Middle East. *See* Gaza V.

Gaza V *World War I*

October 31, 1917, when General Allenby's seven infantry and three cavalry divisions, in all 88,000 men including the Camel Corps, assaulted the 30-mile Turkish Gaza-Beersheba line at Beersheba, in the western foothills of the Judaean Hills, and forced the Turkish 7th Army back to Tel el Sheria. The heavily fortified line was finally reduced after a week's fighting, Gaza fell on November 6–7, Askalon on the 9th, Jaffa on the 16th. Allenby then swung to the east and outflanked Jerusalem from the north. Turkish resistance to the north-west of it, on the Nebi Samwil ridge, was overcome by December 9 and Jerusalem surrendered. Allenby entered on December 11 and read a proclamation guaranteeing religious toleration to all. In Muslim hands for 730 years, the Holy City thus passed into Christian control. This contributed to the later collapse of Turkey. *See* Damascus.

Gazala *World War II*

From May 26, 1942, in Libya, when General Rommel with 332 German and 228 Italian tanks attacked the British in the Gazala Line, a system of minefields and strong boxes 40 miles long and 10 miles deep running from Gazala on the coast to Bir Hakim. Each box was garrisoned by a brigade group with its own artillery and supplies for a week. Rommel advanced on May 26, and in the early hours of May 27 the Panzers refuelled south of Bir Hakim, intending to thrust north east to Tobruk, El Adem and Akroma. General Neil Ritchie's deployment of his forces was tactically unsound however, the three armoured brigades of 30 Corps being widely separated and 7th Armoured Division out of battle positions. They recovered quickly and for a time Rommel, short of petrol, was dangerously placed, until he defeated British infantry in the centre and enabled his supplies to enter through the Trigh Capuzzo. A British counter-attack on his bridgehead failed and after ten days' fighting the French Brigade was forced out of Bir Hakim. Ritchie, believing hopefully that one more armoured fight might exhaust Rommel, clashed with him near the Knightsbridge crossing on June 12 and 13. At the end of it he had only 70 tanks left, against 100 German and 60 Italian. The Battle of Gazala was lost, the 8th Army retreated to the Egyptian border, leaving the 2nd South African Division to hold Tobruk. It fell two days later. Ritchie was relieved by General Auchinleck. *See* Tobruk III, Sidi Rezegh, Mersa Matrûh.

Gebora *Peninsular War*

February 19, 1811, between 8,000 French, under Marshal Soult, and 12,000 Spaniards, under Mendizabal. The Spaniards were routed with a loss of 2,000 killed and wounded, 5,000 prisoners and all their guns. *See* Albuera.

Gelt, The *Anglo-Scottish Wars*

February, 1570, between the rebel Borderers under Leonard Dacre, and the royal troops under Lord Hunsdon. The rebels were completely routed.

Gembloux *Netherlands War of Independence*

January 31, 1578, between the Netherlands patriots, 20,000 strong, under General Goignies, and the Spaniards, in about equal force, under Don John of Austria. The patriots, who were retiring from Namur, were followed by Don John, who sent forward a picked force of 1,600 men, under Gonzaga and Mondragon in pursuit. They attacked the rearguard, under Comte Philip d'Egmont, and dispersed it, and then, falling suddenly upon the main body, utterly routed it, with a loss, it is said, of 10,000 killed and prisoners. The Spaniards lost only a few. *See* Leyden, Maastricht.

Genoa I *Patriotic Rising*

In 1746, the Genoese rose against the Austrian garrison, under General Botta, and after five days' street fighting, lasting from December 6 to 10, drove them out of the city, with a loss of 5,000 men.

Genoa II *French Revolutionary Wars*

March 13, 1795, between a British fleet of 14 sail of the line under Admiral Hotham, and a French fleet of 15. The action lasted throughout the day, and on the following morning the French retired, leaving two line-of-battle ships in the hands of the British. The British lost 74 killed and 284 wounded. *See* Fleurus.

Genoa III *French Revolutionary Wars*

In April, 1800, Genoa, held by the French, under General Masséna, was besieged by the Austrians under General Mélas, and later in the siege under General Ott. The city had for some time been blockaded on the seaward side by the British fleet, under Lord Keith. Provisions were consequently scarce, and notwithstanding some successful sorties, Masséna was forced to capitulate, June 5, the garrison marching out without laying down their arms. *See* Montebello.

Geok Tepe *Russian Conquest of Central Asia*

This place, the stronghold of the Tekke Turcomans (now in Turkman SSR), defended by a garrison of 15,000, was besieged, September 9, 1878, by the Russians, under General Lomakine. After a short bombardment, an attempt was made to storm the fortress, which was repulsed with a loss of 500. The breaching guns were with difficulty saved, and the Russians retired on the following day. About 4,000 Turcomans were killed by shell fire.
In 1881, a second attempt was made by General Skobelev, with 10,000 Russians, the garrison being now nearly 30,000 strong. After a regular siege, lasting from the 8th to the 17th of January, the place was stormed, 6,500 Turcomans falling in the assault, and 8,000 in the subsequent pursuit, ending all resistance. *See* Plovdiv.

Gerberoi *Norman Revolt*

In 1080, between the troops of William the Conqueror, and those of his son Robert, who claimed the Dukedom of Normandy, and was receiving aid from Philip I of France. Robert was defeated and made prisoner, and, obtaining his father's forgiveness, and, resigned his claim to the Dukedom. *See* Hastings.

Gergovia *Gallic War*

52 BC, between the Romans under Julius Caesar, and the Gauls under Vercingetorix. Caesar was besieging the town, but was compelled to retreat. Before retiring, however, he delivered an assault which was repulsed by the Gauls, the Romans leaving over 700 legionaries, and 46 centurions dead on the field. *See* Avaricum.

Germaghah *Tatar Conquest of Central Asia*

Genghis Khan's first battle, fought 1193, when with 6,000 men he defeated the army of his father-in-law, Ung Khan, under Sankun, 10,000 strong, surprising them in a narrow pass, and inflicting heavy loss upon them. *See* Bokhara.

Germantown *American Revolutionary War*

October 4, 1777, between the Americans under Washington, and the British under Sir William Howe. The Americans attacked the British entrenchments, and were repulsed with heavy loss. *See* Stillwater.

Gerona *Peninsular War*

This fortress, held by 3,000 Spanish regulars, under Mariano Alvarez, was besieged, June 4, 1809, by General Verdier, with 18,000 French. Though ill-provided with food, medicines, and money, and receiving but little assistance from outside, Alvarez held out gallantly till December 10, when he capitulated, and the garrison marched out with the honours of war. *See* Talavera.

Gettysburg *American Civil War*

July 1, 2 and 3, 1863, between the Army of the Potomac under General Meade, 88,000, and the Army of Virginia under General Lee, 75,000. On the 1st, Meade's position in front of Gettysburg was attacked by General Ambrose Hill's corps, and the Federals driven in confusion into the town. On the 2nd, Meade took up a fresh position behind Gettysburg, where he repulsed all the Confederate attacks, though at a heavy loss. On the 3rd, Meade succeeded in driving back the Confederate left, but Lee's main attack succeeded in driving the Federals from the ridge. They rallied and retook it, but had lost too heavily to assume the offensive. Lee again offered battle on the 4th, but the Federals declined it, and Lee retired unmolested, having lost about 27,000 men in the three days. The Federal losses were about 23,000. *See* Winchester, Vicksburg.

Ghazni *First British-Afghan War*

This hitherto impregnable fortress, garrisoned by 3,000 Afghans, under Haidar Khan, was captured January 21, 1839, by the British, under General Keane. The besiegers having no siege guns, it was found necessary to blow in the main gate, and the place was then stormed, at a cost of 18 officers and 162 rank and file killed and wounded. The garrison lost 500 killed. The country then came under British rule for three years. *See* Khoord Kabul.

Gherain *British Conquest of Bengal*

August 2, 1763, between the army of Mir Kasim, the deposed Nawab of Bengal, and the British under Major Adams. A severe engagement, lasting four hours, ended in a signal victory for the British. *See* Buxar, Plassey.

Ghoaine *First British-Afghan War*

August 30, 1842, between General Nott's force, on its march from Kandahar to Ghazni, and the Afghans, under Shems-ud-din, Governor of Ghazni. The Afghans were totally defeated, losing all their guns, tents and baggage. *See* Jellalabad.

Gibbel Rutts *Irish Rebellion*

May 26, 1798, when the regulars, under Sir James Duff, attacked the camp of the rebels on the Curragh, and dispersed them at the point of the bayonet, with a loss of 350 killed.

Gibraltar I *War of the Spanish Succession*

This fortress was captured, July 24, 1704, by a combined British and Dutch fleet, under Sir George Rooke, from the Spaniards under the Marquis de Salinas. The resistance of the garrison lasted two days only, during which the allies lost 12 officers and 276 men killed

and wounded. The subsequent possession of Gibraltar sustained Britain's naval power. *See* Vigo Bay.

Gibraltar II *American Revolutionary War*

From June 24, 1779, to February 7, 1783, Gibraltar sustained a siege at the hands of a combined French and Spanish force, who, though provided with powerful floating batteries, were unable to make any impression on the defences. In the course of the siege, the garrison, under General Elliot, were several times reinforced and revictualled by British fleets, which ran the gauntlet of the blockade. *See* Grenada.

Gihon, The *Wars of Tamerlane*

In 1362, between the Getes under their Khan, and the Tatars under Timur (Tamerlane). The Tatars were defeated, and the Getes marched upon Samarkand, but sickness robbed them of nearly all their horses and they were forced to retire.

Gingi *Mughal Invasion of the Deccan*

This place was besieged by the Mughals in 1689, and was defended by Rajah Ram. The siege was carried on in desultory fashion, first by Zulfikar Khan, then by Kambakoh, son of Aurungzebe, and then again by Zulfikar Khan. After three years had been wasted, Aurungzebe took command in person, and after conniving at the escape of Rajah Ram, carried the place by storm.

Gislikon *War of the Sonderbund*

November 23, 1847, when the Federals, under General Dufour, attacked the troops of the Sonderbund, under Colonel Salis-Soglio, strongly posted at Gislikon, near Lake Zug, and drove them from their position. The losses were very small. On the following day the Federals entered Lucerne, and the Civil War, which had lasted 20 days only, came to an end.

Gisors *Anglo-French Wars*

In 1197, English knights led by King Richard

I, Coeur de Lion, attacked Philip II of France's forces and drove them from this town 18 miles north west of Paris. Later, while besieging the castle of Chaluz, Richard was killed by a crossbow bolt on April 6, 1198.

Gitschin *Seven Weeks' War*

June 29 and 30, 1866, between the Prussians, 16,000 strong, under Prince Frederick Charles, and the Austrians and Saxons, 30,000 strong, under Count Clam-Gallas. The Austrians were defeated, and driven from all their positions with a loss of 3,000 killed and wounded, and 7,000 prisoners.

Gladsmuir,

see Prestonpans

Glen Fruin *Scottish Civil Wars*

In 1604, between the royal troops under the Duke of Argyll, and the Macgregors and other clans, when the Highlanders gained a complete victory.

Glenlivet *Huntly's Rebellion*

October 4, 1594, between the troops of James VI, 10,000 strong, under the Earl of Argyll, and the rebel Earls of Errol and Huntly. Though inferior in numbers, the rebels gained a complete victory, driving off the royal troops with a loss of 500 men.

Glen Malone *Colonization of Ireland*

1580, between the English settlers, under Lord Grey de Wilton, and the Irish septs. The English suffered a serious defeat, among the slain being Sir Peter Carew.

Glenmarreston *Angles' Invasion*

683, when the Scots under Donald Bree, King of Dalriada, utterly routed the invading Angles.

'Glorious First of June',

see Ushant

Goa I *Portuguese Conquest*

In 1511, Goa, held by a Portuguese garrison under Albuquerque, was invested by Kumal Khan, General of the Rajah of Bijapur, at the head of 60,000 men. After a siege of 20 days Albuquerque found his communication with his fleet threatened, and withdrew the garrison. In the same year, however, having collected a force of 1,500 men with 23 ships at Cananore, he attacked Goa, and at once forced an entrance. After severe fighting in the streets, the Deccanis fled in confusion to the mainland, with a loss of 6,000. The Portuguese lost 50 only.

Goa II *Portuguese Conquest*

This fort, which was held by a Portuguese garrison of 700, under the Viceroy, Luis de Ataida, was attacked by Ali Adil Shah, Rajah of Bijapur, with 135,000 men and 350 guns, in 1570. Aided by the civilians, and 1,300 monks, the garrison made so strenuous a defence, that the Rajah was beaten off, after losing 12,000 men.

Goits *Italian Wars of Independence*

May 30, 1848, between the Piedmontese under Charles Albert of Savoy, and the Austrians under General Radetsky. The Austrians were completely defeated, and Radetsky compelled to take refuge behind the line of the Adige. *See* Custoza, Venice.

Golden Rock *Carnatic War*

August 7, 1753, between 1,500 British under Major Stringer Lawrence, together with 5,000 Tanjore troops under Monacji, and a detachment of French and Mysoris, forming part of the army besieging Trichinopoly. The Golden Rock was taken by assault, and the enemy driven off in confusion, but the victory would have been more decisive had the Tanjore horse pursued with more vigour. *See* Calcutta.

Goodwins, The *Anglo-Dutch Wars*

July 1, 1666, between a British fleet of 60 sail, under the Duke of Albemarle, and a Dutch fleet of 71 sail-of-the-line, and 30 smaller vessels, under Admirals van Tromp and de Ruyter. The action lasted two days, and was desperately contested, but the Dutch being reinforced in the morning of the 3rd, Albemarle bore away. On the 4th, having been joined by Prince Rupert's squadron, he renewed the attack, but without success. The English lost 10 ships, while most of the others were disabled. The killed and wounded amounted to 1,700, while 2,000 were taken prisoner. *See* North Foreland.

Goraria *Indian Mutiny*

November 23 and 24, 1857, between a British column, about 3,000 strong, under Brigadier Stuart, and a body of 5,000 rebels. The mutineers occupied a strong position, and the British were unable to dislodge them on the 23rd. On the following day the attack was renewed, and the rebels were driven out and dispersed, with a loss of over 1,500. *See* Cawnpore.

Gorlice *World War I*

From April 28, 1915, when Marshal von Hindenburg, pursuing his policy of crushing Russia first, assaulted the Russian 3rd Army with the combined German 11th and Austrian 4th armies. After a tactical forward move on Gorlice, General von Mackensen on May 1 showered the Gorlice-Tarnów sector with 700,000 shells. Gorlice and Ciezkowice (south-east of Cracow) fell on May 3, the Russian line was shattered and 200,000 prisoners taken. Withdrawing to keep their forces intact, the Russians evacuated Przemyśl on June 1.
General Brusilov tried to make a stand on a 40-mile front on the Dniester, threw the Germans back and claimed that they had lost 150,000 men in their attempts to cross. But this temporary stand was followed by the fall of Lemberg (Lvov) on June 22 and, in the north, of Warsaw, August 4–5; and of Brest-Litovsk three weeks later. The Russians had no means of combating the masses of German heavy artillery, and by mid-September the Germans held a line running from Vilna in the north, to Pinsk and Luminetz in the centre, east of the Pripet Marshes, to Dubno and the Rumanian frontier in the south. Russia lost about a million men killed and wounded, another million prisoners and thousands of square miles of food-producing territory, all largely as a result of inadequate military equipment. It was a disaster which lengthened the war and contributed to the Bolshevik revolution. *See* Naroch Lake.

Gorni-Dubnik *Russo-Turkish War*

October 24, 1877, between the 2nd Division of the Russian Guard, under General Gourko, and the Turks, who were holding the redoubt of Gorni-Dubnik, under Achmet Hefzi Pasha. After very heavy fighting, the Russians succeeded in dislodging their opponents, with a loss of 1,500 killed and wounded, and 53 officers and 2,250 men captured, including the Pasha. The Russians lost 3,300 killed and wounded, including 116 officers of the Guards. *See* Plevna.

Gorodeczno *Napoleonic Wars*

August 12, 1812, between 36,000 French and Austrians, under General Reynier and Prince Schwartzenberg, and the Russians, in equal force, under General Tormazoff. The Russians were defeated and driven from their positions, with a loss of 4,000 men. The French and Austrians lost about 2,000. *See* Borodino.

Gothic Line *World War II*

By August 1944, the Allied 5th Army (General Mark Clark) and the British 8th Army (General Oliver Leese), after their 250-mile drive north since the end of May from the Gustav Line, were held at Kesselring's Gothic Line, stretching from Pisa in the west across Italy to Rimini on the Adriatic. On August 26 Alexander attacked with the 8th Army on a 20-mile front by the Adriatic. Rimini fell on September 20, but elsewhere the Line held and the Allied offensive died away during the winter months. It began again on April 9, 1945, the Line was breached and Bologna fell to the Polish Corps on April 20. The Po River was crossed three days later and soon the German retreat turned into a rout. *See* Gustav-Cassino Line.

Graf Spee *World War II*

December 12, 1939, between the British cruiser squadron *Exeter*, *Ajax* and *Achilles*, and the formidable German pocket battleship *Graf Spee*, in the South Atlantic. The *Exeter*, although herself crippled, had badly damaged the *Graf Spee*, which put into Montevideo for repairs. Having been given 72 hours to leave by the Uruguayan government, Captain Langsdorf sailed, then at once scuttled his warship outside the harbour and killed himself rather than face internment. British convoys across the Atlantic were henceforward somewhat safer. *See* Atlantic I.

Grampians, The *Roman Invasion of Scotland*

84 AD, probably on the Moor of Ardoch, between the Romans under Agricola, the military governor, and the Caledonians, 30,000 strong, under Calgacus. The Caledonians attacked with great bravery, but were beaten by the superiority of the Roman discipline, and retired with a loss of 10,000 men. The Romans also lost heavily.

Granada I *Spanish-Muslim Wars*

In 1319, when a Spanish army, under the Regents Pedro and John of Castile, appeared under the walls of Granada. A sortie of 5,000 picked Moors under Said Othman routed the Christians, both the Regents being slain.

Granada II *Spanish-Muslim Wars*

On April 26, 1491, Ferdinand the Catholic, with an army of 50,000 Spaniards, besieged Granada, the last stronghold of the Moors in Spain. The siege was carried on in somewhat desultory fashion, and in the early days one serious sortie was made by the inhabitants and garrison, who were, however, defeated, with a loss of 2,000 killed. The city held out until November 25, when Abdallah, the last king of Granada, capitulated, thus ending the Muslim occupation. *See* Baza, Malaga.

Grandella *Italian Wars*

1266, between the troops of the Two Sicilies, under Manfred, son of the Emperor Frederick II, and the French, under Charles of Anjou. Manfred was defeated, and fell in the battle, Charles seizing the crown of the double kingdom.

Grangam *Russo-Swedish Wars*

Fought 1721, between the Swedes, and the Russian fleet under Admiral Golitshin. The Swedes were completely defeated, losing four line-of-battle ships captured.

Granicus, The *Alexander's Asiatic Campaigns*

May, 334 BC, between 35,000 Macedonians, under Alexander the Great, and 40,000 Persians and Greek mercenaries, under Memnon of Rhodes, and various Persian satraps. Alexander crossed the Granicus in the face of the Persian army, leading the way himself at the head of the heavy cavalry, and having dispersed the Persian light horse, he brought up the phalanx, which fell upon and routed the Greek mercenaries. The Persians lost heavily, while the Macedonians' loss was very slight. *See* Issus, Thebes.

Granson *Burgundian Wars*

March 2, 1476, between the Swiss, 18,000 strong, and 36,000 Burgundians, under Charles the Bold. Charles, trying to entice the Swiss into the plain, ordered a retreat. He was followed by the Swiss, and his rearguard being attacked, was seized with panic, and fled. In the end Charles was completely defeated, his camp captured. *See* Héricourt.

Grant's Hill *Seven Years' War*

September 14, 1758, when Major Grant, with 800 Highlanders, and Provincials, attacked a body of Indians in the French service near Fort Duquesne. He was repulsed, and in turn attacked by the garrison of the Fort, 3,000 strong, under M. de Ligneris. Grant was totally defeated, losing 273 in killed, wounded and prisoners, and was himself captured. *See* Fort St David.

Graspan *Second Boer War*

November 25, 1899, between Lord Methuen's division, with a naval brigade, 400 strong, and a Boer commando of about 2,500 men. The Boers occupied a strong position, the key of which, a high kopje, was attacked in front and flank, and carried, with a loss of nine officers and 185 men. The marines, who numbered 200, lost three officers and 86 men of this total. The Boers lost about 100. This is also called the battle of Enslin. *See* Kimberley.

Gravelines *Franco-Spanish Wars*

July 13, 1558, between 8,500 French and Germans, under Marshal de Thermes, and about 10,000 Spanish, Germans and Flemings, under the Comte d'Egmont. De Thermes' right rested on the sea, and a cavalry charge, headed by d'Egmont, broke his line, after severe hand-to-hand fighting. The French fled in confusion, leaving 1,500 dead on the field, while as many more were driven into the sea, and drowned. Large numbers were cut down in the pursuit, and de Thermes was captured. In 1559, Henri II and Philip II signed the Peace of Cateau-Cambrésis. *See* St Quentin.

Gravelotte *Franco-Prussian War*

August 18, 1870, between the French, 113,000, under Marshal Bazaine, and the combined German army under the supreme titular command of William of Prussia, 187,000. The battle was most hotly contested, but while the French held their ground in the neighbourhood of Gravelotte, the Germans, under General von Moltke, turned their right flank at St Privat, and they were eventually obliged to abandon all their positions, and retire into Metz, where they were subsequently blockaded. The German losses amounted to 899 officers and 19,260 men killed and wounded. The French losses were somewhat less. This battle is also known as the battle of St Privat. The Germans were now able to destroy the French at Sedan. *See* Sedan.

Grenada *American Revolutionary War*

July 6, 1779, between a British fleet of 24 sail, under Admiral Byron, and a French fleet of 25 sail of the line, and 10 frigates, under the Comte d'Estaing. Admiral Byron attacked the French with a view to recapturing Grenada, but was unsuccessful, though he inflicted upon them a loss of 1,200 killed and 1,500 wounded. The British lost 183 killed and 346 wounded. *See* Porto Praia Bay.

Grochów *Second Polish Rising*

February 25, 1831, between the Poles, 90,000 strong under Prince Michael Radziwill, and 120,000 Russians, under General Dubitsch.

After a bloody engagement, the Russians were defeated, with a loss of 10,000 killed and wounded. The Poles lost about 5,000. *See* Warsaw.

Gross-Beeren *Napoleonic Wars*

August 23, 1813, between the French army of the north, under Marshal Oudinot, and the allies, 80,000 strong, under the Crown Prince of Sweden, who was covering the road to Berlin. General Reynier, whose corps formed the centre of Oudinot's army, captured Gross-Beeren, which was retaken by the Prussians under General Baron von Bülow, and again recovered by Generals Fournier's and Guilleminot's divisions, but Oudinot was not sufficiently strong to press his advantage, and retired with a loss of 1,500 men, and eight guns. *See* Bautzen.

Gross-Jägersdorf *Seven Years' War*

July 30, 1757, between 28,000 Prussians, under Marshal Lehwaldt, and a largely superior force of Russians, under General Apraxin. The Prussians were defeated, but Apraxin failed to follow up his victory, and recrossed the frontier. *See* Kolin.

Grozka *Ottoman Wars*

1739, between the Austrians, under Count Neipperg, and the Turks, under the Grand Vizier. The Austrians were defeated, with heavy loss.

Grunnervaldt *German-Polish Wars*

1404, between the Poles, under Vladislas IV, and the Teutonic Knights, under their Grand Master. The Poles gained a complete victory, and it was said that 50,000 knights perished, though it is more than doubtful whether their whole army amounted to so many.

Guadalajara *Spanish Civil War*

March 8, 1937, when 22,000 of General Franco's regular troops and 30,000 Italian Fascist motorized troops under General Roatta attacked this town, 35 miles from partially encircled Madrid. After at first giving way, the Republicans counter-attacked, March 16–17, aided by Soviet tanks and aircraft and routed the Italians, killing 2,000 and wounding 4,000. The Nationalist attack on Guadalajara came to a standstill. *See* Madrid.

Guadalcanal *World War II*

The five-month battle between US forces and Japanese forces for the control of this island, 1,000 miles north-east of Queensland, Australia. After seizing the island, the Japanese began building an airfield in July, 1942. Some 6,000 US Marines under General Vandegrift landed on August 7 and seized it, but Japanese reinforcements attacked the Americans strongly, while their warships blasted them from the sea. Both sides landed reinforcements, the Japanese forces being 36,000 strong. Fighting in the malarial jungles was unrelenting, but gradually the Japanese were worn down and driven back as the US established naval superiority, and by the end of January, 1943, American victory was assured. The Japanese Navy evacuated 12,000 troops at night, but 14,000 Japanese were killed or wounded, 9,000 died of disease or starvation and 1,000 were taken prisoner. About 1,600 Americans were killed, 4,200 wounded and a few thousand died from disease, mainly malaria. *See* New Guinea, Rabaul, Guadalcanal, Naval Battles.

Guadalcanal, Naval Battles *World War II*

Six separate battles, during the land battle in 1942, for control of the seas for reinforcement and supply. Savo Island, August 9: Eastern Solomons, August 24–25: Cape Esperance, October 11–12: Santa Cruz Islands, October 26: Guadalcanal, November 13–15: Tassafaronga, November 30, by which time the US Navy had established a narrow margin of superiority. Both sides lost 24 warships: Japan two battle ships, four cruisers, one light carrier, 11 destroyers, six submarines and over 150 aircraft: the Allies eight cruisers, two heavy carriers, 14 destroyers and almost as many aircraft. *See* Guadalcanal, Solomon Islands.

Guadeloupe *French Revolutionary Wars*

This island was taken by a British force under Sir John Jervis, July 3, 1794, with a loss of three officers and 33 men killed and wounded. It was recaptured by the French, on December 10, of the same year.

Guad-el-Ras *Spanish-Moroccan War*

March 23, 1860, when 25,000 Spaniards, under Marshal O'Donnell, routed a large force of Moors, entrenched in a very strong position behind the Guad-el-Ras. This victory ended the war.

Guam *World War II*,

see Mariana Islands

Gubat,

see Abu Kru

Guilford Courthouse *American Revolutionary War*

March 15, 1781, between 1,900 British, under Lord Cornwallis, and a largely superior force of Americans, under General Greene. The Americans occupied a strongly entrenched position in and round Guilford, and the battle consisted of a series of independent actions, in which the British were uniformly successful, driving out the Americans with heavy casualties, and the loss of all their guns and ammunition. The British lost 548 killed or wounded, but the victory served little purpose, as Lord Cornwallis was too weak to pursue his advantage. *See* Porto Praia Bay.

Guinegate *Anglo-French Wars*

August 16, 1513, when a body of French cavalry, who aimed at relieving Thérouanne, which was besieged by the English, under Henry VIII, and the Imperialists, under Maximilian I, were put to flight by the allies without striking a blow. The French fled so precipitately that the action was dubbed the Battle of the Spurs. *See* Flodden.

Gujerat *Second British-Sikh War*

February 22, 1849, between the British, 25,000 strong, under Lord Gough, and 50,000 Sikhs, under Shir Singh. The British artillery, numbering 84 pieces, broke the Sikh lines, and after resisting infantry attack for over two hours, they fled, losing many in the pursuit. Fifty-three guns were taken. The British lost 92 killed and 682 wounded. This battle completed the conquest of the Punjab and put an end to the Sikh State. *See* Chilianwala.

Gumbinnen *World War I*

Having invaded East Prussia on August 17, 1914, General Rennenkampf's 200,000 strong Russian 1st Army advanced towards Gumbinnen (now Gusev, USSR), before which was deployed General von Prittwitz's German 8th Army. On August 20 the German counter-attack pressed back the Russian right wing, but the line held and stopped the German centre and right with heavy artillery fire. The German advance turned into a somewhat disorderly retreat of nearly 17 miles and the Russians entered Gumbinnen. General von Hindenburg was now brought out of retirement to take over in this sector. *See* Lódź.

Günzburg *Napoleonic Wars*

October 9, 1805, when Marshal Ney's corps carried the three bridges over the Danube, at or near this town, driving off the Austrians with a loss of 300 killed and wounded, and 1,000 prisoners. *See* Ulm.

Gustav-Cassino Line *World War II*

Field Marshal Kesselring in 1943 had fortified a natural line of defence running across Italy from a point north of Ortona, on the Adriatic, to the mouth of the Garigliano river on the west coast, where a total of 18 divisions opposed General Alexander's 5th Army (General Mark Clark) and 8th Army (General Oliver Leese), in their winter attacks. General McCreery's British X Corps crossed the lower Garigliano, but the Germans held them, while the US 36th Infantry Division was repulsed at the Rapido. General Alexander sent in three separate offensives against Cassino from early February to March 15, but dug in around the monastery on the hill the Germans held. By March 23 the offensive had stalled. Alexander then concentrated his forces, bringing the 8th Army to the Cassino front, after very heavy aerial bombing attacked again and on May 17 the Polish II Corps fought its way into Cassino. The two allied armies then broke through the Gustav Line and the Adolf Hitler Line behind it and raced north. Rome fell on June 4 and by August 4 they had swept north 250 miles as far as Kesselring's Gothic Line, stretching east from Pisa to Florence and thence to Ancona on the Adriatic. *See* Cassino, Salerno, Anzio, Gothic Line.

Gwalior I *First British-Maratha War*

This strong fortress was captured from the Marathas, August 3, 1780, by a British force of about 2,000 men, mostly sepoys, under Captain Popham. The wall was scaled by two companies of sepoys, under Captain Bruce, supported by 20 Europeans, and followed by two battalions. The garrison was completely surprised, and an entrance effected without opposition, whereupon the place was surrendered to the assailants, who had not lost a man.

Gwalior II *Indian Mutiny*

June 17, 18 and 19, 1858, between a British column under Sir Hugh Rose, and a large body of rebels, led by the Rani of Jhansi in person. On the 17th the mutineers were driven out of the cantonments with heavy loss, while on the following days the important positions in the town were captured in succession, until by the evening of the 19th, the British were in undisputed possession of Gwalior. The Rani was known to be amongst the slain, though her body was never found. *See* Delhi.

H

Haarlem *Netherlands War of Independence*

This city was invested by the Spaniards, 30,000 strong, under Don Federico de Toledo, December 11, 1572. It was held by a garrison of 4,000 under Colonel Ripperda, including a corps of Amazons, led by a widow named Kenau Hasselaer. The batteries opened fire on the 18th, and on the 21st an assault was repulsed, the assailants losing 400, the garrison three or four only. A second assault, on January 31, 1573, was also repulsed, while a brilliant sortie, on March 25, captured a large and welcome convoy of provisions. On May 28, however, the patriot flotilla of 150 vessels under Martin Brand, on the lake, was defeated by 100 Spanish ships, under Count Bossu. From this point the reduction of the city by famine was inevitable, and the place was surrendered, July 12, 1573. The garrison, reduced to 1,800, was massacred, with the exception of 600 Germans, and altogether 2,300 persons perished after the capitulation. Ripperda was hanged. The Spaniards lost 12,000 men in the course of the siege. *See* Alkmaar.

Habbaniyah *World War II*

On April 18, 1941, the British landed a brigade at Basra to defend treaty rights threatened by the pro-Nazi Iraq government of Rashid Ali, who on May 2 attacked the vital RAF air base Habbaniyah, 38 miles west of Baghdad, with 9,000 troops and 50 guns. The British, 250 infantry, 1,000 RAF personnel, and 1,000 local troops, were supported by the RAF, whose bombing was so effective that after four days Rashid Ali's troops began to withdraw. A British counter-attack drove them across the Euphrates with the loss of 400 prisoners. Reinforced by a motorized unit, the British captured Baghdad on May 30. The victory led to Allied power over the entire Middle East.

Hadranum *Sicilian Wars*

344 BC between Timoleon, the deliverer of Sicily, with 2,000 followers, and Hiketas, Tyrant of Leontini, with 10,000 men. The two had been summoned to the assistance of the rival factions in Hadranum, and Hiketas, who arrived first, was resting his men under the walls, when he was surprised by Timoleon, and totally routed. This was Timoleon's first exploit, and Hadranum became his headquarters. *See* Himera.

Hadrianople I *War of the Two Empires*

July 3, 323, between Constantine, Emperor of the West, with 120,000 troops, and Licinius, Emperor of the East, with 165,000. Licinius, by the skilful manoeuvring of Constantine, was enticed from his entrenched camp into the open plain, and his raw levies being powerless against the Western veterans, he was totally defeated. It is said that 34,000 perished in the battle. *See* Cibalis.

Hadrianople II *Second Gothic Invasion of the East*

August 9, 378, between the Romans, under the Emperor Valens, and the Goths, under Fritigern. The Roman cavalry fled from the field, and the legionaries were surrounded and ridden down by the overwhelming masses of the Gothic horse. Two-thirds of the legionaries, and nine great officers and tribunes perished. Valens was carried off the field wounded, but the hut in which he was lying was fired, and he perished in the flames. The battle foretold the supremacy of cavalry over infantry and the destruction of Rome. *See* Aquileia.

Hahozaki *Tatar Invasion of Japan*

1274, between the troops of the province of Kiushiu and the Tatars forming the expedition, despatched by Kublai Khan, under Lin Fok Heng. After severe fighting, in which the Japanese suffered heavily, Lin was severely wounded, and withdrew to his ships. A heavy gale destroyed a large number of the Tatar and Korean vessels, and finally the remnant of the invading force made good its escape.

Haliartus *Wars of Greek City-States*

395 BC, when Lysander, at the head of a Spartan force, without waiting as had been arranged to effect a junction with Pausanius, attacked the town of Haliartus. The Haliartians made a sortie, and the Spartans, attacked simultaneously in front and rear, were routed, and Lysander slain. *See* Cnidus.

Halidon Hill *Wars of Scottish Independence*

July 19, 1333, in the course of an attempt by Archibald Douglas, the Regent, to relieve Berwick, which was besieged by King Edward III. The Scots were powerless against the English archers, and were defeated with heavy loss, including the Regent, and four Earls. Edward de Baliol, who had been crowned at Scone, paid homage to King Edward, but the Scots did not submit. *See* Neville's Cross.

Hallue *Franco-Prussian War*

December 23 and 24, 1870, between 40,000 French, under General Faidherbe, and 22,500 Germans, under General von Manteuffel. The French lost heavily in the village lying in front of their position, but the Germans were unable to carry the entrenchments on the heights. After their attack had been repulsed, the French assumed the offensive, but with no decisive result. The Germans lost 927 killed and wounded; the French over 1,000, besides 1,300 prisoners. *See* Gravelotte, Metz, Sedan.

Hampton Roads *American Civil War*

March 8 and 9, 1862, between the Confederate armoured frigate, *Merrimac*, and five gunboats, under Captain Buchanan, and five Federal warships, under Captain Marston. On the 8th, the *Merrimac* destroyed two Federal vessels, and drove one ashore, but on the 9th, the Federals were reinforced by the arrival of the turret-ship *Monitor*, and after an indecisive action, the *Merrimac* drew off. In the two days, the Confederates lost only 10 killed and wounded, but the Federal losses were far heavier, the *Cumberland* alone losing 150 out of a crew of 400. *See* Roanoke Island.

Hanau *Napoleonic Wars*

October 30 and 31, 1813, between 80,000 French, the survivors of Leipzig, under Napoleon, and 45,000 Austrians and Bavarians, under General Wrede, who had occupied a position at Hanau, barring Napoleon's retreat to France. On the 30th Napoleon attacked Wrede's left, which was astride the road, and driving it back continued his retreat with the main body, leaving three divisions to secure his rearguard. On the 31st, the rearguard, under Marshal Mortier, attacked Hanau, and Wrede being dangerously wounded, his successor, General Fresnel, drew off, leaving the road clear. The French lost 6,000, the allies 10,000 men in the two days. *See* Leipzig.

Hardenberg *Netherlands War of Independence*

June 15, 1580, between the Dutch Patriots, under Count Philip Hohenlohe, and the Royalists, under Martin Schenck. Fatigued by a long march, the Patriots were no match for Schenck's fresh troops, and after an hour's fighting, were broken and almost annihilated. *See* Antwerp.

Harlaw *Scottish Civil Wars*

July 24, 1411, between the rebel Highlanders, under Donald, Lord of the Isles, and the Lowland Scots, under the Earl of Mar, together with the town militia of Aberdeen, led by their Provost. After a most bloody battle, the Lowlanders were utterly routed. Among the slain were the Provost, many knights, 500 men-at-arms, and the majority of the burghers forming the militia. The Highlanders lost 500 only. *See* Arkenholm.

Harper's Ferry *American Civil War*

September 15, 1862, when the Confederates, three divisions, under General 'Stonewall' Jackson surrounded the Federal garrison of Harper's Ferry, 11,000 strong, with 73 guns, and forced them to surrender. *See* Antietam.

Hashin *British-Sudan Campaigns*

March 20, 1885, when 8,000 British troops, under General Graham, defeated a detachment of Osman Digna's army, inflicting upon them a loss of about 1,000 killed. The British lost 48 killed and wounded. *See* Khartoum.

111

Haslach *Napoleonic Wars*

October 11, 1805, when General Dupont, with 6,000 French, marching upon Ulm, was suddenly confronted with an army of Austrians, 60,000 strong, posted on the Michelberg. Dupont at once seized and entrenched the village of Hanau, which he held until dark against 25,000 Austrians, under the Archduke Ferdinand. After nightfall he withdrew, carrying off 4,000 prisoners. *See* Hanau, Ulm.

Hastenbeck *Seven Years' War*

July 26, 1757, between 36,000 Hanoverians and others, under the Duke of Cumberland, and 60,000 French, under Marshal d'Estrées. The Duke, who had taken post on the Weser, to protect Hanover, was overpowered by d'Estrées, and driven back to Slade, on the Elbe, with a loss of several hundred men. This defeat was followed by the signature of the Convention of Closter-Zeven, under which Cumberland's army was disbanded. *See* Kolin, Rossbach.

Hastings *Norman Conquest*

October 14, 1066, a fortnight after the landing of William the Conqueror, with a 9,000-strong army. The English, about 10,000 infantry, under Harold, fought entirely on the defensive, at first with success, but were at last lured from their position and were then totally routed. Harold was among the fallen. This battle is also known as the Battle of Senlac. It led to Norman rule in England. *See* Stamford Bridge.

Hatvan *Hungarian Rising*

April 2, 1849, when the Austrians, 15,000 strong under Marshal Schlick, attacked the 7th Hungarian Corps, of about equal strength, and after a severe engagement, were totally defeated.

Havana I *War of the Austrian Succession*

October 12, 1748, between a British squadron of seven ships, under Admiral Knowles, and a Spanish squadron of equal strength. The action was fought with little determination, and though the British captured one ship, the result was far from decisive. The Spaniards lost 298, the British 179 killed and wounded. *See* Bergen-op-Zoom.

Havana II *Seven Years' War*

On June 5, 1762, the Earl of Clanwilliam landed with 11,000 British troops, supported by a squadron, under Admiral Pococke, and laid siege to Havana. Moro Castle, the key of the defences, was taken by storm, and after a siege of two months and eight days the city was captured. It was returned to Spain next year in exchange for part of Florida. *See* Pondicherry.

Heathfield *Conquest of Britain*

633, between the Mercians, under Penda, and the Northumbrians, under Edwin. The latter were defeated and Edwin slain. *See* Heavenfield.

Heavenfield *Conquest of Britain*

634, between the Anglo-Saxons, under the Bretwalda, Oswald of Northumbria, and the Britons, under Cadwallon. The Britons were totally routed. *See* Heathfield.

Hedgeley Moor *Wars of the Roses*

April 25, 1464, between the Lancastrians, under Margaret of Anjou and Sir Ralph Percy, and the Yorkists, under Lord Montague. The Lancastrians were totally defeated, Percy falling in the battle. *See* Towton, Hexham.

Heiligerlee *Netherlands War of Independence*

May 23, 1568, between the 'Beggars', under Louis of Nassau, and 5,000 veteran Spaniards, under Count Aremberg. Louis occupied a very strong position on a wooded height, near the monastery of the Holy Lion, his front being protected by a morass crossed by a narrow causeway. The Spanish infantry traversed this to the attack, but were repulsed, and Count Aremberg, leading a charge of horse, in the hope of restoring the day, fell mortally wounded. Upon this the Spaniards broke and fled, having suffered a loss of 1,600 men. *See* Maastricht.

Heilsberg *Napoleonic Wars*

June 10, 1807, between 30,000 French, under Marshal Soult, and 80,000 Russians, under General Bennigsen. The Russians occupied the heights on both sides of the Alle, and the plains below, being in greater force on the left bank. The French attacked and drove the Russians into the entrenchments, but could make no further progress, and night put an end to an obstinate but inconclusive conflict, in which the Russians lost about 10,000, the French 8,000 killed and wounded. *See* Friedland.

Hekitai-Kan *Japanese Invasion of Korea*

1595, between the Japanese, under Kobayagawa Takakage, and the Chinese, under Li Chin. The Chinese were utterly routed, Li's army being almost annihilated, and he himself escaping with difficulty from the field. *See* Hemushagu.

Heligoland *Napoleonic Wars*

This island was captured, August 31, 1807, from the Danes, by a small British squadron, under Admiral Thomas Russell.

Heligoland Bight *World War I*

August 27–28, 1914, as a bait to lure German warships, a flotilla of submarines under Commodore Keyes sailed close in to Heligoland Bight, off Germany's north-west coast, with two flotillas of destroyers and two light cruisers, *Arethusa* and *Fearless*, behind them. A battle cruiser force under Admiral Beatty waited some miles over the horizon. A German squadron of two cruisers and some destroyers sailed out and attacked, but were driven off, mainly by the *Arethusa*. Believing no bigger warships to be there, the German heavy cruisers *Mainz*, *Köln* and *Yorck*, came out and began shelling the *Arethusa* and *Fearless*, which, however, evaded a head-on conflict. Beatty's battle cruisers then came through the German minefields safely, led by the *Lion*, whose 13·5 inch guns sank the *Mainz* and *Köln*, another heavy cruiser and one destroyer, while crippling three other cruisers. Nearly 1,000 enemy sailors were killed or drowned and 200 taken prisoner. About 50 British were killed and 30 wounded. Admiral von Tirpitz was ordered henceforward to 'avoid any action which might lead to heavy losses'. *See* Jutland, Coronel.

Heliopolis *French Revolutionary Wars*

March 20, 1800, between 10,000 French, under General Kléber, and about 70,000 Turks, under Ibrahim Bey. The Turks were utterly routed, with a loss of several thousand men, while the French only lost about 300 killed and wounded. *See* Malta.

Hellespont *War of the Two Empires*

In 323, between the fleet of Constantine the Great, consisting of 200 small galleys, under Crispus, and that of Licinius, numbering 350 sail, under Amandus. After two days' hard fighting, Crispus forced the passage of the Hellespont, and totally routed the Eastern fleet, with a loss of 130 ships and 5,000 men. *See* Cibalis.

Helorus *Wars of Sicily*

492 BC, between Hippocrates, Tyrant of Gela, and the Syracusans. The Syracusans were totally routed, and were so weakened by this defeat, that Syracuse fell an easy prey to Gelon, Hippocrates' successor, in the following year. *See* Himera.

Helsingborg *Danish-Swedish Wars*

In 1710, between 20,000 Swedes, of whom 12,000 were raw recruits, under General Steinbock, and the Danish invading army. The Swedes won a signal victory, and the invaders were compelled to take refuge under the walls of Helsingborg, and a few days later to embark for Denmark. Besides killed, they left 4,000 wounded prisoners in the hands of the Swedes. *See* Stralsund.

Hemushagu *Japanese Invasion of Korea*

In 1595, between the Japanese, under Konishi Yukinaga, and the Chinese, under Li Chin. The Japanese were defeated, and forced to retire upon the capital. *See* Hekitai-Kan.

Hengestesdun *Danish Invasions of Britain*

837, when the men of Wessex, under Egbert, totally defeated the Danes and Cornish Britons. *See* Ashdown.

Hennersdorf *War of the Austrian Succession*

November 24, 1745, between 60,000 Prussians, under Frederick the Great, and 40,000 Austrians and Saxons, under Prince Charles of Lorraine. Frederick surprised Prince Charles on the march, and utterly routed his vanguard, comprised of Saxons, with enormous loss. The Austrians were compelled in consequence to retire into Bohemia. *See* Madras.

Heraclea I *Pyrrhus' Invasion of Italy*

280 BC, between the Epirots, 30,000 strong, under Pyrrhus, and about 35,000 Romans, under P. Laverius Laevinus. The Romans crossed the Siris in the face of the enemy, when they were attacked by Pyrrhus, and after a furious conflict, were at last broken by his elephants, and fled in disorder, losing about 7,000 men. *See* Asculum.

Heraclea II *Roman Civil Wars*

In 313, between the Illyrians, under Licinius, afterwards Emperor of the East, and the troops of the reigning Emperor Maximinus. Licinius was marching with 30,000 men to the relief of Heraclea, when he was attacked by Maximinus, with 70,000. Licinius was at first driven back by weight of numbers, but the steadiness of his troops enabled him to rally, and Maximinus was defeated. *See* Cibalis.

Herat I *Tatar Invasion of Afghanistan*

This city was captured, 1220, by 20,000 Tatars, under Sudah Bahadur. The Governor, Emin Malek, was entirely unprepared to stand a siege and surrendered when the Tatars appeared before the walls. Having meanwhile been retaken by a *coup-de-main*, by Shems-ed-din, who held it as an independent chieftain, Herat was again besieged by the Tatars, under Tuli Khan, in 1221. After a brief, but resolute resistance, during which Shems-ed-din fell, the inhabitants opened the gates to the besiegers. All were put to the sword. *See* Samarkand.

Herat II *Perso-Afghan Wars*

On November 22, 1837, Mohammed, Shah of Persia, laid siege to the city, which was held by an Afghan garrison, under Yar Mohammed. After a somewhat desultory siege, an attempt was made to storm the place, June 24, 1838, when the Persians were repulsed with a loss of 1,700 men. From this time a tacit armistice existed till September 9, when the Shah withdrew his army.

Herdonea *Second Punic War*

210 BC, when the Carthaginians, under Hannibal, defeated and practically destroyed an army of 25,000 Romans, under Cnaeus Fulvius. Fulvius was among the slain. *See* Metaurus.

Héricourt *Burgundian Wars*

November 13, 1474, between the Swiss, 18,000 strong, and the Burgundians, 10,000 in number. The Burgundians were totally defeated, the town of Héricourt taken. *See* Granson.

Hermanstadt *Ottoman Wars*

In 1442, and notable as being the first appearance of John Hunyadi in arms against the Turks. With an army of Hungarians he totally defeated Mejid Bey, who was besieging Hermanstadt, inflicting on the Turks a loss of 20,000 men, and relieving the place. The Hungarians lost 3,000. *See* Kossova.

Hernani I *First Carlist War*

August 29, 1836, between the British legion, under General Evans, and the Carlists. Evans was defeated. *See* Huesca.

Hernani II *First Carlist War*

March 15 and 16, 1837, between the British legion, and a small contingent of Cristinos, under General Evans, and about 17,000 Carlists, under Don Sebastian, strongly posted on the Hernani road. On the 15th, Evans attacked the Carlists on the Venta heights, and after five hours' fighting occupied the position. On the 16th, when the conflict was resumed, the Carlists retired into

Hernani, but reinforcements arriving, they took the offensive, and forced Evans to retreat. *See* Huesca.

Herrera *First Carlist War*

August 23, 1837, between the Carlists, under Don Carlos, with General Moreno in actual command, and the Cristinos, under General Buerens. Don Carlos, who was marching upon Madrid, attacked Buerens before he could effect a junction with Espartero, and severely defeated him, the Cristinos losing 50 officers, and 2,600 men killed, wounded and missing. Don Carlos, after this victory, advanced to within twelve miles of Madrid, when the appearance of Espartero, at the head of 20,000 troops, obliged him to retire. *See* Huesca.

Herrings, The *Hundred Years' War*

Fought at Rouvray-St-Denis, February 12, 1429. Sir John Fastolfe was in charge of a convoy of salt fish for the English army before Orléans, and hearing of the approach of a French force, under the Bastard of Orléans, entrenched himself at Rouvray. Here the French attacked him, and were repulsed with heavy loss, the Bastard being severely wounded. *See* Orléans.

Hexham *Wars of the Roses*

May 15, 1464, when the Yorkists, under Lord Montague, surprised the Lancastrians, under the Duke of Somerset, in their camp at Linnels, near Hexham. The Lancastrians were practically in a trap, and had no option but to surrender. Somerset and many other important leaders were taken, and promptly executed. This success secured Edward IV on the throne. *See* Hedgeley Moor.

Hill 875,
see Vietnam War

Hill 881,
see Vietnam War

Himera I *First Carthaginian Invasion of Sicily*

480 BC, between the Syracusans and Agrigentines, 557,000 strong, under Gelon, Tyrant of Syracuse, and the Carthaginians,

said to number 300,000, under Hamilcar. The Carthaginians were totally routed, and Hamilcar slain. Syracuse became paramount in Sicily. *See* Himera II.

Himera II *Second Carthaginian Invasion of Sicily*

This place was besieged by the Carthaginians, under Hannibal, 409 BC. A first assault was repulsed, and Diocles arriving in the harbour with 25 ships, rescued half the inhabitants. Three days later he returned for the remainder, but too late, for before he could reach the harbour the breach was stormed. The town was sacked, and 3,000 prisoners were sacrificed to appease the shade of Hamilcar, who had fallen in the battle of 480. *See* Selinus.

Hippo *Wars of the Western Roman Empire*

Siege was laid to this city (Bône) in May, 430, by the Vandals, under Genseric. It was defended by Boniface, Count of Africa, who having command of the sea, was able to keep the city well provisioned, and after fourteen months Genseric retired. Among those who died during the siege was St Augustine. *See* Rome II.

Hochkirch *Seven Years' War*

October 14, 1758, between 30,000 Prussians, under Frederick the Great, and 35,000 Austrians, under Count Daun. Frederick, who was encamped on the heights of Hochkirch, was surprised in the early morning by the Austrians, who broke into his camp and seized his artillery. He succeeded, however, in forming up his troops, and descending into the plain, made good his retreat to Bautzen. The Prussians lost 9,000 men, including the Prince of Brunswick and Marshal Keith, all their tents and baggage, and 101 guns. The Austrians lost 8,000 killed and wounded.

Höchst *Thirty Years' War*

June 22, 1622, between 20,000 Palatinate troops, under Christian of Brunswick, and 33,000 Imperialists, under Field Marshal Tilly. Christian, having failed to join forces with General von Mansfeldt, was in retreat, and was engaged in holding a bridge over the Main. While thus employed he was overtaken by Tilly, and though a village covering the bridge was held gallantly for five hours, he was at last overpowered, losing about 12,000 in killed, wounded and prisoners. The Imperialist loss was comparatively small. *See* Wimpfen.

Höchstädt *French Revolutionary Wars*

June 19, 1800, between 60,000 French, under General Moreau, and about 70,000 Austrians, under General Baron von Kray. Moreau crossed the Danube with the object of cutting off the Austrians from their base, and forcing them to evacuate Ulm. In a battle which lasted 18 hours, he succeeded in establishing himself upon the left bank, and making Ulm untenable. The French took 5,000 prisoners and 20 guns, but the losses on both sides in killed and wounded were small for the numbers engaged. *See* Bergen-op-Zoom.

Hogland *Russo-Swedish Wars*

In 1789, between the Russian fleet, under Admiral Greig, and the Swedes, under the Duke of Sudermanland. Each side lost a ship, but strategically the affair was a Russian victory, for the Swedes were compelled to seek the protection of the forts of Vyborg.

Hohenfriedberg *War of the Austrian Succession*

June 4, 1745, between 85,000 Austrians and Saxons, under Charles of Lorraine, and the Prussians, 65,000, under Frederick the Great. The Saxons, who were encamped at Strigau, were attacked in the early morning, and defeated before the Austrians could come to their aid. Frederick then turned upon the Austrians, and routed them, after desperate fighting. The Austrians and Saxons lost 4,000 killed and wounded, 7,000 prisoners, including four generals and 66 guns. The Prussians lost 2,000. *See* Louisbourg.

Hohenlinden *French Revolutionary Wars*

December 3, 1800, between the French, 60,000 strong, 100 guns, under Moreau, and 70,000 Austrians, 150 guns, under the Archduke John. Moreau occupied the small clearing of Hohenlinden, and the surrounding

forest, while the Austrian army marched by five distinct routes to rendezvous at Hohenlinden. The Archduke's attack on the village was repulsed, and meanwhile Moreau had fallen upon his advancing columns at various points, after severe fighting defeating them. The Austrians lost 7,000 killed and wounded, 12,000 prisoners and 87 guns. *See* Höchstädt.

Hollabrunn *Napoleonic Wars*

A rearguard action to protect the retreat of the main Russian army, under General Kutuzov, November 16, 1805, between 7,000 Russians, under Prince Bagration, and the French, under Marshal Lannes. Bagration did not retire until he had lost half his force. *See* Ulm, Austerlitz.

Homildon Hill *Anglo-Scottish Wars*

September, 1402, when the Percies lay in wait for a Scottish force, under Murdach Stewart, and Archibald, Earl of Douglas, who were returning from a foray into England. The Scots were totally routed, losing Stewart, four Scottish peers, and 80 gentlemen of rank. *See* Shrewsbury, Bramham Moor.

Honain *Conquest of Arabia*

629, between 12,000 Muslims, under Mohammed, and a force of pagan Arabs, 4,000 strong. The Muslims were lured into the valley of Honain, and were assailed by slingers and archers from the surrounding heights. They were, however, rallied by the Prophet, and totally routed the pagans, who submitted to the rule of Mohammed. *See* Medina.

Hondschoote *French Revolutionary Wars*

September 6, 1793, between the Austrians, under General Freytag, and the French, under General Houchard. The Austrians occupied a strong position from which they were driven in disorder, and with heavy loss. As a consequence of this victory, the siege of Dunkirk was raised. *See* Toulon.

Hong Kong *World War II*

December 8, 1941, when the Japanese 38th Division attacked three British battalions defending the New Territories on the mainland. After warding off heavy ground and air attack for four days, General Maltby withdrew his outnumbered forces to the island and combined with three other British battalions. The Japanese invaded the island six days later and the British governor, Mark Young, surrendered the island to the Japanese on December 25. The Japanese took 11,000 prisoners. *See* Malaya, Singapore.

Hooghly, The *Anglo-Dutch Conflict in India*

November 24, 1759, between three British ships, under Commodore Wilson, and a Dutch squadron of seven sail, in Bengal. After two hours' fighting, the Dutch were completely defeated, and all their ships captured. Meanwhile a force of 700 Europeans and 800 Sepoys landed from the Dutch fleet, and was defeated with heavy loss by 330 British troops and 800 Sepoys, under Colonel Forde.

Horns of Hattin,

see Tiberias

Hué,

see Vietnam War

Huesca I *Spanish-Muslim Wars*

1105, when the Moors attacked the Spaniards, who, under Alfonso VI of Castile, were besieging Huesca. They were utterly routed, losing 10,000 killed in the battle. *See* Zalaka.

Huesca II *First Carlist War*

May 23, 1837, between 20,000 Carlists, under Don Carlos and Don Sebastian, and 12,000 Cristinos and British under General Irribarreu. The British legion behaved unsteadily and the Cristinos were driven from the field, though the pursuit was checked by a brilliant cavalry charge in which Irribarreu fell. The Cristinos lost over 1,000 killed and wounded, of which number the British legion lost 227. *See* Hernani, Herrera.

Humaita I *Paraguayan War*

May, 1866, between the Paraguayans, under Francisco López, and the Argentinians, under Mitre. Mitre attacked the Paraguayan entrenchments, but was repulsed with heavy loss.

Humaita II *Paraguayan War*

February, 1868, between the Paraguayan batteries, and a flotilla of Brazilian gunboats, endeavouring to force the passage. Their attempt was a complete failure, and the whole flotilla was sunk.

Humaita III *Paraguayan War*

September, 1868, between the Paraguayans, under López, and the allied armies of Brazil, Argentina and Uruguay. The allies largely outnumbered López's forces, and forced him to abandon his entrenchments at Humaita, and retire to Tebienari. *See* Aquidaban.

Humblebeck *Danish-Swedish Wars*

1700, when Charles XII, with a small force of Swedes, landed in the face of the Danish army, which was strongly entrenched close the shore, and drove them headlong from their position with heavy loss. *See* Narva.

Hwai-Hai *Chinese Civil War*

From November 7, 1948, when 500,000 Chiang Kai-shek Nationalists were defeated by an equal number of Communist People's Liberation Army troops in 65 days' fighting. The battle ended on January 12, 1949. Tientsin, in the north, fell three days, and Peking six days after. *See* Tsinan, Nanking.

Hydaspes, The *Alexander's Asiatic Campaigns*

326 BC, in the Punjab, between 65,000 Macedonians and 70,000 Asiatics, under Alexander the Great, and the army of the Indian king Porus, numbering 30,000 infantry, with 200 elephants and 300 war chariots. Alexander crossed the river Hydaspes (now the Jhelum) a few miles above Porus'

entrenchments, and utterly routed him, with a loss of 12,000 killed and 9,000 prisoners, including Porus himself. The Macedonians lost 1,000 only. *See* Granicus, Issus.

Hyderabad *Conquest of Sind*

March 24, 1843, between 6,000 British troops under Sir Charles Napier, and 20,000 Beluchis, under Shir Mohammed. The latter was strongly entrenched behind the Fullali, but the Beluchis, being thrown into disorder by a heavy artillery fire, were overthrown by a charge of cavalry on their exposed flank, and a frontal attack by the 22nd Regiment. This defeat put an end to the resistance of the Sind Emirs to the forward march of the British in India. *See* Dubba, Meeanee.

Hysiae

Fought, approximately, 668 BC, between the Spartans and the Argives. The former were totally defeated, and Argos was left in undisputed possession of the supremacy of the Peloponnesus.

I

Ichinotani *Taira War*

In 1189, between the troops of the Shogun Minamoto Yoritomo, under his brothers Noriyori and Yoshitsune, and the forces of the Taira clan. The Taira were signally defeated.

Iclistavisus *Germanic Wars*

Fought AD 16, between eight Roman legions, under Germanicus, and the Germans, under Arminius, at this place (now Minden). The Germans attacked the Romans in the open plain, but failed against the superior discipline of the legionaries, and were routed with enormous loss. Arminius with difficulty cut his way out of the press and escaped.

Île de France *Napoleonic Wars*

This island, now known as Mauritius, was captured from the French, December 3, 1810, by a fleet of 19 ships, under Admiral Bertie, convoying a number of transports, carrying 19,000 troops, under General Abercromby. The British lost 167 killed, wounded and missing. Seven frigates and ten sloops were taken, as well as 21 French and three captured British merchantmen.

Immac *Revolt of Elagabalus*

June 7, 218, between the Syrian legions, under Elagabalus, and the Imperial troops and Pretorians, under the Emperor Macrinus. The Pretorians, by their superior valour and discipline, broke the legions opposed, and the victory would have been theirs, but at the crisis of the fight, Macrinus fled, and this so discouraged his troops, that in the end they were totally defeated.

Imola *French Revolutionary Wars*

February 3, 1797, when 8,000 French and Italians, under Marshal Victor, defeated the Papal troops, 7,000 strong, under General Colli. Victor took the Papal army in the rear, and routed them with a loss of a few hundred only, as no stand was made. *See* Rivoli.

Inchon *Korean War*

General Almond's US 10th Corps, having made a surprise landing behind enemy lines on September 15, 1950, at Inchon, the Korean west-coast port about 50 miles west of Seoul, drove the North Korean forces inland, routed them and cut their lines of communication, taking 125,000 prisoners. They seized nearby Kimpo airfield on September 19 and continued their advance towards Seoul. *See* Pusan Perimeter, Seoul.

Indo-Pakistan War, 1965

Started by a series of new violations of the cease-fire in the disputed regions of Jammu and Kashmir from August 5, 1965, when armed civilians crossed from Pakistan to the Indian side for military action. On August 14, Pakistan attacked across the Jammu border in battalion strength. India closed the Haji Pir Pass on August 28 to seal entry routes. On September 1, Pakistan launched a big tank attack supported by air cover over the boundary between Pakistan and Jammu. Both air forces then went into action. On September 6 India crossed the border and attacked in the Lahore sector of west Pakistan, and the next day made two new thrusts, from Jammu towards Sialkot and from Rajasthan into Sind. Tank battles among the heaviest since World War II were fought. Fighting stopped on September 22 after a Security Council resolution to that effect, which both sides accepted, withdrawing to their positions of August 5. Indian losses in the seven-week war were 2,759 killed, 7,636 wounded and 1,500 missing. Eighty Indian tanks and 28 aircraft were destroyed. Estimated Pakistan losses were 5,800 killed or wounded, 475 tanks destroyed and 73 aircraft lost. Under the terms of the Tashkent Agreement of January 10, 1966, both sides agreed thenceforward to settle their disputes through peaceful means.

Indus, The *Tatar Invasion of Central Asia*

1221 BC, between 300,000 Tatars, under Genghis Khan, and the army of Jellalladin, Sultan of Kharismia (Khorezm), 30,000 strong. Jellalladin fought with his back to the river, and after an obstinate conflict, in which he inflicted heavy loss on his assailants, was driven across the Indus, having lost 19,000 men killed and drowned. The Tatars lost 20,000. *See* Bamian.

Ingavi *Bolivian-Peruvian War*

November 18, 1841, between the Bolivians, under President Ballivían, 3,800 strong, and the Peruvians, 5,200 strong, under President Gamarra. The Peruvians were routed, and their army dispersed, Gamarra being among the killed.

Ingogo *First Boer War*

February 8, 1881, when a small British column, consisting of five companies of infantry, four guns, and a small mounted force, attacked the Boer position, and were repulsed with a loss of 139 killed and wounded. The Boers admitted a loss of 14 only. *See* Majuba.

Inhlobane Mountain *Zulu War*

March 28, 1879, when a British force of 1,300 men, under Colonels Buller and Russell, attacked a strong Zulu kraal, and after severe fighting, were repulsed with considerable loss.

Inkerman *Crimean War*

November 5, 1854, when 50,000 Russians, under Prince Mentschikov, attacked the Franco-British position at Inkerman, held by about 15,000 troops, under Lord Raglan and General Pélissier. There was a dense fog, and the battle was chiefly a series of detached hand-to-hand combats, some of the most serious fighting being round the Sandbag Battery, where the Russians lost 1,200 killed. At 10 o'clock, French reinforcements arrived on the scene, and the Russians were soon in full retreat, having suffered very heavy loss. *See* Balaclava, Sevastopol.

Inverkeithing *Anglo-Scottish Wars*

1317, between the English invaders, and the Scots, under the Earl of Fife. The first onslaught of the English drove the Scots from their positions, but they were rallied by William Sinclair, Bishop of Dunkeld, and forced the English to retire to their ships.

Inverlochy *English Civil War*

February 2, 1645, when the Marquis of Montrose, with 1,500 Royalist Highlanders, defeated 3,000 Campbells and Lowland Covenanters, killing or wounding 1,700 of them. The Marquis of Argyll left the command of his forces to Campbell of Auchinbrech, taking refuge in a vessel on Loch Linnhe. This defeat broke the power of the Campbells in the Highlands for many years. *See* Tippermuir.

Ipsus *Wars of Alexander's Successors*

306 BC, between the Syrians, 32,000 strong, under Seleucus, and 30,000 Macedonians, under Antigonus. Seleucus utterly routed the Macedonians, Antigonus being among the slain. Demetrius Poliorcetes, who now took command, only succeeded in rallying 8,000 men, after fleeing for 200 miles. *See* Corupedion.

Irun *First Carlist War*

This fortress was captured, May 18, 1837, by 10,000 Cristinos and British, under General Evans. Evans appeared before the place at noon, and summoned it to surrender. On the Carlists refusing, an assault was ordered; by 11 pm the fortress was taken, with very small loss to the assailants. *See* Huesca, Hernani.

Isandhlwana *Zulu-British War*

January 22, 1879, when six companies of the 24th Regiment, with two guns and a small force of Natal volunteers, under Colonel Durnford, were overwhelmed and massacred by the spear-throwing Zulus, under Matyana. Of the regulars, 26 officers and 600 men were killed, in addition to 24 officers, and a large number of men in the Colonial force. *See* Rorke's Drift.

Isaszcq *Hungarian Rising*

April 6, 1849, between the Hungarians, 42,000 strong, under General von Görgey, and the Croats, under Jellachich. The Hungarian First Corps, under Klapka, was put to flight, but the rest stood their ground, and repulsed the Croat attack. Both armies bivouacked for the night on the ground they held, but early on the following morning Jellachich retired, the Hungarians thus being entitled to claim a victory. Hungary proclaimed itself a republic, but on August 9 was defeated by Russia and Austria at Timisoara and made part of the Austrian Empire. *See* Waizan.

Isly *Abd-el-Kader's Rebellion*

August 14, 1844, between 8,000 French, under General Bugeaud, and 45,000 Algerines, chiefly cavalry, under Abd-el-Kader. The French infantry repulsed all the charges of the Algerine Horse, and aided by the artillery, inflicted heavy loss upon them. When they were sufficiently shaken, a charge of the French cavalry completed the rout, and the Algerines fled, leaving 1,500 dead on the field. Abd-el-Kader was captured. *See* Constantine.

Ismail *Ottoman Wars*

This fortress was taken by assault by the Russians, under Suvorov, December 22, 1790. The Russians lost enormous numbers in the storm, and in revenge they massacred the garrison and inhabitants without mercy. *See* Rimnitz, Focsani.

Isonzo *World War I*

Having declared war against Austria-Hungary May 23, 1915, Italy assembled 25 divisions under General Cadorna along the Isonzo River and on June 23 assaulted the Austrian 14 divisions under General Hötzendorf, in the hope of winning substantial territorial gains, especially Trieste. It was the first of 12 battles along the Isonzo. Four of them in 1915 cost the Italians 66,000 killed, 185,000 wounded and 22,000 prisoners without any worthwhile gains. Five equally fruitless battles were fought in 1916, two more in 1917, until, in October 1917 Germany took over and imposed the crushing defeat of Caporetto. *See* Asiago, Caporetto.

Israel,

see Jerusalem, Six-Day War, Sinai Peninsula, Yom Kippur

Issus I *Alexander's Asiatic Campaigns*

333 BC, between 35,000 Macedonians, under Alexander the Great, and a vast horde of Asiatics, with 30,000 Greek mercenaries, under Darius, King of Persia. The Persians were drawn up on the right bank of the Pinarus, which crosses the plain of Issus. Alexander led his heavy cavalry to the attack on the left, crossing the river, and routing the Persian cavalry. The phalanx in the centre was opposed to the Greek mercenaries, and after heavy fighting, the Macedonians made good their footing on the right bank. Alexander meanwhile led his squadron against the bodyguard of Darius, who fled from the field followed by the whole of the Asiatics, and the victory was complete. *See* Granicus, Tyre.

Issus II *Ottoman Wars*

1488, between the Turks, under Bajazet II, and the Egyptians, under the Sultan of Egypt. The Turks were defeated. *See* Cairo, Rhodes.

Itabitsu *Hirotsuke's Rebellion*

October, 740, between the Japanese rebels, under Hirotsuke, 13,000 strong, and the troops of the Emperor Shommu Tenno under Ono-no-Atsuma. The Imperial troops, who were only 8,000 in number, attacked the rebels as they were crossing the river, and routed them with heavy loss. Hirotsuke was killed.

Ivry *French Religious Wars*

March 14, 1590, between the Huguenots, 11,000, under Henri IV, and the Catholics, 19,000, under the Duc de Mayenne. Henri gained a complete victory, and marched forward to invest Paris, but failed. *See* Arques.

Iwo-Jima *World War II*

About 700 miles south of Tokyo, Iwo-Jima, 4½ miles by 2½, provided a base for Japanese aircraft intercepting US B29s bombing Japanese cities. The Japanese, under General Kuribayashi, had garrisoned it with 21,000 troops and built hundreds of strongly fortified bunkers and underground pillboxes. These were hit by 22,000 shells and 6,800 bombs before General Schmidt's US 4th and 5th Marine Divisions assaulted the south-eastern beaches on February 19, 1945. On that first day some 600 marines were killed and 2,400 wounded. A week later they were reinforced by the 3rd Division, for the Japanese defended every yard and fought to the death. The Americans secured Iwo-Jima finally on March 26, at the cost of 6,821 dead and 18,000 wounded. *See* Okinawa, Mariana Islands.

J

Jalula *Muslim Invasion of Persia*

In 637, between the Muslims, under Said, and the Persians, under Yezdegerd. Yezdegerd fled from the field and his troops, discouraged, were totally routed with heavy loss.

Jamaica *Anglo-Spanish Wars*

This island was captured from the Spaniards, May, 1655 by a combined English naval and military force, under Admiral Penn and General Venables. War, hitherto undeclared between England and Spain, became official. *See* Dunes.

Jarnac *Third French Religious War*

March 13, 1569, between the Catholics, under the Seigneur de Tavannes, and the Huguenots, under the Prince de Condé. The brunt of the action was borne by the Huguenot cavalry, who were overpowered by the Catholics, and Condé slain. *See* Montcontour.

Jassy *Ottoman Wars*

September 20, 1620, between the Poles under Gratiani, and the Turks, under Osman II. The Poles were completely defeated. *See* Kotzin.

Java Sea *World War II*

In February 1942, after their seizure of Malaya and Borneo, in December, 1941, the Japanese, under Admiral Takagi, bore down on Java, garrisoned by 120,000 European and Indonesian troops, but lacking aircraft and supported only by a scratch force of 14 British, American and Dutch warships—five cruisers and nine destroyers. On February 27, under its Dutch C-in-C Rear Admiral Doorman, this force intercepted a Japanese squadron of 14 destroyers and four cruisers north of Sourabaya. In a five-hour battle Doorman was killed, his flagship *De Ruyter*, another cruiser and three destroyers sunk and the *Exeter* crippled. One enemy destroyer was badly damaged. Next day, the US cruiser

Houston and the Australian destroyer *Perth*, coming suddenly upon a group of Japanese transports, sank two of them, but were in turn sunk by Japanese warships with the loss of nearly 1,000 men. March 1 the enemy sank the damaged *Exeter* and two more destroyers. Only four destroyers made Australia safely, while the Japanese secured Java by March 9. *See* Coral Sea.

Jellalabad *First British-Afghan War*

This fortress was besieged by the Afghans, under Mohammed Akbar Khan, March 11, 1842, after the destruction of General Elphinstone's force in the Khoord Kabul pass. It was defended by a small British garrison, under General Sale. Akbar led his whole army to the assault, but was repulsed, and then sat down to besiege the place in form. An attempt to relieve it by Brigadier Wyld, in January, 1843, failed, Wyld being defeated in the Khyber Pass by the Khyberis. The garrison meanwhile made several successful sorties, and on April 7 drove Akbar Khan out of his entrenchments, with a loss of all his guns, and many men, forcing him to raise the siege. All chance of a renewal of the investment was ended by the arrival on the 18th, of a strong relieving force, under General Pollock, who was to avenge the massacre in 1842 of the British army occupying Kabul. *See* Ghazni, Khoord Kabul Pass.

Jemappes *French Revolutionary Wars*

November 6, 1792, between the Austrians, under the Archduke Albert, and the French, under General Dumouricz. The Austrians occupied a very strong position on the heights above Jemappes, from which they were driven with heavy loss, the French gaining a signal victory and later taking Brussels and the Austrian Netherlands. *See* Neerwinden.

Jena *Napoleonic Wars*

This name is generally given to the two battles fought October 14, 1806, by the two wings of the French army under Napoleon, at Auerstadt, and Jena. At Auerstadt the Prussian left, 54,000 strong, 230 guns, under the Duke of Brunswick, was encountered by the French right, under Marshal Davout,

26,000, with 44 guns, and after very severe fighting, were defeated, the Duke of Brunswick being mortally wounded. At Jena, Napoleon, with 56,000 men, 70 guns, attacked the Prince of Hohenlohe, with 50,000 Prussians, 120 guns, and after a sternly fought engagement, drove him from the field. The two defeated armies, retiring by converging routes upon Weimar, the retreat became a rout, and Napoleon's pursuing cavalry caused them further heavy losses. The Prussians in the two actions lost 22,000 killed and wounded, 18,000 prisoners and 200 guns. Twenty generals were killed, wounded or captured. The French lost 11,000 killed and wounded, 7,000 of whom fell at Auerstadt. By mid-November all Prussia was under Napoleon's control. *See* Saalfeld, Pultusk.

Jenkins' Ear *War of*

On October 19, 1739, Captain Jenkins told the House of Commons that his ear had been cut off by Spaniards and his ship had been pillaged, after Spain began seizing British ships and exercising the right of search when an illicit trade began with Spanish America. Walpole gave in to the demand for war against Spain. Admiral Vernon then captured Porto Bello, next year unsuccessfully raided Cartagena. Anson circumnavigated the world in quest of Spanish ships and treasure. The War of the Austrian Succession (1740–8) in which Spain and Britain were enemies absorbed the smaller conflict. *See* Porto Bello II.

Jersey *Anglo-French Wars*

In 1550, when an English squadron, under Sir William Winter, attacked a French fleet, which was besieging St Helier. The French were completely routed, losing 1,000 killed and wounded, and the siege was raised.

Jerusalem I *Jewish Wars of Roman Empire*

This city was besieged by Titus, with 60,000 Romans, in March, AD 70. It was defended with the utmost heroism by the Jews, who were led by the Zealot faction. At the end of six weeks Titus gained possession of the suburb of Bezetha, and then by hard fighting, captured position after position, until on September 8, the resistance of the defenders

was finally overcome. Josephus says that 1,100,000 persons perished in the siege, but this is doubtless an exaggeration. The Romans, after the capture, sold 97,000 into slavery. *See* Jotapata.

Jerusalem II *Muslim Invasion of Syria*

Early in 637 Jerusalem was besieged by the Muslims, at first, under Abu Obeidah, and later by the Caliph Omar. After a defence of four months, during which scarcely a day passed without a sortie or an assault, the city was surrendered by the Patriarch Sophronius. *See* Aleppo.

Jerusalem III *First Crusade*

The Crusaders, under Godefroi de Bouillon, laid siege to the city, June 7, 1099, and on July 15, it was taken by assault. For three days it was the scene of a massacre, in which 70,000 Muslims perished. *See* Antioch.

Jerusalem IV *Crusader-Turkish Wars*

On September 20, 1187, the Holy City was besieged by the Saracens, under Saladin, and after a siege lasting fourteen days, in the course of which several determined sorties were repulsed, the Muslims forced an entrance, and Guy de Lusignan, the last King of Jerusalem, surrendered. The Christians were given forty days to evacuate the city. *See* Acre, Tiberias.

Jerusalem V *World War I,*

see Gaza IV

Jerusalem VI *Israeli-Arab Wars*

May 15, 1948. The British mandate over Palestine having ended at midnight May 14, the United Nations Organization partitioned the country, the Jews formed the state of Israel and fighting broke out between the Arabs of Palestine, aided by those of other Middle Eastern countries, and Jewish troops. The Arabs cut the Tel-Aviv/Jerusalem road and besieged the city, isolating the Old City by military action, Jewish troops surrendering on May 28 to the Arab Legion after sharp fighting. A UN cease-fire became effective on

June 11, but fighting began again on July 9, until the 17th in Jerusalem and the 19th elsewhere. A UN resolution calling for Jerusalem to be made an international city was passed, but Israel blocked it by officially incorporating it, and in 1950 making it her capital, although Jordan kept the Old City, the boundary running between the Old and the New Cities. *See* Sinai, Six-Day War.

Jhansi *Indian Mutiny*

This town, which fell into the hands of the mutineers in June, 1857, was recaptured by Sir Hugh Rose, who invested it in March, 1858, and carried the city by assault, April 2.

Jidballi *Somali Expedition*

January 10, 1904, between the Somalis, 5,000 strong, and a small British and native force, under Sir Charles Egerton. The Somalis' camp was attacked, and after a brisk action they were driven out and pursued by the cavalry for twelve miles, losing 1,000 killed in the fight and pursuit. The British losses were small.

Jiron *Peruvian-Colombian War*

February 28, 1829, between the Peruvians, under Lamar, and the Colombians, under Antonio de Sucre. The battle was indecisive, both sides claiming the victory, and it was followed by the signature of peace, September 23.

Jitgurh *British-Gurkha War*

January 14, 1815, between 4,500 British troops, under General Wood, and 1,200 Gurkhas, occupying a strong stockade. The British were led unexpectedly into the zone of fire by a treacherous guide, and though Wood fought his way to a position from which he could have carried the stockade, he retired, having suffered considerable loss, just when the Gurkhas were about to abandon their works. *See* Kalunga.

Jotapata *Jewish Wars of Roman Empire*

This place was besieged by Vespasian, with 60,000 Romans, December, AD 67, and was defended by the Jewish army under Josephus.

The fortress held out for 47 days, when it was stormed and sacked. Josephus gave himself up to Vespasian. *See* Jerusalem I.

Jugdulluk *First British-Afghan War*

In this mountain pass the remnant of General Elphinstone's army, evacuating Kabul, made their last stand, January 12, 1842, against the Afghans and Ghilzais. Of the few who escaped the massacre at this point, only one, Dr Brydon, succeeded in safely reaching Jellalabad. *See* Khoord Kabul Pass.

Julian's Defeat by the Persians *Persian Wars*

June 28, 363, between the Romans, under Julian, and the Persians, under Sapor II. Julian had advanced against Ctesiphon, the Persian capital, but finding himself too weak to attack it, was retreating along the left bank of the Tigris. In the course of the retreat he was attacked by the Persians, and worsted in an action unimportant in itself, but resulting in the death of Julian, who was mortally wounded in the skirmish. The election of Jovian as Emperor was followed by a peace which restored to Shapur almost all the Roman conquests in Persia. *See* Amida.

Junín *Peruvian War of Independence*

1824, between the Spanish Royalists, under General Canterac, and the Peruvian Patriots, under Antonio de Sucre. The Spaniards were completely defeated, August 6, Peruvian independence having been proclaimed three years earlier on July 28, 1821. *See* Ayacucho.

Jutland *World War I*

May 31, 1916, when the German High Seas Fleet under Admiral Scheer deliberately or by accident met the British Fleet engaged in a sweep of the North Sea. Admiral von Hipper commanded five battle cruisers, while Scheer followed 50 miles behind with 16 new and eight old battleships. There were also 11 light cruisers and 63 destroyers. The British Fleet, under Admiral Jellicoe, consisted of the northern group of three battle cruisers and 24 battleships commanded by Jellicoe himself; and the southern fleet, Admiral Beatty, six battle cruisers and four battleships. In addition there were 34 light cruisers and 80 destroyers. Beatty and Hipper sighted each other, and Hipper turned to link up with Scheer, after which the two groups shelled each other. Beatty then turned back to lure the Germans into Jellicoe's hands and in the process lost two of his battleships, but the manoeuvre accomplished, the entire British fleet soon formed a line east and south-east into which the Germans were sailing as into a net. Just when their destruction seemed certain, the weather closed down and rescued the Germans, who later, under cover of darkness, skilfully made their escape. The Royal Navy lost three battle cruisers, three light cruisers and eight destroyers; Germany four cruisers and five destroyers, but the morale of the German navy had been destroyed. Thenceforward it avoided battle, for the sailors threatened mutiny at the prospect. *See* Heligoland Bight, Falkland Isles, Coronel.

K

Kagoshima *Satsuma Rebellion*

On August 18, 1877, the rebels, who were closely besieged in their lines at Enotake, succeeded in passing through the Imperial troops, and making a forced march, under Saigo Takamori, seized the city of Kagoshima. They were quickly followed by the Imperial army, under Prince Taruhito, and an engagement followed which lasted for ten days, at the end of which time the insurgents were driven out and retired to Shirogama, both sides having suffered heavy loss. Saigo committed *hara-kiri*.

Kagul *Ottoman Wars*

August 3, 1770, between 17,000 Russians, under General Roumiantsov, and 90,000 Turks under Halil Pasha. The Russian rear was threatened by a force of 80,000 Tartars, but Roumiantsov boldly attacked the Turkish lines, and after severe fighting drove the Turks out of their entrenchments in headlong flight, capturing all their artillery and baggage. *See* Çeşme.

Kaiping *Sino-Japanese War I*

January 10, 1895, when a Chinese force in a strongly entrenched position was attacked and driven out by a Japanese brigade under General Nogi. The fighting lasted three hours, the Chinese showing more steadiness than usual, and inflicting on the assailants a loss of 300 killed and wounded.

Kalisch *Russo-Swedish War*

In 1706, between 10,000 Swedes, under General Meyerfeld, and 30,000 Russians and Poles, under Prince Mentschikov. The Swedes were defeated with considerable loss. *See* Thorn.

Kalpi *Indian Mutiny*

This town, which had fallen into the hands of the mutineers, was besieged by Sir Hugh Rose, May 19, 1858. The garrison made two ineffectual sorties, in which they were repulsed with heavy loss, and on the 23rd the town was entered without further resistance, the mutineers having fled. *See* Delhi.

Kalunga *British-Gurkha War*

This fort was attacked by the British under General Gillespie, in October, 1814, and was defended by the Gurkhas under Bulbuddur Singh. An unsuccessful assault cost the besiegers 260 officers and men, and after waiting a month for the arrival of heavy guns, a breach was made, and a general assault ordered. This also failed, 680 men being killed and wounded. The fortress was then shelled for three days, at the end of which time the survivors of the garrison, 70 only out of 600, made their escape and the place was captured. *See* Jitgurh.

Kamarut *First Burma War*

July 8, 1824, when a small British force, under Sir Archibald Campbell, stormed a series of stockades held by 10,000 Burmans, under Tuamba Wangyee. The Burmans left 800 dead on the field, including their leader. *See* Kemendine.

Kambula *Zulu War*

March 29, 1879, when Colonel Wood, with 2,000 British and native auxiliaries, was attacked in his lager by three Zulu impi. The Zulus were repulsed with very heavy loss, and pursued for seven miles. The British lost 81 killed and wounded. The defeat practically broke Cetewayo's power.

Kandahar I *Tatar Invasion of Afghanistan*

This city was besieged by the Tatars, under Tuli Khan, in 1221. The Tatars possessed themselves of the city, and were investing the citadel, when Jellalladin, Sultan of Khwarizm, fell upon them with a large force and cut them to pieces. *See* Biruan.

Kandahar II *Mughal Invasion of Afghanistan*

Siege was laid to Kandahar in March, 1545, by the Mughals, under Humayun. The town, which was defended by an Afghan garrison

127

under Mirza Askari, held out for five months, when, weakened by famine and desertion, the garrison was forced to surrender. In 1555 Humayun took Delhi and Agra.

Kandahar III *Perso-Afghan Wars*

In the autumn of 1648 the Persians, under Abbas II, laid siege to the city, which was defended by a Mughal garrison. An attempt to relieve it was made by the Emperor Aurungzebe, but he arrived to find it already in the hands of the Persians. He in turn laid siege to it, but was unsuccessful, and after four months was compelled to retire. Subsequent attempts to recapture the city were made by Said Ullah, the Vizier, and Dara Sheko, the eldest son of Shah Jehan, but without success.

Kandahar IV *Afghan Tribal Wars*

July 29, 1834, when Shah Sujah, the expelled Amir of Afghanistan, attempted to take the city. His successor, Dost Mahomed, and Kohandil Khan sallied forth at the head of their troops, and totally defeated Shah Sujah, dispersing his followers.

Kandahar V *Second British-Afghan War*

September 1, 1880, between the British, under Lord Roberts, and the Afghans, under Ayub Khan, immediately after the completion of the famous march from Kabul. Ayub was completely defeated, with a loss of 2,000 men, and his army dispersed. The British losses were 248 killed and wounded. *See* Maiwand.

Kapolna *Hungarian Rising*

February 26 and 27, 1849, between four Hungarian divisions, under General Dembiński, and the Austrians, under Prince zu Windischgrätz, of whom only General Schlick's corps, 15,000 strong, was seriously engaged. The Hungarians held their own on the 26th, but on the evening of the 27th Schlick captured the key of the position at Kapolna, whereupon the Hungarians retired, though unpursued. *See* Schwechat.

Kappel *Swiss Religious Wars*

October 10, 1531, between the army of the Swiss Catholic Cantons, 8,000 strong, and 1,300 Zürichers, under George Göldli, reinforced later in the day by a similar number under Rudolf Lavater. Göldli attacked in defiance of orders, and was totally defeated, among those who fell being Zwingli.

Kara Burur *Ottoman Wars*

August 11, 1791, when the Russian fleet, under Admiral Ouschakov, totally defeated the Turks after a bloody engagement. *See* Focsani.

Karaku *Tatar Invasion of Khwarizm*

1218, between the Tatars, 400,000 strong, under Genghis Khan, and 200,000 Khwarizmians under the Sultan Mehemet. At nightfall the battle was undecided, and the armies withdrew to their camps, but Mehemet who had lost 90,000 refused to renew the conflict on the following day, and Genghis Khan, having suffered too severely to attack his entrenchments, withdrew.

Karamuran *Mongul Conquest of Central Asia*

Fought during the winter of 1225, between 200,000 Tatars under Genghis Khan, and 350,000 Turks, Chinese and others under Shidasker of Tangat. Shidasker was totally routed, with a loss, it was said, of 200,000 men.

Karee *Second Boer War*

March 29, 1900, when a Boer force holding a line of hills about eighteen miles north of Bloemfontein, were driven from their entrenchments by a British division under General Tucker. The British lost 10 officers and 172 men killed and wounded. *See* Ladysmith.

Kargaula *Cossack Rising*

In 1774, between the insurgent Cossacks of the Don, under Pugatchev, and the Russians, under Prince Galitzin. The insurgents were routed with great slaughter, and Pugatchev fled to the mountains. *See* Kazan.

128

Kars I *Crimean War*

This fortress, held by a Turkish garrison under General Williams, was besieged by the Russians in the course of the Crimean war. The place was bravely defended, but was finally forced by famine to capitulate, November, 1855. *See* Sevastopol.

Kars II *Russo-Turkish War*

This fortress, garrisoned by 24,000 Turks under Hussein Pasha, was stormed by the Russians under General Count Loris-Melikov, on the night of November 17, 1877. The attacking force was led by General Lazarev, which, after severe fighting, captured all the eastern forts. Hussein then endeavoured to cut his way through to the west, but the bulk of his force was driven back, and only he and a few of his officers succeeded in the attempt. The Russians lost 2,273, killed and wounded; the Turks, 2,500 killed, 4,500 wounded, 17,000 prisoners, and 303 guns. *See* Plevna, Tashkessen.

Kashgal *British-Sudan Campaigns*

On November 3, 1883, an Egyptian force, 11,000 strong, under Hicks Pasha (General William Hicks), with several British officers, was led by a treacherous guide into a defile at El Obeid, 225 miles south-west of Khartoum, where they were attacked by the Mahdists, and after fighting for three days, were unable to break out and were massacred almost to a man. Gladstone's government decided to withdraw from the Sudan. *See* Khartoum.

Kassassin *Egyptian Revolt*

August 28, 1882, between the British, under General Graham, and the Egyptians, under Arabi Pasha. Arabi attacked the British position, Graham remaining on the defensive throughout the day, but towards evening he launched his heavy cavalry, under Sir Baker Russell, against the enemy, who broke and fled. The British losses were only 11 killed and 68 wounded. *See* Tel-el-Kebir.

Kasserine Pass *World War II*

On February 14, 1943, Rommel's Afrika Korps, having dug in behind the Mareth Line, on the Tunisian-Libyan frontier, after their defeat at the hands of the British 8th Army in Libya, suddenly attacked with the 10th and 21st Panzer divisions the US 1st Armoured Division and 168 Regimental Combat Team. The US forces were driven back over 20 miles, losing 192 killed, 2,624 wounded and 2,459 prisoners. A counter-attack by the British 6th Armoured Division with strong air support dealt Rommel heavy casualties and on February 22 he began to withdraw to his first positions behind the Mareth Line. *See* Mareth Line.

Katzbach I *Napoleonic Wars*

August 22, 1813, between 130,000 French, under Napoleon, and 100,000 Prussians, under General Blücher. Blücher, who had on the previous day retired behind the Haynau, was pressed hard by Napoleon, and driven across the Katzbach, with considerable loss. *See* Dresden, Katzbach II.

Katzbach II *Napoleonic Wars*

August 26, 1813, between the French, under Marshal Macdonald, and the Prussians, under General Blücher. Macdonald crossed the Katzbach, and while waiting for his left wing and cavalry under General Souham, was attacked by Blücher, and driven back. As Macdonald was retiring Souham appeared on the field, but before he could deploy he was attacked and routed with great slaughter, while the centre under Lauriston also suffered severely in recrossing the river. The French lost 15,000 killed and wounded, and over 100 guns. *See* Gross-Beeren, Dresden.

Kazan *Cossack Rising*

1774, between the rebel Cossacks, under Pugatchev, and the Russians, under General Michelson. The Cossacks were utterly routed. *See* Kargaula.

Kemendine *First Burma War*

June 10, 1824, when 3,000 British troops, under Sir Archibald Campbell, stormed a series of stockades, occupied by a large force of Burmans, and drove out the defenders with heavy loss. *See* Kamarut.

Keresztes *Ottoman Wars*

October 24 to 26, 1596, between the Turks, under Mohammed III, and the Imperialists and Transylvanians, under the Archduke Maximilian and Prince Sigismund of Transylvania. The battle at first went badly for the Turks, and Mohammed would have fled but for the remonstrances of the Grand Vizier. In the end, however, they gained the upper hand, and the Archduke was totally defeated. Under peace terms signed after 10 more years of frontier warfare, Austria was freed from the payment of tribute and recognized as an equal. *See* Lepanto.

Kharismia *Tatar Invasion of Central Asia*

This city, the capital of Khorezm (now Uzbek S.S.R.), was besieged by the Tatars under the three sons of Genghis Khan, in the summer of 1220. It was most obstinately defended for a period of seven months by the inhabitants, under Himartekin, but in February the Tatars mastered the place, massacring thousands. *See* Samarkand.

Kharkov I *World War II*

May 12, 1942, when the Russian 6th, 9th and 57th armies under Marshal Timoshenko launched a counter-offensive towards German-held Kharkov with the object of encircling and liberating it. But lacking the necessary reserves, the Russians were helpless when the Germans cut their communications and encircled a great part of their forces. Russian tank reserves were thrown in too late. The Russian offensive ended May 30, 1942, with the rout of three armies of the South-Western and Southern Fronts. The Germans claimed to have taken 200,000 prisoners and hundreds of guns. Khrushchev blamed Stalin for persisting in the offensive when it had clearly failed and his generals wished to pull out. *See* Stalingrad.

Kharkov II *World War II*

After Marshal von Manstein withdrew Army Group Don to the Donetz and Mius River line, the Russians took Kharkov, February 14-16, 1943, but four days later von Manstein, with the 1st and 4th Panzer Armies defeated General Popov's Army Group, threw them out of Kharkov by March 11, and advanced to Belgorod, about 50 miles north, on the southern flank of the Russian-held salient at Kursk. After the disastrous German defeat at Kursk in July, 1943, General Zhukov advanced the Russian armies on a broad front towards the Dnieper and took Kharkov finally on August 23. *See* Kursk.

Khartoum *British-Sudan Campaigns*

Defended by an Egyptian garrison under General Gordon, this town was invested by the Mahdi in the early part of 1884, and, after a gallant defence, was stormed January 26, 1885. Gordon was cut down and killed. The forerunners of the relieving force, consisting of the river gunboats under Lord Charles Beresford, arrived off the city on the 28th, two days too late, and after a brief engagement with the Mahdist batteries, returned down the river. *See* Tamai, Atbara.

Khelat *First British-Afghan War*

This place, which was defended by a garrison of Beluchis, under Mehrab Khan, was captured by a British force, 1,000 strong, under General Willshire, November 13, 1839. The defenders lost 400 killed, including their leader and 2,000 prisoners. The British lost 37 killed and 107 wounded. *See* Ghazni.

Khe Sanh,

see Vietnam War

Khojah Pass *First British-Afghan War*

March 28, 1842, when General England, in an endeavour to relieve General Nott in Kandahar, marched into the pass with 500 men only, without waiting for the rest of his brigade, and was defeated by the Afghans with a loss of 100 killed and wounded, and compelled to retire to Quettah. *See* Khoord Kabul Pass.

Khoord Kabul Pass *First British-Afghan War*

While passing through this defile, the British

force, under General Elphinstone, retreating on Jellalabad, was attacked by the Afghans, January 8, 1842, and lost 3,000, including followers. *See* Jellalabad.

Kiev *World War II*

By September 9, 1941, General Guderian's Panzers were advancing on Nezhin, 100 miles north-east of Kiev, while Field Marshal von Kleist's had penetrated the Dnieper bend near Pereyaslav, about 60 miles south-east. Budienny and Khrushchev decided to withdraw to avoid encirclement, but Stalin allegedly countermanded the order and replaced Budienny by Marshal Timoshenko. On September 13, when Timoshenko arrived, the bottleneck, from inside which the four Russian armies could still be withdrawn, was 20 miles wide, but with Stalin still adamant, Guderian's and von Kleist's tank formations closed it on September 16. Late on September 17, in response to further entreaties, Stalin authorized the abandonment of Kiev, but made no mention about breaking out across the River Pysol, where the Germans had not yet then consolidated their line. Consequently, a few units tried to break out, while the remainder stayed and fought on against great odds. About 150,500 managed to escape, while some 526,000 officers and men, including generals, fought on, suffered heavy losses, or were taken prisoner. A brilliant tactical success though it was, the Kiev encirclement nevertheless held up the German advance to Moscow at a critical time. *See* Moscow, Stalingrad.

Killiecrankie *Jacobite Rising*

July 27, 1689, between 3,400 Royal troops, loyal to William of Orange, under General Mackay, and 2,500 Highland Jacobites, under Dundee. Dundee allowed Mackay to enter the plain below the pass of Killiecrankie, and then, descending from the heights, fell upon and utterly routed the Royalists, with a loss of over 2,000 killed and 500 prisoners. The Jacobites lost about 900, but among them was Dundee. Mackay on reaching Stirling had only 400 men with the colours. *See* Boyne.

Kilsyth *English Civil War*

August 15, 1645, between the Royalists, under the Marquis of Montrose, and the

Covenanters, under General Baillie. The Royalists won a signal victory, Baillie's infantry, 6,000 in number, suffering heavy losses. *See* Langport, Alford.

Kimberley *Second Boer War*

This town, defended by a garrison of 4,000 (including armed townsmen), was besieged October 15, 1899, by the Boers, under Commandant Wessels, and later under General Cronje. It withstood a severe and continuous bombardment till February 15, 1900, when it was relieved by a force of cavalry, 5,000 strong, under General French. The losses of the garrison during the siege amounted to 18 officers and 163 men. *See* Ladysmith, Mafeking.

Kineyri *Second British-Sikh War*

June 18, 1848, between 8,000 Bhawalpuris, under Futteh Mohammed Khan, aided by 3,000 Mercenaries, under Lieutenant Edwardes, and the Sikhs, 8,000 strong, under Rung Ram. The Bhawalpuris were repulsed in an attack on the Sikh positions, but the timely arrival of Lieutenant Edwardes' guns turned the scale, and at a second attempt the entrenchments were stormed and captured, with a loss to the victors of 300 men. The Sikhs lost 500 killed in the action, and many more during their flight to Multan. *See* Chilianwala, Gujerat.

Kinloss *Danish Invasion of Scotland*

In 1009, between the Danes under Sweyn of Denmark, and the Scots, under Malcolm II. The Danes were besieging Nairne, and Malcolm attempting to raise the siege, they attacked and defeated him after hard fighting, in which Malcolm was wounded. *See* Mortlack.

Kinnesaw Mountain *American Civil War*

June 27, 1864, between 90,000 Federals, under General Sherman, and 50,000 Confederates, under General Johnston. Sherman attacked Johnston in a strong position and was repulsed with a loss of about 3,000, the Confederates losing 500 only. *See* Peach Tree Creek.

131

Kinsale *O'Neill's Rebellion*

This town, which had been seized in
September, 1601, by 5,000 Spaniards, under
Juan d'Aguila, sent to support the rebels,
was besieged by the Royal troops, under
Lord Mountjoy and the Earl of Thomond.
On December 24 an attempt by Sir Hugh
O'Neill to relieve the place, culminating in a
three-hour battle, was defeated, whereupon
d'Aguila surrendered and was permitted to
ship for Spain.

Kiöge *Northern War*

July, 1677, between the Danish fleet, under
Admiral Juel, and the Swedes, under
Admiral Horn. The Swedes suffered a
disastrous defeat, losing eleven ships of the
line sunk or captured. *See* Fehrbellin.

Kirbekan *Sudan Campaigns*

February 10, 1885, when the British, about
1,000 strong, under General Earle, stormed
the heights of Kirbekan, which were held by
a strong Mahdist force, and totally routed
them, with heavy loss. The British lost 60,
among whom was General Earle, killed. *See*
Khartoum.

Kirch-Denkern *Seven Years' War*

July 16, 1761, between the Prussians, under
Prince Ferdinand, and the French, under
Marshal dè Soubise and the Marshal Duc de
Broglie. The French attacked the strong
Prussian position in and around
Kirch-Denkern, and after severe fighting
were repulsed with a loss of 4,000 killed and
wounded. *See* Torgau.

Kirkee *Third British-Maratha War*

November 5, 1817, between the Marathas
under Baji Rao, and a British force of one
European and three sepoy regiments, under
Colonel Burr. On moving out of his
entrenchments, the flanks of Burr's force
were attacked by the Maratha horse, but
their charge was repulsed, and the British
advancing drove off the enemy with a loss of
over 500. The British loss was 75 killed and
wounded. *See* Farrukhabad.

Kiso *Taira War*

September, 1180, between the adherents of
the Minamoto clan, under Yoshinaka, and the
troops of Taira-no-Kiyomori. The Taira men
attacked the position of Yoshinaka at Kiso,
but were defeated and driven from the field
with heavy loss.

Kissingen *Seven Weeks' War*

July 10, 1866, between the Prussians, under
General Falkenstein, and the Bavarians, under
General Zoller. The Bavarians were defeated
and driven out of Kissingen with heavy loss.
See Koeniggrätz.

Kiuchau,

see Nanhan

Kiu-lien-Cheng *Russo-Japanese War*

May 1, 1904, between 40,000 Japanese, under
Marshal Kuroki, and the Russians, about
30,000 strong, under General Sassulitch.
After four days of skirmishing, the Japanese
crossed the Yalu, April 30, and on the
following day attacked the Russian position
at Kiu-lien-Cheng, driving out the
defenders with a loss of 4,000 killed and
wounded, 30 officers and 500 men prisoners,
and 48 guns. The Japanese lost 898 killed and
wounded. *See* Tsushima Strait, Te-li-ssu.

Kizil-Tepe *Russo-Turkish War*

June 25, 1877, between the Russians, under
General Loris-Melikov, and the Turks, in
superior numbers, under Mukhtar Pasha.
The Russians were defeated, and forced to
raise the siege of Kars. *See* Kars, Plevna.

Klausenburg *Ottoman Wars*

May, 1660, between the Turks, under the
Grand Vizier, Mahomet Köprili, and the
Transylvanians, under the Voivode, George
Ragotski II. The Turks gained a complete
victory, Ragotski being mortally wounded.
See Szigeth.

Klonchino *Russo-Polish Wars*

July 4, 1610, between the Russians, under
Basil Choniski, aided by a contingent of
5,000 Swedes, under James de la Gardie, and

the Poles, under Sigismund III. The Russians were totally defeated, and, as a result, the usurper, Choniski, was deposed.

Koeniggratz *Seven Weeks' War*

July 3, 1866, between 170,000 Austrians, with 600 guns, under Marshal Benedek, and the Prussian armies of Prince Frederick Charles and the Crown Prince, together about equal to the Austrians in number. The Austrians, who occupied a very strong position, were attacked in the early morning by Prince Frederick Charles, who, however, made little impression upon them, and it was not till the arrival of the Crown Prince on their right flank at 2 pm that any advantage was obtained. Then, however, the Prussians succeeded in piercing the Austrian lines, and seized the key of the position, after which further resistance being hopeless, the Austrians retired, with a loss of 20,000 killed and wounded, 20,000 prisoners, and 174 guns. The Prussians lost 10,000. The victory helped to create the German Empire. *See* Sedan.

Koenigswartha *Napoleonic Wars*

May 19, 1813, when General Peyri's Italian division, about 8,000 strong, was attacked and defeated by 15,000 Russians, under General Barclay de Tolly, with a loss of 2,000 killed and wounded. The opportune arrival of the cavalry of Marshal Ney's corps saved the division from destruction. *See* Berezina.

Kojende *Tatar Invasion of Central Asia*

This fortress, now Leninabad, was besieged in 1219, by the Tatars, under Tuchi Khan, and defended by a Kharismian garrison, under Timar Malek. After an obstinate resistance, Timar, finding he could hold out no longer, embarked with his officers and his best troops and sailed down the Jaxartes, pursued by the Tatars, whom, however, after heavy fighting, he succeeded in escaping. The city surrendered the day after Timar's departure. *See* Karaku.

Kokein *First Burma War*

December 12, 1824, when 1,800 British troops, under Sir Archibald Campbell, stormed and captured two large stockades, garrisoned by about 20,000 Burmans, under

Maha Bandoola. *See* Kemendine.

Kolin *Seven Years' War*

June 18, 1757, between 32,000 Prussians, under Frederick the Great, and 40,000 Austrians, under Marshal Daun. Daun occupied the heights between Kolin and Chotzewitz, where he was attacked by Frederick, who had nearly succeeded in turning his right flank when the Prussian right broke and fled. The Prussian cavalry charged gallantly six times, but could make no impression on the Austrian defence, and Frederick was beaten back with a loss of 14,000 men and 43 guns. The Austrians lost 9,000. Frederick was forced to raise the siege of Prague and withdraw to Saxony. *See* Prague, Olmütz.

Komatsu *Japanese Nine Years' War*

September 5, 1062, between the Japanese rebels, under Sadatoki, and the Imperial troops, under Yoriyoshi. Sadatoki, who was besieged in his camp, made a vigorous sortie at the head of 8,000 men, but after a severe conflict was repulsed. The fighting was renewed on subsequent days, and on the 16th Sadatoki was slain, and the rebellion came to an end.

Komorn *Hungarian Rising*

An action fought by General von Görgey, April 26, 1849, for the relief of Komorn, which was besieged by the Austrians. In the early morning two Hungarian corps, under Generals Klapka and Damjanics, surprised the Austrian entrenched camp, taking six guns and 200 prisoners. The Austrians retired, though not energetically pursued, and the fortress was relieved. *See* Kapolna.

Koniah *Mehemet Ali's First Rebellion*

In 1831, between the Turks, under Reschid Pasha, and the Egyptians and Syrians, under Ibrahim Pasha. After a severe engagement, the Turks were totally defeated, and fled in disorder. Reschid was severely wounded, and captured. *See* Nizib.

133

Korea,

see Pusan Perimeter, Inchon, Seoul, Sinuiju, Thirty-Eighth Parallel

Kornspruit,

see Sanna's Post

Korygaom *Third British-Maratha War*

January 1, 1818, when a small British force of under 1,000 men, chiefly Indian troops, under Captain Staunton, was attacked by 25,000 Marathas, under the Peshwa, Baji Rao. The British held their ground gallantly all day, and the approach during the night of large reinforcements under General Smith determined the Peshwa to retreat, with a loss of 600. The British lost 275, including five out of eight British officers.

Kossova I *Ottoman Wars*

June 15, 1398, between the Turks, under Murad I, and the combined army of the Serbians, Bosnians, and Albanians, under Lazar, Despot of Serbia. The Turks gained a signal victory, though Murad was mortally wounded in the battle. This success secured the Turkish domination over Serbia and the neighbouring states. *See* Nicopolis.

Kossova II *Ottoman Wars*

October 17, 1448, and two following days, between the Hungarians and Wallachians, 80,000 strong, under John Hunyadi, and a vastly superior Turkish army, under Murad II. The Hungarians left their entrenchments to attack the Turks, and throughout the day the battle was evenly contested. On the 18th, however, the Wallachians deserted to the Turks, and the Hungarians, assailed in front and rear, were hard pressed, while on the 19th they were unable to maintain their position, and were forced to retire, defeated, with a loss of 17,000 killed and wounded. The Turks are said to have lost 40,000 men in the three days, but now they turned their gaze on Constantinople. *See* Constantinople.

Kotah *Indian Mutiny*

This place, which had been seized by the rebellious troops of the Rajah of Kotah, 5,000 in number, was besieged by General Roberts, March 22, 1858. The Rajah, who held the citadel, joined forces with the British, and after a short bombardment the town was stormed, March 30. *See* Delhi.

Kotzin I *Ottoman Wars*

September 22, 1622, between the Poles, 60,000 strong, under General Chodkiewicz, and 200,000 Turks, under Osman II. Chodkiewicz, old and worn out by fatigue, was forced to retire to his tent in the middle of the battle, and on his death-bed handed over the command to Prince Lubomirski, by whom the Turks were totally routed, with a loss of 30,000 men. *See* Candia.

Kotzin II *Ottoman Wars*

November 11, 1673, between 40,000 Poles and Lithuanians, under John Sobieski III, and 80,000 Turks, under Hussein Pasha. The Turks occupied a strongly entrenched position, which was stormed by the Poles, and the Turks driven into the river, losing over 40,000 killed. In consequence of this signal victory, Kotzin capitulated, and Caplan Pasha, who was approaching with a large army, recrossed the frontier. *See* Vienna.

Kovel-Stanislav *World War I*

Began June 3, 1916, with a bombardment by General Brusilov's Southwest Army Group along the entire Russian front from the Pripet Marches to the Rumanian frontier, as the Russian part of the combined Allied offensive against the Central Empires. Russian infantry attacked on June 4 and in barely two weeks had advanced 50 miles towards Kovel, in the north, while in the south Bucovina fell on June 17. By June 30 Russia had inflicted 700,000 casualties on her enemies. To stop this danger on the eastern front, von Hindenburg, from June 30 to the beginning of September, transferred no fewer than 16 German divisions from the western front; the Austrians sent seven, the Turks two. By the end of September, Russia, held at Kovel in the north and Stanislav in the south, was exhausted and the battle ended. Each side had lost about one million killed, wounded and prisoners. Germany had stopped the Russian advance, but her ally Austria was seriously weakened. *See* Naroch Lake.

Krakovicz *Ottoman Wars*

On January 17, 1475, 40,000 Moldavian peasants, aided by 7,000 Hungarian and Polish regulars, under Stephen of Moldavia, fell upon Suleiman Pasha, with 100,000 Turks, in an untenable position near Lake Krakovicz, and totally defeated them, driving them into the lake. Very few of the Turks escaped death, either by the sword or by drowning. *See* Scutari.

Krasnoi *Napoleonic Wars*

November 17, 1812, when the Russians, 50,000 strong, under Marshal Kutuzov, after a series of combats on the two preceding days, during which they had inflicted heavy losses on the retreating French army, were defeated by the corps of Marshal Davout and the Young Guard. The French losses amounted to 5,000 killed and wounded, and about 8,000 missing. *See* Berezina.

Kringellen *Danish-Swedish Wars*

August 29, 1612, when a force of Scots in the Danish service, under Colonel George Sinclair, were ambushed in the mountains by the Norwegians, and massacred, notwithstanding a strenuous resistance. Only two of the Scots succeeded in escaping.

Kronia *Ottoman Wars*

1738, between the Imperialists under Counts Wallis and Neipperg, and the Turks. The latter were defeated, but at very heavy cost, and the Imperial army was so weakened that it was unable to prevent the Turks capturing Semendala, Orsova, and other important fortresses.

Krotzka *Ottoman Wars*

July 23, 1739, between 56,000 Austrians, under Count Wallis, and over 100,000 Turks, under El Hadj Mohammed Pasha. The Austrian vanguard was attacked by the Turks when approaching Kotzin and driven back, but the main body withstood the Turkish onslaught from 5 am to sunset, when Wallis retired, with a loss of 5,700 killed and 4,500

wounded, including nine generals. The Turkish loss is unknown, but was very heavy. *See* Çeşme.

Kulevcha *Ottoman Wars*

1829, between the Russians, under General von Diebitsch, and 40,000 Turks, under Reschid Pasha. The Russians were lying in wait for Reschid in the Kalevtcha defile, and after a severe struggle, totally routed the Turks, with a loss of 5,000 killed and wounded, and all their guns. The Pasha himself escaped with difficulty. Diebitsch took Adrianople on August 20 and the Treaty of Adrianople was signed on September 14, by which the Russians gained much territory. *See* Varna II.

Kulm *Napoleonic Wars*

August 29 and 30, 1813, between the French, 32,000 strong, under General Vandamme, and the 45,000 Austrians, and Russians, with a small force of Prussians, under the Prince Schwartzenberg, who were retreating after their defeat at Dresden. To check the pursuit they occupied Kulm, from which they were driven by Vandamme on the 29th. On the 30th, however, not having received his expected reinforcements, Vandamme was compelled to remain on the defensive, and being attacked in front by the Austrians and Russians, and in the rear by the Prussians, he was totally routed, with a loss of 6,000 killed, 7,000 prisoners, and 48 guns, being himself wounded and captured. The allied lost about 5,000. *See* Dresden, Dennewitz.

Kumai *Moronoshi's Rebellion*

February, 1355, between the troops of the Emperor Go Murakami, under Yoshinori, and the rebel Japanese, under Moronoshi and Tokiushi. The rebels were defeated, and Moronoshi severely wounded.

Kumamoto *Satsuma Rebellion*

The castle in this town was besieged February 22, 1876, by the Satsuma rebels, 15,000 strong, under Saigo. The place was gallantly defended by the garrison under General Tani Tateki, though many Samurai deserted to the rebels, and strenuous efforts were made by the Imperial army under Prince Taruhito to come to its relief. In the course of March, Saigo was attacked in the rear by a force under General Kuroda, but still maintained the siege, and it was not till April 14, when the garrison was on the verge of starvation, that Kuroda, bringing up every available man, succeeded in driving off the rebels and raising the siege.

Kumanovo *1st Balkan War*

October 24, 1912, when King Peter Karageorgevich's Serbian army clashed with Mohammed V's Turkish troops and in a three-day battle at this place, drove them back and seized Monastir on November 18. An armistice was agreed on December 3. At the same time Mohammed's Turks were defeated in Thrace by the Bulgarians. *See* Lülebürgaz.

Kunersdorf *Seven Years' War*

August 12, 1759, between 40,000 Prussians, under Frederick the Great, and 80,000 Austrians and Russians, under Generals Landon and Soltikov. Frederick first attacked the Russians in flank, driving them out of their entrenchments, and capturing 180 guns. Then, against the advice of General Seidlitz, he attacked the Austrian position on the left of the allies, and, though deserted by the Russians, the Austrians held their ground, and, bringing all their artillery to bear on the Prussians at close quarters, totally routed them, with a loss of 20,000 men and 179 guns. The allies lost 18,000. *See* Maxen, Minden.

Kunobitza *Ottoman Wars*

1443, between the Turks, under Amurath II, and the Hungarians, under John Hunyadi. The Turks were utterly routed, and in consequence Amurath concluded with them a ten years' truce. *See* Varna.

Kurdlah *Maratha Wars*

March 11, 1795, between the army of the Maratha Confederacy, under the Peshwa, Madhao Rao II, and Hari Pant, and the forces of the Nizam of Hyderabad. The troops of the Nizam gained an advantage in the fight, but the Nizam being persuaded to leave the field, his troops followed him, and were soon in headlong flight. The Nizam was captured a few days later.

Kursk Salient *World War II*

July 5 to 13, 1943, when General von Kluge's German Army Group Centre launched a massive offensive with 37 divisions, 18 infantry, two motorized and 17 armoured, including nearly 3,000 tanks, against the north (General Rokossovski) and south (General Vatutin) sides of the Russian-held salient of Kursk, 400 miles south of Moscow. By July 9, after heavy tank losses, the Germans had only forced the Russians back ten miles in the north and 30 miles in the south, so that they still had 100 miles to go to complete their encirclement. The Russians counter-attacked and by July 11, Soviet tanks and anti-tank guns had destroyed 40 per cent of the German armour. By July 13, the German offensive came to a standstill. German losses were 70,000 killed, 2,900 tanks, 195 mobile guns and 1,392 aircraft. It was the last German offensive on the eastern front. On July 12 the Russian General Popov counter-attacked the German wedge at Orel, about 100 miles north. *See* Stalingrad, Ukraine, White Russia, Orel.

Kut-el-Amara *World War I*

September 28, 1915, General Townshend's Anglo-Indian corps, 12,000-strong, campaigning against the Turks in Mesopotamia (now Iraq), at this town on the Tigris, defeated General Nur-ud-din's 10,500 strong Turkish force, and then marched on north to Baghdad, only to fail in an attack against the reinforced Turks at Ctesiphon, 24 miles south. Pursued by the Turkish force, the British withdrew again to Kut by December 3. Here, Marshal von der Götz, reinforced by another Turkish division, assaulted but failed to penetrate the British defences, and began a blockade. General Aylmer's relief force failed to penetrate the Turkish lines. General Gorringe, who succeeded him, carried much of their defences, but a flood then swept down and he was turned back with a loss of 6,000 men. By the middle of April the besieged force was weak with hunger, and on April 29, after a 5-month siege, General Townshend surrendered, about 2,000 British and 6,000 Indian troops being taken prisoner. Of the British more than half died in captivity; of the Indian at least one third. *See* Baghdad.

Kwajalein-Eniwetok *World War II*

January 29, to February 6, 1944, four US carrier task groups attacked the Marshall Islands, about 2,200 miles north-west of north Australia, in reconquest of the Pacific. Kwajalein, one of them, held by Rear-Admiral Yakiyama and 5,000 men, was heavily bombarded on February 1, stormed by General Corlett's US 7th Infantry division, and taken after three days' fierce fighting, during which more than 3,800 of the enemy were killed, for 177 Americans killed and about 950 wounded. Eniwetok, about 390 miles to the north-west, was stormed February 19 and cleared in three days. The remaining strategically important Marshalls were secured soon after, when the Americans turned to Truk. *See* Truk, Tarawa-Makin, Mariana Islands.

L

La Belle Famille,

see Niagara

Lade I *Ionian War*

494 BC, between a Persian fleet of 600 sail, which was blockading Miletus under Artaphernes, and 353 Lesbian, Chian and Samian ships, which attempted to raise the siege. The Samians, bribed by the Persians, deserted at the beginning of the action, with the exception of 11 vessels, and the Greeks were totally defeated, with heavy loss. The Chians made a specially gallant fight. *See* Marathon.

Lade II *Macedonian Wars*

201 BC, between the Rhodian fleet, under Theophiliscus, and the Macedonians, under Heraclides. The Macedonians had rather the better of the encounter, though both sides claimed the victory. *See* Cynoscephalae.

Ladysmith *Second Boer War*

Sir George White, with about 12,000 troops, was shut up in Ladysmith by the invading army, under General Joubert, November 2, 1899. The Boers, who were well provided with heavy guns, contented themselves in the main with a continuous bombardment. On January 6, 1900, however, a picked force, under Commandant Villiers, supported by several thousand Boer marksmen posted on the heights, made an attempt to force the British lines at Waggon Hill and Caesar's Camp. The battle lasted throughout the day, and more than once the defenders were very hard pressed, but they held their ground till nightfall, when the Boers withdrew, having lost about 800 men. From this date the Boers again contented themselves with bombarding the town, until it was finally relieved by Sir Redvers Buller, February 27. In addition to deaths by disease, the garrison lost during the siege 89 officers and 805 men, more than half of whom fell in the battle of January 6. *See* Mafeking, Kimberley.

La Favorita *French Revolutionary Wars*

January 16, 1797, between the French, under Napoleon, and the Austrians, under General Provera. Provera moved upon Mantua to succour the beleaguered garrison, and was aided by a sortie in force. Napoleon, making a forced march from the field of Rivoli, fell upon Provera and totally routed him, while the sortie was repulsed by the French besieging force at the point of the bayonet. Provera surrendered, with 5,000 men. *See* Lodi, Brig of.

La Fère Champenoise *Allied Invasion of France*

March 25, 1814, between Marshal Marmont's and Marshal Mortier's corps, 30,000 strong, and the allied army marching on Paris. The French were defeated and forced to retire, with a loss of about 5,000 men and many guns. This was the last action fought in the north before the first abdication of Napoleon. *See* Toulouse.

Lagos *War of the English Succession*

June 17, 1693, when a squadron of 23 Dutch and English ships, under Sir George Rooke, was attacked by Admiral de Tourville's French fleet of 71 sail, while convoying 400 merchantmen to the Mediterranean. The French destroyed 90 merchant ships, and one English and two Dutch warships. The skilful manoeuvring of Rooke, however, saved the rest of the convoy from destruction. *See* La Hogue, Neerwinden.

La Hogue *War of the Revolution*

May 19 and 20, 1692, between a combined Dutch and English fleet of 96 sail, under Admirals Russell and Almonde, and a French fleet of 64 sail of the line and 47 smaller vessels, under Admiral de Tourville. After heavy loss on both sides, the French fleet was dispersed, with a loss of three ships. On the 22nd Admiral Rooke destroyed 15 French sail of the line and a number of transports. *See* Beachy Head, Steenkerke.

Lahore *First Tatar Invasion of India*

1296, between the Monguls, 100,000 strong,

under Amir Daood, and the army of Ala-ud-Din, King of Delhi, under his brother, Alaf Khan. The Monguls were routed, with a loss of 12,000 men.

Lake Erie *The War of 1812*

September 10, 1813, between the English flotilla of six schooners, under Commodore Barclay, and a largely superior American squadron, under Commodore Perry. The whole British flotilla was destroyed, with a loss of 134 killed and wounded. The Americans lost 27 killed and 96 wounded. The British were obliged to withdraw from Detroit. *See* Queenston Heights.

Lake George *Seven Years' War*

September 8, 1755, between 1,500 French and Italians, under Baron Dieskau, and 2,500 New England militia, under Colonel William Johnson. A small force sent by Johnson to the relief of Fort Lyman was ambushed by the French and driven back to camp, but Dieskau pursuing, was repulsed in his attack upon the camp, with a loss of about 400. Dieskau himself was wounded and captured. The loss of the New England men during the day was 216 killed and 96 wounded, most of whom fell in the ambush. *See* Beauséjour.

Lake Kerguel *Tatar Invasion of Russia*

July, 1391, between 300,000 Russians, under Tokatmich, and an equal force of Tatars, under Timur (Tamerlane). The battle began at daybreak, and by midday the Russians were utterly routed, and fled in disorder, leaving their camp in the hands of Timur. *See* Baghdad, Delhi.

Lake Regillus *Rise of Rome*

In 497 BC, the first authentic date in the history of Rome. The details handed down, however, belong to the domain of legend rather than to that of history. According to the chroniclers, this was the last attempt of the Tarquinian family to recover the throne of Rome. They were, however, totally routed by the Romans, under Aulus Postumius, and all the sons of Tarquinius, and his son-in-law, Mamilius, were slain in the battle. The legend avers that the Romans, when victory

was trembling in the balance, found at their head two young men on white horses, whom they claimed to be Castor and Pollux.

Lake Vadimon *Gallic Invasion of Italy*

283 BC, between the Romans, under P. Cornelius Dolabella, and the Gauls and their Etruscan allies. Dolabella attacked the Etruscans as they were crossing the Tiber close to the lake, and destroyed the flower of their army. He then fell upon the Gauls, whom he also defeated with heavy loss, with the result that in the following year they made peace and withdrew from Italy. *See* Sentinum, Heraclea I.

Landau *War of the Spanish Succession*

This fortress, held by a French garrison under M. de Melac, was besieged by the Imperialists, under Prince Louis of Baden, July 29, 1702. The garrison made a gallant defence, but was forced to surrender, September 12. The Comte de Soissons, elder brother of Prince Eugène, fell during the siege. *See* Vigo Bay, Luzzara, Cremona.

Landen,

see Neerwinden I

Landskrone *Danish-Swedish Wars*

July 14, 1676, between the Swedes, under Charles XI, and the Danes, under Christian V, in which the Danes suffered a serious defeat. *See* Fehrbellin.

Langensalza *Seven Weeks' War*

June 27, 1866, between 12,000 Prussians, under General Flies, and the Hanoverians, in about equal strength, under George, King of Hanover. The Prussians attacked the Hanoverian position, and after severe fighting were repulsed with a loss of about 1,400 killed and wounded, and 900 prisoners. The Hanoverians lost 1,392. The victory, however, was fruitless, as the Prussians in the neighbourhood were in overwhelming numbers, and the King was compelled to surrender on the 29th. This is the last appearance of Hanover in history as an independent state. *See* Münchengrätz, Koeniggrätz.

Langport *English Civil War*

July 10, 1645, between the Parliamentarians, under Sir Thomas Fairfax, and the Royalists, under Lord Goring. The Royalists were routed, and driven by Cromwell's horse nearly into Bridgwater, with a loss of 300 killed and 1,400 prisoners. *See* Naseby.

Langside *Scottish Rising Against Mary*

May 13, 1568, when the army of Mary Queen of Scots, 6,000 strong, was defeated and dispersed by the forces of the Regent, Murray. The Queen's troops were broken by a cavalry charge, in which they lost 300, while only one man of the victorious horse was killed, and fled in confusion from the field. Mary escaped to England and was imprisoned by Elizabeth until she was executed in 1587.

Lang's Neck *First Boer War*

January 28, 1881, when a British column, 1,100 strong, under General Colley, attacked the Boers in a strong position at Lang's Neck. The British were repulsed with a loss of 198 killed and wounded. The Boers lost 14 killed and 27 wounded.

Lannoy *Netherlands War of Independence*

January, 1567, between 3,000 Flemish Protestants, under Pierre Cornaille, and a small force of the Duchess of Parma's troops, under Novicarmes. The Flemings, mostly half-armed peasants, were cut to pieces by the Spaniards, 2,600 being killed in one hour's fighting. *See* Alkmaar, Leyden.

Lansdowne *English Civil Wars*

July 5, 1643, between the Royalists, under Sir Ralph Hopton, and the Parliamentarians, under Sir William Waller, who was endeavouring to prevent Hopton's advance upon Bath. The Royalists stormed Waller's entrenchments and forced him to retreat, though at a heavy cost to themselves. *See* Stratton, Roundway Down.

Laon *Napoleonic Wars*

March 9–10, 1814, when Napoleon, with about 46,000 men, the 6th corps east of the town along the road to Reims, and 3rd corps with the Guard south of it, astride the Soissons road, was attacked by Marshal Blücher with an 85,000-strong allied force in the southern sector, thrown back in disorder and only saved by the Guard, who in turn drove back the allies. Late in the afternoon, Napoleon's 6th corps arrived to support him in the southern sector and he attacked and took the village of Arden. Fighting stopped at nightfall, the French camping on the ground they had gained. Blücher then attacked and drove Napoleon's right wing, the 6th corps, back along the road to Reims. Fearing to retreat in the face of such a strong enemy, Napoleon ordered his weak forces in the southern sector to advance, a move which could have led to their destruction. But the stratagem succeeded, for Blücher, seeing his enemy's confidence, ordered his left wing to cease pursuit of the 6th corps and to return. Engaging the allies throughout the day, Napoleon drew off his troops at 4 pm and after dark retired along the Soissons road. He had lost about 6,000 killed or wounded to the allies' 4,000. *See* Reims, Craonne, Arcis-sur-Aube, Paris.

La Paz *Bolivian Civil War*

January, 1865, between the partisans of General Belza and those of Colonel Melgarejo, each of whom had proclaimed himself Provisional President of Bolivia. Belza's forces were totally defeated, and himself slain.

La Placilla *Chilean Civil War*

August 28, 1891, between 10,000 Congressists, under General Del Canto, and 14,000 Balmacedists, under General Barbosa. The latter were routed with a loss of 3,363 killed and wounded, including Barbosa, while thousands laid down their arms on the field. The Congressists, who lost 1,609, at once occupied Valparaiso, and a few days later Balmaceda committed suicide.

La Puebla I *Franco-Mexican War*

May 5, 1862, between the French, 7,500 strong, under General Lorençez, and about 12,000 Mexicans, under General Zaragoza. The French endeavoured to carry the ridge of the Cerro de Guadalupe, commanding the town, but were repulsed by General Negreti, with 1,200 men, losing 456 killed and wounded, and forced to retire from La Puebla. The Mexicans lost 215 only.

La Puebla II *Franco-Mexican War*

On May 4, 1863, the French army, 25,000 strong, under General Forey, laid siege to La Puebla, which was held by a Mexican garrison under General Ortega. Forey's force was too small for a complete investment, and in March he had besieged the Fort of San Xavier. On the 29th March this post was taken by storm, the French losing 230, the defenders 600 men. From this point the French obtained foothold in the town, and then proceeded to capture the houses block by block. So determined was the resistance, however, that by April 7 they had made next to no advance, though they had lost a further 600 men. Later in the month an attack on the Convent of Santa Cruz was repulsed with a loss of 480. On May 8 a relieving force of 10,500 men, under General Comonfort, was defeated by a small French column under General Bazaine, losing 8 guns and 1,000 prisoners, and from this point further resistance was useless. Ortega, therefore, after a most gallant defence, surrendered with 1,455 officers and 11,000 men, May 17, 1863. The French put Archduke Ferdinand on the throne. *See* Calpulalpam, Acultzingo.

Larcay *Chilean Revolution*

December, 1829, between the Federalists, or Government Party, under General Zastera, and the Pelucones, or Unitarians, under General Priefo. The Pelucones gained a signal victory, following which they drove out the Government and abrogated the constitution of 1828.

Largs *Norse Invasion of Scotland*

October 2, 1263, between the Norsemen, under Haco, and the Scots. The Norse fleet of 160 ships was driven ashore off Largs by a violent storm, and many of them wrecked, and Haco landed a force to protect the shipwrecked crews. This force was attacked by the Scots, and utterly routed, and Haco was forced to withdraw, and abandon the project of invasion. The only name on the Scottish side which has come down to us as taking part in the battle is that of Sir Pierce Curry.

Larissa *Third Macedonian War*

171 BC, between the Romans, 40,000 strong, under P. Licinius Crassus, and 43,000 Macedonians, under Perseus. The Romans were defeated with a loss of 2,200 killed and 600 prisoners. *See* Pydna.

Larissus, The *Wars of the Achaean League*

209 BC, between the Achaeans, under Philopoemen, and the Ætolians and Eleians. The allies were defeated and cut to pieces, the Eleian general being among the slain. *See* Mantinea.

La Rochelle I *Hundred Years' War*

June 22, 1372, when an English fleet, under the Earl of Pembroke, intended for the relief of La Rochelle, was intercepted by a greatly superior Spanish fleet, under Don Ambrosio Bercenegra, and after very hard fighting was entirely destroyed or captured. *See* Sluys, Navarrete, Margate.

La Rochelle II *French Religious Wars*

This fortress, the principal Huguenot stronghold in France, was besieged by the Royal troops, under Cardinal Richelieu, in November, 1627. The garrison, under the mayor, Guiton, made a gallant defence, but the assassination of the Duke of Buckingham prevented the arrival of the promised English aid and the town surrendered, October 28, 1628, after holding out for eleven months. The Huguenots were thereafter subjugated. *See* Arques.

La Rothière *Napoleonic Wars*

February 1, 1814, between 42,000 French,

under Napoleon, and 100,000 Prussians, Russians and Württembergers, under Marshal Blücher. Napoleon held a strong position, where he was attacked by Blücher, whom he succeeded in holding at bay till late in the afternoon, when Blücher captured the village of La Rothière. Napoleon with the Young Guard retook the village, but the Russian Guards drove them back, and the battle ended with the allies in possession of the field. The French lost 5,000, the allies about 8,000, and Napoleon was enabled to continue his retirement. *See* Montereau.

Las Navas de Tolosa *Moorish Empire in Spain*

July 10, 1212, between a huge army of Moors, said by the chroniclers to have amounted to 600,000, under Mohammed al Nasin, and the allied armies of the Kings of Castile, León, Aragon, Navarre, and Portugal. The Moors were utterly routed, very few of their enormous host escaping from the field. *See* Alarcos, Cordova.

Las Salinas *Conquest of Peru*

April 20, 1538, between the forces of Francisco Pizarro and those of Almagro. The latter were totally routed, and Almagro captured and executed.

Laswari *Second British-Maratha War*

November 1, 1803, between the British, 10,000 strong, under General Lake, and Sind's army, consisting of 9,000 infantry and 5,000 cavalry. Sind's veteran infantry made a most gallant defence, standing their ground until 7,000 had fallen, when the survivors laid down their arms. The cavalry also suffered heavily. The British loss amounted to about 800. Seventy-two guns and a large quantity of ammunition and stores were captured. *See* Aligarh, Assaye, Farrukhabad.

Lauffeld *War of the Austrian Succession*

July 2, 1747, between 90,000 allied Austrians and British, under the Duke of Cumberland, and 12,000 French under Marshal General Saxe. The village of Lauffeld was thrice carried by the French and thrice recaptured, but about noon the British centre was driven in, and defeat was imminent, when a cavalry charge, headed by Sir John Ligonier, saved the day, and enabled the Duke to retire in good order. The allies lost 5,620 killed and wounded, the French about 14,000. It was a victory, though costly, for Saxe. *See* Bergen-op-Zoom.

Laupen *Burgundian Wars*

June 21, 1339, between 5,000 Swiss of Berne and the Forest Cantons, under Rudolf von Erlach, and 15,000 Burgundians, under the Counts of Kiburg and Nidau. Despite their superior numbers, the mounted Burgundians were unable to withstand the charge of the Swiss pikemen, and were utterly routed and forced to raise the siege of Laupen. *See* Sempach.

Lautulae *Second Samnite War*

316 BC, between the Samnites under Pontius and the Romans under Q. Fabius Maximus. The Romans were defeated with great slaughter. *See* Sentinum.

Le Bourget *Franco-Prussian War*

A determined sortie by the French from Paris, October 27, 1870, in which they carried the village of Le Bourget. They held their ground there until October 30, when they were driven out by the Prussian Guard Corps, leaving 1,200 prisoners in the hands of the Germans, who lost 34 officers and 344 men. *See* Metz, Sedan, Gravelotte, Le Mans.

Le Cateau *World War I*

August 26, 1914, after the Mons defeat of the British Expeditionary Force on August 23, Field Marshal Sir John French retreated south-west on the left of General Joffre's five French armies. His 2nd Corps (General Smith-Dorrien) was overtaken by General von Kluck's 1st Army at Le Cateau, 35 miles south-west of Mons. Cut off from the 1st Corps by the River Oise, General Smith-Dorrien was forced to accept battle and for an entire day his three and a half divisions fought off the masses of von Kluck's army, losing 8,000 men and 36 guns before he managed to withdraw in the night and retreat

142

to St Quentin about 12 miles south-west. The delay enabled the BEF to get clear of the German armies wheeling south-east into France. *See* Battle of the Frontiers, Marne.

Leck, The *Thirty Years' War*

April 5, 1632, between 26,000 Swedes and German Protestants, under Gustavus Adolphus, and 20,000 Imperialists, under Count Tilly. Gustavus had prepared a bridge to cross the river, and immediately after daybreak his engineers started to fix it, the Swedish artillery meanwhile keeping the Imperialists in check. In the artillery duel Tilly was mortally wounded, and his troops retired, leaving the Swedes to effect the passage unmolested. *See* Nördlingen, Lützen.

L'Ecluse *Hundred Years' War*

1340, when the English fleet surprised the French in a narrow channel, and totally routed them, with a loss of 90 ships and 30,000 men. *See* Sluys, Crécy.

Leghorn *Anglo-Dutch Wars*

Fought off Leghorn March 31, 1653, when six English ships under Commodore Appleton were destroyed by a Dutch fleet of 16 sail under Admiral van Gelen. Only a sloop escaped the destruction. Van Gelen was mortally wounded during the action. *See* Texel.

Legnano *Wars of the Lombard League*

May 29, 1176, between the infantry of the Lombard League, aided by Venice and the Pope, and the Imperialists, mounted German knights, under Frederick Barbarossa. Frederick was utterly routed, and fled from Italy in disguise, after a victory which foreshadowed the rise of foot soldiers. *See* Corte Nuova.

Leipzig I *Thirty Years' War*

September 17, 1631, between 40,000 Swedes and an equal force of Saxons, under

Gustavus Adolphus and John George, Elector of Saxony, and 32,000 Imperialists, under Field Marshal the Count of Tilly. The Imperialist right totally routed the Saxons, who fled from the field, headed by the Elector. Meanwhile the Swedes had completely defeated the left of the Imperialists, under Pappenheim, and repulsed the centre under Tilly, and on the return of the right from pursuing the Saxons, they were attacked by the Swedish left and driven from the field, only four regiments holding their ground in a wood until nightfall. The Imperialists lost 8,000 killed and wounded and 5,000 prisoners; the allies 2,700, of whom only 700 were Swedes. Gustavus captured the whole of Tilly's artillery, and his victory was the salvation of the Protestant cause, which was trembling in the balance. *See* Lützen.

Leipzig II *Napoleonic Wars*

October 16, 17 and 18, 1813, between the French, under Napoleon, and the forces of the Great Coalition. Napoleon, who held Leipzig with 185,000 men, 600 guns, was faced by 160,000 Austrians and Russians, under the Prince Schwartzenberg, and 60,000 Prussians, under General Blücher, with some 1,400 guns. On the 16th Schwartzenberg attacked, being faced by Napoleon with 115,000 men, and, after an obstinate engagement, which lasted till nightfall, the French had gained a little ground. At the same time Blücher attacked Marshal Marmont, who, with 24,000 men, held his own throughout the day. The French lost 27,000; the allies about 35,000. Both sides receiving reinforcements during the night, Napoleon on the morning of the 17th was at the head of 150,000 troops, while the allies numbered nearly 300,000, including the Swedes under Crown Prince Bernadotte. Little was done on the 17th, but on the 18th Napoleon moved out to drive back the allies and leave a road of retreat open. He was repulsed at all points and driven back into Leipzig, whence during the night of the 18th to 19th the French retired by the only serviceable bridge. The corps under Prince Josef Poniatowski left to cover the retreat was almost annihilated and Poniatowski drowned when the Elster bridge was blown. The French lost in the three days 60,000 killed and wounded, and 11,000 prisoners, while the losses of the allies were said to be over 50,000. *See* Dennewitz, Hanau.

Leitskau *Napoleonic Wars*

August 27, 1813, between 5,000 French, under General Girard, and a Prussian division, under General Hirschberg, aided by some Cossacks, under General Czernitchev. Girard was defeated, losing heavily in killed and wounded, besides 1,500 prisoners and six guns. *See* Dresden, Leipzig II.

Le Mans *Franco-Prussian War*

January 10, 11 and 12, 1871, between the Germans, 50,000 strong, under Prince Frederick Charles, and the French, an irregular force of about 150,000, under General Chanzy. The French army was completely routed, and the whole force so completely demoralized as to be no longer an effective fighting unit. The Germans inflicted 10,000 casualties, took 20,000 prisoners, 17 guns, and great quantities of war material, at a cost to themselves of 200 officers and 3,200 men. *See* Metz, Sedan, Gravelotte, Le Bourget.

Leningrad *World War II*

January 15, 1944, four Russian armies launched an offensive along a front of 120 miles from Leningrad south to Lake Ilmen. The German front, though strongly defended with minefield and pillboxes, collapsed after five days' fighting. Leningrad's remaining 600,000 people, blockaded by the Nazis for 30 months, were relieved. Russian estimates of the deaths in the city directly owing to the blockade vary from 600,000 to 900,000. *See* White Russia.

Lens *Thirty Years' War*

August 2, 1648, between the French, 14,000 strong, under the Great Condé, and the Austrians, in somewhat superior force, under the Archduke Leopold. Condé feigned a retreat, to draw the enemy from their lines, and then turning upon them, decisively defeated them, with a loss of 4,000 killed, 6,000 prisoners, and all their baggage and artillery. This battle, and the Treaty of Westphalia on October 24, ended the Thirty Years' War. *See* Rocroi, Lerida.

Leontini *Second Punic War*

This city, the stronghold of the National party in Sicily, held by a garrison of Syracusans and Roman deserters, was stormed and sacked, 211 BC, by three Roman legions under M. Marcellus. Two thousand Roman deserters captured in the place were put to the sword. Hippocrates succeeded in escaping. *See* Capua.

Lepanto *Cyprus War*

October 7, 1571, between a fleet of 250 Spanish and Venetian ships, under Don John of Austria, and a Turkish fleet of 270 sail, under Piale, the Captain Pasha. The Turkish left wing met with some success, but the centre and right were almost destroyed, the Turks losing 200 vessels, and, it is said, 30,000 men. Piale was killed. The allies lost between 4,000 and 5,000 men, including 15 Venetian captains. Oar-driven ships were used in a naval battle for the last time at Lepanto, which ended Turkish naval supremacy in the Mediterranean. *See* Keresztes.

Lerida I *Thirty Years' War*

September, 1642, between the Spaniards, under Leganez, and the French, under Lamothe-Houdancourt. The Spanish army was defeated, and this victory, in conjunction with the fall of Perpignan, gave the French possession of Roussillon. *See* Lens.

Lerida II *Thirty Years' War*

This city, held by a garrison of 4,000 Spaniards, under Don Jorge Britt, was besieged by the French, under the Great Condé, May 12, 1647. The defence was vigorous, the garrison making constant sorties, and about the middle of June the appearance of a large Spanish army at Fraga forced Condé either to deliver an assault or to raise the siege. He chose the second alternative and withdrew his troops June 17. *See* Lens, Rocroi.

Lesno *Russo-Swedish War*

A series of actions, fought 1708 between 40,000 Russians, under Peter the Great, and 15,000 Swedes, under General Levenhaupt, who was escorting a convoy of 8,000 waggons

144

to the army of Charles XII. The battle lasted over five days, at the end of which time the remnant of the Swedes, though defeated, were permitted to retire in good order, but without their convoy. The Swedes lost in this series of actions two-thirds of their numbers. The Russians lost 10,000 men. *See* Stralsund, Fredrikshald.

Leucopetra *Wars of the Achaean League*

146 BC, between a Roman Consular Army, under Lucius Mummius, and the forces of the Achaean League, under Diacus. The Greeks, who were only half as strong as their opponents, were routed, and all resistance came to an end, the Greek cities, one after another, opening their gates to the Romans.

Leuctra *Wars of the Greek City States*

371 BC, July, between 10,000 Spartans, under Cleombrotus, and 6,000 Thebans, under Epaminondas. The principal fighting took place on the Theban left, where Epaminondas had massed his best troops, and after a fierce encounter the Spartans were driven back, leaving 1,000 dead, including Cleombrotus, on the field. As a result of this defeat, the Spartans evacuated Boeotia. *See* Mantinea II, Cynoscephalae.

Leuthen *Seven Years' War*

December 5, 1757, between 33,000 Prussians, 71 guns, under Frederick the Great, and 60,000 Austrians, 65 guns, under Prince Charles of Lorraine and Count Daun. Frederick made a feigned attack on the Austrian right wing, and then under cover of the ground withdrew the major part of his force, and strongly attacked in oblique order the exposed Austrian left, which was driven back and finally overthrown by a charge of cavalry. The Austrians lost 7,000 killed and wounded, 20,000 prisoners, including three generals, and 134 guns. The Prussians lost 5,000 killed and wounded. In consequence of this victory, Breslau surrendered to Frederick, with over 18,000 troops, on December 10. *See* Breslau.

Lewes *English Barons' War*

May 14, 1264, between the Barons, under Simon de Montfort, and the Royalists, under Henry III and Prince Edward. The king was completely defeated, and the two parties signed an agreement, known as the Mise of Lewes, to submit the points in dispute to arbitration. *See* Evesham.

Lexington I *American Revolutionary War*

April 19, 1775, between 700 Royal troops, under Lt. Col. Francis Smith and a small force of American militiamen. After a brief engagement the Americans were defeated and retired. The losses on both sides were small. This was the first engagement of the war. *See* Ticonderoga, Bunker's Hill.

Lexington II *American Civil War*

This town was invested September 18, 1861, by the Confederates, 8,000 strong, under General Price, who having cut off their supplies, forced the Federal garrison of 3,000, under Colonel Mulligan, to surrender, September 20. The Confederates lost 100 men only. *See* Wilson's Creek, Ball's Bluff.

Leyden *Netherlands War of Independence*

This city was invested May 26, 1574, by 8,000 Walloons and Germans under General Valdez, who in the course of a few days had erected 62 batteries round the place. There was no garrison, with the exception of a few 'freebooters' and a burgher guard, under Jan van der Does. The Prince of Orange, in order to save the city, determined to open the dykes, and on August 3 the gates at Schiedam and Rotterdam were opened, and the dykes broken along the course of the Yssel. Meanwhile the citizens had come to an end of their bread, but by strenuous efforts the fleet under Admiral Boisot succeeded in throwing relief into the city at the beginning of October. By this time it was on the verge of starvation, and 8,000 of the inhabitants had died of disease. The Spaniards, however, had been driven from work after work, and on October 3 the last of their redoubts was mastered, and Valdez was forced to raise the siege. *See* Alkmaar, Gembloux.

Leyte *World War II*

As the first step towards the complete liberation of the Philippines from Japanese rule, General Krueger's 6th US Army invaded the central island of Leyte on October 20, 1944, against strong opposition by the 35th Japanese Army (General Suzuki). The US forces made some progress, but were slowed by heavy rains and Japanese reinforcements 45,000-strong landing between October 23 and early December. The port of Palampan fell on December 25, but not until March 1945 were all the enemy pockets of resistance finally cleared. Japanese losses in this important battle totalled over 70,000 to the Americans' 3,500 killed, 12,000 wounded. *See* New Guinea, Leyte Gulf, Philippine Sea, Peleliu-Angaur.

Leyte Gulf *World War II*

The Japanese planned to destroy the US fleet protecting the Leyte invasion and on October 22 sent a flotilla of four carriers, two battleships, three cruisers and eight destroyers under Admiral Ozawa to lure away Admiral Halsey's 3rd fleet, then sink or drive off Admiral Kinkaid's 7th fleet and destroy the defenceless invasion fleet. A complex battle made up of three separate engagements followed on October 25, 1944: Surigao Strait; Cape Engano, and Samar. Japan was defeated, losing three battleships, four carriers, ten cruisers and nine destroyers, and failing to stop the Leyte landings. The Japanese sank three US carriers, one of them by suicide dive-bomber, two destroyers, and one destroyer escort. *See* Leyte, New Guinea, Philippine Sea.

Liaoyang *Russo-Japanese War*

August 25, 1904, between General Kuropatkin's 100,000 strong Russian army and Marshal Oyama's seven Japanese divisions, when after seven days' inconclusive fighting Kuropatkin withdrew to the north, having suffered 16,500 casualties to the 25,000 of the Japanese. *See* Port Arthur, Nanhan.

Liège *World War I*

August 4, 1914, when General von Emmerich's Army of the Meuse invaded neutral Belgium to attack France from the north, and by August 6 had filtered through the system of 12 protective underground forts and was marching on Liège. General von Ludendorff personally received the surrender of the city from the burgomaster the next morning. General Leman's Belgian army had meantime retreated across the River Gette, where it skirmished with advance units of the main German force and hopefully awaited the arrival of its French and British allies. On August 12, the German 420 mm siege guns arrived and began pounding the forts into submission. Leman was taken prisoner, unconscious, from one of them, but heroically they held up the main enemy advance for 11 days altogether, thus enabling the British and French to deploy before the main German armies arrived. On August 17 these were beginning their Schlieffen Plan wheeling manoeuvre through Belgium into France. *See* Antwerp III, Namur.

Liegnitz *Seven Years' War*

August 15, 1760; Frederick the Great with 30,000 Prussians was posted near Liegnitz, and expecting to be attacked by the Austrians, 90,000 strong, under Count Daun, commenced a retreat towards Parchwitz, and took up a position which according to Daun's plan was to have been occupied by Landon's corps. Landon, quite unconscious of the presence of the Prussians, marched into the middle of Frederick's lines, and was utterly routed, with a loss of 4,000 killed and wounded, 6,000 prisoners and 82 guns. *See* Torgau.

Ligny *Napoleon's Hundred Days*

June 16, 1815, between 84,000 Prussians, with 224 guns, under Blücher, and 75,000 French under Napoleon, with 218 guns. The French attacked Field Marshal General Blücher's position, and met with a stout resistance, especially at the village of Ligny, but by sundown the Prussians had exhausted their last resources, and Napoleon, bringing up the Guard, and a division of heavy cavalry, drove them from their positions, with a loss of about 12,000. The French lost 7,000 killed and wounded. *See* Waterloo.

Lille *War of the Spanish Succession*

This city was besieged August 12, 1708, by the Imperialists, under Prince Eugène, and defended by a French garrison under Marshal de Boufflers, which after repulsing several determined assaults, surrendered October 25.

The besiegers lost in the course of the siege 3,632. The French lost about 7,000. *See* Oudenarde, Tournai.

Lilybaeum *First Punic War*

This fortress in Sicily was besieged 250 BC, by the Romans, under C. Attilius and L. Manlius, and was defended by a Carthaginian garrison, 10,000 strong, under Hamilcar. The Romans invested the place both by sea and land, but the superior seamanship of the Carthaginians enabled them from time to time to throw succour into the place. The first line of the defences was soon carried but the Romans were then confronted with a second rampart, equally strong, and the siege was begun anew. In 249 P. Claudius took over command, but a defeat of the Roman fleet at Drepanum (Trápani) gave the Carthaginians complete command of the sea, and though the Romans continued to blockade the fortress on the land side, it held out till 241. After the naval battle of Ægusae Carthage sued for peace. *See* Panormus, Drepanum.

Lincoln, Fair of *First Barons' War of England*

Fought in the streets of Lincoln, May 20, 1217, between the Royal troops, under the Earl of Pembroke, and the adherents of the Dauphin Louis, Pretender to the English throne, under the Comte de la Perche. The Royalists were victorious, the French leader was killed, and many of the barons gave in.

Lindley *Second Boer War*

A force of 500 yeomanry, under Colonel Spragge, after holding out for four days against a largely superior Boer force, surrendered May 27, 1900. *See* Ladysmith, Mafeking.

Linköping *Swedish-Polish Wars*

In 1598, between the Poles, under Sigismund III, King of Poland and Sweden, and the Swedes, under Charles the Regent. The Poles were surprised and totally defeated, with a loss of 20,000 men, the Swedes losing, it is said, only 240. This victory was shortly followed by the dethronement of Sigismund and the accession of Charles as King of Sweden. *See* Riga.

Liparaean Islands *First Punic War*

The scene of a naval battle, 257 BC, in which the Roman fleet, under the Consul, C. Attilius, completely defeated the Carthaginians. *See* Mylae, Panormus.

Lippe *Germanic Wars*

11 BC, between the Romans, under Drusus, and the Sicambri, Suevi and Cherusii. The Romans were largely outnumbered and surrounded, and so certain were the Germans of victory, that they had already apportioned the spoil among the various tribes. Drusus, however, attacked the barbarians vigorously, and totally routed them with very heavy loss. *See* Main.

Lissa *Seven Weeks' War*

July 20, 1866, between the Austrian fleet of seven armoured ships and some obsolete wooden vessels, under Admiral Tegethov, and the Italian fleet of 10 armour-clads, under Admiral Persano. Tegethov attacked in wedge formation, with his flagship as the apex, and broke the line of the Italian fleet, which was steaming, line ahead, across his bows. He rammed and sank the Italian flagship, and the rest of the action was a mêlée in which the Italians were defeated and driven off, with a loss of three ships and over 1,000 men. This defeat forced the Italians to raise the siege of Lissa. *See* Münchengrätz, Koeniggrätz.

Little Big Horn *Sioux Rising*

On June 25, 1876, General Custer, with the 7th United States Cavalry, 700 strong, attacked the village of the Sioux chief, Sitting Bull. He divided his force into three columns, one of which, led by himself, marched into an ambush, and was massacred to a man. The other two columns were vigorously attacked by the Sioux, and forced to retire. The cavalry lost on this occasion 265 killed.

Lobositz *Seven Years' War*

October 1, 1756, between 24,000 Prussians, under Frederick the Great, and a somewhat superior force of Austrians, under Marshal Brown. Brown was marching to relieve the

Saxons penned up in Pirna, when he was attacked by the Prussians, who, after hard fighting, forced him to retire. Each side lost about 3,000, but the victory was of great importance to Frederick, as it led to the surrender at Pirna of 17,000 Saxons and 80 guns, whom he forced to fight in his own army. *See* Oswego, Prague.

Locninh,

see Vietnam War

Lodi, Brig of, *French Revolutionary Wars*

May 10, 1796, during Napoleon's pursuit of the retiring Austro-Sardinian army under General Baron de Beaulieu. The bridge over the Adda was defended by the Austrian rear-guard of 10,000 troops, with some 20 guns, commanding passage. Napoleon sent a force of cavalry round by a ford to take the defenders in rear and then rushed the bridge, the 6,000 stormers being led by Berthier and Masséna, while Napoleon himself was in the thick of the fighting. The French loss is said not to exceed 400, while the Austrians lost in the action and subsequent pursuit, 2,000 killed and wounded, 1,000 prisoners, and 20 guns. *See* Mantua, Castiglione.

Lódź *World War I*

A few days before the Germans made their final charge at Ypres, Field Marshal von Hindenburg began moving troops east to oppose the Russian invasion of Silesia, by an attack up the Vistula on the Russian right flank, and to threaten Warsaw, then part of Russia. The Germans under General von Mackensen attacked on November 18, 1914, and the Russian centre was broken, the left pushed back on the Polish industrial capital of Lódź. But the Russian general Russki began to close the end of the wedge the Germans had made, threatening them with encirclement, and it took them three days, November 24–26, to fight their way out. On December 6, the Russians withdrew from Lódź, straightening their line to protect Warsaw. The German offensive had saved Silesia. *See* Masurian Lakes.

Loftcha *Russo-Turkish War*

September 3, 1877, between 20,000 Russians, under Prince Imeretinsky, and 15,000 Turks, under Adil Pasha. The actual attack on the Turkish positions was made by Skobelev, at first with 5,000, and afterwards with 9,000 men, and the Turks were driven out of Loftcha with a loss of 5,200 killed. The Russians lost 1,500 killed and wounded. *See* Plevna.

Loigny-Pouprey *Franco-Prussian War*

December 1, 1870, between the Germans, 34,000 strong, under the Grand Duke of Mecklenburg, and about 90,000 French, forming the army of the Loire, under General d'Aurelle de Paladines. The Germans gained a signal victory, completely breaking the aggressive power of the Army of the Loire. The French lost 18,000 killed and wounded and nine guns, the Germans 4,200. The French capitulated on January 28, 1871. *See* Metz, Sedan, Le Bourget, Gravelotte.

Loja *Spanish-Muslim Wars*

July 4, 1482, between the Spaniards, under Ferdinand the Catholic, and the Moors, under Ali Atar. The King, who was besieging Loja, was encamped on the heights of Almohacen, but finding the position insecure, decided upon a retreat. As he was retiring he was vigorously attacked by the garrison, and though, after very heavy fighting, he succeeded in withdrawing in good order, he lost most of his baggage and artillery. *See* Granada, Malaga, Lucena.

Lonato,

see Castiglione

Londonderry *War of the English Succession*

This town in which about 30,000 Ulster Protestants had taken refuge, was besieged by James II, April 19, 1689. It was defended by about 7,000 armed citizens under Major Henry Baker, and held out until July 30, when Colonel Kirke succeeded in forcing the boom at the head of Lough Foyle and reprovisioning the town. The besiegers then withdrew, having lost 5,000 men during the siege. The garrison was reduced to 4,000. Among those who died during the siege was Major Baker. *See* The Boyne.

Loosecoat Field,

see Empingham

Lostwithiel *English Civil War*

August 21 and September 2, 1644, in the First Civil War. The Royalists, 16,000, took Beacon Hill, the key to Lostwithiel, in the first battle, on August 21. The remainder of the Roundheads, at first 10,000, were surrounded and forced to surrender on September 2 at Castle Dore, near Fowey. Not long after this defeat the Roundheads were reorganized as the New Model Army. *See* Marston Moor.

Loudon Hill *Wars of Scottish Independence*

May 10, 1307, between the Scots, under King Robert Bruce, and the English, under the Regent Pembroke. Bruce met the attack of the English cavalry with a line of spearmen, which they were unable to break, and they were driven off with heavy loss. Pembroke thereupon withdrew his army and returned to England. *See* Bannockburn, Methven.

Louisbourg I *War of the Austrian Succession*

This town, the strongest fortress in America, was captured June 17, 1745, by a force of New Englanders, under Pepperel, aided by a naval force under Commodore Warren. *See* Sohr.

Louisbourg II *Seven Years' War*

Louisbourg, having been restored to the French, was invested June 8, 1758, by a force of 11,600 British troops, under General Amherst, and a fleet of 41 ships of war, under Admiral Boscawen. It was defended by 3,800 French regulars, under Chevalier de Drucour, while in the harbour were 12 ships of war,

with crews numbering 3,000 men. Owing to heavy weather no siege guns were landed till the 18th, but by July 26 a practicable breach had been effected, whereupon the garrison surrendered. During the siege the defenders lost 1,200 men killed or died of disease, while the prisoners numbered 5,637, and 239 guns and mortars were taken. Wolfe, who commanded a brigade, especially distinguished himself. *See* Ticonderoga.

Löwenberg *Napoleonic Wars*

August 21, 1813, between 130,000 French, under Napoleon, and 80,000 Prussians, under Field Marshal General Blücher. Blücher, being vigorously attacked, retired behind Haynau without offering any serious resistance to the French advance. The Prussians lost 2,000 killed and wounded. *See* Dennewitz, Gross-Beeren.

Lucena *Spanish-Muslim Wars*

April, 1483, when the Moors, under Abdullah and Ali Atar, who were besieging Lucena, were attacked by a Spanish relieving force under the Conde de Cabra. The Moorish infantry fled, and Ali Atar, heading a charge of cavalry in a gallant attempt to retrieve the day, was slain, whereupon his following broke and fled, pursued by the Christians to the banks of the Xenil, where the majority were cut to pieces. *See* Malaga, Baza.

Lucknow *Indian Mutiny*

On the approach of the rebel Sepoy army, July 1, 1857, the garrison and residents took refuge in the Residency, which had been prepared to stand a siege. On September 19, 1857, a force of 3,179 British troops, under Generals Sir Henry Havelock and Sir James Outram, left Cawnpore to relieve the garrison. On the 23rd they encountered and defeated a force of 12,000 rebels at the Alumbagh, capturing five guns. On the 25th they forced the Charbagh bridge, and captured Secunderbagh, and the main body, after prolonged street fighting, reached the Residency, the rearguard with the wounded getting in on the 26th. The loss during the operations amounted to 535, while the garrison up to this time had lost 483 killed and wounded. Outram now took command and the garrison held out until November 19, when it was relieved, after very heavy fighting, by a column under Sir Colin Campbell, and the whole force withdrawn. On March 1, 1858, the recovery of the city from the rebels began with the capture of the Alumbagh, and was completed on the 21st when the mutineers were finally driven from the place. During the interval the various fortresses and palaces held by the rebels were successively carried by assault, the fighting in many cases being exceedingly severe. *See* Delhi, Cawnpore.

Lugdunum,

see Lyons

Lüleburgaz *Balkan Wars*

King Ferdinand of Bulgaria, having stopped the offensive in Thrace of Mohammed V of Turkey, attacked and routed the Turks on October 28, 1912, at this town 85 miles north-west of Constantinople, in a three-day battle. The Turks having retreated to Catalca, a fortified line across the peninsula near the Bosphorus, the Bulgars attacked again, but were repulsed. Ferdinand, with Russian mediation, agreed to an armistice on December 3. The Turks suffered 30,000 killed and the Bulgars 15,000 killed and wounded. *See* Adrianople, Kumanovo.

Luncarty *Danish Invasions of Scotland*

980, between the Scots, under Kenneth III, and the Danish corsairs, who had landed on the Tay to attack Dunkeld. After a furious hand-to-hand fight the Danes were defeated and driven to their ships. *See* Kinloss, Mortlack.

Lunden *Danish-Swedish Wars*

1676, between the Swedes, under Charles XI, and the Danes, under Christian V. Both sides claimed the victory, but the advantage rested with the Swedes, for Christian had to fall back upon Copenhagen, while Charles forced the Danes to raise the siege of Malmö. *See* Kiöge.

Lundy's Lane *War of 1812*

July 25, 1814, between 5,000 Americans, under General Jacob Brown, and 3,000 British, under Sir George Drummond. Drummond occupied high ground on each side of Lundy's Lane, where he was attacked by the Americans. The fighting lasted till far into the night, when a final assault was repulsed, and the Americans retired to Chippewa with a loss of 858. The British lost 878. *See* Lake Erie, Chippewa.

Lutter *Thirty Years' War*

August 27, 1626, between the Imperialists, under Tilly, and the Danes and Germans, under Christian IV of Denmark. The allies were retreating before Field Marshal the Count of Tilly, who came up with them in an open plain near the Castle of Lutter, where the king had taken up a strong position. Tilly attacked, and notwithstanding Christian's personal courage, his infantry were overwhelmed, while the German cavalry refused to take any part in the fight. The Danes left 4,000 dead on the field, and Tilly captured 2,000 prisoners, 22 guns and 60 standards. The King with difficulty cut his way through the enemy's horse, and escaped. *See* Stralsund, Dessau.

Lützen I *Thirty Years' War*

November 16, 1632, between 19,000 Swedes with 20 guns under Gustavus Adolphus, and 19,200 Imperialists with 30 guns under General von Wallenstein. The Swedes attacked with success on their right, but their left was driven back by Count zu Pappenheim, and Gustavus, hurrying off to rally them, fell mortally wounded. The fall of their king, however, did not dishearten the Swedes, and a fresh charge, in which Pappenheim was killed, gave them a complete victory. A dense fog, however, came on, which enabled Wallenstein to effect an orderly retreat, though he left all his guns on the field. Casualties: 5,000–6,000 Swedes; 6,000 Imperialists. *See* Nördlingen.

Lützen II *Napoleonic Wars*

May 2, 1813, between the French, 120,000 strong, under Napoleon, and the Russians and Prussians, 75,000 strong, under Prince Wittgenstein and General Blücher. The King of Prussia and the Russian Emperor were present on the field. Napoleon held five villages in front of Lützen, round which the battle centred. They were taken and re-taken several times during the day. The French infantry bivouacked in squares and were fired on by Allied artillery and charged by cavalry, but having no cavalry themselves were unable to oppose. During the night, despite Blücher's opposition the two allied kings ordered a retirement. The allies lost about 20,000; the French about 18,000. *See* Berezina, Bautzen.

Luzon *World War II*

January 9, 1945, when General Krueger's 6th US Army landed at Luzon, held by General Yamashita's 250,000-strong 14th Army, to liberate the Philippines. Pressing 20 miles inland by January 20, the Americans then met stronger Japanese resistance. Despite bitter fighting Clark Field air base was taken by January 23, and by February 3–4 XIV Corps fought their way to the outskirts of Manila, the capital, which they were not, however, able to take for another month, owing to strong enemy opposition. Baguio, the summer capital, fell on April 27. The Americans faced more hard fighting in southern Luzon before finally on July 4 General MacArthur declared Luzon secure. The Luzon battle lasted 173 days and cost 37,854 American killed or wounded, apart from some 2,000 killed or wounded through Kamikaze (suicide dive-bomber) attacks on US and Australian warships during the invasion period. Japanese casualties were very much greater. *See* Leyte.

Luzzara *War of the Spanish Succession*

August 15, 1702, between the French, 35,000 strong under the Duc d'Anjou, and 25,000 Imperialists under Prince Eugène. The Prince attacked the French in their entrenchments in front of Luzzara, Tuscany, and after a stubborn resistance, drove them out with a loss of about 4,000 men. The Imperialists lost 27,000 killed and wounded. *See* Cremona, Landau, Vigo Bay.

Lynn Haven Bay *American Revolutionary War*

September 5, 1781, between a British fleet of 19 ships of the line and seven frigates, under Admiral Thomas Graves, and a French fleet of 25 line-of-battle ships. Admiral Graves attacked the French as they were lying in Lynn Haven Bay but was unsuccessful, and

drew off after two hours' hard fighting, with a loss of 79 killed and 230 wounded. The French lost 22 officers and 200 men killed and wounded. Their navy was now able to land troops to support the Americans at Yorktown. *See* Yorktown, Guilford Courthouse.

Lyons *Roman Civil Wars*

Fought 197 between the legions of Britain, under Clodius Albinus, and the legions of Pannonia, under Severus, both generals having been proclaimed Emperor by their respective troops on the death of Pertinax. Albinus was defeated and slain.

Lys River *World War I*

After General von Ludendorff had failed to break through on the Somme in March 1918, he prepared to attack the sparsely held British front in Flanders and to roll it up from the north. The River Lys, about 100 feet wide, formed the boundary between the British 1st and 2nd armies. After a heavy bombardment with gas and high explosive shells from 7 pm April 7 to 4 am April 9, General Quast's 6th Army attacked a Portuguese division in the British centre, which gave way, forcing back five miles the whole of General Horne's 1st Army. April 11, General von Arnim's 4th Army joined the offensive and pushed back General Plumer's 2nd Army. Encouraged by success, von Ludendorff turned what had been planned as a secondary into a major operation, hoping to take Dunkirk, Calais and Boulogne, but five British and one Australian reinforcement divisions managed to help slow down the pace of the German advance, though the situation remained dangerous in the extreme. April 17, the Belgians threw back an attack near the Ypres salient, inflicting extremely severe casualties upon the enemy, while the British and Canadians defeated an attack on La Bassée Canal. By April 21, Foch at last sent French reinforcements to help offset the great German numerical superiority. Final German attacks with 11 divisions in mass formation were repulsed, the battle ending on April 29. The Germans had gained ten miles, a tactical success, but at a cost of 350,000 casualties. Allied losses, nine-tenths British, were 305,000. *See* Somme, Aisne III.

M

Maastricht *Netherlands War of Independence*

This city, the German Gate of the Netherlands, was besieged by the Spaniards, under Prince Alexander of Parma, March 12, 1579. It was held by a garrison of 1,000 troops and 1,200 armed burghers under Melchior, while the besiegers numbered 20,000. Two unsuccessful assaults were made April 8, which cost the Spaniards 670 officers and 4,000 men, but finally the place was taken by surprise, and a massacre followed, in which 6,000 of the inhabitants perished. *See* Gembloux, Antwerp.

Macalo *Italian Wars*

October 11, 1427, when the Venetians, under Francesco Bussone, known as Carmagnola, in a strong position near Macalo, were attacked by the Milanese, under Malatesta. The Venetians repulsed the attack, and assuming the offensive, surrounded Malatesta, and compelled him to surrender with his whole force, numbering about 10,000 men. The French signed a truce with Austria. *See* Solferino.

Madonna dell'Oleno *War of the Austrian Succession*

September 30, 1744, between the French and Spaniards, under Prince Louis de Conti and Don Philip of Spain, and the Imperialists, under the King of Sardinia. With a view to relieving Cuneo, which the allies were besieging, the King attacked their lines, and though he was defeated in the battle, he gained his object for Conti was compelled by lack of supplies to raise the siege, October 22, having suffered heavy losses from famine, flood and battle. *See* Bergen-op-Zoom, Lauffeld, Madras.

Madras I *War of the Austrian Succession*

This city was invested by the French under the Comte de la Bourdonnais, with nine ships and about 3,700 troops, mostly Europeans, September 14, 1746. It was defended by a garrison of 200, and after a week's

bombardment, surrendered September 25. The garrison lost five men only; the French not a single man. In 1748 Madras was returned to Britain in exchange for Louisbourg, Nova Scotia. *See* Louisbourg, Arcot.

Madras II *Seven Years' War*

On December 16, 1758, Madras was invested by the Comte de Lally-Tollendal with 2,000 European and 4,000 Indian troops. The garrison consisted of 4,000 men, more than half of whom were Sepoys, under Colonel Stringer Lawrence. After a bombardment lasting from January 2, 1759, to February 16, de Lally-Tollendal was on the point of ordering an assault, when the arrival of the British fleet caused him to raise the siege and retire. The garrison lost during the siege 1,341 killed and wounded. The French losses amounted to 700 Europeans besides Sepoys. *See* Wandiwash.

Madrid *Spanish Civil War*

November 7, 1936, when Nationalist General Mola's regular troops, aided by German and Italian aircraft, attacked Republican General Miaja's forces holding the capital, supported by Soviet aircraft. Most of the University City was taken by November 21, after which both sides dug in and a stalemate followed until July 6, 1937, when the Republicans launched an offensive, but were driven back with the loss of some 15,000 killed or wounded. Franco continued to besiege the city while the Nationalists fought the war throughout Spain for the next two years. March 26, 1939, after anti-communist fighting had started in Madrid, he attacked again and Republican forces quickly collapsed. The Nationalists entered Madrid March 31, ending the Civil War which began July 18, 1936. *See* Barcelona.

Mafeking *Second Boer War*

This small township was invested October, 1899, by a force of 5,000 Boers, under General Cronje, and defended by a garrison of about 700 irregulars and armed townsmen, under Colonel Baden-Powell. Later in the siege Cronje withdrew a large part of his force, leaving about 2,000 under Snyman to prosecute it. Though the bombardment was continuous, only one resolute attempt was made to penetrate the defences; when on May 12, 1900, 300 Boers under Sarel Eloff succeeded in getting within the lines, but were surrounded and forced to surrender. On May 17, the place was relieved by a cavalry column under Colonel Mahon. The garrison lost 273, the Boers about 1,000, in the course of the siege. *See* Kimberley.

Magdeburg *Thirty Years' War*

This city, held by a small Swedish garrison, under von Falkenberg, was besieged by the Imperialists, 22,000 strong, under Field Marshal Tilly, March, 1631. In May, Tilly was forced by the approach of King Gustavus Adolphus II of Sweden either to raise the siege or to attempt a storm. Choosing the latter course, an assault was delivered on May 20 under Count zu Pappenheim, and after two hours' severe fighting, in the course of which von Falkenberg was killed, the garrison was overpowered. The victory was sullied by a massacre of the unarmed inhabitants, thousands of whom perished at the hands of the Croats and Walloons. *See* Werben, Frankfort-on-Oder.

Magenta *Italian Wars of Independence*

June 4, 1859, between the 2nd French Corps d'Armée, under General MacMahon, 49,500, and the main Austrian army, under Marshal Gyulai, about 53,000. MacMahon crossed the Ticino River, attacked the Austrian position and after hard fighting drove them out of Magenta and totally defeated them with a loss of about 6,000 killed and wounded. The French lost 4,400. *See* Solferino, Venice.

Magersfontein *Second Boer War*

December 11, 1899, between 9,000 Boers, under General Cronje, and Lord Methuen's division, with the addition of the Highland Brigade. Cronje's position was exceedingly strong, and an attempt to turn it by a flank march undertaken at night led to a disaster to the Highland Brigade, who came under a heavy fire before they were extended, and lost 57 officers and over 700 men, including their brigadier, General Wauchope. Eventually the attacking force was withdrawn, without having made any impression on the Boer position. The total British losses were 68 officers and 1,011 men. The Boers admitted a loss of 320, but it was probably much heavier. *See* Modder River, Stormberg.

Magnesia *Wars of the Hellenistic Monarchies*

190 BC, between Antiochus the Great, with 80,000 troops, and 40,000 Romans under Cnaeus Domitius. Antiochus, leading the right wing, drove back the Roman left and penetrated to their camp, which he nearly succeeded in capturing. His left wing, however, was routed, and his elephants becoming unmanageable, broke the ranks of the phalanx, whereupon his whole army fled in confusion, with a loss, it is said, of 50,000 killed. The Romans lost 300 only. Antiochus ceded Asia Minor to Rome and paid an indemnity. *See* Thermopylae II.

Maharajpur I *Gwalior Campaign*

December 29, 1843, between the British, 14,000 strong with 40 guns under General Sir Hugh Gough, and the troops of Bhagerat Rao Sindhia, 18,000 strong with 100 guns. The Marathas occupied a strong position at Maharajpur, the exact locality of their lines being unknown to Sir Hugh until his troops came under fire. The British at once charged and carried the batteries, and finally routed the Gwalior infantry at a cost of 787 killed and wounded. The Marathas lost 3,000 killed and wounded, and 56 guns. *See* Punniar.

Maharajpur II *Indian Mutiny*

July 16, 1857, between 5,000 rebels under Nana Sahib and the British relieving force under General Sir Henry Havelock. Nana was entrenched across the Grand Trunk Road, and his position being too strong for a frontal attack, Havelock turned his left flank. After severe fighting the rebels were defeated, though Havelock was left with only 800 Europeans available for further service. On the following day Cawnpore was reoccupied. *See* Delhi, Cawnpore.

Mahidpur *Third British-Maratha War*

December 21, 1817, between the British, under Sir Thomas Hislop, and the army of Holkar of Indore. The Marathas, with 70 guns, were strongly posted behind the Sipra, which Sir Thomas crossed in the face of a heavy fire, and completely defeated them. The British lost 778 killed and wounded, the Marathas about 3,000.

Maida *Napoleonic Wars*

July 6, 1806, between the British expeditionary force in Calabria, 5,100 strong under Sir John Stuart, and the French 6,440-strong under General Reynier. The British fired volleys then charged with the bayonet, and the French, though veterans, failing to withstand the onslaught, broke and fled, losing very heavily in the pursuit. *See* Saalfeld, Jena.

Maidan *First British-Afghan War*

September 14, 1842, between the British, under General Nott, and 12,000 Afghans, under Shems-ud-din, who occupied the heights commanding the road to Kabul. Nott attacked and carried the Afghan position, the Afghans being driven off with heavy loss. *See* Ghazni, Jellalabad.

Main, The *Germanic War*

9 BC, when the Romans under Drusus attacked and totally routed the Marcomanni, driving them to the eastward and occupying their territory. *See* Lippe.

Maiwand *Second British-Afghan War*

July 27, 1880, between a small British force with six guns under General Burrows and the Afghan army under Ayub Khan. A Bombay native regiment was broken by a Ghazi rush, and although the 66th Regiment fought magnificently, the British were routed, with a loss of 32 officers and 939 men killed, and 17 officers and 151 men wounded. The survivors escaped with difficulty to Kandahar. *See* Kandahar.

Majuba *First Boer War*

February 27, 1881, when a British column 647 strong under Sir George Colley, posted on the summit of Majuba Hill, was attacked and driven off by the Boers under General Joubert. A strong party of young Boers stormed the hill while the fire of the defenders was kept down by a picked body of marksmen, and the British were driven from their position with heavy loss, especially during the retirement down the hillside. The casualties amounted to 223 killed and wounded, Sir George Colley being killed, and 50 prisoners. The Boer losses were very small. After this disaster an armistice was agreed to, and peace soon afterwards concluded. *See* Mafeking, Kimberley.

Malacca *Portuguese Conquests*

This city, which was defended by 30,000 Malays under Sultan Mohammed, was captured by Albuquerque, with 19 ships and 1,400 Portuguese regulars, after a very feeble defence, in 1513.

Malaga I *Spanish-Muslim Wars*

This city, defended by a Moorish garrison, under Hamet Zeli, was besieged by the Spaniards, 50,000 strong, under Ferdinand the Catholic, April 17, 1487. After an obstinate resistance, lasting for four months, the garrison was forced to surrender, and Ferdinand and Isabella entered the city August 18. The inhabitants were sold into slavery. *See* Granada, Loja, Baza.

Malaga II *War of the Spanish Succession*

August 24, 1704, between the combined British and Dutch fleets, consisting of 45 sail of the line, under Admiral Sir George Rooke, and the French fleet of 53 line-of-battle ships under Admiral the Comte de Tourville. The French admiral was endeavouring to effect a junction with the Spanish fleet, which was engaged in the siege of Gibralter, and was brought to action by Sir George Rooke off Malaga. The fighting was severe, and though no ships were lost on either side, the British gained an important strategic victory as the junction of the two hostile fleets was prevented. The British lost six officers and 687 men killed, and 18 officers and 1,645 men wounded. The French lost 191 officers and 3,048 men killed and wounded. *See* Gibraltar, Barcelona.

Malakand Pass *Chitral Campaign*

April 3, 1895, when the British expedition, under General Low, 15,000 strong, forced the pass, in northern India, which was held by about 12,000 tribesmen, with a loss of eight officers and 61 men killed and wounded. The Chitralis lost about 500.

Malakov *Crimean War*

This fort, forming an important part of the southern defences of Sevastopol, was stormed by 30,000 French under General Pélissier, September 8, 1855. The Russians, being taken by surprise, made but a feeble resistance. *See* Sevastopol.

Malavilly *Third British-Mysore War*

March 20, 1799, when the camp of the British force under Lord Harris, marching on Seringapatam, was attacked in force by Tippu Sahib. The enemy was thrown into confusion by a charge of cavalry, under General Floyd, and retired with a loss of about 1,000. The British losses were trifling. *See* Seringapatam.

Malaya *World War II*

December 8, 1941, the day after Pearl Harbor, three Japanese divisions, later increased to four, landed at Kota Bharu, north-western Malaya (now Malaysia), on Penang and in southern Thailand, and pushing General Percival's 9th and 11th Indian divisions south in a lightning jungle war, took Ipoh, 150 miles south, three weeks later. General Percival made a short stand at Kuala Lumpur, but not even British and Australian reinforcements increasing his combatant strength to 70,000 enabled him to counter the enemy's efficient jungle fighting. He evacuated the Peninsula entirely on January 31, 1942, and retired to Singapore island. The Japanese campaign had lasted seven weeks. *See* Singapore.

Maldon *Danish Invasions of Britain*

991, between the Anglo-Saxons, under Brihtnoth, and the Danes, under Olaf Triggvason and Guthmund. The Anglo-Saxons were completely defeated and Brihtnoth slain. *See* Ethandun.

Malegnano *Second War of Italian Independence*

June 8, 1859, between three French divisions, under Marshal Baraguay d'Hilliers, and the Austrians, in about equal force. After three hours' hard fighting, the Austrians were defeated and driven out of Malegnano, with heavy loss including 1,000 prisoners. The French lost 850 killed and wounded. *See* Milazzo.

Malnate,

see Varese

Maloyaroslavets *Napoleonic Wars*

October 24, 1812, between the Russians, under Marshal Kutuzov, and part of the corps of Eugène de Beauharnais, Napoleon's son-in-law, under General Delzons, about 20,000 strong. On October 19, Napoleon evacuated Moscow and marched south-west to Kaluga, de Beauharnais leading the advance. Unaware of this, and believing the force sighted at Forminskoie, 40 miles south-west of Moscow, was a foraging party, Kutuzov sent General Docturov with 12,000 infantry, 3,000 cavalry and 84 guns to surprise it. While on the road, Docturov learned this force was the Grand Army and decided to hold out until reinforcements came at the road junction and town of Maloyaroslavets, on the Lutza River.
Docturov entered the town from the south and found the French spearhead had seized a bridgehead. Fierce fighting began; the town changed hands five times. General Raevski arrived with 10,000 more Russians; once more they took the town, though not the bridgehead. De Beauharnais threw in his 15th (Italian) division, under General Pino, and by evening they had again expelled the Russians. Marshal Kutuzov arrived, decided against a pitched battle with the Grand Army next day, and to retire instead to Kaluga. The French claimed a victory, but it was a Russian strategical success, for now wishing to avoid battle Napoleon changed his line of march to the north, through Mozhaisk and Smolensk, the route of his advance that he had wished to avoid. French casualties were about 5,000, including Delzons killed; and Russian 6,000. *See* Borodino, Berezina.

Malplaquet *War of the Spanish Succession*

September 11, 1709, between the British and Imperialists, 110,000 strong with 100 guns under the Duke of Marlborough and Prince Eugène, and the French, 80,000 strong with 60 guns under Marshal Villars. Villars offered battle with the object of relieving Mons, which the allies were besieging, but while they were waiting for reinforcement from Tournai, he was enabled to entrench himself strongly on the ground he had chosen. After desperate fighting, however, the French position was carried from end to end, and they were driven out with a loss of 12,000 killed and wounded. The allies lost more than 24,000 men in the bloodiest battle of the 18th century. *See* Tournai, Brihuega.

Malta I *Ottoman Wars*

Besieged May 19, 1565, by 30,000 Turks, under Mustapha Pasha, aided by a fleet of 185 sail, under Piale, the Captain Pasha. It was defended by the Knights of Malta, under their Grand Master La Valette, and though St Elmo was taken, Valletta held out against numerous assaults until September 11, when Mustapha raised the siege. The garrison lost 5,000 men, the Turks 20,000. *See* Rhodes.

Malta II *French Revolutionary Wars*

The town of Valletta and the island of Malta seized by Napoleon on June 12, 1798, prior to the invasion of Egypt, were captured from the French on September 5, 1800 by a combined British naval and military force, under Captain George Martin, RN, and Major-General Pigott. Two line-of-battle-ships and three frigates were seized in the harbour. *See* Nile, Abukir I.

Malta III *World War II*

This British naval and air base, from which Mediterranean convoys were defended and warships were repaired, was under siege and constant air attack by Axis air forces often 250-strong from November 1940 until the end of 1942. By May 1942, the island had endured 2,470 heavy air attacks; supply convoys were blasted and many ships were sunk. The situation was often critical, but the British defeat of Axis forces in North Africa and Egypt reduced the scale of the attacks. The island held out and was awarded the George Cross. *See* Sidi Barrâni, El Alamein II.

Malvern Hill,

see Seven Days' Battle

Mandonia *Macedonian Wars*

338 BC, between the Italian Greeks of Tarentum (Taranto) under Archidamus III, King of Sparta, and the Lucanians. The Greeks were defeated and Archidamus slain. *See* Pandosia.

Mangalore *First British-Mysore War*

Besieged June 20, 1783, by Tippu Sahib with his whole army, and defended by a small British garrison, under Colonel Campbell. On the conclusion of peace between France and England, the French officer assisting Tippu withdrew, and on August 2 an armistice was arranged, during which the garrison was to receive regular supplies. This article was evaded and the defenders half starved, and after some delay Tippu renewed the siege. No attempt, however, was made to relieve the place, and after a gallant defence, Campbell surrendered January 26, 1784. *See* Porto Novo.

Manila *Spanish-American War*

May 1, 1898, between the American squadron of six ships, under Admiral Dewey, and 11 Spanish vessels, chiefly small, and unarmoured. The Spanish fleet was totally destroyed, the Americans suffering no loss. *See* Santiago de Cuba, El Caney.

Mannerheim Line *Russo-Finnish War, 1939-40*

Russia declared war against Finland, November 30, 1939, took Petsamo in the north, but was held at the Mannerheim Line, a system of concrete and steel fortifications between the Gulf of Finland and inland lakes. February 11, 1940, after a massive artillery bombardment, Marshal Timoshenko attacked with 27 divisions supported by tanks, and broke through on an 8-mile front, February 21. The Finns, whose army totalled 100,000 against the Russians' estimated one million were eventually compelled to surrender, ceding the Karelian Isthmus and Viborg. Russian casualties were about 200,000; Finnish, 24,900 killed or missing, 43,500 wounded.

Mansfield *American Civil War*

April 8, 1864, between 20,000 Federals, under General Banks, and about 8,000 Confederates, under General Taylor. Banks, while marching through difficult country, was attacked by Taylor, and utterly routed, at a cost to the assailants of less than a thousand men. Besides heavy losses in killed and wounded, the Federals lost 3,500 prisoners, 22 guns, and 220 waggons of stores and ammunition. This battle ended the fighting west of the Mississippi. *See* Port Hudson.

Mansûra *Seventh Crusade*

In 1250, between the French under Louis IX and the Muslims. The town of Mansûra was seized by the Comte d'Artois, but being surrounded, he and the knights with him were killed. The king meanwhile had seized the Saracen camp but was unable to hold his ground, and was driven back to Damietta. In the course of his retreat, however, he was surrounded and taken prisoner by the Saracens, with his whole army. *See* Tunis.

Mantinea I *Peloponnesian War*

418 BC, between 10,000 Spartans and Tegeans, under Agis, and an equal force of Athenians, under Laches and Nicostratus. The Spartan left was completely routed, but the Athenian centre and left failed to withstand the Spartan attack, and but for the defeat of Agis' left wing, would have been surrounded and captured. In the end the Spartans gained a signal victory. Laches and Nicostratus both fell in the action. *See* Syracuse.

Mantinea II *Wars of the Greek City States*

362 BC, between the Boeotians, under Epaminondas, and the combined forces of Athens, Sparta, and Mantinea. Epaminondas attacked strongly with his left, holding back his right in reserve, and after the driving back of the Mantineans, routed the Spartans in the centre. The Athenians were hardly engaged, but the Boeotian victory was

complete. In the pursuit Epaminondas fell and the loss of the great leader so disheartened the Boeotians that they did not further press their victory. *See* Cynoscephalae I.

Mantinea III *Wars of the Achaean League*

208 BC, between the Achaeans, under Philopoemen, and the Spartans, under Machanidas. The Achaeans drove the Spartans into a ravine in great disorder, and routed them with a loss of 4,000 killed, among whom was Machanidas. *See* Larissus.

Mantua *French Revolutionary Wars*

This city was invested by Napoleon June 4, 1796, and was defended by 14,000 Austrians, 500 guns, under General Canto d'Irles. The siege was vigorously prosecuted, but the approach of Field Marshal Count von Wurmser with an Austrian army of 30,000 forced Napoleon to concentrate his forces, and he raised the siege July 31. After a brief campaign, which resulted in the dispersal of von Wurmser's army, that general, with the remnant of his forces, was shut up in the city which was again closely invested on September 19. Von Wurmser held out till his provisions were exhausted, when, on February 2, 1797, he surrendered, with 20,000 men, of whom only 10,000 were fit for service. It was computed that 27,000 perished during the siege. Having practically finished his conquest of northern Italy, Napoleon marched against Austria. *See* Lodi, Brig of; Rivoli.

Maogamalcha *Persian Wars*

This fortress, defended by a Persian garrison, and considered impregnable, was besieged by the Romans under the Emperor Julian in 363. A mine was carried from the trenches under the ramparts, and three cohorts broke through into the streets, whereupon the garrison deserted the ramparts and the besiegers entered. The place was sacked, and afterwards razed to the ground. All Roman claims to territory east of the Tigris were ceded. *See* Amida.

Marathon *Persian-Greek Wars*

September, 490 BC, between the Athenians and Plataeans, 10,000 and 1,000 strong respectively, under Miltiades, and the army of Darius Hystaspes, about 60,000 in number, under Datis, 20,000 in action. Being greatly outnumbered, Miltiades altered the usual arrangement of the Greek line, so as to extend his wings across the whole width of the valley in which the battle was fought, and thus escape being outflanked. To effect this he was forced to weaken his centre, which was repulsed, but both his wings drove back the invaders, and then fell upon and routed the victorious Persian centre. The Persians fled in confusion to their ships, which they succeeded in launching, and escaped with a loss of 6,400. The Athenians lost 192 only, and inspired other Greek states to resist. *See* Thermopylae.

Marcianopolis *Gothic Invasion of Thrace*

376, between the Romans, under Lupicinus, and the Goths, under Fritigern. The Romans were totally defeated, but stood their ground to the last, and were cut to pieces almost to a man. Lupicinus fled as soon as the ultimate success of the Goths became apparent. *See* Hadrianople.

Mardis *War of the Two Empires*

In 315, shortly after the battle of Cibalis, between Constantine, Emperor of the West, and Licinius, Emperor of the East. Constantine moved a body of 5,000 men round his opponent's flank, and attacked him simultaneously in front and rear. The Illyrian veterans formed a double front, and held their ground, though with heavy loss, till nightfall, when Licinius, having lost thousands of his best troops, drew off his army towards the mountains of Macedonia. The consequence of this defeat was the acquisition by Constantine of Pannonia, Dalmatia, Dacia, Macedonia and Greece. *See* Cibalis.

Marengo *French Revolutionary Wars*

June 14, 1800, between 28,000 French with 15 guns, under Napoleon, and 31,000 Austrians, under General Mélas, with 100 guns. The Austrians attacked, and drove back in disorder the first line under General Victor, and, following up their success, a serious defeat for Napoleon seemed inevitable, when the arrival of the reserve division under General Desaix turned the scale. Under cover of his attack, the broken divisions reformed, and overwhelmed by General Kellermann's cavalry attacks, the Austrians were finally repulsed at all points, and fled in disorder. Desaix was killed at the head of his troops. Some 7,000 French and 6,000 Austrians were killed and wounded. About 8,000 Austrian prisoners were taken. France regained control of much of northern Italy. *See* Montebello, Höchstädt.

Mareth Line *World War II*

Field Marshal Rommel had deployed his Axis forces behind the old French frontier position known as the Mareth Line after his defeat in Libya. From here he broke out to defeat the US 1st and 34th divisions at Kasserine Pass (February 20) and then, on March 6–7, attacked the 8th Army at Medenine, only to lose 52 tanks and have to pull back. On March 20, General Sir Bernard Montgomery attacked frontally with 30th Corps, having sent General Freyberg's NZ division, the 8th Armoured Brigade and General Leclerc's Free French forces on a 200-mile southerly flanking movement which turned the Mareth Line at El Hamma on March 26. The first frontal attack having failed, Montgomery reinforced his southerly attack with the 1st Armoured Division supported by aerial bombardment, and attacked frontally again. Threatened with encirclement the Axis forces withdrew to Wadi Akarit, with the loss of 2,500 prisoners. Shortly after, Rommel was ordered home, being replaced by the Italian General Messe, who retreated to Enfidaville. *See* Tunisia, El Alamein II.

Margate *Hundred Years' War*

March 24, 1387, when Richard II's naval commanders, the earls of Arundel and Nottingham, defeated in a naval battle off this Kentish seaport a combined Franco-Castilian fleet sent to invade England, seizing nearly 100 ships and ending the invasion menace. This and Arundel's other successes made his and the Duke of Gloucester's party a threat to

King Richard and his followers. *See* La Rochelle, Radcot Bridge.

Margus *Roman Civil Wars*

May 285, between the legions of the Emperor Carinus and those of Diocletian, who had been raised to the purple by his soldiers. The troops of Diocletian, wasted by the Persian War, were all but overpowered by the fresher legions of Carinus, but the defection during the battle of one of his generals turned the scale, and Carinus himself being killed by an officer whom he had wronged, Diocletian gained a complete victory. *See* Palmyra.

Mariana Islands *World War II*

June 15, 1944, having retaken New Guinea, General MacArthur, making a 1,000-mile jump to the north, landed 20,000 US troops on Saipan, most northerly of the three biggest islands, which were headquarters of Japan's Central Pacific fleet, held by the 31st Army, under General Obata. The Japanese attacked in strength at once, but were driven back by the early hours and the Americans extended their beachhead. Reinforced by the 27th Infantry division, the Americans took Aslito airfield on June 18, support aircraft starting to use it by June 23. The southern half of Saipan was cleared of Japanese by June 27 and US forces then drove on towards the northernmost part. Resistance ended with the *hara-kiri* of Admirals Nagumo and Saito and the mass *hara-kiri* of Japanese soldiers on July 6 off Marpi Point. Only 1,000 Japanese prisoners were taken. US casualties were about 14,000 killed or wounded.

Guam, southernmost island, held by 19,000 Japanese, was invaded by two US divisions on July 21 and retaken by August 10 at the cost of 7,800 casualties. Tinian, south of Saipan, held by 9,000 Japanese, was invaded by two Marine divisions on July 24 and occupied by July 31, with just over 2,000 Americans killed or wounded. More than 40,000 Japanese were killed or committed *hara-kiri* in the Mariana battles, while simultaneously the battle of the Philippine Sea was waged. *See* Philippine Sea, Tarawa-Makin, Kwajalein-Eniwetok.

Maria Zell *Napoleonic Wars*

November 8, 1805, during the French advance on Vienna, between Marshal Davout's corps and the Austrian corps under General von Meerfeld. The Austrians were defeated and driven off in disorder, leaving 4,000 prisoners in the hands of the French.

Mariendahl *Thirty Years' War*

May 2, 1645, between the French under Marshal Vicomte de Turenne and the Imperialists under Field Marshal Baron von Mercy. Turenne, who had 3,000 infantry and eight regiments of horse, was surprised in his camp by Mercy at 2 am and compelled to beat a disastrous retreat, with the loss of almost all his infantry, 1,200 cavalry and all his artillery and baggage. *See* Lens.

Marignano *Italian Wars*

September 13 and 14, 1515, between 32,500 French, under Francis I, and about 22,200 Swiss. The Swiss attacked the French camp, and forcing the lines, fought till midnight without decisive result. On the morning of the 14th the battle was renewed, and the Swiss were on the point of success, when the arrival of a small force of Venetians obliged them to withdraw. The French lost 6,000 men, and the Swiss 12,500, including 1,200 who perished in the flames of a village they were defending after the repulse of the attack. Marshal Trivulzio, who commanded a wing of the French army, called the action the 'Battle of Giants'. The French recovered the Duchy of Milan. *See* Novara.

Marne I *World War I*

Five German armies surged forward into France from near Amiens to Verdun, during August 20–24, 1914, after the Battle of the Frontiers, led by General von Kluck's 1st Army on the right (north). Defending France were: left, between Paris and Amiens, General Maunoury's 6th Army, then to his right Sir John French's British Expeditionary Force, General Franchet d'Esperey's 5th, the 9th, General Foch, the 4th, General de Langle de Cary and the 3rd, General Sarrail. On August 30, Maunoury's 6th was withdrawn to reinforce the Paris garrison, then on September 1, in face of increased German pressure, Marshal Joffre, Allied C-in-C, ordered the retreat to go on to a line south of the Seine. On September 3, General Galliéni, Military Governor of Paris, learned through aviation reports that the German army had altered course to swing east of Paris instead of west as planned, thus moving across his front and exposing their right flank.

This departure from the Schlieffen Plan proved the Germans' undoing. Galliéni at once urged upon the reluctant Joffre a swift counter-attack upon the exposed enemy flank. At first refusing, Joffre agreed later and Galliéni issued orders to Maunoury's 6th Army at 0830 on September 4. Six hundred Paris taxis were commandeered to help move a division to the front, but Joffre's orders were not received by the other generals until the early hours of September 5. By then both Sir John French and General Franchet d'Esperey felt it was too late and went on retreating while Maunoury's 6th Army was already moving forward against the enemy flank.

The British finally turned round to join in the attack next day, September 6. General Kluck's 1st Army had fallen back at Galliéni's attack, leaving a gap of 30 miles between him and von Bülow's 2nd Army, into which on the 9th the British were moving. On top of untrue rumours that British and Russian armies were landing on the Belgian coast in their rear, this stampeded the German high command into ordering von Bülow's and von Kluck's armies to withdraw. Meanwhile, in the east, near Nancy, an attack by General Prince Rupprecht's 6th Army was defeated by accurate French artillery fire and called off on September 8. General Sarrail's army held on at Verdun and threw back the German 5th Army. But in the centre, General Foch gave way before a German counter-attack by von Hausen's right and Bülow's left at Marais de St Gond. It looked dangerous until fortunately the German High Command ordered a general retirement. The chance of a quick end to the war had gone. Casualties: German about 800,000; French and British 1,080,000. See Aisne.

Marne II *World War I*

July 15, 1918, when in a last effort to try to overwhelm the Allies, Ludendorff launched an all-out offensive with three armies on each side of Reims to try to cross the Marne with two converging attacks, one on General Gouraud's 1st Army on the 26-mile front east of Reims; the other on a 22-mile front south-west of the city above Château-Thierry, both with 15 divisions. Gouraud's 1st Army stopped the enemy with skilful artillery fire, but south-west General von Boehn's 7th Army battled forward across the Marne between Rueil and Château-Thierry, until they were finally held by General Mitry's French 9th Army aided by American, British and Italian divisions. By the evening of July 17 the Entente forces were counter-attacking all along the line. The next day General Foch, Allied C-in-C, launched a massive offensive with four French armies and 14 Allied divisions supported by 350 tanks. It forced a retreat upon the Germans which ended only when four months later they sued for peace. See Amiens.

Marosch, The *Conquest of Dacia*

Fought 101, between the Dacians, under Decebalus, and the Roman, under Trajan. The Dacians were utterly routed, and driven across the river with heavy loss.

Marsaglia *Wars of Louis XIV*

October 4, 1693, between the French, under Marshal de Catinat, and the Austrians, Spanish, and English, under the Duke of Savoy. The allies, who were inferior in numbers, were attacked by the French, and after severe fighting driven across the Po River with a loss of about 6,000. The Duke of Schomberg and Lord Warwick were taken prisoners. The loss of the French was slightly less. See Neerwinden.

Mars-la-Tour *Franco-Prussian War*

August 18, 1870, between 80,000 French, under Marshal Bazaine, and the 3rd and 10th German Army corps, of about equal numbers, under General von Alvensleben. The Germans, though at times very hard pressed, succeeded in holding their ground, and prevented the French breaking through to the west. The battle is chiefly remarkable for the desperate charges of the German cavalry, and especially of von Bredow's brigade, against the French infantry, under cover of which the shattered German infantry was enabled to re-form. That night Bazaine withdrew to Metz, giving the Germans a tactical victory. The losses were about equal, amounting to about 16,000 killed and wounded on each side. The action is also known as the Battle of Vionville. *See* Gravelotte, Sedan.

Marston Moor *English Civil War*

July 2, 1644, between 18,000 Royalists, under Prince Rupert, and 27,000 Parliamentarians and their Scottish allies, under Manchester, Leven and Lord Fairfax. For the first time in the war, Rupert's cavalry were repulsed by Cromwell's Ironsides, and though the right wing under Sir Thomas Fairfax was broken, the left and centre were victorious, and the Royalists were totally defeated, with a loss said to be about 4,000. This victory gave Parliament complete control of the north. *See* Cropredy Bridge, Lostwithiel.

Martinesti *Ottoman Wars*

September 23, 1789, between the Austrians and Russians, 27,000 strong, under the Prince of Coburg and General Suvorov, and the Turks, 70,000 strong, under Osman Pasha. The allies stormed the Turkish entrenchments, and drove out the defenders, of whom 7,000 were killed and wounded, while 8,000 were drowned in crossing the Rymna. The victors lost 617 killed and wounded. *See* Rimnitz, Focsani.

Martinique I *French Revolutionary Wars*

This island was re-taken from the French in 1794, by a combined naval and military force under Admiral Sir John Jervis and General Sir George Grey, with a loss to the victors of six officers and 37 men killed and wounded. *See* Belle-Île-en-Mer III.

Martinique II *Napoleonic Wars*

Having been restored to France at the Peace of Amiens, Martinique was again taken by the British, February 24, 1809, the force engaged being under Admiral Sir A. J. Cochrane and Lieut.-General Beckwith. It was restored to France in 1814.

Maserfield *Teutonic Invasion of Britain*

642, between the Northumbrians, under Oswald, and the Mercians, under Penda. The latter were defeated, and Penda slain. *See* Heavenfield.

Masulipatam *Seven Years' War*

This fortress about 200 miles north of Madras, held by a French garrison, under Marshal de Conflans, was besieged by the British, about 2,500 strong, under Colonel Forde, in March, 1759. After a fortnight's bombardment the place was taken by storm, the resistance being very feeble, and de Conflans surrendered with his whole force, which considerably outnumbered the besiegers. One hundred and twenty guns were taken in the fortress. *See* Wandiwash, Pondicherry.

Masurian Lakes I *World War I*

September 5, 1914, when Field-Marshal von Hindenburg's reinforced German 8th Army counter-attacked General Rennenkampf's Russian 1st Army's offensive against East Prussia between Königsberg (now Kaliningrad) and the Masurian Lakes. Rennenkampf ordered a general withdrawal, counter-attacked the German centre on September 10, and held their advance, many Russian troops thus escaping encirclement. By September 13, they had withdrawn from East Prussia, but Russia lost about 120,000 troops; the Germans 10,000. General Jilinski was removed for having mismanaged the Russian offensive in East Prussia. *See* Tannenberg, Galicia.

Masurian Lakes II *World War I*

February 7, 1915, as part of a plan to knock Russia out of the war, two German armies attacked from East Prussia the Russian 10th Army north of the Masurian Lakes. The Russian XX Corps held the Germans in Augustov Forest while the rest of the army escaped. Russian casualties were heavy; the Germans suffered badly from exposure. *See* Gorlice.

Matapan, Cape *World War II*

March 27–28, 1941, when an Italian fleet under Admiral Riccardi trying to intercept a

British convoy to Greece, encountered Admiral Cunningham's battle fleet of three battleships, four cruisers, and an aircraft carrier. After damaging and slowing down the Italian fleet by air attack, the British warships surprised them at 10.25 pm on March 28 and opened fire at 3,800 yards. The battleship *Vittorio Veneto*, damaged by air attack, managed to escape, but the British sank three 8-inch-gun cruisers, two smaller cruisers and two destroyers. The British lost two naval aircraft, but no seamen. They rescued 900 Italian sailors from the water. Italian losses were some 2,400. The action guaranteed Allied naval superiority in the Mediterranean. *See* Taranto.

Matchevitz *First Polish Rising*

October 10, 1794, between the Russians, under Baron de Fersen, and the Poles, under Kosciusko. The Poles, after hard fighting, were totally defeated, leaving 6,000 dead upon the field, while Kosciusko was severely wounded. *See* Warsaw I.

Matchin *Ottoman Wars*

July 10, 1791, between the Turks, under Yusuf Pasha, and the Russians, under Prince Repnin. The left and centre of the Turkish army held its ground manfully, and the victory was long in doubt, but a brilliant charge of the Russian left, under General Kutuzov, drove back the Turks who were defeated with heavy loss. *See* Rimnitz.

Maxen *Seven Years' War*

November 20, 1759, between the Austrians, under Marshal Daun, and the Prussians, under General Finck. Daun surrounded Finck's position, and after comparatively little fighting compelled him to surrender with over 15,000 men including 17 generals. Seventeen guns were captured. The casualties on both sides were very small. *See* Kunersdorf.

Maya, Colde *Peninsular War*

July 25, 1813, between a British division, under General Stewart, and the French divisions of Generals d'Armagnac, Abbé and Maransin under Marshal Soult. The French,

at a cost of 1,500 men, forced the pass of Maya, driving the British with a loss of 1,400 men and four guns. *See* Vitoria.

Maypo *Chilean War of Independence*

April 5, 1818, between the Chilean Patriots, 9,000 strong, under José de San Martin, and 6,000 Spanish Royalists, under General Osorio. The Spaniards were totally defeated with a loss of 1,000 killed and 2,350 prisoners, the Chileans losing over 1,000 killed and wounded. The battle won the independence of Chile. *See* Chacabuco.

Medellín *Peninsular War*

March 28, 1809, between the French, under Marshal Victor, and 30,000 Spaniards, under Cuesta. The Spaniards soon gave way, and were mercilessly sabred in the pursuit by the French cavalry, losing, it is said, 18,000 killed and wounded. The French lost 300 only. *See* Corunna.

Medenine *World War II*

March 6, 1943, when Field Marshal Rommel's Axis forces having defeated the US 1st and 34th Divisions at Kasserine Pass bore down on the 8th Army at Medenine. General Montgomery had foreseen this possibility and had made ready to fight a defensive battle. When on March 6 the Axis forces attacked, they were caused by a simple stratagem to launch all their three armoured divisions against British positions defended by nearly 500 anti-tank guns. Rommel suffered heavy losses and quickly withdrew. *See* Mareth Line.

Medina *Mohammed's Conquest of Arabia*

Siege was laid to this town in 625 by 10,000 Koreish, under Abu Sophian. It was defended by Mohammed with 3,000 Muslims, and during the space of 20 days several half-hearted assaults were easily repulsed. At the end of this time Abu Sophian withdrew, and the Koreish made no further attempt to interfere with the progress of Mohammedanism. *See* Siffin.

162

Medola *French Revolutionary Wars*

August 5, 1796, between the French, 23,000 strong, under Napoleon, and 25,000 Austrians, under Field Marshal von Wurmser. The Austrians were totally defeated, and driven back to Roveredo, with a loss of 2,000 killed and wounded, 1,000 prisoners and 20 guns. Before this defeat von Wurmser had succeeded in revictualling Mantua, but at very heavy cost, the Austrian losses during the three days' fighting from the 3rd to the 5th amounting to 20,000 men and 60 guns. *See* Caldiero.

Meeanee *Sind Campaign*

February 17, 1843, between 2,800 British and Indian troops, under General Sir Charles Napier, and about 20,000 Beluchis, under the Emirs of Sind. The infantry were at one time almost overpowered by the overwhelming numbers of the enemy, who attacked with great bravery, but they were rescued by a charge of the 9th Bengal cavalry, and in the end the Beluchis were routed with a loss of 5,000 men and several guns. The British lost 256 killed and wounded. Mainly, this war was fought to give the British a much-needed victory after the Afghan disaster. *See* Dubba, Hyderabad.

Meerut *Second Mongul Invasion of India*

Besieged in 1398 by the Tatars, under Tamerlane. It was considered impregnable, and Tamerlane commenced mining operations, but these methods were too slow for his followers, who by means of scaling ladders carried the fortress by storm, and massacred all the inhabitants. Tamerlane afterwards completed his mines and destroyed all the defences. *See* Delhi I, Baghdad.

Megaletaphrus *First Messenian War*

740 BC, between the Messenians, under Aristomenes, and the Spartans. The Messenians were surrounded and cut to pieces, Aristomenes escaping with a few followers.

Megalopolis I *Macedonian Wars*

331 BC, in the attempt of the Spartans, aided by the Arcadians, Achaeans and Eleians, to shake off the Macedonian yoke, during Alexander's absence in Asia. The allies, under Agis, King of Sparta, were besieging Megalopolis, which had declined to join the league, when they were attacked by the Macedonians, under Antipater, and completely routed, Agis falling in the battle, Greek resistance in Alexander's lifetime ending. *See* Thebes, Arbela.

Megalopolis II *Wars of the Achaean League*

226 BC, between the Spartans under Cleomenes and the forces of the Achaean League under Aratus. The Achaeans early gained an advantage, and the Spartans fled, pursued by the light troops. These however being unsupported, the Spartans turned and routed them and then overwhelmed the Achaean hoplites in their turn with enormous slaughter. *See* Megalopolis I.

Melanthias *Sclavonian Invasion*

559, between the Imperial troops, under Belisarius, and the Sclavonians and Bulgarians, under Zabergan, Prince of Bulgaria. The barbarians assailed the Roman lines, but were easily repulsed, and so precipitate was their flight that only about 500 fell. *See* Rome IV.

Melitene *Persian-Byzantine Wars*

578, between the Imperial troops under Tiberius and the Persians under Chosroes. After a somewhat indecisive battle, at the end of which each side had held its ground, Chosroes, owing to his heavy losses, found it necessary to retire during the night. The battle was, however, signalized by an exploit of a Scythian chief, in command of the Roman left wing, who at the head of his cavalry charged through the Persian ranks, plundered the royal tent, and then cut his way out through the opposing hosts. *See* Nineveh.

Memphis I *Athenian Expedition to Egypt*

This city was captured 459 BC by an Athenian fleet of 200 ships, which sailed up the Nile to the assistance of Inaros, who had raised the standard of revolt against Persia. The citadel, however, held out until 456 BC, when a Persian army under Magabyzus defeated the Athenians and drove them out of Memphis. *See* Eurymedon.

Memphis II *Muslim Conquest of Egypt*

In 638, Amrou, lieutenant of the Caliph Omar, with 8,000 Muslims, invested the city, and after a siege of seven months in the course of which the besiegers were nearly overwhelmed by the rising of the Nile, the place was taken by assault. On the site of the Muslim encampment were laid the foundations of Old Cairo.

Memphis III *American Civil War*

A naval action fought June 6, 1862, between eight Confederate armed vessels, under Commodore Montgomery, and 10 Federal gun-boats, under Commodore Davis. Only one of the Confederate vessels escaped destruction, and Memphis fell. *See* Fair Oaks.

Mentana *Italian Wars of Independence*

November 3, 1867, north-east of Rome, between 10,000 Garibaldians, under Garibaldi, and the French and Papal troops, 5,000 strong, under General Kanzler. Garibaldi was totally defeated, a result largely due to the brilliant work of 1,500 Papal Zouaves, who drove them out of position after position. The Garibaldians lost 1,100 killed and wounded, and 1,000 prisoners. The allies' losses were only 182 killed and wounded, of which the Papal troops lost 144. In August 1870, the Franco-German War caused the withdrawal of French troops from Italy. Italian patriots took Rome and it was made the capital of the kingdom. *See* Rome, Venice.

Merida *Spanish-Muslim Wars*

This town was besieged in 712 by 18,000 Moors, under Musa. After a defeat in the open plain before the city, the Spaniards made a long and obstinate defence, which cost the besiegers many lives, but in the end they were forced by famine to surrender. *See* Tours.

Mersa Matrûh *World War II*

June 25, 1942, when Field Marshal Rommel's Axis forces advanced from their victory at Tobruk five days earlier to attack General Auchinleck's four British divisions along a line running from Mersa Matrûh on the Egyptian coast 40 miles south-west into the desert. The German 90th Light Division pushed through the British centre, but was held next day. Auchinleck had given his commanders orders to avoid a standing fight, and to battle the enemy while in retreat between Matrûh and the El Alamein-Qattara depression. General Gott, commanding 13th Corps in the south, unfortunately started the withdrawal when threatened by the 21st Panzer with a mere 21 tanks. The other corps were forced to withdraw as well, so that the position was abandoned and Rommel gained an easy victory. *See* El Alamein I, Gazala, Tobruk III.

Merseburg *Wars of the German States*

In 934, between the Germans under Henry I, the Fowler, and the Hungarian invaders. The Hungarians were completely defeated, with heavy loss, and withdrew from Germany, which they did not again invade for twenty years.

Merta *Mughal Invasion of the Deccan*

This strong fortress, belonging to the Rajput Rajah of Malwar, was besieged in 1561, by Sharf-ud-Din Hussein, one of the generals of Akbar Khan. The place held out for several months, but was then forced by famine to capitulate. One of the Malwar chiefs, however, refused all terms, and cut his way out at the head of 500 men, of whom 250 fell in the enterprise.

Merton *Danish Invasions of Britain*

In 871, between the West Saxons, under Alfred, and the Danish invaders. After a severe battle the Danes were victorious. *See* Reading.

Messina I *Aragonese Conquest of Sicily*

October 2, 1284, between the Sicilian fleet, under the Grand Admiral, Roger de Lauria, and the French fleet, under Charles of Anjou. The Sicilians, who largely outnumbered the French, totally defeated them, burning or destroying practically the whole of their fleet. Charles of Anjou was captured, and henceforth made no further attempt to re-establish his authority in Sicily, which fell to the kingdom of Aragon. *See* Tagliacozzo, Alghero.

Messina II *War of the Quadruple Alliance*,

see Cape Passero

Messines *World War I*

June 7, 1917, when Field Marshal Haig, needing to drive the enemy from Messines ridge in order to break free of the Ypres salient, exploded 19 mines beneath their lines at dawn, to crown 10 days' artillery bombardment. New Zealand troops of the 2nd Army cleared the ruins of the German lines by 7 a.m. and a few days later Australian troops drove the Germans from all their positions in the salient. All in all, it was a limited tactical victory. *See* Ypres II & III, Aisne III.

Metaurus *Second Punic War*

207 BC, between 50,000 Romans under Claudius Nero and Marcus Livius, and the Carthaginians in rather smaller force under Hasdrubal. The Carthaginians were surprised at early dawn while endeavouring to find a ford in the Metaurus, and being vigorously attacked were totally routed, Hasdrubal being slain. The completeness of the victory was due to Nero, who being in command of the right wing, where the ground prevented his getting to close quarters, and seeing the Roman left hard pressed by Hasdrubal's best troops, led the major part of his force round the Roman rear, and fell upon Hasdrubal's right, routing him utterly. The victory gave Rome supremacy over Carthage. *See* Zama.

Methven *Wars of Scottish Independence*

June 19, 1306, when a small Scottish force, under King Robert Bruce, recently crowned at Scone, was attacked and defeated by the English in superior force. *See* Loudon Hill.

Metz *Franco-Prussian War*

This fortress was invested by the Germans after the defeat of Marshal Bazaine at Gravelotte on August 18, 1870, and after several fruitless attempts to break through the German lines had been repulsed, Bazaine surrendered to Prince Frederick Charles on October 26, with three marshals, 6,000 officers, and 173,000 men. The Germans took 56 eagles, 622 field guns, 72 mitrailleuses, 876 pieces of fortress artillery, and about 300,000 rifles. Marshal Bazaine was convicted of treason and sentenced to 20 years' imprisonment after the war. *See* Gravelotte, Sedan.

Meuse-Argonne Forest *World War I*

Marshal Foch, with Field-Marshal Haig, had planned four major operations in mid-September, 1918, in an effort to break the Hindenburg line and bring the war to a close. These were a Belgian attack at Ypres and along the coast; a British thrust between Cambrai and St Quentin, and a French and American associated offensive in the Argonne and on the Meuse. The American front, General Pershing's 1st Army, ran for 17 miles from Forges on the Meuse to the centre of the Argonne, from where General Gouraud's French 4th Army extended to Auberive on the Suippe. By October 31 the US forces had advanced 10 miles and cleared the Argonne Forest, while the French had driven the Germans back 20 miles to the Aisne. Meantime the Belgians had forced the Germans to abandon Ostend, Zeebrugge and Bruges. Soon the Germans were in retreat all along the western front. US losses were over 110,000, the Germans' about 100,000. *See* Cambrai-St Quentin, St Mihiel, Marne II.

Mexico *Conquest of Mexico*

June 20, 1520, when the Spaniards under Cortés, who were evacuating Mexico during the night, were attacked by the Aztecs, and suffered heavy loss. The Spaniards called this event the 'Noche Triste'.

Michelberg *Napoleonic Wars*

October 16, 1805, when Marshal Ney's corps stormed the heights of the Michelberg at the same time that Lannes carried the Frauenberg, driving the Austrians back into Ulm, where on the 17th General Mack capitulated with 30,000 men. *See* Ulm.

Middelburg *Netherlands War of Independence*

This fortress, the last stronghold in Walcheren to hold out for the Spanish king, was besieged by the Patriots in the winter of 1593. It was defended by a garrison under Colonel Mondragon, who in spite of a gallant resistance and numerous attempts to relieve him, was forced by famine to surrender, February 18, 1594. *See* Zutphen, Turnhout.

Midway Island *World War II*

June 4, 1942, when Japan bore down on this US base 1,000 miles north-west of Pearl Harbor in the Central Pacific, with the object of defeating the remnants of the US Pacific Fleet and extending the chain of islands which safeguarded her conquests. The biggest naval operation mounted by the Japanese navy, it gave Admirals Yamamoto and Nagumo a force of 162 warships and auxiliaries, including 12 transports with 5,000 troops, and four carriers, against US Admiral Nimitz's 76, with three carriers, though he could also call on about 100 Midway-based aircraft.
US experts' breach of the Japanese naval cypher had revealed Yamamoto's plans. These were to draw the US fleet north by a diversionary attack on the western and eastern Aleutians, especially Dutch Harbour, while the main fleet bore down on Midway Island. Having safeguarded the landings there, it would await and destroy the US fleet returning from the Aleutians. But refusing to be drawn, Nimitz left the Aleutians to the North Pacific Force and awaited the Japanese north-east of Midway.
Unaware of this, on June 4, then 240 miles north-west, Nagumo sent 108 aircraft on a preliminary attack on Midway. An American reconnaissance pilot spotted the fleet. 100 US bombers took off from Midway in three waves against Nagumo, but scored no hits, lost about half their number. Just as his aircraft had returned from Midway for refuelling and re-arming, Nagumo learned that a fleet of 10 US warships was approaching. By midday the aircraft from *Yorktown* and *Enterprise* had sunk all four Japanese carriers with 250

aircraft, their full complement. Lacking air cover for his battleships, Yamamoto was compelled to withdraw. The US lost *Yorktown*, 150 aircraft and one destroyer; the Japanese lost 275 aircraft, four carriers, the cruiser *Mikuma*. American casualties were 307 men; Japanese over 4,000. The battle was a turning point in the war, since it opened the way for an American counter-attack in the Pacific. *See* Aleutian Islands, Coral Sea, Solomon Islands.

Milazzo *Italian Wars of Independence*

July 20, 1860, between the Italian Volunteers, under Garibaldi, and the Neapolitans, under General Bosco. The Neapolitans occupied a strongly entrenched position, which Garibaldi succeeded in turning, the Neapolitans being totally defeated. *See* Castelfidardo.

Miletopolis *First Mithridatic War*

86 BC, between the Romans, under Flavius Fimbria, and the Pontic troops, under Mithridates. The Romans gained a complete victory. *See* Orchomenus.

Millesimo *French Revolutionary Wars*

April 13, 1796, when the divisions of generals Augereau, Masséna and Laharpe attacked the Austrians, strongly entrenched, under General Colli, and after severe fighting, drove them back, thus cutting Colli's communications with General Beaulieu, the Austrian Commander-in-Chief. The Austro-Sardinians lost about 6,000 men and 30 guns, and all effective co-operation between the two wings was at an end. Also called the Battle of Monte Lezino. *See* Montenotte, Lodi.

Mill Springs *American Civil War*

January 19, 1862, between the Federals, about 4,000 strong, under General Thomas, and 4,500 Confederates, under General Crittenden. The Confederates attacked, and at first drove back the Federals, but reinforcements arriving, Thomas repulsed the assailants with considerable loss, capturing 12 guns. The Federals lost 246 only. This was the first considerable defeat suffered by the Confederates in the war. *See* Fort Donelson.

166

Minden *Seven Years' War*

August 1, 1759, between the French, 54,000 strong, 170 guns, under Marshal the Marquis de Contades, and the Hanoverians, British and Prussians, 42,500 strong, 187 guns, under Ferdinand of Brunswick. Ferdinand detached a force of 10,000 men to threaten de Contades' rear, and then, attacking strongly, broke the first line of the French. But for the failure of the allies' cavalry to advance, the French would have been routed. As it was, they were able to rally, and effect an orderly retreat, though with a loss of 7,086 killed, wounded and prisoners, 43 guns and 17 standards. The allies lost 2,762, fully a half of this number being in the ranks of the six English regiments present, who bore the brunt of the battle. The victory saved Hanover. *See* Kunersdorf.

Minorca I *Seven Years' War*

This island, garrisoned by 2,800 British troops under General Blakeney, was invested by the French under the Marshal Duc de Richelieu, May, 1756. On May 20, a British squadron of 15 line-of-battle ships and three sloops, under Admiral Byng, attacked Richelieu's blockading squadron of 12 sail of the line and five frigates. The attack, however, was conducted with so little resolution that Byng failed and withdrew. Blakeney was shortly afterwards forced to surrender, Byng was tried by court-martial, condemned and shot and Minorca was occupied by the French. *See* Lobositz.

Minorca II *American Revolutionary War*

Having been restored to England by the Treaty of Paris in 1762, Minorca was again recaptured in 1782 by a force of 12,000 French and Spaniards, the garrison, under General Murray, being only 700 strong. Murray made a sturdy defence, but was forced to surrender on February 5, 1782, after six months. *See* Gibraltar.

Miohosaki *Oshikatsa's Rebellion*

September, 764, between the Japanese rebels, under Oshikatsa, and the Imperial troops, under Saiki-no-Sanya. The rebels were totally routed, and Oshikatsa and his son slain.

Miraflores *Peruvian-Chilean War*

January 15, 1881, between the Chileans, under General Baquedano, and the Peruvians, under General Caçeres. The Peruvians were totally defeated, losing 3,000 killed and wounded, while the victors lost 500 killed and 1,625 wounded. Following up their victory, the Chileans occupied Lima on the 17th and the war came to an end. *See* Tacna.

Missionary Ridge,

see Chattanooga

Missolonghi *Greek War of Independence*

Besieged in 1821 by a force of 11,000 Turks under Omar Brionis Pasha, and defended by a small Greek garrison under Mavrocordatos. The little garrison made so gallant a defence that at the end of two months Omar was forced to raise the siege. On April 27, 1825, the town was again besieged by the Turks and was again most obstinately defended by the garrison and inhabitants. So little progress was made that it was found necessary to call for the aid of the Egyptian army, under Ibrahim, son of Mehemet Ali. It was not, however, till three months after his arrival that it was finally taken by storm, April 23, 1826, having held out for all but a year. Britain, France and Russia now sent aid to Greece. *See* Navarino.

Mita Caban *Mongul Wars*

1362, between the Tatars under Tamerlane and the Getes under the Khan Elias. The Getes were routed with heavy loss. *See* Baghdad.

Miyako I *Moronoshi's Rebellion*

June, 1353, between the revolted Moronoshi, and the troops of the Japanese Emperor of the South, Go Murakami, under Yoshinori. Moronoshi gained a complete victory, and Yoshinori and the Emperor fled into the Eastern provinces. *See* Miyako II.

Miyako II *Mitsuyaki's Revolt*

December 30, 1391, between the troops of the provinces of Idzumo and Idzumi, under

Mitsuyaki, and those of the Japanese Emperor of the South, Go Kameyama. A series of engagements took place in and around Miyako, and in the end Mitsuyaki was driven off with heavy loss, among the killed being the Daimio of Idzumi. *See* Miyako I.

Modder River *Second Boer War*

November 28, 1899, between a Boer force, about 9,000 strong, under General Cronje, and the British under Lord Methuen. Cronje held a strong position on both banks of the river which was not accurately known to Lord Methuen who was marching to the Modder. His columns came under fire about 7 am and the action lasted till evening, when a turning movement enabled him to drive Cronje from his entrenchments. The British losses were 24 officers and 461 men killed and wounded, those of the Boers being about the same. *See* Kimberley, Magersfontein.

Mogilev *Napoleonic Wars*

July 23, 1812, between 26,000 French under Marshal Davout and 49,000 Russians under Prince Bagration. Bagration attacked Davout in a strong position which counter-balanced the great disparity of numbers, and the Russians were repulsed with a loss of about 4,000. The French lost barely 1,000. *See* Smolensk.

Mohacz I *Ottoman Wars*

August 29, 1526, between 30,000 Hungarians under King Lewis and Tomore, Bishop of Kolocz, and over 100,000 Turks, with 300 guns, under Suleiman the Magnificent. The Hungarians made a heroic resistance against overwhelming numbers, but were finally routed, leaving 22,000 dead on the field, including the king, seven bishops, 28 magnates and over 500 nobles. This disaster placed Hungary at the mercy of Suleiman, and was quickly followed by the fall of Budapest. *See* Vienna I.

Mohacz II *Ottoman Wars*

On the battlefield where 160 years previously Suleiman had gained so decisive a victory, the Austrians and Hungarians signally defeated the Turks, under Mohammed IV, on August

12, 1687. In consequence of this disaster, following upon a long series of reverses, Mohammed was deposed by the discontented soldiery and succeeded by Suleiman III. *See* Focsani, Rimnitz.

Mohrungen *Napoleonic Wars*

January 25, 1807, between 10,000 French under Field Marshal Prince Bernadotte and 14,000 Russians under General Marhof. The French were defeated with a loss of about 1,000 killed and wounded. *See* Eylau.

Molinos del Rey *Peninsular War*

December 21, 1808, between 26,000 French under General St Cyr and the Spaniards, about equal in strength, under Reding. The Spaniards were routed with a loss of 10,000 killed, wounded and prisoners, and 50 guns, at very slight cost to the victors. *See* Corunna.

Mollwitz *War of the Austrian Succession*

April 10, 1741, between the Prussians, 22,000 strong under Frederick the Great, and 18,000 Austrians under Marshal Neipperg. Frederick surprised the Austrian general and, after severe fighting, drove him from his entrenchments, with a loss of about 5,000 killed, wounded and prisoners. The Prussians lost 2,500. The European nations now took sides in the war. *See* Chotusitz.

Monarda *Moorish Insurrection*

March 18, 1501, between the Spaniards, under the Count di Cifuentes and Alonso de Aguilar, and the insurgent Moors. The Spaniards were largely outnumbered, and were overpowered by the rebels, suffering a disastrous defeat. De Aguilar was killed, fighting to the end.

Monongahela River *Seven Years' War*

July 9, 1755, between 900 French and Indians, under Captain Dumas, and about 1,400 British and Virginians, under General Braddock. The British were attacked shortly after crossing the river, and though the officers and the Virginians fought gallantly, the troops, ignorant of Indian warfare, gave way to panic, and after three hours' fighting were driven across the Monongahela, with a loss of 877 killed and wounded. Of 86 officers, 63 fell, including Braddock, who was mortally wounded. The French lost 16 only; their Indian allies somewhat more heavily. *See* Lake George, Beauséjour.

Mons-en-Pévèle *Flemish War*

1304, between the French, under Philip IV, and the Flemings. The Flemings, unable to withstand the charge of the French cavalry, broke and fled, leaving 6,000 dead on the field. *See* Courtrai.

Montcontour *Third French Religious War*

October 3, 1569, between the Huguenots, under Henri le Béarnais, and the Catholics, under the Duc d'Anjou and General de Tavannes. The Huguenots occupied an untenable position, and at the end of half an hour were utterly routed and almost exterminated, some 700 only remaining with the colours after the battle. *See* Arques, La Rochelle II.

Monte Aperto *Guelfs and Ghibellines*

September 4, 1260, between the Florentine Guelfs and the Ghibellines, who had been driven from the city, under Manfred of Sicily. The Guelfs were totally routed, and the victors took possession of Florence, and re-established their rule.

Montebello I *French Revolutionary Wars*

June 9, 1800, between the French under Napoleon and the Austrians under General Ott. Napoleon, being ignorant of the fall of Genoa, was marching to the relief of that city, when his advanced guard under General Lannes was attacked by Ott, with 17,000 men, who was endeavouring to effect a junction with Mélas. Lannes held his ground until reinforcements arrived, when he assumed the offensive and drove the Austrians from the field with heavy loss, capturing 5,000 prisoners. *See* Marengo, Stockach.

Montebello II *Italian Wars of Independence*

May 20, 1859, between the Austrians under General Stadion and about 8,000 French under General Forey. The Austrians were defeated and driven back to Stradella with a loss of 2,000 killed and wounded, and 200 prisoners. *See* Palestro.

Monte Caseros *Argentine Civil War*

February 3, 1852, between the Argentine Government troops under President Rosas, the leader of the Gaucho party, 25,000 strong, and 20,000 insurgents under Justo de Urquiza. Rosas was totally defeated and compelled to sail for England, thus ending the long domination of the Gauchos in the Argentine Republic. *See* Montevideo.

Monte Lezino,

see Millesimo

Montenotte *French Revolutionary Wars*

April 10 and 11, 1796, when General d'Argenteau with the central division of the Austro-Sardinian army attacked the French position at Montenotte, held by General Cervoni's division. Cervoni was driven back but the key to the position was held throughout the day by Tampon with 1,500 men, and on the 12th d'Argenteau found himself outflanked by General Augereau and Masséna and was compelled to fall back with a loss of 1,000 killed, 2,000 prisoners, and some guns. This was Napoleon's first victory. *See* Lodi, Brig of.

Montereau *Napoleonic Wars*

February 18, 1814, between the rearguard of the French army, under Napoleon, and the Württembergers, under Prince Eugène of Württemberg. Eugène attacked Napoleon's position, but was repulsed with a loss of about 2,000 killed and wounded and 4,000 prisoners. *See* Craonne.

Monterrey *American-Mexican War*

This town in southern California was captured from the Mexicans, September 23,

1846, by the Americans under General Taylor and this success was followed by the occupation of the whole of Northern Mexico by the American army. *See* Buena Vista, Chapultepec.

Montevideo I *Napoleonic Wars*

This city was taken by assault February 3, 1807, by 3,000 British troops under Sir Samuel Auchmuty. The capture was preceded by an action outside the town in which the Rifle corps, later the Rifle Brigade, especially distinguished itself. The British losses amounted to about 600. *See* Buenos Aires.

Montevideo II *Uruguayan Civil War*

This city was besieged February 16, 1843, by Argentine troops under Oribe, leader of the Uruguayan Blancos party, and was defended by the Uruguayan Colorados party and a number of foreign residents, among others Garibaldi, under General Paz. In the course of the siege, Garibaldi, at the head of 160 Italians, made a sortie in which he held his own for a whole day against 12,000 Argentines and eventually effected a retreat in good order. The intervention of France and England eventually forced Oribe to raise the siege temporarily in November, 1845.

Montevideo III *Uruguayan Civil War*

October 8, 1851, between the combined forces of Uruguay, Brazil and Paraguay, under Justo de Urquiza, and the Argentines, under Manuel Oribe. The Argentines were besieging Montevideo, and Oribe was hemmed in in his lines by the allies, forced to capitulate, and the siege, eight years long, was ended.

Montevideo IV *Uruguayan Civil War*

August, 1863, between the Colorados, or Liberal party, of Uruguay, under General Venancio Flores, and the Blancos, under General Medina. The Blancos were victorious.

Montfaucon *Norman Invasion of France*

In 886, between the French, under Eudes, and the Norman invaders. The latter were totally defeated, losing 19,000 men in the battle, and were forced to retire from before the walls of Paris, which they were besieging. *See* Saucourt.

Montiel *Castilian Civil War*

In 1369, between the French under Bertrand du Guesclin and the Spaniards under Pedro II of Castile. Pedro was routed and taken prisoner and Henry de Trastamara placed on the throne of Castile. *See* Navarrete.

Montlhéry *Franco-Burgundian War*

In July 1465, between the forces of the Ligue du Bien Publique under the Comte de Charolais and the Royal troops under Louis XI. Louis was totally defeated after a fierce engagement and driven from the field. *See* Héricourt, Granson.

Montmirail,

see Champaubert

Montmorenci *Seven Years' War*

July 31, 1759, during the siege of Quebec, when General Wolfe with 5,000 men attacked the entrenched camp of the French which was defended by 12,000 men under Marquis de Montcalm. As the British were landing 13 companies of grenadiers advanced to the attack without waiting for the main body. They were repulsed with heavy loss which so weakened Wolfe that he decided not to press the attack further. The British loss amounted to 443, almost the whole of which fell upon the grenadiers. The French losses were very small. *See* Torgau.

Montreal *Seven Years' War*

This city was surrendered to the British, under General Amherst, by Vaudreuil, Governor-General of Canada, September 8, 1760. One of the conditions of the surrender was that the whole of the French army in Canada and its dependencies must lay down their arms. Canada thus became a part of the British dominions, under the Treaty of Paris. *See* Quebec.

Mont Valérien

see Buzenval

170

Mookerheide *Netherlands War of Independence*

April 14, 1574, between the Dutch Patriots, 8,000 strong, under Count Louis of Nassau, and 5,000 Spaniards, under Don Sancho d'Avila. The village of Mookerheide was held by the Dutch infantry, who were driven out by the Spaniards and totally routed, with a loss of at least 4,000. Among the slain were the Counts Louis and Henry of Nassau. *See* Leyden.

Morat *Burgundian Wars*

June 22, 1476, between the Burgundians, 35,000 strong, under Charles the Bold, and 24,000 Swiss under Hans Waldmann. After a few hours' hard fighting the Burgundians were driven into the plain where the Swiss utterly routed them, no less than 8,000 falling. The Swiss chroniclers aver that the victors only lost 500 killed. *See* Granson.

Morawa *Ottoman Wars*

November 3, 1443, between the Hungarians under John Hunyadi, with 12,000 horse and 20,000 foot, and a greatly superior Turkish army under Amurath II. The Turks were defeated with a loss of 2,000 killed and 4,000 prisoners. This battle is also called the Battle of Nissa. *See* Varna.

Morazzone *Italian Wars of Independence*

1848, between 1,500 Garibaldian volunteers, under Garibaldi, and 5,000 Austrians, under General d'Aspre. After a resistance lasting eleven hours, Garibaldi, hopelessly outnumbered, withdrew his force from the town and executed a masterly retreat to Arona. *See* Custoza.

Morella *First Carlist War*

This fortress, the last stronghold of the Carlists, was besieged by Espartero with 20,000 Cristinos, May 23, 1840. It was defended by a garrison of 4,000 veterans under Cabrera, who on the 30th attempted to break through the besiegers' lines. His plan, however, had been betrayed and he was met and driven back, whereupon the place surrendered. Cabrera, however, with a portion of the garrison, made a second and this time a successful attempt to cut his way out. *See* Huesca.

Morshedabad *British Conquest of Bengal*

July 24, 1763, between the troops of Mir Kasim, the deposed Nawab of Bengal, and a British force of 750 Europeans and a large body of Indian troops under Major Adams. The British stormed Kasim's entrenchments, driving out his army in confusion, and followed up their victory by the occupation of Morshedabad without further opposition. *See* Buxar.

Mortara *Italian Wars of Independence*

March 21, 1849, between the Piedmontese under the Duke of Savoy (Victor Emmanuel) and General Darando, and the main Austrian army under Field-Marshal Radetsky. No steps had been taken by the Piedmontese to render Mortara defensible and little guard was kept, with the result that they were surprised by Radetsky and driven out of the town in confusion, with a loss of 500 killed and wounded, 2,000 prisoners and five guns. The Austrians lost 300 only. *See* Novara.

Mortgarten *First Swiss-Austrian War*

November 15, 1315. The men of Schwyz, 1,400 in number, took post in the Pass of Mortgarten, and lay in wait for the Archduke Leopold, who, with 9,000 Austrians was marching into Schwyz. Having disordered the Austrian ranks by rolling down boulders upon them the Swiss then fell upon them with their halberds and totally routed them, with a loss of 1,500 killed. *See* Laupen, Sempach.

Mortimer's Cross *Wars of the Roses*

February 2, 1461, when Edward, Duke of York, defeated the Lancastrians, under the Earls of Pembroke and Wiltshire, and drove them back into Wales, thus preventing a concentration of the Lancastrian forces. *See* St Albans, Wakefield.

Mortlack *Danish Invasions of Scotland*

1010, between the Danes under Sweyn and

the Scots under Malcolm II. After a long and obstinate engagement the Danes were totally defeated and forced to flee to their ships. A victory for them on this occasion would probably have given them a permanent lodgment in Scotland as Malcolm had his last available man in the field. *See* Kinloss.

Mortmant *Napoleonic Wars*

February 17, 1814, between the Russian advance-guard under the Count de Pahlen and the French rearguard under Marshal Victor. The Russians were repulsed with a loss of 3,000 killed and wounded, and 11 guns. *See* Montereau, Craonne.

Moscow *World War II*

Three phases: 1st German offensive, September 30, 1941, to October 31: 2nd German offensive, November 16 to December 5: Russian counter-offensive, December 6 to Spring, 1942. By October 6 German tanks had smashed through the Rzhev-Viazma defence line towards the fortified Mozhaisk line, 50 miles west of Moscow, running from Kalinin to Kaluga. Zhukov was then appointed C-in-C of the entire front. Outflanking the Mozhaisk line from the south, Guderian's 2nd Panzer Groups captured Kaluga on October 12, while the 3rd Panzer and the 9th Army, General Hoth, by-passed it in the north and took Kalinin. The *Luftwaffe* dominated the air, while German tanks forced the Russians to retreat constantly to avoid encirclement, closing in on Moscow from all directions. By mid-October nearly two million people had been evacuated from Moscow, and near panic reigned among civilians. But by October 18 deep mud and Russian counter-attacks slowed down the Germans. In a desperate attempt to reach Moscow before the full fury of winter, the Germans started their second offensive on November 16 in the Kalinin-Volokolmsk sector and by November 22 they had battled forward in the freezing cold to Istra, 15 miles west of Moscow. Tula, an arms centre, 100 miles south of the capital was encircled on December 3, but did not fall, while 4th Army infantry battered on to within sight of the Moscow suburbs, only to be flung back by armed workers' units, who lost heavily in two days' combat. Bitter cold, shortage of petrol and Russian tenacity

finally stopped the Germans on December 5. Zhukov launched a counter-attack with 100 divisions on the next day, December 6, and after the bitterest fighting retook Kalinin, Klin, Istra and Yelets by December 15 and Kaluga by December 30. By January 15, the Red Army had advanced by about 200 miles in the north and about 180 miles in the south, but barely 100 miles west of Moscow the Germans held on to the line Viazma-Gzahtsk-Rzhev; and here, approximately, the Russian counter-offensive ended at the end of January, but far short of the plans to encircle and destroy all German forces between Moscow and Smolensk.
Official Russian figures for German losses in the 2nd offensive alone were 55,000 dead, over 100,000 wounded, 777 tanks, 297 guns and mortars, 244 machine guns. General Halder's *Diary* gives 192,000 killed and wounded from September 30 to November 26. Russian losses were at least twice as high. *See* Leningrad, Ukraine.

Möskirch *French Revolutionary Wars*

May 5, 1800, between 50,000 French under General Moreau and 60,000 Austrians under General Baron Kray. The French advance-guard under Lecourbe approaching Möskirch found the heights strongly held by the Austrians and attempted to carry them, but without success. The arrival of the main body, however, turned the scale and the Austrians were obliged to abandon all their positions with a loss of about 5,000 men. The French lost about 3,500. *See* Höchstädt.

Moskowa,

see Borodino

Motya *Carthaginian Invasion of Sicily*

This city, the chief stronghold of the Carthaginians in Sicily, was besieged by Dionysius of Syracuse, with 83,000 men, 398 BC. Having built a mole to connect the mainland and the island on which Motya stood, he erected thereon his new engines of war, the catapults, used for the first time in this siege. He also built large moving towers to enable him to cope with the lofty defences of the place, and by these devices succeeded in effecting an entrance. Every house,

172

however, was in itself a small fortress and after days of street fighting, which cost the assailants a heavy price, the city was still unsubdued. At last by a night surprise he mastered the quarter which still held out, and the inhabitants were massacred or sold as slaves. *See* Himera, Selinus.

Mount Lactarius *Wars of the Byzantine Empire*

March 553, between the troops of the Emperor Justinian, under Narses, and the Goths, under Teias, the last Gothic king of Italy. The Romans gained a signal victory, and Teias was slain, the Goths thereupon accepting the rule of Justinian. *See* Casilinum.

Mount Seleucus *Civil Wars of the Roman Empire*

August 10, 353, between the rebels under Magnentius and the Imperial legions under Constantius. Constantius forced the passage of the Cottian Alps and defeated Magnentius in a bloody battle which dispersed his army and finally broke his power, Gaul and Italy being thus again brought under the Imperial sway. *See* Singara.

Mount Tabor *French Revolutionary Wars*

April 15, 1799, when Napoleon defeated and dispersed the Syrian army raised to create a diversion in favour of the beleaguered garrison of Acre. General Kléber's division bore the brunt of the fighting. *See* Nile, Pyramids.

Mount Taurus *Muslim Invasion of Asia Minor*

In 804, between the Muslims under Haroun-al-Raschid and the Greeks under the Emperor Nicephorus I. The Greeks were totally defeated with a loss of 40,000 men, and Nicephorus, wounded in three places, with difficulty escaped from the field. *See* Amorium.

Mount Tifata *Civil War of Marius and Sulla*

83 BC, when the legions of Sulla defeated the army of the Consul, Norbanus, with heavy loss, and drove them to take refuge in Capua.

See Orchomenus.

Mouscron *French Revolutionary Wars*

1794, between the French, under Generals Moreau and Souham, and the Austrians, under General Clerfayt. The French were victorious. *See* Fleurus.

Mudki *First British-Sikh War*

December 18, 1845, between the British, 12,000 strong with 42 guns, under Sir Hugh Gough, and the Sikhs, 16,000 strong with 22 guns, under Tej Singh. Gough, at the end of a long march, was surprised by the Sikhs, but he succeeded in driving them from the field, capturing 17 guns. The British loss was 872 killed and wounded, among the former being Generals M'Caskill and Sir Robert Sale *See* Ferozeshah, Sobraon.

Mühlberg *German Reformation Wars*

April 24, 1547, between the German Protestants, 9,000 strong, under the Elector Frederick of Saxony and the Landgrave of Hesse, and the Imperial army, together with 3,500 Papal troops, 13,000 in all, under Charles V. The Protestants were totally defeated, and their two leaders taken prisoners. The Imperialists lost 50 only. *See* Sievershausen.

Mühldorf *Civil War of the Holy Roman Empire*

1322, between the Imperial troops under the Emperor Louis the Bavarian and the German malcontents under Frederick, Duke of Austria. Louis won a signal victory and put an end to the resistance to his rule. *See* Mortgarten.

Mühlhausen *Gallic War*

58 BC between the Romans, 36,000 strong, under Julius Caesar and the Sequani under Ariovistus. The Romans occupied two camps, one of which was held successfully by two legions against a determined attack of the Gauls. The attack having been repulsed, Caesar united his forces and led them against the Sequani whom he totally routed with

173

enormous loss. *See* Bibracte.

Mukden I *Russo-Japanese War*

February 21, 1905, when Field-Marshal
Orama bore down with 300,000 troops on a
47-mile front, against Mukden, Manchuria,
defended by General Kuropatkin's Russian
forces. On March 10 Oyama encircled the city
but Kuropatkin had withdrawn his remaining
forces intact. Japanese losses were about
50,000 and those of the Russians nearly
90,000. *See* Port Arthur, Tsushima Strait,
Nanhan.

Mukden II *Chinese Civil War*

September 17, 1948, when 200,000 of Mao
Tse-tung's troops under General Lin Pao
during their campaign in Manchuria,
encircled this city and defeated those of
General Liao Yao-hsiang's Nationalist forces
who tried to escape. The city surrendered on
November 1, giving Mao Tse-tung power
throughout Manchuria. *See* Sungari River,
Nanking.

Mukwanpur *British-Gurkha War*

February 27, 1816, when a village forming
part of Sir David Ochterlony's position was
attacked by 2,000 Gurkhas. The village was
defended by three companies of Sepoys and 40
men of the 87th Regiment, and the defenders
were hard pressed, but the arrival of
reinforcements enabled them after severe
fighting to beat off the assailants with very
heavy loss.

Multan *Second British-Sikh War*

This fortress, defended by the Sikhs under
Dewan Mulraj, was besieged by Lieutenant
Edwardes with about 15,000 men in July,
1848. After an ineffectual bombardment, the
siege was raised September 22, but was
renewed December 27 by General Whish,
with 16,000 regular and 17,000 mercenary
troops and 64 guns. After a heavy
bombardment the city was stormed and
pillaged January 2, 1849, and on the 22nd of
the same month Mulraj surrendered the
citadel. The British, prize agents and
soldiery, seized gold and silver worth some
£5,000,000. Their loss during the siege was

210 killed and 910 wounded. *See* Gujerat.

Münchengrätz *Seven Weeks' War*

June 28, 1866, between the advance-guard of
Prince Frederick Charles' army and the
Austrians under Count Clam-Gallas. The
Austrians were defeated with a loss of about
300 killed and wounded, and 1,000 prisoners.
The Prussian losses were very small.
See Koeniggrätz, Langensalza.

Munda *Civil War of Caesar and Pompey*

March 17, 45 BC, between the Pompeians,
under Gnaeus Pompeius, and the Caesareans,
under Julius Caesar. The Pompeians were
totally defeated, losing 30,000 men including
Labienus and Varro, while the Caesareans lost
1,000 only. Gnaeus Pompeius was wounded.
This defeat put an end to the resistance of the
Pompeian faction in Spain, and the action is
further notable as being Caesar's last battle.
See Mutina.

Muret *Albigensian Crusade*

In 1213, between the Catholics under Simon
de Montfort and the Albigenses under the
Count of Toulouse, aided by Pedro II of
Aragon. The Albigenses were routed, and this
defeat put an end to their organized
resistance. Pedro fell in the battle.
See Bouvines.

Murfreesboro *American Civil War*

December 31, 1862, between 35,000
Confederates under General Bragg and 45,000
Federals under General Rosecrans. Bragg
attacked and drove back the Federal right, but
the centre and left held their ground and
prevented the defeat degenerating into a rout.
Both sides lost heavily but the Confederates
captured a large number of prisoners and over
20 guns. On the following day the Federal
right retook the ground it had lost on the 31st
and at the end of the day both armies
occupied their original positions. Early on
January 2, 1863, however, Bragg retired in
good order. Each side lost about 12,000
killed, wounded and missing in the two days'
fighting. *See* Perryville, Chickamauga.

Mursa *Civil Wars of the Roman Empire*

September 28, 351, between the usurper Magnentius with 100,000 troops and the Emperor Constantius with 80,000. The battle was severely contested but finally the legions of Magnentius were driven from the field with a loss of 24,000, that of the victors amounting to 30,000. *See* Singara.

Musa Bagh *Indian Mutiny*

March 19, 1858, when a British force under General Sir James Outram totally routed a body of mutineers 7,000 strong under Huzrat Mahul, Begum of Oude, which was holding the Musa Bagh, a fortified palace in the outskirts of Lucknow. *See* Lucknow.

Muta *Muslim Invasion of Syria*

August 20, 636, between the Muslims, under Zaid, and the troops of the Emperor Heraclius. Zaid was slain, and so successively were Jaafar and Abdullah, who followed him in the command, but the banner of the prophet was then raised by Khaled, who succeeded in repulsing the onslaught of the Imperial troops and on the following day led the Muslims undefeated from the field. This is the first battle between the Mohammedan Arabs and a foreign enemy. *See* Medina, Aiznadin, Aleppo.

Muthul, The *Jugurthine War*

108 BC, between the Numidians under Jugurtha and the Romans under Metellus Numidicus. The Numidians were strongly posted on the heights above the river but were driven out by the legionaries with heavy loss. Jugurtha did not again face the Romans in the field, contenting himself with a guerrilla warfare. He was captured and died in prison in Rome.

Mutina *Mark Antony's First Rebellion*

April 14, 43 BC, between the adherents of Antony, and three Consular armies under Hirtius, Octavius, and Vibius Pansa. Antony, who was besieging Mutina, was attacked simultaneously by the three armies. That of

Pansa was routed and Pansa slain, but Octavius and Hirtius gained some small success. Antony, however, was undefeated, and continued the siege. On the 27th Octavius and Hirtius made a combined attack on his lines and succeeded in forcing their way through into the town, though Hirtius fell in the action. *See* Philippi.

Mycale *Persian-Greek Wars*

August 479 BC, between the Greeks under Leotychides the Spartan and a large Persian army. The Greeks effected a landing near Cape Mycale and drove the Persians back upon their entrenchments, which they then carried by storm, whereupon the Persian auxiliaries fled. The fugitives were slaughtered in detail by the revolted Ionians and the whole army destroyed. Greece had overcome the Persian threat. *See* Plataea I.

Mylae *First Punic War*

260 BC, when the Roman fleet under Caius Diulius defeated the Carthaginians under Hannibal, with loss of 50 ships, 3,000 killed and 7,000 prisoners, at Mylae (Milazzo). Diulius had introduced the boarding bridge which was lowered on to the deck of the opposing galley, and this gave full scope to the superior powers of the Romans in hand-to-hand fighting. The Carthaginian threat to Italy was frustrated. *See* Eonomus.

Mylex *Civil War of Caesar and Pompey*

36 BC, between the Pompeian fleet under Sextus Pompey and the fleet of the Triumvirs under Agrippa. The Pompeians were defeated, Pompey was captured a year later and executed. *See* Actium.

Myonnesus *Wars of the Hellenistic Monarchies*

190 BC, between the Roman fleet under Caius Livius and the fleet of Antiochus under Polyxenides, who had an advantage of nine ships. He was, however, defeated by the superior seamanship of the Romans, with a loss of 42 vessels. *See* Thermopylae II.

175

Mytilene I *Great Peloponnesian War*

This city, which had revolted against Athens, was invested in the autumn of 428 BC by the Athenians under Paches, with 1,000 hoplites and a fleet of triremes. A feeble attempt at relief by a Peloponnesian squadron under Alcidas was unsuccessful and in May, 427, the city surrendered and all the male inhabitants were condemned to death. In the end, however, only the leaders of the revolt were executed. *See* Plataea II.

Mytilene II *Great Peloponnesian War*

A naval action fought 406 BC between 140 Peloponnesian vessels under Callicratidas and 70 Athenian triremes under Conon. Conon was defeated with the loss of 30 ships, the rest of his fleet being driven into Mytilene where it was blockaded. *See* Naupactus.

Mytton *Wars of Scottish Independence*

September 20, 1319, a year after the English under Edward II laid siege to Berwick-on-Tweed, King Robert Bruce sent Sir James Douglas to counter-attack into Yorkshire where he defeated a force composed largely of armed monks under Archbishop William Melton of York at Mytton. The defeat compelled Edward to raise the siege of Berwick. *See* Bannockburn.

N

Nachod *Seven Weeks' War*

June 27, 1866, between the 5th Prussian Corps under General Steinmetz and the Austrians under General Ramming. The Austrian cavalry, which was considerably superior in number, was defeated by the Prussian Uhlans and the action resulted in the retreat of the Austrians with a considerable loss in killed and wounded. The Prussians, who lost 900, captured 2,000 prisoners and 5 guns. *See* Münchengratz.

Naefels *Swiss-Austrian Wars*

April 9, 1388, between 6,000 Austrians under Tockenburg and 500 men of Glarus with a few Schwyzers. The Swiss were driven from their first position behind the 'Letzi' at the entrance to the valley but, retiring to the heights of the Rauhberg, disordered the advancing columns by rolling boulders upon them, and, then attacking, utterly routed them. The Austrians lost 80 knights and 2,200 soldiers. *See* Sempach, Vögelinseck.

Nagy-Sarlo *Hungarian Rising*

April 19, 1849, between the Hungarians, 25,000 strong under General Görgey, and the Austrians who endeavoured to prevent Görgey constructing bridges over the Gran. The Austrians were defeated and the river successfully bridged. *See* Kapolna.

Naissus *Gothic Invasion of the Roman Empire*

269, between the Imperial troops under the Emperor Claudius Gothicus and the invading Goths. The Romans were hard pressed, when the Gothic lines were attacked in the rear by a force of 5,000 men which Claudius had concealed for this purpose in the neighbouring mountains, and being thrown into confusion were totally routed. Fifty thousand men are said to have fallen in the battle. *See* Philippopolis, Placentia.

Nájara,

see Navarrete

Nam Dong,

see Vietnam War

Namur *World War I*

August 20, 1914, when the 1st, 2nd and 3rd German armies, about 25 divisions, with cavalry and some 500 Skoda 420-mm mortars and howitzers, all commanded by Generals Kluck, Bülow and Hausen, bore down on the angle of the Sambre and Meuse Rivers in neutral Belgium, against General Lanrezac's 5th French Army, partially in position on the Sambre, two British corps on his left, and Namur, garrisoned by the Belgian 14th division under General Michel. Ten supposedly impregnable forts, minefields, electrified barbed wire and trenches guarded Namur, which barred the way to France. On the evening of August 20, the German guns heavily bombarded the entrenched Belgian infantry. Whole regiments were decimated and the next day the 2-ton shells crashed down on the forts at the rate sometimes of 20 a minute. By that night five had fallen, while the Belgian infantry were pushed back in a fierce battle. By the 25th the last forts had gone, the Belgians had withdrawn and the city surrendered with 50,000 prisoners. *See* Antwerp, Liège, Battle of the Frontiers.

Nanhan *Russo-Japanese War*

May 26, 1904, between three Japanese divisions under General Oku and a Russian division, with a large force of artillery, under General Stoessel. The Russians occupied a very strongly entrenched position on the heights of Nanhan. After an artillery preparation the Japanese attempted to storm the heights, eight successive attacks failing before the concentrated fire of the Russian guns, though the last survivors of the assailants got within 30 yards of the trenches. The infantry were then withdrawn and after a further bombardment, aided by the Japanese fleet in Kiuchau Bay, the whole force attacked simultaneously and, penetrating the defences on the Russian left, drove them from their positions with heavy loss, the defenders leaving 500 dead on the field. The Japanese lost 4,304 killed, wounded and missing. Seventy-eight guns were taken, and the Russians penned up in Port Arthur. *See* Port Arthur, Mukden, Tsushima Strait.

Nanking *Chinese Civil War*

April 22, 1949, when Communist troops drove Chiang Kai-shek's Nationalists out of this city. It led to the fall of Shanghai on May 27, the departure of the Nationalist government to Formosa, the end of the war and the installation of Mao Tse-tung's government at Peking. *See* Mukden II.

Naroch Lake *World War I*

March 18, 1916, when Czar Nicholas II in an offensive designed possibly to frustrate an attack on Riga, assaulted with the Russian 10th Army German forces led by Field Marshal Hindenburg. After a short artillery bombardment the infantry carried the German first and second lines, but the Russian gunners then departed with their weapons. Hindenburg heard of the move, shelled the Russian trenches heavily and sent in his infantry to take back all that they had lost, and much more. The Russians lost more than 80,000 men. *See* Gorlice, Kovel-Stanislav.

Narva *Great Northern War*

November 30, 1700, between 8,000 Swedes under Charles XII and 50,000 Russians under General Dolgorouky. The Russians were besieging Narva, but driving in two large bodies who occupied advanced positions, Charles boldly attacked their entrenched camp. Following a brief cannonade, the Swedes stormed the trenches, and though the Russian artillerymen stood to their guns, after three hours' hard fighting the defenders were driven out in disorder, having lost 10,000 in the trenches, while many more fell in the fight. The Swedes lost 600 only. *See* Pultusk.

Naseby *English Civil War*

June 14, 1645, between 13,000 Parliamentarians under Fairfax and 9,000 Royalists under King Charles I, with Prince Rupert in actual command. Prince Rupert's first charge broke the Parliamentary left wing,

but as usual the pursuit was carried too far, and before the cavalry returned Cromwell on the right had turned the scale, and the battle was over. The Royalist infantry, overwhelmed by superior numbers, were almost annihilated, 5,000 prisoners and all the artillery being captured. *See* Marston Moor.

Nashville *American Civil War*

December 15 and 16, 1863, between 50,000 Federals under General Thomas and 31,000 Confederates under General Hood. Thomas attacked the left of Hood's lines before Nashville, and after hard fighting in which Hood lost 1,200 prisoners and 16 guns, the Confederates withdrew during the night to a position a few miles in the rear. Here they were again attacked on the 16th, and, though at first holding their ground, were in the end driven from the field in confusion, with 1,500 killed and wounded besides 4,460 prisoners and 54 guns. The Federals lost 380 killed, 2,500 wounded. *See* Franklin.

Naulochus *Wars of the Second Triumvirate*

September 3, 36 BC, between the Pompeian fleet of 300 ships under Sextus Pompeius and the fleet of the Triumvirs, of equal strength, under Agrippa. The action was severely contested, but in the end Agrippa was victorious and Pompeius fled with 17 vessels only. *See* Actium.

Naupactus *Great Peloponnesian War*

429 BC, between 20 Athenian ships under Phormio and 77 Peloponnesian ships under Cnemas. The Athenians were entrapped by Cnemas at the entrance to the Bay of Naupactus, and nine of their vessels driven ashore. The remaining 11 fled towards Naupactus, closely pursued by the Peloponnesians, when the rearmost of the flying Athenians suddenly turned and rammed the leading ship of Cnemus' squadron. The pursuers hesitated and the rest of the Athenians then returned and gained a complete victory, taking six ships and recovering eight of the nine which had run ashore. *See* Mytilene, Plataea II.

178

Navarino *Greek War of Independence*

October 20, 1827, when the allied fleets of Great Britain, France and Russia under Admirals Codrington, de Rigny and Heiden respectively, and numbering in all 24 ships, annihilated the Turkish and Egyptian fleets, 60 vessels being entirely destroyed and the remainder driven ashore. The allies lost 272 in killed and wounded; the Turks over 4,000. This battle is noteworthy as the last general action fought between wooden sailing ships. The London Protocol, March 1829, recognized Greek independence. *See* Missolonghi.

Navarrete *Hundred Years' War*

April 3, 1367, between 24,000 English under Edward the Black Prince and 60,000 French and Spaniards under Bertrand du Guesclin and Henry de Trastamara. The English, mainly owing to the skill of their archers, completely defeated their opponents with heavy loss, du Guesclin being made prisoner. Also known as the Battle of Nájara. *See* Montiel.

Naxos *Wars of the Greek City States*

September, 376 BC, between 80 Athenian triremes under Chabrias and 60 Spartan ships under Pollio, who was endeavouring to waylay the Athenian grain ships from the Euxine. Pollio was totally defeated, with a loss of 49 triremes. *See* Leuctra.

Nechtan's Mere *Northumbrian Invasion of Scotland*

May 20, 685, between the Picts under Brude and the Northumbrians under Ecgfrith. The latter was defeated and the Picts by their victory freed themselves from the Northumbrian domination.

Neerwinden I *War of the English Succession*

July 29, 1693, between the English under William III and the French in superior force under Marshal Luxembourg. The French attacked the English entrenchments and were at first repulsed, but after eight hours' hard fighting they succeeded in driving them back all along the line, though owing largely to the personal bravery of the King the retirement was in good order. This victory, which cost the French 10,000 men, was a barren one, for William's retreat was unmolested, and he was almost at once in a condition to renew the conflict. Also called the Battle of Landen. *See* Steenkerke.

Neerwinden II *French Revolutionary Wars*

March 18, 1793, between the French under Geberal Dumouriez and the Austrians under the Prince of Coburg. The Austrians won a signal victory and in consequence of his defeat Dumouriez was compelled to evacuate Belgium. *See* Toulon III.

Negapatam I *War of the Austrian Succession*

1746, off the Madras coast, between a British squadron of six ships under Captain Peyton and nine French ships under the Comte de la Bourdonnais. The fight was conducted almost entirely at long range and was indecisive, but after the action Peyton sheered off and made for Trincomalee, thus practically admitting defeat, though the French had in fact suffered the heavier loss. *See* Madras.

Negapatam II *Second British Mysore War*

Siege was laid October 21, 1781, by a British force, 4,000 strong, under Colonel Braithwaite. The garrison, partly Dutch and partly Mysore troops, though 8,000 in number, did not wait for a bombardment, but surrendered November 3.

Negapatam III *American Revolutionary War*

A naval action was fought off this town in 1782 between a British squadron under Sir Edward Hughes and a French squadron under Admiral Suffren. The opposing forces were of about equal strength and the action was indecisive, but the French designs on Negapatam were frustrated and Suffren drew off to the southward. *See* Trincomalee IV.

179

Nehavend *Muslim Invasion of Persia*

AD 641, between the Muslims under Said, the lieutenant of the Caliph Omar, and a Persian army 150,000 strong. The Persians were utterly routed, this being the last stand made against the conquering Muslims. *See* Tripoli.

Neon *Sacred War*

354 BC, between the Phocians and certain mercenary troops, 10,000 in all, under Philomelus, and the Thebans and Locrians. The Phocians were totally defeated, and Philomelus, driven fighting and covered with wounds to the edge of a precipice, preferred death to surrender, and sprang over the cliff.

Neuwied *French Revolutionary Wars*

April 18, 1797, between the French, 80,000 strong, under General Hoche, and the Austrians, under General Werneck. Hoche won a signal victory, driving the Austrians beyond the Lahn, with a loss of 8,000 men and 80 guns. *See* Camperdown.

Neville's Cross *Anglo-Scottish Wars*

October 17, 1346, between the Scottish invading army under David II and the northern levies under Henry de Percy and Ralph de Neville. The Scots were completely routed with a loss of 9,000 men, and David and many of his nobles captured and held to ransom. *See* Halidon Hill, Otterburn.

Newburn *Anglo-Scottish Wars*

August 28, 1640, between 4,500 English under Lord Conway and the Scottish army, 22,500 strong, under Field Marshal Leslie. Conway endeavoured to hold the ford of Newburn, near Newcastle, but his raw levies, after a cannonade of three hours, fled in confusion. Conway was consequently obliged to evacuate Newcastle which was occupied by the Scots. The losses on both sides were small. Known as the Bishops' War, Scottish rejection of Anglican episcopacy having caused it.

Newbury I *English Civil War*

September 20, 1643, between the Royalists under Charles I and the Parliamentarians under Robert Devereux, Earl of Essex, both about 14,000 strong. Charles's aim, which failed, was to stop Essex's march on London, and though his troops held their ground throughout the day, he could not be said to have gained a victory, as during the night he felt himself obliged to abandon his position.

Newbury II *English Civil War*

A second indecisive battle was fought at Newbury, October 27, 1644, when 9,000 Royalists under Charles I again sustained throughout the day, without giving ground, the attacks of the Parliamentary army, 17,500, under Sir William Waller, Lord Manchester, and others, but, as on the previous occasion, retired during the night. The action gave impetus to the formation of the New Model Army. *See* Naseby.

New Guinea *World War II*

A series of battles by Australian and American forces against the Japanese, lasting two years, from August 26, 1942, to the end of September, 1944, to rid this island of the enemy threat to Australia and to prepare the way for liberation of the Philippines. Japanese 18th Army troops under General Adachi landed in the Papua area of New Guinea on July 21–22, 1942, but the 7th Australian division and the US 32nd and 41st divisions cleared them by January 23, 1943, at a cost of 8,500 casualties to the 12,000 of the Japanese. Clearing the New Guinea region and West New Guinea involved bitter fighting by the Australian 5th, 9th and 7th divisions and the US 6th Army aided by the 7th and 5th US fleets from the spring of 1943 to the end of September 1944. The Japanese lost over 20,000 killed. *See* Coral Sea, Rabaul, Solomon Islands, Leyte, Peleliu-Angaur.

New Market *American Civil War*

May 15, 1864, between 5,200 Federals under General Sigel and 3,500 Confederates under General Breckenridge. The Confederates, by a rapid flank movement, fell upon Sigel's force while on the march, and drove them to seek shelter in a wood behind their artillery. The guns were then most gallantly attacked and taken by 250 boys, pupils of the Lexington Military School, who lost 80 of their number in the charge. Sigel retired, having lost very heavily in men, and leaving six guns in the enemy's hands. *See* Spotsylvania.

New Orleans I *War of 1812*

This city, held by a garrison of 6,000
Americans under General Jackson, was
attacked December, 1814, by a British force
of 6,000 men under General Keane, aided by
the fleet. On the 13th the American warships
lying in the Mississippi were captured by a
boat attack, and by the 21st the whole of the
troops were disembarked. After a few
skirmishes General Sir Edward Pakenham
arrived and took command on the 25th, and
on January 1, 1815, a determined attack was
made upon the American position. This
failed and owing to supply difficulties the
British retired. On the 8th they attacked
again with 5,300 men but were again
repulsed, with a loss of 1,500, including
Pakenham. The expedition then withdrew. At
the time of the action peace had already been
concluded, though neither side knew it. *See*
Bladensburg.

New Orleans II *American Civil War*

On April 16, 1862, the Federal fleet of 30
armed steamers and 21 mortar vessels under
Commodore Farragut began the attack on this
city by the bombardment of Fort Jackson.
After this fort and Fort Mary had been
shelled with little intermission until the 25th,
Farragut forced the passage and anchored
off New Orleans. The city at once
surrendered. The forts, however, still held
out, but a mutiny broke out in Fort Jackson,
and on the 28th they surrendered to
Commodore Porter. *See* Yorktown II.

New Ross *Irish Rebellion*

June 5, 1798, between 30,000 rebels under
Father Roche and Bagenal Harvey and about
1,400 regulars under General Johnstone. The
rebels attacked the troops posted in New
Ross and penetrated into the centre of the
town, but were then driven back with the
bayonet and totally routed, with a loss of
2,600 killed. *See* Arklow.

Newtown Butler *War of the English Succession*

July 31, 1689, between 5,000 Catholics under
Maccarthy and 3,000 Protestants under
Colonel Wolseley, in defence of Enniskillen.

The Catholics were totally routed and fled in
disorder, losing 1,500 in the action and 500
drowned in Lough Erne. *See* Londonderry,
The Boyne.

Niagara *Seven Years' War*

This fort was besieged in June, 1759, by
2,500 British with 900 Indians, under General
Prideaux, the garrison consisting of 600
French under Captain Pouchot. Prideaux was
killed by the premature explosion of a shell
and Sir William Johnson succeeded to the
command. On July 24 when the garrison were
almost *in extremis*, an attempt to relieve the
fort was made by 1,300 French and Indians
under Ligneris, but he was repulsed by
Johnson with considerable loss at La Belle
Famille, and Pouchot at once surrendered.
See Minden.

Nicaea *First Crusade*

This city, now Iznik, Turkey, was
besieged by the Crusaders, under Godefroi de
Bouillon, May 14, 1097. The Saracens were
greatly aided in their defence by the
possession of Lake Ascanius, but with great
labour the crusaders transported boats from
the sea to the lake, and thus completed the
investment of the place. Two determined
attempts to relieve it were made but both
were repulsed, and Nicaea surrendered June
20. *See* Dorylaeum.

Nicholson's Nek,

see Farquhar's Farm

Nicopolis I *Third Mithridatic War*

66 BC, between the Romans under Pompey
and the army of Mithridates. The Romans
had occupied the heights in front of the
retreating Asiatics and Mithridates encamped
under their position. In the night the Romans
attacked him in his camp and utterly routed
him. This was the last battle fought by
Mithridates against the legions of Rome. *See*
Tigranocerta.

Nicopolis II *Third Mithridatic War*

47 BC, when Domitius Calvinus, with one
Roman legion and a contingent of Pontic and
other Asiatic troops, encountered the

181

Bosporans under Pharnaces. Calvinus' Asiatic troops fled at the first onset, and he was completely defeated, only the steadiness of the Romans saving him from disaster. *See* Tigranocerta.

Nicopolis III *Ottoman Wars*

September 28, 1396, between 10,000 French and 50,000 Hungarians, under the Duc de Nevers and Sigismund of Hungary, and the Turkish army of Bajazet I, near this Bulgarian city, now Nikopol. The French charged the Turkish lines without waiting for the Hungarians, and penetrated the two first lines, killing 1,500 Turks, but were then overpowered by the Janissaries in the third line and 3,000 killed, while all the survivors were captured. Bajazet then turned upon the Hungarians, who fled without striking a blow. Bajazet massacred all his prisoners excepting 25 nobles. Timur's invasion of Asia Minor stopped further Turkish conquests in Europe. *See* Kossova.

Nicopolis IV *Russo-Turkish War*

This place, now Nikopol, was captured July 16, 1877 by the 9th Russian Army Corps under General Krüdener, after two days' bombardment, when the garrison of 7,000 Turks surrendered. The Russians lost 1,300 killed and wounded. *See* Plevna.

Nieuwpoort *Netherlands War of Independence*

July 2, 1600, between the Dutch under Maurice of Orange and the Spaniards under the Archduke Albert of Austria. Prince Maurice was surprised by the Archduke in a very critical position but succeeded in holding his own and after a long and evenly-contested engagement, ultimately defeated the Spaniards with heavy loss. *See* Turnhout.

Nikko *Japanese Revolution*

In 1868, between the followers of the Shogun under Otori Keisuke and the Imperial army under Saigo Takamori. The rebels were defeated and fled to the castle of Wakamatsu.

Nile *French Revolutionary Wars*

August 1, 1798, Admiral Brueys, with 13 ships of the line and four frigates, was anchored in Abukir Bay. Nelson, with 13 line-of-battle ships and one 50-gun ship, penetrated with half his squadron between the French line and the shore, while his remaining ships engaged them on the outside. Thus caught between two fires, the French were utterly routed, only two of their vessels escaping capture or destruction. Admiral Brueys was killed and his ship *L'Orient* blown up. This battle is also known as the Battle of Abukir. It ended the projected French conquest of the Middle East. *See* Ushant, Pyramids.

Nineveh *Persian Wars*

December 12, 627, between the Imperial troops under the Emperor Heraclius and the Persians under Rhazates, the general of Chosroes II. The Persians stood their ground manfully throughout the day and far into the night and were almost annihilated before the surviving remnant retreated in good order to their camp. The Romans also lost heavily, but the victory opened the way to the royal city of Destigerd, which fell into the hands of Heraclius, and peace was made the following year. *See* Aiznadin.

Niquitas *Colombian War of Independence*

In 1813, when the Colombian Patriots, under Bolívar, completely defeated the Spanish Royalists.

Nisibis *Persian Wars of the Roman Empire*

This fortress, known as the Bulwark of the East, was thrice besieged in 338, 346 and 350 by Sapor II, King of Persia. In the two former years he was compelled to retire after a siege of 60 and 80 days respectively. In 350 the city was defended by a garrison under Lucilianus, and Sapor, finding the ordinary methods unavailing, diverted the course of the Mygdonius and by building dams formed a large lake, upon which he placed a fleet of armed vessels and attacked the city almost from the level of the ramparts. Under pressure of the water a portion of the wall gave way, and the Persians at once delivered an assault, but were repulsed; and by the following day the garrison had rebuilt the wall. At the end of about three months, Sapor, having lost 20,000 men, raised the siege. *See* Singara.

Nissa *Scandinavian Wars*

A naval action, fought at the mouth of the Nissa in 1064, between the Danish fleet under Sweyn II and the Norwegians under Harold Hardrada. Sweyn was totally defeated and his fleet destroyed, he himself escaping with difficulty to Zealand.

Nive *Peninsular War*

December 13, 1813, between 35,000 French under Marshal Soult and 14,000 British and Portuguese under General Lord Wellington. Having crossed the Nive on the 10th Wellington took up a strong position on the heights near the village of St Pierre. Here he was attacked by Soult, but repulsed him and occupied the French position in front of the Adour. The French losses in this battle and the combats which preceded it amounted to 10,000 men. The British lost 5,019 killed and wounded. *See* Orthez.

Nivelle *Peninsular War*

November 10, 1813, when the French, under Marshal Soult, were driven from a very strong position by the British, under General Lord Wellington, and forced to retire behind the Nivelle. The French lost 4,265, including about 1,200 prisoners, 51 guns, and all their field magazines. The British lost 2,694 killed and wounded. *See* Vitoria, Nive.

Nizib *Mehemet Ali's Second Rebellion*

June 24, 1839, between 30,000 Turks under Hafiz Pasha and Mehemet Ali's Syro-Egyptian army, under his son Ibrahim. Ibrahim was far the stronger in artillery, and his fire so shattered the Turks that when he finally advanced his infantry they made no stand, but turned and fled. Von Moltke, as a captain in the Turkish service, was under fire in this action for the first time. *See* Koniah, Acre IV.

Noisseville *Franco-Prussian War*

A sortie of the French, under Marshal Bazaine, from Metz, August 31, 1870, in the endeavour to break through the investing line of the Germans, under Prince Frederick Charles. The French had some slight success at first, and maintained the ground they had won during the day, but on September 1 their further efforts to advance were fruitless and they were driven back into Metz with a loss of 145 officers and 3,379 men. The Germans lost 126 officers and 2,850 men. *See* Gravelotte, Mars-la-Tour.

Nördlingen I *Thirty Years' War*

September 6, 1634, between 40,000 Imperialists under Ferdinand of Hungary and a numerically inferior force of Germans and Swedes under the Duke of Weimar and Count Horn. The action was fought to relieve Nördlingen which Ferdinand was besieging, and resulted in the total defeat of the allies who lost 10,000 killed, 6,000 prisoners including Horn, and 80 guns. As a result France entered the war. *See* Lützen.

Nördlingen II *Thirty Years' War*

August 3, 1645, between 15,000 French under Louis II, the Great Condé and 12,000 Imperialists under Field Marshal Baron Franz von Mercy. The French attacked the village of Allerheim where the Imperialists were strongly entrenched, and after very severe fighting the left under the Vicomte de Turenne succeeded in expelling them, with a loss of 6,000 killed, wounded and prisoners and almost all their guns. Field Marshal von Mercy was killed. The French loss amounted to about 4,000. *See* Zusmarshausen, Lens.

Northallerton,

see Standard

Northampton *Wars of the Roses*

July 10, 1460, between the Lancastrians under King Henry VI and the Yorkists under the Earl of Warwick. The king's entrenchments were betrayed by Lord Grey de Ruthyn and the Lancastrians were defeated with a loss of 300 killed, including the Duke of Buckingham, the Earls of Shrewsbury, Egremont, and other prominent men. The king was made prisoner. *See* Wakefield.

North Foreland *Anglo-Dutch Wars*

August 4, 1666, between the English fleet

under the Duke of Albemarle and Prince Rupert, and the Dutch under Admirals Van Tromp and de Ruyter. The English gained a complete victory, capturing or burning 20 ships. The Dutch had 4,000 men killed or drowned. The Treaty of Breda ended this war in 1667. *See* The Downs.

Norway *World War II*

April 9, 1940, when six German battle groups including parachutists, aided by Quisling's 5th column, seized Oslo, Kristiansand, Trondheim, Bergen and Stavanger. Britain's Royal Navy intervened, sinking in two actions off Narvik ten German destroyers for the loss of two. Britain then hastily launched an ill-planned counter-invasion, April 14 to 19, with landings at Namsos and Aandalsnes, near Trondheim, and in the north near Narvik. The lack of a large port through which to pour in war supplies and an airfield from which to give air cover against the *Luftwaffe*, made it clear that the invasion could not be sustained and two weeks later Britain was forced to retreat and disembark. At Narvik too, having seized the port and driven the German defenders into the mountains, she was compelled by the sudden débâcle in northern France to abandon the campaign, the last troops being re-embarked on June 9, together with King Haakon, who established a London government-in-exile. Germany had obtained sea and air bases in Norway and a secure northern flank, but she lost a heavy cruiser, two light cruisers, ten destroyers, 11 transports, eight submarines and 11 auxiliary ships, against the British loss of a carrier, two cruisers, nine destroyers and six submarines. *See* Atlantic II.

Notium *Peloponnesian War*

407 BC, between the Peloponnesian fleet under Lysander and the Athenian fleet of Alcibiades, which was lying at Notium. Alcibiades was not present during the action, which was the result of a surprise, and the Athenians were defeated with a loss of 15 ships. *See* Cyzicus.

Nova Carthago *Second Punic War*

This city, defended by a small Carthaginian garrison under Mago was stormed by 27,500 Romans under Scipio, 209 BC. *See* Metaurus.

Novara I *French Wars in Italy*

June 6, 1513, between 10,000 French under Louis de la Trémoille and 13,000 Swiss. The French camp was surprised by the Swiss, who, after hard fighting, totally routed the French with a loss of 6,000 men. The Swiss losses were also heavy. *See* Marignano.

Novara II *Italian Wars of Independence*

March 23, 1849, between 47,000 Piedmontese under Chrzanowski and three Austrian army corps, 45,000, under Field Marshal Radetsky. After hard fighting the Piedmontese were completely defeated and driven from the field in disorder. Under the peace treaty the defeated paid a huge indemnity to Austria. *See* Venice.

Novi *French Revolutionary Wars*

August 15, 1799, between the French under General Joubert and the Russians and Austrians under General Suvorov. Early in the action Joubert fell, General Moreau succeeding to the command. The result was disastrous to the French, who were defeated with a loss of 7,000 killed and wounded, 3,000 prisoners and 37 guns. The allies lost 6,900 killed and wounded and 1,200 prisoners. *See* Nile, Montebello.

Nujufghur *Indian Mutiny*

August 24, 1857, between 6,000 rebels under Mohammed Bukht Khan and a small British force under John Nicholson. The rebels were defeated at small cost with a loss of over 800 men and all their guns. *See* Cawnpore, Delhi.

Numantia *Lusitanian War*

This city, defended by the inhabitants under Megaravicius, was besieged 142 BC by a Roman consular army. In the course of 141 the Romans were twice defeated under the walls, and though negotiations for a surrender were entered into in the following year, they were not concluded, and in 139 the new Roman commander, Popilius Laenas, refused to ratify the terms. Shortly afterwards he was again defeated by the Numantians, as was his successor Mancius in 137. It was not till the arrival of Scipio Æmilianus in 134 that the lengthy resistance of the inhabitants was at last overcome, and fifteen months after he took command the city fell, in the autumn of 133 BC. *See* Carthage.

O

Obligado *Uruguayan Civil War*

November, 1845, between the Argentine fleet under Oribe and the combined French and British squadrons. The allies were victorious and Oribe was forced to raise the siege of Montevideo, while the waters of the Parana were opened to the shipping of all nations. *See* Montevideo, II and III.

Ocean Pond *American Civil War*

February 20, 1864, between 5,000 Confederates under General Finnegan and 6,000 Federals under General Seymour. The Confederates occupied a strong position, protected by swamps and forests, near Lake City, where they were attacked by Seymour, whom they defeated with a loss of 1,200 killed or wounded and five guns. The Confederates' loss amounted to 930. *See* Spotsylvania.

Ockley *Danish Invasions of Britain*

851, between the Danes and the West Saxons under Ethelwulf. The Danes were completely defeated. *See* Reading.

Oczakov *Ottoman Wars*

This fortress, defended by 10,000 Turks and Bosnians, was besieged 1737 by the Russians under Count Münnich, and after the magazine had been blown up was stormed by the besiegers and the garrison cut to pieces.
In 1788 the place was again besieged by the Russians, under General Potemkin, and after a strenuous resistance of six months, was taken by storm, December 17. In the massacre which followed, 30,000 of the garrison and inhabitants were put to the sword. *See* Peterwardein, Çeşme.

Odawara *Hojo Rebellion*

The castle of Odawara, the last stronghold of the Hojo family, was besieged in 1590 by the Japanese Imperial troops under Hideyoshi. The castle held out for over three months, but at last finding that they could hope for no support from without, the garrison surrendered, and the power of the Hojo family came to an end.

Œnophyta *First Peloponnesian War*

457 BC, between the Athenians, under Myronides, and the Thebans and other Boeotian states. The Boeotians were totally defeated and were in consequence compelled to acknowledge the headship of Athens, and to contribute men to her armies. *See* Tanagra.

Ofen *Hungarian Rising*

This fortress, held by an Austrian garrison under General Hentzi, was besieged by the Hungarians under General Görgey, May 4, 1849. After an unsuccessful assault a siege was begun, and several further assaults having also failed, the place was finally taken by storm on the 21st. General Hentzi was mortally wounded. *See* Schwechat.

Ohud *Mohammed's War with the Koreish*

In 623, between 950 Muslims under Mohammed and 3,000 Koreish of Mecca under Abu Sophian. The latter were victorious, 70 Muslims being slain, and the Prophet himself wounded, but Abu Sophian did not feel himself strong enough to follow up his victory by an attack upon Medina. *See* Medina.

Okinawa *World War II*

April 1, 1945, after heavy B29 bombardments, 50,000 men of US General Bruckner's 10th Army landed on the western coast, Hagushi Bay, of this island, 67 miles long by up to 20 wide, in the Ryuku chain, midway between Formosa and Japan, defended by General Ushijima's 100,000-strong 32nd Army. Within 24 hours the Americans seized Yontan and Kadena airfields. Their troops in the northern parts of the island advanced swiftly, but those in the south met bitter resistance. A Japanese relief force, the giant battlecruiser *Yamato* (72,908 tons), one light cruiser and eight destroyers, was intercepted and attacked in the Van Diemen Strait by US aircraft. The *Yamato*, a cruiser and four destroyers were sunk, seriously weakening Japanese naval forces. Meanwhile, despite the most determined Japanese resistance, General

186

Bruckner with 160,000 men had won
four-fifths of the island by April 19. A
Japanese counter-attack in the south on May
4–5 cost them 6,200 killed. The Americans
finally assaulted the Oroku Peninsula in the
south on June 4 and cleared it in ten days'
fighting. The battle for Okinawa was won on
July 2 when resistance ceased. Both generals
died, Bruckner from artillery fire and Ushijima
through *hara-kiri*. Nearly 100,000 Japanese
were killed, including suicide pilots who
dived on the US and British warships in this
three-month battle. The victory cost the US
8,000 killed and 35,500 wounded. The
Japanese navy was now so weak as to be
ineffective, while her air force lost some
7,000 planes. *See* Iwo Jima.

Olmedo *War of the Castilian Succession*

1467, between the Spanish adherents of the
Infante Alfonso, a claimant to the throne,
under the Archbishop of Toledo, and the
Royal troops under Henry of Castile. After an
action which began late in the afternoon and
lasted for three hours without any very
decisive result, the Archbishop, whose troops
were considerably inferior in numbers,
withdrew, leaving Henry in possession of the
field. *See* Toro.

Olmutz *Seven Years' War*

This place was besieged by Frederick the
Great, May, 1758. Having insufficient troops
to invest the place completely, Frederick's
task was a difficult one, and Marshal Daun
was able to keep communications open and
supply the town with provisions. After a siege
of seven weeks the Austrians captured a
convoy of 4,000 waggons, under the escort of
Landon, destined for the Prussian army, and
Frederick was forced by this loss to raise the
siege and retire, on July 1. *See* Crefeld.

Olpae *Great Peloponnesian War*

426 BC, between a small Athenian force under
Demosthenes and a force of Ambraciots, with
3,000 Spartan hoplites, under Eurylochus.
Demosthenes gained a complete victory by
means of an ambuscade, and Eurylochus was
slain. *See* Pylos.

Oltenitza *Crimean War*

November 4, 1853, when General Omar
Pasha's Turkish army crossed the Danube
and defeated at Oltenitza the Russian army
of Czar Nicholas I that had invaded
Wallachia (now Rumania), part of the
disintegrating Ottoman Empire. Turkey had
declared war against the invaders on October
4. *See* Sinope.

Omdurman *British-Sudan Campaigns*

September 2, 1898, between the British and
Egyptians, 23,000 strong, under Sir Herbert
Kitchener, and 50,000 Dervishes, under the
Khalifa. The Dervishes attacked the British
zareba, and were repulsed with heavy loss.
Kitchener then advanced to drive the enemy
before him into Omdurman and capture the
place. In the course of the operation,
however, the Egyptian Brigade on the British
right, under General Macdonald, became
isolated and was attacked in front by the
centre of the Dervish army, while his flank
and rear were threatened by the Dervish
left, which had not previously been engaged.
The position was critical, but through the
extreme steadiness of the Sudanese, who
changed front under heavy fire, the attack
was repulsed. The 21st Lancers, among whom
was Winston Churchill, made the last full-scale
cavalry charge of modern warfare. The British
and Egyptian losses were 500 killed and
wounded. The Dervishes lost about 15,000.
See Atbara.

Onao *Indian Mutiny*

July 28, 1857, between General Havelock's
relieving force, and the rebels, who occupied
a strong position near Onao, so protected on
the flanks that a frontal attack was necessary.
This was successful and after the town had
been passed a further attack by the
mutineers was repulsed with a loss of 300
men and 15 guns. *See* Cawnpore, Delhi.

Onessant *American Revolutionary War*

July 27, 1778, between 30 British ships of the
line under Admiral Keppel and a French
squadron of equal force under the Comte
d'Estaing. After a fight which lasted
throughout the day, the two fleets drew off to

repair damages, neither side having lost a ship. *See* Negapatam.

Oondwa Nullah *British Conquest of Bengal*

September, 1763, when 3,000 British and Indian troops under Major Adams carried by storm the entrenchments and the fort held by Mir Kasim's Bengal army of 60,000 men with 100 guns. Mir Kasim fled and his army was entirely dispersed. *See* Calcutta, Buxar.

Ooscata *First British-Mysore War*

August 23, 1768, when the camp of the Maratha contingent, under Morari Rao, forming a part of Colonel Donald Campbell's column, was attacked by a detachment of Hyder Ali's army. The Marathas repulsed the Mysore cavalry with a loss of about 300, at a cost to themselves of 18 only. *See* Madras, Seringapatam.

Opequan *American Civil War*

September 19, 1864, between 13,000 Confederates under General Early and 45,000 Federals under General Sheridan. Success at first inclined to the side of the Southerners, but their left wing was broken by a charge of 7,000 cavalry under Lieut.-Colonel Custer, and the Confederates were completely routed and fled in confusion. *See* Franklin, Nashville.

Oporto *Peninsular War*

March 28, 1809, when the French under Marshal Soult completely defeated the Portuguese under Lima and Pareiras, outside the city of Oporto. Soult followed up his success by storming Oporto, with horrible slaughter, it being computed that 10,000 of the inhabitants perished. The French lost 500 only. Taking command of the British troops in Portugal in April, General Lord Wellesley (later the Duke of Wellington) made a surprise crossing of the Douro and on May 12 advanced on Oporto. Soult retreated, Wellesley took the city and the French lost heavily. *See* Corunna, Talavera.

Oran I *Spanish Invasion of Morocco*

May 17, 1509, between the Moors and the Spaniards, under Navarro. The Spaniards, late in the evening, attacked and drove off the Moors from a strong position on the heights above the city. They then stormed the city itself, escalading the walls by placing their pikes in the crevices of the stones. The Moors lost, in the battle and the storm, 4,000 killed and about 8,000 prisoners, while the losses of the victors were very small. *See* Granada.

Oran II *World War II*

July 3, 1940, when Admiral Sir James Somerville's Royal Navy Task Force H sailed up to Oran harbour and issued an ultimatum to Admiral Gensoul's French fleet of two battle cruisers, two battleships, eight light cruisers and a number of destroyers and submarines, to join forces with the Allies, sail to North America, or be scuttled. When Admiral Gensoul refused the ultimatum, the British warships and naval aircraft sank or damaged practically the entire French fleet in ten minutes' devastating attack. This much-criticized action prevented the French fleet possibly collaborating with the Germans on the orders of the pro-Nazi Vichy Government. *See* Atlantic II.

Orchomenus *First Mithridatic War*

85 BC, between the Pontic army under Archelaus and the Romans under Sulla. The Asiatic cavalry attacked and drove back the Roman line, but Sulla himself rallied his troops and led them in a charge which totally routed the enemy with heavy loss. *See* Cyzicus, Tigranocerta.

Orel *World War II*

After the disastrous German defeat at Kursk in July 1943, Russian General Popov's army group on July 12 counter-attacked the German-held salient round the city of Orel, 100 miles north, and by July 15 had broken through the main German defences, following an intense artillery bombardment heavier than anything the Germans had yet experienced. The city fell on August 5 after desperate house-to-house fighting. Russian casualties were very heavy, owing especially to the hundreds of thousands of mines with which the Germans had ringed the city. *See* Kursk, Kharkov.

Orléans *Hundred Years' War*

This city was besieged by the English under the Regent, the Duke of Bedford, and the Earl of Salisbury, on October 12, 1428. In April, 1429, a French force, 7,000 strong, under the Comte de Dunois and Joan of Arc, succeeded in entering, it having been found impossible to invest the place completely. After various successful attacks on the batteries erected by the besiegers, Joan, on the 6th and 7th of May, led the garrison to victory against the English lines, and on the 8th Bedford was compelled to raise the siege. The battle was decisive in the 100 years' war. *See* Verneuil.

Orthez *Peninsular War*

February 27, 1814, between the British under General Lord Wellington and the French under Marshal Soult. The French were driven out of Orthez and across the Luy de Béarn with a loss of 4,000 killed and wounded and six guns. *See* Nive, Nivelle.

Oruro *Bolivian Civil War*

In 1862, between the Bolivian Government troops under the President, General Acha, and the rebels under General Perez, who had proclaimed himself President. Perez was utterly routed.

Ostend *Netherlands War of Independence*

This town was besieged, July 5, 1601, by the Spaniards under the Archduke Albert. The town made a most remarkable defence, holding out for more than three years, but Spinola having taken command of the besiegers, it was finally captured, September 14, 1604, by which time scarcely a house was left standing. The Spaniards lost 70,000 men in the course of the siege. *See* Nieuwpoort.

Ostia *French Wars in Italy*

This town, held by a French garrison under Menaldo Guerri, was besieged in 1500 by the Spaniards under Gonsalvo de Cordova. After five days' bombardment an attack was made upon the town on the opposite side by a small party of Spaniards resident in Rome, under Garcilasso de la Vega. Thus between two fires, Guerri surrendered. *See* Cerignola.

Ostrolenka *Crimean War*

In November 1853, between the Turks under Omar Pasha and the Russian army which had invaded the Danubian Principalities. The Turks, who were considerably superior in numbers, gained a complete victory. *See* Sinope.

Ostrowno *Napoleonic Wars*

July 25 and 26, 1812, between the French corps of Marshal Ney and Prince Eugène, with Marshal Murat's cavalry, and the Russian corps of Count Osterman and General Konownitzyn. The Russians were defeated and driven back on both days, with a loss of 3,000 killed and wounded, 800 prisoners and eight guns. The French loss was about the same. *See* Borodino, Smolensk.

Oswego *Seven Years' War*

This village, in French North America, held by a garrison of 1,400 Provincial troops under Colonel Mercer, was besieged by the French under the Marquis of Montcalm, August 11, 1756. After a bombardment of three days in the course of which Mercer was killed, it surrendered. The losses on both sides were very small. *See* Lake George, Beauséjour.

Otrar *Tatar Invasion of Khorezm*

This city (now Uzbek SSR) was besieged 1219, by 200,000 Tatars under Oktai and Zagatai, sons of Genghis Khan, and defended by a garrison of 60,000 under Gazer Khan. It was entered after a four months' siege, by which time the garrison was reduced to 20,000 men, but with this remnant Gazer Khan held out in the citadel for another month. *See* Bamian.

Otterburn *Wars of Scottish Independence*

August 15, 1388, between 9,000 English under Henry Percy (Hotspur) and a greatly inferior force of Scots under Earls Douglas and Murray. Hotspur attacked the Scottish entrenchments and was totally defeated, with a loss of about 2,000. The battle is celebrated in the old ballad of *Chevy Chase*. *See* Neville's Cross.

Otumba *Spanish Conquest of Mexico*

July 8, 1520, between 200 Spaniards, with some thousands of Tlascalan auxiliaries, under Cortés, and a force of about 200,000 Aztecs. The Spaniards, wearied by a long march on their retreat from Mexico, were intercepted by the Aztecs, and after many hours' fighting were on the verge of defeat, when a charge of a few cavaliers, headed by Cortés, into the very heart of the Aztec army so discouraged them that they fled in disorder.

Oudenarde *War of the Spanish Succession*

July 11, 1708, between 80,000 British and Imperialists under the Duke of Marlborough and Prince Eugène, and 85,000 French under the Duke of Burgundy and the Duc de Vendôme. The French, who were besieging Oudenarde, raised the siege on the advance of the allies and marched to meet them, but were totally defeated with a loss of 3,000 killed, 7,000 prisoners and ten guns. The allies lost 2,000. *See* Lille, Tournai.

Overlord, Operation,

see D-Day

P

Paardeberg *Second Boer War*

February 18, 1900, between 5,000 Boers under
Cronje and the British, numbering four
Infantry Brigades with four batteries, under
Lord Kitchener. Cronje had taken refuge in
the bed of the Tugela river and an attempt
was made to dislodge him. The absence of
cover for the attacking force however rendered
this impossible, but he was surrounded and
on the arrival of Lord Roberts, subjected to a
sustained artillery fire, which lasted until he
surrendered on the 27th. The British losses
during the operations amounted to 98 officers
and 1,437 men of whom 1,100 fell in the
battle of the 18th. The prisoners taken
numbered 3,000 Transvaalers and 1,100 Free
Staters with six guns. *See* Kimberley,
Bloemfontein.

Pagahar *First Burma War*

The only occasion during the war when the
Burmans met the British in the open. In 1825
Sir Archibald Campbell with 1,300 men
encountered 15,000 Burmans under
Zay-ya-Thayan, but the battle was almost a
bloodless one for the Burmans failed to make
any stand, their general being the first to flee.
See Kemendine, Kamarut.

Pagasaean Gulf *Sacred War*

352 BC, between the Phocians under
Onomarchus and the Macedonians under
Philip. Philip's infantry was about equal in
numbers to that of the Phocians but he was
far superior in cavalry, and in the end the
Phocians were completely defeated with the
loss of a third of their number. Onomarchus
was slain.

Palais Gallien *War of the Fronde*

September 5, 1649, between the Royal troops,
8,000 strong under the Marshal de la
Meilleraic, and 7,000 Bordelais under the
Ducs de Bouillon and de la Rochefoucauld.
The Bordelais successfully repulsed four or
five assaults, but by nightfall were driven from

their entrenchments into the city with a loss of
about 120. The assailants lost over 1,000
killed and wounded.

Palermo *Italian Wars of Independence*

May 26 and 27, 1848, when Garibaldi with
750 of his 'Thousand Volunteers' and about
3,000 Sicilian 'Picciotti', succeeded in
surprising one of the gates of Palermo which
was garrisoned by 18,000 Neapolitans under
General Lanza. The 'Picciotti' fled at the first
shot but Garibaldi penetrated into the city
where, being joined by the citizens, he erected
barricades, and after some severe fighting in
which the Neapolitans suffered heavily,
General Lanza surrendered. The last of the
Neapolitan troops were withdrawn on June 20.
See Novara.

Palestrina *Italian Wars of Independence*

May 9, 1849, between 4,000 Italian Patriots
under Garibaldi and 7,000 Neapolitans under
King Ferdinand. After three hours' fighting
the Neapolitans were totally routed. Garibaldi
was wounded in the action. *See* Novara,
Palermo, Palestro.

Palestro *Italian Wars of Independence*

May 30, 1859, between the Sardinians under
General Cialdini and the Austrians under
General Stadion. The Austrians attacked the
Sardinians while they were crossing the Sesia
but were repulsed, and Cialdini effected the
passage successfully and drove the Austrians
out of Palestro with considerable loss.
See Palestrina, Palermo, Novara.

Palmyra *Roman Empire Wars*

This city was besieged by the Romans, under
Aurelian, after the defeat of Zenobia at
Emesa in 272. An obstinate defence was made
by the Queen, but Aurelian being reinforced
by Probus early in 273, Zenobia fled from the
city and the place was captured. Zenobia
failed to escape and was brought into
Aurelian's camp. During his return march
Aurelian learnt that the citizens had risen and
massacred the Governor and the garrison he
had left in the place. He thereupon retraced
his steps and destroyed the city, sparing
neither young nor old. *See* Emesa.

191

Palo Alto *American-Mexican War*

May 8, 1846, between the Americans under General Taylor and the Mexicans under Arista. The Mexicans were completely routed at very small cost to the victors.
See Monterrey, Buena Vista.

Panama I *Raids of the Buccaneers*

On December 16, 1670, Morgan the Buccaneer sailed from Hispaniola with 37 ships and about 2,000 men to plunder this town. Having captured the castle of San Lorenzo at the mouth of the Chagre, an exploit which cost the assailants 170 out of 400 men engaged, while two-thirds of the garrison were killed, Morgan started to cross the Isthmus at the head of 1,200 men, January 18, 1671. The garrison of Panama, 2,400 strong, met him outside the city and were defeated with heavy loss, the Buccaneers losing 600 men. Morgan then sacked the place and on February 24 withdrew with 175 mule loads of plunder and 600 prisoners. *See* Panama II.

Panama II *Raids of the Buccaneers*

April 23, 1680, between the Buccaneers, with three ships, under John Coxon, and three Spanish vessels. The Spaniards were defeated after a hard fight in which two Spanish vessels were captured by boarding. The Spanish commander was killed. The Buccaneers then entered the Bay, and captured six vessels lying in the roads.

Pandosia *Macedonian Conquests*

331 BC, between the Italian Greeks under Alexander of Epirus and the Lucanians. During the battle Alexander was stabbed by a Lucanian exile serving in the Greek army, and the Greeks were in the end defeated.
See Hydaspes, Issus.

Pandu Naddi I *Indian Mutiny*

July 15, 1857, between a British relieving force under General Havelock and the Indian troops who were opposing his advance to Cawnpore. By a forced march in the heat of the day Havelock succeeded in seizing the bridge over the Pandu Naddi, which the rebels were engaged in mining, thus securing an open road to Cawnpore. The rebels were driven off after a short engagement.
See Cawnpore.

Pandu Naddi II *Indian Mutiny*

November 26, 1857, between 1,400 British under General Windham and the advance guard of the mutineers and the Gwalior contingent, under the Nana Sahib. The rebels were posted beyond the river and the British, crossing the dry bed, drove them from their entrenchments, capturing three guns. Windham then finding himself close to the main body of mutineers, retired towards Cawnpore. *See* Cawnpore, Delhi.

Panion *Wars of the Hellenistic Monarchies*

198 BC, between the Syrians under Antiochus the Great and the Greeks and Egyptians under Scopas. Scopas was routed, and Antiochus took possession of all the territory held by Egypt in Asia, up to the frontier of Egypt proper. *See* Thermopylae II.

Panipat I *Third Mughal Invasion*

April 21, 1526, between the Delhi Mohammedans, 10,000 strong with 100 elephants, under Ibrahim, and the Mughals, about 2,000 picked men under Babur. Ibrahim was totally defeated, being himself among the slain. The battle marked the end of the Afghan dynasty of Delhi and the start of the Mughal Empire. *See* Panipat II.

Panipat II *Hindu Revolt*

November 5, 1556, between Akbar Khan, with about 20,000 troops, and the forces of the revolted Hindu Rajahs, 100,000 strong with 1,500 elephants, under Hemu. The Hindus attacked, and the onslaught of the elephants being repulsed, their ranks were thrown into disorder and the Mughals gained a complete victory. Hemu was wounded in the eye, captured and executed. By this victory Akbar recovered Delhi, which had fallen into the hands of the rebels. According to custom, a tower was built with the heads of the fallen enemy. *See* Panipat I.

Panipat III *Afghan-Maratha Wars*

1759, between the Marathas, 85,000 strong under Sedashao Rao Bhao, cousin of the Peshwa, and the Duranis, numbering with

Hindu allies about 90,000, under Ahmed Shah. The Bhao attacked and dispersed Ahmed's Indian troops, but on the Duranis coming into action, the Marathas were broken and utterly routed, with enormous loss. The Bhao and the son of the Peshwa were among the slain.

Panormus *First Punic War*

251 BC, between 25,000 Romans under L. Caecilius Metellus and the Carthaginian army in Sicily, under Hasdrubal. Hasdrubal offered battle in front of Panormus and Metellus sent out his light troops to engage him. They ran back into the town before a charge of the elephants which, following closely, were driven into the ditch surrounding the place, where many were killed. Meanwhile Metellus sallied out with his legionaries and taking Hasdrubal in flank completely routed him. All the Carthaginian elephants in Sicily were killed or captured in this battle. *See* Tunis.

Paraetakene Mountains *Wars of Alexander's Successors*

316 BC, between the Macedonians, 30,000 strong under Antigonus and an equal force of Asiatics under Eumenes. Eumenes attacked the Macedonian camp, and after a severe engagement in which the Asiatics held the advantage, Antigonus, by successful manœuvring, withdrew his army without serious loss, leaving Eumenes a barren victory. *See* Cynoscephalae II.

Parana *Paraguayan War*

1866, between the Paraguayans under Francisco López and the Brazilians under Porto Alegre. López was victorious. *See* Aquidaban, Humaita.

Paris I *Napoleonic Wars*

On March 30, 1814, Paris, which was defended only by 20,000 regulars and National Guard under Marshals Mortier and Marmont, was attacked by the Grand Army of the allies under Prince Karl von Schwartzenberg. Three columns assaulted the French positions at Vincennes, Belleville and Montmartre while a fourth attacked the extreme left of the French line in order to turn the heights of Montmartre. The two first positions were carried and Montmartre turned,

whereupon Napoleon's brother King Joseph fled and Marmont surrendered. The French lost over 4,000 men; the allies about 8,000. Napoleon was exiled to Elba. *See* Toulouse.

Paris II *Franco-Prussian War*

Paris was invested by the main German army of 240,000 with 240 siege guns, under the King of Prussia and General von Moltke, September 20, 1870. The garrison, 400,000 strong, under the command of General Trochu, made a gallant defence, several sorties taking place, but the Germans gradually mastered the outer defences, and finally, threatened with famine, the city surrendered January 28, 1871, when Bismarck and Jules Favre, French Foreign Minister, met at Versailles to sign an armistice and end the war. The French lost 10,000 killed or wounded, the Germans 16,000 killed or wounded. *See* Sedan, Metz, Coulmiers.

Parkany *Ottoman Wars*

August, 1663, between 200,000 Turks under the Grand Vizier, Achmet Köpriali Pasha, and the Hungarians in far smaller force under Count Forgacz. The Hungarians were defeated and driven into Neuhäusel, which, after a valiant resistance of six weeks, capitulated September 24. *See* Vienna II.

Parma *War of the Polish Succession*

June 29, 1734, between the French under Marshal de Coigny and the Imperialists, 30,000 strong under Field-Marshal Count Claudius de Mercy. The Imperialists were defeated with a loss of 6,000, including de Mercy, who was killed. The French loss was almost as heavy. *See* Philippsburg.

Paso de la Patria *Paraguayan War*

1866, between the Paraguayans under López and the Brazilians under Porto Alegre. The Paraguayans gained a signal victory. *See* Parana.

Passchendaele *World War I*

October 30, 1917, the last operation in the third battle of Ypres, when the Canadian 3rd and 4th Divisions and the British 58th and

63rd under Field-Marshal Sir Douglas Haig moved off at dawn through deep mud and flooded shell holes to engage in a desperate struggle with the 5th and 11th Bavarian Divisions for this main ridge of West Flanders. Heavy rain and unyielding enemy resistance slowed then stopped the attack until November 6, when at dawn the 1st and 2nd Canadian Divisions staggered forward and carried the entire objective. The ridged salient from which German guns for three years had dominated British positions was eliminated at last. *See* Ypres III.

Patay *Hundred Years' War*

June 18, 1429, between the French under Joan of Arc and the Duc d'Alençon and the English under Talbot, Earl of Shrewsbury, and Sir John Fastolfe. The English were retiring after the siege of Orléans, and their advanced guard under Talbot being attacked by the French, was seized with a panic and refusing to meet the charge of the French cavalry broke and fled. The main body under Fastolfe, however, maintained its formation and made good its retreat to Etampes. Talbot was made prisoner. This victory, and Joan of Arc, stimulated French nationalism. *See* Formigny, Castillon.

Patila *Tatar Invasion of Persia*

1394, between the Tatars under Tamerlane and the Persians under Shah Mansur. The Persians vigorously attacked the Tatar centre and Tamerlane was nearly overwhelmed, but rallying his troops he led a charge which restored the battle and gained a complete victory. The complete subjugation of Persia followed. *See* Delhi II.

Pavia I *Invasion of the Alemanni*

In 271, between the Romans under Aurelian and the German invaders. Aurelian gained a signal victory and the Alemanni recrossed the frontier. *See* Placentia, Emesa.

Pavia II *Lombard Conquest of Italy*

This city was besieged in 568 by the Lombards, under Alboin, and after a gallant defence, lasting over three years, was at last subdued, rather by famine than by force of arms, and surrendered to the besiegers. Pavia then became the capital of the Lombard kingdom of Italy. *See* Taginae, Casilinum, Ravenna.

Pavia III *Italian Wars*

May 22, 1431, on the Ticino, near Pavia, between 85 Venetian galleys under Nicolas Trevisani and a somewhat superior number of galleys in the pay of the Milanese. The Venetians were defeated with a loss of 70 galleys and 3,000 men. *See* Pola, Chioggia.

Pavia IV *Wars of Charles V*

February 25, 1525, between 28,000 Swiss, Italian and French under Francis I and 23,000 Imperialists, mostly Spanish pikemen, under Lannoy. Francis, who was besieging Pavia, awaited the attack of the Imperialists on his lines, and his artillery caused great havoc in their ranks, then, charging at the head of his cavalry, he was repulsed by Lannoy's infantry, and the Swiss mercenaries being taken in flank and thrown into disorder, the battle was lost. Francis was captured. This is the occasion on which he wrote to his mother, 'Rien ne m'est demouré, excepte l'honneur et la vie qui est sauvé.' This defeat led to the period of Spanish control of Italy. *See* Rome VII.

Peach Tree Creek *American Civil War*

July 20, 1864, in the course of the operations round Atlanta, between the Federals under General Sherman and the Confederates under General Hood. Hood attacked the Federal position, and drove off their left wing, capturing 13 guns and some prisoners; being reinforced, however, the Federals rallied and recovered the lost ground. The Confederates however claimed the victory. The Federals lost 3,722, including General McPherson; Confederate losses were about the same. *See* Cedar Creek, Fisher's Hill.

Pea Ridge *American Civil War*

March 7 and 8, 1862, between 17,000 Confederates under General von Dorn and the Federals, 11,000 strong under General Curtis. On the 7th the Confederates drove back the Federal right wing and nearly succeeded in cutting their communications, though they lost General McCulloch in the course of the action. On the 8th the Federals drove back the Southerners and recovered the ground they had lost. Federal casualties totalled 1,300, Confederates' 800. This is also called the Battle of Elk Horn. *See* Shiloh.

Pearl Harbor *World War II*

On December 7, 1941, when an armada of 350 Japanese carrier-launched aircraft attacked the US Pacific Fleet in Pearl Harbor, Oahu, Hawaii, the first wave of 183 aircraft at 7.55 am, the second at 8.40 am For the loss of 29 aircraft and five midget submarines, the Japanese destroyed 247 aircraft, mostly on the ground, sank three battleships and capsized another, damaged still another four, sank 11 warships, killed 2,330 military personnel and wounded 1,145. Luckily not a single US carrier was touched; all were out on an exercise, and lacking battleships the United States fought the Pacific war in a new way, largely with carriers and aircraft. On December 7 the Japanese also attacked Hong Kong and invaded Malaya. Pearl Harbor was followed by a declaration of war on the US by both Germany and Italy, and that nation was thus brought into the war. *See* Guam, Luzon, Philippine Sea.

Peiwar Kotal *Second British-Afghan War*

December 2, 1878, between a British force, 3,200 strong under Sir Frederick Roberts, with 13 guns, and about 18,000 Afghans wih 11 guns strongly posted in the Kotal. The pass was crossed and the Afghans completely defeated. The British lost 20 killed and 78 wounded. *See* Kandahar, Maiwand.

Peking *Tatar Invasion of China*

This city was besieged by the Tatars under Genghis Khan in 1214 and after a long and obstinate defence was taken by stratagem. *See* Bokhara, Samarkand.

Pelekanon *Ottoman Conquest of Asia Minor*

1329, between the Turks under Orkhan and the forces of Andronicus the Younger, Emperor of the East. The Imperialists were defeated. This is the first occasion in which the Byzantines met the Ottoman invaders in battle. *See* Kossova I.

Peleliu-Angaur *World War II*

September 15, 1944, when the 1st Division US Marines (General Rupertus) landed on the south-west corner of the tiny island of Peleliu, six miles by two, about 500 miles east of the Philippine Islands, and a forward air base which the Japanese had fortified and garrisoned with 10,000 troops. September 17, General Mueller's US 81st Infantry Division invaded and in three days overwhelmed nearby Angaur, then sent reinforcements to Peleliu on September 24. The battle there, with the Japanese fiercely contesting every yard, lasted until November 25 when resistance ended. US forces lost 1,460 killed and about 6,100 wounded in this battle which partially cleared the way to the Philippines. About 13,000 Japanese were killed in the entire operation. *See* Philippine Sea, New Guinea, Leyte.

Pelischat *Russo-Turkish War*

August 30, 1877, when the Turks, 25,000 strong with 50 guns, made a sortie from Plevna and attacked the Russian lines in front of Poradim. The Russians, 20,000 strong under General Zotov, succeeded in repulsing all the Turkish attacks with a loss of about 3,000 killed and wounded. The Russians lost 1,000. *See* Plevna.

Pelusium I *Persian Conquest of Egypt*

525 BC, between the Persians under Cambyses and the Egyptians under Psammeticus. The Egyptians were totally defeated and this victory was followed by the complete subjugation of Egypt which became a Persian satrapy.

Pelusium II *War of Alexander's Successors*

321 BC, between the Macedonians under the Regent, Perdiccas, and the Egyptians under Ptolemy Lagus. Perdiccas attacked the fortress but was driven off with heavy loss including 1,000 drowned in the Nile. *See* Hydaspes.

195

Pena Cerrada *First Carlist War*

This fortress, held by a Carlist garrison under Gergue, was captured by Espartero with 19,000 Cristinos, June 21, 1838. After shelling the place for seven hours Espartero attacked the Carlists who held the heights outside the town and dispersed them, capturing 600 prisoners and all their guns. The remainder of the garrison then abandoned the place. *See* Huesca.

Penobscot Bay *American Revolutionary War*

July 14, 1779, when a British squadron of 10 ships under Sir George Collier completely destroyed an American squadron of 24 ships and captured the 3,000 crew.

Pen Selwood *Danish Invasions of Britain*

1016, between the English under Edmund Ironside and the Danes under Knut, shortly after Edmund's election as King by the Witanegemot. This was the first of the series of engagements which ended with the Peace of Olney. *See* Mortlack.

Pered *Hungarian Rising*

June 21, 1849, between the Hungarians, 16,000 strong under General Görgey, and the Austrians and Russians under Prince zu Windischgrätz. The allies attacked the Hungarian position and after severe fighting drove them out, with a loss of about 3,000. *See* Kapolna.

Perembacum *First British-Mysore War*

September 10, 1780, when a Mysore force, 11,000 strong under Tippu Sahib, surrounded and cut to pieces a detachment of Sir Hector Monro's army, 3,700 in number, under Colonel Baillie. Only a few, including Baillie himself, escaped the massacre. *See* Porto Novo.

Perisabor *Persian Wars*

This fortress, defended by an Assyrian and Persian garrison, was captured May, 363 by the Romans under Julian. The fortress was dismantled and the town destroyed. *See* Tigris.

Perpignan *Franco-Spanish War*

This town was besieged by the French, 11,000 strong under the Seigneur du Lude, at the end of 1474, and was defended by a Spanish garrison. The Spanish army could not succeed in relieving the place, and after holding out with great gallantry until March 14, 1475, the garrison, reduced to 400 men, surrendered, and was allowed to march out with the honours of war. The capture of Perpignan gave France possession of Roussillon.

Perryville *American Civil War*

October 8, 1862, between 55,000 Federals under General Buell and a Confederate army of 23,000 under General Bragg. The Confederates attacked and drove back the Federals, but no decisive result was arrived at, and during the night Bragg withdrew, having inflicted a loss of 4,000 on the enemy and captured an artillery train. The Confederates lost about 2,500 killed and wounded. *See* Shiloh, Richmond.

Persepolis *Wars of Alexander's Successors*

316 BC, between the Macedonians, 31,000 strong with 65 elephants under Antigonus, and 42,000 Asiatics with 114 elephants under Eumenes. At the first onslaught Antigonus's infantry was overwhelmed, but his cavalry retrieved the day and seizing the enemy's camp, threw Eumenes's phalanx into confusion. Upon this the Macedonian infantry rallied and gained a complete victory, Eumenes being captured. *See* Hydaspes, Corupedion.

Peshawar *Afghan Invasion of India*

In 1001, between 10,000 Afghans under Sultan Mahmud of Ghazni, and 42,000 Punjabis, with 300 elephants, under the Rajah Jaipal of Lahore. The Rajah was totally defeated and captured with 15 of his principal chiefs. *See* Somnath.

Petersburg I *American Civil War*

June 15 to 18, 1864, forming an episode in the Federal attack on Richmond. General

Beauregard with 14,000 men was charged with the defence of Petersburg and at the same time had to contain General Butler at Bermuda Hundred. His entrenchments before Petersburg were attacked on the 15th by General Smith with 13,600 men, and a portion of the first line carried. On the 16th reinforcements brought the Federal strength up to 48,000. The same day Beauregard withdrew the force masking Bermuda Hundred and concentrated his troops in front of Petersburg, but after holding out till the afternoon the defenders panicked and were driven from the first line. Beauregard however rallied them and retook the entrenchments. During the night he withdrew to a second and stronger line of defences, and on the 17th and 18th, reinforced to a strength of 38,000, repulsed with terrible slaughter all the efforts of the Federals to carry it. They lost more than 10,000 killed or wounded. *See* Petersburg II.

Petersburg II *American Civil War*

On July 30, 1864, a mine was exploded under the Confederate defences in front of Petersburg, killing or wounding 278 men, and an attempt was made by the Federals to carry the entrenchments during the confusion. The Confederates, however, stood their ground, repulsing all attacks with heavy loss and of the Federals who succeeded in entering the breastworks, nearly 4,000 were killed or captured. The Confederates lost about 1,500. Both the generals commanding, Lee and Grant, were present during the action. The siege wore on until the night of April 2, 1865, when the 30,000 Confederates retreated to the west along the Appomattox and Lee surrendered the Confederate army on April 9. Total casualties in the 10-month siege were Federals 42,000, Confederates 28,000. *See* Coldharbour, Five Forks.

Peterwardein *Ottoman Wars*

August 5, 1716, when Prince Eugène, with 80,000 Imperialists, mostly veterans from the Flanders campaign, signally defeated 110,000 Turks under Darnad Ali Pasha. The Turks lost 20,000 killed, 50 standards and 250 guns. The Imperialists lost about 3,000. *See* Belgrade.

Petra *Persian Wars*

This strong fortress (Jordan), garrisoned by 1,500 Persians, was besieged by the Romans, 8,000 strong under Dagisteus in 549. After a series of unsuccessful assaults the Romans succeeded in bringing down a large portion of the outer wall by mining. By this time the garrison was reduced to 400, but Dagisteus delaying to storm the fortress, the Persians succeeded in throwing in reinforcements which brought the garrison up to 3,000. Meanwhile all the breaches had been repaired and the Romans had to undertake a second siege. At last a breach was effected and after very severe fighting the besiegers effected a lodgement. Of the defenders 700 fell in the second siege and 1,070 in the storm, while of 700 prisoners only 18 were unwounded. Five hundred retreated to the citadel and held out to the last, perishing in the flames when it was fired by the Romans. *See* Rome V, Melitene.

Pharsalus I *Civil War of Caesar and Pompey*

August 9, 48 BC, between the Pompeians, 50,000 strong under Pompey, and Caesareans, 25,000 strong under Caesar. The Pompeian cavalry drove back that of Caesar, but following in pursuit were thrown into confusion by the legionaries, whereupon they turned and fled from the field; the infantry followed and the battle became a rout in which 8,000 Pompeians and only 200 Caesareans fell. After the battle 20,000 Pompeians surrendered. *See* Dyrrachium.

Pharsalus II *Greco-Turkish Wars*

May 6, 1897, when Edhem Pasha with three Turkish divisions drove the Greeks from their entrenchments in front of Pharsalus (Thessaly) at a cost of about 230 killed and wounded. Greek losses were light. A peace treaty placing Crete, the cause of the war, under international control, and indemnifying Turkey, was signed on September 20.

Philiphaugh *English Civil War*

September 13, 1645, when 4,000 Covenanter horse under General David Leslie surprised and cut to pieces the Marquis of Montrose's force of Highlanders, encamped

197

near Selkirk. Montrose escaped with a few followers, and the Royalist cause in Scotland was finished. *See* Langport, Preston.

Philippi *Rebellion of Brutus*

42 BC, between the Republicans under Brutus and Cassius, 100,000 strong, and the army of the Triumvirs, about equal in numbers, under Octavius and Mark Antony. Brutus on the right repulsed the legions of Octavius and penetrated into his camp. Cassius however was overthrown by Antony and would have been overwhelmed but for the arrival of aid from the successful right wing. The action was renewed on the second day, when the Triumvirs were completely victorious and the Republican army dispersed. Brutus committed suicide on the field of battle. These two battles decided that Rome would be ruled by an autocracy. *See* Mutina, Dyrrachium.

Philippine Sea *World War II*

Japan's Admiral Toyoda sent 18 battleships and cruisers with nine aircraft carriers to attack the US fleet safeguarding the landing on Saipan, Mariana Islands, in the Philippine Sea, on June 15, 1944. Fifteen carriers of Admiral Mitscher's US Task Force 58 intercepted the Japanese fleet between the Philippines and the Marianas on June 19, when 430 Japanese aircraft fought with 450 from Task Force 58 in an 8-hour aerial battle. American aircraft destroyed 330 of the Japanese and lost 30, while their submarines torpedoed and sank two Japanese carriers. The others fled and on the night of June 20 were pursued and attacked by more than 200 US aircraft. These sank another Japanese carrier and 40 more enemy aircraft for a loss of 20. The battle decisively weakened the Japanese carrier and aircraft fleet. *See* Mariana Islands, Leyte Gulf.

Philippopolis I *First Gothic Invasion of the Roman Empire*

This city was besieged, 251, by the Goths under Cuiva and after a gallant defence, and the defeat of an attempt by Decius to relieve it, was stormed and sacked. It is said that 100,000 of the garrison and inhabitants perished in the siege and subsequent massacre. *See* Naissus.

Philippopolis II *Russo-Turkish War*

January 17, 1878, between the Russians under General Gourko and the Turks under Fuad and Shakir Pashas. The Turks made a stubborn defence of the approaches to Philippopolis but were overpowered by superior numbers and forced to retreat with a loss of 4,500 killed and wounded, 2,000 prisoners and 114 guns. The Russians lost 1,200. *See* Plevna, Schipka Pass.

Philippsburg *War of the Polish Succession*

This fortress near Karlsruhe, held by the Imperialists, was besieged in 1734 by the French under the Duke of Berwick. The Duke was killed by a cannon ball while visiting the trenches, but the place fell soon afterwards notwithstanding the efforts of Prince Eugène to relieve it. The battle had no effect upon the succession to the Polish throne. *See* Parma.

Piave River *World War I*

June 15, 1918, when the reinforced Austrian armies (58 divisions) commanded by General von Bojna on the left (east) and Field-Marshal von Hötzendorf in Trentino, on the right, attacked the 57 divisions of General Diaz's Italian army in a final effort to push Italy out of the war. Von Bojna attacked across the Piave between the Montello and the sea; von Hötzendorf in the mountains to try to turn the entire Italian front on the Piave. After a small initial advance he was stopped by the five Anglo-French divisions. Von Bojna forced a crossing of the lower Piave with 100,000 troops and advanced six miles, but heavy rain then carried away 10 out of the 14 bridges he had thrown across the Piave, stopping the arrival of his supplies. The Italians counter-attacked on June 18, three days later turning the Austrian left flank. The next day von Bojna ordered a general retreat, re-crossing the river with inevitable losses. The Austrian offensive, a failure, cost 130,000 killed or wounded, but General Diaz perhaps too cautiously did not follow up with an attack across the Piave. *See* Caporetto, Vittorio Veneto.

Pieter's Hill *Second Boer War*

The scene of the severest fighting in the course of Sir Redvers Buller's final and successful attempt to relieve Ladysmith. The operations commenced with the capture of Hlangwane on February 19, 1900, which gave the British command of the Tugela which was crossed on the 21st. On the 22nd a steady advance was made up to the line of Pieter's Hill, which was attacked by the Irish Brigade under General Hart on the 23rd. At a cost of nearly half their numbers they succeeded in establishing themselves under cover close to the Boer trenches, but could not dislodge the defenders. It was not till the 27th, when Buller had turned the Boer left, that a general assault was successful and the Boers evacuated the position. The British losses during the operation were 1,896 killed and wounded. *See* Ladysmith.

Pinkie Cleugh *Anglo-Scottish Wars*

September 10, 1547, between the Scots under the Earl of Huntly and the English under the Protector Somerset. The Scots crossed the Esk and attacked the English lines, at first with success, but were fired at by warships in the bay and thrown into confusion by a charge of cavalry; and in the end fled from the field with heavy loss. Somerset occupied Edinburgh. *See* Solway Moss.

Pirot *Serbo-Bulgarian War*

November 26 and 27, 1885, between 40,000 Serbians under King Milan and 45,000 Bulgarians under Prince Alexander. After some desultory fighting the Bulgarians seized the town of Pirot in the course of the afternoon. At dawn on the 27th the Serbians by a surprise attack recovered Pirot, which was later retaken by the Bulgarians, though the Serbians continued to hold a position to the south of the town till nightfall. Early next morning an armistice was concluded. The Bulgarians lost 2,500, the Serbians 2,000 killed and wounded. *See* Slivnica.

Pittsburgh Landing,

see Shiloh

Placentia *Invasion of the Alemanni*

271, between the Romans under Aurelian and the invading Alemanni. The barbarians attacked the Romans in the dusk of evening,

after a long and fatiguing march, and threw them into disorder, but they were rallied by the Emperor and after severe fighting succeeded in beating off the invasion. *See* Pavia I.

Plains of Abraham *Seven Years' War*

September 13, 1759, when General Wolfe, who was lying on shipboard in the St Lawrence above Quebec with 4,000 troops, effected a landing secretly in the night of the 12th to the 13th and took up unperceived a strong position on the plateau above called the Plains of Abraham. Next morning he was attacked by the Marquis de Montcalm with about equal numbers, but notwithstanding the most desperate efforts the French were unable to carry the position and were driven back into Quebec with a loss of about 1,500. Both Wolfe and Montcalm fell mortally wounded. The British loss amounted to 664 killed and wounded. The French immediately afterwards evacuated Quebec. *See also* Quebec.

Plassey *Seven Years' War*

June 23, 1757, between 800 British, with 2,200 Indians and eight guns, under Robert Clive, and the army of Siraj-ud-Daula, Nawab of Bengal, aided by a small force of Frenchmen. Clive was encamped in a grove of mango-trees, where he was attacked by the Nawab. He beat off the attack and then stormed the Nawab's lines, totally routing his army, which fled in panic with a loss of about 500. The British lost 72 only. The East India Company now became supreme in Bengal. *See* Calcutta, Buxar.

Plataea I *Third Persian Invasion*

479 BC, between the Greeks, about 80,000 strong, under Pausanias the Spartan, and 120,000 Persians, with 50,000 Greek auxiliaries, under Mardonius. The Persians fought bravely but were overborne by the superior discipline and heavier armour of the Greeks, and Mardonius falling, a panic ensued and they fled to their entrenched camp. This was stormed by the Athenians and no quarter was given, with the result, it is said, that with the exception of a body of 40,000 which left the field early in the battle,

only 3,000 Persians escaped. Greece was freed from invasion. *See* Salamis.

Plataea II *Great Peloponnesian War*

In 429 BC, this city, held by a garrison of 400 Plataeans and 80 Athenians, was besieged by the Spartans under Archidamus. All the useless mouths were sent out of the place, only 110 women being retained to bake bread. The garrison repulsed numerous assaults and the siege soon resolved itself into a blockade, but provisions becoming scarce an attempt was made to break through the enemy's lines, which half the garrison succeeded in doing with the loss of one man. The remainder held out till 427 when, being on the verge of starvation, they surrendered. The survivors were tried for having deserted Boeotia for Athens at the outbreak of the war, and 200 Plataeans and 25 Athenians were put to death. *See* Mytilene, Naupactus.

Plei Me,

see Vietnam War

Plescow *Russo-Swedish Wars*

This fortress was besieged by the Swedes under Gustavus Adolphus, August 20, 1615, and defended by a Russian garrison. It is notable as marking a departure from the established practice of surrounding a besieged city with walls of circumvallation. For these Gustavus substituted a series of entrenched camps, communications between which were maintained by strong patrolling forces. Little progress was made owing to a delay in the arrival of the Swedish breaching guns, and through the mediation of England negotiations were opened with Russia, and the siege raised, October 14, 1615. *See* Riga.

Plevna *Russo-Turkish War*

Four battles were fought in the course of the siege of Plevna, the first three being attacks on the Russian defences, and the fourth Osman Pasha's final attempt to cut his way through the besiegers' lines.

On July 20, 1877, the advance guard of

General Krüdener's corps, 6,500 strong, attacked the defences to the north and east of Plevna. The Russians lost two-thirds of their officers and nearly 2,000 men.

The second battle took place July 30, when General Krüdener with 30,000 Russians in two divisions assailed the Turkish redoubts to the north and east of the town. General Schakovsky had command of attack, Krüdener himself leading the assault on the Gravitza redoubt to the north. Krüdener was absolutely unsuccessful. Schakovsky by 5.30 pm was in possession of two of the eastern redoubts, but before nightfall these were retaken by the Turks, and the Russians retired, defeated all along the line.

Their losses amounted to 169 officers and 7,136 men, of whom 2,400 were left dead on the field. On the 11th and 12th of September the investing army, 95,000 strong under the Grand Duke Michael, attacked Plevna on three sides, Osman Pasha having now 30,000 men under his command. On the 11th an attack on the Omar Tabrija redoubt was repulsed with a loss to the Russians of 6,000 men.

On the south-west, Skobelev captured two of the six inner redoubts which protected that angle of the fortress. On the 12th, the attack on the second Gravitza redoubt was repulsed, and the two redoubts captured by Skobelev were retaken after a terrible struggle. The losses in the two days' fighting amounted to 20,600 including 2,000 prisoners on the Russian side, on that of the Turks to 5,000. On December 10, Osman Pasha, at the head of 25,000 Turks, accompanied by 9,000 convalescents and wounded in carts, attempted to cut his way through the Russian army, now 100,000 strong, under the King of Rumania, with General Totleben as Chief of Staff. Having successfully crossed the Vid, Osman charged down upon the Russians on a line two miles in length and carried the first line of entrenchments. Totleben, however, hurried up reinforcements, and the Turks were in turn attacked and driven back in confusion across the river, Osman being severely wounded. Here they made their last stand but were overpowered and driven into Plevna, which before evening capitulated, after a defence lasting 143 days. In this engagement the Turks lost 5,000, and the Russians 2,000 killed and wounded. The Russians resumed their advance into the Balkans. *See* Kars, Schipka Pass.

Plovdiv *Russo-Turkish War*

January 17, 1878, when after earlier successes at Schipka Pass and Plevna, a Russian army led by General Gourko marched on to the fortified city of Plovdiv (Philippopolis) and took it by storm. Some 4,500 of General Suleiman Pasha's troops were killed or wounded, 2,000 made prisoner. The Russians lost about 1,200. Turkish retreats towards Constantinople led to British mediation and the Russo-Turkish Treaty of San Stefano. *See* Plevna, Schipka Pass.

Podhajce *Polish-Turkish Wars*

1667, between 10,000 Poles under John Sobieski and 80,000 Cossacks and Tartars who were besieging Kaminiec. They were routed and forced to evacuate Poland, but attacked again later.

Podol *Seven Weeks' War*

June 26, 1866, between the advance-guard of Prince Frederick Charles's army and the Austrians under General Clam-Gallas. The Austrians were defeated and driven out of Podol after severe fighting in which they lost heavily. The Prussians took 500 prisoners. *See* Langensalza.

Poitiers I *Gothic Invasion of France*

In 507, between the Franks under Clovis and the Visigoths under Alaric II. Clovis and Alaric met in single combat and Alaric was slain, following which the Goths were utterly routed. By this decisive victory the province of Aquitaine was added to the Frankish dominions. *See* Tolbiac, Vouillé.

Poitiers II *Hundred Years' War*

September 19, 1356, between 6,000 English under Edward the Black Prince and 20,500 French under King John of France. The English occupied a strong position behind lanes and vineyards, in which their archers were posted. The French cavalry, charging up the lanes, were thrown into confusion by the bowmen and were then taken in flank by the English knights and men-at-arms, who completely routed them with a loss of 4,500 and many prisoners, including the King. The English losses were very small. They were

able to retreat safely to Bordeaux. *See* Auray, Calais.

Pola *War of Chioggia*

In 1380, when Luciano Doria with 22 Genoese galleys offered battle to the Venetian fleet under Vittorio Pisano, which was lying at Pola (now Yugoslavia). Pisano sallied out with 20 galleys and captured the Genoese flag-ship, Doria being killed. The Genoese however rallied, drove Pisano back and defeated him with a loss of 2,000 killed, and 15 galleys and 1,900 men captured. *See* Chioggia.

Poland *World War II*

September 1, 1939, when without warning Germany invaded Poland with 44 infantry and 14 armoured divisions, against the Polish Army's 30 infantry and cavalry divisions and one motorized brigade. The 1,400-strong *Luftwaffe* destroyed the 900-strong Polish Air Force, largely obsolete aircraft, within two days, mostly on the ground. Encircling and annihilating the Polish forces piecemeal according to *blitzkrieg* principles, the Nazi formations reached Warsaw in one week and battered it until September 27, when it surrendered. Meanwhile, having invaded eastern Poland on September 17, and thrust 110 miles forward up to the Curzon Line in two days, the Soviets shared Poland with the Nazis. German losses: 10,600 killed, 30,200 wounded, 3,000 missing. *See* Norway, Poland-East Prussia.

Poland-East Prussia *World War II*

Starting the 1944 Russian summer offensive, General Chernyakovski's 3rd White Russian Army crossed the River Niemen in three places, took Grodno on July 26, Kaunas (Kovno) on August 1 and bore down on the eastern frontier of East Prussia. Earlier on July 18 Bialystok had fallen jointly to the 2nd and 3rd White Russian Armies, and Brest Litovsk on July 28 to General Rokossovski's 1st White Russian Army, which then swept westwards and reached the outskirts of Warsaw on July 31. In the south Generals Koniev and Petrov also bore westward, capturing Stanislav, Lvov and Przemyśl by July 28. Koniev's forces then crossed the Vistula on August 1 at Baranow, south of Warsaw.

201

Russia launched her last great offensive along a 750-mile front on January 12, 1945, by-passing Warsaw which fell, a ruin, on January 17, and by January 30 Marshal Koniev's armies (32 infantry divisions, eight armoured corps) had begun to cross the German frontier about 105 miles east of Berlin. In the north Rokossovski's 2nd White Russian Army drove through to the Baltic west of Danzig on January 26, 1945 and cut off the Germans holding out in East Prussia. On April 9 the 90,000 Nazi defenders of Königsberg surrendered. *See* Ukraine, White Russia, Warsaw.

Pollentia *Wars of the Western Roman Empire*

April 6, 402, between the Goths under Alaric and the Romans under Stilicho. Stilicho attacked the Gothic camp at Pollentia (Pollenza) while they were celebrating the festival of Easter, and owing to the surprise the charge of the Roman cavalry threw them into confusion. They were however soon rallied by Alaric and the Romans driven off with heavy loss, but Stilicho, advancing at the head of the legionaries, forced his way into the camp and drove out the Goths with enormous slaughter. Alaric's wife was among the captives. *See* Rome II.

Pollicore *First British-Mysore War*

August 27, 1781, between 11,000 British under Sir Eyre Coote and the Mysoris, 80,000 strong under Hyder Ali. Coote seized the village of Pollicore, turning Hyder's flank and forcing him to retreat, after an action lasting eight hours. The British lost 421 killed and wounded, the Mysoris about 2,000. *See* Porto Novo.

Polotsk I *Napoleonic Wars*

August 18, 1812, between 33,000 French and Bavarians under General St Cyr and 30,000 Russians under Count Wittgenstein. The Russians were taken by surprise and after an action which lasted two hours only were driven back with a loss of 3,000 killed, 1,500 prisoners and 14 guns. The French lost a little over 1,000 killed and wounded. *See* Borodino.

Polotsk II *Napoleonic Wars*

October 18, 1812, when General St Cyr

with 30,000 French and Bavarians was attacked and defeated by the Russians, in slightly superior force, under Count Wittgenstein, and forced to evacuate Polotsk. *See* Maloyaroslavets.

Ponani *First British-Mysore War*

November 19, 1780, when a force of British and native troops about 2,500 strong under Colonel Macleod, entrenched near Ponani, were attacked before daybreak by a strong force of Mysoris under Tippu Sahib. The Mysoris were repulsed at the point of the bayonet with a loss of 1,100. The British loss was 87. *See* Porto Novo, Pollicore.

Pondicherry I *War of the Austrian Succession*

This town was invested by the British under Admiral Boscawen with a fleet of 30 sail and a land force of 6,000 men, August 30, 1748, and was defended by a French garrison of 4,800 under Dupleix. The siege was grossly mismanaged and in October Boscawen was forced to withdraw, having lost by sickness or in action nearly a third of his land force. The French lost 250 only during the siege. *See* Madras.

Pondicherry II *Seven Years' War*

In August 1760, Colonel Coote with about 8,000 British and Indian troops invested this town, held by a French garrison 3,000 strong under the Comte de Lally-Tollendal. Coote was almost immediately superseded by Colonel Monson, but the latter having been wounded Coote resumed the command. Fire was not opened from the breaching batteries till December 8, and on the 31st a terrific hurricane wrecked all the land batteries and drove ashore six ships of the blockading squadron. On January 10, 1761, however, fire was reopened and the town surrendered on the 15th. *See* Wandiwash.

Pondicherry III *American Revolutionary War*

Having been surrendered to the French by the Peace of Paris, 1763, Pondicherry was again besieged by a British force, under Sir Hector Monro, in conjunction with a squadron of ships under Sir Edward Vernon, August 8, 1778. It was gallantly defended by the French under M. Bellecombe until the middle of October, when after a month's bombardment it surrendered. *See* Trincomalee.

Pondicherry IV *American Revolutionary War*

A naval action was fought off Pondicherry, August 10, 1778, during the third stage, when a French squadron of five ships under M. Tronjolly issued from the roads and offered battle to the five ships of Sir Edward Vernon. The French were worsted and driven back to their anchorage. *See* Cuddalore.

Pondicherry V *American Revolutionary War*

A second naval action off this town was fought June 20, 1783, between a British squadron of 18 ships of the line and 12 frigates, under Sir Edward Hughes, and a French squadron under Admiral de Suffren. The British ships were much damaged and unable to chase when de Suffren sheered off. The British loss was 520 killed and wounded. *See* Cuddalore.

Pontevert *Gallic War*

In 57 BC, between 50,000 Romans under Caesar and the Suevi, 300,000 strong under Galba. The Suevi attacked the Roman entrenched camp but were repulsed with very heavy loss and their army dispersed.

Pont Valain *Hundred Years' War*

In 1370, between the French under Bertrand du Guesclin and the English under Sir Thomas Granson. The French surprised the English camp, but the English rallied and a severe conflict followed in which the French attack was at first repulsed. A flank movement of the French however threw the English into disorder and they were defeated with a loss of nearly 10,000 in killed, wounded and prisoners, among the latter being Sir Thomas Granson. *See* La Rochelle.

Poona *Maratha Wars*

October 25, 1802, between the forces of Jeswunt Rao and the united armies of the Peshwa and Sindhia of Gwalior. After an evenly contested action Jeswunt Rao got the upper hand and gained a complete victory, Sindhia fleeing from the field, leaving behind all his guns and baggage.

Port Arthur I *Sino-Japanese War I*

This place, held by a Chinese garrison of 9,000 men, was attacked and stormed on November 21, 1894, by the Japanese, after a short bombardment. The Chinese made but a feeble resistance, the Japanese losing only 270 killed and wounded. *See* Yalu River, Sino-Japanese War I.

Port Arthur II *Russo-Japanese War*

February 8, 1904, between a Japanese fleet of 16 warships under Vice-Admiral Togo and the Russian fleet of six battleships and 10 cruisers under Vice-Admiral Stark, lying at anchor off Port Arthur, held by some 40,000 Russians. The Japanese attacked with torpedo boats and succeeded in seriously damaging two battleships and a cruiser which were beached at the mouth of the harbour. They then opened a bombardment in which they damaged a third battleship and four more cruisers, sustaining no damage to their own ships. The Russians lost 56 killed and wounded, the Japanese 58, chiefly in the torpedo boats.

On April 13 the Japanese torpedo flotilla attacked the Russian squadron under Admiral Makarov. The battleship *Petropavlovsk* was torpedoed and sunk, Makarov and 700 officers and men being drowned. The battleship *Pobieda* and a destroyer were also torpedoed but managed to reach the harbour. The Japanese suffered no material loss.

The Japanese on May 2 sent in a fleet of merchant steamers accompanied by the torpedo flotilla. Of these, eight succeeded in reaching the outer harbour, and two of them broke the boom guarding the inner harbour, and were blown up by their commanders in the fairway. Several others were sunk near the harbour entrance. Of the 179 officers and men forming the crews of the merchant steamers, only 42 were rescued by the Japanese.

Five Japanese divisions landed near Port Arthur on May 5, attacked the nearby hill of Nanhan and after repeated assaults took it with the aid of a naval bombardment on May 27. General Nogi was thus able to surround Port Arthur by land and shell Russian ships in the harbour, sinking the only four remaining battleships. The Russians surrendered on January 2, 1905. The Japanese won Port Arthur, but at a cost of 58,000 killed or wounded and 30,000 sick. *See* Tsushima Strait, Nanhan.

Porte St Antoine *War of the Fronde*

July 2, 1652, between the Royal troops under Marshal de Turenne and 5,000 insurgents under the Great Condé. Condé occupied a position round the gate, protected by . barricades and fortified houses, where he was attacked by de Turenne. The barricades were taken and retaken several times, but at last after heavy fighting Condé abandoned all idea of penetrating into Paris and retired. His losses were heavy, especially in officers, among the severely wounded being the Duc de Nemours and the Duc de la Rochefoucauld. *See* Arras, Lens.

Port Hudson *American Civil War*

This fortress was invested, May 25, 1863, by five Federal divisions under General Banks, and defended by 16,000 Confederates under General Gardner. An assault on the 27th was repulsed and a regular siege commenced. After a second unsuccessful assault on June 14 the garrison, having no hope of relief, surrendered, July 9, having lost 1,700 during the siege. The losses of the besiegers were far heavier, the two unsuccessful assaults showing a heavy list of casualties. *See* Vicksburg.

Portland *Anglo-Dutch Wars*

February 18, 1653, between an English fleet of about 70 sail under Admirals Blake, Deane and Monck, and a Dutch fleet of 73 ships, convoying 300 merchantmen, under Admirals Van Tromp, de Ruyter and Evetzen. In the early part of the engagement, which was very severely contested, three English ships were carried by the board, and that portion of the fleet which had come into action was nearly overwhelmed. At this crisis, however, the rest of the English ships engaged, the battle was restored and the captured ships retaken. On the 19th the battle was renewed off the Isle of Wight, five Dutch ships being captured or destroyed. On the 20th the Dutch sheered off defeated, having lost during the three days' fighting 11 men-of-war, 40 merchant ships, 1,500 killed and wounded and 700 prisoners.

The English losses were also heavy. *See* North Foreland, Dover.

Porto Bello I *Raids of the Buccaneers*

This Spanish-American fortress was captured in 1665 by 460 Buccaneers under Morgan. The walls were scaled, the town sacked and atrocities inflicted upon the people.

Porto Bello II *War of the Austrian Succession*

This settlement on the Isthmus of Panama was captured from the Spaniards, November 21, 1740, by a British fleet of six ships under Admiral Vernon. The British loss was trifling. *See* War of Jenkins' Ear.

Porto Novo *First British-Mysore War*

July 1, 1781, between 8,500 British troops under Sir Eyre Coote and about 65,000 Mysoris under Hyder Ali. Hyder occupied a strongly entrenched camp, blocking the British advance upon Cuddalore. Here he was attacked by Coote and after a day's hard fighting the position was stormed and Hyder forced to retreat. The British lost 306 while the Mysoris were computed to have lost many more. *See* Seringapatam, Madras.

Porto Praia Bay *American Revolutionary War*

April 16, 1781, when Commodore Johnstone, in command of a British squadron of five ships of the line and five frigates, repulsed a determined attack of a French squadron of 11 sail, under Admiral de Suffren, in this harbour in the Cape Verde Islands. The loss in the British squadron amounted to 36 killed and 147 wounded. *See* Minorca.

Port Republic *American Civil War*

June 9, 1862, between the Federals, 12,000 strong under General Shields and an equal force of Confederates under General Jackson. The Federals were completely defeated, a portion of their army being driven from the field in disorder and with heavy loss. *See* Crosskeys.

Potosi *Bolivian War of Independence*

April, 1825, between the Bolivians under Bolívar, and the Spanish Royalists under Olaneta. The Spaniards were completely defeated.

Prague I *Thirty Years' War*

November 8, 1620, when the Imperialists, under Maximilian of Bavaria and Count Tilly, drove 22,000 Bohemians, under Frederick of Bohemia, up to the walls of Prague, and signally defeated them, with a loss of 5,000 men and all their artillery. Frederick was obliged to take refuge in the city, and soon afterwards capitulated. The battle only lasted an hour, and the Imperialists lost no more than 300 men. *See* Wimpfen.

Prague II *Seven Years' War*

May 6, 1757, between 60,000 Austrians under Charles of Lorraine and 64,000 Prussians under Frederick the Great. The Austrians occupied a very strong position on the Moldau, which was attacked and carried by Frederick, Charles being driven back into Prague with a loss of 8,000 killed and wounded and 9,000 prisoners. Field-Marshal von Browne was mortally wounded. The Prussians lost 13,000, including Marshal von Schwerin. The Prussians laid siege to Prague. *See* Lobositz.

Prairie Grove *American Civil War*

A fierce but indecisive action, fought December 7, 1862, between the Confederates under General Hindman and the Federals under General Herron. The losses were Confederates 1,300, Federals 1,250. *See* Pea Ridge.

Preston I *English Civil War*

August 17–19, 1648, when Sir Marmaduke Langdale, with 4,000 Royalists, was deserted by the main body of the Scottish invading army and left to face the attack of about 9,000 Roundheads under Cromwell. The Royalists fought desperately for four hours but were overpowered and nearly the whole force killed or captured. This battle and the surrender of Colchester on the 28th ended the Second Civil War. *See* Rathmines, Drogheda.

Preston II *Jacobite Rebellion of the Fifteen*

November 13, 1715, between 4,000 Jacobites under General Forster and a small force of Royal troops, chiefly dragoons, under General Wills. The Jacobites had barricaded the approaches to the town, and held their ground throughout the day, but reinforcements arriving, Wills was able to invest the place completely; and early on the morning of the 14th Forster surrendered. Many of the rebels having left the town on the night of the 12th, the prisoners numbered 1,468. The Jacobite loss in killed and wounded was 42, that of the Royalists about 200. *See* Prestonpans.

Prestonpans *Jacobite Rebellion of the Forty-five*

September 21, 1745, between 2,300 Royal troops under Sir John Cope and a slightly superior force of Jacobites under the Young Pretender, Prince Charles Edward Stuart. Cope's infantry failed to stand up against the charge of the Highlanders under Lord George Murray and fled in confusion, losing about 400 in killed and wounded and 1,600 prisoners, including 70 officers. The Highlanders lost about 140 killed and wounded. This action, which helped the Jacobite cause, is also known as the Battle of Gladsmuir. *See* Culloden, Preston.

Primolanó *French Revolutionary Wars*

September 7, 1796, when Napoleon surprised and totally routed the vanguard of Marshal von Wurmser's army. The Austrians lost over 4,000 killed, wounded and prisoners. *See* Mantua.

Princeton *American Revolutionary War*

January 3, 1777 between the Americans under Washington and the British under General Lord Cornwallis. The British were defeated and this victory enabled Washington to regain possession of New Jersey. *See* Brandywine.

205

Pruth, The *Ottoman Wars*

August 2, 1770, when the Russians under General Romanzov stormed the triple entrenchments held by the main Turkish army, 120,000 strong, under Halil Bey, and drove out the Turks with a loss of 20,000 killed and wounded. *See* Çeşme.

Puente *Colombian War of Independence*

February 16, 1816, between the Colombian Patriots under Lorrices and the Spanish Royalists under Morillo. The Royalists gained a complete victory. *See* Boyacá.

Puente de la Reyna *Second Carlist War*

October 6, 1872, between 50,000 Carlists under Ollo and about 9,000 Republicans under Moriones. The Republicans were defeated after hard fighting and were at last driven in disorder from the field by a bayonet charge. The Carlists lost 113 only; the losses of the Republicans were far heavier. *See* Huesca.

Pultava *Great Northern War*

June 28, 1709, between the Swedes, 17,000 strong under Charles XII, and 80,000 Russians under Peter the Great. After some successes early in the battle the Swedes were overwhelmed by the Czar's great superiority in artillery and were defeated with a loss of 7,000 killed and wounded and 3,000 prisoners. Charles with difficulty made his escape from the field. After the victory Russia, which lost only 1,300 killed or wounded, became a major power in Europe. *See* Fredrikshald.

Pultusk I *Great Northern War*

1703, between 10,000 Swedes under Charles XII and an equal force of Saxons under Marshal von Stenau. The Saxons made practically no resistance but fled from the field, losing only 600 killed and 1,000 prisoners. Charles then attacked the Polish fortress of Thorn (Toruń). *See* Thorn.

Pultusk II *Napoleonic Wars*

December 26, 1806, between 60,000 Russians with 120 guns under General Bennigsen, and 35,000 French under Marshal Lannes. Lannes endeavoured to pierce the Russian left and cut them off from the town but did not succeed in getting through, and in this part of the field the action was indecisive. On the left the French did little more than hold their own, but the Russians retired during the night, having lost 3,000 killed and wounded, 2,000 prisoners and a large number of guns. The French admitted a loss of 1,500 only; Russian accounts estimate the French losses at 8,000. *See* Eylau.

Puna *Raids of the Buccaneers*

On April 27, 1687, three buccaneering vessels under Captain Davis engaged two Spanish men-of-war off Puna. The action was entirely one of long-range firing and lasted till May 3 when the Spanish commander withdrew his ships. In the seven days only three or four Buccaneers were wounded.

Punniar *Gwalior Campaign*

December 29, 1843, between the left wing of Sir Hugh Gough's army under General Grey and a force of 12,000 Marathas with 40 guns. The Marathas were routed. *See* Maharajpur I.

Pusan Perimeter *Korean War*

After the Communist forces of the People's Democratic Republic of Korea had attacked across the 38th Parallel on June 25, 1950, they forced back the ill-prepared troops of the Republic of South Korea, occupied Seoul and, spearheaded by Soviet T-34 tanks, swept southward. US forces, newly arrived under UN auspices, fought delaying actions alongside South Korean forces, fell back to Pohang on August 11, then dug in in a perimeter round Pusan, about 25 miles to the west of it, 55 miles to the north-west at Taegu and 60 miles to the north. North Korean forces now lost their impetus, having had 58,000 men killed or wounded in their battles to the south, and General MacArthur planned an amphibious landing behind the enemy lines on the west coast. *See* Inchon.

Pydna *Third Macedonian War*

June 22, 168 BC, between the Romans under Æmilius Paulus and the Macedonians under Perseus. The Macedonian phalanx attacked the Roman line and drove them back on their camp, but becoming disordered by the uneven ground, was broken by the legionaries and cut to pieces. The result was a total defeat of the Macedonians, with a loss of 20,000 killed and 11,000 prisoners. The phalanx here fought its last fight and perished to a man. The empire created by Alexander the Great had fallen. *See* Raphia.

Pylos and Sphacteria *Great Peloponnesian War*

The promontory of Pylos, which is separated by a narrow channel from the island of Sphacteria, was seized and fortified by an Athenian force under Demosthenes, 425 BC. Here he was besieged by the Spartans under Thrasymelidas, with a land force and a fleet of 43 ships, the crews of which occupied Sphacteria. Demosthenes repulsed an attack on Pylos, and Eurymedon, arriving with 50 Athenian vessels, defeated the Spartan fleet and blockaded Sphacteria. After a contracted siege, the arrival of reinforcements under Cleon enabled the Athenians to land 14,000 men in the island, and the garrison, reduced from 420 to 292, surrendered. *See* Mytilene I, Delium.

Pyongyang *Sino-Japanese War I*

September 16, 1894, between the Japanese, 14,000 strong under General Nodzu and 12,000 Chinese, entrenched in a strong position. After severe fighting the Chinese were driven from their entrenchments with heavy loss. The Japanese lost 650 killed and wounded. *See* Yalu River.

Pyramids *French Revolutionary Wars*

July 21, 1798, when the Mameluke army under Murad Bey endeavoured to block Napoleon's march on Cairo. The Mameluke infantry, numbering about 20,000, took little part in the fight but their cavalry charged the French squares with great gallantry. They were however repulsed time after time, with great slaughter, and were eventually driven into the Nile where the shattered remnants escaped by swimming. Napoleon went on to occupy Cairo. *See* Nile, Malta.

Pyrenees *Peninsular War*

The engagements fought between Lord Wellington's 40,000-strong allied forces and Marshal Soult's army, which was endeavouring to relieve San Sebastian, are known as the Battles of the Pyrenees. They include the fighting from July 25 to August 2, 1813, and especially the actions of Roncesvalles, Maya and Buenzas. The British loss in these battles amounted to 7,300, while the French lost almost double that number. *See* Roncesvalles, Maya, Vitoria.

207

Q

Quatre Bras *Napoleon's Hundred Days*

June 16, 1815, between the advance guard of the 36,000 strong British army under the Duke of Wellington and the left wing of the French army, 25,000 strong under Marshal Ney. Napoleon's object was to prevent the junction of the British and the Prussians, and Ney's orders were to drive back the British while Napoleon with his main body engaged the Prussians. Ney attacked at 3 pm, but the British held their own till evening when Ney, not receiving the reinforcements he expected, began to fall back. Wellington then attacked vigorously all along the line, retaking all the positions occupied by the French during the day. Both sides lost over 4,000 men. Next morning Wellington withdrew to his position at Waterloo. *See* Waterloo, Ligny.

Quebec I *Seven Years' War*

This city was besieged June 27, 1759, by 9,000 British troops under General Wolfe, assisted by a fleet of 22 ships of war under Admiral Saunders. It was defended by about 14,000 French under General Marquis de Montcalm. Wolfe was too weak numerically for an investment and his object was to draw Montcalm into an engagement. On July 31 he was defeated in an attack on Montcalm's lines outside the city, but on September 13, having landed on the Plains of Abraham above Quebec, he met and defeated the French who evacuated the place on the 17th. The city surrendered next day. *See* Ste Foy.

Quebec II *Seven Years' War*

After defeating General Murray, April 27, 1760, General François de Lévis laid siege to Quebec with about 8,000 French and Canadians. The garrison consisted of no more than 2,500 effectives, but owing to the superiority of their artillery Lévis was unable to make any impression on the defences. On May 15 a small British squadron anchored off the city and on the following day attacked and destroyed the French ships carrying de Lévis's supplies and reserve of ammunition,

whereupon he hastily raised the siege, leaving behind him 40 siege guns and all his sick and wounded. The battle of Quebec was important in that it decided the future of Canada. *See* Plains of Abraham.

Queenston Heights *War of 1812*

October 13, 1812, between 4,000 British (chiefly Canadian volunteers) under General Brock and about 5,000 Americans under General Van Rensselaer. The Americans attacked the British position on Queenston Heights and after very severe fighting in which General Brock was killed, were totally defeated. The exact losses are unknown, but the British took 1,000 prisoners and the American column was practically annihilated. *See* Lake Erie.

Quiberon Bay *Seven Years' War*

November 20, 1759, between the British fleet, 23 sail of the line and 10 frigates, under Admiral Hawke, and 21 French line-of-battle ships and three frigates, under Marshal de Conflans. The action was fought in a heavy gale on a lee shore and resulted in the French being driven to take refuge in Quiberon Bay, with a loss of two ships sunk and two captured. Notwithstanding the gale, Hawke followed up his advantage and standing in, succeeded in capturing or destroying all but four of the ships which had taken refuge in the bay, though in so doing he lost two of his own ships which were driven ashore and wrecked. The British lost in the action only one officer and 270 men killed and wounded. *See* Warburg, Torgau.

Quipuaypan *Conquest of Peru*

Fought 1532, between the rival Peruvian chiefs Atahualpa and Huascar. Huascar was totally routed and taken prisoner.

Quistello *War of the Polish Succession*

July, 1734, between the Imperialists under Prince Eugène and the French under the Marshal Duc de Broglie. Prince Eugène gained a signal victory. *See* Parma, Philippsburg.

R

Raab *Napoleonic Wars*

June 14, 1809, between 44,000 French under Eugène de Beauharnais and about 40,000 Austrians under the Archduke John. The French attacked the Austrian position and, driving them successively from the villages of Kismeyger and Szabadhegy, totally defeated them. Under cover of night however the Archduke was able to make an orderly retirement, with a loss of about 3,000 killed and wounded and 2,500 prisoners. The French lost something over 2,000. De Beauharnais besieged Raab and took it on June 25, then joined Napoleon's army near Vienna. *See* Wagram.

Rabaul *World War II*

After destructive air attacks, Japanese troops invaded this Australian base in North New Britain Island, Bismarck Archipelago, on January 23, 1943, crushed the small Australian force there and constructed a formidable air and naval base. Its recapture began on December 15, 1943, with a landing at Arawe on the south-west coast. The US 1st Marine Division under General Rupertus took the Gloucester airstrip on December 30 and Talasea on March 6. The occupation of neighbouring islands and their use as airfields finally neutralized Rabaul. *See* Solomon Islands, Tarawa-Makin, New Guinea.

Radcot Bridge *Barons against Richard II*

In 1387, between the troops of Richard II under De Vere, Earl of Oxford, and the forces of the Lords Appellant under the Earl of Derby (Henry IV). De Vere and his troops fled almost without striking a blow and the King was thus left entirely in the power of the Barons. *See* Margate.

Ragatz *Armagnac War*

In March, 1446, between the Austrians and the Swiss Confederation. The Swiss gained a brilliant victory which was followed by peace with Austria and the Armagnacs.

Rajahmundry *Seven Years' War*

December 9, 1758, between 2,500 British troops under Colonel Forde, in conjunction with about 5,000 Indian levies, and the French, 6,500 strong under Marshal de Conflans. The Indian troops did little on either side but Forde's 500 Europeans routed Conflans' Frenchmen and the latter fled with considerable loss. *See* Madras II, Pondicherry II.

Rakersberg *Ottoman Wars*

1416, between 20,000 Turks under Ahmed Bey and 12,000 Austrians and others under Duke Ernest of Styria. Duke Ernest marched to the relief of Rakersberg, which the Turks were besieging and drove them from the field utterly routed. It is said that the Turkish losses amounted to more than the whole Christian army. Ahmed Bey was among the slain. *See* Varna I.

Ramillies *War of the Spanish Succession*

May 23, 1706, between the British and Imperialists, under the Duke of Marlborough and Prince Eugène, about 62,000 strong with 120 guns, and the French, in about equal force but only 70 guns, under Marshal Villeroy. The allies drove the French out of Ramillies, their resistance on the whole being unworthy of them, and in the end they were disastrously defeated with heavy loss, 15,000 being killed and wounded while 6,000 prisoners and 50 guns were taken. The allies lost less than 3,000. *See* Turin, Stolhoffen, Blenheim.

Ramla *Crusader-Turkish Wars*

In 1177, between the Saracens under Saladin and the Christians of Jerusalem under Renaud de Châtillon. The Christians won a complete victory. *See* Tiberias.

Ramnuggur *Second British-Sikh War*

November 22, 1849, when Lord Gough attempted to dislodge Shir Singh, who with about 35,000 Sikhs had occupied a position behind the River Chenab opposite Ramnuggur. The attempt was made by a brigade under General Campbell, with a cavalry force under General Cureton, and failed owing to the strength of the Sikh artillery which was well posted and served. General Cureton was killed. *See* Chilianwala, Gujerat.

Raphia *Wars of the Hellenistic Monarchies*

217 BC, between the Egyptians under Ptolemy Philopator and the Syrians under Antiochus the Great. Antiochus at first held the advantage, but pressing too far in the pursuit was overpowered and totally routed. The Syrians lost 14,000 killed and 4,000 prisoners. But within four years Antiochus won back much of Asia minor. *See* Pydna.

Rastadt *French Revolutionary Wars*

In 1796, between the French under General Moreau and the Austrians under the Archduke Charles. After a severe engagement Moreau succeeded in seizing the heights held by the Austrians and forced Charles to retreat to the Danube. *See* Arcola, Mantua.

Raszyn *Napoleonic Wars*

April 19, 1809, between 30,000 Austrians under the Archduke Ferdinand and about 20,000 French and Poles under Prince Josef Poniatowski. The Archduke was marching on Warsaw when Poniatowski, to whom the defence of that city had been entrusted, came out to meet him and after a stubborn fight in the woods and marshes round Raszyn, was driven back upon Warsaw with a loss of 2,000 killed and wounded. A few days later he surrendered to the Austrians to save Warsaw from a bombardment. *See* Abensberg, Eckmühl.

Rathenow *Swedish Invasion of Brandenburg*

June 25, 1675, between the Brandenburgers, 15,000 strong under the Elector Frederick William, and the Swedes under Charles XI. The Swedes, wearied by a long march, were surprised by the Elector in their camp and suffered a serious reverse. *See* Fehrbellin.

Rathmines *Cromwell's Campaign in Ireland*

August 2, 1649, between the Royalists under the Marquis of Ormonde and the Roundhead garrison of Dublin under Colonel Jones. Ormonde having ordered a night attack upon Dublin the Roundheads made a sortie and, driving back the assaulting column attacked the main body of the Royalists in their camp, totally routing them, with a loss of 4,000 killed and wounded, and 2,000 prisoners. All Ormonde's artillery was captured. Cromwell meanwhile continued with his plans to subdue Ireland. *See* Drogheda.

Ravenna I *Byzantine Empire Wars*

In 729, between the Byzantine troops of Leo the Iconoclast and a force of Italians, raised by Pope Gregory II in defence of image worship. After a severe struggle the Byzantines were routed and in their flight to their ships were slaughtered by thousands.

Ravenna II *War of the Holy League*

April 11, 1512, between the troops of the Holy League and the French under Gaston de Foix. The French gained a signal victory in this bloody struggle, but Gaston de Foix fell in the moment of his triumph, pierced with sixteen wounds, and the Holy Roman Empire now joined the coalition against Louis XII's France. *See* Agnadello, Novara.

Ré, Île de *Anglo-French Wars*

St Martin, the capital of this French island in the Bay of Biscay, was besieged by the English under the Duke of Buckingham from July 17 to October 29, 1627. An assault on October 27 was repulsed and the landing of the Duke of Schomberg with 6,000 French on the island made the English lines untenable, whereupon Buckingham raised the siege. While returning to his ships Buckingham was attacked by the French and suffered considerably. The English losses during the operations amounted to about 4,000 men. *See* La Rochelle II.

Reading *Danish Invasions of Britain*

In 871, between the Danish invaders and the West Saxons under Æthelred and Alfred. The West Saxons after a stubborn resistance were defeated and driven from the field with great slaughter. *See* Chippenham.

Rebec *Wars of Charles V*

In 1524, between the Imperialists under Constable de Bourbon and the French under Bonnivet. The French were totally defeated with heavy loss, among those who fell being the Chevalier de Layard. *See* Pavia IV.

Redan, The Great *Crimean War*

This fort, forming part of the southern defences of Sevastopol, was attacked by 1,900 troops of the British Second and Light Divisions, under Sir William Codrington, September 8, 1855. The ramparts were stormed but the assailants were unable to make good their footing and were eventually repulsed in confusion with heavy loss. The fall of the Malakov however rendered the southern side of Sevastopol untenable and the Russians retired during the night. The British losses amounted to 2,184 killed and wounded. *See* Sevastopol.

Reddersberg *Second Boer War*

April 3, 1900, when five companies of British infantry were surrounded by a force of Boers with five guns, and after holding out for twenty-four hours were compelled by want of water to surrender, having lost four officers and 43 men killed and wounded. The prisoners numbered 405. *See* Kimberley, Ladysmith

Reims *Napoleonic Wars*

March 13, 1814, when Napoleon with 30,000 French, after his defeat at Laon, surprised and routed 13,000 Prussians and Russians under General Saint-Priest, with a loss of 6,000 killed, wounded and prisoners. The French lost a few hundreds only and re-occupied the city. *See* Laon, Arcis-sur-Aube, Paris.

Reval *Russo-Swedish Wars*

This port was attacked in the spring of 1790 by the Swedish fleet under the Duke of Sudermanland. The Russian batteries, however, aided by the fleet under Admiral Chitchagov, drove them off with considerable loss.

Revolax *Russo-Swedish Wars*

April 27, 1808, when General Klingspoor with about 8,000 Swedes surprised an isolated Russian column of about 4,000 men under General Bonlatov. The Russians were surrounded and tried to cut their way through but failed, less than 1,000 succeeding in escaping from the trap. General Bonlatov fell fighting.

Rheinfelden *Thirty Years' War*

March 2, 1638, between the Protestant Germans under Duke Bernard of Saxe Weimar and the Imperialists under Jean de Wert. The Duke was besieging Rheinfelden when he was attacked by de Wert and forced to raise the siege and retire. After retreating, however, a short distance only, unpursued, he suddenly retraced his steps and taking the Imperialists by surprise inflicted upon them a severe defeat, dispersing their army and capturing de Wert. In this action fell the veteran Duc de Rohan. *See* Breitenfeld.

Rhine and the Ruhr Pocket, The *World War II*

March 23 to 28, 1945. The 9th US Army was deployed from Worringen, 12 miles south of Düsseldorf to the River Lippe, just above Wesel, an important communications centre; 2nd British Army from Lippe to the Dutch frontier, eight miles south of Emmerich; 1st Canadian Army from here to the North Sea coast, holding the northern flank; Field-Marshal Montgomery commanding all three. To the south were the 1st, 3rd and 7th US armies, followed by the 1st French Army, down to the Swiss frontier. The main Rhine crossing was to be north of the Ruhr between Rheinberg and Rees, where it was about 500 yards wide at low water, chief initial objective being Wesel. Field-Marshal Kesselring had become enemy C-in-C in place of General von Rundstedt, the German 25th Army holding from Emmerich across north-west Holland to the sea; 1st Parachute Army from near Krefeld to west of Emmerich; four parachute divisions from there to Essen and between Essen and

Cologne four infantry divisions; 47th Panzer Corps and 116th and 15th Panzer Grenadier divisions in reserve.

The British 2nd Army comprised four armoured, two airborne, eight infantry divisions, with five independent armoured brigades, one Commando brigade and one independent infantry brigade. 9th US Army comprised nine infantry and three armoured divisions. The River Lippe was the boundary between the two armies. Field-Marshal Montgomery launched the operation at 1530 hours March 23 with a barrage from 900 guns. All initial crossings were successful, casualties light. Airborne landings followed; the Rhine was bridged and by March 28 enemy resistance was crumbling.

The US 1st Army (General Hodges) battled east from Remagen on March 25, 75 miles to Marburg, where VII Corps swung north towards Lippstadt, joining forces here with XIX Corps of the US 9th Army (General Simpson) and encircling Field-Marshal Model's 5th and 15th Panzer armies and some 100,000 infantry. US forces detached from the 9th and 1st armies' eastward drive attacked the pocket and split it on April 4. Resistance ended two weeks later, when 317,000 prisoners surrendered, including 30 generals.

The French 1st Army crossed the Rhine at Philippsburg on April 1, captured Karlsruhe on April 4, cleared the Black Forest and advanced along the Swiss frontier. In the north Montgomery's armies, instead of sweeping on towards Berlin, were ordered to advance through Holland and northern Germany. The 2nd Army crossed the Elbe on May 2, Hamburg surrendered May 3, followed the next day by all German troops in north Germany. Meanwhile, on April 25 advance units of the US 1st Army had linked up with Russian advance units at Torgau on the Elbe. Germany surrendered unconditionally on May 8, 1945. *See* Rhineland, The.

Rhineland, The *World War II*

February 8 to March 21, 1945, when General Eisenhower's 21st, 12th and 6th Army Groups (85 divisions) began the advance to the Rhine, against General Karl von Rundstedt's Army Groups 'H', 'B' and 'G', a total of 60 weak divisions, which were to stand and fight west of the Rhine along the Siegfried Line. Field-Marshal Montgomery

moved off on February 8 with British 30th Corps and the 1st Canadian Army, nearly 500,000 strong, through and around the Reichswald Forest down through Goch to Geldern.

In the south, the 9th US Army being held up until February 23 by floods caused by enemy destruction of the Roer River dams, the 1st German Parachute Army was thrown in against the British and Canadians, who faced in this sector appalling weather, extensive minefields and intense enemy resistance. When the US 9th Army (General Simpson) started on February 23 it advanced so rapidly that the enemy was threatened with encirclement and was forced to retire quickly across the Rhine.

March 3, the British 2nd and the American 9th armies combined to thrust the 1st Parachute Army across the river, while in the south General Bradley's 1st US Army had advanced with such speed that by March 5 it was approaching the Rhine from Cologne to the Moselle River. March 7, advance units of the US 9th Armoured Division found the Remagen bridge across the Rhine still standing and managed to get five divisions over it. By March 21 9th Army had established a bridgehead eight miles deep by 20 long. German resistance in the south began to give way and in the last week of March, the British and Canadians, who had suffered 15,000 casualties in their sector, closed to the Rhine from Emmerich to Wesel, having taken 23,000 prisoners. Enemy losses were 40,000. The stage was now set for the advance across the Rhine. *See* Rhine and Ruhr Pocket, The.

Rhodes *Ottoman Wars*

This place, defended by the Knights of St John of Jerusalem, under their Grand Master Pierre d'Aubusson, was besieged May 23, 1480, by a Turkish army under Meshid Pasha, aided by a fleet of 160 ships. The siege lasted three months and was raised after the failure of the second assault, the Turks having by that time lost 10,500 killed and wounded.

A second and successful siege was begun July 28, 1522, by Suleiman the Magnificent. The Knights, under Villiers de L'Isle Adam, held out until December 21, repulsing numerous attacks, but at last, worn by famine, they were compelled to surrender. The Turks were said to have lost by disease and battle over 60,000 men. This siege is notable as being the first in which explosive bombs were used. *See* Belgrade I, Constantinople III.

Riachuela *Paraguayan War*

June 11, 1865, between the fleets of Paraguay and Brazil. After a fierce engagement the advantage rested with the Brazilians.

Richmond *American Civil War*

August 30, 1862, between the Confederates, about 9,000 strong under General Kirby Smith, and 8,000 Federals under General Morgan. The Federals were routed and driven headlong into Richmond where 5,000 prisoners, nine guns and 1,000 stand of arms were captured. The Confederate losses were slight. *See* Shiloh, Perryville.

Rich Mountain *American Civil War*

July 11, 1861, between 15,000 Federals under General McClellan and 6,000 Confederates under General Garnett. The Federals stormed the heights of Rich Mountain and Laurel Hill and drove the Southerners from their positions, with a loss of about 1,000, including prisoners. During the pursuit on the following day General Garnett was killed in a cavalry skirmish. *See* Bull Run.

Rietfontein *Second Boer War*

October 24, 1899, between 4,000 British under Sir George White and the Free Staters who were advancing to interrupt the retreat of Colonel Yule from Dundee. The enemy occupied a range of hills about seven miles from Ladysmith, where they were attacked by White. After an indecisive action the British retired to Ladysmith with a loss of 111 killed and wounded, but the object aimed at was attained, for the Boers were prevented from interfering with Colonel Yule's march. *See* Ladysmith.

Rieti *Italian Wars of Independence*

March, 1821, between 10,000 Neapolitans under General Pepe and the Austrian invading army, 80,000 strong. As long as he was opposing only the advance guard Pepe made a most resolute resistance, but on their being reinforced from the main body, the Neapolitans were overpowered by superior numbers and finally driven in confusion from the field. Two days later the Austrians entered Naples and reinstated Ferdinand on the throne. *See* Tolentino.

Riga *Swedish-Polish Wars*

This town was invested by the Swedes under Gustavus Adolphus II in the early part of August, 1621, and defended by a garrison of 300 Poles. A resolute defence was made and several determined assaults repulsed, but a large breach having been effected by September 11, the garrison, now reduced to a handful, had no option but to surrender and the town was entered by the Swedes, September 15, 1621. *See* Linköping.

Rimnitz *Ottoman Wars*

September 22, 1789, when 25,000 Austrians and Russians under the Duke of Coburg and General Suvorov, routed an army of 60,000 Turks under the Grand Vizier. The Turkish losses were enormous, the whole army being killed, captured, or dispersed. *See* Focsani, Martinesti.

Rio Seco *Peninsular War*

July 14, 1808, when Marshal Bessières, with about 14,000 French, defeated 26,000 Spaniards under Cuesta. The Spaniards lost about 6,000 while the French loss was only 370 killed and wounded. Following upon this victory, Joseph Buonaparte entered Madrid. *See* Vimeiro.

Rivoli *French Revolutionary Wars*

January 14, 1797, when the Austrians with five divisions under General Alvinzi attacked Napoleon's position on the heights of Rivoli, where he had deployed 30,000 men and 60 guns. Finding himself under severe pressure Napoleon sent a flag of truce to Alvinzi, and gaining an hour's respite by this ruse, re-deployed his army, which then totally defeated the enemy. The fifth Austrian division, which had not taken part in the frontal attack, appeared in the rear of the French position after the battle was over, but being faced by overwhelming numbers laid down its arms. General Masséna, who had specially distinguished himself, took his title of Duc de Rivoli from this battle when later ennobled by Napoleon. The destruction of the Austrians sealed the fate of Mantua, under siege. *See* Mantua.

Roanoke Island *American Civil War*

This island, which commanded the entrance to Albemarle Sound, North Carolina, and which was defended by 1,800 Confederates under General Wise, was attacked February 7, 1862, by three brigades of Federals under General Burnside, aided by 20 gunboats. On the 8th the Federals landed, overpowered the garrison and occupied the island, losing 235 killed and wounded. The Confederates lost 150 killed and wounded. Of seven Confederate gunboats employed in the defence, five were captured or destroyed. *See* Pea Ridge.

Rocroi *Thirty Years' War*

May 19, 1643, between the French, 22,000 strong under Louis II Condé (later called the Great Condé) relieving Rocroi, and 26,000 Spaniards under Don Francisco de Melo. The battle was sternly contested and at first went against the French, their left wing being repulsed and the centre shaken. Want of cavalry however prevented Melo pressing home his advantage and the French, rallying, broke the Spanish line and severely defeated them. The Spaniards lost 8,000 killed and 6,000 prisoners in the infantry alone, the flower of their army. The French only admitted a loss of 2,000, but it was doubtless considerably heavier. France was now paramount in the war; but the battle marked the decline of Spanish military power. *See* Breitenfeld, Freiburg.

Rolica *Peninsular War*

August 17, 1808, when Wellington with 14,000 British and Portuguese, of whom only 4,000 came into action, attacked the French, 3,000 strong under Delaborde, around this village in Portugal and drove them from their position with a loss of 500 men. The allies lost about 400 in this first British engagement of the Peninsular campaign, and now marched on Vimeiro. *See* Vimeiro.

Rome I *First Invasion of the Gauls*

The first siege of Rome by the Gauls, under Brennus, took place 387 BC. No attempt was made to defend the city, which was seized and burnt by the barbarians, the greater part of the population fleeing to Veii and other neighbouring cities. The Capitol, however, was held by the leading Patrician families, and it is said withstood a siege of six months, when Brennus accepted a heavy ransom and withdrew his army. *See* Veii.

Rome II *Wars of the Western Roman Empire*

The city was besieged in 408 by the Goths under Alaric, and after being brought to the verge of starvation and losing many thousands from famine, the Romans capitulated, but retained their freedom on payment of a heavy ransom, whereupon Alaric retired northward in 409. In the course of the year, however, Alaric seized Ostia, the port of Rome, and summoned the city to surrender. In the absence of the Emperor Honorius, the populace forced the authorities to yield; and Alaric, after deposing Honorius and bestowing the purple on Attalus, withdrew his troops. In 410, during the month of August, Alaric for the third time appeared before the walls and on the night of the 24th the Salarian gate was opened to the besiegers by some sympathizers within the city, and Rome was given over to pillage and massacre, in which thousands perished. *See* Hippo.

Rome III *Ricimer's Rebellion*

The rebel Count Ricimer, with a large army of Burgundians, Suevi and other barbarians, laid siege to Rome in 472, and after a defence of three months the besiegers entered the city by storming the Bridge of Hadrian, and sacked it.

Rome IV *Wars of the Byzantine Empire*

In March, 537, the city was besieged by some 30,000 Goths under Vitiges and defended by Belisarius. After a determined resistance, during which a vigorous assault was repulsed and several successful sorties made, with heavy loss to the besiegers, Vitiges in March, 538, was compelled to raise the siege. *See* Rome V.

214

Rome V *Wars of the Byzantine Empire*

In May, 546, Totila, King of Italy, at the head of an army of Goths, laid siege to Rome, which was defended by a garrison of 3,000, under Bassas. An attempt to relieve it by Belisarius was on the point of success, but Bassas failed to co-operate with the relieving force, and Belisarius was forced to retire, whereupon the city surrendered, December 17, 546.

It was recovered by Belisarius in the following February but was again besieged by Totila in 549. On this occasion it was defended by a garrison of 3,000 troops under Demetrius who, aided by the inhabitants, made a gallant resistance, but the Gate of St Paul was opened to the besiegers by some Isaurian sympathizers within the walls, and Totila thus made himself master of the last Italian city excepting Ravenna, which had resisted his victorious army.

In 552, after the defeat of Totila at Tagina, Rome was invested by the Imperial army under Narses, who after a brief siege stormed the defences and finally delivered the city from the Gothic domination. *See* Rome IV, Taginae.

Rome VI *Norman Seizure*

In the course of dispute with Pope Gregory VII who had refused to recognize him as emperor, Henry IV of Germany laid siege to Rome in 1082. After two interruptions to the siege, the city was finally surrendered to him by the Roman nobles, March, 1084. Gregory had employed a Norman mercenary, Robert Guiscard, to expel the Germans, but instead he sacked the city.

Rome VII *Wars of Charles V*

The city was taken by storm May 9, 1527, by 30,000 Spanish troops and German mercenaries under the Constable de Bourbon, who fell in the assault. A massacre followed in which 8,000 of the inhabitants perished. Pope Clement VII retired to the Castle of St Angelo where he held out until November 26, when a treaty between him and Charles V put an end to the conflict. *See* Pavia IV.

Rome VIII *Italian Wars of Independence*

After the proclamation of a Roman republic on February 9, 1849, by Garibaldi and his adherents, a French army under General Nicolas Oudinot was sent to restore the papal rule. On April 30, 1849, the French, 7,000 strong, attacked the Porta San Pancrazio, where they were encountered by the Republicans under Garibaldi and repulsed, with a loss of 300 killed and wounded and 500 prisoners. The Garibaldians lost 100.

On June 3 of the same year the French, under Oudinot, 20,000 strong, made a night attack upon the Garibaldians, who brought up about 8,000 men to oppose them. The Garibaldians were repulsed, with a loss of over 2,000, including 200 officers. Oudinot then laid siege to the city which, after a terrible bombardment, surrendered July 2, 1849. *See* Venice.

Romerswael *Netherlands War of Independence*

January 29, 1574, between the 'Beggars of the Sea' under Admiral Boisot and a Spanish fleet of 75 ships under Julian Romero. The 'Beggars' grappled the enemy's ships in a narrow estuary and after a very severe encounter, in which the Spaniards lost 15 vessels and 1,200 men, Romero retreated to Bergen-op-Zoom. *See* Mookerheide.

Roncesvalles I *Charlemagne's Conquests*

August, 778, between the Franks under Charlemagne and the Basques and Gascons under Loup II. The army of Charlemagne, retreating from Spain, was caught in the defile of Roncesvalles in the Pyrenees, and the rearguard was totally annihilated, among those who fell being the famous Paladin, Roland.

Roncesvalles II *Peninsular War*

One of the actions known as the 'Battles of the Pyrenees', fought July 25, 1813. Marshal Soult, at the head of Clausel's division, attacked the British, consisting of three brigades under General Byng, but was unable to carry their position and after severe fighting was repulsed with a loss of 400. The British lost 181 killed and wounded. *See* Vitoria, Nivelle.

Rorke's Drift *Zulu-British War*

On the night of January 22, 1879, after the

disaster of Isandhlwana, this outpost, held by a company of the 24th Regiment and details, in all 139 men, under Lieutenants Chard, R.E., and Bromhead, was attacked by a force of Zulus estimated at 4,000. After a determined defence in which many acts of heroism were performed, especially in the removal of the sick from the hospital which was fired by the spear-throwing Zulus, they were beaten off by rifle and gunfire, leaving over 400 dead on the field. The little garrison lost 25 killed and wounded. Eight Victoria Crosses and nine Distinguished Conduct Medals were awarded for this affair, a battle of spears against firearms. *See* Isandhlwana, Ulundi.

Rosbecque *Flemish-French Wars*

In 1382, between 40,000 Flemings under Philip van Arteveldt and the French under Charles VI. The Flemings at first drove back the French but were overwhelmed by the charges of the French cavalry on their flanks, and were in the end utterly routed. Thousands fell in the action and subsequent pursuit, amongst them van Arteveldt.
See Mons-en-Pévèle.

Roseburgh *Anglo-Scottish Wars*

This town, defended by an English garrison, was besieged by the Scots under James II of Scotland in 1460, and after a stubborn defence was captured and destroyed. This is the first occasion on which artillery was used by the Scots. During the siege the Scottish king was killed by the bursting of a gun of large calibre, August 3, 1460. *See* Otterburn.

Rossbach *Seven Years' War*

November 5, 1757, between 41,000 French and Austrians under Lt. General Prince de Soubise and 22,000 Prussians under Frederick the Great. Frederick, who occupied the heights of Rossbach, was attacked by the allies. The Prussian cavalry, however, under General von Seidlitz, charged down upon the Austrians and threw them into disorder, and the infantry falling upon the broken columns utterly routed them, with a loss of 3,000 killed and wounded, 5,000 prisoners, including 11 generals and 63 guns. The Prussians lost 540 only. Frederick marched off to Silesia to defeat the Austrians at Leuthen in December. *See* Leuthen, Breslau, Olmütz.

Rostock *Danish-Swedish Wars*

June, 1677, between the Danish fleet under Admiral Juel and the Swedes under Admiral Horn. The Swedes were completely defeated. *See* Fehrbellin.

Rotto Freddo *War of the Austrian Succession*

July, 1746, when the rearguard of the retreating French army under Marshal Maillebois was attacked by the Austrians under Prince Lichtenstein, and after a gallant resistance defeated with heavy loss. In consequence of this defeat the French garrison of Placentia, 4,000 strong, surrendered to the Imperialists. *See* Lauffeld.

Roucoux *War of the Austrian Succession*

October 11, 1746, between the French under Marshal Maurice de Saxe and the Imperialists under Charles of Lorraine. The French won a signal victory, as the result of which they occupied Brabant. *See* Cape Finisterre II, Lauffeld.

Rouen *Hundred Years' War*

This city was besieged 1418, by the English under Henry V. After a gallant defence the garrison surrendered January 19, 1419, the city paying a ransom of 300,000 crowns. *See* Agincourt.

Roundway Down *English Civil War*

July 13, 1643, when the Parliamentarians under General Sir William Waller and Heselrige were attacked by the Royalists under Lord Wilmot and Prince Maurice who were advancing to the relief of Devizes. The Parliamentarians were totally defeated, their attack on Prince Maurice being repulsed, while at the same time they were taken in the rear by a sortie of Sir Ralph Hopton's infantry from the town. Of 1,800 infantry, 600 were killed and the rest taken prisoners. The Royalists went on to take Bristol. *See* Newbury.

Rouvray-St-Denis,

see Herrings

Roveredo *French Revolutionary Wars*

September 4, 1796, between 25,000 Austrians under General Baron Davidovich and the main body of Napoleon's army, 30,000 strong. Napoleon attacked the Austrian entrenched position and in spite of a determined defence carried it, driving the enemy out of Roveredo with heavy loss, including 7,000 prisoners and 15 guns. This victory enabled Masséna to occupy Trent, and the remnants of the Austrian army were driven headlong into the Tirol. *See* Primolano, Mantua.

Rowton Heath *English Civil War*

September 24, 1645, when a body of Royalist cavalry under Sir Marmaduke Langdale, which was endeavouring to prevent the investment of Chester, was attacked by the Parliamentary horse under General Poyntz. The first attack was repulsed with loss but Poyntz, receiving infantry support, rallied his troops and drove the Royalists from the field with a loss of 300 killed and wounded and several hundred prisoners. *See* Marston Moor, Naseby.

Ruhr Pocket *World War II*

The Ruhr was surrounded on April 1, 1945, by the US 9th Army in the north and the 1st Army in the south. Encircled were Field-Marshal Model and the 5th Panzer and 15th armies as well as almost 100,000 other troops. While these two US armies pushed on eastwards, two corps from each attacked, and by April 14 had split the enemy in two. The Germans began surrendering, and by April 18 some 317,000 with 30 generals gave themselves up, the biggest surrender in the war. Model killed himself. *See* Rhine and Ruhr Pocket.

Rullion Green *Covenanters' Rising*

November, 1666, between 900 Covenanters under Colonel Wallace and the Royal troops under General Dalziel. The Covenanters were defeated. *See* Bothwell Bridge.

Rumani *World War I*

After a Turkish force of 20,000 commanded by Colonel von Kressenstein was beaten off in an attack across the Sinai desert against the Suez canal on February 2, 1915, by British and French naval artillery, General Archibald Murray led an army of Australians and New Zealanders in an offensive from Egypt towards Palestine (now Israel), in July 1916. Von Kressenstein's Turks manoeuvred to attack them at Rumani on their right flank, but General Murray countered by deploying his troops to the south and attacking the Turkish right flank, routing them, killing or wounding 6,000 and taking 4,000 prisoners for the loss of only 1,100. The British continued their advance. *See* Gaza III.

Rumania *World War I*

Expecting Russian support, ill-armed Rumania belatedly declared war with the Allies against Germany on August 27, 1916. After two weeks' initial success in advancing through the Transylvanian Alps in the north into Hungary, her armies were checked by the Austrians. Field-Marshal von Mackensen meanwhile attacked from the Bulgarian Black Sea coast early in September, and on September 18 General von Falkenhayn attacked the Rumanian armies through Transylvania with the German 9th Army. By the middle of November he was advancing on Bucharest from the west while von Mackensen bore down from the east, and entered Bucharest on December 6. The remnants of the Rumanian armies retreated to Moldavia, holding out with Russian help. Rumania lost about 350,000 men, Germany about 50,000, while she gained the vital supplies of Rumanian wheat and oil.

Rumersheim *War of the Spanish Succession*

August 26, 1709, between the French under Marshal Villiers and the Imperialists under General Count de Mercy. De Mercy was defeated and driven out of Alsace. *See* Denain.

Ruspina *Civil War of Caesar and Pompey*

January 3, 46 BC, between Julius Caesar, with three legions, and a force of Pompeians, composed entirely of cavalry and archers, under Labienus. Caesar's troops were surrounded, but behaving with extreme steadiness, were able to retire to Ruspina in good order, though with very heavy loss. *See* Thapsus.

Rynemants *Netherlands War of Independence*

August 1, 1578, between the Dutch Patriots, 20,000 strong under Count Bossu and François de la Noue, and the Spaniards, numbering about 30,000, under Don John of Austria. Don John crossed the Demer and attacked Bossu in his entrenchments. He was however repulsed after severe fighting and retired, leaving 1,000 dead on the field. He offered battle in the open on the following morning but Bossu declined to leave his lines, and Don John was indisposed to renew the attack and fell back upon Namur. *See* Leyden, Gembloux.

S

Saalfeld *Napoleonic Wars*

October 10, 1806, between 7,000 Prussians under Prince Louis of Prussia and a division of Lannes' corps under the Marshal himself. The Prussian infantry was broken and driven under the walls of Saalfeld, whereupon the Prince put himself at the head of his cavalry and charged the advancing French. The charge was repulsed and the Prince, refusing to surrender, was cut down and killed. The Prussians lost in this action 400 killed and wounded, 1,000 prisoners and 20 guns. *See* Austerlitz, Maida, Jena.

Sabugal *Peninsular War*

April 3, 1811, between three British divisions under Lord Wellington and the French, consisting of General Reynier's corps. Reynier held the salient angle of the French position on the Coa and was driven back after less than an hour's fighting with a loss of about 1,500. The British lost 200 only. *See* Albuera.

Sacile *Napoleonic Wars*

April 16, 1809, between 40,000 Austrians under the Archduke John, and 36,000 French and Italians under Eugène de Beauharnais, Regent of Italy. After hard fighting in which little generalship was shown on either side, an Austrian flank movement, which menaced the French line of retreat, forced Eugène to retire, victory thus resting with the Austrians. The losses were about equal on the two sides. *See* Abensberg, Raab.

Sacripontus *Civil War of Marius and Sulla*

82 BC, between the legions of Sulla and the army of the younger Marius, 40,000 strong. Sulla's veterans were too steady for the newer levies of Marius and the latter was routed, with the loss of more than half his army killed or captured. After this victory Sulla occupied Rome. *See* Mount Tifata, Orchomenus.

Sadowa,

see Koeniggrätz

Sadulapur *Second British-Sikh War*

December 3, 1848. After the failure of his frontal attack on the Sikh position at Ramnuggur in November, Lord Gough despatched a force under Sir Joseph Thackwell to cross the Chenab and turn the Sikh left. An indecisive action followed, which Lord Gough claimed as a victory, but though the Sikhs retired it was only to take up a new position at Chilianwala, on the Jhelum, which Gough did not consider himself strong enough to attack, without reinforcements. *See* Chilianwala, Gujerat.

Sagunto *Peninsular War*

This fortress, held by a Spanish garrison, was besieged by the French, 22,000 strong under Marshal Soult, September 23, 1811. Built on the heights above Murviedro, the place was accessible on one side only, and an attempt to escalade this was repulsed September 28. A regular siege was then begun and a second unsuccessful assault was made on October 18. On the 25th General Blake with 30,000 Spaniards made an attempt to relieve the place but was defeated with a loss of 1,000 killed or wounded and 4,000 prisoners, the victory costing the French about 800 men. On the following day the garrison surrendered. *See* Albuera.

Saigon,

see Vietnam War

St Albans I *Wars of the Roses*

Two engagements were fought here in the course of the war. On May 22, 1455, 2,000 red-rose Lancastrians under Henry VI, posted in the town, were attacked by 3,000 white-rose Yorkists under the Duke of York. The Duke pierced the Lancastrian centre and drove them out of St Albans with heavy loss, among those who were killed being the Earls of Somerset and Northumberland.

St Albans II *Wars of the Roses*

The second battle took place February 17, 1461, when the army of Margaret of Anjou,

219

led by Somerset, Exeter and others attacked the Yorkists under the Earl of Warwick. Warwick withdrew his main body, leaving his left unsupported to withstand the Lancastrian attacks, and these troops, after a feeble resistance, broke and fled. Henry VI, who was a prisoner in Warwick's camp, escaped and rejoined the Queen, and a rapid advance on London would probably have led to his reinstatement. Warwick, however, took such prompt measures as to render the Lancastrian victory practically fruitless. *See* Wakefield, Mortimer's Cross.

St Charles *French-Canadian Rising*

1837, between the Loyalists under Colonel Wetherall and the Canadian rebels. The latter were defeated. *See* St Denis II.

St Denis I *French Religious Wars*

November 10, 1567, between the Catholics under the Constable Montmorency and the Huguenots under the Prince de Condé. Victory rested with the Catholics, but at the cost of the Constable, who was killed, and the battle had no decisive effect upon the course of the war. *See* Jarnac.

St Denis II *French-Canadian Rising*

In 1837, between the Canadian rebels and a force of British and Canadian troops under Colonel Gore. The rebels were victorious but the results of their victory were unimportant. *See* St Charles.

Ste Croix *Napoleonic Wars*

This island in the Caribbean, held by a small Danish garrison, was captured by a British naval and military force under Admiral Sir A. J. Cochrane and General Bowyer, December 25, 1807, little resistance being offered.

Ste Foy *Seven Years' War*

April 27, 1760, between 3,000 British troops under General Murray and 8,000 French under General François de Lévis, who was approaching from Montreal with the object of recapturing Quebec. Murray marched out to attack de Lévis but was defeated and driven back into Quebec with a loss of over a third of his force. The French lost about 800. One could say that this was more decisive than Wolfe's victory over Montcalm the previous year. *See* Quebec II.

St Eustache *French-Canadian Rising*

In 1837, between the rebels under Girod and the Government troops under Sir John Colborne. The rebels were defeated and the rebellion suppressed. *See* St Charles, St Denis II.

St George *Ottoman Wars*

This town, the capital of the island of Cephalonia, now Kaffalinia, was besieged in October, 1500, by the Spaniards and Venetians under Gonsalvo de Cordova and Pesaro. The garrison consisted of 400 Turks only, but being veteran soldiers they made a most gallant defence. At the end of two months the place was stormed from two quarters simultaneously, and the survivors of the garrison, some 80 only, laid down their arms. *See* Lepanto.

St Gothard *Ottoman Wars*

August 1, 1664, between 80,000 Turks under Achmet Köpriali Pasha and 60,000 French and Germans under General Count Montecucculi, who occupied a strong position behind the Raab. On the Turks advancing to the attack, a young Turk rode out and challenged a Christian to single combat. The challenge was accepted by the Chevalier de Lorraine, who killed his adversary. The Turks then assaulted Montecucculi's entrenchment but could make no impression, and after hard fighting were beaten off with a loss of 8,000 killed. *See* Candia.

St Jakob an der Birs *Armagnac War*

August 26, 1444, between 30,000 Armagnacs, under the Dauphin, and 1,300 Confederate Swiss. The Swiss being hard pressed occupied the hospital of St Jakob an der Birs, where they maintained the unequal fight until the last man had fallen. The Armagnacs however had lost 2,000 killed and the Dauphin felt compelled to abandon the invasion of Switzerland. *See* Héricourt.

St Kitts *Anglo-Dutch Wars*

May 10, 1667, when Admiral Sir John Harman, commanding an English squadron of 12 frigates, fell in with a combined Dutch and French fleet of 22 sail under Commodore Kruysen and M. de la Barre, off St Kitts. Notwithstanding his inferiority, Harman boldly attacked and gained a signal victory, burning five and sinking several more of the enemy's vessels. The allies took refuge in the harbour of St Kitts and Sir John, following them in, destroyed the rest of their fleet at a cost of 80 men only. *See* Southwold Bay, North Foreland.

St Lô *World War II*

On July 25, 1944, after 4,200 tons of bombs were dropped in 90 minutes over an area one and a half by two and a half miles, General Lawton Collins's US VII Corps launched General Montgomery's Operation Cobra to break out of the restricted region 20 miles inland from the Normandy invasion beaches, stretching from Caen and St Lô to Lessay. General Dempsey's 2nd British Army (14 divisions) had already thrust towards Caen and was engaged with 14 German divisions. Six 2nd Army divisions now thrust southwards to set behind the Germans. The US 1st Infantry and 3rd Armoured Divisions, after bitter fighting with little progress on the first two days, broke through towards Coutances, and by dusk on the 28th were 15 miles south of their start line. Two days later they had stormed on to Avranches. On August 1, General Patton's US 3rd Army tore through the Avranches gap and VII Corps raced into Brittany. Hitler now ordered five Panzer divisions to reinforce the German 7th Army in an attempt to break through to the coast via Avranches and smash the US forces in Brittany, but tremendous Allied air attacks broke their columns and they succeeded only in capturing Mortain. German armour and troops were eventually surrounded and destroyed in the Mortain–Falaise pocket, while the US 3rd Army drove eastwards towards the Seine from Dreux, Chartres and Orléans. *See* D-Day.

St Lucia *French Revolutionary Wars*

This island was captured from the French,
April 4, 1794, by a British squadron under Sir John Jervis. *See* Toulon.

St Mary's Clyst *Arundel's Rebellion*

August 4, 1549, when Lord Russell, marching with the Royal army to the relief of Exeter, was attacked by 6,000 rebels, detached from the besieging force. The rebels were defeated with a loss of 1,000 killed and Arundel was forced to raise the siege of Exeter. *See* Sampford Courtney.

St Mihiel *World War I*

On 12 September, 1918, when 16 divisions of the US Army under General Pershing, supported by French tanks and artillery and the 2nd Colonial Corps, attacked this German-held salient south-east of Verdun from the north and the south, after 36 hours' heavy fighting forcing the enemy back. Some 15,000 prisoners were taken and about 200 guns. The salient was eliminated. Pershing lost about 7,000 killed or wounded. *See* Marne II, Amiens, Meuse-Argonne Forest.

St Privat,

see Gravelotte

St Quentin I *Franco-Spanish Wars*

August 10, 1557, between 20,000 French and Germans under the Constable Montmorency, and about 5,000 Spanish and Flemish cavalry of the Duke of Savoy's army under Count Egmont, supported by a small force of infantry. The French in attempting to throw reinforcements into St Quentin were entrapped in a narrow pass, and were utterly routed with a loss of 15,000 killed, wounded and captured, and all but two of their guns. The Spaniards only lost 50 men. *See* Gravelines.

St Quentin II *Franco-Prussian War*

January 19, 1871, between the French, 40,000 strong under General Faidherbe, and 33,000 Germans under General von Goeben. The French were decisively defeated with a loss of 3,000 killed and wounded, 9,000 prisoners and six guns. The Germans lost 96 officers and 2,304 men. *See* Bapaume, Le Mans, Paris.

221

Saints, The,

see Dominica

St Thomas *Napoleonic Wars*

This island in the Caribbean, was captured from the Danes, December 21, 1807, by a combined British naval and military force under Admiral Sir A. J. Cochrane and General Bowyer. *See* Ste Croix.

Salado *Spanish-Muslim Wars*

October 30, 1340, between the Portuguese and Castilians, under Alfonso IV of Portugal and Alfonso XI of Castile, and the Moors under Abu Hamed, Emir of Morocco. The Christians won a signal victory, and Alfonso IV so distinguished himself in the battle as to earn the title of the 'Brave'.

Salamanca I *Peninsular War*

July 22, 1812, when Wellington, with 50,000 men, including cavalry, 14,000 Portuguese, 3,000 rebel Spaniards, 54 guns, encountered Marshal Auguste Marmont's 49,000 French troops, with 78 guns. Since July 15 Marmont had manoeuvred to cut Wellington off from his base in Salamanca, but Wellington gave ground and prevented this, his army being about 6 miles and Marmont's 7 miles south of the city. On July 22, believing that Wellington, whose army was mainly out of sight, was retreating, Marmont sent his leading division on the left, 4,500 men, ahead to envelop Wellington's right. When it was a mile ahead of the main army, Wellington pounced, ordering his 3rd Division, on the right, under Edward Pakenham, to overcome it. Surprised on the march, the French lost about 2,500 killed or wounded, all their guns and General Thomières, being then driven back in confusion.
Meanwhile, Wellington's centre, the 4th and 5th Divisions, with cavalry, breasted a ridge to assault Marmont's centre with first a deadly volley, then a bayonet charge. Dragoons decimated the survivors, Marmont was killed and altogether a third of the French were eliminated in 45 minutes. But Wellington's Portuguese, on the left, storming a steep hill, were thrown back, exposing the British 4th Division, which was then vigorously assaulted by two French

Divisions under Generals Bonet and Clausel. Three British reserve divisions arrived in time and routed them, but 27,000 enemy escaped the field. French losses were 15,000 killed or wounded, 7,000 prisoners, 25 guns. Wellington had won a great victory and destroyed one of the three French armies in Spain at cost to himself of 5,000 killed or wounded. *See* Badajoz, Vitoria.

Salamanca II *Mexican Liberal Rising*

March 10, 1858, between the Government troops under Miguel Miramón and the Liberals under Doblado. Doblado's raw levies could not face Miramón's trained troops and were utterly routed.

Salamis I *Third Persian Invasion*

In 480 BC between the Greek fleet of 370 sail under Themistocles and the Persian fleet of over 1,000 galleys. The Greeks at first hesitated to attack in face of the overwhelming numbers of the Persian ships, but an Athenian trireme commanded by Aminias dashed in, followed by the rest of the Athenians and the Æginetans in good order, and the Persians were, after a hard struggle, totally defeated with the loss of more than half their fleet. Xerxes and his army witnessed the rout from the shores of Salamis. He was forced to postpone his land offensive. *See* Thermopylae, Plataea, Mycale.

Salamis II *Wars of Alexander's Successors*

307 BC, between the Macedonian fleet under Demetrius Poliorcetes and the Egyptians under Ptolemy Soter. The Egyptians were routed with the loss of 100 ships captured and the rest sunk, and 30,000 prisoners. *See* Corupedion.

Salankemen *Ottoman Wars*

August 19, 1691, between 80,000 Turks under the Grand Vizier, Mustapha Köpriali Pasha, and 45,000 Imperialists under the Margrave Louis. The Turks were signally defeated and Köpriali slain. *See* Peterwardein.

Saldanha Bay *French Revolutionary Wars*

August 17, 1796, when Sir Keith Elphinstone

with a British squadron entered the bay, and after capturing a Dutch ship of war lying in the harbour, landed a force, to which the garrison surrendered after a brief resistance. *See* Cape St Vincent.

Salerno *World War II*

September 9–16, 1943, when the Allied 5th Army made an amphibious landing around Salerno, south of Naples, in order to secure this port. After initial gains, the British and American forces on September 12 faced strong German attacks which, in some places, drove them back to within two miles of the coast. Reinforcements, the US 82nd Airborne and the British 7th Armoured, counter-attacked and stopped the Germans on September 15. Next day 8th Army troops drove up from the south and joined forces. Marshal Kesselring retreated, and Naples fell to the Allies on October 1. *See* Gustav-Cassino Line.

Salo,

see Castiglione

Salum-Halfaya Pass *World War II*

June 15–17, 1941, when General Beresford-Peirse counter-attacked Marshal Rommel's advancing Afrika Korps with two divisions at Salum, on the coast, and at Halfaya Pass inland. The British armour was decisively beaten with the loss of 100 tanks by the skilful German use of their new 88-mm gun in its first role as an anti-tank weapon. The British lost about 1,000 killed or wounded.

Samaghar *Rebellion of Aurungzebe*

June, 1658, between the Army of the Great Mogul, Shah Jehan, under Dara, and the forces of his rebellious sons, Aurungzebe and Marad. Dara was totally defeated and his army dispersed, and three days later the rebels occupied Agra, where Shah Jehan was imprisoned and Aurungzebe seized the crown.

Samarkand *Tatar Invasion of Khorezm*

This city, which was defended by a garrison of 110,000 under the Governor, Alub Khan, was besieged by the Tatars under Genghis Khan in June, 1220. The garrison harassed the Tatars by numerous sorties and little progress was made with the siege, but some of the inhabitants, hoping to save the city from pillage, opened the gates to the besiegers. After heroic efforts to defend the city against the overwhelming hordes of the enemy, Alub Khan put himself at the head of 1,000 picked horsemen and cut his way out. The survivors of the garrison, now reduced to 30,000, were put to the sword. *See* Kharismia.

Sampford Courtney *Arundel's Rebellion*

The final engagement with the rebels, fought August 17, 1549, when Arundel was defeated by the Royal troops under Lord Russell, with a loss of 700 killed and many prisoners, including most of the ringleaders in the rising. *See* St Mary's Clyst.

San Giovanni *French Revolutionary Wars*

June 17, 1799, between the French under General Jacques Macdonald and the Russians under General Count Suvorov. After three days' hard fighting, the French were forced to retreat, having suffered a loss of 6,000 killed and wounded and 9,000 prisoners. The Russian losses were about 6,000. *See* Marengo.

Sangro *World War II*

From November 19 to December 3, 1943, in the river valley of the Sangro, in the Abruzzi Mountains, about 80 miles east of Rome, when General Montgomery, with three infantry divisions and an armoured brigade of the 8th Army, defeated two infantry divisions and one Panzer division of General Victinghoff's 10th Army by forcing a crossing of the Sangro under heavy fire. *See* Gustav-Cassino Line.

San Isodoro *Paraguayan War*

April, 1870, between the Paraguayans under López and the allied army of Brazil, Argentina and Uruguay, under General Camera. Camera attacked López's entrenchments and drove him out, forcing him to take refuge in the mountains with the small remnant of his troops. *See* Aquidaban, Parana.

223

San Jacinto I *Texan Rising*

April 21, 1836, when the Mexican army under General Santa Anna, about 2,000 strong, was routed and almost destroyed by the Texans under General Houston. The survivors, with Santa Anna and his staff, were taken prisoners. Santa Anna agreed to recognize the independence of Texas which in 1845 was admitted into the United States. *See* Alamo.

San Jacinto II *Franco-Mexican War*

February 12, 1867, between the adherents of the Emperor Maximilian, under Miramón, and the Mexican Constitutionalists, under General Escobedo. Miramón was defeated, and his army surrendered, he himself escaping with difficulty from the field. *See* La Puebla.

San Juan,

see El Caney

San Lazaro *War of the Austrian Succession*

June, 1746, between the Austrians, 40,000 strong under Prince Lichtenstein, and the French and Spaniards under Marshal Maillebois. The allies attacked the Austrian entrenched camp and after an obstinate conflict, lasting nine hours, were repulsed with a loss of 8,000 killed and wounded. *See* Roucoux.

Sanna's Post *Second Boer War*

March 31, 1900, when a force of cavalry with two R.H.A. batteries and a considerable convoy, under Colonel Broadwood, was ambushed by a party of Boers under De Wet. The guns were just entering a donga when the Boers opened fire, and four guns of Q battery succeeded in getting clear, and opening fire, stuck to their work till only ten men of the battery were left standing. Broadwood succeeded in extricating his force, but at a cost of 19 officers and 136 men killed and wounded, 426 prisoners, seven guns, and the whole of his convoy. General Colville's column was within a few miles, but though the firing was heard, he failed to relieve. This is also known as the action of Kornspruit. *See* Vaalkranz.

San Sebastian I *Peninsular War*

This town was besieged July 10, 1813, by the Allies, some 10,000 strong, under General Graham, and defended by a French garrison under General Rey. An assault on July 25 was repulsed, and pending the arrival of heavy guns from England, the siege resolved itself into a blockade. Active operations were resumed, and on the 31st the town was taken by storm. Rey, however, still held out in the citadel, and it was only after further bombardment that he surrendered on September 9. The besiegers' losses amounted to 3,700 killed and wounded. *See* Vitoria, Nivelle.

San Sebastian II *First Carlist War*

This fortress, held by a garrison of Cristinos and a small detachment of the British legion under Colonel Wylde, was besieged by the Carlists under Sagastibelza, February, 1836. The siege was carried on in desultory fashion, with constant fighting between the outposts, till June, 1836, when General Evans, with 10,000 British and Spanish troops, occupied the advanced Carlist positions and forced them to withdraw. *See* Huesca.

Santa Lucia *Rio Grande Rising*

In 1842, between the Brazilian Government troops under General Caxias, and the rebels, 6,000 strong, under Feliciano. The rebels were totally defeated.

Santander *Spanish Civil War*

August 14, 1937, when 106 battalions of Nationalists under General Davila advanced against about 52,000 Republican troops led by the Basque General Ulíbarri in Santander. Artillery and air bombardment forced the Republicans back until by August 23 they surrendered. *See* Bilbao.

Santarem *Portuguese Civil War*

February 18, 1834, when the Portuguese Government troops, under Marshal Saldanha, totally defeated the 'Miguelists', under Dom Miguel, who gave up all claims to the Portuguese throne.

Santa Vittoria *War of the Spanish Succession*

July 26, 1702, when four regiments of Prince Eugène's army under General Visconti were attacked by 15,000 French and Spaniards under the Duc de Vendôme. The Imperialists were forced to abandon their camp and retire with the loss of their baggage, but lost only 500 men, while their qualified success cost the allies nearly 2,000 killed and wounded. *See* Landau, Luzzara.

Santiago de Cuba *Spanish-American War*

July 3, 1898, between the American fleet of four battleships and three cruisers under Admiral W. T. Sampson, and the Spanish fleet of four armoured cruisers and three torpedo-boats under Admiral Cervera. The Spaniards endeavoured to escape from the blockaded harbour of Santiago but were unsuccessful, the whole squadron being destroyed. The Americans suffered hardly any damage, the Spanish gunnery being very inefficient, and lost only one man killed. *See* Manila, El Caney.

Sapienza *Ottoman Wars*

In 1490, between the Turkish fleet under Kemal Reis, and the Venetians. The Venetians suffered a severe reverse, this being the first naval victory of the Turks in the Mediterranean. *See* Rhodes, Belgrade I.

Saragossa I *War of the Spanish Succession*

August 20, 1700, between 25,000 Spaniards and a force of 23,000 Austrians, British, Dutch and Portuguese troops under the Archduke Charles. The Portuguese in the right wing gave way, leading a large force of Spaniards in pursuit, but the left and centre stood their ground and finally repulsed the enemy, with a loss of 4,000 prisoners besides killed and wounded. The Archduke at once took possession of Saragossa. *See* Cremona.

Saragossa II *Peninsular War*

In June, 1808, siege was laid to this city by the French under Marshal Lefebvre. A successful defence was made and the marshal's forces being insufficient to effect a prompt capture, he raised the siege in August. In December of the same year it was again besieged by the French, under Marshals Moncey and Mortier, and defended by a Spanish garrison under General de Palafox. A most heroic defence was made, notable for the bravery of Agostina, the legendary Maid of Saragossa, who took the place of her wounded lover on the ramparts and helped to serve the guns, but despite all the efforts of de Palafox the place was stormed and, after very severe house-to-house fighting, captured, February 21, 1809. *See* Vimeiro.

Saratoga,

see Stillwater

Sardis *Wars of Alexander's Successors*

Fought 280 BC between the troops of Pergamus under Eumenes and the Syrians under Antigonus Soter. Eumenes gained a signal victory and annexed a large part of the dominions of Antigonus. *See* Sentinum.

Sárkány *Hungarian Rising*

December 30, 1848, between the Austrians under Prince zu Windischgrätz and the Hungarians under General Perczel. Perczel had been entrusted by General Görgey with the defence of the Sárkány defile, but on being attacked by the Austrians his division made little resistance and fled in disorder, thus forcing Görgey to retire from the line he had chosen to defend. *See* Schwechat, Kapolna.

Sauchie Burn *Rebellion of the Barons*

June 18, 1488, between the rebel Barons under Angus 'Bell-the-Cat', and the troops of James III of Scotland, under the king. The royal army was totally defeated and James slain.

Saucourt *Norse Invasion of France*

In 861, between the Neustrians under Louis III and the invading Norsemen, when Louis gained a brilliant victory.

Savage's Station,

see Seven Days' Battle

Savandroog *Second British-Mysore War*

Siege was laid to this place December 10, 1791, by a column of General Lord Cornwallis' army about 4,000 strong. It was defended by a strong garrison of Mysoris and was considered impregnable, but a practicable breach having been effected, was taken by storm eleven days later, the garrison offering little resistance. The assailants did not lose a man. *See* Seringapatam.

Saxa Rubra *Revolt of Maxentius*

October 28, 312, between the Imperial troops under Constantine and the legions of Italy under Maxentius. The Italian cavalry, posted on the wings, was routed by Constantine's horse; the infantry, thus left unsupported, fled from the field, only the Pretorians making a brave resistance, dying where they stood. Maxentius escaped, but crossing the Tiber into Rome by the Milvian Bridge, was forced by the crowd of fugitives into the river and drowned. *See* Verona, Heraclea.

Scarpheia *War of the Achaean League*

146 BC, between the Romans under Metellus and the Achaeans under Critolaus. The Greeks were totally defeated with heavy loss, Critolaus being killed.

Schipka Pass *Russo-Turkish War*

August 21, 1877, and following days, when the Russians, 7,000 strong under General Darozhinsky, holding the pass, were attacked by 25,000 Turks under Suleiman Pasha. The Russians were driven from point after point of their defences and were on the verge of being overwhelmed, when the arrival of reinforcements enabled them to assume the offensive and recover their lost positions, and on the 26th fighting ceased. The Russian losses amounted to 4,000, including Darozhinsky, while the Turks lost about 11,500.

On September 16 Suleiman, reinforced to 40,000 men, made an attempt to carry the Russian position on Mount St Nicholas, but was repulsed with a loss of 3,000, the Russians losing 31 officers and about 1,000 rank and file.

By January 8, 1878, the Russian force in the Schipka had been increased to 60,000 men under General Radetski, while the Turks, numbering 40,000, were under Vessil Pasha. General Mirsky with 25,000 men attacked the Turkish entrenchments and drove them out of all their positions, and on the following day Vessil Pasha surrendered with 36,000 men and 93 guns. The Russians lost 5,000. *See* Plevna, Plovdiv, Philippopolis, Kars.

Schwechat *Hungarian Rising*

October 30, 1848, between the Austrians under Prince zu Windischgrätz and the Hungarians under General Móga. The Hungarian militia made a very feeble stand against the Austrian regulars, and were driven back all along the line with considerable loss. *See* Sárkány, Kapolna.

Scio *Ottoman Wars*

July 5, 1769, between a Russian fleet of ten sail of the line under Admiral Spiritov, and 15 Turkish ships, with some small vessels, under the Captain Pasha. After a severe engagement in which both the flagships were blown up, the Turks were driven into the Bay of Ceşme where a few days later their fleet was destroyed by fire-ships. *See* Cesme.

Scutari *Ottoman Wars*

This town (Shkoder, Albania), held by a Venetian garrison under Antonio Loredano, was besieged by the Turks under Suleiman Pasha, May, 1474. The garrison held out stoutly till the middle of August, when Suleiman raised the siege.

Four years later in June 1478, Mohammed II invested it, the garrison now being under the command of Antonio di Lezze. Though few in numbers the Venetians withstood a continuous bombardment, repulsing two serious attacks, until September 8, when Mohammed retired, leaving behind him only a blockading force. When on the conclusion of peace the place was handed over to the Turks only 450 men and 150 women were alive in the town. *See* Cairo.

Sealion, Operation,

see Britain, Battle of

Secchia, The *War of the Polish Succession*

September 14, 1734, when the Imperialists under Count Koningsegg surprised the camp of the French army under the Duc de Broglie, capturing 5,000 prisoners, 100 guns and the whole of the stores, baggage and ammunition. *See* Parma, Philippsburg.

Secessionville *American Civil War*

June 15, 1862, when 6,000 Federals under General Benham attacked the strong position of Secessionville, covering the road to Charleston, which was held by 2,000 Confederates under General Evans. The Federals were repulsed with a loss of 600 men, the Confederates losing 200. *See* Fair Oaks, Seven Days' Battle.

Secunderbagh *Indian Mutiny*

November 16, 1857, during the second relief of Lucknow, by Sir Colin Campbell. The Secunderbagh, a walled enclosure of strong masonry, held by a large body of rebels, was after a bombardment of about an hour and a half taken by storm by the 93rd Highlanders and the 4th Punjabis, with very heavy loss to the enemy, over 2,000 dead being afterwards carried out of the enclosure. *See* Cawnpore.

Sedan *Franco-Prussian War*

This battle, the most decisive of the war, was fought September 1, 1870. The French, 20,000-strong, with 564 guns, under Marshal de MacMahon, who was wounded early in the action, were driven from all their positions by the 200,000 Germans, with 774 guns, under General von Moltke, and compelled to retire into Sedan where they laid down their arms. The Emperor Napoleon III was among the prisoners, and one of the results of the surrender was his dethronement and the proclamation of a republic in Paris. The battle is remarkable for the desperate charge

of the Chasseurs d'Afrique under General Margueritte. The brigade was cut to pieces and the general killed. The Germans lost in the action 460 officers and 8,500 men; the French 3,000 killed, 14,000 wounded and 21,000 prisoners, while 83,000 subsequently surrendered in Sedan. The Germans took 419 guns, 139 fortress guns and 66,000 rifles, and marched on Paris. *See* Metz, Paris.

Sedgemoor *Monmouth's Rebellion*

July 6, 1685, between the 2,500 Royal troops under the Earl of Feversham, and the rebels, 3,700 strong under James, Duke of Monmouth. Monmouth attempted a night attack on Feversham's camp, but the alarm was given and the Royal troops, falling upon their assailants, put Monmouth's cavalry to flight, and though his infantry made a sturdy resistance they were at length overpowered and routed with heavy loss. This defeat put an end to the rebellion. *See* Bothwell Bridge.

Segewár *Hungarian Rising*

July 31, 1849, between the Hungarians under General Nem and the Russians under General Lüders. The Russians after a severe engagement were totally defeated. *See* Sárkány, Kapolna.

Seine Mouth *Hundred Years' War*

August 15, 1416, when the English fleet under the Duke of Bedford sailed into the Seine with the object of revictualling Harfleur, which the French were besieging. The blockading force, consisting of eight large Genoese carracks, besides smaller vessels, attacked the English fleet and after six hours' hard fighting were totally defeated, with a loss of five carracks and five other ships, while Bedford succeeded in throwing supplies into the town. *See* Agincourt, Rouen, Castillon.

Sekigahara *Rebellion of Hideyori*

September 16, 1600, between the troops of the Japanese Shogun Tokugawa Iyeyasu, 80,000 strong, and 100,000 rebels under Mitsunari. The rebels were utterly routed, with the loss of 30,000 killed, among whom was Mitsunari, and the rebellion was suppressed. The Tokugawa shogunate lasted until 1867.

227

Selby *English Civil War*

April 11, 1644, between the Royalists, 3,300 strong under Colonel John Bellasis, and a slightly superior force of Parliamentarians under Sir Thomas Fairfax. Bellasis had occupied Selby with the object of preventing a junction between Fairfax's troops and those of the Scots from Durham. He was attacked by Fairfax and totally defeated, with the loss of 1,600 men and all his artillery and baggage. *See* Adwalton Moor, Marston Moor.

Selinus *Second Carthaginian Invasion of Sicily*

This city was besieged by the Carthaginians, 60,000 strong under Hannibal, 409 BC. An attempt by the Syracusans under Diocles to relieve came too late, for after resisting stubbornly for nine days, the garrison, hopelessly outnumbered, were overpowered; and the place stormed and sacked, all the survivors being carried off into captivity. *See* Himera, Syracuse.

Seminara *French Wars in Italy*

1495, between 6,000 Spaniards and Neapolitans under Gonsalvo de Cordova and Ferdinand of Naples, and a largely superior French army under d'Aubigny. The Neapolitans fled almost without striking a blow, and though the Spaniards fought well they were overpowered by numbers and in the end totally routed, only Gonsalvo with 400 Spanish cavalry making an orderly retreat. *See* Garigliano, Cerignola.

Sempach *Swiss War of Independence*

July 9, 1386, between 4,000 Austrians under Duke Leopold and 1,500 Swiss Confederates. The Swiss gained a complete victory, the Austrians losing 1,500 killed and wounded, while only 120 Swiss fell. The battle is celebrated for the heroic action of Arnold von Winkelried, who broke the line of the Austrian spearmen at the cost of his life, and enabled his followers to penetrate their phalanx. *See* Laupen.

Seneffe *Wars of Louis XIV*

August 8, 1674, between the French, 45,000 strong under the Great Condé and the Flemings and Spaniards, 50,000, under the Prince of Orange. Orange, finding Condé's position too strong to attack, began a retreat towards Le Quesney, thereby exposing his flank. Condé took instant advantage of this error and dispersed the vanguard of the allies, but the Prince took up a strong position at Seneffe from which Condé was unable to dislodge him, and the conflict ended in a drawn battle after seventeen hours' hard fighting. *See* Sinsheim.

Senekal *Second Boer War*

May 29, 1900, when a British force under General Rundle attacked the Boers, strongly posted on the Biddulphsberg. The attack was made amidst great bush fires, in which many of the wounded perished, and was unsuccessful, the British losses amounting to seven officers and 177 men killed and wounded. *See* Vaalkranz, Sanna's Post.

Sentinum *Third Samnite War*

298 BC, between five Roman legions under Q. Fabius Maximus and Publius Decius, and the Samnites and Gauls under Gellius Equatius. The Roman left was disordered by the war-chariots of the Gauls, but was rallied by Decius, who restored the battle, but at the cost of his life. On the right the Samnites were routed, Fabius then fell upon the Gauls in flank and broke them. Meanwhile the Samnite camp was attacked and Equatius slain, the Romans gaining a signal victory. The losses of the victors amounted to 8,200, while the Gauls and Samnites lost 25,000 killed and 8,000 prisoners. *See* Camerinum, Bovianum.

Seoul *Korean War*

The US 1st Marine Division with two battalions of South Korean infantry crossed the Han River under fire on September 20, 1950, after the amphibious landing at Inchon and advanced towards Seoul from the west. Meanwhile, General Walker's US 8th Army having broken out of the Pusan perimeter on September 16, its 7th Infantry Division and the 17th South Korean Regiment encircled Seoul from the north, south and east. A battle lasting nine days began on September 20 and the city was destroyed with many civilians killed before it fell on September 29.

As a result of this and the Pusan perimeter battle, six enemy divisions were trapped in South Korea and thousands of prisoners taken.

UN forces, composed now of American, British, Australian, Canadian, French, Greek and Philippino units, crossed the 38th Parallel into North Korea on October 8. Pyongyang, 50 miles north of the 38th Parallel, was captured by the US 1st Cavalry Division on October 19. Soon after, the vital line of the Yalu River on the Chinese–Korean frontier was reached and the town of Changjin taken. China now warned that she would be forced to intervene and on November 24 about 180,000 Chinese troops entered the war and began to drive the UN forces back. *See* Thirty-Eighth Parallel, Sinuiju.

Sepeia *Argive War*

494 BC, between the Spartans under Cleomenes and the Argives. The Spartans, by a ruse, succeeded in surprising the Argives while the soldiers were dining and totally routed them. This defeat deprived Argos of the paramountcy in the Peloponnesus, created rivalry with Athens and led to the Peloponnesian Wars. *See* Aegina.

Seringapatam I *Second British-Mysore War*

This city was besieged, February 5, 1792, by 22,000 British and Indian troops with 86 guns, under Lord Cornwallis, and defended by a Mysori garrison under Tippu Sahib. On the 6th an assault upon the outlying works was successful, all the redoubts commanding the city being carried, at a cost to the assailants of 530, while the Mysoris lost heavily. On the approach of reinforcements under General Abercromby on the 16th, Tippu consented to treat, and peace was signed in the following month, when he gave up half his territory to the British. *See* Seringapatam II.

Seringapatam II *Third British-Mysore War*

The second siege by General Harris opened April 6, 1799, when the city was defended by a garrison of 20,000 under Tippu. On May 3 the breach was declared practicable and the place was stormed by 4,000 men under General Baird. Tippu was slain in the rout which followed the assault. The British losses during the siege amounted to 1,464. About 6,000 Mysoris fell in the assault. The victory gave the British supremacy in southern India. *See* Seringapatam I, Sidassir.

Seringham *Carnatic War*

In 1753, between 1,000 British troops under Major Stringer Lawrence and the French, with their Maratha and Mysori allies, under M. Astruc. The French attacked in force an isolated post near Madras, held by 200 Sepoys, and carried it before Major Lawrence could come up. He then attacked and in turn carried the position, driving off the French and the Marathas who came up to their support, and captured three guns. *See* Madras II, Trincomalee I.

Seskar *Russo-Swedish Wars*

In 1790, between the Swedish fleet under the Duke of Sudermanland and a Russian squadron under Admiral Kruze. The Swedes were totally defeated after a severe engagement which lasted from daybreak till far into the night.

Seta *Yoshinaka's Rebellion*

In 1183, between the army of Yoritomo under his brothers Noriyori and Yoshitsune, and that of Yoshinaka. The rebels were completely defeated and Yoshinaka killed. Having banished Yoshitsune, Minamoto Yoritomo became the real ruler of Japan in 1185.

Sevastopol *Crimean War*

This fortress was besieged by the allied French and British armies, under General Canrobert and Lord Raglan, September 28, 1854. It was defended by a large force of Russians under Prince Mentschikov, with General Totleben as his principal engineer officer. The besiegers were too few for a complete investment, and though the harbour was closed by the British fleet under Sir Edmund Lyons, the Russians were throughout the siege able to obtain reinforcements and provisions from the north side. The batteries opened fire on October 17, and from that time till September 8, 1855, the town was more or less continuously bombarded. On that day the Malakov, an important part of the southern defences, was stormed by the French and the place became untenable, the allies entering it unopposed on the following day. The 54,000 Russians are said to have lost during the later days of the bombardment as many as 3,000 men a day. Peace was signed at the Congress of Paris, March 30, 1856. *See* Balaclava, Inkerman, Kars.

Seven Days' Battle *American Civil War*

A series of actions fought by General Lee, with 100,000 Confederates, against General McClellan, with 95,000 Federals, Lee's object being to relieve Richmond. On June 26, 1862, General Hill with 1,400 Confederates attacked McCall's division in a strong position at Beaver's Dam Creek, which attack McCall repulsed at small cost to his force. On the 27th General Porter, 30,000 strong, posted on the Chickahominy at Gaines' Mill, was attacked by 65,000 Confederates under Lee in person. The Southerners advanced under a heavy artillery fire, and after severe fighting drove the Federals across the river with 6,800 losses, and captured 20 guns. On the 28th McClellan prepared to withdraw to the James River, his centre having been pierced, and began his retreat. On the 29th four Confederate divisions under Longstreet, aided by an armoured train, came up with Sumner's corps at Savage's Station but were repulsed, Sumner thus inflicting a serious check upon the pursuing columns.
On the 30th three divisions under General Jackson overtook the Federal rearguard under General French near the White Oak Swamp, and an artillery duel followed which cost the Federals some guns. Two divisions under Longstreet also attacked McCall's division and routed it, McCall being captured. By the evening of the 30th, McClellan reached Malvern Hill, overlooking the James River, and determined to oppose here the further advance of the Confederates. On July 1st the Confederates attacked, but the Federals held their ground throughout the day and on the 2nd retired in good order and practically unmolested. The Federals admitted a loss of

15,249 men and 25 guns during the operations, but Confederate accounts put the figure much higher and claim 51 guns. The losses of the Southerners, about 20,000, were also very heavy, especially at Malvern Hill, but Lee's object was accomplished and Richmond was relieved. *See* Cedar Mountain, Fair Oaks.

Sevenoaks *Cade's Rebellion*

June 18, 1450, between the rebels, under Jack Cade and the royal troops under Sir Humphrey Stafford. The force under Stafford was quite inadequate for the work in hand . and was routed, Stafford being killed. Cade's men were defeated at London Bridge on July 5 and he was later killed. *See* Southwark.

Seven Pines,

see Fair Oaks

Shahjehan *Tatar Invasion of Khorezm*

This city was besieged 1221, by the Tatars under Tuli Khan, and was obstinately defended by the garrison under a Turkish general named Bugha. For twenty-one successive days the besiegers delivered assaults which were repulsed, but finally the inhabitants made terms with Tuli Khan and opened the gates. *See* Kharismia, Samarkand.

Shaldiran *Ottoman Wars*

August 24, 1514, between 120,000 Turks under Selim I and about 80,000 Persians under the Shah Ismael. The wing led by the Shah in person was victorious but the Persian left was totally routed, and in endeavouring to restore the battle on that side Ismael was wounded, whereupon the army was seized with panic, and took to flight. *See* Lepanto, Cairo.

Shanghai *Sino-Japanese War II*

August 13, 1937, when 200,000 Japanese troops in this 'special undeclared war' attacked this principal Chinese port with the aid of naval and air force. The Chinese held out for three months, until November 8.

Shannon and Chesapeake *War of 1812*

A famous frigate action, fought May 29, 1813, between the British frigate *Shannon*, of 38 guns, commanded by Captain Broke, and the American frigate *Chesapeake*, also of 38 guns, under Captain John Lawrence. The *Chesapeake* sailed out of Boston Harbour to attack the *Shannon*, and after a brisk action was taken by the board by the British. The *Shannon* lost four officers and 21 men killed, and three officers and 56 men wounded; the *Chesapeake*, eight officers and 39 men killed, and nine officers and 106 men wounded. Captain Lawrence was killed and Captain Broke wounded. *See* Lake Erie.

Sharqat *World War I*

October 29, 1918, when General Cobbe, with the object of taking the Mosul (Iraq) oilfields, attacked the Turkish forces of General Hakki with a strong Anglo-Indian force of cavalry and horse-drawn artillery. The Turks were routed, Cobbe took altogether 18,000 prisoners and the Mosul oilfields were occupied November 14. *See* Damascus.

Sheerness *Anglo-Dutch Wars*

June 7, 1667, and following days, when the Dutch fleet under Admiral de Ruyter, sailed up the Medway as far as Upnor Castle and destroyed seven ships of war. *See* The Downs, North Foreland.

Sheriffmuir *Jacobite Rebellion of the Fifteen*

November 13, 1715, between 3,500 royal troops under the Duke of Argyll and 9,000 Highlanders under the Earl of Mar. Argyll's right wing was routed by the Macdonalds, and his left and centre, though at first they held their own, were in the end compelled to retire, and Argyll effected a retreat in good order to Stirling. *See* Preston.

Sherstone *Danish Invasion*

1016, between Edmund Ironside and Knut, the rival claimants to the throne. The battle was indecisive. *See* Pen Selwood.

Shijo Nawate *War of the Northern and Southern Empires*

In 1339, between the army of the Northern Japanese Emperor, and the troops of the Southern Emperor under Kusunoki Masatsura. Masatsura was attacked at Yoshino, which place was temporarily the Imperial residence. Feeling that he was too weak to defend it, he marched out with his whole force to meet his assailants, and fell fighting to the last, the Northern troops gaining a complete victory. Not for 55 years was Japan again united, under the rule of the Northern line.

Shiloh *American Civil War*

April 6 and 7, 1862, between the Confederates, 40,000 strong, under General Johnston, and 42,000 Federals under General Grant. The Confederates attacked Grant's position on the west of the Tennessee River and surprised the Federals, driving back the first line in confusion. By nightfall Grant was practically defeated, but Johnston failed to take advantage of his opportunity, and Grant being reinforced by 20,000 men during the night, was able on the 7th to assume the offensive. After severe fighting the Southerners were driven from the field with a loss of 10,690 killed and wounded and 959 prisoners, General Johnston being among the killed. The Federals lost 10,150 killed and wounded, and 4,044 prisoners, and were able to undertake the conquest of the Mississippi. *See* New Orleans.

Shinowara *Yoshinaka's Rebellion*

April, 1183, between the troops of the rebel Daimio Yoshinaka, and the Japanese Imperial army, consisting of 100,000 horsemen, under Taira-no-Kore. The Imperial troops were defeated with a loss of 20,000 killed. *See* Shijo Nawate.

Shirogawa *Satsuma Rebellion*

September 24, 1876, when the last remnants of the rebels, under Saigo, were defeated by the Imperial army under Prince Taruhito. The rebels were practically annihilated and most of the leaders of the revolt killed. Saigo, after the defeat, committed *hara-kiri* on the field. *See* Tansara Saka, Tayeizan.

231

Sholapur *Third British-Maratha War*

May 10, 1818, when a body of cavalry under General Pritzen, forming part of General Monro's force, attacked and dispersed the retreating remnant of the Peshwa's army. Sholapur surrendered on the 15th, the operations having cost the British only 97 killed and wounded, while the loss of the Marathas exceeded 800 killed. *See* Kirkee.

Sholingur *First British-Mysore War*

September 27, 1781, between the British, 10,000 strong, under Sir Eyre Coote, and the Mysoris, numbering about 60,000, under Hyder Ali. Hyder was surprised in the act of striking camp, and though a series of cavalry charges enabled him to withdraw his guns in safety, it was at a cost of 5,000 men that he eventually made good his retreat. The British loss did not exceed 100. *See* Aligarh.

Shrewsbury *Percy's Rebellion*

July 21, 1403, when the royalists under Henry IV, met and defeated the insurgents under Sir Henry Percy, known as Hotspur. Hotspur was killed, the earls of Douglas and Worcester taken prisoners. The battle was the baptism of fire of Henry, Prince of Wales (Henry V), who displayed great bravery, and was severely wounded. This is the battle treated by Shakespeare in *Henry IV Part II*. *See* Homildon Hill, Bramham Moor.

Shropshire *Roman Conquest of Britain*

AD 50, between the Romans under Ostorius Scapula and the Britons under Caractacus. The Britons occupied the slope of a hill, where they were attacked by the Romans and totally routed. Caracactus fled to the Brigantes, by whom he was surrendered and sent a captive to Rome.

Sicily *World War II*

The 38-day battle for this Italian island began on the night of July 9–10, 1943, when 160,000 British and US forces of General Alexander's 15th Army Group landed by parachute, glider and landing craft on the south and south-east coasts. The port of Syracuse fell to the 8th Army on July 12, and Augusta the next day. Palermo fell to US forces under General Patton on July 22, but Axis troops, including the Hermann Goering Division, dug in on the slopes of Mount Etna, held up the advance on the east coast for nearly three weeks. When these positions were taken, the Axis command fought a delaying action while they evacuated some 60,000 troops across the Straits of Messina. The campaign ended on August 16, having cost the Germans 7,000, and the Italians 140,000 prisoners and 31,000 killed or wounded. Allied casualties were 31,158, including a large number of malaria cases. *See* Salerno.

Sidassir *Third British-Mysore War*

March 6, 1799, between the advance guard of General Stuart's force, composed of three regiments under Colonel Montresor, and 12,000 Mysoris under Tippu Sahib. Montresor's small force withstood the attack of Tippu's troops for over six hours and their ammunition was all but exhausted, when Stuart came up and drove back the enemy with a loss of 2,000 men. The British lost 143 killed and wounded. *See* Seringapatam I and II.

Sidi Barrâni *World War II*

Marshal Graziani invaded Egypt in September 1940 with 80,000 men, 120 tanks and numerical superiority in aircraft, establishing several miles over the border around Sidi Barrâni a chain of seven forts, defensible only from the east. General O'Connor, whose force of 31,000 men and 275 tanks lay about 70 miles to the east, decided to make a five-day raid on the forts, advancing 30 miles during the night of December 7, and another 40 miles the next night, attacking at dawn on December 9. Entering the Italian lines through a 20-mile gap between the forts, the British attacked from the rear and flank. By the end of the third day they had utterly routed the Italians, putting five of their divisions out of action, and taking 39,000 prisoners at a cost of 600 casualties. *See* Bardia, Beda Fomm.

Sidi Rezegh *World War II*

November 18, 1941, when the 118,000-strong

8th Army's XIII Corps (infantry) attacked General Rommel's Axis forces along the coast road east of Tobruk, and XXX Corps (armoured) attacked Sidi Rezegh from the south in an attempt to relieve the besieged garrison at Tobruk, 50 miles to the north-east. Rommel's forces beat off the British attack and counter-attacked strongly. During November 22–23 a furious tank battle raged around Sidi Rezegh, which eventually fell. Rommel next attacked the British rear with two Panzer divisions. After much confused desert fighting, during which General Cunningham, who wished to withdraw, was replaced by General Ritchie, Rommel himself withdrew to the west on December 2 and Tobruk was relieved. The British lost 18,500 men, the Axis 24,500, as well as 36,000 prisoners, but two weeks later Rommel attacked again. *See* Gazala, Tobruk.

Sievershausen *German Reformation Wars*

July 9, 1553, between the Germans, under Maurice, Elector of Saxony, and the Brandenburgers, under the Margrave Albert. The Brandenburgers were defeated, but Maurice was wounded in the action and died two days later. In 1555, Charles V granted religious toleration to Protestants. *See* Mühlberg.

Siffin *Muslim Civil Wars*

A series of actions extending over a hundred days, in 657, between the Muslims, under the Caliph Ali, and the adherents of Moawiyeh, the son of Abu Sophian, a pretender to the Caliphate. In the course of these engagements Ali lost 25,000, and Moawiyeh 45,000 men, but the latter was undefeated, and the conflict was ended by an unsatisfactory compromise. Ali was assassinated in 661, and Moawiyeh succeeded him. *See* Bosra, Medina, Basra.

Sikajoki *Russo-Swedish Wars*

April 18, 1808, between the Swedes under General Klingspoor and the Russians under General Bouxhoevden. The Russians endeavoured to outflank the Swedes by moving out on to the ice at the mouth of the Sikajoki river, at the same time assailing them in front. Both attacks were repulsed and, after

eight hours' fighting, Klingspor took the offensive and drove the Russians from the field with heavy loss. The Swedes lost 1,000 killed and wounded. Sweden ceded Finland to Russia in 1809.

Silistra *Crimean War*

March 20, 1854, when, following the Turks' victory at Oltenitza, and their defeat by the Russian fleet at Sinope in 1853, Russian forces under Field-Marshal Paskevich crossed the Danube and besieged this Turkish fortress (now in Bulgaria). Two English officers, Captain Buller and Lieutenant Nasmyth, gave the garrison valuable assistance and it stubbornly repulsed the Russian attacks. Though the Turks made no efforts to relieve the defenders they held out until June 22. Field-Marshal Paskevich, who had lost 10,000 men, then raised the siege. Russia, meanwhile, had ignored the British and French requests of February 27, 1854, to evacuate the Danubian Principalities within a month. During the siege France therefore declared war on March 27, Britain on March 28 and the ill-fated Crimean War began. *See* Oltenitza, Sinope, Alma.

Silpia,

see Elinga

Sinai Peninsula *Israeli-Arab War*

Tension between Britain, France and Israel on the one hand, and Egypt on the other, followed President Nasser's nationalization of the Suez Canal, on July 26, 1956. On October 29, the Israeli Army crossed the frontier and invaded the Egyptian Sinai Peninsula with 10 brigades commanded by General Dayan. Two days later Franco-British air forces bombed Egyptian airfields and dropped parachute troops who occupied Port Said and Port Fuad, at the Canal's northern end. In response to UN resolutions and, possibly, Soviet threats, Britain and France, who claimed they were merely enforcing a cease-fire, halted their military action. But by November 4, the Israeli Army had utterly routed Egyptian forces throughout Sinai at a loss of 172 killed and about 900 wounded.

Many thousands of Egyptian prisoners were taken as well as hundreds of Russian tanks, self-propelled guns and lorries, huge quantities of ammunition and supplies. A UN force was sent to the region and the Anglo-French troops were withdrawn in December. The Israeli Army moved out of Sinai in March, 1957. *See* Six-Day War.

Singapore *World War II*

Defeated by General Yamashita's Japanese forces on the Malaya Peninsula, the British under General Percival retreated across the Johore Strait, dynamited the causeway on January 31, 1942, and hoped for a breathing space after their retreat down Malaya. The Japanese, however, began to shell Singapore island, repaired the damaged causeway and began crossing 25,000 troops and light tanks on February 9. Spearheads advanced inland, and seized the reservoirs in the centre of the island. Lacking ammunition and food, and with the water supply denied him, General Percival surrendered his 16,000 British, 14,000 Australian and 32,000 Indian troops on February 15. Winston Churchill described it as the worst disaster in British history. *See* Malaya.

Singara I *Persian Wars of the Roman Empire*

In 348, between the Romans under Constantius and the Persians, in largely superior force, under Sapor II. The Persian king, having posted the major part of his army on the heights overlooking Singara, engaged the Romans with a comparatively small force of light-armed troops who were easily routed by the legionaries. The pursuit however was carried too far, and when night fell the Romans, exhausted by their efforts, bivouacked under the heights. During the night Sapor led his best troops to the attack and routed the weary Romans, with terrible slaughter. *See* Mursa.

Singara II *Persian Wars of the Roman Empire*

This fortress, held by a Roman garrison, was captured after a brief siege by the Persians, under Sapor II, in 360. The garrison was sent

into captivity and the fortress dismantled. *See* Tigris.

Sinnaca *Parthian War*

At this place the remnants of the army of Crassus, after the battle of Carrhae, 53 BC, surrendered to the Parthians. Only 5,000 men were with the Roman eagles. *See* Carrhae, Alesia.

Sino-Japanese War I

July 27, 1894, when rivalry for ownership of Korea led to a Japanese declaration of war against China. Chinese troops were routed and on April 17, 1895, Japan imposed the Treaty of Shimonoseki upon China, which gave the Pescadores, the Liaotung Peninsula, Formosa and a big indemnity to Japan, while declaring Korea independent. *See* Yalu River, Port Arthur I.

Sino-Japanese War II

July 7, 1937, when, having established the puppet state of Manchukuo in Manchuria in 1932, Japanese troops clashed with those of China at the Marco Polo bridge near Peking. Without a declaration of war, Japan launched a major campaign to overrun all China. This 'special undeclared war' became part of World War II when Japan attacked the US fleet at Pearl Harbor on December 7, 1941. It went on until Japan surrendered on August 14, 1945, after the Hiroshima and Nagasaki atomic bomb attacks. In this eight years' war Chinese killed and wounded amounted to 3,200,000. *See* Shanghai.

Sinope *Crimean War*

November 30, 1853, when following the Turkish victory three weeks earlier at Oltenitza, Czar Nicholas I, having sent a Russian fleet across the Black Sea, destroyed nine Turkish ships in harbour at Sinope during a heavy bombardment. About 4,000 Turks were killed aboard and ashore and the harbour installations were wrecked. Great Britain and France, who had sent fleets to Constantinople in moral support of Turkey, at once ordered them into the Black Sea with the avowed aim of protecting Turkish shipping. Indignation arose in Britain and France over the Russian action and the war would soon spread. *See* Silistra.

Sino-Vietnamese War

February 17, 1979, when China launched a major offensive with 5 army corps comprising 15 divisions, infantry, armoured and artillery, about 120,000 men, along her frontier with Vietnam. China's declared object was 'to teach the Vietnamese a lesson' for repeated attacks on people and villages in her frontier regions for the past 12 months. In overall command of this punitive operation, for which ammunition, fuel and supply dumps had been secretly built up for three months, were Vice-Premier Teng Hsaio-ping, as Chief of Staff, and Hsu Shih-yu, chief of the Canton military region. The Chinese armoured divisions employed World War II Russian tanks, the T-34s, and a few of the late 1950s T-54s. Their supporting infantry, discarding the 'human wave' tactics advocated by Mao Tse-tung, used more orthodox tactics and, lacking air support, relied on long-range bombardment of Vietnamese positions. Fighting was concentrated in the mountainous provinces of Lang Son, Hoang Lien Son, Cao Bang, and Mon Cai near the coast, respectively north-west, north and north-east of Hanoi. The provincial capital of Mon Cai and the towns of Dong Dang and Muong Khuong, about 12 miles inside Vietnam, were occupied by February 19, as regional Vietnamese units there retreated.

Fighting stiffened after February 28 when three regular divisions from Vietnamese occupying forces in Cambodia arrived, equipped with 105mm and 130mm guns. Fighting subsequently developed into long-range artillery duels with armoured and infantry assaults by the Chinese on key objectives. By March 1 Chinese units had advanced through the mountains to Ngan Son township on the road to Hanoi. Another column by passed the fiercely contested town of Lang Son to reach Dinh Lap, then two days later, Quang Uyen, on the coast, about 100 miles from Hanoi. After intense fighting, Lang Son, a road, rail and river communications centre and a fortress vital for the control of the northern provinces, fell to the Chinese on March 3. Meanwhile, limited Vietnamese counter-attacks across the border into China's Guangxi-Yunnan border provinces had been repelled by border units. China, which had always declared the operation was punitive, with strict military limits, announced on March 6 that 'having attained the goals set for them' her troops had begun to withdraw. This fighting withdrawal was completed by March 16. Vietnam, which in December 1978, had occupied Cambodia and overthrown its government, denied accusations that it was attempting to extend its borders into China, or trying to set up an Indo-Chinese Federation, with Soviet backing. Soviet Russia made repeated threats to intervene in the Sino-Vietnamese battles, under its treaty obligations with Vietnam, all of which came to nothing. China contended that she had dented Russian credibility and shown the West how to deal with surrogate aggression by Russian client states.

Sinsheim *Wars of Louis XIV*

June 16, 1674, between the French under Marshal de Turenne and the Imperialists under General Caprara and Charles V, Duke of Lorraine. The French gained a signal victory. *See* Seneffe.

Sinuiju *Korean War*

April 12, 1951, the world's biggest jet air battle to date, when 115 USAF fighters of the UN forces, escorting 32 Super Fortress bombers, engaged 80 Russian MIG 15 jet fighters and destroyed or damaged 46 at small loss to themselves. *See* Thirty-Eighth Parallel.

Sitabaldi *Third British-Maratha War*

November 24, 1817, between a small force of Madras troops and some Bengal cavalry, in all about 1,300 men, under Colonel Scott, and the army of Nappa Sahib, Rajah of Nagpur, 18,000 strong with 36 guns. The Sepoys held their ground for 18 hours and eventually beat off their assailants, at a cost to themselves of about 300 men. *See* Kirkee.

Six-Day War *Israeli-Arab War*

June 5-10, 1967, when Israel won a total victory in 80 hours over the United Arab Republic, Syria and Jordan. In the first few hours of June 5 Israel's air force, flying in a wide arc over the Mediterranean to Egypt, destroyed some 360 UAR aircraft on the ground and won mastery of the air. By June 7, after fierce tank battles, Israeli armoured units had taken the entire Sinai peninsula, advanced to the Suez Canal and captured the Gaza Strip. At the same time, in fierce fighting, they defeated Jordanian tank units by air attack, seized the Old City of Jerusalem and over-ran all Jordan west of the Jordan River, taking Bethlehem, Hebron, Jericho, Nablus, Ramallah and Jenin.

Winning mastery of the strongly fortified high ground on the Syrian border, on June 9–10, Israeli armour and infantry advanced 12 miles into Syria and took the garrison town of Kuneitra, only 12 miles from Damascus, the capital. Israel had extended its territory to four times its size before the war, half conquest, half self-defence, began.

The United Arab Republic army lost 80,000 to 100,000 men killed, wounded or prisoner, mostly the latter, and some 800 Russian tanks, as well as some 10,000 lorries and hundreds of guns. About 258 Migs, 60 Ilyushin bombers and 28 Hunters were destroyed. Jordanian casualties totalled 12,000 to 15,000 out of a strength of 55,000. Israel claimed to have lost only 61 tanks and 679 men killed, 2,563 wounded. The Israeli capture of Sharm-es-Sheikh opened the Straits of Tiran and the Gulf of Aqaba to international shipping. *See* Sinai Peninsula.

Skalitz *Seven Weeks' War*

June 28, 1866, between the 5th Prussian Army Corps under General Steinmetz and the 6th and 8th Austrian Corps under General Ramming. The Austrians were defeated and Skalitz occupied by the Prussians, who captured 4,000 prisoners and eight guns. *See* Langensalza, Koeniggrätz.

Slivnica *Serbo-Bulgarian War*

November 17, 18 and 19, 1885, between the Serbians, 28,000 strong, under King Milan, and Bulgarians, at first 10,000 in number, but reinforced on the night of the 17th and during the 18th by a further 5,000, under Prince Alexander. On the 17th Prince Alexander, who occupied a position strong against a frontal attack but very vulnerable on his left, made a strong attack on the Serbian left to distract attention from his weak flank. This attack was repulsed and on the following day the Serbians attacked Alexander's left. Having been reinforced however he was able

to beat them off, while a frontal attack was also repulsed with loss. On the 19th the Serbian attacks were again unsuccessful, and by 3 pm they were in full retreat, pursued by the Bulgarians. The Serbians lost about 2,000, the victors 3,000 in killed and wounded, in the three days. *See* Pirot.

Sluys *Hundred Years' War*

June 24, 1340, when the English fleet of 200 sail, under Sir Robert Morley and Richard Fitzalan, attacked the French fleet of about 70, under Hugues Quieret, lying in Sluys harbour. Practically the whole of the French fleet was captured or destroyed, and Quieret was killed. *See* Halidon Hill, Crécy.

Smolensk I *Great Northern War*

September 22, 1708, when Charles XII of Sweden, with 4,000 infantry and six regiments of cavalry, attacked a force of 16,000 Cossacks and Tartars. The king, with one regiment, was in the course of the action cut off from the rest of his troops by a body of Tartars, and had a narrow escape. His immediate following was reduced to five men, when he was rescued by a cavalry charge. In the end the Swedes routed the Cossacks with heavy loss. *See* Fredrikshald.

Smolensk II *Napoleonic Wars*

August 17, 1812, between 175,000 French under Napoleon and 130,000 Russians under Prince Bagration, of whom about 50,000 and 60,000 respectively were actually engaged. Bagration's corps occupied the town of Smolensk, which Napoleon attacked, carrying two of the suburbs. During the night the Russians set fire to the place and evacuated it, having lost in the action about 10,000 killed and wounded. The French lost 9,000. *See* Mogilev, Borodino.

Smolensk III *World War II*

July 16, 1941, when Field-Marshal von Bock's Central Army Group (42 infantry divisions, nine armoured, seven motorized, one cavalry) encircled this town, defended by 26½ Russian infantry divisions, seven armoured and one cavalry. The 10th Panzer division battled into the town on the night of July 18. Strong Russian counter-attacks from the south against

236

the German salient enabled several Russian divisions to escape encirclement. The Russian counter-offensive mounted in intensity; German reserves were thrown in, yet more Russians cut their way out at Yeremolino. Smolensk fell on August 6, but fighting continued in the region to the east for another two weeks. The Germans were held at the line 25 miles east of Yartsevo-Yelna-Desna. About 100,000 Russians were killed or wounded and probably more than 150,000 taken prisoner as well as thousands of tanks and guns lost. But here for the first time the Russians succeeded in bringing the German *blitzkrieg* to a halt, thus upsetting Hitler's timetable and giving themselves time to make ready for the defence of Moscow. *See* Moscow, Stalingrad.

Sobraon *First British-Sikh War*

February 10, 1846, between the British, about 15,000 strong, and 25,000 Sikhs under Runjur Singh. The Sikhs were strongly entrenched in a bend of the Sutlej, and Sir Hugh Gough, with feigned attacks on their centre and right, succeeded in pushing home his assault on their left and after hard fighting drove the defenders to the river, where many perished. The British lost 2,383, the Sikhs about 8,000. This was the last battle of the First British-Sikh War. *See* Aliwal, Ferozeshah, Mudki.

Soczawa *Ottoman Wars*

In 1676, between the Poles under John Sobieski and the Turks under Mohammed IV, who wished to reduce Poland to vassalage. The Poles, who had been reinforced by the Lithuanians under Paz, totally routed the Turks, who were greatly superior in numbers, and drove them in confusion into Kaminiec, with the exception of which fortress the whole of Poland was thus freed from the Ottoman invaders. *See* Zurakow, Vienna II.

Sohr *War of the Austrian Succession*

September 30, 1745, between 18,000 Prussians under Frederick the Great and 30,000 Austrians under Prince Charles of Lorraine. The Prussians attacked the Austrian position and the Austrians, failing to display their usual courage, made no stand against the steady advance of the Prussian infantry, and were driven back in confusion with a loss of 6,000 killed, wounded and prisoners, and 22 guns.

The Prussians lost between 3,000 and 4,000 men. *See* Louisbourg, Hennersdorf, Madras.

Soissons *Rise of France*

In 486, and notable as the first military exploit of Clovis, the founder of the Merovingian dynasty, who here defeated Syagrius, Count of Soissons, and annexed his dominions. *See* Tolbiac.

Solferino *Italian Wars of Independence*

June 24, 1859, between 120,000 Austrians, with 451 guns, under the Emperor Franz Josef, with Generals Wimpffen and Scholick in actual command, and the French and Piedmontese, 118,000, with 320 guns, under Napoleon III and Victor Emmanuel. The French attacked the Austrian position on the heights round Solferino, which were held by Scholick, and after very hard fighting they were captured by the corps of Generals MacMahon and Baraguay d'Hilliers. Meanwhile Wimpffen, with three Army Corps, attacked the French left, but was held at bay throughout the day by Marshal Niel's corps, and when night fell, the Austrian centre being broken, Franz Josef had no option but to retreat, and he recrossed the Mincio. The Austrians lost 22,000 killed, wounded and missing. The allies' losses were 18,000, of which number the Piedmontese corps of 25,000 lost 4,000. Austria ceded all Lombardy except Mantua and Peschiera to Italy and a unified Italy began to emerge. *See* Magenta.

Solomon Islands *World War II*

Japan followed up her gains in the western Pacific by capturing the Solomon islands of Buka on March 13, 1942, Bougainville on April 7, Tulagi on May 3 and Guadalcanal on July 6. The struggle of the US and her Pacific Allies to retake them began on August 7, 1942, when the 1st Marines Division landed on Guadalcanal, and ended over two years later on November 25, 1944 with the US naval victory at Empress Augusta Bay. *See* Guadalcanal, New Guinea, Rabaul.

Solway Moss *Anglo-Scottish Wars*

December 14, 1542, between the Scottish invading army under Oliver Sinclair and a band of 500 English borderers under Thomas

Dacre and John Musgrave. The Scots were totally defeated and many important nobles captured. *See* Flodden.

Somme I *World War I*

July 1 to November 18, 1916, when the 4th British Army in the north of the western front, and the 16th and 10th French armies in the south, tried to achieve a major breakthrough between Arras and St Quentin, in the low hills where the Germans had dug in after their retreat from the Marne in 1914. After a week's heavy shelling, the British attacked on July 1 over a 15-mile front towards Bapaume with 18 divisions, and the French with 16 divisions towards Péronne. Hit by a hurricane of German fire, the British lost some 60,000 officers and men on this first day for an advance of 1,000 yards. Though the French 6th Army (General Fayolle) penetrated von Bülow's lines, it soon became clear to the Allies that a major breakthrough of the German in-depth defences was impossible. They settled for a battle of attrition and for 10 weeks hammered the German lines, but even the first tank attack in the war, on September 15, failed to dislodge them. The battle ended on November 18, with an Allied advance of seven miles only along a 20-mile front at a cost of 418,000 British and 195,000 French casualties. The Germans lost 650,000 killed or wounded. *See* Verdun, Arras II.

Somme II *World War I*

The biggest offensive of all, by Ludendorff, against on the left (north) General Gough's 5th Army (11 divisions in line) and on the right General Byng's 3rd Army (10 divisions in line), together holding a 50-mile front south of Arras. On March 21, 1918, after a bombardment by 6,000 guns and a heavy gas attack, Ludendorff in the first wave hurled in 37 divisions and successively another 24, with the major aim of splitting and quickly defeating the Allied forces by first breaking the British right centre.

The German armies (17th, von Bülow, 2nd, von der Marwitz, 18th, von Hutier, making 71 divisions with reserves), advanced only three miles during the first three days, despite their great superiority, but the 5th Army, weakened through heavy losses, then gave way, uncovering Byng's 3rd Army's left

flank, which had then to fall back to Le Sars, nearly half way to Albert. By the evening of March 25th, the 5th Army's losses had reduced it to two corps, but though it had held the Germans to a 14-mile advance, they now threatened to break through the link of the British-French armies at Roye, some 35 miles south-east of Amiens.

Divided command weakened the Allies, and on March 26 Marshal Foch was appointed General-in-Chief. Albert, 20 miles north-west of Amiens fell on 26/27 April; Montdidier, a railway junction 28 miles south-east of Amiens on the 27th.

Exhaustion now slowed both Allies and Germans, the latter being 38 miles from their start point, short of food and ahead of their heavy guns. Ludendorff now made an all-out effort both to cut the vital Calais–Paris railway and to capture Amiens. The 3rd Army repulsed a big attack at Arras, in the north, but in the south the Germans drove back the French, and by April 3 had captured Hangard and the railway station at Moreuil, 12 miles from Amiens.

On April 4 General von Hutier's 18th Army made a last desperate attempt to break through the French and British link near Hangard, forcing the French back to within two miles of the Paris railway. But the French held and Ludendorff's great offensive ended between April 4th and 6th, his armies exhausted. Allied losses during the 16 days' severe fighting totalled nearly 230,000, those of the Germans nearly as great. It was the first battle in the last German offensive. *See* Lys.

Somnath *Mahmud's Twelfth Invasion of India*

This city, one of the holy places of India, was captured by the Afghans under Sultan Mahmud of Ghazni, in 1024. According to tradition, he carried off the great gates of the city to Ghazni; and certain gates purporting to be the same, but which afterwards proved to be of later date, were brought back to India with a flourish of trumpets, after the capture of Ghazni by the British in 1839, and the end of the 1st Afghan War in 1842. *See* Ghazni.

Son-Tai *Tongking War*

This fortress, defended by a garrison of 25,000 Chinese, including 10,000 'Black

Flags', under Lin Yung Ku, was attacked by the French under Admiral Courbet, with seven river gun-boats and force of 7,000 men, December 14, 1883. On this day the outer defences were carried and the garrison driven into the citadel. During the night the French were surprised by a sortie, which however they repulsed after severe fighting. On the 16th they stormed the citadel, losing in the three days 92 officers and 318 men killed and wounded. The Chinese lost about 1,000. *See* Taku Forts.

Sorata *Inca Rising*

Besieged, 1780, by the revolted Peruvians under Andrés. The fortifications, well provided with artillery, proved impregnable, but Andrés diverted certain mountain torrents against the walls and thus opened a large breach, through which the Peruvians entered the city and massacred the whole of the garrison and inhabitants. Of 20,000 souls, it was said that only one priest escaped.

Sorauren *Peninsular War*

July 28, 1813, between the French, 25,000 strong under Marshal Soult, and the British, 12,000 strong under General Lord Wellington. Soult attempted to turn the British left in order to drive them from a strong position, but after severe fighting was repulsed with a loss of about 3,000. The British losses were about 2,600. Soult renewed his attempt to force Wellington's lines on the 30th, but was again repulsed, with a loss of 2,000 killed and wounded and 3,000 prisoners. The British loss amounted to 1,900. *See* Vitoria.

South Mountain *American Civil War*

September 14, 1862, between the Federals under General McClellan and the Confederates under General Lee. Lee's object was to hold McClellan in check while Jackson captured Harper's Ferry, and to this end he posted General D. Hill with 15,000 men on South Mountain. Here Hill was attacked and driven to the upper slopes, but being reinforced by a portion of Longstreet's command, he maintained his position there, withdrawing on the morning of the 15th. Each side lost about 2,500 men, but Lee had

gained his object, as the delay to McClellan ensured the capture of Harper's Ferry. *See* Antietam.

Southwark *Cade's Rebellion*

July 5, 1450, between the rebels under Jack Cade and the citizens of London under Matthew Gough. The Londoners endeavoured to hold London Bridge, to prevent the plundering expeditions of Cade's followers into the city, but were driven back, and the central drawbridge set on fire. The Londoners lost heavily, among the killed being Gough. *See* Sevenoaks.

Southwold Bay *Anglo-Dutch Wars*

June 7, 1672, between the English and French fleet of 101 ships, under the Duke of York, and the 91 ships of the Dutch fleet, under Admiral de Ruyter. The English and French fleets having divided, the Dutch attacked the English. The battle was indecisive for though the Dutch lost five ships and the English one ship only, their fleet was too crippled to take the offensive for a month. *See* Texel.

Spanish Armada,
see Armada, The

Spanish Galleons,
see Vigo Bay

Sphacteria,
see Pylos

Spicheren *Franco-Prussian War*

August 6, 1870, between the Germans, under General von Alvensleben, 35,000 strong, and a French force of 28,000, under General Frossard. After an obstinate encounter, the French were driven from all their positions with heavy loss, and compelled to retreat on Metz. The Germans lost 223 officers and 4,648 men. The battle is remarkable for the storming of the Rote Berg by one company of the 39th Regiment and four companies of the 74th Regiment, under General von François, who was killed. These five companies maintained their position

239

throughout the afternoon, in face of a vastly superior force. This action is also known as the Battle of Forbach. *See* Colombey, Wörth.

Spion Kop *Second Boer War*

General Buller's second attempt to break through the Boer lines on the Tugela, and relieve Ladysmith, is known by this name. The operations began on January 19, 1900, some 24,000 men being employed. On that day Sir Charles Warren's division started to turn the Boer right, and gradually drove them from ridge to ridge till the evening of the 22nd, when by a night surprise, Spion Kop, the centre of the position, was seized. It was however found impossible to get artillery up the steep slopes, and the brigade holding the hill lost about a third of their strength in the course of the 23rd, including the Brigadier, General Woodgate. At nightfall, Colonel Thorneycroft, who had been appointed to the command, abandoned the hill, and on the following day General Buller decided to recross the Tugela. The British losses during the operations amounted to 87 officers and 1,647 men. *See* Vaalkranz, Ladysmith.

Spira *War of the Spanish Succession*

November 15, 1703, between the French under Marshal Tallard and the Imperialists under the Prince of Hesse, each side being about 20,000 strong. After a severe engagement, the Imperialists were overpowered by the French cavalry, and totally defeated with a loss of 6,000 killed, wounded and missing. Among the prisoners was the Prince of Hesse. *See* Donauwörth, Blenheim.

Splitter *Swedish Invasion of Brandenburg*

January, 1679, between 16,000 Swedes under Field-Marshal Horn and 10,000 Brandenburgers under the Elector Frederick William. The Swedes were utterly routed, Horn being taken prisoner, and not more than 1,500 succeeded in making their way to Riga. *See* Kiöge, Fehrbellin.

Spotsylvania *American Civil War*

A continuation of the Battle of the Wilderness, fought May 10 to 12, 1864, between the 56,000 Confederates under General Lee and the 101,000 Federals under General Grant. Lee's position covering Richmond was attacked on the 10th by Grant, and the day ended with both armies in their original positions, while the losses were heavy. On the 12th Grant renewed the attack, and General Hancock on the right surprised the first line of the Confederate defences and compelled General Johnson and his division to surrender. With this exception, entailing the loss of about a mile of ground, Lee held his own throughout the day, and Grant had suffered too severely to renew the attack. The losses from the 5th, the date of the first Battle of the Wilderness, to the 12th, inclusive, were: Federals, 35,000 killed and wounded; Confederates, 12,000. *See* Wilderness.

Spurs I *Flemish War*,

see Courtrai

Spurs II *Anglo-French Wars*,

see Guinegate

Stadtlohn *Thirty Years' War*

August 9, 1623, between the army of the Protestant Princes of Germany, about 16,000 strong under Duke Christian of Brunswick, and the Catholic League forces under Tilly. The Protestants were utterly routed and dispersed, Christian fleeing to Holland. *See* Fleurus, Dessau.

Staffarda *War of the English Succession*

August 18, 1690, between the French under Marshal Catinat and the Imperialists under Victor Amadeus of Savoy. The Imperialists met with a crushing defeat. *See* Marsaglia.

Stalingrad *World War II*

General von Paulus's 6th Army forced the Russians back into Stalingrad (now Volgograd) in August, 1942, and early in September attacked the western suburbs, where General Zhukov's 62nd Army fought a desperate house-to-house defence. By mid-October all but three sectors had fallen. The Don Army Group, General Rokossovski, the Stalingrad Army Group, General Yeremenko, and the South-West Army Group, General Vatutin, had all been secretly reinforced and in September together had 1,050,000 men, 900 tanks, 13,000 guns, 1,100 aircraft, against about the same number of Germans, Italians, Rumanians and Hungarians, with 700 tanks, 10,000 guns, and 1,200 aircraft.

A Russian 3-pronged counter-offensive started on September 21, when from the north they entered the bottleneck between the Don and Volga. On November 1, another prong crossed the Volga south of Stalingrad, towards Kalach. Then on November 19 the major offensive began with a massive artillery barrage. Vatutin's troops routed the Rumanian 3rd Army, the 8th Italian and the 2nd Hungarian, and advanced 75 miles in three days, reaching Kalach on November 22, linking up there with General Yeremenko's forces. General Rokossovski's troops at the same time broke through to General Gorokhov's bridgehead on the Volga north of Stalingrad. By November 23 the Russians had encircled 22 German and satellite divisions, between 200,000 and 300,000 men. General von Manstein launched a relief attack with three infantry and three tank divisions from the south, on December 12, approaching to within 25 miles of General Paulus's perimeter, but Hitler refused to allow the 6th Army to break out. The relief force was defeated and withdrew on December 28. Paulus then spurned the Russian surrender offer on January 8. On January 10, the Russians attacked behind an artillery barrage of 7,000 guns and mortars from two sides and split the Germans into sectors. Six days later the last airfield was taken, and the Germans were squeezed into a pocket nine miles by 15. On January 25 the Russians crossed the Volga and joined forces with their 62nd Army in Stalingrad west. Hitler ordered the encircled troops to fight to the last man, but under the ruthless Soviet attacks von Seydlitz (51st Corps) surrendered on January 31, followed by von Paulus's battered 6th Army later that day. The last German force, the 11th Panzer Corps, was finally wiped out by noon on February 2. The battle was the great turning point of World War II. More than 200,000 German troops were killed or

had died since the November encirclement and 91,000, including 24 generals, taken prisoner. *See* Ukraine.

Stamford Bridge I *Norse Invasion of Britain*

September 25, 1066, between the English under King Harold II and the Norse invaders under King Harold Hardrada and Tostiq. The Norsemen were surprised by Harold in their camp near York and totally defeated, both Hardrada and Tostiq being killed. Three days later came the Norman invasion. *See* Hastings.

Stamford Bridge II *Wars of the Roses*

An encounter between the retainers of Sir Thomas Neville and Lord Egremont, which developed into a pitched battle in August, 1453. It is considered the beginning of the Wars of the Roses. *See* St Albans.

Standard, The *Anglo-Scottish Wars*

At Luton Moor, near Northallerton, on August 22, 1138, between the Scots under David and the English under Thurstan, Archbishop of York, and Raoul, Bishop of Durham. The Scots were routed and fled in disorder. The battle derives its name from the fact that the banner of St Cuthbert of Durham, which was held to ensure victory, that of St Peter of York and those of other saints, were carried in a waggon in the midst of the English army. *See* Stirling Bridge.

Stavrichani *Ottoman Wars*

August 28, 1739, between 30,000 Russians under General Münnich and the Turkish army under Veli Pasha. The Russians stormed the Turkish entrenched camp, driving the Turks headlong into the Danube where thousands perished, and capturing all their guns and baggage. Münnich followed up this success by the capture of Choczim. *See* Choczim.

Steenkerke *War of the Revolution*

August 3, 1692, between the English under William III and the French under Marshal de Luxembourg. The English attacked the

French camp at daybreak and broke and dispersed a brigade. Luxembourg however rallied his troops and after a severe engagement repulsed the English attack, though William was able to withdraw his forces in good order. *See* Neerwinden I.

Stillwater *American Revolutionary War*

October 7, 1777, between the British, 6,000 strong under General Burgoyne, and the Americans under General Gates. The Americans occupied a strongly entrenched position, which was attacked by Burgoyne. After a severe encounter the attack was repulsed at all points and the British driven back upon their camp at Saratoga with heavy loss, including General Fraser, mortally wounded. The Americans followed up their success by an assault upon the British camp, in which they succeeded in effecting a lodgement, and on the following day Burgoyne withdrew and took up a fresh position on the heights near the Hudson. On October 15, Burgoyne, surrounded by the Americans and finding that no aid could reach him, surrendered with 5,790 men, his total losses during the campaign having amounted to 4,689. This victory marks a turning point in the war, and may therefore be ranked as one of history's decisive battles. *See* Ticonderoga, Bennington.

Stirling Bridge *Wars of Scottish Independence*

September 11, 1297, between the Scots under Sir William Wallace and the English, 50,000 strong, under the Earl of Surrey. Wallace fell upon the English army as it was crossing a narrow bridge over the Forth, and practically annihilated the bridgehead. The rest of the English were driven back to the Tweed, the invasion thus failing. *See* Dunbar, Falkirk.

Stockach *French Revolutionary Wars*

March 25, 1799, between 40,000 French under General Jourdan and the Austrians, 60,000 strong, under the Archduke' Charles. The French were defeated and driven back upon the Rhine. *See* Abukir, Zürich.

Stoke *Lambert Simnel's Rebellion*

June 16, 1487, between the royal troops under Henry VII and the rebels under John de la Pole, Earl of Lincoln, who was aided by 2,000 German mercenaries under Martin Schwarz. The King, whose force was superior in numbers, completely defeated the rebels, Simnel and all the rebel leaders being taken prisoners. *See* Bosworth Field.

Stolhoffen *War of the Spanish Succession*

May 22, 1707, when Marshal de Villars with 45 French battalions stormed and captured the lines of Stolhoffen, which were held by the Imperialists under the Marquis of Baireuth. *See* Ramillies, Toulon.

Stone River,

see Murfreesboro

Stormberg *Second Boer War*

December 10, 1899, when General Gatacre with about 3,000 men made a night march to attack the Boer position at Stormberg. He was misled by his guides, and came unexpectedly under a heavy Boer fire. The position was too strong to carry, and Gatacre was forced to retire, with a loss of 89 killed and wounded and 633 prisoners. *See* Magersfontein, Colenso.

Stralsund I *Thirty Years' War*

This port was besieged, July 5, 1628, by the Imperialists under General von Wallenstein, who had sworn to take it in three days. It was defended mainly by the inhabitants, aided by a small garrison of Swedes and Scots. An assault on the 8th was repulsed, and though on the 9th some of the outworks were gained, the town still held out, and finally, after a siege of 11 weeks, Wallenstein was compelled to withdraw his troops, having lost heavily. *See* Dessau, Lutter.

Stralsund II *Great Northern War*

This Pomeranian port was besieged, October

242

19, 1715, by an army of Prussians and Danes, 36,000 strong, under Frederick William III of Prussia and Frederick IV of Denmark, and was defended by a Swedish garrison under Charles XII. At the end of three months the besiegers succeeded in seizing the island of Rügen, which commanded the town, and an attempt by Charles to retake it ended disastrously, the king escaping with difficulty, and severely wounded, while the whole of his force was killed or captured. On October 10 the allies captured the hornwork and on the 20th, the place being no longer defensible, Charles left the town and embarked for Sweden on the only ship remaining in the harbour. The garrison immediately afterwards surrendered. *See* Fredrikshald.

Stratton *English Civil War*

May 16, 1643, between the Parliamentary troops under General Chudleigh and the Cornish Royalists under Sir Ralph Hopton. The Royalists attacked the Parliamentarian position on Stratton Hill, and after severe fighting defeated them, capturing 1,700 prisoners, including Chudleigh, 13 guns and all their baggage and munitions of war. *See* Lansdowne, Roundway Down.

Suddasain *Second British-Sikh War*

July 1, 1848, when a force of Bhawalpuris and Pathan mercenaries 18,000 strong, under Lieutenant Edwardes, encountered 12,000 Sikhs under Mulraj outside the city of Multan. The Sikhs attacked but were beaten off, largely owing to the superiority of Edwardes's artillery, and defeated. *See* Multan, Gujerat.

Sudley Springs *American Civil War*

August 29, 1862, between the Federals under General Pope and the Confederates under General Jackson. Jackson by a forced march had succeeded in taking up a strong position in Pope's rear, and defied all attempts to dislodge him, repulsing the Federal attacks with a loss of over 5,000 men. *See* Cedar Mountain.

Suero, The *Civil War of Sertorius*

75 BC, between the rebels under Sertorius and the Roman army under Pompey. The Roman right, under Pompey, was broken and defeated, but Lucius Afranius turned defeat into victory, capturing the Sertorian camp and routing and dispersing the rebel army.

Suez *Franco-British Invasion,*

see Sinai Peninsula, Six-Day War

Sugar-Loaf Rock *Carnatic War*

September 20, 1753, between the British, about 3,000 strong under Major Stringer Lawrence, and the French army which was besieging Trichinopoly, under M. Astruc. Lawrence attacked before daybreak and the Indian auxiliaries with the French army fled leaving the Europeans unsupported. In the end the French were defeated with a loss of 100 killed and 200 prisoners, including Astruc. The British lost 40 killed and wounded. *See* Seringham, Madras II.

Sungari River *Chinese Civil War*

Mao Tse-tung's People's Liberation Army attacked Chiang Kai-shek's Nationalists across the frozen Sungari River, northern Manchuria, near the USSR border, in January, February and March, 1947, but each time the Nationalists drove them back. In May a force of 270,000 crossed the Sungari, drove back the Nationalists some 150 miles, inflicting heavy casualties and seizing the military initiative in Manchuria. *See* Mukden.

Surinam *Napoleonic Wars*

This colony, held by a Dutch garrison, was captured May 5, 1804, by a British squadron under Commander Hood together with 2,000 troops under Sir Charles Green. *See* Ste Croix.

Sursuti I, The *Mohammed Ghori's Invasion*

In 1191, between the Afghans under Mohammed Ghori and the Hindus under the

243

King of Delhi, with 200,000 horse and 300 elephants. The Afghans, who were greatly outnumbered, were surrounded and utterly routed, Mohammed Ghori escaping with difficulty from the field.

Sursuti II, The *Mohammed Ghori's Invasion*

In 1192, when Mohammed Ghori, on the field where he had suffered defeat in the previous year, encountered the forces of the Hindu league under the Rajah of Ajmir. The Afghans, numbering 120,000, with 10,000 mounted archers, completely routed the Rajputs, captured and killed the Rajah. The victory ensured the success of the Muslim onslaught on Hindustan.

Svistov *Russo-Turkish War*

June 26, 1877, when a Russian force under General Dragomirov crossed the Danube in a fleet of small boats and attacked this Turkish fortress. General Skobelev followed with an attack in force next day and the Turkish garrison surrendered after hard fighting. The Russians now made ready to attack Nicopolis. *See* Nicopolis IV.

Sybota *Peloponnesian Wars*

433 BC, between a Corinthian fleet of 150 sail and a Corcyrean fleet of 110 sail, aided by 10 Athenian triremes. The Corcyrean right wing was defeated and would have been destroyed but for the assistance of the Athenians, and the arrival of a reinforcement of 20 Athenian ships caused the Corinthians to retire. The Corcyreans offered battle on the following day but the Corinthians declined. Both sides claimed the victory but the advantage lay with the Corinthians, who captured several ships.

Syracuse I *Peloponnesian Wars*

Siege was laid to this city by the Athenians, under Alcibiades, Lamachus and Nicias, who with a fleet of 134 galleys took possession of the harbour and effected a landing in the autumn of 415 BC. Alcibiades was soon

recalled, and Lamachus killed in a skirmish, while Nicias proved weak and incompetent. The siege works were not pressed and in the following year Gylippus of Sparta succeeded in getting through the Athenian lines and bringing a considerable force to the aid of the Syracusans, capturing at the same time the advanced positions of the besiegers. Early in 413, Demosthenes arrived from Athens with a fleet of 73 triremes and made a desperate attempt to recover the lost ground. He was however totally defeated, and in a series of sea-fights which followed the Athenian fleet was completely destroyed. This disaster forced the Athenians to raise the siege and was in addition a death-blow to the supremacy of Athens, which eventually gave way to Sparta. *See* Amphipolis, Cynossema.

Syracuse II *Second Carthaginian Invasion of Sicily*

Syracuse was again besieged, 387 BC, by about 60,000 Carthaginians under Himilco, aided by a powerful fleet, and defended by Dionysius with about an equal number of troops. A fleet of 30 Lacedaemonian triremes arrived to the succour of the Syracusans, and meanwhile an epidemic had carried off thousands in the besiegers' camp. At this juncture Dionysius decided on a joint sea and land attack upon the Carthaginians, which was completely successful. Leptinus, with 80 galleys, surprised the Carthaginian fleet while the crews were ashore and completely destroyed it, while Dionysius stormed Himilco's defences and utterly routed the besiegers, Himilco and his principal officers escaping from Sicily, and leaving the army to its fate. *See* Crimisus.

Syracuse III *Second Punic War*

In 213 BC Syracuse, then in the hands of the pro-Carthaginian faction, was besieged by the Romans, 25,000 strong under M. Marcellus, and a fleet under Appius Claudius. The city was defended by a garrison under Hippocrates. The siege is specially notable for the presence in the city of Archimedes, whose military engines played an important part in the defence, especially against the fleet. During the winter the revolt of other Sicilian towns drew off a portion of the besiegers, and during the spring and early summer of 212 only a partial blockade could be maintained. Then, however, taking advantage of a festival in the city, Marcellus stormed and captured the upper portion of the town. An attempt to force the Roman lines by a Carthaginian relieving force under Himilco was repulsed, and shortly afterwards the rest of the city was captured by assault. *See* Capua.

Szigeth *Ottoman Wars*

This small town, held by a Hungarian garrison under Count Zrinyi, was besieged by the Turks under Suleiman the Magnificent, on August 5, 1566. The siege was prosecuted with vigour, but was fatal to the great Sultan, who died on September 5. On the following day, however, the Turks stormed and sacked the town, and Count Zrinyi and his little garrison perished in the flames. *See* Vienna I.

T

Tabraca *Revolt of Gildo*

In 398, between 5,000 picked Roman
legionaries under Mascazel and the revolted
Africans, 70,000 strong, under Gildo. At the
first onslaught of the legionaries all the
Roman soldiers serving under Gildo deserted,
and the Africans taking to flight, Mascazel
gained an almost bloodless victory. Gildo was
captured and committed suicide in prison.

Tacna *Peruvian-Chilean War*

May 26, 1880, between the Chileans under
General Baquedano and the Peruvians, the
Chileans gaining a signal victory. The
Peruvian losses were very heavy, including 197
officers. Following up their victory, the
Chileans captured the fortress of Arica. In
1883, a treaty between the two countries ceded
the nitrate province of Tarapaed to Chile. *See*
Tarapacá.

Tacubaya *Mexican Liberal Rising*

April 11, 1859, between the Mexican
Government troops under Marquez and the
Liberals under Degollado. The Liberals were
completely routed with the loss of all their
artillery and munitions of war. *See*
Calpulalpam.

Taginae *Byzantine Empire Wars*

July, 552, between the Goths under Totila,
King of Italy, and 30,000 Imperial troops
under Narses. The Romans withstood the
charge of the Goths, broke their cavalry and
then drove their infantry from the field, with
a loss of about 6,000. Totila was overtaken
and slain in the pursuit, Rome and Italy were
freed from the Goths. *See* Rome V.

Tagliacozzo *Guelfs and Ghibellines*

August 23, 1268, between the Guelf party
under Charles of Anjou, the usurper of the
throne of Naples, and the Ghibellines under
Conradin, the rightful heir and Frederick,
Duke of Austria. The Ghibellines were
utterly routed and their leaders, including

Conradin and the Duke, captured and
beheaded. *See* Messina, Benevento.

Taiken Gate *Hogen Insurrection*

In 1157, between the Japanese rebels under
Sutoku and the Imperial troops under
Tadamichi. The rebels were defeated. This
battle is remarkable for the fratricidal nature
of the conflict, many of the greatest families
of Japan having representatives in both
armies. Taira Kujomori became the *de facto*
ruler of Japan.

Taillebourg *Anglo-French Wars*

July 21, 1242, between the French under
Louis IX and the English under Henry III,
with whom were allied the rebellious vassals
of the French crown, the Comtes de Marche
and de Foix. The allies were defeated and
Henry withdrew his forces from France.

Takashima *Chinese Invasion of Japan*

After the wreck of the Chinese fleet in 1281,
the survivors under Chang Pak took refuge
on the island of Takashima. Here they were
attacked by the troops of Kiushiu, under
Shoni Kagasuke. They were almost without
exception killed or captured, only three out of
the vast host returning to China.

Taku Forts *Second China War*

June 25, 1859, during the campaign by the
Western Powers to compel the Chinese
emperor to grant trade concessions. The
British attempted to carry the forts at the
mouth of the Peiho River. Eleven
light-draught gunboats crossed the bar and
tried to silence the batteries, but without
success, and at 5 pm a force of 600 marines
and bluejackets under Captain Vansittart was
landed, but after severe fighting the troops
were driven back to the boats, with a loss of
68 killed and nearly 300 wounded. Six of the
gunboats were sunk or disabled and their
crews also suffered heavily
On August 21, 1860, a second and successful
assault was made on the forts by a force of
11,000 British and 7,000 French troops under
Sir Hope Grant. After a brief bombardment
the small north fort, garrisoned by 500
Chinese, was stormed by 2,500 British and
400 French, 400 of the garrison falling, while

246

the British lost 21 killed and 184 wounded. In the course of the day the remaining forts surrendered without further fighting. Grant then led his force on an 80-mile march to seize Peking on October 12. *See* Son-Tai.

Talana Hill *Second Boer War*

October 20, 1899, between 4,000 Boers under General Lucas Meyer and a British force of equal strength under General Symons. The Boers occupied a strong position on the heights of Dundee, from which they were dislodged by the British infantry, with a loss of about 300. The British lost 19 officers, 142 men killed and wounded, and 331 prisoners, the latter a detachment of cavalry and mounted infantry who were surrounded by a superior force of Boers, and surrendered. General Symons was mortally wounded. Also called the battle of Dundee. *See* Ladysmith, Sanna's Post, Vaalkranz, Spion Kop.

Talavera *Peninsular War*

July 28, 1809, when having driven Marshal Soult's French army from Portugal, General Sir Arthur Wellesley's 20,000 British troops joined forces with 33,000 Spanish forces under General Cuesta and marched up the river Tagus valley to Talavera, 70 miles south-west of Madrid. Here on July 28 they encountered 50,000 French under Marshals Victor and Sebastiani, with the French king of Spain, Joseph Buonaparte, in nominal command. The British bore the entire weight of this hard-fought set-piece battle, for which the Spaniards were untrained, and withstood all the French attacks at a cost of 6,200 killed or wounded. The French lost 7,390 killed or wounded. Many of the wounded on both sides were burnt to death when the dry grass caught fire. To avoid an immediate conflict with Marshal Soult's advancing army, Wellesley retreated into Portugal again. After this battle he was created Viscount Wellington. *See* Oporto, Busaco.

Talkhan *Tatar Invasion of Khorassan*

This fortress was captured, 1221, by the Tatars under Genghis Khan, after an obstinate defence of seven months in which thousands perished on both sides. *See* Samarkand.

Talneer *Third British-Maratha War*

By the treaty of January 6, 1818, this fortress was surrendered by Holkar to the British, but when Sir Thomas Hislop with a British force arrived to take possession on February 17, the commandant refused to hand it over. He fired upon the British, whereupon Hislop opened fire, and in the afternoon of the same day the place surrendered. By some misunderstanding, however, the Arab garrison of 300 were drawn up at one of the gates, and on the approach of two British officers and some Sepoys, cut them down. No quarter was then given, the garrison being killed to a man and the commandant hanged. *See* Kirkee.

Tamai *British-Sudan Campaigns*

March 13, 1884, when 4,000 British under General Graham attacked and defeated the Mahdists under Osman Digna, destroying their camp. The British fought in two squares, one of which was momentarily broken by the Mahdists who captured the naval guns. The second square however moved up in support, and the Mahdists were repulsed and the guns recovered. The British lost 10 officers and 204 men killed and wounded; the Dervishes over 2,000 killed. *See* Khartoum, Omdurman.

Tanagra *Peloponnesian Wars*

In 457 BC, between the Spartans with their Peloponnesian allies, and about 14,000 Athenians and others, including a body of Thessalian cavalry. The battle was stubbornly contested, both sides losing heavily, but the desertion of the Thessalians during the action turned the scale, and the Spartans were victorious, though at a cost which deterred them temporarily from their intended attack upon Athens. *See* Coronea, Aegina.

Tanjore I *Seven Years' War*

Besieged, August, 1758, by the French under Lally-Tollendal, and defended by a garrison under the Vizier, Monacji. After five days' bombardment the walls were still insufficiently breached, and owing to lack of ammunition Lally determined to retire. Hearing this

247

Monacji made a sortie and nearly succeeded in surprising the French camp. He was with difficulty beaten off, and the French withdrew with the loss of all their siege guns and heavy baggage. *See* Madras II.

Tanjore II *First British-Mysore War*

This fortress, in India, was besieged, August 20, 1773, by a British force under General Joseph Smith, and defended by a garrison of 20,000 men under the Rajah, Lalijaji, and his Vizier, Monacji. On September 16, a breach having been effected, the besiegers delivered an assault at midday when the garrison were taking their usual noonday rest, and meeting with little opposition made themselves masters of the place. *See* Seringapatam I.

Tannenberg *World War I*

August 26–30, 1914, when the German 8th Army of 12 divisions and 800 guns under General von Hindenburg won a great victory over the Russian 2nd Army, 10 infantry and three cavalry divisions, 620 guns, under General Samsonov, near this village about 110 miles north-west of Warsaw, and then in East Prussia. The Russians invaded East Prussia in August, 1914 at the request of the French, and drove the Germans from Gumbinnen and Insterburg, in the north. General von Prittwitz was superseded by General Hindenburg. Meantime, a gap had grown between General Rennenkampf's 1st Russian Army in the north and General Samsonov's in the south. The Germans moved their forces south-west by rail to exploit this by attacking General Samsonov's force, whose exact dispositions they had learned through uncoded radio messages. General von François encircled the Russian left on August 28, von Bülow defeated the open flank at Allenstein and von Mackensen attacked Samsonov's VI Corps. The sole escape for the Russians was through a narrow strip of land between the marshes leading to Ortelsburg and here they were decimated. Some 30,000 were killed or wounded, over 90,000 prisoners taken. General Samsonov killed himself in the retreat. By September 10 the Russians had been chased out of East Prussia. *See* Gumbinnen, Masurian Lakes I.

Tansara Saka *Satsuma Rebellion*

In 1876, when the rebels in a very strong position were attacked by the Japanese Imperial troops under Prince Taruhito, and after very severe fighting, driven out with enormous loss. The Imperialists also suffered severely. *See* Shirogawa.

Taranto I *Franco-Spanish Wars in Italy*

This fortress, held by a Neapolitan garrison under the Conde di Potenza, was besieged by about 5,000 Spaniards under Gonsalvo de Cordova, in August, 1501. Gonsalvo endeavoured to reduce the place by blockade, but found his forces melting away by desertion and was forced to have recourse to more active measures. The north front of Taranto, being bounded by a lake, was unfortified and Gonsalvo, with incredible labour, transported overland some of the smaller vessels of the Spanish fleet lying in the Bay of Taranto and launched them on the lake. The town was then at his mercy and surrendered, being entered by the Spaniards, March 1, 1502. *See* Cerignola, Garigliano.

Taranto II *World War II*

November 11, 1940, when Admiral Sir Andrew Cunningham, C-in-C the British Mediterranean Fleet, ordered 21 aircraft from the carrier *Illustrious* to attack the Italian fleet in the spacious harbour of Taranto, in the heel of Italy. Torpedoes from the aircraft sank two auxiliary vessels, put three Italian battleships and two cruisers out of action, and disabled much of the Italian battle fleet for four months. Two British aircraft were lost. *See* Matapan.

Tarapacá *Peruvian-Chilean War*

November 17, 1879, resulting in the defeat of the Peruvians with heavy loss. *See* Tacna.

Tarawa-Makin *World War II*

In the Gilbert Islands, just north of the equator, Central Pacific, and target of the start of the US offensive against Japan there. Aircraft and the navy blasted the strongly fortified Tarawa string of atolls, and 5,000 Marines of General Julian Smith's 5th Amphibious Corps 2nd Division landed at Betio atoll on November 20, 1943, to be met by a hurricane of fire from 4,800 Japanese marines in ferroconcrete shelters. The atoll fell after four days' desperate fighting at a cost of nearly 1,000 US dead and 2,311 wounded. The Japanese lost some 4,700 men. Makin Island fell to the 27th Infantry Division at the same time. The US *Lipscombe Bay*, a carrier, was torpedoed and sunk with a loss of some 640 men. *See* Rabaul, Kwajalein-Eniwetok.

Tarragona *Peninsular War*

This city was besieged by the French, 40,000 strong under General Suchet, in May, 1811, and defended by a garrison but little inferior in numbers. The outer defences were stormed one by one, and by June 21 the besiegers had effected a lodgement in the lower town. On the 28th, the upper town was taken by storm and the survivors of the garrison, 8,000 in number, laid down their arms. The French lost about 6,000 during the siege. *See* Albuera, Ciudad Rodrigo.

Tashkessen *Russo-Turkish War*

December 28, 1877, between 2,000 Turks under Valentine Baker Pasha and a Russian division under General Kourlov. To cover Shakir Pasha's retirement from the Shandurnik heights, Baker's greatly inferior force withstood throughout the day the determined onslaughts of the Russians. Baker finally withdrew, having effected his object. He lost 800 men, but inflicted a loss on his assailants of 32 officers and over 1,000 men. *See* Plevna, Kars.

Tauris *Civil War of Caesar and Pompey*

47 BC, between the Pompeian fleet under Marcus Octavius and the Caesareans under Publius Vatinius. The Caesarean fleet consisted of merchant vessels temporarily equipped with beaks but Vatinius, though his ships were inferior both in number and quality, boldly attacked the Pompeians and after severe fighting completely defeated them, compelling Octavius to abandon the Adriatic. *See* Pharsalus, Dyrrachium.

Tayeizan *Japanese Revolution*

In 1868, when the adherents of the Shogun made their last stand in Tokyo at the Tayeizan temple in the Park of Uyeno. They were defeated after a sharp conflict, leaving the Imperialists in undisputed possession of the Shogun's capital. *See* Shirogawa.

Tchernaya *Crimean War*

August 16, 1855, between three Russian divisions under General Gortschakov and three French and one Sardinian division under General La Marmora. The Russians attacked the allies' position on the Tchernaya, and after severe fighting were repulsed with a loss of 5,000 killed and wounded. The allies lost 1,200. *See* Kars, Balaclava.

Tearless Battle *Wars of Sparta*

368 BC, when a force of Arcadians endeavoured to cut off a Spartan army under Archidamus in a narrow defile in Lucania. They were repulsed with heavy loss, and not a single Spartan was killed, so that the engagement came to be called the Tearless Battle.

Tegea *Wars of Sparta*

473 BC, when the Spartans defeated the combined forces of the Arcadian League and the Argives under the walls of Tegea. Though victorious, the Spartans were too much weakened to venture upon the attack of Tegea, which had been the object of the expedition.

Tegyra *Boeotian War*

373 BC, when Pelopidas with the Sacred Band of 300 Thebans routed a large force of Spartans in a narrow pass near Orchomenus, slaying 600, including their two generals. *See* Leuctra.

Telamon *Conquest of Cisalpine Gaul*

225 BC, when the Gauls, marching upon Rome, found themselves caught between two Roman consular armies, and though fighting desperately, were cut to pieces.

Tel-el-Kebir *Egyptian Revolt*

September 13, 1882, Egypt being under British–French rule, the British, 17,000 strong under Lord Wolseley, after a night march across the desert attacked and stormed

Colonel Arabi Pasha's entrenchments, defended by 22,000 Egyptians. The British lost 339 killed and wounded, the Egyptian loss was very heavy. Wolseley entered Cairo two days later on September 15, and joint British–French rule over Egypt was ended. *See* Kassassin, Tel-el-Mahuta, Alexandria.

Tel-el-Mahuta *Egyptian Revolt*

August 24, 1882, when the Egyptians attempted to oppose the march of the British advance guard under General Graham to Kassassin. They made only a feeble resistance, and were driven off with heavy loss. *See* Kassassin, Alexandria, Tel-el-Kebir.

Te-li-ssu *Russo-Japanese War*

June 14 and 15, 1904, between 35,000 Russians under Baron de Stakelberg and about 40,000 Japanese under General Oku. The Japanese attacked the Russian position, but the Russians held their ground throughout the 14th, at a cost of about 350 killed and wounded. On the 15th, however, their flank was turned, and after hard fighting in which they suffered heavily, two batteries of artillery being absolutely cut to pieces, they retreated in some disorder, leaving over 1,500 dead on the field. The Japanese, who lost 1,163 in the two days, captured 300 prisoners and 14 guns. The total Russian losses were about 10,000. *See* Liaoyang, Kiu-lien-Cheng.

Tellicherry *First British-Mysore War*

This place, held by a small British garrison and very imperfectly fortified, was besieged June, 1780, by a Mysore force under Sirdar Ali Khan. Aid was sent to the garrison from Bombay and it held out till January 18, 1782, when reinforcements arrived under Major Abington who stormed the Mysori entrenchments, capturing all their guns, 60 in number, and 1,200 prisoners, among whom was Sirdar Ali. *See* Porto Novo.

Temesvar *Hungarian Rising*

August 9, 1849, between the Austrians under Marshal Haynau and the Hungarians under General Dembiński. The latter was totally routed and his army dispersed, this being the last stand made by the Hungarians in the war. On the 13th, General Görgey and his army surrendered to the Russians at Villágos. *See* Schwechat, Kapolna.

Tergoes *Netherlands War of Independence*

This fortress was besieged, August 16, 1572, by the Dutch Patriots, 7,000 strong, under Jerome de 't Zeraerts, and was defended by a small Spanish garrison. On October 20, a force of 3,000 Spanish veterans under Colonel Mondragon succeeded in crossing the 'Drowned Land' with a loss of only nine men drowned, and relieved the town, 't Zeraerts's troops refusing to face this unexpected attack. *See* Haarlem, Alkmaar.

Tertry *Rise of France*

In 687, between the Neustrians under Thierry III and the Austrasians under Pepin d'Héristal, the Maire du Palais. The Neustrians were routed and Thierry captured. Pepin's son Charles Martel succeeded him. *See* Tolbiac.

Tet Offensive, The

see Vietnam War

Tettenhall *Danish Invasions of Britain*

On August 5, 910, between the Danish invaders and the West Saxons under Edward the Elder. The Danes were defeated and Edward extended his kingdom as far north as the Humber. *See* Maldon.

Tetuán *Spanish-Moroccan War*

February 4, 1860, when 30,000 Spaniards under Marshal O'Donnell stormed the Moorish entrenchments outside Tetuán, held by about 40,000 Moors. Three days later Tetuán was entered by the Spaniards.

Teuttlingen *Thirty Years' War*

November, 1643, between the French under the General de Rantzau and the Imperialists under the Count de Mercy. The Imperialists surprised the French camp and totally routed them, Rantzau being captured, with most of his superior officers and all his artillery and baggage. *See* Breitenfeld, Freiburg.

Tewkesbury *Wars of the Roses*

May 4, 1471, when the white-rose Yorkists under Edward IV defeated the Lancastrians under Prince Edward, Somerset and others, with heavy loss. Prince Edward and other leading Lancastrians were killed, and Margaret of Anjou, who had hoped to put him on the throne, promptly surrendered. *See* Bosworth Field.

Texel *Anglo-Dutch Wars*

June 2, 1653, between a British fleet under General Monck and a Dutch fleet under Admiral Van Tromp. The action was undecided but on the following day Monck, having been reinforced by 18 ships under Admiral Blake, renewed the attack and signally defeated Van Tromp, who was killed, with a loss of 11 ships and 1,300 prisoners taken, and six ships sunk. The British lost 20 ships and 363 killed and wounded. Peace was signed early in 1654. *See* North Foreland, Southwold Bay.

Thala *Numidian Revolt*

In the year ?? this fortress, defended by no more than 500 Roman veterans, was attacked by a large force of nomads under Tacfarinas. The Romans sallied out and inflicted so severe a defeat upon Tacfarinas that his army was dispersed.

Thapsus *Civil War of Caesar and Pompey*

April 6, 46 BC, between the Caesareans, consisting of 10 legions, under Julius Caesar, and the Pompeians, 14 legions in addition to cavalry, light troops and 100 elephants, under Metellus Scipio and Juba. Caesar gained a considerable victory and was nominated dictator for ten years. *See* Ruspina.

Thebes *Macedonian Conquest*

This city was captured by the Macedonians under Alexander the Great, in September,

335 BC. The Thebans were blockading the Macedonian garrison, which held the citadel, and the Cadmea; Perdiccas, one of Alexander's captains, without orders broke through the earthworks outside the city. Before the Thebans could shut the gates Perdiccas effected an entrance into the city and being joined by the garrison of the Cadmea, soon overcame the resistance of the Thebans. Six thousand of the inhabitants were massacred and the city was razed to the ground. *See* Granicus.

Thermopylae I *Third Persian Invasion*

480 BC, when 300 Spartans and 700 Thespians, under Leonidas, defended the pass of Thermopylae, leading southwards out of Thessaly, against the Persian host under Xerxes. They kept the Persians at bay until, a considerable force having passed the mountains by another path, they were attacked in the rear. They then retired to a hillock and fought till the last man fell. The Greeks withdrew behind a wall across the Isthmus of Corinth. *See* Marathon, Salamis.

Thermopylae II *Wars of the Hellenistic Monarchies*

191 BC, between 40,000 Romans under Glabrio and the army of Antiochus the Great of Syria. Antiochus was entrenched at Thermopylae where he was attacked by the Romans, and a post held by 2,000 Ætolians being surprised, his flank was turned and he was disastrously defeated. Antiochus escaped from the field with barely 500 men. *See* Cynoscephalae II.

Thetford *Danish Invasion*

In 870, between the Danish invaders and the East Anglians under Edward, who were defeated, Edward being killed. *See* Ashdown, Reading.

Thirty-Eighth Parallel *Korean War*

Chinese 'volunteers', having forced back General MacArthur's 365,000 UN forces to the 38th Parallel after their drive north from Inchon, attacked in strength with North Korean forces, in all 485,000 men, on January 1, 1951. Seoul and Inchon both fell before General Ridgeway held a line 75 miles south of the parallel on January 24, then next day began a counter-offensive, taking Inchon on February 10, Seoul on March 14 and recrossing the 38th Parallel.

President Truman then removed General MacArthur, who demanded the right to bomb Chinese bases in Manchuria, and replaced him by Ridgeway. April 22–23, about 350,000 Chinese and North Koreans launched another offensive in a vital communications area north of Seoul. Ridgeway was forced to give ground, then, after a pause to regroup, the Communists attacked again on May 15–16, forcing the UN forces back slightly, until after five days of heavy fighting they were checked on May 20. The US 8th Army began a counter-offensive, May 21, drove back the enemy by June 15 to 20 miles north of the 38th Parallel. Fighting stopped on July 10, 1951, after the Communists had suffered an estimated 205,000 casualties. After protracted negotiations, hinging largely on the issue of repatriation of prisoners, sick and wounded, carried out in April, 1953, an armistice was signed on July 27. *See* Pusan Perimeter, Inchon, Seoul, Sinuiju.

Thorn *Great Northern War*

Siege was laid to this fortress near Warsaw by the Swedes under Charles XII, September 22, 1702. It was defended by a garrison of 5,000 Poles under General Robel, but after a month he was compelled by famine to surrender. Charles had Stanislas Leszczynski elected to the throne of Poland. *See* Pultusk.

Thurii *Roman Civil Wars*

282 BC, when a Roman consular army under Caius Fabricius routed the Lucanians and Bruttians, who were besieging Thurii. The siege was raised and the Tarentine coalition temporarily broken up.

Tiberias *Crusader-Saracen Wars*

July 4, 1187, between the Saracens under Saladin and the Christians of Jerusalem under Guy de Lusignan. Saladin gained a signal victory, capturing the King, the Grand Master of the Templars and the Marquis de Montferrat. Following up his success, also known as the Horns of Hattin, Saladin recovered in succession Acre, Jaffa and other important towns and in the month of October of the same year recaptured Jerusalem. *See* Jerusalem IV.

Ticinus *Second Punic War*

218 BC, between 26,000 Carthaginians under Hannibal and 25,000 Romans under P. Cornelius Scipio (the Elder). The Romans were defeated with heavy loss, Scipio being severely wounded. *See* Trebbia.

Ticonderoga I *Seven Years' War*

July 8, 1758, between the Marquis of Montcalm, with 3,600 French and Canadians, and the British, 15,000 strong, including 6,000 regulars, under General James Abercromby. Montcalm was strongly dug in on a ridge in front of Fort Ticonderoga, his position being further strengthened by an abattis. Abercromby made no attempt to turn the position but without waiting for his guns, ordered the regulars to take the lines by storm. Notwithstanding the courage of the troops, who advanced six times to the assault, the position proved impregnable and Abercromby was forced to withdraw, with a loss of 1,944 killed and wounded, the French losing 377 only. The 42nd Regiment (Black Watch) showed conspicuous bravery, losing half the rank and file and 25 officers killed and wounded. On July 22, 1759, a British force of 11,000 men under General Amherst, arrived before Ticonderoga, which was held by about 3,500 French and Canadians, under General Bourlemaque. On the 23rd, Bourlemaque withdrew to the Île-aux-Noix, on Lake Champlain, leaving only 400 men under Hébécourt, with instructions to hold Amherst before the place as long as possible. On the 26th however Hébécourt set fire to the magazine and retired. *See* Louisbourg, Madras II.

Ticonderoga II *American Revolutionary War*

Invested, June 22, 1777, by the British under General Burgoyne and defended by 5,000 Americans under General St Clair. After a brief siege the Americans evacuated the Fort, July 5. *See* Stillwater.

Tiflis *Tatar Invasion of the Caucasus*

In 1386, between the Tatars under Timur and the troops of the Caucasian tribes under the Queen of Georgia. The Queen issued from Tiflis to offer battle to the Tatars, but her forces could not stand against them and were cut to pieces. *See* Delhi II, Meerut.

Tigranocerta *Third Mithridatic War*

Fought 69 BC, when the Romans, 10,000 strong under Lucullus, who was besieging the city, were attacked by 110,000 Pontic and Armenian troops under Tigranes. Tigranes had failed to occupy some high ground which commanded the position of his cavalry. This Lucullus seized, and attacking the Pontic cavalry in rear, broke it. He then attacked and routed the infantry, with a loss according to the Roman account of 100,000. The Romans lost five men only. *See* Cyzicus, Nicopolis.

Tigris *Persian Wars*

In 363, when the Romans under Julian crossed the Tigris in the face of a large Persian army strongly entrenched on the opposite bank. At the first assault, though an attempt at a surprise failed, the Romans stormed the Persian lines and after 12 hours' fighting drove them from the field. The Romans only admitted a loss of 75 men, while they claimed that the Persians lost 6,000 killed. Roman claims to territory east of the Tigris were ceded. *See* Perisabor, Amida.

Tinchebrai *Norman Civil War*

September 28, 1106, between the English under Henry I and the Normans under Robert of Normandy, Henry's brother. Robert was totally defeated and made prisoner for life, and Henry annexed Normandy to the crown of England.

Tippermuir *English Civil War*

September 1, 1644, between the Covenanters, 5,700 strong, under Lord Elcho, and about 3,000 Scottish Royalists under the Marquis of Montrose. The Covenanters were totally defeated, with a loss variously estimated at from 1,300 to 2,000 killed, and 800 prisoners, while the Royalist loss was trifling. Following up his victory Montrose occupied Perth. *See* Marston Moor, Aberdeen.

Toba *Japanese Revolution*

In 1868, between the troops of Aizu and Kuwana, under the Shogun, Yoshinobu, and the army of Satsuma and Choshu. The Shogun was totally defeated and abandoned his invasion of Satsuma, returning with his troops to Yedo by sea, surrendering shortly afterwards to the Imperial forces. *See* Tayeizan.

Tobruk I *World War II*

January 21, 1941, when the 6th Australian and the 7th British Armoured Division during the British campaign in Libya against Italian forces, attacked this port, some 70 miles from the Egyptian frontier, then held by 32,000 troops under General Manella, and at once penetrated the perimeter defences. Tobruk fell the evening of the next day, about 25,000 prisoners and great quantities of stores being taken. *See* Bardia.

Tobruk II *World War II*

March 31, 1941, when General Rommel in his first offensive eastwards first seized Benghazi, which the British General Neame had evacuated, then drove on and attacked Tobruk, April 10–14, with one German and four Italian divisions. The 23,000 defenders, of whom 15,000 were Australian, repelled this attack and another on April 30, subsequently holding out for 240 days, being supplied by the Royal Navy. They were relieved after the British 8th Army's victory at Sidi Rezegh on November 29. The denial of Tobruk as a German base led to the failure of Rommel's offensive against Egypt, which stopped at Sollum, about 12 miles across the frontier. *See* Sidi Rezegh.

Tobruk III *World War II*

Defeating the British at the battle of Gazala, General Rommel pressed on to Tobruk, about 40 miles east, and at dawn on June 20, 1942, Stuka dive bombers and artillery heavily pounded its defences. German infantry and tanks of the 15th and 21st Panzers broke through. That evening General Klopper (2nd South African Division) surrendered with 25,000 men and vast quantities of stores. Units of the Coldstream Guards refused to surrender and escaped in their transport. *See*

Gazala, Mersa Matrûh, El Alamein.

Tofrek *British-Sudan Campaigns*

March 22, 1885, when General McNeill, with
three battalions of Indian and one and a half
of British troops, was surprised in his zariba
by about 5,000 Mahdists. One of the Sepoy
regiments broke and fled, but the Berkshires
and Marines held their ground, though the
zariba was forced, as did the other Sepoy
regiments. After twenty minutes' fighting, the
attack was beaten off, the Mahdists leaving
1,500 dead on the field. The British lost 294
combatants, and 176 camp-followers, killed,
wounded and missing. *See* Khartoum, Abu
Klea, Omdurman.

Tolbiac *Rise of France*

In 496, between the Franks under Clovis and
the Alemanni. The Franks, after a desperate
conflict, began to give way but were rallied by
Clovis, who leading a charge in person utterly
routed the Alemanni. This victory gave the
Franks undisputed possession of the territory
west of the Rhine. *See* Vouillé.

Tolentino *Napoleon's Hundred Days*

May 2, 1815, between 50,000 Italians under
Marshal Murat and 60,000 Austrians under
General Bianchi. The Italians were routed
and dispersed, and Murat fled from Italy.
See Paris, Ligny, Waterloo.

Tolenus *Social War*

90 BC, between the Romans under Lupus and
the revolted Marsians. Lupus was attacked
while crossing the Tolenus, and defeated with
a loss of 8,000 men. *See* Asculum II.

Tondeman's Woods *Carnatic War*

February 14, 1754, when a convoy to supply
Trichinopoly, escorted by 180 British and 800
Indian troops, was attacked by 12,000
Mysore and Maratha horse, under Hyder Ali
and Morari Rao, supported by a small French
force. The Sepoys at once laid down their
arms, but the British fought back until the
arrival of the French force when, hopelessly
outnumbered, they also surrendered. The
convoy and the whole detachment were
captured. *See* Sugar-Loaf Rock, Seringham.

Torgau *Seven Years' War*

November 3, 1760, between the Prussians,
44,000, under Frederick the Great, and the
Austrians, 50,000, under Count Daun. The
Austrians, besides being numerically superior,
occupied a strong position at Torgau.
Frederick divided his forces, and while one
portion, under General Ziethen, attacked in
front, he himself led the rest of his army
round the position and fell upon the Austrian
rear. Both attacks were repulsed, but during
the night Ziethen, finding the heights badly
guarded, gained them and seized the batteries,
turning a defeat into a signal victory. The
Austrians lost 4,500 killed or wounded and
7,000 prisoners; the Prussians, 13,000. The
victory gave Frederick possession of the whole
of Saxony. *See* Liegnitz, Pondicherry II.

Toro *War of the Castilian Succession*

March 1, 1476, between the Portuguese and
Spanish supporters of Joanna for the throne
of Castile, 8,500 strong, under Alfonso of
Portugal, and the adherents of Isabella, about
equal in numbers, under Ferdinand the
Catholic. Ferdinand after a long march
attacked the Portuguese at 4 pm and at the
end of two hours' fighting defeated them with
heavy loss.

Toulon I *War of the Spanish Succession*

An attack was made upon the fortress by a
combined Dutch and British fleet under Sir
Clowdesley Shovell, July 17, 1707. The allies
failed to gain a footing in the town, but eight
French ships lying in the harbour and 130
houses were destroyed by fire. *See* Ramillies,
Stolhoffen.

Toulon II *War of the Austrian Succession*

February 21, 1744, between a British fleet of
27 sail of the line, and eight frigates, under
Admiral Matthews, and a combined French
and Spanish fleet of 28 line-of-battle ships.

The British fleet suffered a serious reverse, in consequence of which the Admiral and four captains were tried by court-martial and cashiered. The British lost 274 killed and wounded, the allies about 1,000. *See* Cape Finisterre I.

Toulon III *French Revolutionary Wars*

On August 29, 1793, Toulon, which had opened its gates to the British, and was held by a small garrison under Lord Mulgrave, was besieged by 11,500 French under General Dugommier. By December 18 most of the landward defences had been carried, and the place having become untenable, Lord Mulgrave carried off his troops by sea. This siege is chiefly memorable as being the first important appearance of Napoleon Bonaparte, who commanded the artillery and was largely responsible for the success of the siege. *See* Neerwinden.

Toulouse *Napoleonic Wars*

April 10, 1814, between 42,000 French under Marshal Soult and 49,000 British and Spaniards under General Lord Wellington. The French entrenchments in front of Toulouse were attacked by the British, who after severe fighting captured some of the outworks. The victory, however, was incomplete and was in effect of no value, as Napoleon had on this date already surrendered to the allies in Paris. The French lost about 3,000 killed and wounded, the allies 4,659, of whom 2,000 were Spaniards. *See* Paris, Ligny, Tolentino, Waterloo.

Tou Morong,

see Vietnam War

Tourcoing *French Revolutionary Wars*

In 1794, between the French under Souham and the British under the Duke of York. The British were defeated and driven back upon Tournai. *See* Ushant, Fleurus II.

Tournai I *Netherlands War of Independence*

This town was besieged, October 1, 1581, by the Royal troops under Alexander of Parma, and in the absence of the Governor, Prince Espinay, was gallantly defended by the Princess who held out until November 30, when by an honourable capitulation she was allowed to march out at the head of the garrison with all the honours of war. *See* Maastricht, Zutphen.

Tournai II *War of the Spanish Succession*

Besieged by the British under the Duke of Marlborough, July 8, 1709, and defended by French garrison under M. de Surville. After 56 days in open trenches the garrison surrendered, having suffered a loss of 3,000 men. *See* Lille, Malplaquet.

Tours *Muslim Invasion of France*

October 10, 732, between the Franks under Charles Martel and the Saracens under Abderrahman Ibn Abdillah. The battle lasted several days—according to the Arab chroniclers, two, while the Christian accounts say seven—and ended when the Saracens, discouraged by the death of their leader, Abderrahman Ibn Abdillah. The battle lasted heavily in the pursuit. The victory checked the Islamic conquest of Europe and is one of the decisive battles of history. *See* Constantinople I.

Towton *Wars of the Roses*

March 29, 1461, when the white-rose Edward IV, immediately after his proclamation, marched 16,000 men against the red-rose Lancastrians, 18,000 strong, under Henry VI, and vigorously attacked their entrenched position at Towton. Aided by a heavy snowstorm, blowing in the faces of the defenders, and the Duke of Norfolk's reinforcements, Edward defeated them all along the line with heavy loss, among the killed being Northumberland, Dacre and de Mauley. Henry and Margaret escaped from the field and fled northward. Edward IV was crowned on June 28 at Westminster. *See* St Albans, Ferrybridge.

Trafalgar *Napoleonic Wars*

October 21, 1805, between the British fleet of 27 sail of the line and four frigates, under

Admiral Lord Nelson, with Admiral Collingwood second in command, and the combined French and Spanish fleets, numbering 33 sail of the line and seven frigates, under Admiral Villeneuve. Nelson attacked in two lines, at right angles to the enemy, leading himself, on board the *Victory*, destroyed the enemy's formation and completely defeated them, 20 ships striking their colours. Nelson fell in the moment of victory, while the Spanish Admiral was killed and Villeneuve captured. Most of the prizes were lost in a heavy gale which sprang up after the battle, but the destruction of Villeneuve's fleet put an end to Napoleon's scheme for an invasion of England and established British naval supremacy for over a century. The British lost 1,587 killed and wounded, the losses of the allies being about 14,000. Napoleon at the same time won an important victory at Ulm, Germany. *See* Ulm.

Trautenau *Seven Weeks' War*

June 27, 1866, between the First Prussian Army Corps under General von Bonin and the 10th Austrian Corps under General Gablenz. The Prussians at first drove back the Austrians but General Gablenz, advancing in force, fell upon the Prussians, wearied with a long march, and compelled them to retreat, with a loss of 1,277 killed and wounded. The Austrians, though victorious, suffered a loss of 5,732. *See* Langensalza.

Travancore *Second British-Mysore War*

December 28, 1789, when Tippu Sahib, with about 15,000 Mysoris, made a night attack upon the British lines. Having thrown down a portion of the ramparts, a small advance party were hastening to open the gate, when they were assailed by a detachment of the garrison and hurled back into the trench. This repulse threw the advancing troops into confusion and they were routed with a loss of over 2,000. *See* Seringapatam.

Trebbia I *Second Punic War*

December, 218 BC, between 26,000 Carthaginians, 6,000 being cavalry, under Hannibal, and 40,000 Romans under the Consul Sempronius. Sempronius' colleague, Scipio, had been wounded a few days before

in a skirmish and Sempronius, contrary to his advice, being in sole command, crossed the Trebbia to attack the Carthaginians. The Romans fought with determination and the issue was for some time in doubt, but finally a charge of the Carthaginian horse under Mago against their left flank threw the legionaries into confusion, and they were routed with enormous loss. *See* Syracuse III.

Trebbia II *French Revolutionary Wars*

June 17 to 19, 1799, between 60,000 French under General Jacques Macdonald and 25,000 Russians under General Suvorov. After a severe conflict the French were totally defeated and driven beyond the Apennines, being obliged shortly afterwards to evacuate Italy. *See* Abukir, Montebello, Stockach.

Trebizond *Ottoman Wars*

This city, where the last representative of the family of Comnenus had taken refuge after the fall of Constantinople, was besieged by the Turks under Mohammed II in 1461. After a brief resistance the city surrendered and the last vestige of the Empire of the East was swept away. *See* Belgrade.

Treveri *Gallic War*

55 BC, between the Romans, 50,000 strong, under Julius Caesar, and 200,000 Asipetes, a German tribe, who had made a raid into Gaul. The Germans were routed with enormous loss, the action being less a battle than a massacre, and very few succeeded in recrossing the Rhine. *See* Cremona II.

Tricameron *Invasion of the Vandals*

November, 533, between the Romans under Belisarius and the Vandals under Gelimer and Zano. The Romans were drawn up behind a stream and were attacked by the Vandals, though only the wing under Zano displayed any vigour in the assault. In the end the Vandals were defeated with a loss of 800, the Romans losing 50 only. This defeat put an end to the Vandal domination in Africa. *See* Carthage II.

Trincomalee I *Seven Years' War*

August 10, 1759, between a British squadron

of 12 sail under Admiral Pococke and a French fleet of 14 sail under the Comte d'Ache. After an engagement lasting two hours the French were worsted, but sailing better than the British, as usual at this period, eluded pursuit and lost no ships. *See* Madras II.

Trincomalee II *First British-Mysore War*

September 3, 1767, between the British under Colonel Smith and the Mysore army under Hyder Ali. Hyder attacked the British camp but was beaten off with a loss of 2,000 men while the British lost 170.

Trincomalee III *First British-Mysore War*

On September 26, 1767, a second engagement took place near Trincomalee when Colonel Smith, with 12,000 British and Indian troops, came unexpectedly upon the united armies of Hyderabad and Mysore, 60,000 strong, under Hyder Ali, while rounding a hill which separated them. The superior discipline of the British enabled them to take full advantage of the surprise, and they inflicted an overwhelming defeat upon their opponents' disordered masses. Hyder Ali lost over 4,000 men and 64 guns, the British loss being 150 killed and wounded, but in 1769 he secured a favourable treaty, including mutual restitution of conquests. *See* Porto Novo.

Trincomalee IV *American Revolutionary War*

A naval action was fought off this place April 12, 1782, between 11 British ships under Sir Edward Hughes and 12 French vessels under Admiral Suffren. After a bloody action with no decisive result the two fleets, both too seriously damaged to renew the conflict, separated, the British making for Trincomalee and the French for their base to repair damages.

Trincomalee V *American Revolutionary War*

On September 3, 1782, another indecisive fight took place between the same Admirals off Trincomalee, the British having 12 and the French 15 sail. Both squadrons were compelled after the action to return to their respective bases to refit. *See* Cuddalore, Pondicherry V.

Trinidad *French Revolutionary Wars*

This island was captured from the French without resistance by a naval and military expedition under Admiral John Harvey and Sir Ralph Abercromby, February 17, 1797. *See* Ste Croix.

Trinkitat *British-Sudan Campaigns*

March 29, 1884, when the British, 4,000 strong, under General Graham, totally defeated 6,000 Mahdists, under Osman Digna, after five hours' severe fighting. The British casualties amounted to 189 killed and wounded; the Mahdists lost about 2,000. Also known as the Battle of El Teb. *See* Khartoum, Atbara.

Tripoli *Muslim Conquest of Africa*

In 643, between the invading Muslims, under Abdallah, and 120,000 besieged Imperial troops and African levies, under the Prefect, Gregory. The Muslims gained a signal victory, Gregory being among the slain in this start of the Muslim invasion of North Africa. *See* Alexandria.

Troy

The siege and destruction of this city by the Hellenes, though all the details are legendary, may be accepted as a historical fact, and the date may be put approximately at 1100 BC.

Truk *World War II*

February 17–18, 1944, when the tiny Caroline island of Truk, 1,200 miles north-east of New Guinea, seized by the Japanese after Pearl Harbor and made into an air and naval base, was blasted by US naval forces under Admiral Spruance and Task Force 58, Admiral Mitscher. Two Japanese light cruisers, four destroyers and 24 merchant vessels were sunk at a loss of 25 US aircraft. Again on April 28–29, Task Force 58 pounded Truk, sinking all vessels in the harbour and destroying 93 aircraft. Forty-six US aircraft were shot down. The elimination of Truk opened the way to

257

further operations in the Central Pacific. *See* Tarawa-Makin, Mariana Islands.

Tsinan *Chinese Civil War*

September 14, 1948, when Mao Tse-tung's People's Army attacked the key city of Tsinan, on the Yellow River, in Shantung Province, held by a garrison of 80,000 Chiang Kai-shek Nationalists, who surrendered after ten days, many going over to the Communists. *See* Mukden II.

Tsingtao *World War I*

Japan saw World War I as an opportunity for territorial gains, declared war with the Allies against Germany and on September 18, 1914, landed some 23,000 troops near the model German colony and fortress of Tsingtao, on the Chinese Shantung Peninsula. Britain fearing Japanese aggrandizement, sent a token force of some 1,500 troops and units of her Far East fleet. Held by 4,000 German troops, the fortress was bombarded by land and sea until November 6 when, with 700 casualties, it surrendered.

Tsushima *Mongul Invasion of Japan*

In 1419, between the Chinese and Koreans, and the ships of the Barons of Kiushiu. The Japanese gained a signal victory, and from that time were no more troubled by foreign invasion.

Tsushima Strait *Russo-Japanese War*

May 27–28, 1905, when Czar Nicholas II sent 45 warships of his Baltic fleet, including seven battleships and six cruisers, through the Tsushima Strait between Korea and Japan, to challenge Admiral Togo's supremacy there. Togo, with a fleet equal in size but greater in speed and firepower, met the Russian fleet in the afternoon of May 27, and had soon sunk four battleships and badly damaged another without loss to himself. When the Russians tried to flee towards the harbour of Vladivostok, the Japanese attacked with destroyers and torpedo boats, sinking three ships during the night. The battle continued next day, until all but 12 of the Russian fleet were either captured, driven aground or sunk. Admiral Togo lost three

torpedo boats only. The greatest naval battle since Trafalgar, practically 100 years before, it led to both sides accepting US President Theodore Roosevelt's peace terms. *See* Mukden I, Port Arthur.

Tudela *Peninsular War*

November 23, 1808, between 30,000 French under Marshal Lannes and 45,000 Spaniards under Generals Castaños and Palafox. The Spaniards were totally defeated with a loss of about 9,000 killed and wounded, 3,000 prisoners and 30 guns. The French losses were small. *See* Saragossa, Vimeiro.

Tunis I *First Punic War*

255 BC, between 15,000 Romans under Regulus and 16,000 Carthaginians, of whom 4,000 were cavalry, with 100 elephants, under Xanthippus the Spartan. The Romans were broken by a cavalry charge and their rout was completed by the elephants, and all but 2,500 fell on the field. Regulus was captured and Tunis at once occupied by the Carthaginians. *See* Panormus.

Tunis II *Eighth Crusade*

This city was besieged by the French Crusaders under Louis IX in 1270. While before the walls of the place, which offered an obstinate resistance, Louis died of a fever, and the crusaders at once raised the siege and retired. Thus ended the last crusade. *See* Acre II.

Tunisia *World War II*

Operation *Torch*, the Anglo-American landings at Algiers, Casablanca and Oran on November 8, 1942, aimed to take Tunis and Bizerta and thus to trap Rommel's *Afrika Korps*, then in retreat after its defeat by General Montgomery's 8th Army at El Alamein. Speedy German reinforcements of 15,000 troops and numerous aircraft frustrated the quick accomplishment of this aim. After a winter lull, General Rommel's 10th and 21st Panzers attacked and defeated US 1st Armoured and 168th Regimental Combat Team on February 14, 1943, at Kasserine Pass, killing or wounding nearly

3,000 and taking 2,460 prisoners. The British 6th Armoured (1st Army) counter-attacked and by February 23 had driven Rommel back to his start line. On March 6, three Panzer divisions attacked the 8th Army at Medenine, but were driven off with the loss of 52 tanks. On March 26, the 8th Army broke through Rommel's Mareth Line, took Gabes on April 6 and linked up with the 1st Army on April 7. Mateur fell on May 3, Bizerta and Tunis on May 7. The Axis forces retreated into the natural fortress of the Cape Bon peninsula, chased furiously by the British 6th Armoured Division. On April 12, some 250,400 German and Italian troops surrendered. Allied losses totalled 70,000, of whom 20,000 were Americans. *See* Mareth Line, El Alamein.

Turbigo *Italian Wars of Independence*

June 3, 1859, when the advance guard of Marshal MacMahon's corps, under the Marshal, was attacked by a portion of the Austrian Division of General Clam-Gallas, while simultaneously 4,000 Austrians assailed the bridge over the canal near the Ticino, which the French main body was crossing. After severe fighting both attacks were repulsed with considerable loss. *See* Magenta.

Turin I *Civil Wars of the Roman Empire*

In 312, between the legions of Gaul, 40,000 strong, under Constantine, and the troops of Maxentius, considerably superior in number. The charge of Maxentius's heavy cavalry failed, and he was driven back into Turin with enormous loss. *See* Verona.

Turin II *War of the Spanish Succession*

This city, held by an Imperialist garrison, 10,000 strong, under the Duke of Savoy, was besieged by a French army of 68 battalions and 80 squadrons, with artillery and engineers, under the Duc de la Feuillade, May 26, 1706. On June 17 the Duke of Savoy left the city to organize a relief force, Count Daun taking the command. The garrison held out stoutly till September 7, when the attacks of a large relieving force under Prince Eugène forced the French to raise the siege. About 5,000 of the garrison died either in action or by disease. In the action which preceded the retirement of the French, the Imperialists lost 1,500, the French 2,000 killed and wounded and 6,000 prisoners. The French defeat led to the eventual recapture of all northern Italy. *See* Ramillies.

Turnhout *Netherlands War of Independence*

August 22, 1597, between the Dutch under Prince Maurice of Nassau and the Spaniards under the Archduke Albert. The Spaniards were totally defeated, and this victory may be said to have set the seal of the Independence of the Netherlands. *See* Zutphen, Nieuwpoort.

Tyre *Alexander's Asiatic Campaigns*

This strongly fortified city, built on an island separated from the mainland by a channel 1,000 yards wide, was besieged by the Macedonians under Alexander the Great, 332 BC. Alexander at once began the construction of a mole across the channel but was much hampered by the Phoenician galleys, which issued from the two fortified harbours and destroyed his military engines. He therefore collected in Sidon a fleet of 250 ships from the captured Phoenician cities, and holding the Tyrian galleys in check, completed his mole. It was some time, however, before a breach could be effected, but in August, 332, an assault was delivered, headed by Alexander in person, and the city was stormed and taken. Eight thousand Tyrians fell in the storm, and about 30,000 were sold into slavery. *See* Gaza.

U

Ucles *Spanish Muslim Wars*

In 1109, between the Spaniards under Don Sancho of Castile and the Moors under Ali. The Spaniards were defeated with a heavy loss of the Christian chivalry, among the killed being Don Sancho. *See* Alarcos.

Uji *Taira War*

In 1180, between the Taira clan under Shigehira and the Japanese who had risen against the domination of the Taira at the Court of the Emperor Antoku, under Prince Yukiiye and Yorimasa. The Taira gained a complete victory, Yukiiye being killed, while Yorimasa committed *hara-kiri* in the field.

Ukraine *World War II*

Early in October, General Vatutin (1st Ukrainian Front) pushed his armies across the Dnieper north and south of Kiev, and on November 6, 1943, liberated this capital of the Ukraine and pressed on 100 miles west to retake Zhitomir, only to lose it temporarily to General von Manteuffel's counter-attack. By January 4, 1944, Vatutin's 1st Ukrainian Front had advanced on a wide front to 125 miles west of the Dnieper; General Koniev's 2nd Ukrainian Front, to the south, had advanced about 90 miles west of it; General Malinovski's 3rd Ukrainian Front had crossed the Dnieper, liberated Dnepropetrovsk on October 25 and pushed on towards Krivoi Rog, while General Tolbukin's 4th Front had passed the Perekop Isthmus to the Black Sea estuary of the Dnieper, cutting off the Germans in the Crimea.

Apparently on Hitler's orders, the Germans had held on grimly in a 30-mile salient on the Dnieper some 50 miles south of Kiev, between Korsun and Shevchenkovo, but by February 3 troops of the 1st and 2nd Ukrainian Fronts had linked up at Zvenigorodka and trapped 10 divisions and a brigade. A 14-day battle began, ending on February 17, with the loss to the Germans of 55,000 dead, 18,000 prisoners, 500 tanks, 300 aircraft and much else. Nikopol had fallen to Tolbukin on February 8, while Malinovski's

3rd Front took Krivoi Rog on February 22. Koniev's 2nd Front now pressed on into northern Rumania; north of it Zhukov's 1st Front (Vatutin had been killed) overcame stiff resistance to take Rovko and advance almost as far as Lvov; Malinovski's 3rd Front took Kherson and Odessa at the beginning of April, while Tolbukin's 4th Front liberated the Crimea. By mid-April the battle of the Ukraine was over except for the city of Lvov, which fell on July 27 after the Red Army began its next offensive. *See* White Russia, Stalingrad, Poland, Warsaw.

Ulm *Napoleonic Wars*

In 1805, England, Austria, Sweden and Russia formed the 3rd Coalition to overthrow the French Empire. When Bavaria sided with Napoleon, the Austrians, 72,000-strong under General Baron Mack von Liebereich, prematurely invaded her, while the Russians were still marching through Poland. It brought the Austrians into conflict with the French before the Russians could come into line, Napoleon had 180,000 troops of the Grand Army at Boulogne, ready to invade England. They marched south on August 27 and by September 24 were in position facing General Mack, around Ulm, from Strasbourg to Weissenburg. On October 7, Mack learned that Napoleon planned to march round his right flank so as to cut him off from the Russians who were marching via Vienna. He accordingly changed front, placing his left at Ulm and his right at Rain, but the French went on and crossed the Danube at Neuburg. Trying to extricate himself, Mack attempted to cross the Danube at Günzburg, but clashed with the French 6th corps, lost 2,000 men and returned to Ulm. By October 16 Napoleon had surrounded his entire army at Ulm and three days later Mack surrendered with 30,000 men. Some 20,000 escaped, 10,000 were killed or wounded and the rest made prisoner. About 6,000 French were killed or wounded. Mack was court-martialled and sentenced to 20 years' imprisonment. On October 21 the French were defeated at Trafalgar. *See* Caldiero, Trafalgar.

Ulundi *Zulu-British War*

The last battle of the year, July 4, 1879, between 5,000 British under Lord Chelmsford and about 20,000 Zulus. The

Zulus were routed with a loss of over 1,500, the British losing 15 killed and 78 wounded. The great chief Cetewayo was captured on August 28. *See* Rorke's Drift.

Uppsala I *Danish-Swedish Wars*

In 1520, between the Danes under Otho of Krumpen and the Swedes under Christina Gyllenstierna, widow of the Administrator, Sten Sture. The Danes, in superior force, were strongly entrenched at Uppsala. They were vigorously attacked, but the advantage of position and numbers enabled them to beat off their assailants with heavy loss, though only after severe fighting. *See* Uppsala II.

Uppsala II *Danish-Swedish Wars*

In 1521, when 3,000 Swedes under Gustavus Vasa defeated the troops of the Bishop of Uppsala, who was holding the city in the Danish interest. After his victory Gustavus occupied the city. *See* Uppsala I.

Urosan *Japanese Invasion of Korea*

This town, held by a Japanese garrison under Kiyomasa, was besieged 1595 by the Chinese and Koreans, under Tik Ho. The garrison was so short of food that they had eaten their horses, when the approach of a relieving force, under Toyotomo Hideaki and Mori Hidemoto, forced Tik Ho to withdraw. While retreating, however, he was attacked by the Japanese and totally routed.

Ushant *French Revolutionary Wars*

This action, generally known as the 'Glorious First of June', was fought June 1, 1794, between a British fleet of 25 sail of the line under Lord Howe, and 26 French ships under Admiral Villaret de Joyeuse. After four

hours' fighting the French were defeated, with a loss of six ships captured and one, the *Vengeur*, sunk. The sinking of this ship was elaborated by the French into a fable, to the effect that she refused to surrender and went down with all hands and colours flying. She had, however, undoubtedly struck her colours, and her captain and over 200 of her crew were rescued by the boats of the British fleet. The French admitted a loss of 3,000 men, besides prisoners, while the British lost 922 killed and wounded. *See* Cape St Vincent.

Utica I *Civil War of Caesar and Pompey*

49 BC, between the Pompeians under Varus and the Caesareans under Curio. Varus sallied from his entrenchments to attack the Caesareans but was signally defeated, his troops fleeing in disorder, opening the way for the occupation of Utica by Curio. *See* Pharsalus, Dyrrachium.

Utica II *Muslim Conquest of Africa*

694, between 40,000 Muslims under Hassan and a large force of Greeks and Goths in the Imperial service. The Imperialists were defeated and driven out of Africa, and Hassan followed up his victory by the destruction of Carthage, which thenceforth ceased to exist except as an obscure village. *See* Tripoli, Alexandria.

Utsonomiya *Japanese Revolution*

In 1868, between the forces of the Shogun under Otori Keisuke and the Imperial troops under Saigo Takamori. The Imperialists were completely victorious. *See* Shirogawa, Tayeizan.

V

Vaalkranz *Second Boer War*

General Buller's third attempt to pierce the Boer lines on the Tugela. On February 5, 1900, he seized Vaalkranz, under cover of a feint attack at Brakfontein towards the Boer right. The hill was held by a brigade during the 6th and 7th, but finding further progress impossible, Buller again recrossed the Tugela. The British losses amounted to 374 killed and wounded. *See* Ladysmith, Sanna's Post.

Valenciennes I *Netherlands War of Independence*

Siege was laid to this place in December, 1566, by a force of Spaniards, and German mercenaries, under General Noircarmes. The operations were somewhat idly conducted, insomuch that he and his six lieutenants were derided as the 'Seven Sleepers', but towards the end of February, 1567, he began to press on his siege works, and on March 23 his batteries opened fire, the city surrendering on the following day. *See* Alkmaar, Haarlem.

Valenciennes II *Franco-Spanish Wars*

Defended by a Spanish garrison under Francisco de Manesses, Valenciennes was besieged June, 1656, by the French, under Marshal Vicomte de Turenne and General La Ferté. The French deployed in two divisions on the opposite side of the Scheldt, and when the city was on the point of surrendering, La Ferté's division was attacked by 20,000 Spaniards, under the Great Condé, on July 16, and totally routed with a loss of 400 officers and 4,000 men, before de Turenne could come to his assistance. In consequence of this defeat, de Turenne was forced to abandon the siege and retire.
See Arras I.

Val-es-Dunes *Rise of Normandy*

In 1047, between the Normans, under William of Normandy, with aid from Henri I of France, and the rebel Norman Barons. The rebels were totally defeated, William becoming paramount. *See* Hastings.

Valletta *French Revolutionary Wars*

The capital of Malta, held by a French garrison, 60,000 strong, under General Vaubois, was besieged September, 1798, by a force of British and Maltese, under Sir Alexander Ball. Vaubois held out for two years, but on September 5, 1800, was forced by famine to surrender. The Maltese lost 20,000 men during the siege. *See* Abukir, Nile, Marengo.

Valmy *French Revolutionary Wars*

September 20, 1792, between the French, 36,000-strong, under Dumouriez, and 34,000 Prussians, under the Duke of Brunswick. The battle consisted in the main of an artillery duel, in which the French had the upper hand, and after nightfall the Prussians retired, recrossing the frontier two days later. This retreat secured the Revolutionary government, which led to the European upheaval. *See* Jemappes, Neerwinden.

Valutino *Napoleonic Wars*

August 19, 1812, between Marshal Ney's corps, about 30,000 strong, and a strong rear-guard of General Barclay de Tolly's army, about 40,000 strong, under Barclay de Tolly in person. The Russians were strongly posted in marshy ground, protected by a small stream. The French, attacking resolutely, carried the Russian position in the face of enormous natural difficulties. Each side lost about 7,000 men, but the Russian army retreated in good order. *See* Smolensk, Borodino.

Van Tuong Peninsula,

see Vietnam War

Varaville *Rise of Normandy*

In 1058, between the Normans, under William of Normandy, and the French and Angevins, under Henri I of France. The Normans gained a complete victory, and the French king shortly afterwards made peace. *See* Val-es-Dunes, Hastings.

Varese *Second War of Italian Independence*

May 25, 1859, between 3,000 Garibaldians, under Garibaldi, and 5,000 Austrians, under General Urban. The Austrians were repulsed after hard fighting, and suffered considerable loss. This action is also known as the Battle of Malnate. *See* Solferino.

Varmas *Colombian War of Independence*

1813, between the Colombian Patriots, under Bolívar, and the Spanish Royalists, who were defeated.

Varna I *Anti-Turkish Crusade*

November 10, 1444, between the Turks, under Amurath II, and the Poles and Hungarians, under King Ladislaus and John Hunyadi. The Hungarians and Poles attacked the Turkish camp, but were beaten off with heavy loss, the King being killed. On the following day Amurath stormed the Crusaders' entrenchments, practically the whole of the defenders being put to the sword. *See* Nicopolis.

Varna II *Ottoman Wars*

This fortress, held by a Turkish garrison of 20,000 men, was besieged July, 1828, by the Russians, under Prince Mentschikov, and though a feeble attempt to relieve it was made by Omar Vrione Pasha, the place was taken by storm on October 11. *See* Navarino.

Varus, Defeat of *Germanic Wars*

The site of this famous battle is supposed to be between the rivers Ems and Lippe, not far from the modern Detmold. In AD 9, the Roman army under Quintilius Varus was attacked, while on the march and encumbered by a heavy baggage-train, by the Germans, under Arminius or Hermann. The country was thickly wooded and marshy, and the Romans could make but little defence, with the result that they were almost annihilated. Varus committed suicide on the field to avoid falling into the hands of the victors.

Vasaq *Ottoman Wars*

In 1442, between 80,000 Turks under Shiabeddin Pasha and 15,000 Hungarians under John Hunyadi. The Turks were defeated with a loss of 20,000 killed and wounded; and 5,000 prisoners, including the Pasha. *See* Varna I.

Vauchamps,

see Champaubert

Veii *Rise of Rome*

This city was besieged 405 BC by the Romans, the siege being carried on in a desultory fashion for ten years. At the end of this period the citizens of Capua and Valerii made an attack upon the Roman camp, and defeated the besiegers. M. Furius Camillus was then appointed dictator, and a determined attempt was made to end the siege, with the result that Veii fell 396 BC. Rome's greatest rival in Italy was thus destroyed. *See* Rome I.

Velencze *Hungarian Rising*

September 29, 1848, between the Hungarians under General Móga and the Croats under Jellachich. The battle was indecisive, and was followed by a brief armistice. *See* Waizan.

Velestinos *Greco-Turkish War*

May 5, 1897, between a Turkish division under Hakki Pasha, and the Greeks, 9,000 under Colonel Smolenski. The Greeks occupied a strong position at Velestinos, where they were attacked by the Turks but held their own throughout the day. After nightfall however, his line of retreat being threatened, Colonel Smolenski withdrew to Volo where he embarked his troops on the 7th. An armistice was signed May 18 and Greece paid a £3½m. indemnity.

Velletri *Italian Wars of Independence*

May 19, 1849, between 10,000 Garibaldians under Roselli and the Neapolitans, 12,000 strong under Ferdinand, King of Naples. The advance guard under Garibaldi attacked the town of Velletri, which made a poor

263

defence and was evacuated during the night. *See* Rome VIII, Venice.

Venice *Italian Wars of Independence*

Proclaimed the Republic of St Mark on March 22, 1848, Venice was besieged by Marshal Radetsky's Austrian troops on July 20, 1849, after risings in Rome, Lombardy and Sicily had been crushed. The citizens surrendered on August 28, owing to bombardment, a cholera epidemic and near starvation. *See* Novara, Magenta, Rome VIII.

Vercellae *Cimbric War*

Fought July 30, 101 BC, between 50,000 Romans under Marius and the Cimbri under Boiorix. The Cimbri were almost annihilated.

Verdun *World War I*

February 21, 1916, when General von Falkenhayn launched the 5th Army (1m. men) on a massive offensive against the salient before this city held by the French 2nd Army. Aware that the French for reasons of national pride would fight to the last there, von Falkenhayn planned a war of attrition and launched the offensive with a day-long bombardment heavier than anything before, which obliterated the outer ring of French defences and enabled the Germans to occupy them with little opposition. Owing to the new policy of *attack* many French forts, including Douaumont, had been deliberately left unmanned. This fort fell on February 25. French counter-attacks and accurate artillery fire checked the German advance temporarily, but the village of Vaux fell on March 29 and Fort Vaux on June 6. A desperate German assault on the heights commanding Verdun was repulsed on July 11, after which exhaustion checked them. In six months' fighting they had failed to take the city and lost 280,000 men, to France's 315,000. After a three-month build-up the French, under General Nivelle, launched a counter-offensive on October 24, forced back the Germans and retook forts de Vaux and Douaumont by November 2. Another counter-offensive won back more ground. The longest of the war, the battle ended on December 18 in stalemate,

with 542,000 French and 434,000 German casualties. *See* Somme I.

Verneuil *Hundred Years' War*

August 17, 1424, between 3,000 English, under the Duke of Bedford, and 18,000 French and Scots, under the Constable Buchan and the Earl of Douglas. The men-at-arms on both sides fought dismounted, but the French could make no impression upon the English archers, who were protected by a barricade of stakes, and in the end the French were utterly routed, leaving over 4,000 dead on the field, among them Buchan and Douglas. The Duc d'Alençon was taken prisoner. *See* Orléans.

Verona *Civil Wars of the Roman Empire*

This city was besieged in 312 by Constantine, with the legions of Gaul, and was defended by a body of rebels under Pompeianus. After a sortie had been repulsed, Pompeianus escaped through Constantine's lines and raised a force for the relief of the city. He was, however, met and defeated by Constantine, many thousands of the Italians, including their leader, falling, and Verona at once surrendered. *See* Turin.

Veseris *Latin War*

Fought near Mount Vesuvius, 339 BC, between the Romans under Manlius Torquatus and Decius Mus, and the Latin army. The Roman left was repulsed but Decius Mus, sacrificing himself for the army, sprang into the midst of the enemy and was slain, and his soldiers following him, renewed the conflict. Manlius now brought up his veteran reserve and the Romans, breaking the Latin line, slew or captured nearly three-fourths of their opponents. The Roman loss, however, was so heavy that they were unable to pursue. *See* Caudine Forks, Bovianum.

Vicksburg *American Civil War*

This city, held by a Confederate garrison, was invested June 24, 1862, by a fleet of 13 Federal gunboats under Admiral Farragut, aided by a land force of 4,000 men under

General Williams. After a bombardment which made no impression on the defences, Farragut reimbarked the troops and withdrew, July 24. In the course of the siege Captain Brown with the *Arkansas*, a small river steamer, armour-plated and carrying eight guns, attacked the Federal flotilla, which mounted 200 guns, and ran the gauntlet successfully, losing 14 men killed and wounded. The Federals lost 82.

On January 9, 1863, the city was again invested, by two Federal corps under General McClernand, aided by a flotilla of gunboats under Admiral Porter. It was defended by a garrison of 3,000 Confederates under General Churchill. On the 11th an attack by the combined forces overpowered the garrison of the fort, but the town defences still held out and the siege was not pressed. On May 18, the siege was renewed by three army corps of General Grant's army, the garrison being now commanded by General Pemberton. On the 22nd an unsuccessful assault cost the Federals 3,200, and a regular siege commenced, with the result that on July 4 Pemberton surrendered with 25,000 men and 90 guns. This victory cost Grant 9,362 killed or wounded, but it split the Confederacy in two. *See* Gettysburg, Chattanooga.

Vienna I *Ottoman Wars*

This city, held by a garrison of 16,000 men under Count de Salm, was besieged by Suleiman the Magnificent at the head of 120,000 Turks, in September, 1529. From the 27th of that month till October 14, the garrison withstood a series of assaults, culminating in an attempt to storm the breach, which were repulsed with heavy loss. Suleiman thereupon raised the siege and withdrew, marking the ebb of the Muslim tide in eastern Christendom. *See* Mohacz I.

Vienna II *Ottoman Wars*

September 12, 1683, between 138,000 Turks under Kara Mustapha Pasha and 70,000 Christians under John Sobieski III of Poland. The Turks were besieging Vienna and Sobieski marched to its relief with 30,000, bringing up the available forces to 70,000, of which he was given the command. With this army he attacked the Turkish lines and after a fierce engagement, lasting throughout the day, routed the Turks with enormous loss. Six

Pashas were killed and Mustapha only escaped capture by running away. Vienna was saved. *See* Soczawa, Zurakow.

Vietnam War

The Communist victory over the French at Dien Bien Phu in 1954 led to the setting up by international agreement of the States of North and South Vietnam on either side of the 17th Parallel, North Vietnam becoming a one-party people's (Communist) republic, South Vietnam a democratic republic with a National Assembly and president elected by universal suffrage. The attempt of Communist Vietcong guerrillas to dominate South Vietnam led in 1961 to US military aid and military advisers. Warfare began in 1963 between South Vietnamese and US forces on the one hand and Vietcong supported by North Vietnamese regular troops on the other, aided by China and the USSR. US air bombing began in mid-1964 and became permanent by early 1965. During these operations almost the whole of South Vietnam became a battle-ground; towns and villages were devastated.

In 1966, American bombing of enemy targets was greatly intensified, Hanoi, the capital, and Haiphong being bombed for the first time on June 29. In a raid on April 12 on Mugia Pass the main supply route from North Vietnam to Laos and thence to South Vietnam, nearly 1,400,000 tons of bombs were dropped. The first air battle over North Vietnam took place on April 23, when two Mig-21s and 14 Mig-17s were engaged by 14 US Phantoms. In what was then reported to have been the largest single air raid of the war, the Yen Bay arsenal, 75 miles north-west of Hanoi, was attacked on May 31, 1966, and set afire. Twenty-five out of 30 batteries were said to have been knocked out, while two Thunderbolts were lost. North Vietnam claimed on August 20, 1966, that 132 US aircraft had been shot down since July 17. It also protested about the bombing of civilian targets.

By November 1967, according to US official figures, enemy involvement in the fighting had grown to between 223,000 and 228,000, consisting of 118,000 North Vietnamese regulars, 70,000 to 90,000 guerrillas and 35,000–40,000 support troops. Mr McNamara, US Defense Secretary, claimed that during 1967 enemy losses totalled 88,000 killed in action, 30,000 dead or disabled from wounds, 6,000 taken prisoner, while 18,000 defected to South Vietnam and another 25,000 were either missing or disabled by disease. American losses by early 1971 were 44,459 dead and about 290,000 wounded. Main battles were Nam Dong (1964); Van Tuong Peninsula, Plei Me, Chu Pong-Ia Drang River, (1965); An Lao Valley, A Shau, Tou Morong, (1966); Hill 881, Locninh, Dak To, Hill 875, (1967); this last battle being up till then one of the heaviest of the war, lasting 23 days and costing 281 American and 1,400 enemy lives. During the 1967 bombing, large areas of the port of Haiphong were reduced to ruins. By January 1968 South Vietnamese forces totalled 732,000; American, 485,000; South Korean, 48,000; Australian, 8,000; New Zealand, 450; Thai, 2,500; Philippine, 2,100. About 60 per cent of US forces were combat troops, remainder auxiliary.

Main battles of 1968 were the siege of Khe Sanh, January 21–April 7; the Tet Offensive, January 30–February 24; Hué, January 31–February 24; Saigon, January 3–February 23. Allied casualties during these battles from January 30–February 26 were: South Vietnamese 10,997 killed or wounded; American and others, 9,300 killed or wounded. Vietcong and North Vietnamese, 38,794 killed, 6,991 captured. During the first half of 1968 and especially from May 28 until June 11, 1968, enemy rockets fell on Saigon regularly, with 40 on June 4 and 16 on June 7, killing or wounding more than 1,000 civilians. Fighting went on in the Central Highlands, the Northern Provinces and the northern front during June–August. The Vietcong took the offensive on August 18 with attacks near the Laotian and Cambodian borders to keep their supply routes clear. From October 15 there came a lull in the fighting and on October 31 President Johnson announced the end of bombing of North Vietnam territory. President Nixon's policy of gradual de-escalation and disinvolvement was initiated with his announcement of the withdrawal of 25,000 American troops by June 8, 1969 and another 35,000 by December 15, 1969. On December 15 he announced the withdrawal of 50,000 more troops by April 15, 1970 and thereafter additional phased withdrawals. But on May 1, 1970, a task force of South Vietnamese troops and 5,000 US infantry supported by massive bombing strikes, tanks and artillery thrust 30 miles into southern

Cambodia in an operation to surround and destroy Vietcong bases, including an important suspected command headquarters. A gamble to bring the war to a speedy end in direct contrast to President Nixon's de-escalation policy, it was followed in February 1971 by a similar move by American-supported Vietnamese troops against Communist supply lines in Laos.

On February 25, North Vietnamese forces counter-attacked at Hill 61 (6 miles inside Laos) with 25 PT-76 tanks backed by infantry and after three days' heavy fighting forced the South Vietnamese troops there back across the border. The North Vietnamese on March 19 attacked the town of Khé San, just over the border in Vietnam, and under cover of an artillery barrage destroyed petrol and ammunition dumps, and several helicopters. The Americans and South Vietnamese withdrew from the town on April 6 with the loss of three to four thousand men plus a number of guns and aircraft.

During the remainder of 1971 fighting was mainly by guerrilla action, both sides having diverted troops to Cambodia and Laos. By the end of the year US troops no longer took an active part in the fighting, except for bombing.

Fighting in 1972 was marked by the much greater use by North Vietnam forces of Soviet tanks, missiles and armoured troop carriers. On March 30 after a heavy bombardment with 122mm rockets and 130mm guns, 15,000 North Vietnamese backed by tanks over-ran all the South Vietnamese strong-points south of the demilitarized zone. Heavy tank battles followed around the town of Dong Ha, 12 miles south of the zone in early April, but the South Vietnamese held it; while the town of Quang Tri, about 30 miles south of the zone fell to the North Vietnamese tanks and infantry on May 1. The garrison retreated in disorder towards the town of Hué.

In the south, An Loc, a provincial capital 60 miles north of Saigon, and the nearby town of Loc Ninh, were heavily attacked by North Vietnamese forces with tanks on April 1, the South Vietnamese withdrawing from Loc Ninh after a sharp battle on April 8. Also on April 8 An Loc was encircled and besieged, the South Vietnamese losing half the town after five days' hard fighting; but on April 14 about 1,000 of their paratroops dropped on to the outskirts and forced the enemy out. Counter-attacking, the North Vietnamese again entered the town. The battle for it went on for the next two or three weeks, often with hand-to-hand fighting, until on May 3 a South Vietnamese relief force from the Mekong delta fought its way through and drove the North Vietnamese four miles out of An Loc, enabling a supply and ammunition convoy to enter. Thus, for the time being, aided as ever by US bombing, the South Vietnamese held this important provincial capital. In another important battle, the North Vietnamese besieged the town of Kontum in the Central Highlands, on April 24.

From May to September 1972 the South Vietnamese forces, generally aided by US bombing, won major successes in five hard battles. At Kontum, they defeated the enemy by June 6, after a five-week battle during which the town was destroyed. Continuous fighting around An Loc also led to the defeat of the enemy and virtually stopped the pressure here too by June 12.

In Binh Din province three smaller towns were re-taken during the last week of July. Finally, Quang Tri, lost in May, was re-captured on September 15 by South Vietnamese Marines, paratroops and helicopter-landed infantry, after heavy bombing by 100 B-52s and shelling by 17 US cruisers and destroyers.

These defeats led to enemy pressure in other areas. The North Vietnamese pressed home attacks in the North on Da Nang and Hué; around Plei Ku in the Central Highlands, in the Mekong delta and towards Saigon in the south. North Vietnamese ports were blockaded by the US Navy at this time, but supplies came in nevertheless by land, sea and air, oil arriving in a newly-completed pipeline from China.

American bombing of North Vietnam, suspended on October 22, began again on December 18. On the 12 days following, Hanoi and Haiphong were bombed more heavily than at any other stage of the war. After a wave of international protests, President Nixon stopped the bombing on January 15, 1973. While the Paris peace talks continued meantime, North Vietnamese and the so-called National Liberation Front forces launched early in January, with the object of strengthening their hand in the talks, no less than 142 strong attacks, mainly

in the Northern and Central Provinces. This was the most since the Tet offensive in 1968. As the chance of a negotiated cease-fire loomed, both North and South battled to consolidate their positions before it took effect, especially between Saigon and the Cambodian frontier; and near the provincial capital of Tay Ninh, part of which the North Vietnamese seized on January 26. When the cease-fire did come into effect on January 28, 1973, the North Vietnamese and National Liberation Front forces were controlling large areas of the country, but the South Vietnamese forces were showing themselves, with American air support, capable of standing up to and holding the North Vietnamese. Under the cease-fire agreement all remaining US forces were to be withdrawn within 60 days.

Fighting began again in the early months of 1973, declined after the second negotiated cease-fire of June 15, 1973, then broke out again in late September. In the Saigon sector the North Vietnamese launched heavy attacks with tanks, forcing back the South Vietnamese, whose air force bombed areas held by the Provisional Revolutionary Government. In January 1974 it was estimated that since the peace treaty some 58,000 troops had been killed.

Both sides having re-equipped, the strategically placed town of Ben Cat, 25 miles north of Saigon, was taken by the North Vietnamese after a battle lasting six weeks, while heavy fighting went on near Kontum, March 16–18, and in the Northern Provinces. On August 6, 1974, the US Congress cut heavily the military aid requested by President Nixon. A blow to South Vietnamese morale and military capability, it led President Thieu to complain that shortages of ammunition, weapons and supplies had tied the hands of his troops while the North Vietnamese and the Vietcong guerrillas were intensifying their attacks in all sectors. The next several months were marked by the gradual erosion of the South Vietnamese positions as their morale declined week by week.

By April 26, after the three-week battle of Xuan Loc, 37 miles east of Saigon, the South Vietnamese were defeated in their effort to stem the enemy's encirclement of the capital and the total occupation of the Central Provinces, and organized South Vietnamese resistance collapsed. The North

Vietnamese occupied Saigon on May 1, 1975, the war ended and the Vietnam Socialist Republic was established.

But peace in Indo-China was shortlived, as the ages-old hostility between Vietnam and Cambodia reasserted itself. Armed conflict started in 1975, worsened in 1977 and grew serious in 1978, though conflicting reports obscured details of the war. But on December 25, 1978, some 12 Vietnamese divisions with tanks and aircraft invaded Cambodia along a 200-mile front. At the same time Vietnam set up the Cambodian Front for National Liberation which, it claimed, was leading the fighting against the Government of Pol Pot and the Cambodian Communist Party. Rapid progress towards the Cambodian capital, Phnom Penh, was made by Vietnamese forces, who occupied it on January 7, 1979, without much opposition, 12 days after they crossed the frontier. Pol Pot escaped via Thailand to China, which backed Cambodia, while Soviet Russia backed Vietnam. A Cambodian Front government was set up, supported by a large Vietnamese army of occupation. Meanwhile China began a build-up of its forces along its southern frontier with Vietnam. *See* Sino-Vietnamese War.

Vigo Bay *War of the Spanish Succession*

October 12, 1702, when the combined fleet of 30 British and 20 Dutch ships, under Sir George Rooke, forced the boom at the entrance to Vigo Harbour and destroyed the French and Spanish fleet anchored there. Of the men-of-war, 11 were burnt and ten captured, while 11 Spanish galleons, with treasure, were taken. This action was called the affair of the Spanish Galleons. *See* Gibraltar.

Villach *Ottoman Wars*

In 1492, between the Turks under Ali Pasha and a Christian army under Rudolph de Khevenhuller. During the battle 15,000 Christian prisoners in the Turkish camp broke out and fell upon the rear of the Turks, who were in consequence defeated. The Christians lost 7,000 killed, the Turks 10,000 killed, including Ali. *See* Varna I.

Villa Viciosa *War of the Spanish Succession*

December 10, 1710, when 13,000 Imperialists under Prince Starhemberg, retreating into Catalonia after the defeat of James, Earl of Stanhope at Brihuega, were attacked by 20,000 French under Philip of Anjou and Marshal Vendôme. Starhemberg's left wing was cut to pieces, but his right and centre more than held their own, driving back the French with considerable loss and capturing some guns. Starhemberg was, however, too weak to take advantage of this partial success and continued his retreat. *See* Denain.

Villeta *Paraguayan War*

December 11, 1868, between the Paraguayans under López, and the armies of Brazil, Uruguay and Argentina. Overwhelmed by vastly superior numbers, López was forced to withdraw his forces to the entrenched camp at Angostura. *See* Aquidaban, Parana.

Villiers *Franco-Prussian War*

A determined sortie from Paris under General Ducrot, on November 30, 1870, directed against the Württembergers. The operations lasted till December 3. The French, who had at first gained some successes, were finally repulsed with a loss of 424 officers and 9,053 men. The Germans lost 156 officers and 3,373 men. *See* Metz, Sedan.

Vimeiro *Peninsular War*

August 21, 1808, between 17,000 British and Portuguese under Sir Arthur Wellesley, and 13,000 French under Marshal Junot. The French were signally defeated, losing 2,000 men and 13 guns, but the victory was not followed up by Sir Harry Burrard who with Sir Hew Dalrymple was in supreme command, and the French were allowed to evacuate Portugal unmolested, in English ships, under the Convention of Cintra. The British lost 720 killed and wounded. *See* Corunna.

Vimy Ridge *World War I,*

see Arras, Artois

Vinaroz *Spanish Civil War*

On March 9, 1938, as part of a general offensive through Aragon into Catalonia, General Franco's Nationalists under General Davila launched an attack backed by bombardment and aerial bombing from Teruel. During the next eight days the Republicans fell back about 60 miles, eventually on April 3 yielding Lerida. Vinaroz, a fishing village half way between Barcelona and Valencia fell to Franco on April 15. He had succeeded in his objective of splitting Republican forces in two. *See* Barcelona, Ebro River.

Vinegar Hill *Irish Rebellion*

June 21, 1798, when the British regulars under General Lake attacked the camp of the Irish rebels, 16,000 strong, under Father Murphy. Little resistance was made and the rebels were driven out of their camp with a loss of 4,000 killed and wounded, and 13 guns.
See Camperdown.

Vionville,

see Mars-la-Tour

Vitoria *Peninsular War*

June 21, 1813, between 75,000 British, Portuguese and Spanish troops, with 90 guns, under Wellington, and 58,000 French with 153 guns under King Joseph Buonaparte and Marshal Jourdan. In July 1812, after the battle of Salamanca, the French had evacuated Madrid, which Wellington's army entered on August 12, 1812. Deploying three divisions to guard the capital's southern approaches, he then marched north with the rest of his army to lay siege to the fortress of Burgos, 140 miles away, but he had underrated the enemy's strength and on October 21 he had to abandon the siege and retreat. By October 31 he had abandoned Madrid too, and retreated first to Salamanca then finally to Ciudad Rodrigo, near the Portuguese frontier, to avoid encirclement by French armies from the north-east and south-east.

Spending the winter reorganizing and strengthening his forces, Wellington marched his troops from northern Portugal across the mountains of northern Spain and the Elsa river, by May 30, 1813, to outflank Marshal Jourdan's army of 58,000 strung out between the Douro and the Tagus. The French retreated to Burgos, with Wellington's forces marching hard to cut them off from the road to France. Finally, Wellington launched his attack at Vitoria on June 21, in three columns. After hard fighting General Picton's 3rd Division broke the enemy's centre and soon the French defence crumbled. Their retreat became a rout, with losses of 8,000 killed or wounded and 2,000 prisoners, compared to Wellington's 4,500 killed or wounded. 152 guns and much booty were also taken in this battle that ended Napoleon's rule in Spain. By December, after detachments had seized San Sebastian and Pamplona Wellington's army was encamped in France. *See* Toulouse.

Vittorio Veneto *World War I*

On October 24, 1918, Italian General Armando Diaz attacked, with 57 divisions and 7,700 guns, the 52 Austrian divisions with 6,000 guns of Archduke Joseph and General von Bojna, which were holding the plains north-east of the Piave River. Together with the British 10th Army (General Lord Cavan) and the French 12th Army (General Graziani), General Caviglia's Italian 8th Army forced three crossings of the Piave River under heavy fire. Vittorio Veneto fell to the Italians on October 30, the British 10th and the Italian 3rd armies crossed the Livenza River at Sacile on November 1. Now hopelessly disorganized, the Austrians fled and by November 3 the ten-day campaign was over. Italian casualties were about 36,000. The Italians claimed 300,000 prisoners and 5,000 guns. The victory led to the collapse of the Austro-Hungarian Empire. *See* Piave River, Caporetto.

Vögelinseck *Appenzel Rebellion*

May 15, 1402, between 5,000 troops of the Swiss Imperial towns and 900 rebels of Appenzel and Schwyz. The rebels were driven from the field. *See* Naefels.

Volturno *Italian Wars of Independence*

October 1, 1860, between 20,000 Italians under

Garibaldi and 40,000 Neapolitans under Afan de Riva. Garibaldi's position in front of Capua was attacked by the Neapolitans who, after hard fighting, were repulsed. The Garibaldian casualties were 2,023 killed and wounded. The Neapolitans lost 2,070 prisoners, but their losses in killed and wounded are unknown. In consequence of this victory Garibaldi almost immediately captured Capua. See Velletri, Rome VIII, Venice.

Vouillé *Rise of France*

In 507, between the Franks under Clovis and the Visigoths under Alaric II. Alaric was trying to effect a junction with Theodoric, King of the Ostrogoths, when he was attacked by Clovis and totally defeated. Alaric fell in the battle. See Tolbiac.

Vyborg *Russo-Finnish War*

After General Mannerheim's Finnish White Army and General von der Goltz's German troops drove Finnish and Russian Bolsheviks from Helsinki on April 13, 1918, they again defeated them at Vyborg (now in USSR) on April 24, and drove them from the country. Finland was proclaimed a republic about a year later. See Mannerheim Line.

W

Wagram *Napoleonic Wars*

July 6, 1809, between 154,000 French under Napoleon with 554 guns, and 158,000 Austrians under the Archduke Charles with 480 guns. Napoleon crossed the lesser arm of the Danube from the Island of Lobau, on the night of the 4th and 5th July, and driving the Austrian advanced posts before him, prepared to attack their main position. An attack upon them on the evening of the 5th was repulsed. On the 6th the Austrians attacked the French right, under Marshal Davout, but were unsuccessful; later, however, the French centre and left were compelled to give ground, but Napoleon, bringing up the artillery of the Guard and General Jacques Macdonald's corps of 8,000 men, checked the Austrian advance, while Davout carried the heights on the Austrian left, outflanking them, and rendering their position untenable. By three o'clock they were in full retreat, having lost about 30,000 killed and wounded, 9,000 prisoners including 12 generals, and 20 guns. The French lost 32,000 killed and wounded. Britain, Spain and Russia only now opposed Napoleon. *See* Aspern.

Waizan *Hungarian Rising*

April 10, 1849, between the 3rd Hungarian corps under Damjanics, about 7,000 strong, and two Austrian brigades under Götz and Jablonowski. Damjanics attacked the Austrians and drove them out of Waizan with heavy loss, among those who fell being General Götz. *See* Veleneze.

Wakamatsu *Japanese Revolution*

The last stand of the Shogun's followers was made at the Castle of Wakamatsu, which was stormed by the Imperialists, September 22, 1868. The resistance to the new régime was thus completely broken. *See* Utsonomiya.

Wakefield *Wars of the Roses*

December 30, 1460, between the red-rose Lancastrians under Somerset and the white-rose Yorkists under Richard, Duke of York. The Lancastrians advanced from Pontefract and offered battle to Richard, who, though weakened by the absence of foraging parties, accepted the challenge. Somerset prepared an ambush into which the Duke fell as he marched out of Wakefield, and the Yorkists were defeated with heavy loss. The Duke and many other nobles were killed and Salisbury captured and beheaded. *See* Mortimer's Cross.

Waltersdorf *Napoleonic Wars*

February 5, 1807, between the French under Marshal Ney and the Prussian corps of General von Lestocq. The Prussians were defeated with a loss of about 3,000 killed, wounded and missing. *See* Eylau.

Wandiwash I *Seven Years' War*

January 22, 1760, between the British, with 1,900 European and 3,350 Indian troops under Colonel Coote, and the French, 2,250 Europeans and 1,300 Indians under Comte de Lally-Tollendal. The French army was accompanied by 3,000 Maratha horse who took no part in the action. After severe fighting Lally was defeated with a loss of 600 Europeans besides Indians, the British losing 190 only. *See* Madras, Pondicherry.

Wandiwash II *First British-Mysore War*

This fort, defended by a small Indian garrison under Lieutenant Flint, who had only one other European with him, was besieged, December, 1780, by the Mysoris under Hyder Ali. Flint held out till January 22, 1781, when the approach of Sir Eyre Coote forced Hyder Ali to raise the siege. The garrison had then only one day's ammunition left. *See* Porto Novo.

Warburg *Seven Years' War*

July 31, 1760, between the French, 35,000 strong under the Chevalier du Muy, and a largely superior force of Prussians and British under Prince Ferdinand. The French were in danger of having their flanks turned, and after a brief engagement retired, having lost 1,500 killed and wounded and 1,500 prisoners. *See* Minden.

Wargaom First British-Maratha War

January 12, 1779, when a British force, 2,600 strong, under Colonel Cockburn, retreating from Poona, was attacked by the Maratha army under Mahadaji Sindhia and Hari Pant. The British succeeded in beating off the attack and making good their position in the village of Wargaom, but at a loss of 352, including 15 officers, and ultimately a convention was signed by Sindhia under which the British retired unmolested. *See* Aligarh.

Warsaw I Second Polish Rising

This city, which was held by a garrison of 30,000 Poles under General Dembiński, was attacked by the Russians, 60,000 strong under General Paskevich, on the 6th September, 1831, and the Poles were driven from their first line. On the 7th a further assault was made, notable for the defence of the Wola redoubt where, when it was finally captured by the Russians, only eleven Polish defenders remained alive out of a garrison of 3,500. On the 8th the last defences were overcome and the city capitulated. The Poles lost 9,000 killed in the defence. The Russians admitted a loss of 63 officers and 3,000 men killed, and 445 officers and 7,000 men wounded. Russian rule over Poland continued, with Paskevich governor.

Warsaw II World War I

In October 1914, to support her Austro-Hungarian allies who were hard-pressed by the Russians, the Germans unified their 9th Army and the Austrian 1st Army under von Hindenburg and advanced on Warsaw, then ruled by Russia. Faced by no less than eight Russian armies, they were heavily outnumbered. The battle for Warsaw, defended by Siberian and Caucasian troops, was fought all along the Vistula. The Germans were defeated and thrust back to Radom on October 25 and to Kielce on November 3. Behind a screen of rearguard actions they then withdrew. After the German breakthrough in the Gorlice-Tarnow sector in May, 1915, Warsaw was taken on August 4, 1915 by von Mackensen. *See* Galicia, Gumbinnen, Gorlice.

Warsaw III Russo-Polish War

Marshal Josef Pilsudski and Polish patriots proclaimed an independent Polish Republic on November 9, 1918, while civil war raged in Russia. Polish troops then fought with Ukrainians against the Bolsheviks, helping to occupy Kiev on May 7, 1920, but were driven back nearly to the suburbs of Warsaw by July 31. On August 15, Pilsudski's 4th Army, advised by the French General Weygand, counter-attacked at Brest-Litovsk, broke through the Russian lines and advanced 200 miles, taking more than 60,000 prisoners. At the Riga armistice on October 12, the Polish-Russian boundaries that stayed until the Soviet invasion of Poland in September 1939 were agreed.

Warsaw IV World War II

Poland was attacked by Germany on August 31, 1939, and by the Russians on September 17. Heavily bombarded and shelled, Warsaw surrendered on September 27. *See* Poland.

Warsaw V World War II

During the Russian summer offensive in 1944 across the Western Ukraine, General Rokossovski advanced an armoured force ahead of the main front, reaching the eastern Warsaw suburb of Praga on July 31. Poland's 40,000-strong Underground Army, led by General Bor-Komarovski, which owed allegiance to the London government in exile, responded to Moscow Radio's call to rise and at 5 p.m. on August 1 in the belief that Soviet forces would soon enter the city, attacked the Germans with small arms and home-made grenades. A desperate gamble— they had food, and weapons for seven days only—the rising depended on Russian relief or parachuted supplies from the Allies. SS Police General von dem Bach-Zelewski was sent to quell the rising, and was reinforced by units of the Hermann Goering division, two SS divisions, the Kaminiski Brigade of Russian turncoat prisoners, and the Dirlewanger SS Brigade of German convicts. After an initial success, the Polish forces were split up and slowly annihilated piecemeal by German tanks, and ceaseless *Luftwaffe* bombing, in fighting that spread soon to the city's sewers. Stalin refused Churchill's and Roosevelt's pleas to fly in aid, calling the Warsaw leaders 'criminals', and denying landing rights to Allied aircraft after their supply-dropping flights to the city. Eventually, without food or ammunition, the Poles were forced to surrender on October 2. Hitler then ordered the destruction of Warsaw.

Some 15,000 Polish fighters were killed and about 200,000 civilians—old people, women and children. The Germans lost 10,000 killed, 9,000 wounded and 7,000 missing. Warsaw was finally liberated by the Soviet forces on January 17, 1945, a ruin. *See* White Russia.

Wartemberg *Napoleonic Wars*

October 3, 1813, when Marshal Blücher with 60,000 Prussians defeated 16,000 French under Bertrand, posted in a very strong position, protected by a dyke and a swamp. Aided by the ground, the French withstood the Prussian attack for over four hours, but finally Blücher turned their right flank and drove them from their position. The Prussians lost about 5,000; the French admitted a loss of 500 only. *See* Dennewitz.

Waterloo *Napoleon's Hundred Days*

June 18, 1815, between 24,000 British and 43,500 Dutch, Belgians and Nassauers, in all 67,655 men with 156 guns, under the Duke of Wellington; and the French, 71,947 strong with 246 guns, under Napoleon. Wellington posted his troops along the line of heights covering the road to Brussels, sheltered from French gunfire behind the slopes, with advanced posts at the farms of Hougoumont and La Haye Sainte. Napoleon's Marshal Ney attacked this position at 2 pm with the utmost resolution, but the British squares held their ground against the French cavalry and artillery.

In a second attack, led by Ney himself, the French captured La Haye Sainte at 6 pm and obtained a footing in Hougoumont, but the arrival of Field-Marshal Blücher with the Prussian army, on the French right, enabled Wellington at last to assume the offensive and drive the enemy headlong from the field. The British lost about 15,000, the Prussians 7,000 in the battle. The losses of the Dutch and Belgians were very small, as they left the field early in the day. The French lost 25,000 killed, wounded and prisoners, and the army

practically ceased to exist as an organized force. *See* Ligny, Wavre.

Watigaon *First Burma War*

November 15, 1825, when Brigadier-General McDonell with four Indian regiments advanced in three columns against a large force of Burmans under Maha Nemyo. The columns failed to keep touch and were repulsed in detail, with a loss of 200 men including the Brigadier. *See* Kemendine.

Wattignies *French Revolutionary Wars*

October 15–16, 1793, when the French under General Jourdan attacked the Austrians under the Duke of Coburg and drove him from his position, forcing him to raise the siege of Maubeuge. *See* Hondschoote.

Wavre *Napoleon's Hundred Days*

June 18, 1815, between the 30,000 French under Marshal Grouchy and the Prussians, 27,000 strong under General Baron von Thielmann, who had been entrusted by Marshal Blücher with the task of containing Grouchy while the main Prussian army marched on Waterloo. Grouchy, who was anxiously expected at Waterloo, mistook his instructions and wasted the day in attacking Thielmann, whom he defeated, but uselessly. *See* Ligny, Waterloo.

Wednesfield *Danish Invasions of Britain*

Fought in 911, between the Danes and the West Saxons, under Edward the Elder. The Danes were defeated. *See* Reading, Ashdown.

Wei-hai-Wei *Sino-Japanese War*

February 4, 1895, the boom protecting Wei-hai-Wei harbour was cut and the Chinese fleet attacked by ten Japanese torpedo-boats, which succeeded in sinking one battleship, at the cost of two torpedo-boats. On the following night the attack was renewed by four boats, and three Chinese ships were sunk. On the 9th another battleship was sunk by the Japanese land batteries, whereupon Admiral Ting, the Chinese commander, surrendered, and he and his principal officers committed suicide. The Japanese occupied Wei-hai-Wei. *See* Port Arthur.

Weissenburg *Franco-Prussian War*

The opening engagement of the campaign, fought August 4, 1870, between the advance-guard of the Third German Army, under the Crown Prince of Prussia, and a portion of Marshal MacMahon's army under General Abel Donay, who fell in the battle. The Germans carried the French position and captured the town of Weissenburg, at a cost of 91 officers and 1,460 men. The French lost 2,300 killed, wounded and prisoners. *See* Sedan.

Wepener *Second Boer War*

This place was invested by a strong force of Boers, under De Wet, April 9, 1900, and was defended by 1,700 men of the Colonial Division under Colonel Dalgety. Notwithstanding the Boers' superiority in artillery and a succession of bold assaults on the trenches, the garrison held out gallantly till April 25, when they were relieved by General Rundle, having lost 300 killed and wounded in the course of the operations. *See* Ladysmith, Vaalkranz.

Werben *Thirty Years' War*

July 22, 1631, between the Swedes, 16,000 strong under Gustavus Adolphus, and 23,000 Imperialists under Field-Marshal Count Tilly. Tilly attacked Gustavus' entrenchments in front of Werben, but his troops could not face the fire of the Swedish batteries and being thrown into disorder, were then charged by the cavalry under Baudissen, and repulsed. The attack was renewed a few days later with a similar result, and Tilly then drew off his forces, having suffered a loss of 6,000 men. *See* Magdeburg.

White Oak Swamp,

see Seven Days' Battle

White Russia *World War II*

Hitler's Operation *Citadel*, an attempt to seize the key city of Kursk, 350 miles south of Moscow, was launched on July 5, 1943, with 17 panzer divisions, General Model's 9th Army attacking from the north and the 4th Panzer, General Hoth, from the south at the base of the Russian salient. Facing the Germans were Marshal Zhukov's five infantry armies and a tank army, supported by 20,000 guns, including 6,000 76mm. anti-tank guns. After an advance of six miles, Model's attack in the north was held, while in the south rain and a swamp stopped Hoth's nine divisions on the first day, Russian guns dealing them heavy losses until they moved again on July 8. By July 11, Hoth's forces had driven a salient 15 miles wide by nine deep in the Russian General Vatutin's line, but there was no breakthrough. Zhukov's 5th Tank Army was still in reserve, and on July 12, when Hoth attacked with 600 tanks, he unexpectedly ran into it. What has been called history's greatest tank battle raged for over eight hours until by evening the Russians had defeated their enemies no less completely than at Stalingrad. The Germans pulled out their depleted Panzer divisions both from the Kursk front, and in the centre and south, where von Kleist retreated towards the River Dnieper. On August 23, the Soviets re-took Kharkov, on September 22 Poltava and on the 25th Smolensk.

They crossed the Dnieper north of Kiev, early in October, taking Zaporozke on October 14, Melitopol on the 23rd, Kiev on November 6. Since their defeat at Kursk on July 12, the Germans had lost 133,000 men. About 3 million strong, they now faced 5,700,000 Russians on the east front.

After re-organizing during the winter, four Soviet armies—146 infantry and 43 armoured divisions—attacked again on June 22, 1944, on a 450-mile front, with 31,000 guns, and mortars, 5,200 tanks and self-propelled guns, and about 6,000 aircraft, while some 140,000 partisans destroyed the rail system, stopping German supplies. After six days' fighting, the Russians had broken the German front in six places. Minsk was taken on July 3. Rokossovski took Pinsk and Kowell on July 5, Vitebsk was encircled and fell on June 27, Mogilev was taken on June 28, Bobruisk on June 29. Advancing 10 to 15 miles a day, the Russians took Vilna (Lithuania) and Dvinsk

(Latvia) on July 13. Crossing the Polish border, they took Lublin on July 23 and Brest-Litovsk on July 28. Hitler replaced Field-Marshal Busch in the centre by Field-Marshal Model, but too late. The Germans had already been driven from Byelorussia into Poland. In an offensive lasting 36 days Soviet Russia had destroyed 25 German divisions and eliminated 350,000 men, a victory greater than Stalingrad. *See* Ukraine, Leningrad, Poland, East Prussia.

Wiazma *Napoleonic Wars*

November 3, 1812, when the corps of Eugène de Beauharnais and Marshal Davout were attacked during the retreat from Moscow, by the Russians, under Kutuzov, and suffered a loss of 4,000 men. *See* Krasnoi, Winkovo.

Wiesloch *Thirty Years' War*

April 16, 1622, between the troops of the Count Palatine, under the Count von Mansfeldt, and the Imperialists under Count Tilly. Tilly attacked and drove in the Palatinate rear-guard, but failing to check the pursuit was confronted by the main body and defeated with a loss of 3,000 killed and wounded and all his guns. This victory enabled Mansfeldt to effect a junction with the army of the Margrave of Baden. *See* Wimpfen.

Wilderness, The *American Civil War*

May 4 to 8, 1864, between the Army of the Potomac, 119,000 strong with 316 guns under General Grant, and 64,000 Confederates with 274 guns under General Lee. Lee's object was to intercept Grant's advance on Richmond, and early on the morning of the 5th he attacked the approaching Federal columns and after a hard-fought day, succeeded in arresting the progress of Grant's right wing. On the 6th, Lee almost succeeded in breaking Grant's centre, but at the critical moment, General James Longstreet, who was to lead the attack, was fired upon and dangerously wounded by his own troops. The Federal right wing however was driven back in confusion, and Lee on his side lost no ground. The two following days minor skirmishes took place, leading up to the great battle of Spotsylvania. The Confederates lost about 8,000 in the two days' fighting. The Federal

losses were far heavier, amounting to 15,000 in the second day alone. *See* Spotsylvania.

Williamsburg *American Civil War*

May 5, 1862, between the Confederates under General Magruder and the Federals under General McClellan. Magruder occupied a very strong position and held the Federals at bay throughout the day, but being greatly outnumbered, withdrew during the night. The Federals lost 2,228 killed, wounded and missing, the Confederates loss being about 1,600. *See* Yorktown.

Wilson's Creek *American Civil War*

August 10, 1861, between 6,000 Federals under General Lyon and 11,000 Confederates under General McCulloch. General Lyon divided his force into two columns, for the attack on McCulloch's position and that led by himself surprised the Southerners, and gained a partial success. They rallied, however, and beat him off, Lyon falling, the other column being also repulsed. The Federals lost 1,236, and the Confederates 1,095 killed, wounded and missing. When the Federals withdrew north-east, the Confederates occupied Springfield. *See* Ball's Bluff.

Wimpfen *Thirty Years' War*

May 6, 1622, between 14,000 Palatinate troops under the Margrave of Baden, and the Imperialists under Count Tilly and Gonsalvo de Cordova. Tilly attacked the Margrave's camp, which was not entrenched, and though a brilliant enemy cavalry charge captured his guns, it was not supported by the Palatine infantry, and the Imperialists rallying, drove off the cavalry in disorder, recovered the guns, and then routed the infantry, with a loss of 2,000 killed and wounded, and all their artillery, baggage and camp equipment. *See* Höchst, Wiesloch.

Winchester *American Civil War*

June 14, 1863, when 7,000 Federals under General Milroy were defeated by three Confederate divisions under General Ewell and forced to retreat with heavy loss, including 3,700 prisoners and 30 guns. *See* Gettysburg.

275

Winkovo *Napoleonic Wars*

October 18, 1812, when Murat, with 30,000 men, forming the advance-guard of the retiring French army, was attacked by the Russians under Count Orloff Dennizov, and driven from his position with a loss of 2,000 killed, 1,500 prisoners and all his baggage and artillery. *See* Wiazma.

Wisby *Danish-Swedish Wars*

A three-day battle, fought 1613, between the fleet of Gustavus Adolphus of Sweden and that of Christian IV of Denmark. The action was very obstinately contested, and finally the fleets separated without any decisive result.

Worcester *English Civil War*

September 3, 1651, between 12,000 Royalists, mostly Scottish, under Charles II, and about 28,000 Parliamentarians under Oliver Cromwell. Charles attacked Cromwell's wing, and was repulsed and driven into Worcester, where he was met by the other wing of the Parliamentary army under Fleetwood. The Royalists were routed and dispersed, losing 3,000 killed and a large number of prisoners, including Lords Derby, Lauderdale and Kenmure, and five generals. The Duke of Hamilton was mortally wounded. Charles himself escaped with difficulty to France. This was the last pitched battle of the Civil War. *See* Carbiesdale, Dunbar II.

Wörth *Franco-Prussian War*

August 6, 1870, between the Third German Army, about 80,000 strong, under the Crown Prince of Prussia, and the French, 37,000 strong under Marshal MacMahon. The war's first battle, it opened Alsace to the German forces. After a closely contested engagement the French were driven from all their positions, and made a hasty retreat beyond the Vosges. The Cuirassier division of General Bonnemain was completely cut to pieces in charging the German infantry, near Elsasshausen. The German losses amounted to 489 officers and 10,153 men, while the French lost 10,000 killed and wounded, 6,000 prisoners, 28 guns and five mitrailleuses. French rifle fire was more effective than that of their enemy, but the new rifled German field guns easily outclassed the obsolescent French artillery. On the same day, the French were also defeated at Spicheren. *See* Spicheren, Colombey, Metz.

Wrotham Heath *Wyatt's Insurrection*

January 1554, when the Kentish insurgents under Sir Henry Isley were totally defeated by the Royal troops under Lord Abergavenny.

Würtzburg *French Revolutionary Wars*

September 3, 1796, between the French under General Jourdan and the Austrians under the Archduke Charles. The Archduke interposed between the armies of Jourdan and General Moreau, who were endeavouring to effect a junction, and inflicted a severe defeat upon Jourdan, forcing him to retire to the Rhine. *See* Bassano.

Wynandael *War of the Spanish Succession*

September 28, 1708, between the British under General Webb and the French under the Comte de la Motte. The French, with 40 battalions and 40 squadrons, attempted to intercept a convoy of supplies for the army besieging Lille, and were totally defeated by a far inferior force, with a loss of 7,000 men.

X

Xeres *Spanish-Muslim Wars*

July 19 to 26, 711, between 90,000 Spaniards under Roderic and 12,000 Muslims, with a numerous force of African auxiliaries, under Tarik. On the fourth day the Muslims suffered a severe repulse, leaving 16,000 dead on the field, but the defection of Count Julian with a large part of the King's forces revived their courage, and finally the Christians were routed and dispersed. Roderic fled from the field but was drowned in crossing the Guadalquivir. This victory marks the fall of the Gothic monarchy and the beginning of the Moorish domination in Spain. *See* Utica.

Y

Yalu River I *Sino-Japanese War I*

September 17, 1894, between the Chinese fleet of two battleships and eight cruisers under Admiral Ting, and the Japanese fleet of ten cruisers and two gunboats under Admiral Ito. The two fleets met at the mouth of the Yalu, the Chinese steaming out in line abreast. Ito attacked in line ahead, using his superior speed to circle round the enemy's ships. Two of the Chinese vessels hauled out of the line and fled without coming into action, while two more were set on fire, and made for the shore. The remaining six ships fought well, and a little before sundown Ito retired, leaving the crippled Chinese fleet to make its way to Port Arthur. The Japanese lost 294 killed and wounded, of whom 107 fell on the flagship, the *Matsushima*, while the *Chiyada*, which was the next ship in the line, had not a man touched. The Chinese losses are unknown. *See* Port Arthur.

Yalu River II *Russo-Japanese War*

see Kiu-lien-Cheng

Yamazaki *Mitsuhide Rebellion*

In 1582, between Vice-Shogun Oda Nobunaga and the followers of the Oda family, and the rebel Akechi Mitsuhide. Mitsuhide sustained a crushing defeat, but later murdered Oda and became dictator.

Yarmuk *Muslim Invasion of Syria*

November, 636, between 110,000 Imperial troops under Manuel, the General of Heraclius, and 50,000 Muslims under Khaled. The Muslim attack was thrice repulsed, but they returned to the charge and after a long and bloody engagement drove their opponents from the field with enormous loss. The Muslims lost 4,030 killed and went on to attack Jerusalem. *See* Jerusalem II.

Yashima *Taira War*

In 1184, between the followers of the Taira family, and the rebels under Yoshitsune. The Taira forces were defeated.

Yawata *War of the Northern and Southern Empires*

January, 1353, between the armies of the Northern and Southern Emperors of Japan. The army of the latter, led by Moroushi, gained a signal victory.

Yenikale, Gulf of *Ottoman Wars*

July, 1790, between the Turkish fleet, and the Russians under Admiral Onschakov. The battle was fiercely contested, but eventually both fleets drew off without any decisive result. *See* Rimnitz.

Yom Kippur *Israeli-Arab War*

October 6–25, 1973, when at 1400 hours along the Golan Heights and the Suez Canal, Syria and Egypt simultaneously launched powerful offensives against unready Israeli forces on the eve of Yom Kippur, Jewish Day of Atonement.

Syria, after an hour's heavy bombardment by 1,000 guns and by aircraft on the 75 Israeli strong-points along the 75-mile cease-fire line, attacked at first with 500 tanks of the 3rd Armoured Division, with infantry, towards Kuneitra, in the north, held by about 100 tanks of the enemy 7th Armoured Brigade, with infantry. At the same time, Syria also hurled another 600 tanks of the 3rd and 1st Armoured Divisions, backed by infantry, against the southern Golan Heights, held by only 60 tanks of an Israeli armoured brigade and accompanying infantry. Here the initial Syrian objective was Naffekh, Israeli operational headquarters.

In the north the Israelis, in desperate fighting, managed to hold the Syrians. But four Syrian tank brigades broke through in the southern Golan towards Tiberias and by Sunday morning had partially surrounded Naffekh, had reached to within two miles of the Benot-Yaakov bridge over the Jordan into Israel, and to within five miles of the El Al road into Israel in the south.

With newly mobilized reserves, the Israelis counter-attacked, aided by the I.A.F. using napalm. By noon on October 10 they had thrown the Syrians back and regained their original lines. Then in the north, Major-General Hofi, Israeli G.O.C., had by October 16 driven the Syrians right out of Israel, to within 24 miles of Damascus. A subsequent battle against 250 Syrian, Iraqi and Jordanian tanks again gave victory to the Israelis, who also made more slight gains until the cease-fire on October 24, when they held about 300 square miles of Syrian territory. Moshe Dayan, Israeli Minister of Defence and Lieut-General David Elazar, Chief of Staff, were in overall command for Israel, with President Asad and Defence Minister Mustafa Tlas for Syria. The Egyptian offensive began with a surprise bombardment of 1,100 guns on Israel's 35 Bar Lev Line strong-points in Sinai along the east bank of the canal, then held by about 500 men. Three Israeli armoured brigades totalling about 280 tanks, British Centurions, American Patton M-48s and M-60s, plus a few modified Russian T-54s and 55s, were moving up from bases 50 miles east. Major-General Gonen was G.O.C. Israel's Southern Command, under the Chief of Staff Lieut-General David Elazar. For Egypt, General Ahmed Ismail, C-in-C., Gen. Saad Shazli, Chief of Staff, Gen. Gamasy, Military Operations.

After the initial bombardment five Egyptian infantry divisions crossed the canal in assault boats and established three separate bridgeheads. More infantry crossed in BTR amphibians while eleven Russian pontoon bridges, built at the rate of six metres a minute, enabled the first tanks and APCs to get over by 1530 hours, so that by early October 7, two armoured divisions had crossed.

Israeli aircraft diving to attack the canal bridges became targets for SAM 2 and 3 and the mobile SAM 6 and 7 ground-to-air missiles, and 11 were shot down before dusk on October 6. Israeli tanks moving up from the east fell victims to the enemy infantry's RPG-7 missiles and Sagger missiles (the 'suitcase' weapon) with the HEAT (heavy explosive anti-tank) armour-piercing warhead, fired from the west bank. By Sunday morning 200 of them lay smashed in the desert.

First objective of the Egyptians was to block the Mittla and Gidi passes through the Sinai mountains to stop the arrival of more Israeli reinforcements, which by Sunday morning had increased their strength to nine armoured brigades, four mechanized brigades and one paratroop battalion. At 1500 hours on Sunday, October 7, the Israelis counter-attacked from north to south along the canal to destroy the enemy bridgeheads, but failed owing to scant air support, no infantry or artillery backing and disregard of enemy anti-tank weapons, with the loss of nearly 100 tanks. When in their turn the Egyptians counter-attacked with a tank brigade and a mechanized brigade, a tank-to-tank battle developed at 600 yards' range, during which more accurate Israeli shooting led to the Egyptian withdrawal, with heavy losses.

By October 10 the Egyptians had lost the advantage of surprise, for Israel's mobilization had reached 17 brigades with 600 tanks and 70,000 men in Sinai. To relieve pressure on Syria, General Ahmed Ismail then ordered reserves to cross the canal to help stage a major battle for Israel's operational headquarters at Bir Gifgafar; Romani, on the coast road and Ras el Sudr in the Gulf of Suez. A tank battle followed at 6 am October 14 but the Egyptians could not match the Israelis for skill and by the evening 264 of their tanks and APCs were counted wrecked in the desert.

In a major counter-stroke on October 15 the Israeli General Sharon's division (2 armoured brigades and 2 paratroop brigades) crossed the canal and established a bridgehead, and by midday October 16 some 60 tanks and an infantry brigade were over. But in a tank battle north of the Great Bitter Lake, where the Israelis tried to establish a supply corridor, they met with heavy losses in fighting that went on till dusk on October 18, when the weary Egyptians withdrew, having lost 90 tanks.

After destroying the SAM bases on the west bank, Sharon's forces cut the Cairo–Suez road, and thus the communications of the Egyptian 3rd Army, then fanned out into Egypt. A Security Council cease-fire on October 21 was disregarded by Israeli units on the outskirts of Suez, where they were then cut off and lost heavily. When the second cease-fire began on October 25, the Israelis held some 1,500 square miles of Egypt, including the port of El Abadiya, on the western side of the Gulf of Suez.

Israel had by then decisively beaten the Egyptians, mainly through more accurate tank gunnery. Altogether in Syria and Sinai, Egypt lost 580 tanks, Syria 860, Israel 780, Iraq 125, Jordan about 25. There were also heavy losses of APCs. Losses in men killed or wounded were said to be 12,000 Syrians, 7,800 Egyptians and 2,700 Israelis, the latter being probably less than the fact.

Yorktown I *American Revolutionary War*

The entrenched position of General Lord Cornwallis, with 6,000 British troops, was invested by Washington, with 7,000 French under Rochambeau and 8,850 Americans, in September, 1781. The British held out until October 19 when, surrounded and outnumbered, Cornwallis surrendered, having lost during the operations 12 officers and 469 rank and file, killed and wounded. This surrender, due to the temporary loss by the British of command of the sea, ended the war and American independence was acknowledged in a treaty signed September 3, 1783. *See* Minorca.

Yorktown II *American Civil War*

This once small village gave its name to the entrenched position occupied by General Magruder with 13,000 Confederates, which was invested by General George McClellan's 60,000 Federal troops with 103 siege guns, April 5, 1862.

On the 16th an unsuccessful attack was made upon Magruder's lines, and both sides having been reinforced, McClellan set about the erection of batteries. On May 4, the Federals were about to open fire when it was found that the Confederates had abandoned the position and retired. *See* Williamsburg.

Youghioghenny *Seven Years' War*

A skirmish of no importance in itself, but notable as being 'the shot fired in America which gave the signal that set Europe in a blaze' (Voltaire, *Louis XV*), and was in a sense the cause of the Seven Years' War. On May 27, 1754, Washington with 40 Virginians surprised a small French detachment under Coulon de Jumonville, despatched probably as a reconnaissance by Contrecoeur from Fort Duquesne. The entire detachment, with one exception, was killed or captured. *See* Minorca I, Lobositz.

Ypres I *World War I*

Last major battle in 1914 on the Western front, when on October 14 General von Falkenhayn attacked the BEF (Sir John French) with the 4th and 6th German armies at Ypres, where the British linked with the Belgian army. The German initial advance of several miles, French reinforcements and the Belgians' flooding of their front from the sea to Dixmude, halted. After a British counter-attack and another German attack, the battle ended on November 11 in rain and snow with the British still holding the ruins of Ypres at the base of a 6-mile eastward salient into the German lines. About 80 per cent of the original BEF died here, no less than 2,368 officers and 55,787 men. French losses were 50,000, German 130,000. *See* Aisne.

Ypres II *World War I*

April 22, 1915, and the first use ever of lethal chlorine gas when General von Falkenhayn loosed it into the British-held salient here, killing or incapacitating thousands of troops in a four-mile front. General Smith-Dorrien's 2nd Army stopped the German advance there by bringing in Canadian reserves, who held during another chlorine gas attack on April 24. The British then withdrew to a stronger position on the outskirts of Ypres, which they held at great cost until the battle ended on May 25. The British and Allies lost 60,000 officers and men, against 35,000 German, a reversal of the usual defence-attack ratio probably due to chlorine. *See* Artois.

Ypres III *World War I*

On June 7, 1917, the British and New Zealand troops captured Messines ridge after it had been blown up by the explosion of 19 huge mines beneath the German lines there, thus making the Ypres salient the base for an advance. On July 21, 1917, General Gough's 5th Army attacked north-east after a heavy ten-day bombardment which, after two miles' advance, torrential rain stopped in a maze of flooded shell holes and quagmires. General Plumer's 2nd Army then advanced another five miles, while French troops also made limited advances. Weather held up the battle until September 20, after which the Australians and Canadians finally took Passchendaele on November 6. Total advance in five months' fighting with losses amounting to 240,000 officers and men was less than five miles, the costliest of all British advances. *See* Messines, Cambrai.

Z

Zab, The *Bahram's Revolt*

In 590, between the troops of the Persian usurper Bahram and the army of the Emperor Maurice under Narses. The usurper's forces were defeated and Chosroes II restored to the throne of Persia. *See* Nineveh.

Zalaka *Moorish Empire in Spain*

October 23, 1086, between 40,000 Moors, under Yusuf ibn-Tashfin, and a stronger Spanish army under Alfonso VI of Castile. The Spaniards were routed with enormous loss. Alfonso, at the head of 500 horse, cut his way out and with difficulty escaped. Ibn-Tashfin ruled all Spain south of Toledo, except Valencia, home of El Cid, for 20 years.

Zama *Second Punic War*

202 BC, between the Carthaginians under Hannibal and the Romans under Scipio Africanus. The Carthaginians began to attack with their elephants, 80 in number, but some of these became unmanageable and fell back upon the cavalry, throwing them into disorder, while the legionaries opened out and allowed the others to pass down the lanes between their ranks. The infantry then closed, and after severe fighting the Romans gained a complete victory, 20,000 Carthaginians falling, while as many more were made prisoners. Hannibal escaped from the field at the end of the day and Carthage ceded Spain to Rome. *See* Carthage.

Zamora *Spanish-Muslim Wars*

In 901, between the Spaniards under Alfonso the Great, King of the Asturias, and the Moors under Abdullah, King of Cordova. The Moors were utterly routed with heavy loss, Alfonso thereby extending his dominions as far as the Guadiana. *See* Alhandega.

Zeim *Russo-Turkish War*

April 20, 1877, between the Russians under General Loris-Melikov and the Turks under Mukhtar Pasha. Melikov attacked the Turks in a strongly entrenched position, but was repulsed with considerable loss. *See* Plevna.

Zela I *Third Mithridatic War*

67 BC, between the Romans under Triarius and the Pontic army under Mithridates. The King attacked the Roman camp and practically annihilated them, though himself dangerously wounded in the assault. *See* Nicopolis I.

Zela II *Wars of the First Triumvirate*

August 2, 47 BC, between seven Roman legions with some Asiatic auxiliaries, under Julius Caesar, and the Bosporans under Pharnaces. Pharnaces attacked the Romans while they were pitching camp, but the legionaries quickly formed up and routed their assailants. This is the occasion of Caesar's famous despatch, 'Veni, vidi, vici'. *See* Ruspina.

Zendecan *Turkish Invasion of Afghanistan*

In 1039, between the Seljuks under Moghrul Beg and the Afghans under Musrud, Sultan of Ghazni. The Afghans were defeated and Musrud compelled to retire on his capital.

Zenta *Ottoman Wars*

September 11, 1679, between the Austrians under Prince Eugène and the Turks under Elwas Mohammed, the Grand Vizier. Eugène attacked the Turkish army as it was crossing a temporary bridge over the Theiss, the cavalry being already across, Eugène cut the bridge in two and completely routed the infantry, driving them into the river. The Turks lost 29,000 men, the Austrians 500 only. *See* Vienna II.

Zeugminum *Hungarian War*

1168, between the Greeks under Manuel I, Emperor of Constantinople, and the Hungarian invaders. The Hungarians were signally defeated and the war, which had lasted for five years, came to an end.

281

Ziezicksee *Flemish War*

In 1302, when the Genoese galleys in the service of Philip IV of France, under Grimaldi and Filipo di Rieti, destroyed the Flemish fleet.

Zlotsow *Ottoman Wars*

In 1676, between the Poles under John Sobieski, and 20,000 Turks and Tartars under Mohammed IV. The Turks were signally defeated. *See* Vienna II.

Znaim *Napoleonic Wars*

July 14, 1809, when Marshal Masséna with 8,000 French attacked 30,000 Austrians, under the Prince of Reuss, and drove them into Znaim with considerable loss, including 800 prisoners.

Zorndorf *Seven Years' War*

August 25, 1758, between the Prussians, 25,000 strong under Frederick the Great, and a 40,000 strong Russian army under Fermor, which was besieging Custria. Frederick attacked the Russian entrenchments and drove them out with a loss of 10,000, forcing them to relinquish the siege. The Prussians lost about 11,000. *See* Olmütz, Hochkirch, Crefeld.

Zurakow *Ottoman Wars*

In 1676, John Sobieski with 10,000 Poles was besieged by 150,000 Turks and Tartars, under Ibrahim Pasha (Shaitan). Having 63 guns, Sobieski made a sturdy defence and by constant sorties inflicted enormous loss on the besiegers. At last, being unable to make any impression on the defence and finding his army wasting away, Ibrahim consented to treat and withdrew his forces from Polish territory. The Turks lost enormous numbers during the siege; the Poles 3,000. *See* Vienna II, Soczawa.

Zürich *French Revolutionary Wars*

June 4–7, 1799, about 14 months after France had created the Helvetian Republic in Switzerland, Archduke Charles Louis, brother of Francis II of the Holy Roman Empire, marched in and attacked with an army of 40,000, about 25,000 French troops under General Masséna. After a costly four-day battle, Masséna withdrew and Zürich fell to the Second Coalition powers.

Soon after, the Archduke fell sick and General Korsakov with 30,000 Russian troops superseded him, while in northern Italy Russia's Marshal Suvorov, having defeated the French, began marching his forces towards the St Gothard Pass for Switzerland to combine with Korsakov against Masséna. With an army of about 40,000, Masséna sent a force to harass Suvorov in the Pass, then attacked Korsakov on September 26, defeating and scattering the Russians, killing or wounding 8,000, taking many prisoners and guns and forcing them to withdraw from Switzerland. He then turned and fell on Suvorov, who turned back, a prey in the mountains to French ambushes and lack of food. These cost him some 14,000 men, half his army, before he too withdrew from the country. These two defeats caused Czar Paul I to resign from the Second Coalition. *See* Alkmaar.

Zusmarshausen *Thirty Years' War*

In 1647, when the French and Swedes, under Vicomte de Turenne and General Wrangel, inflicted a decisive defeat upon the Imperialists and marched into Bavaria up to the River Inn. *See* Nördlingen.

Zutphen *Netherlands War of Independence*

September 22, 1586, between the Spaniards under Prince Alexander of Parma and the English under the Earl of Leicester. The Spaniards endeavoured to throw a convoy of provisions into Zutphen, which Leicester was besieging. He attempted to intercept it, but without success, and was forced to retire after suffering considerable loss. Among those who fell on the English side was Sir Philip Sidney. *See* Turnhout.

Zuyder Zee *Netherlands War of Independence*

October 11, 1573, between 30 Spanish ships under Bossu and 25 Dutch ships under Admiral Dirkzoon. The Spanish fleet fled after losing five ships, only Bossu resisting. His ship, however, was eventually captured, after losing three-fourths of her crew. *See* Alkmaar.

Index

Note:
The names of battles are not included in the index, as these are listed alphabetically through the text.
Personal names, ships and wars are listed.
Where a person is referred to under more than one battle heading on a page of text, or more than one battle of the same war occurs on a page, the number of battles concerned is given in brackets after the page number in the index.

284

287

148, 156, 157, 158, 161,
163, 166, 169(2), 172,
173(2), 179, 180, 182,
184, 205, 207, 221, 222,
213-14, 217, 221, 222,
223, 242, 255(2), 256,
257, 261, 262(2), 273,
282
Fresnel, Gen., 111
Freyberg, Gen., 158
Freyre, 66
Freytag, Gen., 116
Friant, Gen., 9
Friedrich Wilhelm, Crown
Prince, 24
Fritigern, 110, 158
Fronde, War of the, 64, 191, 204
Frossard, Gen., 239
Fuad Pasha, 198
Fulvius: Cnaeus, 41, 114
Q., 58
Futtah Mohammed Khan, 131

Gabes, 259
Gablenz, Gen., 256
Gage, Gen., 51
Gaines' Mill, 230
Galba, 203
Gallic Invasions:
I, 18, 214
II, 72
IV, 24
of Asia, 89
of Italy, 139
Revolt, 44
Tribal Wars, 11
Wars, 11, 12, 16, 32, 38, 50,
102, 173, 203, 256
Galliéni, Gen., 160
Galitzin, Prince, 66, 81, 128
Gallus, Cestius, 43
Galway, Lord, 15, 19
Gamarra, Pres. of Peru, 120
Gamasy, Gen., 278
Gardiner, Col., 19
Gardner, Gen., 204
Garibaldi, Guiseppe, 30, 54, 164,
166, 170, 171, 191(2),
215, 263(2), 270
's Rising, 30
Garnett, Gen., 213
Gatacre, Gen. Sir W., 242
Gates, Gen., 56, 242
Gazer Khan, 189
Gelen, Adm. van, 143
Gelimar, 59, 256
Gellius: Equatius, 56, 228
Statius, 47
Gelon, 113, 115
Genghis Khan, 35, 46, 102, 119,
128(2), 195, 223, 247
Genseric, 57, 115
Gensoul, Adm., 188
George: II, King of England, 79
King of Hanover, 139
Georgia, Queen of, 253
Gergue, 196
German:

Invasion of Italy, 73
—Polish Wars, 107
Reformation Wars, 173, 233
States' Wars, 85, 164
See also Franco-Prussian War
Germanic Wars, 119, 147, 154,
263
Germanicus, 119
Gerow, Gen. Leonard, 25
Getes, the, 103
Giap, Gen., 80
Gilbert Islands, 249
Gildo, Revolt of, 246
Gillespie, Gen., 127
Ginkel, Gen. de, 31
Girard, Gen., 144
Girod, 220
Glabrio, 251
Glasgow, 71
'Glorious First of June', 261
Gloucester, Duke of, 158
Gneisenau, 31, 71, 91
Go Kameyama, 168
Go Murakami, Emp., 135, 167
Goddard, Gen., 12, 37
Godefroi de Bouillon, 22, 28,
124, 181
Goeben, Gen. von, 36, 221
Goering, Hermann, 49, 232
Goignies, Gen., 101
Göldli, George, 128
Golitshin, Adm., 106
Goltz, Gen. von der, 270
Gonen, Maj.-Gen., 278
Gonsalvo de Cordova, 62,
100(2), 189, 220, 228,
248, 275
Gonzaga, 101
Francisco de, of Mantua, 94,
100
Good Hope, 71
Gordon, Gen., 23, 130
Gordon Highlanders, the, 77
Gore, Col., 220
Görgey, Gen. von, 10, 120, 133,
177, 186, 196, 225, 250
Goring, Lord, 140
Gorokhov, Gen., 241
Gorringe, Gen., 136
Gortschakov, Gen., 249
Gothic invasions of:
the East, 110
France, 201
the Roman Empire, 95, 177,
198
Thrace, 158
Gott, Gen., 164
Götz, Gen. von der, 136, 271
Gough: Gen. (World War I),
238, 280
Sir Hugh, 65, 92, 108, 153,
173, 206, 209, 219, 237
Matthew, 239
Gouraud, Gen., 160, 165
Gourko, Gen., 81, 105, 198, 201
Gracchus, Tiberius, 41
Graf Spee, 106
Graham, Gen.: (of Penisular
War), 36, 224

(of Egyptian Wars), 111, 129,
247, 250, 257
Grailli, Jean de, 68
Grammont, Gen. de, 79
Grand Alliance, Wars of the, 93
Granson, Sir Thomas, 203
Grant: Gen. U.S., 23, 64, 65, 68,
94, 197, 231, 240, 265, 275
Sir Hope, 246-7
Major, 106
Grasse, Comte de, 81
Gratiani, 123
Gratianus, 26
Graves, Adm. Thomas, 151
Graziani, Marshal, 36, 232, 269
Great Irish Rebellion, 40, 83, 84
Great Northern War, 14, 96, 178,
206(2), 236, 242-3, 252
Great Peloponnesian War see
under Peloponnesian Wars
Greathed, Col., 12
Greco:
—Persian Wars, 158, 175
—Turkish Wars, 197, 263
Greece: Crown Prince of, 82
Roman Invasion of, 26
Greek: City States, Wars of the,
68, 75, 111, 145, 157, 179
War of Independence, 82, 167,
179
Green, Sir Charles, 243
Greene, Gen., 90, 108
Gregory: II, Pope, 210
VII, Pope, 215
Prefect, 257
Greig, Adm., 116
Grenville, Sir Richard, 33
Grey: Gen., 206
Sir George, 161
de Ruthyn, Lord, 183
Griffin, Gen., 25
Grimaldi, 282
Groener, Gen., 55
Grouchy, Marshal, 273
Guderian, Gen., 93, 95, 131, 172
Guelfs and Ghibellines, 19, 56,
71, 169, 246
Guerri, Menaldo, 189
'Guglers', Invasion of the, 96
Guilleminot, Gen., 107
Guiscard, Robert, 68, 85, 215
Guise: Duc de, 54
François de, 83
Guiton, Mayor, 141
Gurkha War, 19, 174
Gustavus Adolphus, 67, 77,
143(2), 150, 200, 274, 276
II, of Sweden, 19, 95, 153, 213
Gustavus Vasa, 261
Guthmund, 155
Guthrum, 66, 90
Guy de Lusignan, 124, 252
Guyeaux, Gen., 61
Gwalior Campaign, 153, 206
Gylippus of Sparta, 244
Gyllenstierna, Christina, 261
Gyulai, Marshal, 153

Mousson, Oglou, 50
Mueller, Gen., 195
Mughal: -Hindu Wars, 67
    Invasions: III, 192
        of Afghanistan, 127-8
        of the Deccan, 13, 103, 164
Mukhlis Khan, 20
Mukhtar Pasha, 14, 88, 132, 281
Mulgrave, Lord, 255
Mulligan, Col., 145
Mulraj, 243
Munemori, 77
Münnich, Gen. Count, 186, 241
Munro, Gen., 99
Münzer, Thomas, 95
Murad: I, of Turkey, 134
    II, of Turkey, 134
    Bey, 207
Murat, Marshal, 21, 83, 92,
        189, 254, 276
Murphy, Father, 35, 269
Murray: Earl, 190
    Lord George, 205
    Gen.: (c.1760), 167, 208, 220
    Archibald, 100, 101, 217
    Sir John, 60
    Regent of Scotland, 140
Mus, P. Decius, 28, 264
Musa, 164
Musgrave, John, 238
Muslim:
    Civil Wars, 233
    Conquest of Africa, 257, 261
    Invasions of: Egypt, 16, 164
        Europe, 69
        France, 255
        Persia, 53, 123, 180
        Syria, 15, 46-7, 175, 277
    See also Spanish-Muslim
        Wars
Musrud, Sultan of Ghazni, 281
Mussolini, Benito, 15, 35
Mustapha: II, 39
Mustapha Pasha, 91
    IV, 9
    Kara, 265
    Köpriali Pasha, 222
Mutaguchi, Gen., 51
Muzuffer Jung, 20
Mygdonius, River, diverted, 182
Myronides, 186
Mysore Wars, see British-
        Mysore Wars

Nabis of Sparta, 26, 36
Nadir, Shah, 59
Nagasaki, 234
Nagumo, Adm., 159, 166
Namsos, 184
Namur, Guy de, 72
Nana Sahib, 61, 153, 192
Napier, Gen. Sir Charles, 84,
        118, 163
Napoleon Bonaparte, 9, 10,
        24(2), 29, 32, 38, 41,
        46(2), 49, 54, 61, 63, 72,
        75, 83, 85, 87, 90, 97,
        123-4, 129, 138, 140, 142,

143, 146, 148, 150, 155,
156, 157, 158, 163,
169(3), 173, 205, 208,
211, 213-14, 217, 236,
255(2), 256, 260, 271, 273
    first appearance of, 255
    Hundred Days of, 92, 146,
        208, 254, 273(2)
    Italian Campaigns of, 54
Napoleonic Wars, 9, 21, 24(2),
        29-30, 32, 37, 38, 41, 42,
        45, 46, 47, 49, 50(2), 54,
        57, 61, 63, 70, 72, 75,
        77(2), 79, 83, 85, 86, 87,
        88, 90, 97, 105, 107, 109,
        111, 112, 113(2), 116,
        123-4, 129(2), 133,
        135(2), 140, 141-2, 143,
        144, 149, 150-1, 154, 155,
        159, 161, 165-6, 168(2),
        169, 170, 172, 189, 193,
        202(2), 206, 207, 209,
        210, 211, 219(2), 220,
        222, 236, 243, 255(2),
        260, 262, 271(2), 273,
        275, 276, 282
Napoleon III, 227, 237
Nappa Sahib, 235
Narses, 60, 215, 246, 281
Narvik, 184
Nasmyth, Lieut., 233
Nassau: Count Henry of, 171
    Count Louis of, 171
Nasser, Col. Gamal Abdul, 233
Navarre, Gen., 80
Navarro, 188
Ndlambi, 19
Neame, Gen., 253
Needham, Gen., 26
Negreti, Gen., 141
Neipperg, Count, 107, 135, 168
Nelson, Adm. Lord Horatio, 58,
        70, 182, 256
Nem, Gen., 227
Nemours, Ducs de, 62, 204
Nero, Claudius, 165
Netherlands War of
    Independence, 18, 22, 49,
        101, 110, 111, 112, 140,
        145, 152, 166, 171, 182,
        189, 215, 218, 250, 255,
        259, 262, 282(2)
Nevers, Duc de, 182
Neville: Ralph de, 180
    Sir Thomas, 241
Nevilles, the, 87
New Zealand, 81
Newcastle, Earl of, 11
Ney, Marshal, 38, 52, 72, 79, 88,
        109, 133, 165, 189, 208,
        262, 271, 273
Nicephorus I, Emp., 173
Nicholas: I, Czar, 187, 234
    II, Czar, 172, 258
Nicholson, Gen. John, 78, 184
Nicias, 244
Nicolls, Col., 19
Nicostratos, 157
Nidau, Count of, 142

Niel, Marshal, 237
Nikopol, 260
Nimitz, Adm., 166
Nivelle, Gen., 13, 27-8, 264
Nixon, Richard, US President,
        267
Nizam-al-Mulk, 59
Noailles, Duc de, 79
'Noche Triste', 165
Nodzu, Gen., 207
Nogi, Gen., 127, 203
Noircarmes, Gen., 262
Norbanus, Consul, 92, 173
Norfolk, Duke of, 47, 255
Norfolk, 44
Noriyori, 77, 119, 229
Norman: Civil War, 253
    Conquest of England, 112
    Invasion of: France, 170
        Italy, 68, 85
    Revolt, 102
    Seizure of Rome, 215
Normandy: John, Duke of, 13
    Robert of, 102, 253
    William of, 262(2)
Normandy, Rise of, 262(2)
Norse Invasions of:
    Britain, 98, 241
    France, 225
    Ireland, 68
    Scotland, 141
North-West Frontier Campaign,
    British, 77
Northern and Southern
        Empires, Wars of the, 231,
        278
Northern Wars, 89, 132
    Great, 14, 96, 178, 206(2), 236,
        242-3, 252
Northumberland, Earls of:
    (d.1408), 48
    (d.1455), 219
    Siward, 84-5
Northumberland's Rebellion, 48
Northumbrian Invasion of
        Scotland, 179
Nott, Gen., 103, 130, 154
Nottingham, Earl of, 158
Noyan, 94
Nudo, Rutilius, 62
Nugent, Gen., 48
Numidian Revolt, 251
Nuñez, Blasco, 21
Nürnberg, 91
Nur-ud-din, Gen., 136

Obata, Gen., 159
Ochterlony, Sir David, 174
O'Connor, Gen., 36, 39, 232
O'Connors, the, 30
Octavius, 10-11, 175, 198
    Marcus, 74, 249
Oda Nobunaga, 277
Odessa, 260
O'Donnell, Marshal, 108, 250
Oktai, 189
Oku, Gen., 177, 250
Olaf Triggvason, 155

296

298

300

301

302